FOURTEENTH EDITION

The Enjoyment
of Music

FOURTEENTH EDITION

The Enjoyment of Music

Kristine Forney

Professor Emerita of Music

California State University, Long Beach

Andrew Dell'Antonio

Distinguished Teaching Professor of Music

The University of Texas at Austin

Joseph Machlis

Late of Queens College of the City University of New York

W. W. NORTON & COMPANY

Independent Publishers Since 1923

W. W. Norton & Company has been independent since its founding in 1923, when William Warder Norton and Mary D. Herter Norton first published lectures delivered at the People's Institute, the adult education division of New York City's Cooper Union. The firm soon expanded its program beyond the Institute, publishing books by celebrated academics from America and abroad. By midcentury, the two major pillars of Norton's publishing program—trade books and college texts—were firmly established. In the 1950s, the Norton family transferred control of the company to its employees, and today—with a staff of five hundred and hundreds of trade, college, and professional titles published each year—W. W. Norton & Company stands as the largest and oldest publishing house owned wholly by its employees.

Editor: Chris Freitag
Project editor: Michael Fauver
Media editor: Steve Hoge
Production manager: Jane Searle
Managing editor, college: Marian Johnson
Managing editor, college digital media: Kim Yi
Assistant editor: Julie Kocsis
Media assistant editor: Ellie Shirocky
Market research and strategy manager, music: Trevor Penland
Design director: Rubina Yeh
Designer: Lissi Sigillo
Photo editor: Mike Cullen
Director of college permissions: Megan Schindel
Permissions associate: Patricia Wong
Copyeditor: Jodi Beder
Proofreader: Debra Nichols
Indexer: Heather Dubnick
Composition: Graphic World, Inc.
Manufacturing: Transcontinental—Beauceville

Library of Congress Cataloging-in-Publication Data

Names: Forney, Kristine, author. | Dell'Antonio, Andrew, author. | Machlis,
    Joseph, 1906-1998, author.
Title: The enjoyment of music / Kristine Forney, Andrew Dell'Antonio,
    Joseph Machlis.
Description: Fourteenth edition. | New York : W. W. Norton & Company, 2021.
    | Includes index.
Identifiers: LCCN 2021032461 | ISBN 9780393543025 (paperback)
Subjects: LCSH: Music appreciation.
Classification: LCC MT90 .M23 2021 | DDC 780--dc23
LC record available at https://lccn.loc.gov/2021032461

W. W. Norton & Company, Inc., 500 Fifth Avenue, New York, NY 10110
wwnorton.com

W. W. Norton & Company, Ltd., 15 Carlisle Street, London W1D 3BS

1 2 3 4 5 6 7 8 9 0

Contents

Preface xvi

PART 1
Materials of Music

PART 2

The Middle Ages and Renaissance

PART 3
The Baroque Era

PART 4

Eighteenth-Century Classicism

PART 5

The Nineteenth Century

PART 6

Twentieth-Century Modernism

PART 7

Postmodernism: The Mid-Twentieth Century and Beyond

Preface

The Enjoyment of Music continues to be at the forefront of pedagogical innovation for introductory college music classes; for more than half a century, it has remained both classic and cutting edge. We constantly update both its contents and approach to offer an exceptionally appealing repertory and the latest scholarship, all integrated with unparalleled media resources. Organized chronologically by historical eras, the book is modular, with short chapters featuring one or (at most) two works. These make for easier reading and will help you master the material more quickly. You will also find the language direct and engaging, with comments focused toward you, the student.

What's new in this 14th edition, you might ask? Most significant is our innovative chapter on musical repertories and canons: that is, works that have been deemed timeless or worth preserving over generations. Here, we explore how canons are formed and how they change. We have woven a new feature throughout the book called **Many Voices**, focused on music outside the established canon—much of it by individuals historically underrepresented in narratives of "great" musicians—as well as popular and global music. Your continued exploration of the ever-evolving canon is encouraged by our **Online Gallery of New Voices**, which features music by younger composers who are just gaining attention for their innovative approaches and new soundscapes. Finally, we have included a new pedagogical feature at the beginning of each part that lays out clear **Learning Objectives**. These, along with **Key Points** in each chapter, should help guide your studies.

In addition to listening, you are likely to be asked to write about music in your class. To assist you in this endeavor, we have a chapter at the end of Part 1 entitled **Putting Music into Words**, which provides ideas and resources for using effective prose to express what you hear. Furthermore, each historical section ends with an opportunity to try your hand at writing about a new musical work (**Music in Words**), applying terms and concepts you have learned in that section. Here we continue our focus on alternative interpretations of selected works, and on the essential role that performers have played in the development of musical styles.

This new edition embraces a wide diversity of repertories and approaches. **Your Turn to Explore** boxes at the end of each chapter encourage you to discover music from different traditions and repertoires, and **Interface** boxes make connections between music and other subjects you may be studying. You'll see all these items described below, along with the other main features in the text and online. Understanding these resources will greatly enhance your listening, help with study skills, and improve your overall performance in class. Most importantly, we hope that these features will encourage your continued *Enjoyment of Music*.

BOOK AND MEDIA HIGHLIGHTS

The Enjoyment of Music is designed to help you discover for yourself the joy of studying music.

- A **varied repertory** broadly represents current and past classical composers, as well as jazz, musical theater, film music, popular and traditional music, and non-Western styles.

- **Key Points** at the beginning of each chapter briefly summarize the terms and main ideas in that chapter.

- **Marginal sideheads** and **boldface type** identify key terms defined in the text and focus attention on important concepts.

44

Sounding Literature: Orchestral Program Music by Mendelssohn and Grieg

"I dipped into the rich treasures of native folk song and sought to create a national art out of this hitherto unexploited expression of the folk soul of Norway."

—*Edvard Grieg*

KeyPoints

- Prominent types of Romantic program music include the **concert overture**, **incidental music** to a play, and the **symphonic poem** (a one-movement work).

- Felix Mendelssohn drew on his passion for Shakespeare's plays in writing a concert overture that he felt encapsulated the story and expressive qualities of *A Midsummer Night's Dream*.

- Political unrest throughout Europe stimulated schools of nationalistic composers in Russia, Scandinavia, Spain, England, and Bohemia.

- Edvard Grieg looked to the folklore of his native Norway in many of his works. His incidental music for *Peer Gynt* was written to accompany a play by Henrik Ibsen about this folk legend, then was excerpted into an independent suite.

One of the most important roles that music plays in all human societies is building community cohesion. Since the nineteenth century, the notion of community has been strongly tied to the concept of nationality: a distinctive culture and heritage shared by people who live in a common territory. But although individuals are associated with a nation by birth or immigration, they can choose whether or not—and how—to highlight that association through their music. Literary references are also a powerful way to express shared heritage, whether national or cross-cultural, and the nineteenth century saw increasing interest in the linking of instrumental music and literature. In this chapter, we will explore two contrasting orchestral approaches to such linking: Felix Mendelssohn's *A Midsummer Night's Dream* and Edvard Grieg's *Peer Gynt*.

Varieties of Orchestral Program Music

One type of program music came out of the opera house, where the overture, a rousing orchestral piece in one movement, served as an introduction to an opera (or a play). Some operatic overtures became popular as separate concert pieces, which in turn pointed the way to a new type of **overture** not associated with opera: a single-movement concert piece for orchestra that might evoke a land- or seascape, or embody a patriotic or literary idea, like Tchaikovsky's *Romeo and Juliet*.

Another type of program music, **incidental music**, usually consists of an overture and a series of pieces performed between the acts of a play and

Program overture

Incidental music

273

Example of Harmony 🔊

Yankee Doodle (Revolutionary War song)

Melody — Yan - kee Doo - dle went to town → horizontal plane (melody)

Harmony (chords) → vertical plane (harmony)

Scale — do re mi fa sol la ti do / 1 2 3 4 5 6 7 8

- **Audio icons** in the text and listening guides alert you to online resources including short examples, full audio selections, or Metropolitan Opera video clips.

■ **Interface** boxes help you make interdisciplinary connections, linking music to other studies you may undertake (including science, technology, philosophy, religion, politics, history, literature, and more).

■ **Many Voices** features highlight music from underrepresented or lesser-known composers as well as global and popular music traditions.

---

180   PART 4 EIGHTEENTH-CENTURY CLASSICISM

Inter*face*

Science, Philosophy, and Music in the Age of Enlightenment

In a major intellectual and cultural shift, the eighteenth century looked toward the advancement of knowledge through reason and science. Among those who spearheaded change were the philosopher Voltaire and the physicist who developed the laws of gravity, Isaac Newton. These thinkers embraced a new philosophy that sought to understand all things according to nature and mathematics rather than religion. Scholars assiduously collected information to increase the overall body of knowledge, and society in general embraced a focus on learning. One result was the great French *Encyclopédie*, a thirty-five-volume reference source purporting to systematize all knowledge, written by the leading intellectuals of the day, including Voltaire and Jean-Jacques Rousseau. Musicians took part in this effort to amass learning: Rousseau (also a composer) published a comprehensive dictionary of musical terms; Jean-Philippe Rameau wrote an important music theory treatise; and in 1776, the Englishman Charles Burney penned the first music history text (the ancestor of your textbook), which sought to record all knowledge about musicians and their works.

Some of the most celebrated technological achievements were connected to music: for example, "music boxes" with rotating cylinders and other mechanical means of plucking strings or striking metal plates when wound up. (Many of these musical machines were created by clock makers, who were making tremendous technological strides in miniaturizing time-keeping devices in the 1700s.) Some musical machines, known as automata, were made to resemble humans: a life-size human flute player played twelve separate melodies, and there's a famous automaton, now in the museum of Art and History in Neuchâtel, Switzerland, of a woman playing an organ, pressing the keys of the instrument with her fingers. While the "robotic" performer's bodily movements may seem less convincing to us in an age of sophisticated CGI animation, they were certainly among the most humanlike mechanical actions that had ever been seen at the time, and they demonstrated the power of human ingenuity.

Across the Atlantic, the statesman and scientist Benjamin Franklin was central to the American Enlightenment through his scientific experiments

A glass armonica from Boston, c. 1830.

with electricity and his diverse inventions, including the lightning rod, bifocal glasses, the Franklin stove, and the glass armonica—a musical instrument made of tuned water glasses, for which both Mozart and Beethoven composed works. Franklin was a musician himself (he played harp and guitar), and he wrote a treatise on musical aesthetics, in which he espoused a philosophy of simplicity in melody and harmony.

We can easily relate the Enlightenment's goals of reasoned thought and simplicity to the music we are studying from this period. Both the individual musical elements—melody, rhythm, and harmony—and the overall structures are designed to embody a clarity, balance, and logic new to composition. This was truly intended as a "universally understandable" language of sound, and it is partly because of this quasi-scientific clarity that many still point to the music of the Classical era as the most straightforward pathway into understanding the musical logic of the European tradition.

An automaton of a mandolin player, built by P. Gaultier (eighteenth century).

— MANY VOICES —

Masters—and Non-Masters

Part 4 of this book focuses exclusively on the works of three "master" composers—Haydn, Mozart, and Beethoven. Indeed, these musicians' compositions have been understood as defining the canon of the "Classical style" even since their own lifetimes. But of course there were many other Europeans at the time whose music was highly valued, though their place in the canon was not enshrined by subsequent generations. We will here consider two musicians whom Haydn and Mozart recognized as worthy peers, but who have been excluded from the music canon at least to some extent because of their identity and social role.

Joseph Boulogne (Bologne), Chevalier de Saint-Georges (1745–1799), was a champion fencer as well as violinist, composer, and conductor. A native of the French Caribbean colony of Guadeloupe and illegitimate son of a French plantation owner and his enslaved Senegalese servant Nanon, Saint-Georges was educated in France, where he obtained his earliest musical training. He began his career as a violin soloist, performing with the newly formed Concert des Amateurs in his early twenties; shortly thereafter, he was named the director of this celebrated orchestra. He was further recognized by his nomination in 1776 as the director of the Paris Opéra; unfortunately, this appointment was blocked by several influential prima donnas who petitioned the Queen, writing that they found it degrading to have to "submit to the orders of a mulatto." He was then named the director of a private opera theater belonging to Madame de Montesson, wife of the Duke d'Orléans, at which he presented several of his own operas. He eventually founded another orchestra in Paris that achieved great success: Le Concert de la Loge olympique. As director of his ensemble, he commissioned and conducted the premiere of Joseph Haydn's six *Paris* Symphonies (nos. 82–87 of 1785–86, see p. 187).

In addition to operas, Saint-Georges wrote a number of string quartets, violin concertos and sonatas, several symphonies, and vocal music. Wolfgang Amadeus Mozart almost certainly heard him perform when visiting Paris at age 22, and one of the violin works Mozart wrote soon thereafter seems to draw on a distinct virtuosic sequence pioneered by Saint-George, in which the violin climbs to its highest register and then dives to the lowest.

On top of his successes as a performer, composer, and conductor, Saint-Georges had a distinguished military career, serving as colonel of a specially formed regiment of people of color in the 1790s, and standing as France's premier fencer; future US President John Adams, then ambassador to Paris, referred to him as "the most accomplished man in Europe in horse-riding, shooting, fencing, dancing and music." How could so fascinating and talented an individual have been excluded from our histories? Try listening to his three-movement Symphony No. 1 in G Major, Op. 11, or one of his string quartets, and

The composer and champion fencer Joseph Boulogne, Chevalier de Saint-Georges; engraving by American artist **Mather Brown** (1761–1831).

consider what similarities and differences you can hear between his approach and Haydn's or Mozart's.

Another extraordinary biracial musician, George Bridgetower (1778–1860), was recognized in his day as a superb violinist who performed alongside Haydn in the London Salomon concerts; Beethoven wrote a highly virtuosic violin sonata specifically to display Bridgetower's talents alongside his own, and they performed the work to great acclaim. Beethoven even initially dedicated the sonata to Bridgetower, but then changed the dedication to the more famous violinist Rodolphe Kreutzer (the work is now known as the *Kreutzer* Sonata), even though Kreutzer thought it was too difficult to play and never performed it. Does the absence of Boulogne's works from the Classical canon and the omission of any recognition of Bridgetower's musical talents reflect insufficient quality, or might there be other reasons for their noninclusion?

Even geographically closer to the "Classical Masters," we can consider Marianne Martinez (also Marianne von Martinez, 1744–1812), an Austrian composer of Spanish descent who made her way as a single woman in the music world, both as a performer and a composer. Martinez was born into a family well connected with the imperial court, and as such, she was favored by the Empress Maria Theresa, for whom she performed frequently. Martinez's musical training was overseen by none other than Pietro Metastasio, the imperial poet and foremost librettist in Europe, who shared lodgings not only with the Martinez family but also with the young Haydn, who lived in the attic apartment and was Marianne's first voice and keyboard teacher. One of her early compositions, a Mass setting, was performed at the imperial Church of St. Michael on the feast day for the Archangel Michael, to the amazement of "all those who understand the art." Martinez's reputation as a composer extended internationally, and in 1773 she was elected unanimously to the Accademia Filarmonica in Bologna, the first woman to hold this honor since the founding of the esteemed music institution in 1666. Members of the academy lavished praise on her large-scale motet *Dixit Dominus*, written for the organization: they noted in admiration its "beauty, ingenuity, nobility of expression, and astonishing correctness."

Martinez maintained a more private presence than her male colleagues, premiering most of her compositions in the various salons of Vienna—including the one she hosted—rather than in a more public sphere. In the 1790s she established a concert series that attracted Vienna's leading musicians and composers, Haydn and Mozart among them. She also maintained a vocal studio where she trained some excellent singers. Martinez's output of compositions is extensive, including oratorios, Masses, and motets as well as works for solo voice, solo keyboard, and orchestra. The same questions arise: how can a composer, so admired in her day, have been erased from historical record until recently? Was it because the incomparable compositions of towering giants Haydn, Mozart, and Beethoven are more worthy of inclusion in the canon? Or was it because she was a woman, and did not have the public visibility and reputation-building fan base in following generations that the three canonic "Classical Masters" had? You can be the judge, after listening to her inspired Concerto for Cembalo (harpsichord) in G Major (or another of her compositions).

Many Voices Expanded
• Joseph Boulogne, String Quartet, Op. 14, No. 1 in D Major
• Marianne Martinez, Concerto for Cembalo in G major
• Marianne Martinez, Sonata for Cembalo in A Major, Adagio

Austrian composer and singer Marianne Martinez, painted by **Anton von Maron** (1733–1808).

George Gershwin (1898–1937)

Gershwin grew up in Manhattan, where he worked for a Tin Pan Alley publisher, playing and singing new releases for customers. "This is American music," he told one of his teachers. "This is the kind of music I want to write." He had his first big hit in 1920, with the song *Swanee*, recorded by Al Jolson.

During the 1920s, Gershwin won international acclaim with *Rhapsody in Blue*, premiered in 1924 by the Paul Whiteman Orchestra. This was followed by his *Concerto in F* and the tone poem *An American in Paris*. He also had a string of hit musicals, beginning with *Lady, Be Good* (1924), his first collaboration with his brother Ira, who wrote many of his song lyrics. Gershwin wrote enduring film scores, including *Shall We Dance* (featuring the song *They Can't Take That Away from Me*), starring Fred Astaire and Ginger Rogers. His folk opera *Porgy and Bess* is perhaps his masterpiece. He died of a brain tumor in 1937, at not quite thirty-nine.

In his music, Gershwin achieves an appealing rhythmic vitality through the use of syncopation, blue notes, and an "oom-pah" accompaniment typical of jazz piano style. His harmonic language extends from diatonic to very chromatic, with sudden shifts in tonality. His melodies range from declamatory to highly lyrical, and his forms are typical blues and song structures. No master has achieved this union of styles—popular and classical, vernacular and art—more successfully than Gershwin.

MAJOR WORKS: Orchestral works, including *Rhapsody in Blue* (1924, for piano and jazz band), *Concerto in F* (1925), and *An American in Paris* (1928) • Piano music • More than 30 stage works, including *Strike Up the Band* (1927), *Girl Crazy* (1930), *Of Thee I Sing* (1931), and *Porgy and Bess* (1935) • Songs for films, including *Shall We Dance* (1937) • Other songs (such as *Swanee*, *'S Wonderful*, *Embraceable You*, *The Man I Love*).

■ **Composer biographies** are set off from the text's narrative for quick reference, along with a list of each composer's major works by genre.

■ **Music in Words**, at the end of each part, provide a chance to write about a new work in a style you have just studied.

■ A **Style Summary** lists composers and describes elements of the important works written during that era.

Music in Words

Reviewing Modernist Style

The examples of early twentieth-century music featured in Part 6 provide a frame of reference for other modernist-era compositions you may encounter beyond your course. Here are some suggestions for things to listen for when you hear an unfamiliar work from this period.

MELODY: How many important melodic ideas can you identify? Are they lyrical and singable, or wide-ranging with leaps? What expressive elements do you hear in the melodic lines?

RHYTHM/METER: Is the meter clear throughout? Do you perceive elements that might be associated with dance? How does the composer maintain the energy throughout the work?

HARMONY: In this era, tonality is often clouded by chromaticism and dissonance, but there is often a strong sense of a tonal center, or home base. Listen for moments that are more dissonant and unstable; what expressive purpose might they serve?

TEXTURE: How do the various instruments work together? Is the texture more vertical (homophonic), or does it feature independent lines (polyphonic)? Does the texture change as the work progresses, and if so, how?

FORM: Most compositions are built on the basic formal principles of repetition, contrast, and variation. What is the role of repetition in the work? of contrast (that is, new music)? What holds the selection together, or helps it make sense to the listener?

PERFORMING FORCES AND TIMBRE: Some modernist-era works require an orchestra with new instruments and timbres; unlike in earlier periods, the string section may not always be the center of the ensemble. What timbres strike you as new or unusual? Do you hear a blend of instrumental colors, or do individual tone colors stand out?

Listen and Respond

Let's see how you well you can apply what you have learned to a new musical example. Be sure to consult the listening suggestions above and also the style summary chart. Compare this new work with other symphonic works we have heard from the modernist era.

Revueltas, *Homage to Federico García Lorca*, III (*Son*)

1. Create a simple listening outline for the piece. Think about melody, rhythm and meter, levels of dissonance, texture, performing forces, and form. Do you hear repeated sections? What modernist elements do you hear in this work?

2. How might you describe this work to a friend who is not in the class and not familiar with

the terminology we've been developing? What general descriptions can you apply to the melody? rhythm? harmony? texture? overall effect of the piece?

3. Write a short paragraph describing the work as you might for a concert report assignment. Here you can demonstrate your understanding of the terms and concepts you have learned as well as your response to the piece's expressive qualities. Refer back to Chapter 14 for ways to frame your perspective.

Style Summary for Modernist-Era Music (c. 1900–1940)

Composers	Schoenberg, Stravinsky, Boulanger, Berg, Holiday, Ellington, Still, Gershwin, Ives, Copland, Revueltas, Bartók
Melody	Melodies conceived instrumentally; disjunct, wide-ranging lines; elements from folk and traditional music
Rhythm/meter	Changing meter, polyrhythms, much syncopation; influence of jazz styles
Harmony	Atonality, polychords and polyharmony; use of tone rows (serialism); extremes in dissonance
Texture	Contrapuntal; linear movement
Vocal genres	Motet, opera, solo song with chamber ensemble
Instrumental genres	Neo-Classical genres (symphony, concerto, suite); ballet suites; film music; jazz band and wind band music
Form	Succinct, tight forms; revival of older forms
Dynamics	Wide-ranging dynamics for expressive purposes
Timbre	Bright, lean sound; winds and percussion favored; quickly shifting instrumental colors
Performing forces	Smaller orchestra, including piano; diverse percussion instruments; unusual combinations of instruments
Virtuosity	New challenges for vocalists and instrumentalists
Expression	Dramatic and emotional, often with high energy

In Their Own Words

66 Music is a science that would have us laugh and sing and dance."

—Guillaume de Machaut

- **In Their Own Words** offer relevant quotes throughout from composers and important historical figures.

At the end of each chapter:

- **Critical Thinking** questions raise issues for further study.
- **Your Turn to Explore** boxes offer suggestions for independent investigation of the issues raised in that chapter, whether within or beyond the confines of the course.

CRITICAL THINKING

1. Why was the piano considered such an important domestic instrument?
2. What difficulties did a woman composer face in this era? What other important roles did women play in music, and why?

Your Turn TO EXPLORE

In contemporary society, are certain musical styles, genres, and/or instruments associated more with women than with men, or vice versa? If so, why? How do different ideals of gender in your community play out in the way music is performed, created, or supported?

- **Timelines** that open each part provide a chronological orientation for composers as well as world events and principal literary and historical figures.
- **Learning Objectives** serve to guide listening and study for each period.

PART 4

Eighteenth-Century Classicism

"In truth, there is nothing like music to fill the moment with substance, whether it attune the quiet mind to reverence and worship, or whether it make the mobile senses dance in exultation."

—German poet Johann Wolfgang von Goethe (1749–1832)

Learning Objectives

By the end of Part 4, you will be able to

- recognize that the music has balanced melodic lines and phrases, accompanied by diatonic harmonies in major and minor.
- distinguish the regular rhythmic movement and clear duple or triple meters.
- perceive how the vertical, homophonic texture helps you focus on the melody.
- follow the unfolding of medium- and large-scale forms built around one or two main themes.
- Identify some of the main vocal and instrumental genres and forms in the Classical era, as you become familiar with the most renowned composers of the period.

OVERVIEW

1715
Louis XIV dies; reign of Louis XV begins.

1732
George Washington born.

1751
Benjamin Franklin's experiments with electricity published.

1771
First edition of *Encyclopaedia Britannica*.

1775
American Revolutionary War begins.

1785
Friedrich von Schiller writes "Ode to Joy."

1789
French Revolution begins.

1804
Napoleon crowned emperor of France.

| 1700 | 1710 | 1720 | 1730 | 1740 | 1750 | 1760 | 1770 | 1780 | 1790 | 1800 | 1810 |

1732
Joseph Haydn born.

1741
Antonio Vivaldi dies.

1763
Child prodigy W. A. Mozart tours Europe.

1781
Haydn writes string quartets Op. 33.

1791
Mozart dies, leaving his *Requiem* incomplete.

1801
Ludwig van Beethoven writes his *Moonlight* Sonata.

About the Listening Guides

Listening is at the heart of *The Enjoyment of Music*, and the Listening Guides (LGs) are the book's essential feature; follow along with them as you listen to the recordings. These guides will enhance your knowledge and appreciation of each piece.

1. The composer, title, duration, and other information about the selection are at the top of each guide.

2. The What to Listen For box focuses your listening by drawing your attention to each musical element.

3. The body of the guide includes timed moment-by-moment descriptions that lead you through the selection, often with short musical examples as visual cues. Texts and translations are given for all vocal works.

4. Certain LGs feature an alternative performance of the work—Another Hearing—for comparison.

1

LISTENING GUIDE 17   🔊 7:24

Bach: Orchestral Suite No. 3, Air and Gigue

2

Date: 1731	**Performed by:** Freiburger Barockorchester
Genre: Dance suite for orchestra	**Movements:** Overture Bourrée
	Air **Gigue**
	Gavotte I and II

Gigue   2:47

What to Listen For

3

Rhythm/ Meter	Fast-paced compound (6/8) meter that feels like a propelling duple pattern.	**Texture**	Largely homophonic, with counterpoint created by the basso continuo line.
Harmony	Bright D major; moves to the dominant key (A major), then returns to the tonic; highly consonant.	**Performing Forces**	Festive sound with oboes, trumpets, and timpani added to the strings; alternation of ideas between strings and winds (with percussion).

0:00   **A section:** vigorous dance with continuous motion as the strings and oboes exchange musical phrases with the trumpets.

4

0:27   **A section** repeated.
0:53   **B section:** longer, with some development of musical ideas as the music modulates (returns) to the tonic key.
1:46   **B section** repeated.

Opening of the violin and trumpet melody, played in octaves:

🔊 **AnotherHearing** Now that you have heard this dance performed by a small orchestra using "historically informed" instruments and techniques, listen to an arrangement for digital synthesizer by Herbert Waltl, a composer and producer active in the commercial music industry. How does the digital medium create contrast in ways different from the original "analog" ensemble version? Which do you prefer, and why?

Online listening tools take advantage of the power of technology to blend word and sound together in a rich listening experience. For example:

■ The **What to Listen For** section becomes a **Listen For** tutorial that provides a video walk-through, highlighting the use of musical materials in the selection.

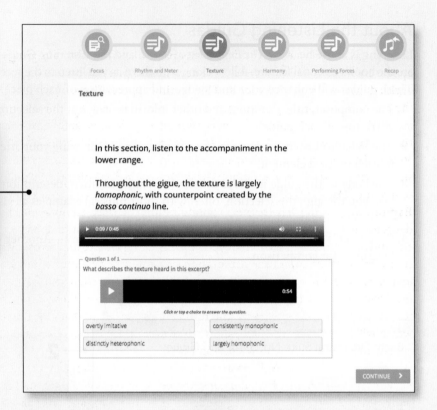

■ The **interactive Listening Guide** (iLG) combines an easy-to-navigate diagram of the form with descriptions and examples that appear in real time as the music plays. The design allows you to interact with the music on computer, phone, or tablet.

■ **Chapter activities** powered by Norton's adaptive InQuizitive engine reinforce learning and develop listening skills with proven results in a fun, gamelike environment. Rich feedback—often with audio examples—helps students improve performance.

FOR INSTRUCTORS: WHAT'S NEW

Students may well question how and why particular musical works are chosen to appear in *The Enjoyment of Music*. This new edition presents an innovative chapter entitled "Many Voices: Creating and Recreating Musical Canons," which considers the notion of canons, how they are formed, and how they are constantly expanding. This discussion raises the timely issue of populations largely excluded from the existing classical music canon and sets up a series of features entitled **Many Voices** that considers, in each historical era, individuals and traditions that are outside the traditional Western canon. These "voices" include historically underrepresented musicians as well as global and popular music traditions. The **Your Turn to Explore** feature in each chapter, continuing from earlier editions, prompts students to think about the music just studied and sends them out to discover repertories and performance traditions beyond the Listening Guides and across all musical styles. In an effort to aid the exploration of contemporary music, our **Postlude** invites readers to the **Online Gallery of New Voices**, where we feature young musicians who may not yet be a part of an established canon but whose voices represent the present—and perhaps the future. This cutting-edge online component, which will be regularly updated, allows us to sample the works of diverse composers and to keep pace with new developments.

Recognizing that for students in introductory classes, writing about music is difficult, even daunting, we introduced, in the previous edition, a pedagogical framework designed to help beginning students learn to write (and talk) about music from a variety of perspectives. The chapter "Putting Music into Words" provides a systematic introduction to our writing pedagogy, with clear suggestions and guidelines that are concrete but not too prescriptive. At the end of each historical part, a **Music in Words** exercise (in the textbook and also online) reviews stylistic traits of music from that era and asks students to describe a different work similar to those they have heard. "Reporting on the Concert Experience," in Appendix III, prepares students for what they will encounter at a classical music concert, and offers a sample student-written concert report, along with possible criteria for evaluation.

The Enjoyment of Music continues to expand its treatment of the most critical musical act: listening. The Prelude for Part 1 newly considers how the brain hears and processes music, with a goal of guiding students toward active listening. Throughout the book, the feature **Performance Matters** directs students to the "big questions" surrounding performance in each historical period. To help students appreciate the important role played by performers, selected Listening Guides in each historical period provide **Another Hearing**—an alternate recording that encourages students to reflect on the expressive effect of a different interpretation of the same work by a different artist.

As always, we have enhanced the featured repertory with new, highly teachable selections that expand and diversify the book's musical landscape. Highlights include the catchy troubadour dance-song *Kalenda maya*; two movements from Bach's Orchestral Suite No. 3 (including the famous Air), and the ever-popular Bach G-minor "Little" Organ Fugue; several scenes from Mozart's comic opera *The Marriage of Figaro*; the dramatic *Revolutionary* Étude by Chopin; the lovely fourth movement from Brahms's *Requiem*; the first movement of the highly melodic *American* String Quartet by Dvořák; a martial-arts fantasy film score selection by Tan Dun; and a movement from a syncretic-style ballet by the Cuban-American composer Tania León.

We have also continued the popular **Interface** boxes, which provide interdisciplinary discussions of music in connection with various fields that make up most general studies or liberal arts curricula—among them science, philosophy, technology, history, religious studies, art, literature, gender studies, and Black studies. The Interfaces are designed to help students integrate their academic work, while responding to a broad pedagogical push toward cultural diversity and creating world citizens.

MEDIA RESOURCES: TOTAL ACCESS

Thanks to **Total Access**, students and teachers can take full advantage of all the book's superb online offerings—audio, video, and assessment content—in a flexible format that's easily integrated with campus learning systems. Look for the unique registration code printed on a card in the book, and register at digital .wwnorton.com/enjmusic14.

Total Access includes a full-featured ebook that is accessible across devices. Music, videos, and interactive Listening Guides (iLGs) are integrated into the text for an immersive listening and learning experience. New to the 14th edition's ebook are *engagement activities* for 25 of the most popular selections. These "pre-listening" exercises build confidence by asking low-stakes questions after students listen to the selection, or a portion of the selection.

A "Materials of Music Tutorial" is assignable for each chapter in Part I. These tutorials combine narrated videos and engagement questions that can be assigned at the beginning of the course and remain available throughout the term for review.

As students encounter featured pieces, they follow a standard online learning pathway. Revised "What to Listen For" tutorials can now be assigned, allowing instructors to confirm that students are prepared for listening. A link to the selection's interactive Listening Guide (iLG) is included at the end of each tutorial.

Every chapter is accompanied by an InQuizitive activity that helps students master historical context and practice their listening skills. These activities offer students a popular and proven approach to further understanding with gamelike questions that include helpful feedback and links to specific ebook content.

Norton Teaching Tools

The Norton Teaching Tools site for *The Enjoyment of Music* 14th edition is your first stop when looking for creative and engaging resources to refresh your syllabus or design a new one. The site also includes Learning Management System course cartridges and prebuilt Norton Test Maker practice quizzes and exams, as well as tips and best practices for assigning Norton's digital learning tools and addressing the most common course challenges.

In addition to chapter outlines, suggested lecture and discussion topics, the Norton Teaching Tools site includes:

- A checklist of learning objectives addressed in the tutorials and InQuizitive activities

- Additional student assignments suitable for individual and group work. Assignments are developed using the Transparency in Learning and Teaching (TILT) framework that outlines the purpose, task, and criteria for success so that students understand the expectations and see how the assignment contributes to learning.

- Image files for the art, photos, and charts from the text, provided in JPEG and PowerPoint formats

- PowerPoint presentations combining text graphics and bulleted outlines for each chapter
- Music Example Bank: 130 additional audio examples indexed by era, composer, musical element, and title
- Model answers for to the Performance Matters and Music in Words assignments, accompanied by a grading rubric
- Model responses to the Your Turn to Explore research prompts at the end of each chapter

Test Bank

Norton Testmaker brings Norton's high-quality testing materials online. Create assessments for your course from anywhere with an Internet connection, without downloading files or installing specialized software. Search and filter test bank questions by chapter, type, difficulty, learning objectives, and other criteria. You can also customize test bank questions to fit your course. Easily export your tests or Norton's ready-to-use quizzes to Microsoft Word or Common Cartridge files for your Learning Management System.

As a new feature, Norton Testmaker now includes questions with embedded music. These questions can be selected to create cross-chapter or "drop the needle" exams, and any excerpt can be added to newly created questions.

ACKNOWLEDGEMENTS

Any project of this size is dependent on the expertise and assistance of many individuals to make it a success. First, we wish to acknowledge the many loyal users of *The Enjoyment of Music* who over many years and editions have taken the time to comment on the text and ancillary package. Their suggestions help us shape each new edition. In particular, we wish to thank those instructors who provided invaluable feedback for this 14th edition: Sandy Abel (Cisco College), Amanda Castellone (College of Charleston), Richard Cavallo (Trident Technical College), Trey Demmond (Moorpark College), Bradley Franklin (Chaffey College), Nicholas Holland (Charleston Southern University), Stephen Kunzer (Auburn University), Daniel McCarthy (University of Akron School of Music), Matthew Parker (Trident Technical College), Paul Sherman (Glendale Community College), Louis Shirer (Midlands Technical College), and Estefania Wilcox (Jacksonville State University)

We also greatly appreciate the creativity and insights of the 14th edition's digital media authors and focus group participants, including Mohamed Belal (Gwinnett Technical College), Sherri Bishop (Indiana University), Erin Walker Bliss (University of Kentucky), Joshua Busman (University of North Carolina, Pembroke), Alicia Doyle (California State University, Long Beach), Sarah Fuchs (Syracuse University), Pamela Haynes (Manchester University), Melissa Lesbines (Appalachian State University), Rebecca Marchand (Boston Conservatory at Berklee), Linell Gray Moss (Blue Ridge Community College), and RaSheeda Waddell (Pitt Community College). Thanks also to Tom Laskey of the Sony BMG Custom Marketing Group for licensing the recordings. Our spouses, William Prizer (professor emeritus, University of California, Santa Barbara) and Felicia Miyakawa, assisted in more ways than can possibly be named.

This new edition could not have been realized without the very capable assistance of the entire Norton team. We owe a profound thanks to our music editor Chris Freitag, for his inspired and sure-handed guidance; to our production team, including Jodi Beder, for her meticulous copyediting, Debra Nichols, for her eagle-eyed proofreading, and Michael Fauver, for overseeing so ably all aspects of its production; to Steve Hoge, Ellie Shirocky, and Meg Wilhoite, for creating and coordinating our stellar digital media package; to Lissi Sigillo, for her stunning design; to Julie Kocsis, for her help with myriad editorial details; to Mike Cullen, for his invaluable assistance with selecting and licensing the illustrations; to Jane Searle, for handling the production of the *Enjoyment of Music* package; to Trevor Penland, for his insightful marketing strategies; to Heather Dubnick, for her index; and to Patricia Wong, for her management of permissions.

We wish finally to express our deep appreciation to four former music editors at Norton—Maribeth Payne, Michael Ochs, Claire Brook, and David Hamilton— who over the years have guided and inspired *The Enjoyment of Music* to its continued success.

Kristine Forney
Andrew Dell'Antonio

FOURTEENTH EDITION

The Enjoyment of Music

Materials of Music

"Musical training is a more potent instrument than any other, because rhythm and harmony find their way into the secret places of the soul."

—Ancient Greek philosopher Plato (c. 428–c. 347 BCE)

OVERVIEW

Middle Ages

- Melodies preserved through notation.
- Harmony developed.
- Rhythmic concepts introduced.

Renaissance

- Metric schemes developed.
- Textures grow more complex, based on imitation.
- Increased emphasis on text expression.

Baroque

- New multimovement genres developed.
- Most orchestra-family instruments developed.
- Expression markings introduced.

400-1450   1450-1600   1600-1750

Learning Objectives

By the end of Part 1, you will be able to

- hear how melodies have varied shapes and how they move in time through rhythm and meter.

- grasp some of the basic precepts of Western harmony and hear how harmony adds depth to the music.

- perceive how different lines can interact to form varied musical textures.

- recognize how simple shapes, or forms, in a piece are created through repetition and contrasting ideas.

- appreciate how changing the tempo and the dynamics (loudness and softness) in music lends expression to a work.

- distinguish the unique sound, or timbre, of each instrument or voice, and learn how voices and instruments are combined in various music ensembles.

- understand how musicians combine these elements in different ways to make one musical work sound different from another.

- consider the concept of canon in musical repertories, how it has developed through time as well as your potential role in its future evolution.

- develop confidence in writing about music as you are introduced to new repertories of music.

Classical

- Balanced melodic phrases accompanied by major or minor harmonies.

- Standardization of forms and genres.

- Pianoforte becomes favored keyboard instrument.

Romantic

- Increased levels of chromaticism and dissonance.

- Expanded concepts of tonality.

- Broadening of formal structures.

Twentieth Century and Beyond

- Revolutionary concepts in harmony and rhythm introduced.

- Experiments in free forms and procedures.

- Technology and global music concepts explored.

1750-1825   1820-1900   1900-

1

The Enjoyment of Music

"Music, in truth, is the mediator between intellectual and sensuous life."

—Ludwig van Beethoven

"You can't mess with people's heads, that's for sure. But that's what music's all about, messing with people's heads."

—Jimi Hendrix

Human beings are wired for the enjoyment of music. Musician-neuroscientist Daniel Levitin asserts that "music is a kind of fuel for the brain," noting that extensive research has demonstrated how music activates nearly every area of the brain. Our brains cause our bodies to respond to rhythm automatically, whether we think we can dance or not. Other aspects of music, like tempo, volume, and tone color, provoke similar involuntary responses.

The influence music can exert on our brain makes it one of the most effective ways to alter our mental state. Listening to a melancholy song can put you in a sad mood, or it can boost your mood, if you feel an affinity with the emotion being conveyed. Levitin explains that music with an upbeat tempo can energize you as "the neurons [in your brain] fire in synchrony to the beat of the music."

Music, like language, creates meaning through predictable patterns; finding and recognizing these familiar patterns contributes to our enjoyment. And just like language, music is a social activity: the ability to sing, dance, move together has increased the connections between humans across time and cultures. Our brains have helped us flourish as a species in part because of our penchant to come together through collective song and other kinds of music-making.

We have a spontaneous response to music on first hearing based largely on the disparate ways in which our brains are "wired" as well as our unique social and cultural backgrounds. But a deeper and richer response is possible when we learn to listen actively to music.

Listening to Music

It takes practice to become an informed listener. We often "listen" to music while performing another activity—perhaps studying, driving, or just relaxing. In these situations, the music tends to stay in the background and get less than our

Listening to music can spark intense emotions, as this image suggests.

full attention. This type of "partial listening" is normal and appealing, but this book aims to help you succeed in your music class by **developing your listening skills**. Why is this necessary you might ask—you probably listen to music all the time. But when we encounter music of an unfamiliar type, or music that's intended to be the center of attention, we need focused listening strategies. Music is a temporal art, meaning that it moves through time. In an art class, you can look at a painting and choose how long to dwell on each element, but music does not hold still. And you will, in this course, listen to works that are much longer than your favorite songs. A symphony, for example, can last more than an hour. How can any music hold our attention for so long? Very easily—as we hope you will discover in the chapters that follow.

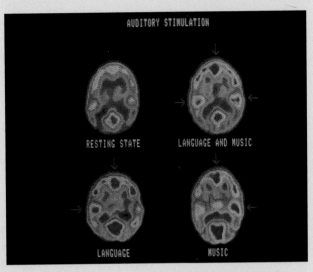

PET scans show the brain's response to auditory stimulations of language and music.

One of the best ways to "study" music is by **repeated listening**. You probably have favorite books, movies, or songs that you like to revisit again and again, and each time you may notice something new, or appreciate even more a moment you have grown to cherish. It's precisely through repeated encounters that we gain both familiarity with and understanding of the touchstones of our culture. And one of the wonders of the present-day world is that we have the opportunity to listen to recorded music almost any time we want. We encourage you to listen repeatedly to the examples this book provides: with this kind of repeated, attentive listening, you will gain skills you can then transfer to new repertories as well as to music you already like.

At the same time, while recordings facilitate repeated listening, it's important to hear music in performance, for nothing can equal the excitement of a live concert. The crowded hall, the visual and aural stimulation of a performance, the audience response, and even the element of unpredictability—what might happen on a particular night—all contribute to the unique communicative powers of people making music. (Be sure to consult Appendix III before you attend a live performance.) At a concert, you will likely hear a work only once, but you can probably find the same composition online and listen again before you try to discuss or write about it. You have undoubtedly heard the expression "practice makes perfect"; this applies to listening as well as to any other activity.

But just hearing the music is not enough; you need to be an **active listener**, rather than a passive one. This means setting aside all distractions and letting the music be the foreground activity, not background. It's also important to develop your **musical memory**. This will initially be easier if you are listening to a song in a language you

The library is a quiet and comfortable place to study music.

understand, especially if there are repeated lyrics. Instrumental music may seem more daunting at first, but you can concentrate on major events, patterns, or memorable moments, and consider if (most likely when!) you hear them return—a principle at the root of Western musical practice as well as other world traditions. Some composers provide a program, or story, to follow in instrumental works: in those cases, you will be able to associate specific musical ideas with elements of that story. If there is no program, you can make up your own if it helps you follow the "plot"—the order of musical events and patterns of repetition and similarity.

Memory will help you develop a **sense of time** while listening. How long is the work? How long from one recognizable event to another? Is there a pattern in the way events return? You might want to **take notes** as you listen, so that you can recall better the sequence and timing of events. As you listen, allow yourself to respond both **objectively** and **subjectively** to the music. You will be applying technical terms to certain aspects of the music, but consider also your personal response, in your own words. When did you have that response, and what musical events triggered it?

Each work studied in the chapters that follow is accompanied by a Listening Guide that outlines **What to Listen For** at the top. You might want to make a similar outline for new works you hear. Be sure to note the **style traits** that help define each composer, era, and type of work discussed in the book; listen for these "markers" when hearing a piece for the first time. We have provided exercises throughout the book that can help you decode a new work's style and formulate your own description and response.

Pianist Beatrice Rana (b. 1993) performs with the Fort Worth Symphony, conducted by Leonard Slatkin, as part of the 2013 Van Cliburn Piano Competition.

Performance Matters

Just as no two compositions are exactly alike, so is each performance of a musical work unique: that is, no two performers or groups will choose exactly the same interpretation. Think of covers of rock songs—you recognize the original song, but you also distinguish aspects of the performance that differ. There are a number of criteria that shape a performer's interpretation—anything from a subtle variation in tempo or dynamics (volume) to changes in the voices or instruments, vastly different ideas of the main lines or melodies, added interpolations between sections, and even the order of sections in a composition.

Throughout the book, we have featured alternate performances of selected works so that you can hear how various musicians reshape the same work; these are noted at the end of the relevant Listening Guides. In some cases, instruments or performance groups may differ significantly from what you heard in the Listening Guide; in other cases, performers have reimagined the original in a dissimilar—and unexpected—musical style. As you learn to discern musical details, take advantage of the varied interpretations we provide, and seek out others; the uniqueness of interpretation, especially in live performance, is at the root of musical expressiveness.

You already enjoy music—that's our starting point. Our goal is to help you expand, deepen, and intensify that great pleasure.

1

Melody: Musical Line

"It is the melody which is the charm of music, and it is that which is most difficult to produce. The invention of a fine melody is a work of genius."

—*Joseph Haydn*

KeyPoints

- A **melody** is a line, or the tune, in music.
- Each melody is unique in **contour** (how it moves up and down) and in **range**, or span of pitches.
- An **interval** is the distance between any two pitches. A melody that moves in small, connected intervals is **conjunct**, while one that moves by leaps is **disjunct**.

- The units that make up a melody are **phrases**; phrases end in resting places called **cadences**.
- A melody may be accompanied by a secondary melody, called a **countermelody**.

We tend to characterize any musical sound as one that has a perceivable and measurable **pitch**, determined by its **frequency** (number of vibrations per second). This pitch depends on the length or size of a vibrating object. For example, a short string vibrates faster (has a higher frequency) than a long string (which has a lower frequency). This is why a violin sounds higher than a cello: its strings are shorter overall. When a musician places a finger on the string of a violin or cello, the vibrating length of the string is shortened, and the pitch/frequency changes accordingly.

In the Western tradition, we represent each pitch with a symbol called a **note** that's placed on a **staff** (five parallel lines; see Appendix I for more on notation). This symbol designates the frequency and the **duration**, or length of time, of the pitch. A pitch also has a certain **volume** (loudness or softness), and a distinct quality known as **tone color**, or **timbre**; this last quality distinguishes voices from instruments, or a trumpet from a clarinet.

Note and staff

A **melody** is a succession of single pitches that we hear as a recognizable whole. We relate to the pitches of a melody in the same way we hear the words of a sentence—not singly but as an entire cohesive thought. We know a good melody when we hear one, and we recognize its power to move us, as do most musical cultures of the world.

Each melody goes up and down in its own distinct way, with one pitch being higher or lower than another; its **range** is the distance between the lowest and highest notes. This span can be very narrow, as in an easy children's song, or very wide, as in some melodies played on an instrument. Although this distance can be measured in the number of notes, we will describe range in approximate

Range

This apartment building in Vejle, Denmark, called *The Wave*, was designed by architect **Henning Larsen** to blend in with the surrounding environment of hills and fjord. Its wavelike shape resembles that heard in many melodies.

Contour terms—narrow, medium, or wide. The **contour** of a melody is its overall shape as it turns upward or downward or remains static. You can visualize a melody in a line graph, resulting in an ascending or descending line, an arch, or a wave (see Melodic Examples below).

Interval The distance between any two pitches is called an **interval**. Melodies that move principally by small intervals in a joined, connected manner (like *Joy to the World*) are called **conjunct**, while those that move in larger, disconnected intervals (like *Ride of the Valkyries*) are described as **disjunct**. A tune's motion need not necessarily remain the same throughout: it may, for example, begin with a small range and conjunct motion and, as it develops, expand its range and become more disjunct.

The Structure of Melody

Phrase The component units of a melody are like parts of a sentence. A **phrase** in music, as in language, is a unit of meaning within a larger structure. The phrase ends in a rest-

Cadence ing place, or **cadence**, which punctuates the music in the same way that a comma or period punctuates a sentence. The cadence may be inconclusive, leaving you

Melodic Examples

Ode to Joy (Beethoven, Symphony No. 9)
Range: narrow (5-note span)
Contour: wavelike
Motion: conjunct

Joy to the World (Christmas carol)
Range: medium (8-note span)
Contour: descending
Motion: conjunct, then a few leaps

Joy to the world, the Lord is come. Let earth

Ride of the Valkyries
  (Wagner, opera *Die Walküre*)
Range: wide (10-note span)
Contour: wavelike
Motion: disjunct (many leaps)

Melodic Phrases and Cadences

Amazing Grace (traditional hymn)
Four text phrases = four musical phrases
Final cadence = end of verse

Phrase 1 (incomplete, turns downward)
A - maz - ing grace, how sweet the sound

Phrase 2 (incomplete, upward inflection and climax)
That saved a wretch like me!

Phrase 3 (incomplete)
I once was lost, but now am found

Phrase 4 (complete, sense of rest)
Was blind, but now I see.

(Note: Our recording elaborates on the original tune.)

with the impression that more is to come, or it may sound final, giving you the sense that the melody has reached the end. The cadence is where a singer or instrumentalist pauses to draw a breath.

If the melody has words, the text lines and the musical phrases will usually coincide. Consider the well-known hymn *Amazing Grace* (above). Its four musical phrases are of equal length, and the **rhyme scheme** of the text (the way the last syllables in each line rhyme) is *a-b-a-b*. The first three cadences (at the end of each of the first three phrases) are inconclusive, or incomplete; notice the upward inflection like a question at the end of phrase 2. Phrase 4, with its final downward motion, provides the answer; it gives you a sense of closure.

In order to maintain the listener's interest, a melody must be shaped carefully, either by the composer or by the performer who invents it on the spot. What makes a striking effect is the **climax**, the high point in a melodic line, which usually represents a peak in intensity as well as in range. Sing through or listen to *Amazing Grace* (music above) and note its climax at the end of the second phrase, when the line reaches its highest point on the text "a wretch like me!"

More complex music can feature several simultaneous melodies. Sometimes the relative importance of one over the other is clear, and the added tune is called a **countermelody** (literally, "against a melody"). You may have heard the high-range countermelody played by the piccolos in the famous *Stars and Stripes Forever* march by John Philip Sousa (Chapter 54). In other styles, each melodic line is of seemingly equal importance. For much of the music we will study, melody is the most basic element of communication between the composer or performer and the listener. It's what we remember, what we whistle and hum.

Rhyme scheme

Climax

Amazing Grace

Countermelody

Stars and Stripes Forever

2

Rhythm and Meter: Musical Time

"I got rhythm, I got music . . ."
—Ira Gershwin (1896–1983)

KeyPoints

- **Rhythm** is what moves music forward in time.
- **Meter,** marked off in **measures** (or **bars**), organizes the **beats** (the basic units) in music.
- Measures often begin with a strong **downbeat**.
- **Simple meters**—duple, triple, and quadruple—are the most common; each beat is divided into two.
- **Compound meters** divide each beat into three rather than two.
- Rhythmic complexities occur with **offbeats, syncopation**, and **polyrhythm**.
- Some music is **nonmetric**, without an identifiable meter or clear beat.

Beat

Music is propelled forward by **rhythm**, the movement of music in time. Each individual note has a length, or duration—some long and some short. The **beat** is the basic unit of rhythm, a regular pulse that divides time into equal segments. Some beats are stronger than others; we perceive these as **accented** beats. In much of Western music, these strong beats occur at regular intervals—every other beat, every third beat, every fourth, and so on—and thus we hear groupings of two, three, or four. These organizing patterns are called **meters** and, in notation, are marked off in **measures** (or **bars**). Each measure contains a fixed number of beats, and the first beat in a measure usually receives the strongest accent. Measures are designated with **measure (bar) lines**, regular vertical lines through the staff (on which the music is notated; see Appendix I).

Meter and measure

Meter organizes the flow of rhythm in music. In Western music, its patterns are simple, paralleling the alternating accents heard in poetry. Consider, for example, this well-known stanza by the American poet Robert Frost. Its meter alternates a strong beat with a weak one (this is iambic meter, da DUM, da DUM, da DUM, da DUM). A metrical reading of the poem will bring out the regular pattern of accented (´) and unaccented (–) syllables:

The woods are love-ly, dark and deep,

But I have prom-is-es to keep,

And miles to go be-fore I sleep,

And miles to go be-fore I sleep.

Metrical Patterns

You will hear the regularly recurring patterns of two, three, or four beats in much of the music we will study. As in poetry, these patterns, or meters, depend on regular accents. The first accented beat of each pattern is known as a **downbeat**, referring to the downward stroke of a conductor's hand (see conducting patterns, p. 51). The most basic pattern, known as **duple meter**, alternates a strong downbeat with a weak beat: ONE two, ONE two; or, if you marched it, LEFT right, LEFT right.

Triple meter, another basic pattern, has three beats to a measure—one strong beat and two weak ones (ONE two three). This meter is traditionally associated with dances such as the waltz and the minuet.

The Gothic arches of this famous long arcade in St. Mark's Square in Venice clearly show duple subdivisions, much like simple meters in music.

Quadruple meter contains four beats to the measure, with a primary accent on the first beat and a secondary accent on the third. Although it is sometimes difficult to distinguish between duple and quadruple meter, quadruple meter usually has a broader feeling.

In **simple meters** (simple duple, simple triple, and simple quadruple), the beat is divided into two (ONE-and, two-and; or ONE-and, two-and, three-and). However, in some patterns, the beat is divided into three; these are known as **compound meters**. The most common compound meter is **sextuple meter** (compound duple), which has six beats to the measure, or two main beats that each divides into three (ONE-and-a, TWO-and-a). Marked by a gently flowing effect, this pattern is often found in lullabies and nursery rhymes:

Lit-tle Boy Blue, come blow your horn, the

sheep's in the mea-dow, the cow's in the corn.

The examples on page 12 illustrate the four basic patterns. Not all pieces begin on a downbeat (beat 1). For example, *Greensleeves*, in sextuple meter, begins with an **upbeat** (beat 6). (Notice that the Frost poem given earlier is in duple meter and begins with an upbeat on "the.")

Like meter in music, basic repeated patterns can be found in nature, such as in this close-up of a spiral leaf pattern.

Rhythmic Complexities

Composers have devised a number of ways to keep the recurrent accent from becoming monotonous. The most common technique is **syncopation**, a deliberate upsetting of the normal pattern of accents. Instead of falling on the strong beat of the measure, the accent is shifted to a weak beat, or **offbeat** (in between the stronger beats). Syncopation is heard in many kinds of music, and is particularly characteristic of the African American dance rhythms out of which jazz developed. The example on page 12 illustrates the technique.

Syncopation is only one technique that throws off the regular patterns. A composition may change meters during its course; certain twentieth-century pieces shift meters nearly every measure. Another technique is the simultaneous use

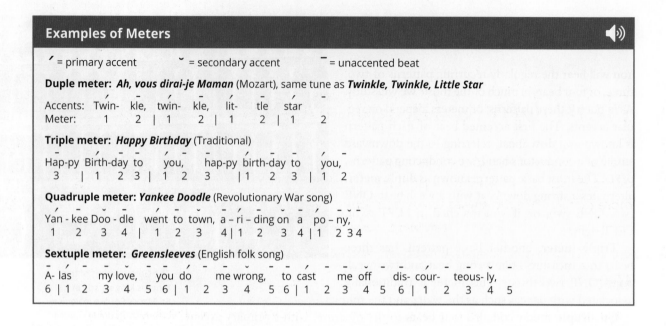

Examples of Meters

ˊ = primary accent   ˘ = secondary accent   ¯ = unaccented beat

Duple meter: *Ah, vous dirai-je Maman* (Mozart), same tune as ***Twinkle, Twinkle, Little Star***

Accents:	Twin-	kle,	twin-	kle,	lit-	tle	star	
Meter:	1	2	1	2	1	2	1	2

Triple meter: *Happy Birthday* (Traditional)

Hap-py Birth-day to you, hap-py birth-day to you,
3 | 1 2 3 | 1 2 3 | 1 2 3 | 1 2

Quadruple meter: *Yankee Doodle* (Revolutionary War song)

Yan - kee Doo - dle went to town, a – ri – ding on a po – ny,
1 2 3 4 | 1 2 3 4 | 1 2 3 4 | 1 2 3 4

Sextuple meter: *Greensleeves* (English folk song)

A- las my love, you do me wrong, to cast me off dis- cour- teous- ly,
6 | 1 2 3 4 5 6 | 1 2 3 4 5 6 | 1 2 3 4 5 6 | 1 2 3 4 5

Syncopation

Swing Low, Sweet Chariot (African American spiritual):
Try singing or speaking this song in time with a regular beat.
(Note that the words in the first measure fall between the beats.)

Swing low,_____ sweet char-   i- ot,___
1   2 | 1   2 |

comin' for to car-ry me home   _____
1   2 | 1   2 |

In Their Own Words

❝ Rhythm and motion, not the element of feeling, are the foundations of musical art."

—Igor Stravinsky

Polyrhythm

Nonmetric

of rhythmic patterns that conflict with the underlying beat, such as "two against three" or "three against four"—in a piano piece, for example, the left hand might play two notes to a beat, while the right hand plays three notes to the same beat. This is called **polyrhythm** ("many rhythms") and characterizes the music of several world cultures, including drum ensembles from Ghana and Uganda (p. 438) and gamelan music of Indonesia (p. 424). Some non-Western cultures create meter through **additive** rhythms, where larger patterns are built from combinations like 2 + 3 + 3 (= 8), rather than recurring patterns of two or three. This is typical of Indian classical music (p. 201).

Some music moves without any strong sense of beat or meter. We might say that such a work is **nonmetric** (this is the case in the chants of the early Christian church): the beat is veiled or weak, with the music moving in a floating rhythm that typifies certain non-Western styles.

Time is a crucial dimension in music. This is the element that binds together the parts within the whole: the notes within the measure and the measure within the phrase. It is therefore the most fundamental element of music.

3

Harmony: Musical Depth

"We have learned to express the more delicate nuances of feeling by penetrating more deeply into the mysteries of harmony."

—Robert Schumann

KeyPoints

- **Harmony** describes the vertical aspects of music: how notes (pitches) sound together.

- A **chord** is the simultaneous sounding of three or more pitches; chords are built from a particular **scale**, or sequence of pitches.

- The most common chord in Western music is a **triad**, three alternate pitches of a scale.

- Most Western music is based on **major** or **minor scales**, from which melody and harmony are derived.

- The **tonic** is the central pitch around which a melody and its harmonies are built; this principle of organization is called **tonality**.

- **Dissonance** is created by an unstable, or discordant, combination of pitches. **Consonance** occurs with a resolution of dissonance, producing a stable or restful sound.

To the linear movement of the melody, harmony adds another dimension: depth. **Harmony** is the simultaneous combination of sounds. It can be compared to the concept of perspective in artworks (see p. 14). Not all musics of the world rely on harmony, but it is central to most Western styles.

Harmony determines the relationships of intervals and chords. Intervals, the distance between any two notes, can occur successively or simultaneously. When three or more notes are sounded together, a **chord** is produced. Harmony describes a piece's chords and the progression from one chord to the next. It is the progression of harmony in a musical work that creates a feeling of order and unity.

Chord

The intervals from which chords and melodies are built are chosen from a particular collection of pitches arranged in ascending or descending order known as a **scale**. To the notes of the scale we assign syllables, *do–re–mi–fa–sol–la–ti–do,* or numbers, 1–2–3–4–5–6–7–8. An interval spanning eight notes is called an **octave**.

Scale
Octave

$$
\begin{array}{cccccccc}
do & re & mi & fa & sol & la & ti & do \\
1 & 2 & 3 & 4 & 5 & 6 & 7 & 8
\end{array}
$$

octave

The most common chord in Western music is known as a **triad**. This particular combination of three pitches may be built on any note of the scale by combining every other note. For example, a triad built on the first pitch of a scale consists of the

Triad

Example of Harmony

Yankee Doodle (Revolutionary War song)

Melody

Yan - kee   Doo - dle   went to town

→ horizontal plane (melody)
↓ vertical plane (harmony)

Harmony (chords)

Scale

do   re   mi   fa   sol   la   ti   do

1   2   3   4   5   6   7   8

first, third, and fifth pitches of that scale *(do–mi–sol);* on the second pitch, steps 2–4–6 *(re–fa–la);* and so on. The triad is a basic formation in most music we know. In the example above, the melody of *Yankee Doodle* is harmonized with triads. You can see at a glance how melody is the horizontal aspect of music, while harmony, comprising blocks of notes (the chords), constitutes the vertical. Melody and harmony do not function independently of one another. On the contrary, the melody suggests the harmony that goes with it, and each constantly influences the other.

The Organization of Harmony

Tonic

In all music, regardless of the style, certain notes assume greater importance than others. In most Western music, the first note of the scale, *do,* is considered the **tonic** and serves as a home base around which the others revolve and to which they ultimately gravitate. We observed this principle at work earlier with

Harmony lends a sense of depth to music, as perspective does in this photograph taken near Bruges, Belgium, of a view down a tree-lined canal.

Just as dissonance provides tension in music, this image of global researchers sunbathing on the edge of a frozen fjord in the Arctic to emphasize the dramatic rate of global warming is discordant to the eye.

Amazing Grace (p. 9): the tune does not reach a final cadence, or stopping point, on the tonic note until its last phrase. It is this sense of a home base that helps us recognize when a piece of music ends.

The principle of organization around a central note, the tonic, is called **tonality**. The scale chosen as the basis of a piece determines the identity of the tonic and the key of the piece. Two different types of scales predominate in Western music written between about 1650 and 1900: major and minor. Each scale has a distinct sound because of its unique combination of intervals, as we will see in Chapter 4.

Tonality

Consonance and Dissonance

The movement of harmony toward resolution is the dynamic force in Western music. As music moves in time, we feel moments of tension and release. The tension results from **dissonance**, a combination of notes that sounds unstable, sometimes harsh, and in need of resolution. Dissonance introduces conflict into music in the same way that suspense creates tension in drama. Dissonance resolves in **consonance**, an agreeable-sounding combination of notes that provides a sense of relaxation and fulfillment. Each complements the other, and each is a necessary part of the artistic whole.

Harmony appeared much later historically (around 900) than melody, and its development took place largely in Western music. In many Asian cultures, harmony is relatively simple, consisting of a single sustained pitch, called a **drone**, against which melodic and rhythmic complexities unfold. This harmonic principle also occurs in some European folk music, where, for example, a bagpipe might play one or more accompanying drones to a lively dance tune.

Our system of harmony has advanced steadily over the past millennium, continually responding to new needs. Composers have tested the rules, changing our notion of what sounds consonant, as they have experimented with innovative sounds and procedures. Yet their goal remains the same: to impose order on sound, organizing the pitches so that we perceive a unified idea.

In Their Own Words

❝ Do you know that our soul is composed of harmony?"

—*Leonardo da Vinci*

Drone

4

The Organization of Musical Sounds

"If only the world could feel the power of harmony."

—Wolfgang Amadeus Mozart

KeyPoints

- An **octave** is the interval spanning eight notes of the scale. In Western music, the octave is divided into twelve **half steps**; two half steps make a **whole step**.

- The **chromatic scale** is made up of all twelve half steps, while a **diatonic scale** consists of seven whole and half steps whose patterns form **major** and **minor scales**.

- A **sharp** (♯) is a symbol that raises a pitch by a half step; a **flat** (♭) lowers a pitch by a half step.

- Other scale types are found around the world, sometimes using **microtones**, which are intervals smaller than half steps.

- The **tonic chord**, built on the first scale note, is the home base to which **active chords** (**dominant** and **subdominant**) need to resolve.

- Composers can shift the pitch level (**key**) of an entire work (**transposition**), or change the key during a work (**modulation**).

Here we consider how melody and harmony, two of the essential building blocks of musical compositions, function together to construct a musical system, both in the West and elsewhere.

Pitches are named using the first seven letters of the alphabet (A through G), which just start over again when you reach an octave. As noted earlier, an **octave** is an interval spanning eight notes of the scale. When we hear any two notes an octave apart, we recognize that they sound "the same." (These two notes take the same pitch name: for example, a C and the C an octave higher.)

Octave

One important variable in the different languages of music around the world is the way the octave is divided. In Western music, it is divided into twelve equal semitones, or **half steps**; from these are built different kinds of scales, which have constituted the basis of this musical language for nearly four hundred years. Some non-Western music features intervals even smaller than half steps, called **microtones**: for example, you can hear "bent," or inflected, pitches in Indian sitar music (p. 201) and microtonal sliding between pitches in Islamic chant (p. 78).

Half step

Microtone

The Chromatic Scale

The twelve half steps that make up the octave constitute what is known as the **chromatic scale**. You can see these twelve half steps on the keyboard (across), counting all the white and black keys from C to the C above it. Virtually all Western music, no matter how intricate, is made up of the same twelve pitches and their duplications in higher and lower octaves.

You will notice that the black keys on the piano are named in relation to their white-key neighbors. The black key between C and D can be called C-sharp (♯) or D-flat (♭), depending on the context of the music. This plan applies to all the black keys. Thus, a **sharp** raises a note by a half step, and a **flat** lowers a note by a half step. The distance between C and D is two half steps, or one **whole step**.

The Major Scale

Chapter 3 introduced the notion that certain notes in music assume greater importance than others; in Western music, the first pitch of the scale, the tonic, is the home base to which the music gravitates. Two main scale types—major and minor—function within this organizational system known as tonality. When you listen to a composition in the **key** of C major, you hear a piece built around the central tone C, using the harmonies formed from the C major scale. Tonality is the basic harmonic principle at work in most Western music written from around 1600 to 1900 and in most popular music still today.

The **major scale** is the most familiar sequence of pitches. You can produce a C major scale (*do–re–mi–fa–sol–la–ti–do*) by playing only the white keys on the piano from one C to the next C. Looking at the keyboard above, you will see that there is no black key between E and F (*mi–fa*) or between B and C (*ti–do*). These notes are a half step apart, while the other white keys are a whole step apart. A major scale is created by a specific pattern of whole (W) and half (H) steps— (W–W–H–W–W–W–H; see chart on p. 19)—and can be built with this pattern starting on any pitch, even a black key.

Within each major scale are certain relationships based on tension and resolution. One of the most important is the thrust of the seventh pitch to the eighth

In Their Own Words

"There are only twelve tones. You must treat them carefully."

—*Paul Hindemith*

Key

(*ti* resolving to *do*). Similarly, we feel resolution when *re* moves to *do; fa* gravitates to *mi;* and *la* descends to *sol.* You can hear some of these relationships at work in the beginning of the well-known carol *Joy to the World.* It starts on the tonic note (*do*) ("Joy"), then descends and pauses on the **dominant** note (*sol*) ("world"), after which it continues downward, feeling a strong pull to the final *do* (on "come"; see melody on p. 8 and chart below).

Dominant

Joy to the World

Tonic			Dominant				Tonic
8	7	6	5	4	3	2	1
do →	*ti*	*la* →	*sol*	*fa* →	*mi*	*re* →	*do*
Joy	to	the	world,	the	Lord	is	come.

The major scale defines two poles of traditional harmony: the tonic, the point of ultimate rest; and the dominant, which is the most important active harmony. Tonic moving to dominant and returning to tonic is a basic progression of harmony in Western music. Songs and pieces in a major key, like this carol, generally sound cheerful or triumphant to our ears (more a cultural convention than an absolute trait).

The Minor Scale

The Art of Fugue

The **minor scale** sounds quite different from the major. One reason is that it has a lowered, or flatted, third note. Therefore, in the scale of C minor, there is an E-flat rather than the E-natural (white-key E) of the major scale; the interval C to E-flat is smaller than the interval C to E. Minor-key pieces sound sadder, darker than those in a major key. In the famous Bach theme to *The Art of Fugue,* you hear the smaller third interval right near the beginning, as the melody outlines a minor chord. The intervals of the minor scale (W–H–W–W–H–W–W) are shown in the table opposite.

Diatonic vs. Chromatic

Music in a major or minor key focuses on the seven notes of the respective scale and is considered **diatonic**. In diatonic music, both the melody and the harmony are firmly rooted in the key. But some compositions introduce other notes that are foreign to the scale, drawing from the full gamut of the twelve half steps that span the octave. These works are considered **chromatic** (from Greek *chroma*, meaning "color"). Romantic-era composers explored the possibilities of chromaticism to charge their music with emotion. In contrast, music of the Baroque and Classical eras is largely diatonic, centering on a tonic note and its related harmonies.

Other Scale Types

Pentatonic scale

The Western musical system is only one way to structure music. The musical languages of other cultures often divide the octave differently, producing different scale patterns. Among the most common is the **pentatonic**, or five-note, **scale**, used in some African, Asian, and Native American musics. (*Amazing Grace,*

Pattern of Major and Minor Scales

One version of a pentatonic scale, as used in *Amazing Grace* (note the gap between the 3rd and 5th scale tone)

on p. 9, is a pentatonic, folklike melody.) Another non-Western scale type is **tritonic**, a three-note pattern also found in the music of some African cultures.

Some scales are not easily playable on Western instruments because they employ intervals smaller than the half step. Such intervals, known as **microtones**, may sound "off-key" to Western ears. One way of producing microtonal music is by an **inflection** of a pitch, making a brief microtonal dip or rise from the original pitch; this technique, similar to that of the "blue note" in jazz (see Chapter 59), makes possible a host of subtle pitch changes.

The musical system and the notes chosen in that system determine the sound and character of each work, whether classical, popular, or traditional. They are what make Western music sound familiar to us and why the music of other cultures may sound foreign.

Sophie Taeuber-Arp (1889–1943), *Composition in Circles and Overlapping Angles* (1930). The overlapping and repeated shapes in this artwork can be compared, in music, to new pitch levels or to modulations to another key.

The Major-Minor System

Tonic (rest) chord (I)

Just as melodies have inherent active and rest notes, the harmonies supporting them have active and rest chords. The three-note chord, or triad, built on the first scale step is called the **tonic**, or **I chord**, and serves as a point of rest. This **rest chord** is counterposed against other chords, which are active. The **active chords** in turn seek to be completed, or resolved, in the rest chord—the dynamic force in Western music, providing a forward direction and goal.

Dominant (active) chord (V)

Subdominant chord (IV)

The fifth scale step (*sol*), the **dominant**, forms the chief active chord (V), which brings a feeling of restlessness and seeks to resolve to the tonic. The triad built on the fourth scale step (*fa*) is known as the **subdominant** (IV). The movement from the subdominant to the tonic (IV to I) is familiar from the "Amen" sung at the close of many hymns.

Rest chord and active chords in C major

These three basic chords are enough to harmonize many simple tunes. The well-known song *Twinkle, Twinkle, Little Star* is a good example:

◀))
Twinkle, Twinkle, Little Star

The Key as a Form-Building Element

The three main chords of a musical work—tonic (I), dominant (V), and subdominant (IV)—are the foundations over which melodies and harmonic progressions unfold. Thus, a piece's key becomes a prime factor for musical unity.

At the same time, contrast between keys adds welcome variety. Composers begin by establishing the home key (for example, C major), then change to a related key, perhaps the dominant (G major), through a process known as **modulation**. In so doing, they create tension, because the dominant key is unstable compared with the tonic. This tension requires resolution, which is provided by the return to the home key.

Modulation

The progression, or movement, from home key to contrasting key and back outlines the basic musical pattern of statement-departure-return. The home key provides unity; the foreign key ensures variety and contrast.

The twelve major and twelve minor keys may be compared to rooms in a house, with the modulations equivalent to corridors leading from one to the other. A composer establishes the home key, then shapes the passage of modulation (the "corridor") into a key area that is not far away from the starting point. Alternately, composers may take an entire work and **transpose** it to a new key (making a transposition). This is convenient when a song's original key is too high or low to sing or play easily. You could begin on a different pitch and shift all the other pitches a uniform distance. In this way, the same song can be sung in various keys by differing voice ranges (soprano, alto, tenor, or bass; see p. 36).

Transposition

Although we are not always conscious of key centers and chord progressions while listening to music, these basic principles are deeply ingrained in our responses. We perceive and react to the tension and resolution provided by the movement of harmony, and we can sense how composers have used the harmonic system to give a coherent shape and meaning to their works.

The windows of this apartment building reflect the idea of transposition, with the same patterns repeating at different heights.

5

Musical Texture

"The composer . . . joins Heaven and Earth with threads of sound."

—Alan Hovhaness (1911–2000)

KeyPoints

- **Texture** refers to the interweaving of the melodic lines with harmony.
- The simplest texture is **monophony**, a single voice or line without accompaniment.
- **Polyphony** describes a many-voiced texture with different melodic lines, based on **counterpoint**—one line set against another.
- **Homophony** occurs when one melodic voice is prominent over the accompanying lines or voices.
- **Imitation**—when a melodic idea is presented in one voice, then restated in another—is a common unifying technique in polyphony; **canons** and **rounds** are two types of strictly imitative works.

Types of Texture

Monophony   Melodic lines may be thought of as the various threads that make up the musical fabric, or the **texture**, of a piece. The simplest texture is **monophony**: a single voice. ("Voice" refers to an individual part or line, even in instrumental music.) Here, the melody is heard without any harmonic accompaniment or other melodic lines; it's you singing in the shower. It may be accompanied by rhythm and percussion instruments that embellish it, but interest is focused on the single melodic line rather than on any harmony. Until about a thousand years ago, the Western music we know about was monophonic, as some music of the Far and Middle East still is today; we will hear an example of monophonic Islamic chant, sung throughout the Muslim world, in the Many Voices feature on page 78.

Heterophony   Another common texture in non-Western cultures is **heterophony**, in which several musicians sing or play the same musical line (as in monophony), but each one varies some element—maybe a pitch or rhythm—so that they're "out of sync" with each other. These are usually subtle, nuanced variations that develop from individual expression. To Western ears, heterophony might sound as though the musicians are having trouble staying together (see the discussion of early American hymn singing in Chapter 27). Jazz (for example, the New Orleans jazz favorite *When the Saints Go Marching In*) and spirituals often depend on heterophonic texture—musicians' individual interpretations result in simultaneous elaborations of the same melody.

🔊
When the Saints Go Marching In

Polyphony   **Polyphony** ("many-voiced") describes a texture in which two or more different melodic lines are combined, thus distributing melodic interest among all the parts.

Examples of Musical Texture

Monophonic: One melodic line, no accompaniment
Gregorian chant: *Kyrie*:

Ky - ri - e_____ e - le - i - son.

Polyphonic: Two independent lines combined
Sousa: *Stars and Stripes Forever* March, Trio

Piccolo countermelody

Main melody

Homophonic: One melody with subordinate accompaniment.
Haydn: Symphony No. 94 *(Surprise)*, II:

Violin 1 — *semplice* — *ten.* — *ten.*
Cello and bass

Homorhythmic: A type of homophonic texture in which all voices move together, with the same words.
Handel: "Hallelujah Chorus," from *Messiah*:

Rhythm			
Soprano	Hal - le - lu-jah,	Hal - le - lu-jah,	Hal-le -	lu - jah,
Alto	Hal - le - lu-jah,	Hal - le - lu-jah,	Hal-le -	lu - jah,
Tenor	Hal - le - lu-jah,	Hal - le - lu-jah,	Hal-le -	lu - jah,
Bass	Hal - le - lu-jah,	Hal - le - lu-jah,	Hal-le -	lu - jah,

Polyphonic texture is based on **counterpoint**: that is, one musical line set against another.

In perhaps the most commonly heard texture, **homophony**, a single voice takes over the melodic interest, while the accompanying lines are subordinate. Normally, the accompanying lines become blocks of harmony, the chords that support, color, and enhance the principal line. Homophonic texture is heard when a pianist plays a melody in the right hand while the left sounds the chords, or when a singer or violinist carries the tune against a harmonic accompaniment on the piano. Homophonic texture, then, is based on harmony, just as polyphonic texture is based on counterpoint. The differences between the two can be subtle, depending

Homophony

As in music, line and texture are the focus of this Kente cloth from Ghana, in Africa.

on whether a listener perceives additional musical lines as equal or subordinate to a primary melody.

Homorhythm

Finally, there is **homorhythm**, a kind of homophony where all the voices or lines move together in the same rhythm. When there is text, all words are clearly sounded together. Like homophony, it is based on harmony moving in synchronization with a melody.

A composition need not use one texture exclusively throughout. For example, a large-scale work may begin by presenting a melody with accompanying chords (homophony), after which the interaction of the parts becomes increasingly complex as more independent melodies enter (creating polyphony).

We have noted that melody is the horizontal aspect of music, while harmony is the vertical. Comparing musical texture to the cross weave of a fabric makes the interplay of the parts clear. The horizontal threads, the melodies, are held together by the vertical threads, the harmonies. Out of their interaction comes a texture that may be light or heavy, coarse or fine.

Contrapuntal Devices

Imitation

When several independent lines are combined (in polyphony), one method that composers use to give unity and shape to the texture is **imitation**, in which a melodic idea is presented in one voice and then restated in another. While the imitating voice restates the melody, the first voice continues with new material. Thus, in addition to the vertical and horizontal threads in musical texture, a third, diagonal line results from imitation (see example opposite).

The duration of the imitation may be brief or it may last the entire work. A strictly imitative work is known as a **canon** (this is a special musical usage of the word); and the simplest and most familiar form of canon is a **round**, in which each voice enters in succession with the same melody that can be repeated endlessly. Well-known examples include *Row, Row, Row Your Boat* and *Frère Jacques* (*Are You Sleeping?*). In the example above, the round begins with one voice singing "Row, row, row your boat," then another voice joins it in imitation, followed by a third voice and finally a fourth, creating a four-part polyphonic texture.

Canon and round

Musical Texture and the Listener

Different textures require different kinds of listening. Monophonic music has only one focus—the single line of melody unfolding in real time. In homophonic music, the primary focus is on the main melody, with subordinate harmonies as accompaniment. Indeed, much of the music we have heard since childhood—including traditional and popular styles—consists of melody and accompanying chords. Homorhythmic texture is easily recognizable as well, in its simple, vertical conception and hymnlike movement; the melody is still the most obvious line. Polyphonic music, with several independent melodies woven together, requires more experienced listening, but a good place to start is the round, the simplest polyphonic texture. With practice, you can hear the roles of individual voices and determine how they relate to each other, providing texture throughout a musical work.

6

Musical Form

"The principal function of form is to advance our understanding. It is the organization of a piece that helps the listener to keep the idea in mind, to follow its development, its growth, its elaboration, its fate."

—Arnold Schoenberg

KeyPoints

- **Form** is the organizing principle in music; its basic elements are repetition, contrast, and variation.

- **Strophic form**, common in songs, features repeated music for each stanza of text. In **through-composed form**, there are no large repeated sections.

- **Binary form (A-B)** and **ternary form (A-B-A)** are basic structures in music.

- A **theme**, a melodic idea in a large-scale work, can be broken into small, component fragments

- (**motives**). A **sequence** results when a motive is repeated at a different pitch.

- Many cultures use **call-and-response** (or **responsorial**) music, a repetitive style involving a soloist and a group. Some music is created spontaneously in performance, through **improvisation**.

- An **ostinato** is the repetition of a short melodic, rhythmic, or harmonic pattern.

- Large-scale compositions, such as symphonies and sonatas, are divided into sections, or **movements**.

Form refers to a work's structure or shape, the way the elements of a composition have been combined by the composer to make it understandable to the listener. In all the arts, a balance is required between unity and variety, symmetry and asymmetry, activity and rest. Nature too has embodied this balance in the forms of plant and animal life and in what is perhaps the supreme achievement—the human form.

Structure and Design in Music

Repetition and contrast

Music of all cultures mirrors life in its basic elements of **repetition** and **contrast**, the familiar and the new. Repetition fixes the material in our minds and satisfies our need for the familiar, while contrast stimulates our interest and feeds our desire for change. Every kind of musical work, from a nursery rhyme to a symphony, has a conscious structure. One of the most common in vocal music, both popular and

Strophic form

classical, is **strophic form**, in which the same melody is repeated with each stanza of the text, as for a folk song (*Greensleeves*) or carol (*Silent Night* or *Jingle Bells*). In this structure, while the music within a stanza offers some contrast, its repetition binds the song together. The direct opposite of strophic form in a song would be

Through-composed

through-composed form, where no main section of the music or text is repeated.

One kind of form that falls *between* repetition and contrast is **variation**, where some aspects of the music are altered but the original is still recognizable. You hear this formal technique when you listen to a new arrangement of a well-known popular song: the tune is recognizable, but many features of the known version are changed.

While all musical structures are based in one way or another on repetition and contrast, the forms are not fixed molds into which composers pour their material. What makes each piece of music unique is the way the composer adapts a general plan to create a wholly individual combination. And performers sometimes participate in shaping a composition. In works based mostly on **improvisation** (pieces created spontaneously in performance—typical of jazz, rock, and certain non-Western styles), repetition, contrast, and variation all play a role. We will see that in jazz, musicians organize their improvised melodies within a pre-established harmonic pattern, time frame, and melodic outline that is understood by all the performers. And in Indian sitar music (see p. 201), improvisation is a refined and classical art, where the seemingly free and rhapsodic spinning out of the music is tied to a prescribed musical process that results in a lacework of variations. Thus, even pieces created on the spot are balanced by structural principles.

This famous painting by **Andy Warhol** (1928–1987), *32 Campbell's Soup Cans*, illustrates the reliance of artists on the basic elements of repetition and variation.

By Andy Warhol: © 2021 The Andy Warhol Foundation for the Visual Arts, Inc. / Artists Rights Society (ARS), New York.

Binary and Ternary Form

Two basic structures are widespread in art and in music. **Binary** (two-part) **form** is based on a statement and a departure, without a return to the opening section. **Ternary** (three-part) **form** extends the idea of statement and departure by bringing back the first section. Formal patterns are generally outlined with letters: binary form as **A-B** and ternary form as **A-B-A** (illustrated in the chart on p. 28).

Both two-part and three-part forms are found in short pieces such as songs and dances. The longer ternary form, with its logical symmetry and its balance of the outer sections against the contrasting middle one, constitutes a clear-cut formation that is favored by architects and painters as well as composers.

In Their Own Words

66 Improvisation is not the expression of accident but rather of the accumulated yearnings, dreams, and wisdom of our very soul."

—*Yehudi Menuhin*

The Building Blocks of Form

When a melodic idea is used as a building block in the construction of a larger work, we call it a **theme**. The introduction of a theme and its elaboration are the essence of musical thinking. This process of growth has its parallel in writing, when an idea, a topic sentence, is stated at the beginning of a paragraph and enlarged upon and developed by the author. Just as each sentence leads logically to the next, every musical idea takes up where the one before left off and continues convincingly to the next. The expansion of a theme, achieved by varying its melody, rhythm, or harmony, is considered **thematic development**. This is one of

Theme

Thematic development

Binary and Ternary Form

Binary form = A-A-B-B: *Greensleeves* (English folk song)

Statement **A** (repeated with varied final cadences):

Departure **B** (with different cadences):

Ternary form = A-B-A: *Simple Gifts* (Shaker hymn)

Statement **A** (repeated):

'Tis the gift to be sim-ple, 'tis the gift to be free, 'Tis the gift to come down where we ought to be, And when we find our-selves__

Departure **B** (ending resembles **A** with new text):

When true sim-pli-ci-ty is gained, To bow and to bend we will not be a-shamed. To turn,__ to__ turn,__ will__ be our de-light,

Repeated statement **A**:

'Tis the gift to be sim-ple, 'tis the gift to be free,

the most important techniques in music and requires both imagination and craft on the part of the creator.

Thematic development is generally too complex a process for short pieces, where a simple contrast between sections and modest expansion of material usually supply the necessary continuity. But it's necessary in larger forms of music, where it provides clarity, coherence, and logic.

Certain procedures help the music flow logically. The simplest is repetition, which may be either exact or varied. Or the idea may be restated at a higher or lower pitch level; this restatement is known as a **sequence**. Within a theme, a small fragment that forms a melodic-rhythmic unit is called a **motive**. Motives are the cells of musical growth, which, when repeated, varied, and combined into new patterns, impart the qualities of evolution and expansion. These building

Sequence and motive

Motive and Sequences

Wagner's famous *Ride of the Valkyries*

(Brackets show repeated **motives** at different pitch levels, or in **sequences**.)

blocks can be heard in the famous *Ride of the Valkyries* by Richard Wagner. The brass instruments announce the five-note motive featuring a dotted rhythmic pattern followed by several longer notes. This is repeated at several different pitch levels in sequence; although the contour of the melody is varied, the motive remains easily recognizable.

Whatever the length or style of a composition, it will show the principles of repetition and contrast, of unity and variety. One formal practice based on repetition and heard throughout the world is **call and response**, or **responsorial music**. In this style of performance, predominant in early Western church music and also in the music of African, Native American, and African American cultures, a singing leader is imitated or answered by a chorus of followers. This is a typical singing style for spirituals and gospel music, as you will hear in a performance of one of the most famous spirituals of all time, *Swing Low, Sweet Chariot* (Chapter 53).

Another widely used procedure linked to the principle of repetition is **ostinato**, the use of a short musical pattern—melodic, rhythmic, or harmonic—that is repeated throughout a work or a major section of a piece. One well-known work that uses this technique is the Pachelbel *Canon in D* (see p. 140), in which rich string lines unfold gradually over an ever-present bass pattern. This unifying technique is especially prevalent in popular styles such as blues, jazz, rock, and rap, which rely on repeated harmonies that provide a scaffolding for musical development.

Music composition is an organic form in which the individual notes are bound together within a phrase, the phrases within a theme, the themes within a section, the sections within a **movement** (a complete, comparatively independent division of a large-scale work), and the movements within the work as a whole (like a symphony)—just as a novel binds together the individual words, phrases, sentences, paragraphs, and chapters into a cohesive whole.

The Gare de Saint-Exupéry, a modern train station in Lyon, France, designed by the Spanish architect **Santiago Calatrava**, shows the importance of symmetrical patterns in architecture.

Movement

7

Musical Expression: Tempo and Dynamics

"Ah, music . . . a magic beyond all we do here!"

—Albus Dumbledore, Headmaster,
Hogwarts School of Witchcraft and Wizardry

KeyPoints

- **Tempo** is the rate of speed, or pace, of the music.
- We use Italian terms to designate musical tempo: some of the most familiar are *allegro* (fast), *moderato* (moderate), *adagio* (quite slow), *accelerando* (speeding up), and *ritardando* (slowing down).

- **Dynamics** describe the volume, or how loud or soft the music is played; Italian terms for dynamics include *forte* (loud) and *piano* (soft).
- Composers indicate tempo and dynamics as a means of expression.

The Pace of Music

Most Western music has steady beats underlying the movement; whether these occur slowly or rapidly determines the **tempo**, or rate of speed, of the music. Consequently, the flow of music in time involves meter patterns (the grouping and emphasis of the beats) and tempo.

Tempo also carries emotional implications. We hurry our speech in moments of agitation or eagerness. Vigor and gaiety are associated with a brisk speed, just as despair usually demands a slow one. Since music moves in time, its pace is of prime importance, drawing from listeners responses that are both physical and psychological.

Because of the close connection between tempo and mood, tempo markings indicate the character of the music as well as the pace. The markings, along with other indications of expression, are traditionally given in Italian. This practice reflects the domination of Italian music in Europe from around 1600 to 1750, when performance directions were established. Here are some of the most common **Tempo markings** **tempo markings**:

grave: solemn (very, very slow)   *moderato*: moderate
largo: broad (very slow)   *allegro*: fast (cheerful)
adagio: quite slow   *vivace*: lively
andante: a walking pace   *presto*: very fast

You frequently encounter modifiers such as *molto* (very), *meno* (less), *poco* (a little), and *non troppo* (not too much). Also important are terms indicating a change

Speed and movement are easily perceived in this photograph of the 2002 Tour de France. Here, the cyclists are racing toward the finish on Paris's famous Avenue des Champs-Élysées.

of tempo, among them *accelerando* (getting faster), *ritardando* (holding back, getting slower), and *a tempo* (in time, or returning to the original pace).

Loudness and Softness

Dynamics denote the volume (degree of loudness or softness) at which music is played. Like tempo, dynamics can affect our emotional response. The main dynamic indications, listed below, are based on the Italian words for soft *(piano)* and loud *(forte)*.

pianissimo (***pp***): very soft	*mezzo forte* (***mf***): moderately loud
piano (***p***): soft	*forte* (***f***): loud
mezzo piano (***mp***): moderately soft	*fortissimo* (***ff***): very loud

Directions to change the dynamics, either suddenly or gradually, are also indicated by words or signs:

crescendo (<): growing louder
decrescendo or *diminuendo* (>): growing softer

Tempo and Dynamics as Elements of Expression

The composer adds markings for tempo and dynamics to help shape the expressive content of a work. These expression marks increased in number during the late eighteenth and nineteenth centuries, when composers tried to make their

In Their Own Words

" Any composition must necessarily possess its unique tempo. . . . A piece of mine can survive almost anything but a wrong or uncertain tempo."

—*Igor Stravinsky*

Tempo and Dynamics in a Music Score

Beethoven: **Symphony No. 5**, opening:
Tempo: Fast (*allegro*), with vigor (*con brio*)

Dynamics: Very loud (*fortissimo*), then soft (*piano*)

intentions known ever more precisely; by the early twentieth century, few decisions were left to the performer at all.

If tempo and dynamics are the domain of the composer, what is the role of performers and conductors in interpreting a musical work? Performance directions can be somewhat imprecise—what is loud or fast to one performer may be moderate in volume and tempo to another. Even when composers give precise tempo markings in their scores (the exact number of beats per minute), performers have the final say in choosing a tempo that best delivers the message of the music.

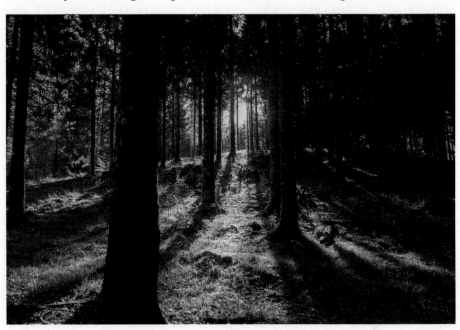

Dynamics in music may be compared to the light and shade in this photograph of the sun shining through a forest of trees.

8

Text and Music

"Rhetoric should govern music, not be its servant."

—Claudio Monteverdi

KeyPoints

- A song's text can convey the meaning of the words or simply sounds. Some composers use the voice as an instrument, as in **vocalise** (melodies sung on a neutral sound like "ah") or **scat-singing** in jazz (to made-up syllables).
- **Secular** (nonreligious) music is generally sung in the language of the people (the **vernacular**). Much Western **sacred** (religious) music is in **Latin**, the language of the Roman Catholic Church.

- Composers may set an already-written text to music, or, as in opera and musical theater, work together with lyricists as a songwriting team.
- Each syllable of a song text may get one note (**syllabic** setting); one syllable may get a few notes (**neumatic** setting); or one syllable may get many notes (**melismatic** setting).
- Composers use **word-painting** to emphasize the text, perhaps with a drawn-out word over many notes (**melisma**) or with a melody that pictorializes a word.

Today, thanks largely to music streaming, many people consider "song" synonymous with any musical selection, with or without words. Though the term correctly refers to a union of music and words—something that is sung—the original Greek word for "music," *mousikas,* implied a union of melody, language, *and* movement. The Greek philosopher Plato considered music without words to be lacking in artistic taste, and it was through language that Greek listeners reacted to the mood of a composition.

There are many facets of text and music we can consider here. For starters, does the text communicate something that can be understood, or are the syllables **nonlexical** (nonsensical)? Examples of nonlexical syllables are "Na na na na, na na na na, na na na na, hey Jude"(from the Beatles' *Hey Jude*) and "Chim chim cher-ee" (from *Mary Poppins*). Jazz singers often launch into **scat-singing**, a vocal improvisation using wordless vocables, like "Shoo-be-doo-be doo-wop" (Louis Armstrong famously invented this technique), and in English madrigals and Christmas carols you'll sometimes hear syllables like "fa la la la la" as a refrain. In all these cases, the sounds and rhythms of the "text" contribute to the music and its broad meaning. The voice can even be used for its timbral characteristics, like any other instrument—as in the technique called **vocalise**, or wordless melody (singing on a neutral vowel like "ah").

Singing without words

Throughout this book, you will encounter music with texts in a variety of languages other than English. Music for worship has been set for centuries in Hebrew, Greek, and Latin, among other languages. Not only was **Latin** the language of the Roman Empire, it was also the language of learning at medieval and Renaissance universities and of the Roman Catholic Church until the Second Vatican Council

This humorous score of *Stripsody*, by soprano Cathy Berberian, features comic-book images that ask the vocalist to make sounds matching the pictures.

Vernacular of 1962, when the church approved the use of the **vernacular** (the language of the people) for the Mass. **Secular** (nonreligious) music has traditionally been in vernacular languages. You will hear most selections sung in their original language (although we provide an English translation), since a sung translation will never fit the musical line as well as the original words. In the case of a famous lullaby by Brahms, though, you probably know the English version better than the original German words:

Brahms, *Lullaby*

In addition to modern European languages (Italian, French, Spanish, and German), you will also hear texts in Arabic, Chinese, and even Nahuatl, a language of the Aztec peoples. As we encounter words in other languages, their translations often have meanings that are slightly different from the original; if you have studied (or grown up with) a language other than English, you know that some terms or concepts really don't translate perfectly from language to language or culture to culture. This is another reason why it's important to consider the texts of songs in their original language even as we also try to grasp the meaning through the translation.

Which comes first in a song, the melody or the words? As we will see, many composers select an already existing poem or prose text to set to music, so clearly those words precede the tune. But great lyricist-composer teams have worked together to come up with enduring songs, and there is no clear formula for their creations. When George Gershwin composed the tune that became *I Got Rhythm*, his partner and brother Ira set out to write lyrics that fit the syncopated rhythms. It took him several tries, and the famous ones they settled on do not rhyme ("I got rhythm, I got music, I got my girl, who could ask for anything more"). Likewise, the lyrics for the Talking Heads' famous song *Burning Down the House* were added after the band had found a set of rhythmic and melodic ideas that they liked.

The text of a song may help organize the tune. Words flow in phrases, just as melodies do, and both are punctuated (by cadences, in the case of music). Poems are often written in rhymed **stanzas**, or **strophes**. As mentioned earlier, the most common type of musical setting, in both popular and art music, is **strophic form**, in which the same music is repeated for each stanza. Or the song might feature a **refrain**, or **chorus**, words and music that recur after each stanza. In sung dramas (like operas), the text may be free (unrhymed, metrical) verse or even prose, as people speak to each other. We will hear a variety of melodic styles in opera: some songlike passages (called arias) are very lyrical, while others are more speechlike.

How the words fit into the flow—both melodic and rhythmic—of a song makes the difference between a memorable song and an easily forgotten one. The simplest way that words and melody can fit together is a one-to-one match called **syllabic**: each syllable gets one note, as in "Happy Birthday." The opposite style of syllabic is **melismatic**, in which a single syllable is elongated by many notes, thereby giving a particular word more emphasis. Both styles, and a middle ground called **neumatic** (with a few notes to each syllable), are represented in the examples above from Handel's *Messiah*. In the last example, you can see how "rejoice" is drawn out in a long **melisma**, not only emphasizing the word, but capturing its joyful meaning through music. This technique is called **word-painting**, and you will hear it frequently in vocal music. Gospel, as well as some pop singers—such as Mariah Carey, Christina Aguilera, Jennifer Hudson, Kelly Clarkson, and Beyoncé Knowles—use melismas as part of their signature style.

The words of a song offer a way for all of us to understand the music, no matter what our cultural or aesthetic backgrounds. But keep in mind that often, especially when the text is a poem, the words themselves have purposefully vague or multiple implications, or are chosen by the poet (or the musician) for their sound and rhythm as much as for their specific meaning. One thing is sure: when words are sung, their power and effect always go well beyond their literal meaning on the page.

Stanza/strophe

Refrain/chorus

Text-setting styles

Happy Birthday

Word-painting

9

Voices and Instrument Families

"It was my idea to make my voice work in the same way as a trombone or violin—not sounding like them but 'playing' the voice like those instruments."

—Frank Sinatra (1915–1998)

KeyPoints

- Properties of sound include pitch, duration, volume, and **timbre**, or **tone color**.

- An **instrument** generates vibrations and transmits them into the air.

- The human voice can be categorized into various ranges, including **soprano, alto, tenor,** and **bass.**

- The world instrument classification system divides into **aerophones** (such as flutes or horns), **chordophones** (violins or guitars), **idiophones** (bells or cymbals), and **membranophones** (drums).

Musical Timbre

Instruments   A fourth property of sound besides pitch, duration, and volume—**timbre**, or **tone color**—accounts for the striking differences in the sound quality of musical **instruments**, mechanisms that generate vibrations and launch them into the air. It's what makes a trumpet sound altogether different from a guitar or a clarinet. Timbre is influenced by a number of factors, such as the size, shape, and proportions of the instrument, the material from which it is made, and the manner in which the vibration is produced. A string, for example, may be bowed, plucked, or struck.

Register   Each voice type and instrument has a limited melodic range (the distance from the lowest to the highest note) and dynamic range. We describe a specific area in the melodic range of an instrument or voice, such as low, middle, or high, as its **register**.

The Voice as Instrument

Voice types   The human voice is the most natural of all musical instruments; it is also one of the most universal—all cultures employ some form of vocal music. Each person's voice displays a particular quality (or character) and range. The standard designations for vocal ranges, from highest to lowest, are **soprano, mezzo-soprano, alto** (short for "contralto"), **tenor, baritone,** and **bass.**

LEFT: Luciano Pavarotti (1935–2007), one of the greatest operatic tenors of all time.

RIGHT: Pan pipe (aerophone) players from Peru.

In earlier eras, Western social and religious customs severely restricted women's participation in public musical events. Thus, young boys, and occasionally men with soprano- or alto-range voices, sang the upper parts in church music and on the stage. In the sixteenth century, women singers came into prominence in secular (nonreligious) music. Tenors were most often featured as soloists in early opera, while baritones and basses became popular soloists later, in the eighteenth century. In other cultures, the sound of women's voices has always been preferred for certain styles of music, such as lullabies.

Throughout the ages, the human voice has served as a model for instrument builders, composers, and players who have sought to duplicate its lyric beauty, expressiveness, and ability to produce **vibrato** (a throbbing effect) on their instruments.

Vibrato

The World of Musical Instruments

The diversity of musical instruments played around the world defies description. Since every conceivable method of sound production is used, and every possible raw material, it would be impossible to list them all here. However, specialists

LEFT: A steel drum band playing steelpans (idiophones) competes in the famous Panorama competition in Trinidad.

RIGHT: A drum (membranophone) ensemble from Burundi in Central Africa.

Composer Ravi Shankar (1920–2012) plays sitar (chordophone) with his daughter Anoushka. He was the most renowned and honored figure in Indian classical music of the twentieth century.

In Their Own Words

❝ If you can walk, you can dance. If you can talk, you can sing."

—*Zimbabwean proverb*

have devised a method of classifying instruments based solely on the way their sound is generated. The system designates four basic categories. **Aerophones** produce sound by using air. Instruments in this category include flutes, whistles, and horns—in short, any wind instrument. One of the most common aerophones around the world is the **bagpipe**, with a somewhat raucous tone and built-in drones for harmony. **Chordophones** produce sound from a vibrating string stretched between two points. The string may be set in motion by bowing, as on a violin; by plucking, as on a guitar or Indian sitar; or by striking, as on a hammered dulcimer.

Idiophones produce sound from the substance itself. They may be struck, as are steel drums from Trinidad (p. 37); scraped or shaken, as are African rattles; or plucked, as is the mbira, or African "thumb piano." The variety of idiophones around the world is staggering. **Membranophones** are drum-type instruments that are sounded from tightly stretched membranes. They too can be struck, plucked, rubbed, or even sung into, to set the skin in vibration.

In the next chapter, we will review the instruments used most frequently in Western music. Throughout the book, however, you will learn about other instruments associated with popular and art music cultures around the world that have influenced the Western tradition.

Listening to Non-Western Instruments

Aerophones: *Los Jilicatas*, Peruvian panpipes
Membranophones and idiophones: *Tabuh Kenilu Sawik*, Indonesian gamelan
Chordophones and membranophones: *Raga Bhimpalasi*, sitar and tabla drums, from North India

10

Western Musical Instruments

"In music, instruments perform the function of the colors employed in painting."

—Honoré de Balzac (1799–1850)

KeyPoints

- The four families of Western instruments are **strings**, **woodwinds**, **brass**, and **percussion**.

- String instruments (chordophones) are sounded by **bowing** and **plucking**. Bowed strings include the violin, viola, cello, and double bass; plucked strings include the harp and guitar.

- Woodwind instruments (aerophones) include the flute, oboe, clarinet, bassoon, and saxophone.

- Brass instruments (aerophones) include the trumpet, French horn, trombone, and tuba.

- Percussion instruments include idiophones (xylophone, cymbals, triangle) and membranophones (timpani, bass drum); some are pitched (chimes), while others are unpitched (tambourine).

- Keyboard instruments, such as the piano, organ, and synthesizer, do not fit neatly into the Western classification system.

The instruments of the Western world, and especially those of the orchestra, may be categorized into four groups of their own: strings, woodwinds, brass, and percussion. Not all woodwinds, however, are made of wood, nor do they share a common means of sound production. Furthermore, certain instruments do not fit neatly into any of these convenient categories (the piano, for example, is both a string and a percussion instrument).

String Instruments

The string family, all chordophones, includes two types of instruments: those that are **bowed** and those that are **plucked**. In the bowed-string family, there are four principal members: violin, viola, violoncello, and double bass, each with four strings (double basses sometimes have five) that are set vibrating by drawing a bow across them. The bow is held in the right hand, while the left hand is used to "stop" the string by pressing a finger down at a particular point, thereby leaving a certain portion of the string free to vibrate. By stopping the string at another point, the performer changes the length of the vibrating portion, and with it the rate of vibration and the pitch.

The **violin** evolved to its present form at the hands of the master instrument makers who flourished in Italy from around 1600 to 1750. It is capable of brilliance and dramatic effect, subtle nuances from soft to loud, and great agility in rapid passages throughout its extremely wide range.

Violin

LEFT: Grammy-Award-winning violinist Hilary Hahn (b. 1979) enjoys a prominent career as a soloist.

RIGHT: Yo-Yo Ma (b. 1955), the revered and wide-ranging virtuoso cellist.

The color coding helps this young harpist position her hands as she plucks the strings.

Viola

The **viola** is somewhat larger than the violin and thus has a lower range. Its strings are longer, thicker, and heavier. The tone is husky in the low register, somber and penetrating in the high. It often fills in the harmony, or it may **double** another part—that is, reinforce another part when it plays the same notes an octave higher or lower.

The **violoncello**, popularly known as **cello**, is lower in range than the viola and is notable for its singing quality and its dark resonance in the low register. Cellos often play the melody, and they enrich the sound with their full timbre.

The **double bass**, known also as a **contrabass** or **bass viol**, is the lowest of the orchestral string instruments. Accordingly, it plays the bass part—the foundation of the harmony. Its deep tones support the cello part an octave lower. These four string instruments constitute the core or "heart" of the orchestra, a designation that indicates the section's versatility and importance.

String instruments can be played in many styles and can produce striking special effects. They excel at playing **legato** (smoothly, connecting the notes) as well as the opposite, **staccato** (with notes short and detached). A different effect, **pizzicato** (plucked), is created when a performer plucks the string with a finger instead of using the bow. **Vibrato**, a slight throbbing, is achieved by a rapid wrist-and-finger movement of the left hand on the string that slightly alters the pitch. For a **glissando**, a finger of the left hand slides along the string while the right hand draws the bow, gathering all the pitches under the left-hand finger in one swooping sound. **Tremolo**, the rapid repetition of a tone through a quick back-and-forth movement of the bow, is associated with suspense and excitement. No less important is the **trill**, a rapid alternation between a note and one adjacent to it.

String instruments are capable of playing several notes simultaneously, thereby producing harmony: **double-stopping** means

LEFT: American Christian McBride (b. 1972) playing the double bass at a jazz festival in East Sussex, England, 2014.

RIGHT: Bass guitarist Ricardo Winandy performs in the Brazilian progressive band Mindflow.

playing two strings at once; playing three or four strings together is called **triple-** or **quadruple-stopping**. Another effect is created by the **mute**, a small attachment that fits over the bridge, muffling the sound. **Harmonics** are eerie, crystalline tones in a very high register that are produced by lightly touching a finger to the string at certain points while the bow is drawn across the string.

Harp

Two popular plucked-string instruments are the harp and the guitar. The **harp** is one of the oldest of musical instruments, with a home in many cultures outside Europe. Its plucked strings, whose pitches are changed by means of pedals, produce an ethereal tone. Chords on the harp are frequently played in broken form—that is, the notes are sounded one after another instead of simultaneously. From this technique comes the term **arpeggio**, which means "broken chord" (*arpa* is Italian for "harp"). Arpeggios can be created in a variety of ways on many instruments.

Guitar

The **guitar**, another old instrument, dating back at least to the Middle Ages, probably originated in the Middle East. A favorite solo instrument, it is associated today with folk and popular music as well as classical styles. The standard **acoustic guitar** is made of wood and has a fretted fingerboard and six nylon or steel strings, which are plucked with the fingers of the right hand or with a pick. The electronically amplified **electric guitar**, capable of many specialized techniques, comes in two main types: the hollow-bodied (or electro-acoustic), favored by jazz and popular musicians; and the solid-bodied, used more by rock musicians. Related to the guitar are such traditional instruments as the **banjo** and **mandolin**.

Woodwind Instruments

Woodwind instruments (aerophones) produce sound with a column of air vibrating within a pipe that has fingerholes along its length. When one or another of these holes is opened or closed, the length of the vibrating air column is changed. Woodwind players are capable of remarkable agility on their instruments by means of an intricate mechanism of keys arranged to suit the natural position of the fingers.

Nowadays woodwinds are not necessarily made of wood. They employ several different methods of setting up vibration: blowing across a mouth hole (flute),

Flutist James Galway (b. 1939), the "man with the golden flute."

blowing into a mouthpiece that has a single reed (clarinet and saxophone), or blowing into a mouthpiece fitted with a double reed (oboe and bassoon). They do, however, have one important feature in common: the holes in their pipes. In addition, their timbres are such that composers think of them and write for them as a group.

The **flute** is the soprano voice of the woodwind family. Its tone is cool and velvety in the expressive low register, and often brilliant in the upper part of its range. The present-day flute, made of a metal alloy rather than wood, is a cylindrical tube, closed at one end, that is held horizontally. The player blows across a mouth hole cut in the side of the pipe near the closed end. The flute is used frequently as a melody instrument—its timbre stands out against the orchestra—and offers the performer great versatility in playing rapid repeated notes, scales, and trills. The **piccolo** (from the Italian *flauto piccolo,* "little flute") is the highest-pitched instrument in the orchestra. In its upper register, it takes on a shrillness that is easily heard even when the orchestra is playing *fortissimo.*

Oboe

The **oboe** continues to be made of wood. The player blows directly into a double reed, which consists of two thin strips of cane bound together with a narrow passage for air. The oboe's timbre, generally described as nasal and reedy, is often associated with pastoral effects and nostalgic moods. The oboe traditionally sounds the tuning note (A) for the other instruments of the orchestra. The **English horn** is an alto oboe. Its wooden tube is wider and longer than that of the oboe and ends in a pear-shaped opening called a **bell,** which largely accounts for its soft, expressive timbre.

Clarinet

The **clarinet** uses a single reed, a small, thin piece of cane fastened against its chisel-shaped mouthpiece. The instrument's tone is smooth and liquid, and its range remarkably wide in both pitch and volume. It too displays an easy command of rapid scales, trills, and repeated notes. The **bass clarinet,** one octave lower in range than the clarinet, has a rich dark tone and a wide dynamic range.

Oboe players in an orchestra.

Bassoon players in an orchestra.

Clarinet player in an orchestra.

The **bassoon**, another double-reed instrument, sounds weighty in the low register and reedy and intense in the upper. Capable of a dry staccato and wide leaps that can sound humorous, it is at the same time a highly expressive instrument. The **contrabassoon** produces the lowest tone of the woodwinds. Its function in the woodwind section of supplying a foundation for the harmony may be likened to that of the double bass among the strings.

The **saxophone**, invented by the Belgian Adolphe Sax in 1840, is the most recent of the woodwind instruments. It was created by combining the single reed of the clarinet with a conical bore and the metal body of the brass instruments. There are various sizes of saxophone: the most common are soprano, alto, tenor, and baritone. Used only occasionally in the orchestra, the saxophone had become the characteristic instrument of the jazz band by the 1920s, and it remains a favorite sound in popular music today.

Brass Instruments

The main instruments of the brass family (aerophones) are the trumpet, French horn (or horn), trombone, and tuba. All these instruments consist of cup-shaped mouthpieces attached to a length of metal tubing that flares at the end into a bell. The column of air within the tube is set vibrating by the stretched lips of the player, which are buzzed together. Going from one pitch to another involves not only mechanical means, such as a slide or valves, but also muscular control to vary the pressure of the lips and breath. Brass and woodwind instrument players often refer to their **embouchure**, the entire oral mechanism of lips, lower facial muscles, and jaw.

Trumpets and horns were prevalent in the ancient world. At first, they were fashioned from animal horns and tusks and were used chiefly for religious ceremonies and military signals. The **trumpet**, highest in pitch of the brass family, asserts itself with a brilliant, clear timbre. It is often associated with ceremonial display. The trumpet can also be muted, with a pear-shaped, metal or cardboard device that is inserted in the bell to achieve a muffled, buzzy sound.

Classical trumpeter Alison Balsom (b. 1978) performs in a Christmas special in London, 2015.

LEFT: Kenny Garrett (b. 1960) plays alto saxophone at a jazz festival in New York City, 2013.

RIGHT: The French horn section of an orchestra.

French horn

The **French horn** is descended from the ancient hunting horn. Its mellow resonance can be mysteriously remote in soft passages and sonorous in loud ones; muted, it sounds distant. The horn is played with the right hand, cupped slightly, inserted in the bell and is sometimes "stopped" by plugging the bell tightly with the hand, producing an eerie and rasping quality. The timbre of the horn blends well with woodwinds, brasses, and strings.

Trombone and tuba

The **trombone**—the Italian word means "large trumpet"—offers a full and rich sound in the tenor range. In place of valves, it features a movable U-shaped slide that alters the length of the vibrating air column in the tube. The **tuba,** the bass instrument of the brass family, furnishes the foundation for the harmony, like the

LEFT: This young woman demonstrates the tuba, largest of the brass family.

RIGHT: Orchestral trombone players in rehearsal.

double bass and contrabassoon. The tuba adds depth to the orchestral tone, and a dark resonance ranging from velvety softness to a rumbling growl.

    Other brass instruments are used in concert and marching bands. Among these is the **cornet**, similar to the trumpet and very popular in concert bands in the early twentieth century. The **bugle**, which evolved from the military (or field) trumpet of early times, sends out a powerful tone that carries well in the open air. Since it has no valves, it is able to sound only certain pitches of the scale, which accounts for the familiar pattern of duty calls (and "Taps") in the army. The **fluegelhorn**, often used in jazz bands, is really a valved bugle with a wide bell. The **euphonium** is a tenor-range instrument whose shape resembles the tuba. And the **sousaphone**, an adaptation of the tuba designed by the American bandmaster John Philip Sousa (see Chapter 54), features a forward bell and is coiled to rest over the shoulder of the marching player.

Percussion Instruments

The percussion instruments of the orchestra accentuate the rhythm, generate excitement at the climaxes, and inject splashes of color into the orchestral sound. This family (encompassing a vast array of idiophones and membranophones) is divided into two categories: instruments capable of producing definite pitches, and those that produce an indefinite pitch. In the former group are the **timpani**, or **kettledrums**, which are generally played in sets of two or four. The timpani has a hemispheric copper shell across which is stretched a "head" of plastic or calfskin held in place by a metal ring. A pedal mechanism enables the player to change the tension of the head, and with it the pitch. The instrument is played with two padded sticks, or mallets. Its dynamic range extends from a mysterious rumble to a thunderous roll. The timpani first arrived in Western Europe from the Middle East, where Turks on horseback used them in combination with trumpets (see p. 88).

Pitched percussion

    Also among the pitched percussion instruments is the **xylophone** family; instruments of this general type are used in Africa, Southeast Asia, and throughout the Americas. The xylophone consists of tuned blocks of wood laid out in the shape of a keyboard. Struck with mallets with hard heads, the instrument produces a dry, crisp sound. The **marimba** is a more mellow xylophone of African origin. The **vibraphone**, used in jazz as well as art music, combines the principle of the xylophone with resonators, each containing revolving disks operated by electric motors that produce an exaggerated vibrato.

Evelyn Glennie (b. 1965) is a virtuoso solo percussionist who is also profoundly deaf.

    The **glockenspiel** (German for "set of bells") consists of a series of horizontal tuned steel bars of various sizes, which when struck produce a bright, metallic, bell-like sound. The **celesta**, a kind of glockenspiel that is operated by means of a keyboard, resembles a miniature upright piano. Its steel plates are struck by small hammers to produce a sound like a music box. **Chimes**, or **tubular bells**, a set of tuned metal tubes of various lengths suspended from a frame and struck with a hammer, are frequently called on to simulate church bells.

    Percussion instruments that do not produce a definite pitch include the **snare drum** (or **side drum**), a small cylindrical drum with two heads (top and bottom) stretched over a shell of wood or metal and

Pianist Yuja Wang (b. 1987) performs with the Rotterdam Philharmonic Orchestra in a festival in Italy (2018).

played with two drumsticks. This instrument owes its brilliant tone to the vibrations of the lower head against taut wire snares. The **bass drum** is played with a large, soft-headed stick and produces a low, heavy sound. **Tom-tom** is a colloquial name given to Native American or African drums of indefinite pitch. The **tambourine** is a round, handheld drum with "jingles"—little metal plates—inserted in its rim. The player can strike the drum with the fingers or knee, shake it, or pass a hand over the jingles. Of Middle Eastern origin, it is particularly associated with music of Spain, as are **castanets**, little wood clappers mounted on wooden boards or, for Spanish dancing, moved by the player's fingers.

The **triangle** is a slender rod of steel bent into a three-cornered shape; when struck with a steel beater, it gives off a bright, tinkling sound. **Cymbals**, which arrived in the West from central Asia during the Middle Ages, consist of two large circular brass plates of equal size; when struck against each other, they produce a shattering sound. The **gong** and the **tam-tam** are both broad circular disks of metal, suspended to a frame so as to hang freely. The tam-tam is a flat gong of indefinite pitch; the gong, on the other hand, with a raised metal center, has a definite pitch and when struck with a heavy stick produces a deep roar. In the Far East and Southeast Asia, the gong is central to the ensemble known as the **gamelan** (see p. 424).

🔊 Keyboard Instruments

Piano   The **piano** was originally known as the *fortepiano*, Italian for "loud-soft," which suggests its wide dynamic range and capacity for nuance. Its strings are struck with hammers controlled by a keyboard mechanism. The piano cannot sustain a tone as well as the bowed-string and wind instruments, but in the hands of a fine performer, it is capable of producing a singing melody.

The piano boasts a notable capacity for brilliant scales, arpeggios, trills, rapid passages, and octaves, as well as chords. Its range from lowest to highest pitch spans eighty-eight semitones, or more than seven octaves. Its several foot pedals govern the length of time a string vibrates as well as its volume.

Organ   The **organ**, one of the earliest keyboard instruments, is also a type of wind instrument. The air flow to each of its many pipes is controlled by the organist from a console containing two or more keyboards and a pedal keyboard played by the feet. The organ's multicolored sonority can easily fill a huge space. Electronic keyboards, or synthesizers, capable of imitating pipe organs and other timbres, have become commonplace. Another early keyboard instrument, much used in the Baroque era,

Harpsichord   is the **harpsichord**. Its sound is produced by quills that pluck its metal strings.

The instruments described in this and the previous chapter form a vivid and diversified group, which can be heard and viewed with your book's online materials. To composers, performers, and listeners alike, they offer an endless variety of colors and shades of expression.

11

Musical Ensembles

"Conductors must give unmistakable and suggestive signals to the orchestra—not choreography to the audience."

—*George Szell (1897–1970)*

KeyPoints

- Choral groups often feature *a cappella* singing, with no accompaniment.
- **Chamber music** is ensemble music for small groups, with one player per part.
- Standard chamber ensembles include **string quartets**, **piano trios**, and **brass quintets**.

- The modern **orchestra** can feature over one hundred players.
- Most **bands—wind**, **marching**, **jazz**, **rock**—feature a core of winds and percussion.
- Large ensembles are generally led by a **conductor** who beats patterns with a baton to help performers keep the same tempo.

The great variety in musical instruments is matched by a wide assortment of ensembles, or performance groups. Some are homogeneous—for example, choral groups using only voices or perhaps only men's voices. Others are more heterogeneous—for example, the orchestra, which features instruments from the different families. Across the world, any combination is possible.

The Washington National Cathedral Girls Choir sings an evening church service.

Choral Groups

Choral music is sung around the world, both for religious purposes (sacred music) and for nonspiritual (secular) occasions. Loosely defined, a **chorus** is a fairly large body of singers who perform together; their music is usually sung in several voice parts. Many groups include both men and women, but choruses can also be restricted to women's or men's voices only. A **choir**, traditionally a smaller group, is often connected with a church or with the performance of sacred music. The standard voice parts in both chorus and choir correspond to the voice ranges described earlier: soprano, alto, tenor, and bass (abbreviated **SATB**). In early times, choral music was often performed without accompaniment, a style of singing known as *a cappella* (meaning "in the chapel"). Smaller, specialized vocal ensembles include the madrigal choir and chamber choir.

A cappella

Standard Chamber Ensembles			
Duos	**Quartets**	**Quintets**	
Solo instrument (e.g., violin or clarinet)	String quartet	String quintet	Woodwind quintet
	Violin 1	Violin 1	Flute
Piano	Violin 2	Violin 2	Oboe
	Viola	Viola 1	Clarinet
Trios	Cello	Viola 2	Bassoon
String trio	Piano quartet	Cello	French horn (a brass instrument)
Violin 1	Piano	Piano quintet	
Viola or violin 2	Violin	Piano	Brass quintet
Cello	Viola	String quartet (violin 1, violin 2, viola, cello)	Trumpet 1
Piano trio	Cello		Trumpet 2
Piano			French horn
Violin			Trombone
Cello			Tuba

The Ying String Quartet, founded in 1988 by four siblings.

Chamber Ensembles

Chamber music is ensemble music for a group of two to about a dozen players, with only one player to a part—as distinct from orchestral music, in which a single instrumental part may be performed by as many as eighteen players or more. The essential trait of chamber music is its intimacy.

Several of the standard chamber music ensembles consist of string players. The most well-known combination is probably the **string quartet**, made up of two violins, viola, and cello. Other popular combinations are the **duo sonata** (solo string, wind, or percussion instrument with piano); the **piano trio**, **piano quartet**, and **piano quintet**, each made up of a piano and string instruments; the **string quintet**; as well as larger groups—the **sextet**, **septet**, and **octet**. Winds too form standard combinations, especially **woodwind** and **brass quintets**. Some of these ensembles are listed above.

Contemporary composers have experimented with new groupings that combine the voice with small groups of instruments and electronic elements with live performers. In some cultures, chamber groups mix what might seem to the Western listener to be unlikely timbres—in India, for example, plucked strings and percussion are standard (see p. 201).

The Orchestra

In its most general sense, the term "orchestra" may be applied to any performing body of diverse instruments—this would include the **gamelan** orchestras of Bali and Java, made up largely of gongs, xylophone-like instruments, and drums (you will hear this ensemble in an Encounter about the Javanese gamelan, p. 424). In the West,

Typical Distribution of Orchestral Instruments				
Strings	16–18	first violins	10–12	cellos
	16–18	second violins	8–10	double basses
	12	violas	1–2	harps, when needed
Woodwinds	2–3	flutes, 1 piccolo	3	clarinets, 1 bass clarinet
	2–3	oboes, 1 English horn	3	bassoons, 1 contrabassoon
Brass	4–6	French horns	3	trombones
	4	trumpets	1	tuba
Percussion	3–5	players	1	timpani player (2–4 timpani)

the term is now synonymous with **symphony orchestra**, an ensemble of strings coupled with an assortment of woodwinds, brass, and percussion instruments.

The symphony orchestra has varied in size and makeup throughout its history but has always featured string instruments at its core. From its origins as a small group, the orchestra has grown into an ensemble of more than a hundred musicians, approximately two-thirds of whom are string players. The chart above shows the distribution of instruments typical of a large orchestra today.

The instruments are arranged to achieve the best balance of tone: most of the strings are near the front, as are the gentle woodwinds, with the louder brass and percussion at the back. A characteristic seating plan is shown on page 51.

Wind, Jazz, and Rock Bands

Band is a generic name applied to a variety of ensembles, most of which rely on winds and percussion. The band is a much-loved American institution. One American bandmaster, John Philip Sousa, achieved worldwide fame with his **wind**, or **concert**, **band** and the repertory of marches he wrote for it.

In the United States today, the **wind band**, ranging in size from forty to eighty or so players, is an established institution in most secondary schools, colleges, and universities and in many communities as well. Modern composers like to write for this ensemble, since directors are usually willing to play new compositions. The familiar **marching band** usually entertains at sports events and parades. Besides its core of winds and percussion, this group often features remnants from its military origins, including a display of drum majors, majorettes, flags, and rifles. The repertory of marching bands is extensive, but almost always includes marches by John Philip Sousa, such as the well-known *Stars and Stripes Forever*.

The precise instrumentation of **jazz bands** depends on the particular music being played but usually includes a reed section made up of saxophones and an occasional clarinet, a brass section of trumpets and trombones, and a rhythm section of percussion, piano, double bass, and electric guitar. **Rock bands** often supplement amplified guitars and percussion with synthesizers, and may also feature winds and brass.

The University of Texas Longhorn Marching Band in the 2006 Rose Parade in Pasadena, California.

Gustavo Dudamel (b. 1981), a graduate of the Venezuelan music education system called El Sistema, was appointed conductor of the Los Angeles Philharmonic in 2009 at the age of twenty-seven.

The Role of the Conductor

Large ensembles, such as an orchestra, concert band, or chorus, generally need a conductor, who serves as the group's leader. Conductors beat time in standard metric patterns to help the performers keep the same tempo; many conductors use a thin stick known as a **baton**, which is easy to see. These conducting patterns, shown in the diagrams opposite, further emphasize the strong and weak beats of the measure. Beat 1, the strongest in any meter, is always given a downbeat, or a downward motion of the hand; a secondary beat is shown by a change of direction; and the last beat of each measure, a weak beat, is always an upbeat or upward motion, thereby leaving the hand ready for the downbeat of the next measure.

Baton

Equally important is the conductor's role in interpreting the music for the group, deciding on the precise tempo (how fast or slow) and the dynamics (how soft or loud) all the way through the piece. In most cases, the composer's markings are relative (how loud is *forte?*) and thus open to interpretive differences. Conductors also rehearse ensembles in practice sessions, helping the musicians to learn their individual parts. String players depend on the conductor, or sometimes the **concertmaster** (the first-chair violinist), to standardize their bowing strokes so that the musical emphasis, and therefore the interpretation, is uniform.

Concertmaster

The Orchestra in Action

A thrilling introduction to the infinite range of the modern orchestra is Benjamin Britten's *Young Person's Guide to the Orchestra,* written expressly to illustrate the timbre of each instrument. The work, composed in 1946 and subtitled *Variations and Fugue on a Theme of Purcell,* is based on a dance tune by the great seventeenth-century English composer Henry Purcell. You can hear Purcell's

Purcell, *Rondeau*

Basic Conducting Patterns

| Duple meter | Triple meter | Quadruple meter | Sextuple meter |

original tune—in a broad triple meter and a minor key—in the online Listening Examples.

In *The Young Person's Guide*, Britten introduces the sound of the entire orchestra playing together, then the sonorities of each instrument family as a group— woodwinds, brasses, strings, percussion—and finally repeats the statement by the full orchestra. With the theme, or principal melody, well in mind, we hear every instrument in order from highest to lowest within each family. Next we encounter variations of the theme, each played by a new instrument (see Listening Guide 1). The work closes with a grand **fugue**, a polyphonic form popular in the Baroque era (1600–1750), which is also based on Purcell's theme. The fugue, like the variations, presents its subject, or theme, in rapid order in each instrument. (For a general discussion of the fugue, see Chapter 30.)

Fugue

A typical seating plan for an orchestra.

The Vancouver Symphony Orchestra rehearsing in the city's Orpheum Theatre, 2008.

LISTENING GUIDE 1   16:36

Britten: *The Young Person's Guide to the Orchestra*
(*Variations and Fugue on a Theme of Purcell*)

Date: 1946

Basis: Dance from Purcell's incidental music to the play *Abdelazar* (*The Moor's Revenge*)

Performed by: Britten–Pears Festival Orchestra; Marin Alsop, conductor

What to Listen For

Melody	Stately theme, based on tune by Baroque composer Henry Purcell.	**Texture**	Homophonic at the beginning; closing fugue is polyphonic.
Rhythm/meter	Slow, triple meter for opening statement of theme, then changing to duple and compound.	**Form**	Theme with many variations.
		Performing forces	Full orchestra, statements by instrument families, then individual instruments.
Harmony	Begins in minor tonality; shifts between major and minor.		

0:00   **I. Theme:** Eight measures in D minor, stated six times to illustrate the orchestral families.

  1. Entire orchestra   4. Strings
  2. Woodwinds   5. Percussion
  3. Brass   6. Entire orchestra

II. Variations: 13 short variations, each illustrating a different instrument.

	VARIATION	FAMILY	SOLO INSTRUMENT	ACCOMPANYING INSTRUMENTS
1:57	1	woodwinds	piccolo, flutes	violins, harp, and triangle
	2		oboes	strings and timpani
	3		clarinets	strings and tuba
	4		bassoons	strings and snare drum
5:00	5	strings	violins	brass and bass drum
	6		violas	woodwinds and brass
	7		cellos	clarinets, violas, and harp
	8		double basses	woodwinds and tambourine
	9		harp	strings, gong, and cymbal
9:34	10	brass	French horns	strings, harp, and timpani
	11		trumpets	strings and snare drum
	12		trombones, tuba	woodwinds and high brass
11:53	13	percussion	various	strings

(Order in which percussion instruments are introduced: timpani, bass drum, and cymbals; timpani, tambourine, and triangle; timpani, snare drum, and wood block; timpani and xylophone; timpani, castanets, and gong; timpani and whip; whole percussion section; xylophone.)

13:47 **III. Fugue:** Subject is based on a fragment of the Purcell theme, played in imitation by each instrument in the same order as the variations.

Woodwinds: (highest to lowest)	piccolo flutes oboes clarinets bassoons	
Strings: (highest to lowest)	first violins second violins violas cellos double basses harp	
Brass: (highest to lowest)	French horns trumpets trombones, tuba	
Percussion:	various	

15:39 Full orchestra at the end with Purcell's theme heard over the fugue.

🔊 **AnotherHearing** Compare the two recordings of this work we provided—a non-narrated audio recording and a narrated video version, both performed by students of the Britten–Pears Young Artist Programme at Aldeburgh, England, and conducted by Marin Alsop. How does the video help you follow the contrasting instrumental timbres? Does it change your understanding of the work? How does the narration affect your listening experience? Does the video enhance your listening of the non-narrated performance? Which do you prefer, and why?

12

Style and Function of Music in Society

"A real musical culture should not be a museum culture based on music of past ages. . . . It should be the active embodiment in sound of the life of a community—of the everyday demands of people's work and play and of their deepest spiritual needs."

—*Wilfrid Mellers (1914–2008)*

KeyPoints

- Most cultures around the world employ **sacred music** for religious functions, and **secular music** for entertainment and other nonreligious activities.

- There are many **genres**, or categories, of music; some works **cross over** categories, borrowing elements of one genre for use in another.

- The **medium** is the specific group (e.g., orchestra, chorus) that performs a piece.

- Some music is not written down, but is known through **oral transmission**.

- The distinctive features of any artwork make up its **style**. A musical style is created through individual treatment of the basic musical elements.

- We organize styles of artworks into historical periods, each with its own characteristics.

In every culture, music is intricately interwoven with the lives and beliefs of its people. Music serves different functions in different societies, though some basic roles are universal. In some cultures, such as in the Western classical tradition, only a few people are involved with the actual performance of music; in others, cooperative work is so much a part of society that the people sing as a group, with each person contributing a separate part to build a complex whole.

There is music for every conceivable occasion, but the specific occasions vary from one culture to another. Thus, musical genres, or categories of repertory, do not necessarily transfer from one society to another, though they may be similar. For example, Japanese *Noh* drama and a Beijing opera like *The Legend of the Red Lantern* (Many Voices, p. 312) serve essentially the same role as Western opera does. And we can distinguish in most cultures between **sacred music**, for religious purposes (like the Islamic chant on p. 78), and **secular music**, for entertainment (such as the Mariachi band on p. 398).

It's important to differentiate between genre and form. A **genre** is a more general term that suggests something of the overall character of the work as well as its function. For example, song is a genre, as is **symphony**— usually designating a four-movement orchestral work. As we will see later, each

LEFT: In Japanese *Noh* drama, performers often wear symbolic masks.

> ### Reviewing Terms
>
> **Title: Symphony No. 5 in C Minor,**
>   **Op. 67** (Op. = Opus = work number)
> **Composer**: Ludwig van Beethoven
> **Genre**: Symphony
> **Form**: Four-movement work for orchestra
> **Medium**: Symphony orchestra
>
> **Title**: *Wiegenlied* (*Lullaby*), Op. 49, No. 4
> **Composer**: Johannes Brahms
> **Genre**: Romantic song (in German, Lied)
> **Form**: Strophic (two stanzas sung to the
>   same music)
> **Medium**: Solo voice and piano

movement of a symphony has a specific internal **form**, or structure. "Symphony" also implies the **medium**, or the specific group that performs the piece—in this case, an orchestra (see box above).

Titles for musical compositions occasionally indicate the genre and key: Symphony No. 94 in G Major, by Joseph Haydn, for example. Another way works are identified is through a cataloguing system, often described by **opus number** (*opus* is Latin for "work"; an example is Nocturne, Op. 48, a piano work by Frédéric Chopin). Other titles are more descriptive, such as *The Nutcracker* (a ballet by the Russian composer Peter Ilyich Tchaikovsky) and *The Trout* (a song by Franz Schubert, an Austrian composer).

Opus number

Just as the context for music—when, why, and by whom a piece is performed—varies from culture to culture, so do aesthetic judgments. For example, the Chinese consider a thin, tense vocal tone desirable in their operas (see p. 312), while the Italians prefer a full-throated, robust sound in theirs.

Not all music is written down. In most cultures of the world, music is transmitted by example or by imitation and is performed from memory. This is even true for some styles of Western music. The preservation of music without the aid of written notation is referred to as **oral transmission**. We will see that in modern times, music scholars known as ethnomusicologists, who study music in its cultural context, have attempted to "capture" music that had never previously been written down through field recordings (an example from East Africa is on p. 438).

Oral transmission

While we will consider how music operates in several different traditions, our Listening Guides focus primarily on Western art music—that is, the

Note the stylistic differences between paintings of similar subject matter from different historical eras.

LEFT: *The Guitar Player,* by **Jan Vermeer** (1632–1675).

RIGHT: *The Old Guitar Player,* by **Pablo Picasso** (1881–1973).

Famed cellist Pablo Casals (1876–1973) working with a student.

notated and cultivated music of European and Euro-American society. We often label art music as "classical" or "serious," for lack of better terms. However, the lines that distinguish art music from other kinds can be blurred. **Vernacular** musics (often called "popular" or "traditional," wrongly understood as spontaneously generated by untrained musicians) are essential traditions in their own right, and both rock and especially jazz are considered new art forms, having already stood the test of time.

The Concept of Style

Style may be defined as the characteristic way an artwork is presented. The word may also indicate the creator's personal manner of expression—the distinctive flavor that sets one artist apart from all others. Thus, we speak of the literary style of Dickens or Hemingway, the painting style of Picasso or Rembrandt, or the musical style of Bach or Mozart (compare the paintings on p. 55).

What makes one musical work sound similar to or different from another? It's the style, or individualized treatment of the elements of music. We have seen that Western music is largely a melody-oriented art based on a particular musical system from which the underlying harmonies are also built. Musics of other cultures may sound foreign to our ears, because they are based on entirely different systems, and many do not involve harmony to any great extent. Complex rhythmic procedures and textures set some world musics apart from Western styles, while basic formal considerations—such as repetition, contrast, and variation—bring musics of disparate cultures closer. In short, a style is made up of pitch, time, timbre, and expression, creating a sound that each culture recognizes as its own.

Musical Styles in History

Each historical period has its own stylistic characteristics; although the artists, writers, and composers of a particular era may vary in outlook, they all share certain qualities. Because of this, we can tell at once that a work of art—whether music, poetry, painting, sculpture, or architecture—dates from the Middle Ages or the eighteenth century. The style of a period, then, is the total language of all its artists as they react to the political, economic, religious, and philosophical forces that shape their environment. A knowledge of historical styles will help you place a musical work within the context (time and place) in which it was created.

The following table lays out the generally accepted style periods in the history of Western music, along with a brief description of forms, genres, and stylistic traits for this period. Several brief listening examples are suggested for each era, allowing you to preview works, genres, and forms to come in each period.

Musical Styles In History

Period	Description	Listening examples
Middle Ages **400–1450**	The earliest notated music; church music prevails; harmony and rhythmic concepts introduced.	Gregorian Chant: *Kyrie* Notre Dame School: *Gaude Maria virgo*
Renaissance **1450–1600**	Printing and distribution of music; musical focus moves from church to palace; development of national styles.	Josquin: *Ave Maria . . . virgo serena* Farmer: *Fair Phyllis*
Baroque **1600–1750**	Invention of opera; development of instrumental music and genres; tonal harmony developed.	Strozzi: *Amor dormiglione* Vivaldi: *Spring Concerto*, from *The Four Seasons*
Classical **1750–1825**	Public concerts featured; symphony orchestra flourishes; large-scale compositions developed.	Haydn: Symphony No. 94 in G Major, II Beethoven: *Moonlight* Sonata, I
Romantic **1820–1900**	Composer as independent artist; rise of virtuoso performer; chromatic harmony and more dissonance featured; programmatic music; nationalism in composition.	Chopin: *Revolutionary Étude* Berlioz: *Symphonie fantastique*, IV
Post-Romantic and Impressionist **1890–1915**	Modal and exotic scales; music influenced by art and literary movements.	Debussy: *Prelude to "The Afternoon of a Faun"*
Early 20th century Modernist	Revolutionary concepts in harmony and rhythm; influence of jazz, traditional, and popular music; unusual instrumental combinations; development of recording.	Stravinsky: *The Rite of Spring*, Part I Gershwin: *Rhapsody in Blue*
Later 20th–early 21st century Postmodernist	Influence of technology; idiosyncratic approaches to music; expanded instrumental techniques and ranges; global music influences.	Cage: Sonata V from *Sonatas and Interludes* León: "Understanding" from *Inura*

13

Many Voices: Creating and Recreating Musical Canons

"Masterpieces are not single and solitary births; they are the outcome of many years of thinking in common, of thinking by the body of the people, so that the experience of the mass is behind the single voice."

—English writer Virginia Woolf

In any creative tradition there are works broadly recognized as extraordinary and worth preserving. A collection of such great works is often referred to as a **canon**, from an ancient Greek term indicating a measure of excellence. You are probably already familiar with the concept of a canon in literature: the books assigned in your English literature classes are most likely among those considered canonic. Shakespeare might lead the list, for example—undoubtedly you have read one or more of his plays or sonnets.

But canons are not static: they are ever-changing, with new or formerly "neglected" works being proposed for inclusion among the declared "masterpieces." Consider the case of women authors: Jane Austen (*Pride and Prejudice,* 1813) was not widely read in her day, and she also wrote anonymously to avoid readers knowing her gender (although this was not a well-kept secret). She had clearly entered the canon by the early twentieth century, when new editions of her novels were published and societies arose to further her work to a wider public. Much more recent additions to the literary canon include women of color, such as Maya Angelou (*I Know Why the Caged Bird Sings,* 1969) and Amy Tan (*The Joy Luck Club,* 1989), among others.

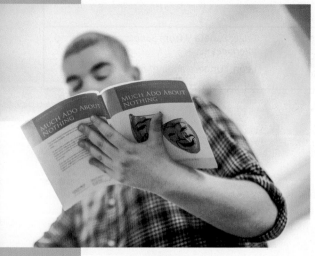

A student is reading Shakespeare's popular play *Much Ado about Nothing,* a work central to the literary canon.

Given the immense variety of styles, traditions, and cultures, it's not possible to speak of a single canon in any art form: any finite list inherently excludes vastly more than it includes, and different genres or repertories have their own canons: we can speak of a rock canon, a jazz canon, a band music canon, and so on. How then do we set about presenting a canon of music for you to hear and study in *The Enjoyment of Music*?

As discussed earlier, the central focus of this book is the Western classical music tradition. The concept of this musical canon began in the late eighteenth century, as public concerts grew and the emerging tradition of music criticism established the notion of "genius," suggesting that some works were worthy of repeated hearings and preservation. Audiences who formerly wanted to hear only "new music" embraced this principle, and the generation of Mozart, Haydn, and Beethoven benefited from this new trend, which grew throughout the following generations. It is striking that the music of Bach, considered so central to the canon today, was not widely performed until a century after his death in 1750! Likewise, some formerly popular works are rarely performed today: Beethoven's bombastic hit *Wellington's Victory* is now viewed as his least sophisticated work.

Canons are controversial because of what they include, what they exclude, and who decides. Is it the concert promoter who decides what music will be performed? Is it the critic who chooses to praise some composers and works and not others? Is it the publisher who decides what music to print, the label executive who decides what music gets recorded, or the programmer who decides what gets played on the radio or added to an online playlist? Or is it perhaps the professor teaching a music appreciation course or the authors writing a textbook?

German composer Richard Wagner (1813–1883) honored Beethoven in 1872, conducting a monumental performance of his revered Symphony No. 9. Color lithograph by **Louis Sauter.**

The means by which music is transmitted also matter. In the Western world we have privileged music that can be shared across time and space; music that is written down, or music that is recorded. And yet oral transmission has long been more important in many cultures around the world. Their great music is transmitted through memory rather than through notation.

As we have said, canons are not static. In addition to preserving the past, most traditions also develop and expand into the present and future. Musicians and their audiences continually broaden categories through new ways of engaging with established repertories, the inclusion of previously excluded individuals or traditions, and the creation of new music. The canon as it exists today—as represented by concert programs, album releases, music journalism, and online playlists—still centers largely around the music of "dead white men." And yet more and more performers and listeners are embracing repertories that are inclusive of previously underrepresented populations, including women and people of color.

Over the years *The Enjoyment of Music* canon has changed: we have added some musical works to the listening guides in this book, and removed others, responding to evolving ideas about canon. We consider each work that we have chosen to present through our Listening Guides a valuable resource for your journey toward greater enjoyment of music, yet we also acknowledge that there are many voices that are not included in the traditional Western canon. By weaving in a new feature called **Many Voices** throughout the book, we give you the opportunity to consider some of the individuals and traditions presently outside the established canon, as well as music and performances that engage with the canon in nontraditional and innovative ways.

As you learn more about musical traditions, you also have the opportunity to create your own canons—each of us can shape a list of what music we consider most valuable, and be open to revisiting that list thoughtfully as our perspectives change. To help in this effort, each chapter ends with a more general set of suggestions, providing **Your Turn to Explore** questions and repertories that are even further afield from the Western canon—but perhaps relevant to its expansion in ways that you will be able to define as a critical listener.

In Their Own Words

66 You have to have a canon so the next generation can come along and explode it."

—*Henry Louis Gates*

14

Putting Music into Words

"Writing about music is like dancing about architecture."

As a nonverbal art, music does not easily translate into words, as the quip above suggests. But people have been writing about music since the time of the earliest literate societies—probably because we want to describe those experiences we find most meaningful, even when we realize that words can't quite convey all the nuances of what we sense, hear, or feel. As an assignment for this course, you may well be asked to discuss or write a report about works you've listened to in class or heard at a concert. If you feel strongly about a favorite song, you will likely want to describe it to a friend. These situations call for different types of explanations and different vocabularies.

The opening chapters of this book have provided you with an idea of how knowledge is constructed in music—and these concepts apply to all styles, popular and classical alike. Let's say that you listened in class to Britten's *Young Person's Guide to the Orchestra* (Chapter 11). You might tell a friend that the end of the work—the fugue—sounded "exciting," and follow up by saying it sounded like a frenzied and intense "wake-up call" at the end of a long piece. But with a knowledge of the building blocks of music, you are equipped not only to understand better but also to elaborate on how and why you had this reaction. You could note the fast tempo, the different instruments entering one after the other with the same tune (starting with those in a high register), how complex or polyphonic the texture became, and how the main tune rose in the brass from under all this musical

An audience enjoying a live performance of an orchestral concert.

activity. These kinds of insights are likely what your instructor would expect from you in a class discussion or a written report, and they also would allow your friend to understand more deeply what was meaningful to you, and perhaps make that friend want to hear the music too.

In this way, your reaction and your ensuing analysis connect the three planes of listening described by composer Aaron Copland: the sensuous, in which the music simply washes over the listener; the expressive, in which the emotional power of the music is at the forefront and the listener is considering the composer's meaning; and the musical, in which the listener delves into the inner workings of the music.

In another scenario, you might want or be asked to analyze a new musical work, one not discussed in the book or in class. Here, you can draw on your developing listening skills to determine its genre, aspects of its style, and perhaps the era in which it was composed. You'll be able to use vocabulary relating to melody, rhythm, harmony, texture, form, and timbre—in short, the materials of music. Here are some tips to help you get started in applying those terms and concepts to what you hear.

To begin, listen to the work several times if possible—this will give you a better chance to perceive individual elements. Then consider the big picture:

Student studying music in the library.

- If you can define the **performing forces** of a work, this can help you determine its **genre**. Works of the same genre (song, symphony, string quartet) often share certain style traits. In particular, the performing forces and timbres you hear should be similar—that is, a symphony generally features strings, and usually brass, woodwinds, and percussion. One helpful clue can be the title of a work, which frequently specifies a genre (e.g., Beethoven, Symphony No. 5 in C Minor).

- If you know the date of a composition or dates of its composer, you can easily place it within a **historical period** (Baroque era, Romantic era, etc.; see p. 57, "Musical Styles in History," to find the dates of each era). Beginning with Part 2, this book is organized chronologically, so that you will encounter eras and styles in historical order. Compositions from the same period generally share style traits, regardless of the genre. For example, you will find that many Romantic-era works, whether for solo voice, solo piano, or orchestra, feature broad-ranging, very lyrical melodies.

- Note the prominent moments, or **signposts**, that catch your ear. Why and how do they do so? You might **take notes** as you listen, so that you can recall better the sequence and timing of events.

- What **organizational features** can you identify? Is there significant repetition or variation of musical ideas? Do you hear new, contrasting music? Does the work sound balanced, or more asymmetrical?

- Is the **overall sound** mostly consonant or dissonant? Do you think the work is based on a major scale, or a more somber minor one?

- Can you describe the **musical conversation** at play in the work? If it has a story (or program) provided by the composer, become familiar with it, as it will help you follow the progression of musical events. Not all works have an explicit story, but each provides a set of musical ideas as a sort of conversation on which you can focus. If it helps for you to create your own story, that's great.

The necessary study tools for music.

- How would you describe the overall **mood** of the piece? Allow yourself to respond both **objectively** and **subjectively** to what you hear. That is, consider both the technical terms you can apply to the music and your personal response. At what points in the music did you have that response, and why?

Artworks from the same historical era, in this case Impressionism, share style traits such as paint strokes, colors, and even subject matter.

TOP: *Young Girl Sewing in a Garden,* by **Mary Cassatt** (1844–1926).

BOTTOM: *Peasant Girl,* by **Camille Pissarro** (1830–1903).

- Do some **research** on the work, if this is appropriate and allowed in the assignment (or for your own interest). This way you can deal with the **ideas of others**, along with your own reactions. If you don't agree with the assessment or description provided by someone else, why not? What descriptors would you use instead, and why?

Now for some finer details:

- Describe how the **main melodies** sound (cheerful? disjunct?) and how they move.
- How pronounced is the **rhythm and meter**? Does the work flow gently, or is it heavily accented? What is the **tempo,** and how does it affect the rhythmic flow?
- Does the **texture**, or interaction of the different parts, seem simple (as in a melody with accompaniment), or complex, with multiple lines occurring simultaneously?

Finding Your Voice and Framing Your Ideas

Don't strive to be comprehensive, since it's not really possible to hear everything that's going on in a piece of music, nor is there only one way to understand it. A blow-by-blow description of a work, whether literary or musical, can be daunting to complete and tiresome to read. Instead, your perspective can focus on the moments that leap out at you, that jolt your senses or seem particularly important. In discussion or in writing, you should try to achieve a balance between descriptive analysis and personal reaction, thus presenting your own "voice" or "spin" on a work.

Your discussion could take one of various forms. Consider how you might use or adapt the templates below in constructing your argument. A comparison with something you already know can be a helpful way to begin.

Perhaps you will be faced with a new symphony, hopefully after having studied Beethoven's famous Fifth Symphony. This template allows a **comparison** of the two works, noting the differences and opening a conversation that can be further developed.

Unlike Beethoven's Fifth Symphony, which is unified by a short, four-note motive, _____ [title of the new work] presents _____ themes that are _____.

In some cases, a piece, let's say a song by Stephen Foster, may share features with one you already know and like, and thus prompt an **evaluative statement** to start:

Like Foster's *I Dream of Jeanie,* _____ [title of the new work] is memorable, for its _____ form and _____ melodies.

Alternately, you might take issue with, or **argue against**, the general description of a genre when you are faced with a new multimovement work from, say, the Classical era. Clearly you will need to develop your argument further.

Although many Classical-era works feature a slow second movement and a dancelike third movement, _____ [title of the new work] changes this standard format to _____.

Yet another approach might be structured by giving some description or **analysis** that then leads you to a conclusion, such as the era of composition:

The composition _____ [title of new work] features _____ harmonies and _____ rhythms, which suggest it was likely written in the twentieth century.

Here are excerpts showing how different authors have written about music. Don't try to imitate these, but do consider how each writer presents an individual perspective. And remember that one listener's perspective will differ from that of another.

For the song *The Trout*, by Franz Schubert, the author (Thomas Forrest Kelly, *Music Then and Now*) considers the text carefully, then writes this:

The piano introduction is charming, . . . bouncy and bright, with an unforgettable rhythmic pattern. . . . The poem paints an innocent outdoor scene of a trout in a brook and the music matches it in sunny simplicity. When the second verse arrives, we are not surprised; there is the same piano introduction, the same melody, but the words have just a hint of something ominous. We suspect the trout may be in trouble. And there it is: the third verse is suddenly very different. What before seemed innocent enough, now is full

In Their Own Words

❝ There is no such thing as music divorced from the listener. Music as such is unfulfilled until it has penetrated our ears."

—*Yehudi Menuhin*

Disco Days at Casa della Musica in Naples, Italy, promote music and the culture of listening, especially among lovers of vinyl.

of bitter humor. In the same way the fisherman lures the trout, Schubert's apparently simple setting lures in the listener.

Here, the critic follows the text of the song through its changing moods as the music follows course. When writing about a song, try to have the words and (if appropriate) a translation handy in order to follow the meaning of the music. Note that this discussion is descriptive and evaluative with a dash of humor.

In discussing the piano piece Prelude in E Minor, Op. 28, No. 4, by Frédéric Chopin, the author (Roger Hickman, *The Norton Scores*) selects his points carefully, rather than trying to be comprehensive:

> The Prelude in E minor is justifiably one of Chopin's most renowned compositions, principally because of its brevity, chromaticism, and emotional potency. The melody . . . moves in a restricted range with simple ornamentation, suggesting the lyricism of a vocal line. . . . The climax occurs near the middle, where the melody suddenly expands, the rhythmic activity increases and the rate of harmonic change accelerates.

The author is evaluative in telling the reader that this is a famous work, and then proceeds to speculate why. He describes the expressiveness of the melody, but then focuses on an important moment in the short work—the climax, detailing what happens here to the melody, rhythm, and harmony.

Listening to contemporary art music can be especially challenging, as twentieth-century composers broke away from many of the established procedures. Here is a discussion of Mexican composer Silvestre Revueltas's orchestral work *Homage to Federico García Lorca,* from an earlier edition of this book.

> This movement, in a rondo-like form, begins explosively, tossing about fragmentary ideas with unrestrained energy. The strings and piano then establish a steady 6/8 pulse, over which the muted trumpet sounds a narrow-ranged theme built from whole tones. Rhythmic confusion and percussive accents lead to the principal theme—a syncopated Mexican dance tune. . . . A rhythmic idea from this theme is then manipulated and developed by various instruments, after which the Mexican tune returns in a full orchestral statement. A frenetic coda is unleashed after two dissonant chords in the piano.

In Their Own Words

" Just listen with the vastness of the world in mind. You can't fail to get the message."

—*Pierre Boulez*

In this case, the authors chose to describe what they perceived as the main events in the order they appear in the work, but because music is not a series of unrelated events, they also noted the return of the main melody. The authors were purposefully vague in some aspects of their description, saying the form was "rondo-like" rather than a rondo. This loose treatment of form is typical of the "rule-breaking" by contemporary composers.

Music and sound are crucial not only to historical multimedia (such as opera, ballet, and musical theater) but to contemporary multimedia as well. The author of this excerpt (Reba Wissner, from the Norton website *The Avid Listener*) describes how musical "codes" in science-fiction TV alert us to something sinister:

> Common malevolent musical techniques include the use of low-pitched instruments, such as organ, cello, and bassoon, played in minor keys; ostinato melodies (melodies that repeat over and over in a single piece); simple and short melodies that move by step or half step; dissonant chords (stacks of notes that sound harsh or tense); rising or falling chromatic melodies (that is, by half steps); alternating minor seconds; and unusual instruments such as the Theremin. Musical codes for impending danger include dissonance,

often paired with a low-pitched drone (a single note or pair of notes that remain static); ominous rising motives; minor second and tritone intervals; and siren-like oscillations. Each of these allows viewers to see with their ears before they see with their eyes.

Here the author describes specific details of timbre, melody, and harmony to convey the effects they create in the science-fiction narrative.

Some final words of advice are in order. In this age of information overload, we are in danger of losing our listening skills. Be aware that active, engaged listening takes not only practice but time. So listen to music—all types of music—often and think about it. Learning more about music can only enhance your enjoyment!

Music fans enjoy a concert with fireworks at the Hollywood Bowl in Los Angeles.

The Middle Ages and Renaissance

"When the words come, they are merely empty shells without the music. They live as they are sung, for the words are the body and the music the spirit."

—German poet, composer, and mystic Hildegard of Bingen (1098–1179)

OVERVIEW

476
Fall of the
Roman Empire.

800
Charlemagne
crowned Holy
Roman Emperor.

1163
Construction
begins on Notre
Dame in Paris.

1271
Marco Polo travels
to the Far East.

500   1000   1200

c. 1150
Hildegard founds
the monastery
in Rupertsberg,
Germany.

c. 1200
Notre Dame organum
composed.

Learning Objectives

By the end of Part 2, you will be able to

- perceive how the free-flowing melodic lines in less familiar scales (modes) and the hollow-sounding, modal harmonies and cadences of medieval and early Renaissance music differ from the fuller sounds resembling major and minor tonality of later Renaissance music.

- understand how the music of this era enhances the words and how the text helps determine repeated sections of music.

- recognize that some of the earliest music (chant) moves with no perceptible pulse (nonmetrically) while other music from this time moves in a clearly metered pattern (whether triple or duple)

- note how the texture becomes more complex as more lines, or voices, are added in a composition and consider how they interact with each other

- define some of the main sacred and secular genres (categories of music) of the Middle Ages and Renaissance, and become familiar with some of the most renowned composers of the era.

1348
Black Death strikes in Europe.

1455
Gutenberg Bible printed.

1492
Columbus lands in the New World.

1504
Michelangelo completes the sculpture *David*.

1517
Martin Luther launches the Protestant Reformation.

1559
Elizabeth I crowned queen in England.

1602
Shakespeare's *Hamlet* produced.

1400   1500   1600

1360s
Guillaume de Machaut composes *Messe de Notre Dame*.

1480s
Josquin des Prez writes motet *Ave Maria*, dedicated to the Virgin.

1551
Tielman Susato publishes *Danserye*, a book of dances.

1554
Palestrina presents his earliest printed Mass to Pope Julius.

1599
John Farmer issues the madrigal *Fair Phyllis*.

1603
Claudio Monteverdi publishes his fourth madrigal book.

2

Music as Commodity and Social Activity

"Nothing exists without music, for the universe is said to have been framed by a kind of harmony of sounds, and heaven itself revolves under the tones of that harmony."

—Isidore of Seville (c. 560–636)

Humans have been using sound to enhance their communication for thousands of years—in fact, some scholars argue that what we call "song" may have been the earliest form of speech. But our story begins when Europeans came up with the idea of putting sound to paper—the concept of musical notation, which is not unique to Western culture (musical notation from China dates back at least 2,500 years) but has defined the development of Western music and allowed for its astonishing variety, diffusion, and staying power.

Musical styles that stem from the European tradition are at the core of music-making throughout the world today, a level of influence that surpasses any language or religion. And this is because of notation, which allows us to think of a song or other musical work as a product or commodity to be preserved, taught and learned, bought and sold. Still, in Western culture as in all world cultures, making music is also a social activity that allows individuals to feel closely connected to a group, and to express their feelings both recreationally and spiritually.

Music notation was invented to further the goals of Christian worship, and social music-making was essential to the early Christian church. Therefore, much of the music we still have from the Middle Ages and Renaissance was intended for **sacred** purposes: sounds designed to inspire the faithful to worship. We will be exploring various ways in which these early worship-music traditions expanded and shifted to meet the needs of a changing society.

Despite the predominance of sacred music, more and more through this period we have evidence of **secular** music, social music-making for entertainment and personal expression. It's especially in the secular context that music becomes both a social activity and a commodity item—already in these early centuries of the Western tradition.

Angel Musicians, from the Ghent (Belgium) altarpiece by **Jan van Eyck** (c. 1390–1441).

From Antiquity to the Middle of Things

While we believe that many ancient civilizations enjoyed flourishing musical cultures, only a few fragments of their music survive today. We do know that ancient Mediterranean cultures provided the foundation of the Western musical heritage, as well as the traditions that it shares with the Middle East.

The fall of the Roman Empire, commonly set in the year 476 CE, marked the beginning of a thousand-year period usually described as the Middle Ages. The first half of this millennium, from around 500 to 1000, was a period of political and cultural consolidation. During this era, all power flowed from kings, with the approval of the Roman Catholic Church. The struggle between these two centers of power, church and state, is at the core of European history and has resonances to this day. The modern concept of a strong, centralized government as the guardian of law and order is generally credited to Charlemagne (c. 742–814), the celebrated emperor of the Franks. A progressive monarch, Charlemagne encouraged education and left behind him an extensive system of social justice. It was during his reign that Europeans started to make systematic use of music notation.

During the later Middle Ages, from around 1000 to 1450, universities were founded throughout Europe, and cities emerged as centers of art and culture. Literary landmarks such as the *Chanson de Roland* (c. 1100) in France, Dante's *Divine Comedy* (1307) in Italy, and Chaucer's *Canterbury Tales* (1386; see illustration on p. 70) in England helped shape their respective languages. This time also witnessed the construction of the great cathedrals, including Notre Dame in Paris, one of the first centers in which **polyphony** (multivoiced music) was notated and integrated into musical worship.

Among the first named composers of the Western tradition, Léonin (who lived in the second half of the 1100s) and Pérotin (who worked around 1200) developed a style known as **organum**, in which plainchant—single-line melodies of the early Christian church—was "decorated" with one or more simultaneous musical lines. The effect was described at the time as astonishing, the same way that the Cathedral of Notre Dame, for which this music was composed, was considered an awe-inspiring tribute to divine power.

Reliquary of the emperor Charlemagne in the form of a portrait bust, c. 1350.

Markets and Courts

In the later Middle Ages, a merchant class that drew its wealth from trade and commerce arose outside of feudal society. Although travel was perilous—the roads were plagued by robbers and the seas by pirates—each region of Europe exchanged its natural resources for those it lacked: the plentiful timber and furs of Scandinavia were traded for English wool and cloth manufactured in Flanders; England wanted German silver and, above all, French and Italian wine; and European goods of all kinds flowed through the seaport of Venice to Constantinople in exchange for Eastern luxuries. Musicians and their works also moved along the trade routes: music became both a necessity (for worship activities) and a desirable recreational ornament, a crucial commodity in the economies of Europe.

In Their Own Words

❝ We may compare the best form of government to the most harmonious piece of music; the oligarchic and despotic to the most violent tunes; and the democratic to the soft and gentle airs."

—*Aristotle (384–322 BCE)*

In an era of violence brought on by deep-set religious beliefs, knights embarked on holy—and bloody—Crusades to capture the Holy Land from the Muslims. Although feudal society was male-dominated and idealized the figure of the fearless warrior, the status of women was raised by the universal cult of Mary, mother of Christ (see illustrations on p. 105), and by the concepts of chivalry that arose among the knights. In the songs of the court minstrels, women were adored with a fervor that laid the foundation for our concept of romantic love. This poetic attitude found its perfect symbol in the faithful knight who worshipped his lady from afar and was inspired by her to deeds of great daring and self-sacrifice, and led to the first great flowering of secular music written in the **vernacular** (the language of the people, as opposed to **Latin**, the formal language of the church and the sacred tradition).

Most prominent in this secular tradition were the **troubadours** of Languedoc (what is now southern France) and the **trouvères** of northern France, who not only left us the first extensive notated tradition of love song, but also helped to introduce increasingly complex instruments into the Western tradition. Many instruments and song styles were adapted from the highly sophisticated Middle Eastern traditions of the time (see illustration below): a number of European courts (notably the court of Alfonso the Wise in what is now Spain) maintained good private relations with Muslim princes, despite their public rejection of Islam.

Two characters—the Miller, playing a bagpipe (top), and the Prioress (bottom)—from the Ellesmere manuscript of Geoffrey Chaucer's *Canterbury Tales* (c. 1400).

Looking Out and Looking In

Though there was significant cultural continuity from the 1400s into the 1500s, a number of important new concerns arose in the early part (1450–1520) of the time frame we now call the Renaissance. Europeans embarked (with the help of the newly developed compass) on voyages of discovery that opened up new horizons, both external and internal. Explorers of this age, in search of a new trade

In this miniature from the *Prayer Book* of Alfonso the Wise, King David is playing a rebec, in the manner of the Middle Eastern rabab.

route to the riches of China and the Indies, stumbled on North and South America. During the course of the sixteenth and seventeenth centuries, these new lands became increasingly important to European treasuries and society.

After the fall of Constantinople to the Turks (1453), ancient Greek and Roman writings, many of which had been tightly guarded by the church during the Middle Ages, were brought to Europe in increasing numbers. They were distributed ever more widely through the medium of print, the European introduction of which (c. 1455) is generally credited to the German goldsmith and inventor Johannes Gutenberg. These writings from classical antiquity encouraged a tendency for individuals to look within, at their personal thoughts, beliefs, and reactions. While this led to increasing interest in human (secular) rather than divine (sacred) concerns, far-reaching religious reformations of the 1500s, both Protestant and Catholic, also gave this inward exploration a religious grounding.

The ideals that the ancient writings exemplified began to have a great influence in architecture, painting, and sculpture. Instead of the Gothic cathedrals and fortified castles of the medieval world, lavish Renaissance palaces and spacious villas were built according to the harmonious proportions of the classical style, which strove for order and balance. This phenomenon first came to flower in Italy, the nation that stood closest to the classical Roman culture. As a result, the great names we associate with Renaissance painting and sculpture are predominantly Italian: Botticelli, Leonardo da Vinci, Michelangelo, and Titian. The nude human form, denied or covered for centuries, was revealed as a thing of beauty and used for anatomical study. Painters also began exploring the beauties of nature and conforming to the laws of perspective and composition.

The printing press, developed by Johannes Gutenberg (c. 1400–1468), brought books to a wide readership throughout Europe.

Musicians in Medieval and Renaissance Society

Musicians were supported by the chief institutions of their society—the church, city, and state, as well as royal and aristocratic courts. They found employment as choirmasters, singers, organists, instrumentalists, copyists, composers, teachers, instrument builders, and, by the sixteenth century, music printers. There was a corresponding growth in a number of supporting musical institutions: church choirs and schools, music publishing houses, civic wind bands. And there were increased opportunities for apprentices to study with master singers, players, and instrument builders. Only a few women can be identified as professional musicians in the Renaissance era, earning their living as court singers.

The rise of the merchant class in the later Middle Ages brought with it a new group of music patrons. This development was paralleled by the emergence,

In *The Concert* (c. 1530–40), three women perform a French secular song with voice, flute, and lute. The Flemish artist is known only as the Master of the Female Half-Lengths.

among the cultivated middle and upper classes, of amateur musicians—men and women alike—who sang secular songs (chansons and madrigals) and played simple dances on instruments. When the system for printing from movable type was successfully adapted to music in the early sixteenth century, printed music books became available and affordable. As a result, music literacy spread dramatically.

The concerns of musicians surrounding worship and play, individuality and community, and music both as commodity and as social activity were grounded in the historical circumstances in which they lived. But such issues also resonate today. In the next few chapters, we will examine how these long-standing concerns became rooted in Western society.

Performance Matters

VARIETY AND FLEXIBILITY

Many aspects of early music performance are open to speculation. What we do know is that in the Middle Ages and Renaissance, there was no one absolutely correct way to perform a work—which gives modern performers a great deal of leeway. Still, there are some basic principles that applied. Sacred genres were generally considered to be ensemble vocal music, usually sung by a small group. Because women were prohibited from singing in church (except within all-female religious communities), the ensemble often included choirboys on the higher parts and men on the lower ones. Secular music had no real restrictions: women and men both sang and played instruments, and it was acceptable to take a song and sing all the parts, play the parts on instruments, or combine voices and instruments depending on the available resources and desired effect. Notational subtleties such as tempo and dynamic markings were absent from early music, but some general principles were understood. For example, the tempo for a sacred work would likely be based on a man's heartbeat (60–80 bpm); in both secular and sacred works, the occasion and text would give performers ideas of how to interpret the piece.

Performing choices today are rich and varied. We might hear medieval and Renaissance music sung by all-male, all-female, or mixed vocal ensembles, or played on modern as well as historical instruments.

CRITICAL THINKING

1. How did society and musical institutions change from the Middle Ages to the Renaissance?
2. How was music-making in sacred (church) and secular (court, marketplace) contexts similar in this period? How was it different?

15

Voice and Worship: Tradition and Individuality in Medieval Chant

"When God saw that many men were lazy, and gave themselves only with difficulty to spiritual reading, He wished to make it easy for them, and added the melody to the Prophet's words, that all being rejoiced by the charm of the music, should sing hymns to Him with gladness."

—St. John Chrysostom (c. 347–407)

KeyPoints

- Sung worship is a shared feature among many world cultures, allowing for a more intense personal and collective connection with the divine.
- Religious communities (monasteries) fostered the extensive development of worship music, starting in the Middle Ages.
- The music of the early Christian church, called **plainchant** (or just **chant**), features monophonic,

nonmetric melodies set in one of the church **modes**, or scales.

- Chant melodies fall into three categories (**syllabic**, **neumatic**, **melismatic**), based on how many notes are set to each syllable of text.
- The expressive music of Hildegard of Bingen exemplifies the tension between an individual, creative response to divine inspiration, and community expectations of worship.

Voices raised in song as people connect to a spiritual power: wherever you are from, you may have encountered this in your own community. This is one of the most widespread purposes of music throughout world cultures—and in medieval Europe, communities of men and women dedicated themselves fully to sung prayer, seeking the salvation of humanity through music.

Plainchant: Music of the Church

The early music of the Christian church is testimony to the highly spiritual nature of the Middle Ages. **Plainchant** consists of a single-line melody; it is thus monophonic in texture, lacking either harmony or counterpoint. Its freely flowing vocal line subtly follows the inflections of the Latin text and is generally free from regular accent. These beautiful melodies, shaped in part by Greek, Hebrew, and Syrian influences, represent the starting point of artistic creativity in Western music.

LEFT: Manuscript illumination of Pope Gregory the Great dictating to his scribe Peter. A dove, representing the Holy Spirit, sits on his shoulder.   RIGHT: A Kyrie chant in Gregorian notation, from the *Liber usualis*.

Liturgy

In time, it became necessary to assemble the ever-growing body of music into an organized **liturgy**, a term that refers to the order of church services and the structure of each service. The task extended over several generations, though tradition often credits Pope Gregory the Great (r. 590–604) with codifying these melodies, known today as **Gregorian chant**.

The Gregorian melodies, numbering more than 3,000, form an immense body of music, nearly all of it anonymous. In fact, tradition held that Pope Gregory had received the melodies of "true prayer" directly from the Holy Spirit in the form of a dove whispering into his ear—therefore, in a very real sense, those who sang Gregorian plainchant in the Middle Ages believed it to have been composed by a divine and not human mind.

Chant melodies

Gregorian chant avoids wide leaps, allowing its gentle contours to create a kind of musical speech. Free from regular phrase structure, the continuous, undulating vocal line is the musical counterpart to the lacy ornamentation typical of medieval art and architecture (see the photo of Notre Dame Cathedral on p. 85). Chant melodies fall into three main classes, according to the way they are set to the text: **syllabic**, with one note sung to each syllable of text; **neumatic**, generally with three to five or six notes sung to a syllable; and **melismatic**, with many notes set to a single syllable (see chart on p. 35). The melismatic style, which descended from the elaborate improvisations still heard in Middle Eastern music today, became an expressive feature of Gregorian chant and exerted a strong influence on subsequent Western music.

At first, chants were handed down through oral tradition from one generation to the next. But as the number of chants increased, church leaders moved to standardize them throughout the European Christian lands. To help singers remember

Neumes

the general shapes of the different melodies, **neumes**, little ascending and descending symbols, were written above the words to suggest the contours of the melody. Neumes eventually developed into a musical notation consisting of square notes on a four-line staff (see above).

Modes

From Gregorian chant through music of the Renaissance, Western music used a variety of scale patterns, or **modes**. The modes codified in the Middle Ages served as the basis for European music for a thousand years. They preceded and overlapped with major and minor scales (scales are also types of modes), which are character-ized by a strong pull toward a tonic note; the earlier modes lacked this sense of attraction. You may find that the melodic shapes of modal music (and the chant ex-amples we will consider) seem unfamiliar. This is because for those of us in Western culture, **tonal** melody and harmony are deeply ingrained in our musical experience. In fact, you may hear similarities between the modal melodies in chant and the melodies and scales used by Middle Eastern sacred traditions (see Many Voices on p. 78)—not surprising, since both developed from the same Eastern Mediterranean religious heritage centuries ago.

The Mass

Ever since the Middle Ages, chanted prayers have been central to two types of services: the daily **Offices**—a series of services celebrated in religious communities at various hours of the day—and the **Mass**, a reenact-ment of Christ's Last Supper with his disciples. The Mass is the primary (and most solemn) ritual of the Roman Catholic Church, and the one generally attend-ed by public worshippers. Its name derives from the Latin words *Ite, missa est* ("Go, it is the dismissal"), recited at the end of the service by the priest.

In this fourteenth-century manuscript illumination, the monks sing during the celebra-tion of Mass, and an altar boy (left) pulls a bell rope.

The prayers that make up the Mass (its liturgy) fall into two categories: the **Proper**, texts that vary from day to day throughout the church year, depending on the feast being celebrated; and the **Ordinary**, texts that remain the same in every Mass. (See the chart on p. 110.) Gregorian melodies, prescribed for each sec-tion, remain central to the celebration of the Mass. Until the middle of the twentieth century, most of the Mass text was in Latin, the language of the ancient Romans, which continued to be a shared language of learning and tradition for Europeans through the Middle Ages and Renaissance and beyond.

A Gregorian Melody: *Kyrie*

We will consider one of many settings of the **Kyrie**, the first item in the Ordinary (fixed portion) of the Mass, as an excellent example of the flowing melodic struc-ture of Gregorian chant (LG 2). The text of the Kyrie is a Greek prayer for mercy taken from the central-Mediterranean Christian tradition; Pope Gregory is often credited with establishing it as part of the Mass. Its three-part form consists of nine invocations to God: three of "Kyrie eleison" ("Lord, have mercy upon us"), three of "Christe eleison" ("Christ, have mercy upon us"), and again three of "Kyrie eleison." The structure is symbolic: the number three evokes the Trinity—Father, Son, and Holy Spirit—and thus represents perfect unity.

The melody of this *Kyrie* moves freely in waves; its range is narrow at first, but grows slightly wider and higher in the second and third sections. You will hear that it's sung *a cappella* (voices alone) and in an **antiphonal** manner, alternating   *A cappella*

Interface

Influences in the Early Christian Church

How did early Christians first establish the rituals of their church, and where did their musical practices come from? Since Christianity descended directly from Judaism—Jesus and his followers were, after all, Jews—the early Christians naturally kept some familiar Judaic traditions. For example, they retained the concept of one God (as opposed to other world religions that worship multiple deities) and many of the same moral codes respected today. Christianity also borrowed from Judaism the use of congregational prayer; a reliance on written texts, including the biblical Tanakh or Hebrew Scriptures (Old Testament); and the practice of reading and discussing sacred texts in a public meeting house—the Jewish synagogue or Christian church. Some Hebrew words, such as "Amen" (in truth) and "Hallelujah" (praise God), remain common in Christian prayer.

Judaism and Christianity are linked musically by the Old Testament Book of Psalms, poems that were sung during ceremonial meals and in the home. "O come, let us sing to the Lord," "O sing to the Lord a new song," and "I will sing of loyalty and justice" are a few opening lines. Some of the Psalms have a refrain of "hallelujah." In Jewish practice, they were sung responsorially by a cantor (a singing leader) and the congregation, using simple repetitive melodies. In the Roman Catholic Church, the simply chanted responsorial recitation of Psalms became the core of the Divine Offices—the daily cycle of services, or hours—and, to a lesser extent, the Mass. Psalm texts were adopted as well into the services of

Jewish folk artist **Samuel Shulman** depicts Zion, the city of David, with biblical instruments and tombs of the kings of the House of David.

the Protestant movements during the Reformation, especially the Calvinist Church (see p. 110).

Other practices in the early Roman Catholic Church came from the East—the Church of Byzantium (Constantinople, or modern-day Istanbul), which gradually separated from Western tradition during the first few centuries of Christianity. Such practices included devotional songs (hymns) as well as ideas about melody and harmony that shaped Western music for centuries. Some prayers of the Roman Church (most prominently the *Kyrie eleison*) retained the Greek language that had defined Christianity since the writing of the Gospels.

Although musical instruments are mentioned in the Hebrew Scriptures (harp, trumpet, and cymbals among others), the music of the early Christian Church was sung rather than accompanied by instruments. For centuries, Christians associated instruments with secular life and felt they did not serve religion. The organ, an invention of the Greeks, was the first instrument to be widely accepted for use in Christian worship.

Over the centuries, early conventions have changed in Jewish as well as Christian faith communities. Texts for devotional music are often in the vernacular (the language of the people) rather than in Hebrew or Latin, so that everyone can understand them. And many styles of music serve religion: whatever moves people spiritually is acceptable, whether instrumental or vocal, new or old, popular or art.

between two groups of singers. At first, they sing only a few notes per syllable (a neumatic text setting); as the second and third phrases grow longer, however, some syllables are stretched over many notes, producing a melismatic setting.

Life and Music in the Medieval Monastery

Chants like the *Kyrie* were the most regularly sung prayers in the Middle Ages, as part of the established repertory. The greatest creativity in musical worship often took place within **monasteries** and other religious communities of individuals who chose to gather in systematic religious practice. Here, both men and women devoted themselves to prayer, scholarship, preaching, charity, or healing the sick, depending on the religious order they had joined. Parents might choose a religious life for a child if they had no land holdings to give a son or no dowry for a daughter's wedding. Others might take this spiritual path as an adult—a widow who did not wish to remarry or a young woman who longed for the education that cloistered life provided.

A life devoted to the church was not an easy one; the discipline was arduous. A typical day began at 2:00 or 3:00 a.m. with the celebration of the first of the daily Offices, the reading of lessons, and the singing of psalms. Each day in the church calendar had its own ritual and its own order of prayers. The members of the community interspersed their religious duties with work in the fields or the library, or producing items that could be sold—wine, beer, or cheese—thus bringing in revenue to the order. Many in religious life dedicated themselves to writing and preserving knowledge from earlier times. Such a person was Hildegard of Bingen, one of the most remarkable women of the Middle Ages, who was renowned in her day as a poet and prophet and whose serenely beautiful music has regained popularity in recent years.

In this vision from Hildegard's *Scivias* (*Know the Ways of the Lord*), the saint listens to choirs of angels praising the Lord.

A Song for Worship by Hildegard

Hildegard set many of her own texts to music; her poetry is characterized by brilliant imagery and creative language. Some of her songs celebrate the lives of local saints such as Saint Rupert, the patron of her monastery, while others praise the Virgin Mary, comparing her to a blossoming flower or branch and celebrating her purity. Our example is an *Alleluia* (LG 2), derived from the Hebrew words for "Praise [be] to God"; to this day, some version of the "Alleluia" is used in most Christian communities to express joyful celebration. Hildegard wrote this chant for a specific occasion—a feast day for the Virgin Mary. Might Hildegard have found particular inspiration as a woman writing in honor of a woman?

The chant is in three parts, beginning and ending with the word "Alleluia" (meant to be sung by the entire worship community) and featuring a **verse** in the middle, sung by a single leader. The leader first sings the opening "Alleluia" phrase of the chant, and then that same phrase is repeated and extended in **unison** by the

Islamic Chant

Many world cultures employ a kind of "intoned speech" in their worship or religious rituals, which is distinct from "music" for entertainment or other purposes. We can hear through the plainchant by Hildegard how this relatively simple style of song enhances Christian prayer. Among other religions that feature intoned prayers is Islam, which is centered on the Quran, the sacred text presenting the word of God as transmitted to the Prophet Muhammad by the Archangel Gabriel. The practice of reciting the Quran is governed by established oral traditions known as *tajweed* that specify the vocal timbre, rhythmic treatment of texts, pronunciation, and a special vibrato (a wavering fluctuation of the pitch). While different branches of Islam view other kinds of music more or less favorably— "haram" (sinful according to Quranic teaching) or "maqruh" (problematic but not explicitly forbidden)—they are united in the ideal of "beautifying" the Quran with one's voice in daily devotion.

One of the most familiar sounds in Islamic culture is the call to prayer, or *Adhan,* which is sounded publicly five times daily—morning, noon, afternoon, sunset, and evening— and helps regulate Muslim life. (You may notice a similarity with the specifically regulated prayer times of medieval Christianity.) The Prophet Muhammad is credited with instituting the practice of the call to prayer, given from the minaret (a tower on the mosque) by the muezzin: a prayer leader chosen for his vocal ability to recite the *Adhan* beautifully and clearly for all to hear. Originally the muezzin began the call without amplification from the top of the tower, but today his voice is broadcast from the minaret via speakers.

The text of the *Adhan* reiterates the Islamic statement of faith: "There is no God but Allah" and "Muhammad is the Messenger of God." There are seven invocations in this recited prayer, and all but the last are repeated. You will hear the careful balance between repetition and contrast in the reciting structure, as the first statement of each phrase is presented quite simply, and then followed by a more ornate, melismatic variation. The *Adhan* is usually sounded slowly and freely, except at sunset, when it is recited more quickly. The pitches are based on an Arabic mode, or scale type, called a *maqam,* which defines patterns of embellishments as well.

The call to prayer is followed by the Blessings on the Prophet, a text from the Quran (chapter 33, verse 56) ending with the words "the opening"— an invitation to all to recite silently the opening chapter of the Quran. We hear a quite different intoning style from the call in this blessing, which is delivered in a syllabic, speechlike rendition.

Archangel Gabriel revealing the Quran to Muhammad (in 610 CE), from the *Siyer-i Nebi,* a Turkish epic by fourteenth-century writer Mustafa.

A muezzin, or crier, sounds the Muslim call to prayer from the minaret of a mosque.

🔊 *Adhan: Call to Prayer*

What to listen for:
- Repetitive structure of the text and *tajweed*, with its subtle variations and rich elaborations in which text syllables are extended through various pitches.
- Free, rhapsodic delivery designed to give the faithful opportunity to reflect on the scriptural text.

Text	Translation	Structure
Allahu Akbar	God is most great.	Sung four times.
Ash-hadu an-la ilaha illa llah	I witness that there is no god but Allah.	Sung twice.
Ash-hadu anna Muhammadarn Rasulullah	I witness that Muhammad is the Messenger of God.	Sung twice.
Hayya ala s-salah	Come to prayer.	Sung twice.
Hayya 'ala 'l-falah	Come to salvation.	Sung twice.
Allahu Akbar	God is most great.	Sung twice.
La ilaha illa-Allah	There is no god but Allah.	Sung once.

🔊 *Adhan: Blessings on the Prophet* (Quran 33:56)

What to listen for: faster, speechlike delivery of text.

Text	Translation
Inna Allaha wamala-ikatahu yusalloona AAala alnnabiyyi ya ayyuha allatheena amanoo salloo AAalayhi wasallimoo tasleeman. Assalatu was salamu alayka ya sayyidi ya liabiba Liah. Al Fatihah.	Verily God raineth blessings, and his angels pray for blessings, upon Muhammad. O ye who believe, pray for blessings and peace upon him. Blessings and Peace upon thee, O my liege-Lord. O beloved of God. The opening.

Hildegard of Bingen (1098–1179)

Hildegard of Bingen was the daughter of a noble German couple who promised her, as their tenth child, to the service of the church as a tithe (the practice of giving one-tenth of what one owns). Raised by a religious recluse from age eight, she lived in a stone cell with one window and took her vows at the age of fourteen. From childhood, Hildegard experienced visions, which intensified in later life. She was reportedly able to foretell the future.

Around the year 1150, Hildegard founded a monastery in Rupertsberg (near Bingen), in Germany. Her reported miracles and prophecies made her famous throughout Europe: popes, kings, and priests sought her advice on political and religious issues. Sainthood came late for Hildegard; she was canonized only in 2012 by Pope Benedict XVI. Her highly original compositional style resembles Gregorian chant but is full of expressive leaps and melismas that clearly convey the meaning of the words.

MAJOR WORKS: A collection of poetry and visions entitled *Scivias* (*Know the Ways*) • A volume of religious poetry set to music (*Symphony of the Harmony of Celestial Revelations*) • A sung morality play (*The Play of the Virtues*) • Scientific and medical writings.

Responsorial singing

full ensemble. This **responsorial singing** practice of group repetition of a leader's text-music phrase has its roots in ancient Jewish practice. It differs from call and response (which we will encounter in a later chapter) because in this case the people are expected to repeat the leader's words and melody precisely, rather than changing the idea. Hildegard elaborates some words with melismas, especially in the last line of the verse, describing the Virgin's purity.

Because we know that Hildegard composed this praise song, it is not "Gregorian" chant—it is not part of the established repertory that was sanctioned in her day. The notion that *new* praise song could be used in the liturgy was very controversial at the time. How could a mere human come up with prayer melodies that would be appropriate for communication with God? This was all the more complicated for Hildegard, since many in the church held that women were unworthy to aspire to connection with the divine. She had to strike a balance between claiming divine inspiration and not appearing to be heretical or even devilish.

In Their Own Words

❝ The words I speak come from no human mouth; I saw and heard them in visions sent to me. . . . I have no confidence in my own capacities—I reach out my hand to God that He may carry me along as a feather borne weightlessly by the wind."

—*Hildegard of Bingen*

CRITICAL THINKING

1. In what ways did composers of chant vary their melodies?
2. How did Hildegard of Bingen instill her music with emotional expression?

Your Turn TO EXPLORE

Consider the way worship music is used in communities around the world (for example, in Chinese or Vietnamese Buddhism, native traditions in both North and South America, Hindu practices in South Asia). How do other experiences of singing to communicate with the divine compare with the examples considered in this chapter?

Two Examples of Chant

Gregorian Chant: *Kyrie*   1:59

Date: 10th century
Genre: Kyrie plainchant, from the Ordinary of the Mass

Performed by: Schola Cantorum of Amsterdam, Wim van Gerven, director

---

What to Listen For

Melody	Conjunct, wavelike motion, small range; neumatic, then melismatic.	**Form**	Three phrases, each sung three times (**A-A-A B-B-B C-C-C′**).
Rhythm	Free-flowing rhythm, nonmetric.	**Performing forces**	*A cappella* choir, alternating between two groups (antiphonal).
Texture	Monophonic (single line).	**Text**	Greek prayer for mercy.

	TEXT	TRANSLATION	MUSICAL FORM
0:00	Kyrie eleison.	Lord, have mercy upon us.	**A**
	Kyrie eleison.	Lord, have mercy upon us.	**A** repeated.
	Kyrie eleison.	Lord, have mercy upon us.	**A** repeated.
0:27	Christe eleison.	Christ, have mercy upon us.	**B**
	Christe eleison.	Christ, have mercy upon us.	**B** repeated.
	Christe eleison.	Christ, have mercy upon us.	**B** repeated.
1:10	Kyrie eleison.	Lord, have mercy upon us.	**C**
	Kyrie eleison.	Lord, have mercy upon us.	**C** repeated.
	Kyrie eleison.	Lord, have mercy upon us.	**C′** repeated (varied).

Opening melody for the first "Kyrie," sung three times:

Hildegard of Bingen: *Alleluia, O virga mediatrix*   3:30
(*Alleluia, O mediating branch*)

Date: Late 12th century
Genre: *Alleluia* plainchant, from the Proper of the Mass on feasts for the Virgin Mary

Performed by: Oxford Camerata, Jeremy Summerly, director

What to Listen For

Melody	Unaccompanied, conjunct line with some expressive leaps and melismas.	**Expression**	Dramatic leaps of a fifth; high-range climaxes on important words.
Rhythm	Free and nonmetric, following the flow of words.	**Performing forces**	*A cappella* choir (voices alone), alternating soloist and choir.
Texture	Monophonic (single line).	**Text**	Prayer to the Virgin Mary, written by Hildegard.
Form	Three-part structure ("Alleluia"–verse–"Alleluia"), performed responsorially.		

continued on next page

	TEXT	TRANSLATION	PERFORMANCE
0:00	Alleluia.	Alleluia.	Solo intonation, then choral response; very melismatic.
0:45	O virga mediatrix sancta viscera tua mortem superaverunt, et venter tuus omnes creaturas illuminavit in pulchro flore de suavissima integritate clausi pudoris tui orto.	O mediating branch Your holy flesh has overcome death, and your womb has illuminated all creatures through the beautiful flower of your tender purity that sprang from your chastity.	Solo verse, with several melismas. Higher range, neumatic text setting. Melismatic at the end.
2:56	Alleluia.	Alleluia.	Choir returns to the opening.

Opening of solo chant, with melismatic setting on "Alleluia":

Expressive leap of a rising fifth and melisma on "mortem" ("death"):

🔊 **AnotherHearing** In recent decades there has been a renewed interest in chant, and especially the works of Hildegard. This performance of Hildegard's *Alleluia* by Sequentia features a solo singer throughout, with an improvised harp accompaniment. How is the character of her chant altered by these improvised additions? Which performance do you find more effective, and why?

16

Layering Lines: Early Polyphony of the Notre Dame School

"When you hear the soft harmonies of the various singers . . . it drives away care from the soul, . . . confers joy and peace and exultation in God, and transports the soul to the society of angels."

—*John of Salisbury (1120–1180)*

KeyPoints

- **Polyphony** (multivoiced music), originally improvised and eventually notated, is an essential feature of the Western musical tradition.

- In the Middle Ages, Paris's Cathedral of Notre Dame was a center for **organum**, the earliest type

of polyphony: two, three, or four vocal lines sung in fixed rhythmic patterns (**rhythmic modes**).

- Preexisting chants formed the basis for early polyphony, including organum.

Monophonic music is the most straightforward kind, and many world traditions focus on a single melodic line in their songs. But other traditions also cultivate greater complexity through the simultaneous sounding of multiple musical lines. This is the case of the Western tradition, which has become distinctive—and popular throughout the globe—because of its potential for layered complexity. From the symphonic hall to the mixing studio, the ability to create and coordinate simultaneous lines—call them melodies, layers, or "tracks"—is a mark of supreme musical craft and professional training.

Early polyphony, including organum, served to praise the Virgin Mary. French school, thirteenth century.

Early Polyphony

Polyphony, or the combination of two or more simultaneous melodic lines, is the single most important feature in the development of Western music. While improvised polyphony likely goes back many centuries, European polyphony is distinctive because it was notated, allowing for more detail and control over the musical texture. Notated polyphony began to emerge toward the end of the Romanesque era (c. 850–1150)—interestingly, around the same time that music notation itself became increasingly sophisticated on the European Continent. Because polyphonic music had to be written down in a way that would indicate precise rhythm and pitch, a more exact notational system developed, the direct ancestor of the one in use today.

LISTENING GUIDE 3   **1:26**

Notre Dame School: *Gaude Maria virgo* (*Rejoice, Virgin Mary*)

Date: Early 13th century   **Performed by:** Lionheart
Genre: Organum

What to Listen For

Melody	Short, repeated ideas exchanged between the upper voices.
Rhythm/ meter	Simple pattern of long-short-long-short in upper voices over the slow-moving bottom voice (Tenor).
Harmony	Open, hollow-sounding cadences on the intervals of fifths and octaves.

Texture	Three-part polyphony, alternating with monophonic chant.
Expression	The opening words "Gaude Maria" are drawn out in a long melismatic setting.
Performing forces	*A cappella*; soloists sing organum; choir sings chant.
Text	Prayer in praise of the Virgin Mary.

	TEXT	TRANSLATION	PERFORMANCE
0:00	Gaude Maria	Rejoice, Mary,	Organum style; upper two voices moving rhythmically over a sustained third voice (Tenor).
1:07	virgo cunctas hereses sola interemisti.	O Virgin, you alone have destroyed all heresies.	Monophonic chant, melismatic, then continuing in a neumatic setting.

Opening of organum, with two rhythmic upper voices over a long chant note:

With the development of notation, music expanded from an art of improvisation and oral tradition to one that was carefully planned and preserved. During the Gothic era (c. 1150–1450), which saw the rise of magnificent cathedrals, individual composers came to be recognized. These learned musicians, mostly clerics in religious communities, mastered the art of writing extended musical works in varied textures and forms.

Organum

The earliest polyphonic music, called **organum**, grew out of the improvisatory custom of adding a second voice to a Gregorian melody at the interval of a fifth or fourth. Soon a polyphonic art blossomed in which the individual voices moved with ever greater independence. In the forefront of this evolution were the composers centered at Paris's Cathedral of Notre Dame during the twelfth and thirteenth centuries. Their leader, Léonin (fl. 1150–c. 1201), is the first composer of polyphonic music whose name we know. He is credited with compiling the *Great Book of Organum* (*Magnus liber organi*), music for the entire church year, in this new musical style. His successor, Pérotin (fl. c. 1200), expanded organum by increasing the voice parts, first to three and then to four.

To the medieval mind, the new had to be founded on the old. Therefore composers of organum based their pieces on preexisting Gregorian chants. While the lower voice sang the fixed melody in extremely long notes, the upper voice or voices sang a freely composed part that moved rapidly above it.

The Cathedral of Notre Dame in Paris, viewed from the Left Bank, with its prominent flying buttresses, was a major composition center for organum. The roof and spire, destroyed by fire in 2019, is being rebuilt.

Gaude Maria virgo (Rejoice, Virgin Mary)

In the organum *Gaude Maria virgo* (LG 3), the opening polyphonic section features two voices singing in a **rhythmic mode**, a fixed pattern of long and short notes that is repeated or varied, over a sustained bottom voice taken from the chant of the same name. The setting, in the style of Pérotin (and possibly by him), is highly melismatic, with many notes sung to each syllable of text, a prayer in praise of the Virgin Mary. The form of this organum is typical in that it alternates polyphony (sung by soloists) and monophonic chant (sung by the choir).

Not all religious communities welcomed polyphony: some saw it as a distraction from the simplicity and equality of communal singing of plainchant. However, the magnificence and complexity of polyphonic music became increasingly sought after, since it was seen to enhance worship on the highest feast days, like Easter. Polyphony became a mark of distinction, both for the musicians who practiced it and for those who sponsored its innovations and expressive potential—and thus the stage was set for the entire unfolding of the Western musical tradition.

A choir of monks in a detail from a fresco on the life of San Nicola, by the fourteenth-century Master of Tolentino.

CRITICAL THINKING

1. Why did composers of early polyphony use chant as the basis for their works?
2. What were considered the advantages and disadvantages of polyphony?

Your Turn TO EXPLORE

Many hip-hop songs are especially multilayered, but most other traditions that feature multiple performers (jazz and heavy-metal bands, for example, as well as several ensemble-based world traditions) are carefully layered as well. Consider a song that has several distinct lines or layers of voice or instrument. How are the voices/instruments/layers kept distinct, and how are they combined? Is one layer the most prominent throughout, or do different ones emerge in turn as leaders?

17

Storytelling through Song: Troubadours and Medieval Court Culture

KeyPoints

- Religious wars (the Crusades) and medieval explorations enabled an exchange of musical instruments and theoretical ideas about music between European and Asian cultures.
- Secular music arose in courts and was performed by aristocratic **troubadours** and **trouvères** in France, and by wandering minstrels in cities.

- Song texts focused on idealized love and the values of chivalry (a code of behavior).
- Songs were sung monophonically and played with improvised instrumental accompaniment. One popular type of dance song was called an **estampie**.

The medieval German courtly love poet Heinrich von Meissen, called Frauenlob (champion of ladies), is pictured here with his musicians (fourteenth century).

You have probably experienced the direct impact of a singer telling his or her emotional story with a simple melody and unobtrusive instrumental accompaniment; it's one of the more compelling images of Western musical culture, and indeed of many world cultures across millennia. It's therefore not surprising that the earliest written records we have in the West of secular music (that is to say, music not designed for worship) are by poet-musicians. These singer-songwriters continued unwritten traditions from centuries before *their* time, and helped to shape the conventions of song text and melody that continue to ours. We will focus on a musician from the songwriting tradition of Occitania, corresponding to present-day southern France: the troubadour Raimbaut de Vaqueiras.

Medieval Minstrels and Court Musicians

Alongside the learned music of the cathedrals and choir schools grew a popular repertory of songs and dances that reflected every aspect of medieval life. Some musicians lived on the fringes of society, wandering among the courts and towns and entertaining audiences with juggling and other tricks as well as songs and dances. While we know of their existence through descriptive accounts, their compositions have not survived, since they most likely didn't write down their music.

On a higher social level were the poet-musicians who flourished at the various courts of Europe and did write down their songs, using the notation systems that were being developed for plainchant. Those who lived in the region of southern France known as Occitania called themselves **troubadours** (or, in the case of women, **trobairitz**); those in northern France called themselves **trouvères**. These terms mean the same thing: finders or inventors (in musical terms, composers). Similar terms were given to singer-songwriters in other regions of Europe. Some songs are attributed to members of the aristocracy and even royalty—among them King Richard the Lionheart of England, whose mother, the legendary Eleanor of Aquitaine (c. 1122–1204), presided over a famous court of poet-musicians.

Music in the singer-songwriter traditions accompanied dancing, banquets, and after-dinner entertainment at medieval courts. It was central to ceremonies, tournaments, civic processions, and military campaigns; music inspired warriors departing on the Crusades and welcomed them on their return. The poems ranged from simple ballads to love songs, political and moral ditties, war songs, chronicles of the Crusades, laments, and dance songs. They praised the virtues of the ruling classes in this age of chivalry: valor, honor, nobility of character, devotion to an ideal, and the quest for perfect love.

Like so many popular songs today, many of the lyrics described a man's unrequited, or unconsummated, passion. The object of his desire was generally unattainable, either because of her higher rank or because she was already wed to another; such love songs expressed idealized objectification-from-afar rather than mutually consensual tenderness. A few of them, attributed to women poet-musicians, express a female point of view and are generally more direct, personal, and emotionally charged. Clearly, the theme of intense unrequited love was especially appealing to listeners, again a tendency that has lasted through the centuries.

In this thirteenth-century manuscript illumination, a French minstrel recites a poem to the lady Blanche of Castile, wife of King Louis VIII of France.

Raimbaut de Vaqueiras and the Troubadour Tradition

Raimbaut de Vaqueiras typifies the tradition of the courtly troubadour. Of his extant works, *Kalenda maya* (*The First of May*) is the most famous. This is a love song addressed to a noble lady—specifically Beatrice, daughter of his patron Boniface of Montferrat; the text celebrates the return of spring but also confirms the poet's pledge of honor, love, and service to the lady (LG 4).

Unlike in many songs we will hear later, the lines of the poem (and therefore the musical phrases) are irregular in length. The poet compares his devotion to that of well-known lovers (Eric and Enide) in an ancient epic poem; and at the end, he identifies the work as an **estampie** (*estampida*), a sung dance form common in late medieval France. The melody is in three sections, each of which is repeated, and the overall form is **strophic**—where the same melody is repeated with every stanza. Notice how the tune is balanced by phrases rising upward at the beginning and downward at the closing.

On our recording, we hear the dance version first, with a **rebec** (an early version of the violin; see p. 70) playing the tune, accompanied by a **pipe** (a three-holed, end-blown flute), **guitarra moresca** (a strummed string instrument introduced into Spain by the Moors), and small drums known as **nakers** (see p. 89). Not only the instruments but also the improvisational style and structure of *Kalenda maya* echo the sounds of Middle Eastern music, which Raimbaut certainly heard on his journey eastward.

In Their Own Words

❝ I have served you . . . with a glad heart; I have wooed ladies with you; and I have ridden at your side at war. . . . All good usage rules in your court: munificence and courting, elegant clothing and handsome armor, trumpets and games and viols and songs."

—*Raimbaut de Vaqueiras*

Inter*f*ace

Opening Doors to the East: The Crusades

A Turkish military (Janissary) band, with mounted players of trumpets, cymbals, and drums. Miniature from Vehbi's *Imperial Festival Book* (c. 1720).

Extending over some two hundred years, from 1095 to 1291, the Crusades were a series of religious wars waged by Western Europeans with the stated goal of conquering the Holy Land of Palestine from the Muslims. Clearly, there were underlying economic and political ambitions as well: European merchants wished to open and ultimately to control rich trade routes to the Middle East and India, while the pope sought to quell the spread of Islam and to increase the power of the papacy by reuniting the Eastern Orthodox Church with the Western church, after a schism in 1054. There were military successes for both sides in the wars; however, in the end, the Europeans' goal of retaking the Holy Land was unsuccessful.

Amidst pillaging and destruction, the interaction of distant cultures had noteworthy results, as both Christian Westerners and Muslims were able to gain a broader knowledge of the world and other ways of life. The crusading knights learned from the expert military skills of the Turkish and Moorish warriors, and the advanced medical and scientific knowledge of the Arab world was imported to Europe. It was at this time too that the Arabic numeral system was adopted in the West (until then, Europeans had used Roman numerals—I, II, III, IV, V— rather than the Arabic numerals 1, 2, 3, 4, 5). With this came a growing interest in numerology, which allowed for mathematics and other pattern-related disciplines, including musical theory, to flourish in the West.

Musicians who had traveled eastward with the crusading armies brought music, theoretical ideas, and instruments of all types back to their homeland. The medieval rebec, a small bowed-string instrument that was a forerunner of the modern violin, derived from the Arab rabab (see p. 70), and military bands adopted the loud, double-reed shawm (pp. 115, 117), the predecessor of the modern oboe, often deployed alongside trumpets and drums, from Turkish armies. Many of our orchestral percussion instruments stem from Turkish models as well, including the cymbals, bells, and bass drum. The foundation of the European system of early scales (modes) also came from Eastern theoretical systems.

Despite the long-standing hostility these wars drew on and fostered between the Christian and Islamic worlds, the Crusades were extremely influential in the cultural life of both regions. Recent studies and televised documentaries have explored the two sides of these military conflicts and the interactions of two differing civilizations.

Christian Crusaders entering Constantinople after the Second Crusade.

Medieval musicians playing a lute and nakers, both instruments of Arabic origin.

The medieval manuscripts of *Kalenda maya* provide the poem, the melody, and an ambiguous indication of rhythm; notation had not yet become standardized. In other performances, you may hear the song in duple rather than triple meter, depending on the musicians' decision about the best "flow" for the music. Further, the original notation gives no indication of instrumental accompaniment: what we hear in performance comes from the historical research and creativity of twenty-first-century musicians. Something similar is true of many of the songs we find most meaningful today: the text and melody may be predominant in our minds, but the singer-songwriters and their collaborators carefully build a web of musical texture and timbre around them to intensify the effect on our emotions.

Raimbaut de Vaqueiras (c. 1155–1207)

This French manuscript shows Raimbaut de Vaqueiras armed for battle.

According to his *vida*, or biography written in the language of the troubadour, Raimbaut was of humble origin, the son of a "poor knight" from Provence, in southern France. As a young man, he entered the service of Marquis Boniface I of Montferrat, whose court was in northwestern Italy; he was later knighted for saving the life of his patron in a battle in Sicily. When Montferrat set off in 1202 on the Fourth Crusade to the Holy Land, Raimbaut did not accompany him, but he later joined the forces in Constantinople, where he wrote a famous epic describing the colorful events. It's likely that he was killed in battle there, alongside his patron. Thirty-five poems by Raimbaut survive, of which seven preserve the music as well.

Raimbaut de Vaqueiras: *Kalenda maya*
(The First of May)

Date: Late 12th century

Genre: Estampie (troubadour dance song)

Performed by: Martin Best Ensemble

What to Listen For

Melody	A mostly conjunct line in a small range (an octave) and wavelike motion.
Rhythm	Performed in a dancelike triple meter; other rhythmic interpretations are possible.
Texture	Monophonic song with elaborations in the improvised instrumental accompaniment.
Form	Strophic song: an instrumental (dance) introduction followed by four verses; the

dance and verses all have the same music, three repeated phrases (**A-A-B-B-C-C**).

Performing forces Solo singer accompanied by a bowed string instrument (rebec), a strummed guitar, a pipe (three-holed end-blown flute), and drums (nakers).

Text Strophic poem in Provençal French.

Instrumental dance: Entire melody played once (**A-A-B-B-C-C**)

0:00 Solo rebec (phrase **A**).

0:07 Accompaniment with strummed guitar (on repeat of **A**).

0:12 Hand drum (nakers) accompaniment enters (on new phrase, **B**).
      Melody continues through phrase **C**, with more complex rhythms in
      the accompaniment; flutelike pipe enters at the end with an ostinato figure.

0:28 **Stanza 1,** with voice

Kalenda maya.	**A**
ni fueills de faia	
ni chans d'auzell ni flors de glaia	
non es qe m plaia,	**A**
pros dona gala	
tro q'un i snell mes sagier aia	
del vostre bell cors, qi.m retraia	**B**
plazer novell q'amors m'atraia	**B**
e jaia e.m traia vas vos	**C**
dona veraia.	
e chaia de plaia .lgelos.	**C**
anz qe.m n'estraia.	

Neither May Day nor the beech tree's leaves nor the song of birds nor gladiolus flowers are
pleasing to me, noble and vivacious lady, until I receive a swift messenger from your fair
person to tell me of some new pleasure that love brings me; and may I be joined to you
and drawn toward you, perfect lady; and may the jealous fall stricken before I must leave you.

Stanza 2

0:56   Mabell'amia, / par Dieu non sia / qe ja.l gelos de mon danria, . . .

My sweet beloved, for the sake of God, may the jealous one never laugh at my pain, for his jealousy would be very costly if it were to separate two such lovers: for I would never be joyful again, nor would joy be of any benefit to me without you; I would set out on such a road that no one would ever see me again; on that day would I die, worthy lady, that I lost you.

Stanza 3

1:23   Con er perduda, / ni m'er renduda / donna, s'enanz non l'ai aguda? . . .

How shall my lady be lost, or restored to me, if she not yet be mine? For a man or woman is not a lover just by thinking so. But when a suitor is accepted as a lover, the reputation that he gains is greatly enhanced, and the attractive appearance causes much stir: but I have not held you naked nor conquered you in any other sense; I have only desired you and believed in you, without any further encouragement.

Stanza 6 (stanzas 4 and 5 not recorded)

1:52   Dona grazida, / qecs lauz'e crida / vostra valor q'es abellida . . .

Worthy lady, everyone praises and proclaims your merit which is so pleasing: and whoever would forget you places little value on life; therefore I worship you, distinguished lady, for I have singled you out as the most pleasing and the best, accomplished in worth, and I have courted you and served you better than Eric did Enide. Lord Engles [Boniface, marquis of Montferrat], I have constructed and completed the estampida.

CRITICAL THINKING

1. What role did secular music play in medieval court life, and what themes were expounded upon in the texts?
2. What ideas did Western European society borrow from the Middle East?

Your Turn TO EXPLORE

Find an example of a stanza-based (strophic) song performed by a single individual—many contemporary singer-songwriters take this approach, but so do folk traditions of the United States and around the world. Pay attention to how (or whether) the singer changes her or his delivery in each stanza—through the melody, dynamics, vocal timbre, accompanying instruments, or other means. How does the musical delivery suit the text and implicit message of each individual stanza? How does it affect the impact of the song's overall story?

18

Symbols and Puzzles: Machaut and the Medieval Mind

"Able was I ere I saw Elba."   —English palindrome referring to Napoleon's exile

KeyPoints

- The development of sacred polyphony inspired new genres of secular polyphonic music.
- Guillaume de Machaut was a poet-composer of the French ***Ars nova*** (new art) who wrote sacred music and polyphonic **chansons** (secular songs) set to fixed text forms (**rondeau**, **ballade**, **virelai**).

- Machaut's chanson *Ma fin est mon commencement* employs a palindromic form and an enigmatic text to display compositional craft and challenge the listener to careful listening and thinking.

In Their Own Words

" Which creature walks on four legs in the morning, two legs in the afternoon, and three legs in the evening?"

—*The Sphinx of Thebes*

The Sphinx's riddle, Fermat's last theorem, cryptography, the "Da Vinci Code": we humans are fascinated by riddles and puzzles, maybe because they challenge us to think of possibilities beyond our current understanding. In the Western tradition, music has been linked with mathematics and geometry since antiquity. Ancient Greek mathematician Pythagoras was renowned for his musical experiments, In medieval times, the four topics (Quadrivium) considered essential to education were music, mathematics, geometry, and astronomy. Since then, musicians have remained involved in exploring the mathematical or geometrical implications of their art and conveying puzzles through sound.

The courtly love-song tradition of the troubadours and trouvères continued into the early 1300s. While some of these songs remained monophonic, the polyphonic developments in sacred music—organum and motet—soon carried over to the secular realm, as we will hear in the works of French composer Guillaume de Machaut; his music forms a bridge between the tradition of the trouvères and a new creative sensibility.

Machaut and the French *Ars nova*

European contacts with Eastern cultures, along with developments in feudal social structure, inspired new concepts of life, art, and beauty. These changes were reflected in the musical style known as ***Ars nova*** (new art), which appeared in the early 1300s in France, and soon thereafter in Italy. The music of the French *Ars nova*, more refined and complex than the music it displaced (which became known as ***Ars antiqua***, old art), ushered in developments in rhythm, meter, harmony, and counterpoint that transformed the art of music.

At the same time, writers such as Petrarch, Boccaccio, and Chaucer were turning from otherworldly ideals to human subjects; painters soon rediscovered the beauty of nature and the attractiveness of the human form. Similarly, composers like the French master Machaut turned increasingly from religious to secular themes. The influence of this last great poet-composer was far-reaching, his music and poetry admired long after his death. He was also the first composer to self-consciously collect his works and leave them for posterity.

Machaut's music introduced a new freedom of rhythm characterized by gentle syncopations and the interplay of duple and triple meters. In his secular works, he favored the **chanson**, which was generally set to a French courtly love poem written in one of several fixed text forms. These poetic forms—the **rondeau**, **ballade**, and **virelai**—established the musical repetition scheme of the chansons.

A polyphonic chanson is performed with voices and lute in this miniature representing the Garden of Love, from a Flemish manuscript of *Le Roman de la Rose* (c. 1500).

We will consider a rondeau by Machaut (LG 5) that presents us with both an enigmatic text and a hidden musical structure involving palindromes, words or phrases that read the same backward or forward. Machaut's text reiterates the refrain "My end is my beginning and my beginning is my end," a sentiment found in several biblical passages (e.g., Ecclesiastes 1:9–10: "The thing that hath been is that which shall be, and that which is done is that which shall be done. There is nothing new under the sun"), and one taken up by various rulers. Two centuries later, for example, while Mary, Queen of Scots, was imprisoned by Elizabeth I, she spent hours embroidering in French "En ma fin est mon commencement," or "In my end is my beginning." Thus, when we investigate the puzzles in Machaut's chanson, we must consider that their purpose was not merely to amuse but to carry a religious connotation as well.

As a priest and a canon at the Reims Cathedral, Machaut was certainly familiar with the famous octagonal labyrinth or maze built into the floor of this church, and with the ritual processions held on Easter and other holy days that traversed the maze, moving to the center and back, with retrograde motion in each direction symbolic of Christ's path through hell to resurrection. With this insight, we can appreciate all the more the palindromic structure of *Ma fin est mon*

Guillaume de Machaut (c. 1300–1377)

Machaut was the foremost poet-composer of the *Ars nova*. He took holy orders at an early age but worked much of his life at various French courts, including that of Charles, duke of Normandy, who subsequently became king of France.

Machaut's double career as cleric and courtier inspired him to write both religious and secular music. His own poetry embraces the ideals of medieval chivalry. One of his writings, a long autobiographical poem of more than 9,000 lines in rhymed couplets, tells the platonic love story of the aging Machaut and a young girl named Peronne. The two exchanged poems and letters, some of which the composer set to music. Machaut spent his final years as a priest and canon at the Cathedral of Reims, admired as the greatest musician and poet of the time.

MAJOR WORKS: Motets, chansons (both monophonic and polyphonic) • A polyphonic Mass (*Messe de Notre Dame*), one of the earliest complete settings of the Ordinary of the Mass.

5:39

Machaut: *Ma fin est mon commencement* (*My end is my beginning*)

Date: Mid-14th century

Genre: Polyphonic chanson (rondeau)

Performed by: Hilliard Ensemble, Paul Hillier, conductor

What to Listen For

Melody	Wavelike, with long melismas.		**Form**	Two sections (**A, B**), repeated **ABaAabAB** (uppercase = refrain; lowercase = verses); palindromes in voices.
Rhythm/ meter	Duple meter, syncopated.			
Harmony	Open, hollow cadences.		**Performing forces**	Three voices.
Texture	Nonimitative polyphony.		**Text**	Rondeau by the composer; puzzle text.

A SECTION	B SECTION
Triplum	
Cantus	
Tenor	

A SECTION	B SECTION
1, 4, 7 Ma fin est mon . . .	2, 8 Et mon commencement . . .
3 Est teneüre . . .	6 Se retrograde . . .
5 Mes tiers . . .	

		TEXT		TRANSLATION
0:00	Refrain	1. Ma fin est mon commencement	A	My end is my beginning
0:42		2. Et mon commencement ma fin	B	and my beginning my end
1:23	Partial verse	3. Est teneüre vraiement.	a	and my true tenor.
2:05	Partial refrain	4. Ma fin est mon commencement.	A	My end is my beginning.
2:47	Verse	5. Mes tiers chans trois fois seulement	a	My third part three times only
		6. Se retrograde et einsi fin.	b	moves backward and so ends.
4:10	Refrain	7. Ma fin est mon commencement	A	My end is my beginning
		8. Et mon commencement ma fin.	B	and my beginning my end.

🔊 **AnotherHearing** In early times, the use of instruments and voices was not prescribed in performance, so that a work could be sung, played by instruments, or a combination of the two. Now that you have heard an all-vocal performance, listen to this version by Ars Cameralis, featuring a solo singer on the cantus line and double reed instruments (shawm and dulcian, early versions of the oboe and bassoon) on the other lines. How is the character of the work altered? Which performance do you find more effective, and why?

commencement, in which the two upper voices trade parts in retrograde at the center of the work (the cantus **B** section is the triplum **A** section in retrograde; the triplum **B** section is the cantus **A** section in retrograde), while the bottom voice, the Tenor, is a retrograde of itself at the midpoint. Although this musical puzzle cannot be easily heard, Machaut provides clues to its structure in his text.

Similar elements of balance and symmetry can be found in his other works as well. Indeed, the secular works of Machaut and his contemporaries in the *Ars nova* reflect a growing interest in both regularity and complexity of musical patterns. These sonic puzzles often require the listener to focus carefully, and listen several times to understand the nuances of both craft and expression. Like all puzzles, they engage the brain in novel ways, and feed our human desire for subtlety and complexity.

The octagonal maze in the marble floor of the Cathedral of Amiens in France (1288) is similar to the one Machaut knew in Reims, which is now destroyed.

CRITICAL THINKING

1. What ideas did Western European medieval society borrow from the Middle East?

2. How does Machaut use the palindromic process in *Ma fin est mon commencement*? Why do you think he does this?

YourTurn TO EXPLORE

Look for another musical work that's built as a puzzle or palindrome—you might search YouTube for "crab canon" or "palindrome." How is the piece organized? What ways have the composer and performer(s) found to make the palindrome or canon audible (or even visible) to a listener? How do the musicians balance intellectual ingenuity with emotional expression?

19

Singing Friendship:
The Renaissance Madrigal

"Come sing to me a bawdy song, make me merry."

—William Shakespeare, Henry IV, Part 1

KeyPoints

- Both professional and amateur music-making expanded in the Renaissance through secular vocal and instrumental genres.

- Jacques Arcadelt was an early master of the **Italian madrigal**, a sixteenth-century tradition that linked music and lyric poetry. Madrigals usually feature

expressive text setting, word-painting, and multiple meanings.

- **English madrigals**, such as those by John Farmer, were often simpler and lighter in style than their Italian counterparts.

When friends get together to celebrate, singing can't be far behind. Spontaneous social song is often monophonic throughout world cultures: everyone sings the same melody (think of "Happy Birthday"). Western culture has also developed a complex and widespread tradition of social part song, in which separate musical lines are combined into a harmonious whole—a fitting sonic image for friendship.

Social Music-Making in the Renaissance

In the Renaissance, while professional musicians entertained noble guests at court and civic festivities, more and more amateurs began making music in their homes. The music could be vocal—both unaccompanied and supported by instruments— or purely instrumental; indeed, in most prosperous homes you would find a lute (see illustrations, pp. 89 and 103) or a keyboard instrument. The study of music was considered part of the proper upbringing for a young girl or, to a lesser degree, boy. Partly as a result, women began to play prominent roles in the performance of music both in the home and at court. During the later sixteenth century in Italy, a number of professional women singers achieved great fame.

Two important secular genres arose from the union of poetry and music: the **French chanson** (an outgrowth of the medieval version we heard by Machaut) and the **Italian madrigal**. The intricate verse structures of French and Italian poetry helped shape these musical forms. The madrigal is known for the expressive

A stylized sixteenth-century painting of four singers performing from music part books. The two singers in back are beating time. *Concert in the Open Air* (Italian School).

device of **word-painting**—that is, making the music directly reflect the meaning of the words. An unexpected harsh dissonance, for example, might coincide with the word "death," or an ascending line might lead up to the word "heaven" or "stars." We will see how these so-called **madrigalisms** enhanced the emotional content of the music.

Word-painting

The Madrigal: Linking Music and Poetry

The sixteenth-century **madrigal**, the most important secular genre of the era, was an aristocratic form of poetry and music that flourished at the Italian courts as a favorite diversion of cultivated amateurs. The text consisted of a short poem of lyric or reflective character, often including emotional words for weeping, sighing, trembling, and dying, which the Italian madrigalists set suggestively. Love and unsatisfied desire were popular topics, but so were humor and satire, politics, and scenes of city and country life. The madrigal literature therefore presents a vivid panorama of Renaissance thought and feeling.

From the beginning, the Italian madrigal was an art form in which words and music were clearly linked. During its early period (c. 1525–50), the composer's chief concern was to give pleasure to amateur performers. As the genre grew in complexity and expanded to five or six voices, professionals were often hired to join the amateurs or even sing on their own. The final phase of the madrigal (1580–1620) extended beyond the late Renaissance into the world of the Baroque. The genre became the direct expression of the composer's musical personality and feelings. One of the most artful and influential composers of this later Italian madrigal tradition was Claudio Monteverdi, who famously declared that his music was designed to serve the expressive power of his texts. Certain traits were carried to an extreme: rich chromatic harmony, dramatic declamation, vocal virtuosity, and vivid depiction of emotional words in music all lead us to the new Baroque style.

In Their Own Words

" A verse without music is like a mill without water."

—*Anonymous troubadour*

Periods of madrigal composition

Claudio Monteverdi (1567–1643)

Born in Cremona, Italy, Monteverdi began publishing his music while still a young man. In 1590, he took a position as court composer to the duke of Mantua, for whom he wrote his first great operatic masterwork, *Orfeo*, based on the famous Greek myth about the power of music. Eventually he won the coveted position of choirmaster at St. Mark's in Venice, where he remained until his death some thirty years later.

Monteverdi wrote madrigals throughout his lifetime, publishing nine books that transformed the genre from polyphonic part music to an emotionally charged soloistic style that highlighted the text through unprepared dissonances and speechlike melodies. He claimed that in his works "rhetoric should govern music, not be its servant." Monteverdi injected into his sacred works, ballets, and especially his late operas an emotional intensity that was new to music. Characters in his music dramas are not stereotypes but men and women who unleash their joy and sorrow through song.

MAJOR WORKS: Nine books of madrigals (published 1587–1651); sacred music, including *Vespers* (1610), Masses, Magnificats, and motets; operas, including *Orfeo* (1607) and *L'incoronazione di Poppea* (*The Coronation of Poppea*, 1643); other dramatic music.

Monteverdi and Vocal Rhetoric

Monteverdi's sensuous *Si ch'io vorrei morire*, from his *Fourth Book of Madrigals* (1603), represents the peak of the Italian madrigal tradition (LG 6). The composer felt that music should follow the words rather than strict rules of harmony or counterpoint, and the changing textures, repetition, and dissonance in this work exemplify his ideas on how to convey words both clearly and passionately. Since references to death in madrigal poetry were usually understood as erotic, death being a conceit for sexual climax, the underlying meaning of this madrigal is fairly

---

LISTENING GUIDE 6   2:54

Monteverdi: *Si ch'io vorrei morire*

Date: Published 1603
Genre: Italian madrigal

Performed by: Les Arts Florissants, William Christie, director

What to Listen For

Melody	Mostly stepwise, ideas passed from voice to voice.
Rhythm/ meter	Flexible, following the structure of the poem.
Harmony	Modal, with affective dissonances.
Texture	Alternates homophony and polyphony.
Form	Through-composed, with a return of the opening phrase.

Expression	Each phrase and some individual words are illustrated through musical detail; some words are repeated for rhetorical effect.
Performing forces	Five voice parts (SAATB).
Text	Poem by 16th-century poet Maurizio Moro.

TEXT	TRANSLATION	DESCRIPTION
0:00 Si ch'io vorrei morire	Truly I want to die,	Homophonic declamation, text repeated three times.
0:16 Hora ch'io bacio, Amore,	now that, Love, I am kissing	Sudden harmonic shift, homophony
La bella bocca del mio amato core.	the beautiful mouth of my beloved.	is less strict.
0:32 Ahi cara e dolce lingua,	Ah dear, sweet tongue,	Imitation in five voices, from lower to upper; dissonances on "Ahi/ah."
0:46 Datemi tant'humore	Give me such nectar	Voices are paired; text overlapping.
0:51 Che di dolcezza in questo sen m'estingua.	that I expire from sweetness on your breast.	All voices have descending lines ("expiring"); text is drawn out slowly with syncopation and overlapping lines.
1:13 Ahi vita mia, a questo bianco seno	Ah my life, to your white breast	Alternating voice groups.
1:31 Deh stringetemi finch'io venga meno.	grasp me until I perish.	Top two voices with syncopation "perish" downward; poetic line is repeated, bottom three voices "perish/climax" upward.
2:20 Ahi bocca, ahi baci, ahi lingua! Torno a dire,	Ah mouth, ah kisses, ah tongue! Again I say,	Staggered homophony: four voices together, one a half beat behind, rising again.
2:31 "Si ch'io vorrei morire."	"Truly I want to die."	Exact repetition of opening phrase.

Three lowest voices begin imitation on "Ahi," with dissonances on the downbeats (*):

Syncopated top voices in descending lines ("I expire"):

clear—all the more so given the references to kissing and bodily interaction as the level of desire escalates. Madrigals were sung as chamber music, with one singer per line, reading from a **part book** (see illustration, p. 97). You can imagine how the double meaning of "death" and the breathless sighs and cries might play in mixed-company social singing! (See Many Voices: Madrigals for Modern Ears, p. 102.)

Part book

John Farmer (c. 1570–1603)

The English composer Farmer was active in Dublin, Ireland, as an organist and master of the choirboys at Christ Church. In 1599, he moved to London and published his only collection of four-voice madrigals. Farmer used clever word-painting in these lighthearted works and helped shape the madrigal into a truly native art form.

MAJOR WORKS: English songs and madrigals (for four and six voices).

The Madrigal in England

Just as Shakespeare adapted the Italian sonnet, so English composers developed the Italian madrigal into a native art form during the late sixteenth century and the reign of Elizabeth I (1558–1603). In their own madrigals, some English composers followed the late Italian model, setting dramatic love poetry in serious, weighty works, while others favored simpler texts in more accessible settings. New humorous madrigal types were cultivated, some with refrain syllables such as "fa la la." One of the most important English madrigal composers was John Farmer.

Farmer's *Fair Phyllis*

A shepherd serenades a shepherdess on an endblown flute. Eighteenth century.

The pastoral text, lively rhythms, and good humor of *Fair Phyllis* (LG 7) make it a perfect example of the English madrigal. The poem tells of a shepherdess (Phyllis) being pursued by her lover, Amyntas (their names are stock ones for such rustic characters). The narrative brings their story to a happy conclusion with their amorous love play. English composers adopted the Italian practice of word-painting, allowing us to "hear" this charming story. While it's fun to listen to these madrigals, more fun is to "tell" the story in interactive social song—remember, this music was designed for friends to sing with each other, rather than for professionals to perform to an audience. The melodies are simple enough that you might be able to sing them yourself after you've heard them a few times. How does your connection to the story change when you tell it, rather than hearing it?

CRITICAL THINKING

1. How did the madrigal tradition change from the early 1500s into the early 1600s?

2. What aspects of *Si ch'io vorrei morire* and *Fair Phyllis* make them suitable for amateur performance?

LISTENING GUIDE 7   🔊 **1:21**

Farmer: *Fair Phyllis*

Date: Published 1599   **Performed by:** Quink Vocal Ensemble
Genre: English madrigal

What to Listen For

Melody	Dancelike, diatonic melody.	**Expression**	Word-painting on opening line ("all alone") and on "up and down."
Rhythm/ meter	Lively rhythms; begins in duple meter, shifts to triple and back.	**Performing forces**	Four voices (SATB), *a cappella*.
Texture	Varied: first monophonic, then some imitation; homorhythmic for last line.	**Text**	Lighthearted pastoral English poem.
Form	Short, repeated sections.		

TEXT

0:00   Fair Phyllis I saw sitting all alone,
        Feeding her flock near to the mountain side.
        The shepherds knew not whither she was gone,
        But after her [her] lover Amyntas hied.

0:24   Up and down he wandered, whilst she was missing;
        When he found her, oh, then they fell a-kissing.

0:48   Up and down . . .

Examples of word-painting

"Fair Phyllis I saw sitting all alone"—sung by soprano alone:

"Up and down"—descending line, repeated in all parts imitatively; shown in soprano and alto:

YourTurn TO EXPLORE

Can you find examples of twenty-first-century part songs (whether in North America or elsewhere) that are designed for social singing rather than concert performance? Does the number of singers in a group affect the performance, in terms of hearing the words clearly or being able to follow the interaction of the voices? Is the effect different if the musical story is sung by a mixed-gender rather than single-gender group?

Madrigals for Modern Ears

The madrigals you just heard—both the Italian and English examples—were performed on our recordings with just one person singing each part, following historical performance practice. Whether sung by professionals at court entertainments or by amateurs at home, madrigals were generally performed a cappella from part books, one for each voice part (see illustration on p. 97). Another manner of madrigal performance in the Renaissance era was, however, as a solo song with instrumental accompaniment, often on a lute.

Today, you may have the occasion to hear madrigals at your school sung by a small group—a chamber choir or a madrigal ensemble—or you might have the opportunity to attend a Renaissance fair, featuring colorfully costumed performers offering up a variety of songs from the era. One of the first such fairs began in California in the 1960s, and continues to celebrate Elizabethan culture and music annually.

Another opportunity to experience madrigals is provided by the contemporary English singer Sting (b. 1951), former front man for the new-wave band Police. In 2006, Sting took up playing the lute while exploring the music of English Renaissance composer John Dowland (1563–1626), perhaps the finest lutenist of his era. Sting recorded some of his favorite selections from Dowland's works, including madrigals and solo songs with lute accompaniment, the latter called **ayres** (or airs). Sting's recording *Songs from the Labyrinth* features works from Dowland's *First Booke of Songs and Ayres* (1597), a highly successful publication of music for home and amateur performance. The Dowland collection included works that could be performed by one person singing the main tune accompanied by a lute, a common household instrument of the Renaissance era, or sung in four parts, like a madrigal, while sitting around a table. The music in Dowland's book, unlike that used for part-book performance, was laid out in table-book format, so that only one copy of the publication was needed, and each person could see her or his part (see illustration). The top, or solo, part is coupled with the lute music, written in a tablature not unlike one used by guitarists today: in the lute part, each

A sample work from Dowland's *First Booke of Songes or Ayres* showing table-book format.

Composer-lutenist John Dowland, working on a new composition.

was imprisoned in the Tower of London and beheaded in 1601. Dowland's music strikes a lighthearted mood that is in stark contrast to the text; it sets a rollicking dance tune—*The Earl of Essex Galliarde*, featuring shifting rhythmic accents that throw off the sense of triple meter.

Sting was drawn to the serious nature of the texts in many of Dowland's songs, including the famous *Flow My Teares*, claiming that "melancholy leads to reflection, . . . to a sense of humility, a sense of kindness, of compassion—so we need it." The modern-day singer takes an innovative approach to these songs, realizing that they were not the high art of the era, but rather "they're pop songs written around 1600. I relate to them in that way: beautiful melodies, fantastic lyrics, great accompaniments" and definitely not needing "a trained operatic voice." Sting recorded Dowland's songs with the assistance of the virtuoso Bosnian lutenist Edin Karamazov, and for his nontraditional performance, Sting overdubbed all the four vocal parts of the madrigal himself. Check out the YouTube video of his performance showing him in all four seats around the table-book music, singing "Can She Excuse My Wrongs."

horizontal line represents a string on the lute, while the letters tell the players on which fret to place their fingers (a = open string, b = first fret, etc.). The rhythms are notated above the lines. The lute part is essentially an instrumental arrangement of the three lower voice parts, so that the same notes can be heard in both a voice-plus-lute and a four-voice performance; it was common for singers to accompany themselves on the lute.

One of the Dowland songs that Sting recorded was "Can She Excuse My Wrongs," set to a poem attributed to Robert Devereux, 2nd Earl of Essex and a favorite courtier of Queen Elizabeth I. This song, with its weighty text, seems to appeal to the Queen for a return to her good graces (and perhaps her bed). The plea fell on deaf ears, and after Devereux staged an unsuccessful *coup d'état* against the government, he

Singer Sting performing on lute at the Classical Brit Awards on May 3, 2007.

Many Voices Expanded

Other interpretations of lute songs:
- "Traditional" Dowland performances by Emma Kirkby, soprano and Anthony Rooley, lute
- John Potter and "The Dowland Project," incorporating jazz and contemporary improvisation approaches to the music of Dowland: https://www.john-potter.co.uk/dowland.php

20

Remember Me: Personalizing the Motet in the Renaissance

"We know by experience that song has great force and vigor to move and inflame the hearts of men to invoke and praise God with a more vehement and ardent zeal."

—John Calvin

KeyPoints

- Renaissance sacred music was generally performed *a cappella* (for unaccompanied voices) and features a fuller, more consonant sound (with "sweet" thirds and sixths) than medieval music. Some works are built on a fixed, preexisting melody (**cantus firmus**).

- Josquin des Prez's *Ave Maria . . . virgo serena* is a **motet** to the Virgin Mary set in varied textural styles, which are designed to convey the changing meanings in the text.

Religious belief continued as a core aspect of identity in the Renaissance, even as the nature of that belief shifted to a more personal connection to the divine. This shift is perhaps most clearly reflected in the different artistic renditions of the Virgin Mary, on whom worshippers began to focus at this time.

Medieval painting presented life through symbolism; the Renaissance preferred realism. Medieval painters posed their idealized figures impersonally, facing frontally; Renaissance artists developed profile portraiture and humanized their

Leonardo da Vinci (1452–1519), whose remarkable *Last Supper* is the most reproduced religious painting of all time, was a contemporary of composer Josquin des Prez.

Medieval and Renaissance artistic approaches to the depiction of the Virgin and child:

LEFT: **Cimabue** (c. 1240–1302) aims to create an ideal effect, using magnificent colors, and there is an emotional distance between the characters that is in keeping with their distance from the worldly.

RIGHT: **Raphael** (1483–1520) shapes a more realistic environment, and the emotional bond between mother and child resonates with the faithful's trust that the Virgin will care for those who believe in her.

subjects. Space in medieval works was organized in a succession of planes that the eye perceived as a series of episodes, but Renaissance painters made it possible to see the whole simultaneously. They discovered the landscape, created the illusion of distance, and focused on the physical loveliness of the world. Echoing the visual arts, musicians helped to reinforce and intensify this newly personal approach to praise through beauty.

Renaissance Sacred Music

The Renaissance marks the passing of European society from a predominantly religious orientation to a more secular one, and from an age of unquestioning faith and mysticism to one of growing reliance on reason and scientific inquiry. A new way of thinking centered on human issues and the individual. People gained confidence in their ability to solve their own problems and to order their world rationally, without relying exclusively on tradition or religion. This awakening, called **humanism**, was inspired by the ancient cultures of Greece and Rome, its writers and artworks.

Humanism

In attempting to reconcile the needs of the individual with the primacy of the divine, musicians expanded their approaches to sung worship. In addition to the monophonic Gregorian chant that defined Catholic prayer, music for church services included hymns, motets, and polyphonic settings of the Mass. These were normally multivoiced and, especially in the early Renaissance era, based on preexisting music. They were sung by professional male singers trained from childhood in cathedral choir schools.

The vocal forms of Renaissance music were marked by smoothly gliding melodies conceived specially for the voice. In fact, the sixteenth century has come to be regarded as the golden age of the *a cappella* style (for voices alone, without

Imitation

instrumental accompaniment). Polyphony in such works was based on the principle of **imitation**: musical ideas are exchanged between vocal lines, the voices imitating one another so that a similar phrase is heard in different registers. (This use of imitation is different from a canon or round in that the phrases sung by different voices in imitation are *similar* but not *identical*.) The result is a close-knit musical fabric capable of subtle and varied effects, in which each voice participates equally in the polyphonic prayer—a way to combine individual action with collaborative worship. In the matter of harmony, composers of the Renaissance leaned toward fuller chords. They turned away from the open fifths (missing the third of a triad) and octaves preferred in medieval times to the "sweeter" thirds and sixths. The use of dissonance in sacred music was carefully controlled.

Cantus firmus

Polyphonic writing offered the composer many possibilities, such as the use of a fixed melody (**cantus firmus**) in one voice as the basis for elaborate ornamentation in the other voices. Triple meter had been especially attractive to the medieval mind because it symbolized the perfection of the Trinity. Renaissance composers, much less preoccupied with religious symbolism, showed a greater interest in duple meter.

Josquin des Prez and the Motet

"[Josquin] is the master of the notes. They have to do as he bids them; other composers have to do as the notes will."

—*Martin Luther*

In the Renaissance, one of the most popular genres was the **motet**—a sacred work with a Latin text, for use in the Mass and other religious services. The ability to combine newly written texts of praise with prescribed prayers was part of the appeal of the motet for composers, who were able to demonstrate their individual creativity through choice of text as well as musical invention. Motets in praise of the Virgin Mary were extremely popular because of the many religious groups all over Europe devoted to her, and also because of the potential for the faithful to identify with the powerful intimacy of the mother-child relationship.

The preeminent composers of motets from the early Renaissance (1450–1520) were from northern Europe, in particular present-day Belgium and northern France. Among these composers, we will consider Josquin des Prez, one of the great masters of sacred music.

Josquin des Prez (c. 1450–1521)

Josquin (as he is known) exerted a powerful influence on generations of composers to follow. After spending his youth in northern Europe, Josquin was employed for much of his varied career in Italy, at courts in Milan and Ferrara and in the papal choir in Rome. In Italy, he absorbed the classical virtues of balance and moderation, the sense of harmonious proportion and clear form, visible in the paintings of the era. Toward the end of his life, he returned to his native France, where he served as a provost at the collegiate church of Condé.

Josquin appeared at a time when the humanizing influences of the Renaissance were being felt throughout Europe. His music is rich in feeling, characterized by serenely beautiful melodies and expressive harmony.

MAJOR WORKS: Over 100 motets • At least 17 Masses • Many French chansons and Italian secular songs.

LISTENING GUIDE 8   4:38

Josquin: *Ave Maria . . . virgo serena* (Hail Mary . . . gentle Virgin)

Date: 1480s?

Genre: Latin motet

Performed by: La Chapelle Royale, Philippe Herreweghe, director

---

What to Listen For

Melody	High vs. low voices, singing in pairs; opening phrase quotes a chant.	**Form**	Sectional according to strophes of the poem (each begins "Ave").
Rhythm/ meter	Duple meter, with shift to triple, then back.	**Expression**	Personal plea from composer at the end.
Harmony	Consonant; hollow-sounding cadences.	**Performing forces**	Four-voice choir; *a cappella*.
Texture	Imitative polyphony, with moments of homorhythm.	**Text**	Rhymed, strophic prayer to the Virgin Mary.

	TEXT	TRANSLATION	DESCRIPTION
0:00	Ave Maria, gratia plena, Dominus tecum, virgo serena.	Hail Mary, full of grace, The Lord is with you, gentle Virgin.	Four voices in imitation (SATB) quote a chant; duple meter.
0:45	Ave cujus conceptio Solemni plena gaudio Caelestia, terrestria, Nova replet laetitia.	Hail, whose conception, Full of solemn joy, Fills the heaven, the earth, With new rejoicing.	Two and three voices, later four voices; more homorhythmic texture.
1:21	Ave cujus nativitas Nostra fuit solemnitas, Ut lucifer lux oriens, Verum solem praeveniens.	Hail, whose birth Was our festival, As our luminous rising light Coming before the true sun.	Voice pairs (SA/TB) in close imitation, then four voices in imitation.
1:59	Ave pia humilitas, Sine viro fecunditas, Cujus annuntiatio, Nostra fuit salvatio.	Hail, pious humility, Fertility without a man, Whose annunciation Was our salvation.	Voice pairs (SA/TB); a more homorhythmic texture.
2:27	Ave vera virginitas, Immaculata castitas, Cujus purificatio Nostra fuit purgatio.	Hail, true virginity, Unspotted chastity, Whose purification Was our cleansing.	Triple meter; clear text declamation; homorhythmic texture.
3:04	Ave praeclara omnibus Angelicis virtutibus, Cujus fuit assumptio Nostra glorificatio.	Hail, famous with all Angelic virtues, Whose assumption was Our glorification.	Imitative voice pairs; return to duple meter.
3:59	O Mater Dei, Memento mei. Amen.	O Mother of God, Remember me. Amen.	Completely homorhythmic; text declamation in long notes, separated by rests.

Rising melodic idea at the opening:

A - ve   Ma - ri -   a,

A choir of men and boys sing sacred music from a choir-book, under the direction of composer Johannes Ockeghem (1410–1497), wearing glasses.

Ave Maria . . . virgo serena (LG 8) is a prime example of how Josquin experimented with varied combinations of voices and textures to highlight different emotional aspects of the text. In this four-voice composition dedicated to the Virgin Mary, high voices engage in a dialogue with low ones, and imitative textures alternate with **homorhythmic** settings (in which all voices move together rhythmically). Josquin opens the piece with a musical reference to a preexisting chant for the Virgin, but soon drops this melody in favor of a freely composed form that is highly sensitive to the text. Notice that the equality and interdependence of the voices is highlighted by the frequent changes in the way voices are grouped, and that smaller groupings of two or three voices tend to build to the full ensemble at the ends of phrases.

Homorhythm

The final two lines of text, a personal plea to the Virgin ("O Mother of God, remember me"), is set in a simple texture that emphasizes the words, proclaiming the humanistic spirit of a new age. How do you think this direct appeal relates to the change in the depictions of the Virgin shown in the images on page 105? How does the full-chord sound that opens this section compare with the sound of the final "Amen," which is instead an open fifth?

In Their Own Words

❝ The better the voice is, the meeter it is to honor and serve God."

—*William Byrd*

CRITICAL THINKING

1. In what way does the "humanist" approach differ from ways of thinking in the Middle Ages?
2. How does Josquin bring his own creativity to the text? Does this combination of individuality and tradition also connect to other examples we have examined?

Your Turn TO EXPLORE

The recording associated with our Listening Guide features a mixed-gender chorus of several voices to a part, but in the Renaissance, sacred music of this sort was almost exclusively sung by small all-male ensembles. Find a recording of this work (or another Josquin motet) by an all-male group (for example: the Hilliard Ensemble, The King's Singers, Chanticleer). How is the effect different from the version on your recording? Which do you find more expressive, and why?

21

Glory Be: Music for the Renaissance Mass

"Our wisest mortals have decided that music should give zest to divine worship. If people take great pains to compose beautiful music for secular songs, they should devote at least as much thought to sacred song."

—Giovanni Pierluigi da Palestrina

KeyPoints

- The most solemn ritual of the Catholic Church is the **Mass**, a daily service with two categories of prayers: the **Ordinary** (texts that remain the same for every Mass) and the **Proper** (texts that vary according to the day).

- Renaissance composers set texts from the Ordinary of the Mass (Kyrie, Gloria, Credo, Sanctus, Agnus Dei) for their polyphonic Masses.

- Reformers such as Luther and Calvin believed that monophonic congregational singing in the vernacular should define Christian worship, while the Catholic establishment preferred trained singers and polyphony.

- Giovanni Pierluigi da Palestrina's *Pope Marcellus* Mass met the Council of Trent's demands for *a cappella* singing with clearly declaimed text.

Does elaborate music in church distract worshippers from their focus on the scriptural text? Or does the sublime power of sound convey ultimate praise, and help the faithful envision the blessings of heaven? To this day, many consider unison song essential for building collective purpose, whether in worship or in other group activity—while others rely on the grandeur of polyphony to convey magnificence and glory, whether in church or in other places of celebration.

The Renaissance Mass

A similar debate was at the core of Christian reform in the 1500s: while Protestants argued for the simple unity of congregational singing, Catholics affirmed the power of professional choirs and complex textures, especially in polyphonic settings of the Mass.

A reenactment of Christ's Last Supper with his disciples (see p. 104), the **Mass**, as we have seen, is the most solemn ritual of the Catholic Church. The collection of prayers that make up the **Ordinary** remain the same in every Mass; the **Proper** texts vary from day to day throughout the church year, depending on the feast being celebrated. While the Kyrie is a Greek text, the remainder of the Mass is Latin, the language of the ancient Romans and the language of learning throughout the

Ordinary and Proper

109

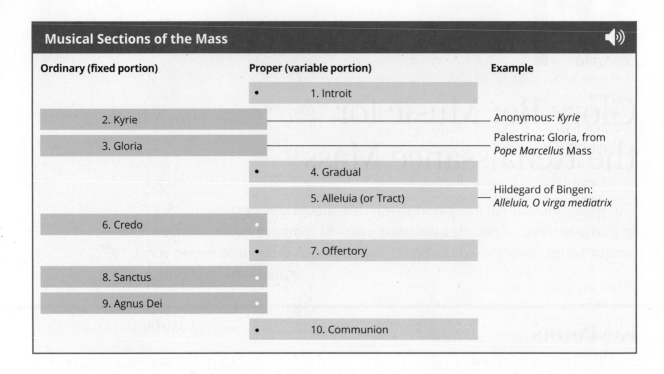

Musical Sections of the Mass

Ordinary (fixed portion)	Proper (variable portion)	Example
	• 1. Introit	
2. Kyrie		Anonymous: *Kyrie*
3. Gloria		Palestrina: Gloria, from *Pope Marcellus* Mass
	• 4. Gradual	
	5. Alleluia (or Tract)	Hildegard of Bingen: *Alleluia, O virga mediatrix*
6. Credo •		
	• 7. Offertory	
8. Sanctus •		
9. Agnus Dei •		
	• 10. Communion	

Middle Ages and Renaissance. You might be surprised to know that the Catholic Church continued to celebrate the Mass in Latin until the middle of the twentieth century.

With the rise of Renaissance polyphony, composers concentrated their musical settings on the Ordinary, the fixed portion that was sung daily. Its five prayers are the Kyrie, Gloria, Credo, Sanctus, and Agnus Dei. (Today, these sections are recited or sung in the vernacular, the language of the country, rather than in Latin—although in recent years there has been a resurgence of interest in the Latin Mass throughout the world.) The **Kyrie** is a prayer for mercy that dates from the early centuries of Christianity, as its Greek text attests. This prayer is followed by the **Gloria** ("Glory be to God on high"), a joyful hymn of praise. The third section, the **Credo** ("I believe in one God, the Father Almighty"), is the confession of faith and the longest of the Mass texts. Fourth is the **Sanctus** ("Holy, holy, holy"), a song of praise, which concludes with "Hosanna in the highest." The fifth and last part of the Ordinary, the **Agnus Dei** ("Lamb of God, Who takes away the sins of the world"), is sung three times, with different words for its conclusion. The order of the Mass, with its Ordinary and Proper prayers, appears above.

In Their Own Words

❝ The Credo is the longest movement. There is much to believe."

—*Igor Stravinsky*

Portrait of the Protestant reformer Martin Luther, painted by **Lucas Cranach** (1472–1553).

The Reformation and Counter-Reformation

Around the time of Josquin's death (1521), major religious reforms were spreading across northern Europe. In 1517, the Augustinian monk Martin Luther (1483–1546) launched the Protestant movement known as the **Reformation** with his Ninety-Five Theses—a list of reforms he proposed for the practices of the Catholic Church. Rather than adopt these new ideas, the church excommunicated him, and the rest is history.

Both Luther and another important reformer, John Calvin (1509–1564), believed that simple, monophonic **congregational singing** in the vernacular should be the basis of Christian worship. Calvin rejected polyphony as distracting from the essential focus on scriptural text: his followers (including the early Puritan colonists who came to North America from England) embraced the idea that worship song should be monophonic and shared by all congregants. But Luther, an admirer of Josquin, encouraged *his* followers to add polyphonic worship music to enhance the congregational unison singing; we will examine the result of his idea through the music of J. S. Bach in a later chapter.

The Catholic Church was undergoing its own reform movement, focused on a return to Christian piety, known as the Catholic Reformation or **Counter-Reformation**. This movement, which extended from the 1530s into the early decades of the next century, witnessed sweeping changes in the church as religious orders increased their efforts to help the poor and combat heresy. The church organized what some view as the longest committee meeting in history: the **Council of Trent**, which met, with some interruptions, from 1545 to 1563.

In its desire to regulate every aspect of religious discipline, the Council of Trent took up the matter of church music. The attending cardinals noted the corruption of traditional chants by the singers, who added extravagant embellishments to the Gregorian melodies. They also objected to the use of certain instruments in religious services, the practice of incorporating popular songs in Masses, the secular spirit that had invaded sacred music, and the generally irreverent attitude of church musicians. In polyphonic settings of the Mass, the cardinals claimed, the sacred text was made unintelligible by the elaborate texture. Some advocated abolishing polyphony altogether and returning to Gregorian chant, but there were many music lovers among them who opposed so drastic a step.

The committee assigned to deal with the music problem issued only general recommendations in favor of a pure vocal style that would respect the integrity of the sacred texts, avoid virtuosity, and encourage piety. We will hear some of these traits in the glorious polyphony by the Italian master Giovanni Pierluigi da Palestrina.

At the Council of Trent, Catholic clergymen worked to reform and clarify the Church's doctrines, including how music should heighten worship.

Council of Trent

Giovanni Pierluigi da Palestrina (c. 1525–1594)

Palestrina (named for the town where he was born) worked as an organist and choirmaster at various Italian churches, including St. Peter's in Rome, where he spent the last twenty-three years of his life. He wrote largely sacred music—his output of Masses exceeds that of any other composer—and his music represents the pure *a cappella* style of vocal polyphony typical of the late Renaissance. He strove to make the words understood by properly accentuating them, thereby meeting the guidelines of the Catholic reform.

MAJOR WORKS: Over 100 Masses (including the *Pope Marcellus* Mass) • Madrigals and motets.

Palestrina worked at the Vatican in Rome, where **Michelangelo** (1475–1564) painted the famous Sistine Chapel ceiling, *The Creation of Adam* (c. 1511).

Palestrina and the *Pope Marcellus* Mass

Palestrina's *Pope Marcellus* Mass was once thought to have been written to satisfy the Council of Trent's recommendations for polyphonic church music, but this is probably not true. Since the papal choir sang without instrumental accompaniment, this Mass was most likely performed *a cappella*. It was written for six voice parts—soprano, alto, two tenors, and two basses, a typical setting for the all-male church choirs of the era. The highest voice was sung by boy sopranos or male falsettists (singing in falsetto, or head voice), and the alto part by male altos, or countertenors (tenors with very high voices).

The Gloria from the *Pope Marcellus* Mass (LG 9) exhibits Palestrina's hallmark style— restrained, serene, and celestial. The opening line, "Gloria in excelsis Deo" ("Glory be to God on high"), is chanted by the officiating priest. For the remaining text, Palestrina constructed a polyphonic setting, balancing the harmonic and polyphonic elements so that the words are clearly audible, an effect that foreshadows the recommendations of the Council of Trent. His music is representative of the pure *a cappella* style of vocal polyphony of the later Renaissance. It reflects the Catholic Church's belief that heavenly sounds produced by trained professionals would be more spiritually powerful than the rough song of an untrained congregation—the precise opposite of Calvin's concept of a "musical priesthood of all the faithful."

In Their Own Words

❝ Among the various things which are suitable for man's recreation and pleasure, music is the first and leads us to the belief that it is a gift of God set apart for this purpose."

—*John Calvin*

CRITICAL THINKING

1. What were some differences and similarities between Protestant and Catholic approaches to musical worship?
2. How did the Council of Trent influence the performance and style of sacred music?

YourTurn TO EXPLORE

Consider public events that involve "community spirit"—sports, political rallies, church services, and so forth. How is music used to foster that spirit? How do songs that are sung by the entire gathering differ from music played by professional musicians to "create the mood" at the event? Have you attended community events in which you were particularly inspired by the music? Was it participatory, listener-directed, or was it a combination of both?

Palestrina: Gloria, from *Pope Marcellus* Mass

Date: Published 1567
Genre: Gloria, from his setting of the Mass Ordinary

Performed by: The Sixteen, Harry Christophers, director

What to Listen For

Melody	Shifts between high- and low-range voices.	**Form**	Through-composed (no major section repeated), with some short ideas exchanged between voices.
Rhythm/ meter	Slow duple meter, weak pulse.		
Harmony	Full, consonant harmony.	**Expression**	Focus on the clarity of the words.
Texture	Monophonic opening; then homorhythmic, with some polyphony; frequent changes in the density of voices.	**Performing forces**	Six-part choir, *a cappella*.
		Text	Hymn of praise; second movement of the Ordinary of the Mass.

	TEXT	NO. OF VOICES	TRANSLATION
0:00	Gloria in excelsis Deo	1	Glory be to God on high,
	et in terra pax hominibus	4	and on earth peace to men
	bonae voluntatis.	4	of good will.
	Laudamus te. Benedicimus te.	4	We praise Thee. We bless Thee.
	Adoramus te.	3	We adore Thee.
	Glorificamus te.	4	We glorify Thee.
	Gratias agimus tibi propter	5/4	We give Thee thanks for
	magnam gloriam tuam.	3/4	Thy great glory.
	Domine Deus, Rex caelestis,	4	Lord God, heavenly King,
	Deus Pater omnipotens.	3	God, the Father Almighty.
	Domine Fili	4	O Lord, the only-begotten Son,
	unigenite, Jesu Christe.	6/5	Jesus Christ.
	Domine Deus, Agnus Dei,	3/4	Lord God, Lamb of God,
	Filius Patris.	6	Son of the Father.
2:44	Qui tollis peccata mundi,	4	Thou that takest away the sins of the world,
	miserere nobis.	4	have mercy on us.
	Qui tollis peccata mundi,	4/5	Thou that takest away the sins of the world,
	suscipe deprecationem nostram.	6/4	receive our prayer.
	Qui sedes ad dexteram Patris,	3	Thou that sittest at the right hand of the Father,
	miserere nobis.	3	have mercy on us.
	Quoniam tu solus sanctus.	4	For Thou alone art holy.
	Tu solus Dominus.	4	Thou only art the Lord.
	Tu solus Altissimus.	4	Thou alone art most high.
	Jesu Christe, cum Sancto Spiritu	6/3/4	Jesus Christ, along with the Holy Spirit
	in gloria Dei Patris.	4/5	in the glory of God the Father.
	Amen.	6	Amen.

🔊 **AnotherHearing** Today, Renaissance music such as this Mass is often heard performed by a mixed choir—that is, with women (sopranos and altos) and men (tenors and basses). But in earlier times, women were not allowed to sing church music, so choirs were made up of men and boys only. Listen to the performance by the Westminster Cathedral Choir, and suggest how the timbres and choir size differ. Which recording do you prefer, and why?

22

Instrumental Movements: Medieval and Renaissance Dance Music

"A time to weep, and a time to laugh; a time to mourn, and a time to dance."

—Ecclesiastes 3:4

KeyPoints

- Dance music has often been both groundbreaking and provocative in the Western tradition.
- Musical instruments in medieval and Renaissance Europe were categorized as soft (*bas*) or loud (*haut*) according to their purpose.

- Both professional and amateur musicians played instrumental dance music, often adding **embellishments**.

In Their Own Words

" I hope his tune will be worthy of the instrument."

—Cicero (106–43 BCE)

Throughout the Western tradition, dance music has both driven expressive change and been accused of fostering social disruption. While we might consider dance music from earlier times odd and stilted, our grandchildren will likewise be amused at what we find provocative or sensuous in dances today. Instrumental music first flourished in conjunction with dance, since the varied layers of wordless sound gave the opportunity for creative interpretation through movement, just as they do in the hands of spinning DJs in the twenty-first century.

Instrumental Music in the Middle Ages and Renaissance

In early times, instrumental music was largely an oral tradition that relied on the improvisation skills of players. Much of our knowledge of the instruments and performing practices comes, then, from artworks and historical documents rather than notated music. We know that early instruments were grouped into the same general families as modern ones—strings, woodwinds, brass, percussion, and keyboard—but unlike today, they were also categorized as soft (*bas*, or indoor) and loud (*haut*, or outdoor), according to their use.

Soft vs. loud instruments

Among the most common soft instruments were the **recorder**, an end-blown flute with a breathy tone; the **lute**, a plucked-string instrument of Middle Eastern origin (p. 89); and various bowed-string instruments, including the **rebec** (see illustration, p. 70). The loud instruments, which played mainly for tournaments or

114

outdoor processions, included the **shawm**, a nasal-sounding ancestor of the oboe (also of Middle Eastern origin); the **sackbut**, an early version of the trombone; and the **cornetto**, a wooden instrument with fingerholes like a recorder but a cup-shaped mouthpiece. These loud instruments made up the civic wind band, a group of three to five players found in most urban centers; the band was often accompanied by percussion instruments, including the **tabor** (a cylindrical drum) and **nakers** (small hand drums played in pairs, p. 89).

Other brass instruments such as trumpets were used to heighten the grandeur during ceremonial processions and were also sounded in warfare, to frighten or confuse the enemy or to signal across the battlefield. Because of their construction and the fact that they played fanfares and other simple combinations of sounds rather than melodies, trumpets served mostly as sonic reinforcement at public events, and were integrated into the orchestra only from the later 1600s.

Our first notated record of instrumental music comes from a mere handful of dances in late medieval manuscripts, but with the advent of music printing in the sixteenth century, books of dance music became readily available for amateur and professional players alike. These publications included a wide variety of dance types, ranging from the slow and stately **pavane** to the showy, fast-paced **saltarello** to the group-oriented **ronde**, a circle or line dance (see illustration on p. 117). Because instruments were not yet specified, there was much flexibility in performance, based on the occasion and what was on hand. Since this was also the time when books describing the latest and most fashionable dances were published, we have a fairly good idea of what patterns of movement were considered most attractive and "trendy" for young Europeans to try out while the musicians played.

A city wind band, with bassoon, shawms, cornetto, and sackbut. Detail from *Procession in Honor of Our Lady of Sablon in Brussels* (1616), by **Denis van Alsloot** (c. 1570–1626).

Dance types

Susato and His *Danserye*

One of the most popular dance collections of the sixteenth century was published in Antwerp (in modern-day Belgium) in 1551 by Tielman Susato (c. 1515–c. 1571), a well-known printer and musician. Susato was a musical jack-of-all-trades: he composed and arranged different styles of secular and sacred works, and unlike modern musicians who generally specialize on a particular instrument, he played virtually all the brass and woodwind instruments of his day. This last talent gained him a position as a member of the Antwerp city band—an esteemed group of five instrumentalists who performed regular town concerts as well as for processions (or parades) held on religious occasions and for the entertainment of visiting dignitaries (see illustration of a civic band above). The music this group played is less clear, but we know they did not rely exclusively on notated music; rather, they were expert improvisers, able to turn a simple dance into an intricate, masterful work, much as a modern jazz band can build from a few standards to keep an audience active and engaged for hours on end.

In Their Own Words

" Music is a science that would have us laugh and sing and dance."

—*Guillaume de Machaut*

LISTENING GUIDE 10 2:29

Susato: Three Dances

Date: Published 1551
Genre: Ronde

Performed by: Convivium Musicum

What to Listen For

Melody	Prominent tunes; short phrases.
Rhythm/meter	Lively duple meter.
Harmony	Full chords, consonant; ronde 2 is modal.
Texture	Mostly homophonic.

Form	Three binary-form dances (each **A-A-B-B**).
Expression	Occasional embellishments.
Performing forces	Four-part instrumental group: loud wind band—shawm, cornetto, sackbut, tabor, dulcian (early bassoon), tambourine.

Ronde 1

0:00	A	Shawm solo
0:06	A	Tabor joins.
0:11	B	Loud band.
0:22	B	Repeat of **B**.

Opening phrase (**A**) of ronde 1:

Ronde 2

0:33	C	Cornetto with instruments.
0:38	C	Repeat of **C**.
0:44	D	Contrapuntal section.
0:55	D	Embellished repeat of **D**.

Opening phrase (**C**) of ronde 2:

Ronde 1 (transition)

1:12	A	Played four times.

Ronde 3

1:23	E	Shawm with loud band.
1:34	E	Repeat of **E**.
1:45	F	New short section.
1:51	F	Repeat of **F**.

Opening phrase (**E**) of ronde 3:

Ronde 1

1:57	B	Played twice.
2:20		Final bow chord.

Embellishments

Susato's collection, called *Danserye,* features a variety of popular dance types, including the set of three rondes we will hear (LG 10). Although originally a country dance, the ronde made its way to the city and to the courts of the nobility. Our recording features the loud, civic-style wind band. The repeated dance sections allowed the musicians to improvise **embellishments**, or melodic decorations, as they saw fit, and the performers in our modern recording follow that custom, making sure that the sound is enriched and varied through the different combinations of instruments. The dances flow from one to another—you can imagine that once this high-spirited dance gets going, no one will want to stop. A final chord brings the gaiety to a close with all the players bowing to each other.

Shawm players accompany an aristocratic group dancing a ronde. From a fifteenth-century French manuscript.

It was through such dance pieces that Renaissance composers began to explore the possibilities of purely instrumental forms, beginning a tradition of finding new ways sound can move us—both physically and emotionally—when words don't get in the way.

CRITICAL THINKING

1. What were the main categories of instruments in the Renaissance? How do they compare with modern Western instrument categories?
2. Who do you think might have performed dances in the Renaissance? Where would they have taken place?

Your Turn TO EXPLORE

Find video recordings of dances from past and/or non-Western traditions. How do the dancers' movements follow the patterns set out by the musicians? What kinds of variation, elaboration, or improvisation do the musicians employ on the basic patterns, whether through melody, texture, or timbre? What do you find most expressive about the union of movement and sound in these dances?

Music in Words

Reviewing Medieval and Renaissance Styles

MUSIC from the Middle Ages and Renaissance—commonly referred to as early music—is quite varied, and distinct in many ways from more recent repertories. Here are some things to listen for when you hear an unfamiliar work from this period.

MELODY is not always the focus of early music (except for single-line music like chant). Rather, multiple melodies are often heard together, forming a complex texture. Consider whether the melody is flowing (wavelike), constructed in long or short phrases, has a small or medium range, is conjunct or disjunct. Is the relationship with the text syllabic or melismatic? Are there expressive leaps?

RHYTHM can be complicated and syncopated and also lack a strong metric sense, sometimes with a barely perceptible beat. But in later Renaissance music, you can often perceive a strong beat. Can you deduce either a duple or triple meter? Does the pattern of accents stay the same throughout?

HARMONY proceeds from one sonority or chord to another using modal scales rather than the more modern major and minor scales. The preferred consonant, or pleasing, harmonies of early times often sound empty and foreign to us because they don't rely on triads (see p. 13). In later Renaissance music, the sonority is more modern. Would you describe the harmonies as open and hollow, or rich and full? as consonant or dissonant? as modal or in a major or minor tonality?

TEXTURE is often dense, with multiple lines moving independently of each other; as more voices (or instruments) enter, it can become harder to focus on any one individual line. Is the texture in this song thick or thin? Is it largely homophonic (with the voices moving together) or polyphonic (with more independent lines)? Do the lines imitate each other, or are they independent?

VOCAL TIMBRE in performances of early music often does not resemble later singing styles. Vibrato was used sparingly at the time, if at all, and in sacred music only male voices—boys and men—were heard. How would you describe the timbre(s) heard in this song? Is the performance *a cappella* (all vocal)? Is the group made up of only male singers? only female singers? Is it a mixed group?

GENRES include sacred vocal music (Mass, organum, motet), secular vocal music (madrigal, chanson), and instrumental music (dances).

Listen and Respond

Let's see how well you can apply what you've learned to a new example of early music. Listen to Thomas Morley's *April is in my mistress' face* (text is below) and complete the exercise that follows.

> April is in my mistress' face,
> And July in her eyes hath place;
> Within her bosom is September,
> But in her heart a cold December.

1. Create a simple listening outline for the song. Think about melody, rhythm and meter, harmony, texture, and genre. How is the short text treated? How do the various lines interact and how does this interaction change throughout the song?

2. Consider how you might describe this song to a friend who is not in the class and not familiar with the terminology we've been developing. What general descriptions can you apply to the melody? harmony? texture? overall effect of the piece?

3. Now write a short paragraph describing the work as you might for a concert report. Here you can demonstrate your understanding of the relevant terms and concepts as well as your response to the meaning and expressive quality of the song. Look back at Chapter 14 to find ways to frame your perspective. How would you compare this song with Farmer's *Fair Phyllis?*

Summary of Medieval and Renaissance Styles

	Medieval (c. 400–1450)	Renaissance (c. 1450–1600)
Composers	Hildegard, Notre Dame composers, Machaut, Raimbaut de Vaqueiras	Josquin des Prez, Palestrina, Susato, Monteverdi, Farmer
Melody	Conjunct, small range; occasional expressive leaps	Arched, smooth, asymmetrical lines, diatonic with expressive chromaticism
Rhythm/meter	Nonmetric, free (early); syncopated (late); triple meter	Regular, gentle pulse; duple meter prevalent; occasional shifts to triple
Harmony	Modal; open-sounding sonorities	Modal, moving toward tonality; consonant sonorities
Texture	Monophonic (early); nonimitative polyphony (late)	Imitative polyphony; homophony to emphasize the text
Vocal genres	Chant, organum, chanson, motet, Mass	Mass, motet, madrigal, chanson, lute ayre
Instrumental genres	Dance music	Dance music; various solo lute and keyboard works, ensemble music
Expression	Pure, *a cappella* performance (sacred), without vibrato	Pure, *a cappella* performance (sacred), without vibrato; word-painting (secular)
Borrowed material	Sacred music based on chant	Sacred music with cantus firmus (early), moving toward freely composed
Performance sites	Church, court	Church, court, home

The Baroque Era

"It is the special province of music to move the heart."

—German composer and organist
Johann Sebastian Bach (1685–1750)

OVERVIEW

1628
Dr. William Harvey
explains the body's
circulatory system.

1667
John Milton's masterpiece
Paradise Lost published.

1687
Sir Isaac Newton's
theory of
gravitation issued.

1611
King James
Version of Bible
printed.

1649
Period of
Commonwealth
begins in England.

1682
French court of Louis XIV
established at Versailles.

1600	1625	1650	1675

1650
Chiara Margarita
Cozzolani and
Barbara Strozzi
publish their music.

1689
Henry Purcell's opera
Dido and Aeneas
performed.

Learning Objectives

By the end of Part 3, you will be able to

- perceive speechlike melodies (in vocal works) with some chromatic inflections for emotional effect, as well as long, continuous melodies (in later instrumental music) with wide leaps.
- note the steady rhythmic pulse within a clear duple or triple meter, and how the rhythm in vocal music may move more freely to better express the words.
- recognize how specific words are emphasized through distinctive musical gestures (such as melismas, embellishments, and leaps), and how instrumental music can be highly virtuosic and dramatic.
- distinguish how the musical lines or voices interact, creating textures that vary from homophonic to highly polyphonic and imitative.
- identify some of the important vocal and instrumental genres of the Baroque, recognize the different formal structures employed, and become familiar with some of the most renowned composers of the era.

1732
George Washington born.

1740
Maria Theresa succeeds to the Austrian throne.

| 1700 | 1725 | 1750 | 1775 |

1731
G. F. Handel begins presenting his English oratorios in London.

1749
J. S. Bach composes *The Art of Fugue.*

1770
Williams Billings publishes *The New England Psalm-Singer.*

1711
Antonio Vivaldi publishes his first collection of concertos.

3

Music as Exploration and Drama

"These harmonic notes are the language of the soul and the instruments of the heart."

—*Barbara Strozzi*

Music intensifies emotion. This may seem self-evident to us in the twenty-first century, but it was in the period that we are about to explore—the 1600s and early 1700s—that Europeans set out to develop musical approaches designed to "ramp up" various emotional states and help listeners experience their diversity more deeply.

Composers and performers became increasingly interested in how music could enhance the expression of words—most prominently through the development of a kind of musical theater called opera, but also through the training of specialized singers whose **virtuosity** (remarkable technical skill) made the amateur singing tradition of the Renaissance seem outdated and bland. Even more novel was a significant focus on the expressive power of musical instruments—not only in conjunction with voices, but on their own. While purely instrumental music existed before the 1600s, in the Baroque era it became much more prominent with the development of several new genres and the refinement of instrument building and performance techniques.

Virtuosity

The Flemish painter **Peter Paul Rubens** (1577–1640) instills his paintings with high energy and drama. His voluptuous nudes, as in *Diana and Her Nymphs*, established the seventeenth-century ideal of feminine beauty.

Renaissance and Baroque sculptural approaches to the depiction of the biblical David:

LEFT: **Michelangelo** shows us David in contemplation (1501–04).

RIGHT: In contrast, **Gian Lorenzo Bernini** captures David about to sling the stone that will bring down the giant Goliath (1623).

During the early part of this period, musicians seemed almost giddy with the possibilities for intense expression, creating works that appear designed to swing between musical extremes. As time passed, such experimentation gave way to a more standardized practice: the later Baroque is characterized by a greater interest in predictable musical forms and procedures.

"Baroque" Art and Culture

The years between 1600 and 1750 represent a period of change, adventure, and discovery. The conquest of the New World stirred the imagination and filled the treasuries of Western Europe. The ideas of Galileo and Kepler in physics and astronomy, of René Descartes in mathematics, and of Spinoza in philosophy were milestones in the intellectual history of Europe. The English physician William Harvey explained the circulation of the blood, and Sir Isaac Newton formulated the theory of gravity. Empires clashed for control of the globe.

There was appalling poverty and wasteful luxury, magnificent idealism and savage oppression. Baroque art—with its vigor, elaborate decoration, and grandeur—projected the pomp and splendor of the era. Indeed, the term "baroque" (applied in retrospect by later writers who saw this period as excessively extravagant) derives from a Portuguese word that originally meant "misshapen" or "distorted."

A comparison between the two depictions of the biblical figure David above, one by Renaissance artist Michelangelo (1475–1564) and the other by Bernini (1598–1680), clearly reveals the Baroque love of the dramatic. The earlier sculpture is balanced, calm, reflective; on David's shoulder is the sling with which he has just slain the giant Goliath, but the overall effect is static, poised. The Baroque David shows the young man in motion, every muscle in his body tensed in the act that will save his people. In like fashion, the Venetian school of painters and Northern masters such as Flemish artist Peter Paul Rubens captured the dynamic spirit of the new age, producing canvases ablaze in color and movement (see illustration opposite).

In Their Own Words

❝ I do not know what I may appear to the world; but to myself I seem to have been only like a boy playing on the seashore . . . whilst the great ocean of truth lay all undiscovered before me."

—*Isaac Newton*

Jan Vermeer is well known for his painting of bourgeois (middle-class) Dutch women playing keyboard instruments. *A Young Lady Seated at a Virginal,* c. 1670.

In Their Own Words

" Music must be supported by the King and the princes."

—Martin Luther

The Baroque was an era of absolute monarchy. Rulers throughout Europe modeled their courts on Versailles, a sumptuous palace on the outskirts of Paris. Louis XIV's famous statement "I am the State" summed up a way of life in which all art and culture served the ruler. Courts large and small maintained elaborate musical establishments, including opera troupes, chapel choirs, and orchestras. Baroque opera, the favorite diversion of the aristocracy, told stories of the gods and heroes of antiquity, in whom the nobility and courtiers saw flattering likenesses of themselves.

The middle classes, excluded from the salons of the aristocracy, created a culture of their own. Their music-making took place in the home. It was for the middle classes that the comic opera and the novel, both genres filled with keen and witty observations on life, came into being. For them, painting abandoned its grandiose themes and turned to intimate scenes of bourgeois life. The Dutch School, embodying the vitality of a new middle-class art, reached its high point with Rembrandt and Jan Vermeer (see illustration at left).

The Baroque was also an intensely devout period, with religion a rallying cry on some of the bloodiest battlefields in history. Protestants were centered in England, Scandinavia, Holland, and northern Germany, all strongholds of the rising middle class. On the Catholic side were two powerful dynasties: the French Bourbons and the Austrian-Spanish Hapsburgs, who fought one another as fiercely as they did their Protestant foes. Religion was an equally important part of life in the New World as well, both in the colonies of Protestant refugees who settled on the East Coast of North America and in the fervently Catholic Spanish and French colonies (Spanish in what is now Mexico, Central America, and the southwestern United States; French in Canada, the Mississippi valley, and the Gulf Coast).

England's John Milton produced the poetic epic of Protestantism (*Paradise Lost*), just as Dante had expressed the Catholic point of view in *The Divine Comedy* three and a half centuries earlier. The Catholic world answered Martin Luther's call for reforms with the Counter-Reformation (see Chapter 21), whose rapturous mysticism found expression in the canvases of El Greco. These paintings were the creations of a visionary mind that distorted the real in its search for a reality beyond.

Creative artists played a variety of roles in Baroque society. Rubens was not only a famous painter but also an ambassador and friend of princes. The composer Antonio Vivaldi was also a priest, and George Frideric Handel an opera impresario. Artists usually functioned under royal or princely patronage, or, like Johann Sebastian Bach, they might be employed by a church or city administration. In all cases, artists were in direct contact with their public. Many musical works were created for specific occasions—an opera for a royal wedding, a dance suite for a court festivity, a cantata for a religious service—and for immediate use.

Main Currents in Baroque Music

"The end of all good music is to affect the soul."
                            —*Claudio Monteverdi*

One of the most significant characteristics of the early Baroque style was a shift from a texture of several independent parts (polyphony) to one in which a single melody stood out (homophony).

A group of Florentine writers, artists, and musicians known as the Camerata (a name derived from the Italian word for "salon") first cultivated this approach, which they called "the new style," around 1600. The members of the Camerata were aristocratic humanists who aimed to resurrect the musical-dramatic art of ancient Greece. Although little was known of ancient music, the Camerata deduced that it must have heightened the emotional power of the text. Thus their "new style" consisted of a melody that moved freely over a foundation of simple chords. Members engaged in excited discussions about their homophonic music, which they also proudly named the "expressive style." The group soon realized that their approach could be applied not only to a short poem but also to an entire drama, fostering the most notable Baroque innovation: "drama through music," or what we now call **opera**.

Florentine Camerata

Opera

A new kind of notation accompanied the new style: since musicians were familiar with the basic harmonies, the composer put a numeral above or below the bass note, indicating the chord required (a kind of notation called **figured bass**), and the performer filled in the necessary harmony. This system, known as **basso continuo**, provided a foundation over which a vocal or instrumental melody could unfold. It led to one of the most significant changes in all music history: the establishment of **major-minor tonality** (see Chapter 4). With this development, the thrust to the key note, or tonic, became the most powerful force in music. Each chord could assume its function in relation to the key center; and the movement between keys, governed by tonality, helped shape a musical structure. Composers were able to develop forms of instrumental music larger than had ever before been known.

Basso continuo

Major-minor tonality

The Hall of Mirrors in the French Royal Palace of Versailles, built by French kings Louis XIII and Louis XIV, exemplifies the Baroque love for elaborate decorations.

Two professional singers of the era: the Venetian mezzo-soprano Faustina Bordoni (1697–1781), painted by **Bartolomeo Nazari**; and the famous castrato singer Carlo Broschi, called Farinelli (1705–1782), by **Jacopo Amigoni** (1682–1752).

The transition to major-minor tonality was marked by a significant technical advance: a new tuning system that allowed instruments to play in any key. Called **equal temperament**, this tuning adjusted (or tempered) the mathematically "pure" intervals within the octave to equalize the distance between adjacent tones, making it possible to play in every major and minor key without producing unpleasant sounds, and greatly increasing the range of harmonic possibilities available to the composer. J. S. Bach demonstrated this range in his two-volume keyboard collection *The Well-Tempered Clavier*: each volume contains twenty-four preludes and fugues, one in every possible major and minor key. Today, our ears are conditioned to the equal-tempered system, since this is how pianos are now tuned.

The elaborate scrollwork of Baroque architecture found its musical equivalent in the principle of continuous expansion of melody. A movement might start with a striking musical figure that would then be repeated and varied with seemingly infinite modifications, driven by rhythms that helped capture the movement of this dynamic age. In vocal music, wide leaps and chromatic tones helped create melodies that were highly expressive of the text.

Baroque musicians used dissonant chords more freely, for emotional intensity and color. In setting poetry, for example, a composer might choose a dissonance to heighten the impact of a particularly meaningful word. The dynamic contrasts achieved in Renaissance music through varied imitative voicings gave way to a more nuanced treatment in the Baroque, allowing for a more precise expression of emotions, especially of the text. Dramatic *forte/piano* contrasts and echo effects were also typical of the era.

Finally, the Baroque inherited from the Renaissance an impressive technique of word-painting, in which the music vividly mirrored the words. It was generally accepted that music ought to arouse the emotions, or "affections"—joy, anger, love, fear. By the late seventeenth century, an entire piece or movement was normally built on a single affection: the opening musical idea established the mood of the piece, which prevailed until the end. This procedure differs markedly from the practice of later eras, when music was based on two or more contrasting emotions.

Performance Matters

THE RISE OF THE VIRTUOSO MUSICIAN

As the great musical instrument builders in Italy and Germany improved and refined their instruments, Baroque performers responded with more virtuosic (remarkably skilled) playing. Composers in turn wrote works demanding even more advanced playing techniques. Out of these developments came the virtuosic violin works of Antonio Vivaldi (see Chapter 29).

Instrumental virtuosity had its counterpart in the vocal sphere. The rise of opera brought with it the development of a phenomenal vocal technique, exemplified in the early eighteenth century by the **castrato**, a male singer who was castrated during boyhood in order to preserve the soprano or alto register of

Castrato

his voice for the rest of his life. What resulted, after years of training, was an incredibly agile voice of enormous range, powered by breath control unrivaled by most singers today. The castrato's voice combined the lung power of the male with the brilliance of the female upper register. Strange as it may seem to us, Baroque audiences associated this voice with heroic male roles. When castrato roles are performed today, they are usually sung in a lower register by a tenor or baritone, or in the original register by a countertenor or a woman singer in male costume.

Women, particularly singers, began to expand their role in music. Two early seventeenth-century Italian singers, Francesca Caccini and Barbara Strozzi (p. 132), were among the earliest female composers to publish their works. Caccini stands out as the first woman to write an opera, and Strozzi was a prolific composer of both secular and sacred music. Some opera singers reached the level of superstars, such as the Italian sopranos Faustina Bordoni (see illustration at left) and Francesca Cuzzoni, who engaged in a bitter rivalry. As we will see, another, perhaps less expected, venue for women was the cloister, or convent.

Improvisation played a significant role in Baroque music. In addition to elaborating on the simple harmonic foundation that was part of almost every musical work, musicians were expected to be able to improvise and add embellishments to what was written on the score, much like jazz or pop musicians today. Baroque music sounded quite different in performance from what was on the page.

In Their Own Words

" Music is the universal language of mankind."

—*Henry Wadsworth Longfellow*

Improvisation

An All-European Art

As great voyages of exploration opened up unknown regions of the globe, exoticism became a discernible element of Baroque music. A number of operas looked to faraway lands for their settings—Persia, India, Turkey, the Middle East, Peru, and the Americas—offering picturesque scenes and dances that may not have been authentic but that delighted audiences through their appeal to the imagination.

Paradoxically, alongside the interest in exotic locales and regional traditions, the Baroque was a period in which there was significant exchange among national cultures. The sensuous beauty of Italian melody, the pointed precision of French dance rhythm, the luxuriance of German polyphony, the freshness of English choral song—these characteristic local traditions eventually blended into an all-European art that absorbed the best of each national style. For example, we will see how Handel, a German, wrote Italian opera for English audiences and gave England the oratorio. And it was precisely through this internationalization that, in the end, the Baroque gave way to a new set of stylistic priorities. An era of discovery and experimentation in which diversity and variety of musical expression was the ultimate goal eventually resulted in commonality of purpose and style, as Europeans became more and more interested in the elements that made humans equal rather than different.

An exotic Chinese dancer in a Venetian opera, c. 1698–1700.

CRITICAL THINKING

1. How did Baroque artists and composers bring drama to their works?

2. What was new about the so-called new music at the beginning of the Baroque period?

Voicing Gender: Women Composers in Baroque Italy

"These harmonic notes are the language of the soul and the instruments of the heart."

—Barbara Strozzi

KeyPoints

- Creative women musicians had limited career choices in the Baroque era. Only a few managed to maintain professional lives in the public sphere, and they were often viewed as women of ill repute.

- One suitable choice for unmarried women was to enter the convent, where singing and sometimes composing formed an integral part of their role as spiritual advocates.

- Chiara Margarita Cozzolani, a Benedictine nun who was a musician and composer, was able to have her works—including her impressive *Magnificat*—published and circulated beyond the convent.

- Singer-composer Barbara Strozzi was one of the few women of her day to pursue a composing career in the secular world; she also received public recognition for her published compositions, including arias for solo voice and basso continuo.

In Their Own Words

" Loving shepherds, while they feed their beloved flocks, often entertain them with the harmony of instruments and the melody of songs. . . . In the same way, so as to imitate the talents shared by the best shepherds . . . I wanted to compose and dedicate this *armonia* to your extraordinary taste and merit."

—Chiara Margarita Cozzolani, dedication of a work to the Bishop of Crema

In the twenty-first century, we are accustomed to enjoying open access to the arts—in museums, at concert venues, and on the Internet. But in earlier times, the arts were largely cultivated within restricted environments, such as aristocratic courts, elite salons or academies where intellectuals met to try out new ideas, and religious institutions.

The Baroque era offered few possibilities for creative women. Generally speaking, women musicians who did not choose the traditional role of wife and mother and wanted to maintain an upstanding reputation had the option of either joining a convent—an honorable choice—or making their way within the insular world of a court or a male-dominated academy. While a handful of singers made a name for themselves as professionals on the operatic stage and other public venues, their character and morality were often in question because women who participated in the public world tended to be courtesans—educated women who entertained men musically, intellectually, and sexually.

In this chapter, we will meet two Italian women who worked to leave their creative mark within a male-dominated society: Chiara Margarita Cozzolani, a nun whose sacred compositions and religious dialogues set to music won the praise of her male peers; and Barbara Strozzi, one of the most prolific singer-composers—male *or* female—of secular music in her era, who not only performed her own music at a salon hosted by her father but also published it for a wider audience. It's extremely fortunate that the works of both women were circulated in their day, allowing modern listeners to hear the distinct voice each projected to the world.

A Nun's Life in Baroque Italy

In recent years, scholars have unearthed sheaves of documents and music that reveal a "secret" musical world within the confines of convents. Though convents were generally considered to be private places for spiritual retreat from outside influences, this was far from the case in seventeenth-century Italy, where they played a major societal role for women and allowed those who desired one a public voice through music.

Music-making at the Benedictine convent of St. Radegunda in Milan was, by all accounts, famous. Dignitaries and other visitors filled the church on special occasions to hear the nuns' angelic voices. In 1670, the Augustinian priest Filippo Picinelli lavished praise on the convent and on one nun in particular:

A chorus of nuns sings in the French Abbey of Port-Royal-des-Champs, as depicted by **Louise-Magdeleine Hortemels** (1688–1767).

> The nuns of St. Radegunda of Milan are gifted with such rare and exquisite talents in music that they are acknowledged to be the best singers in Italy . . . they seem to any listener to be white and melodious swans, who fill hearts with wonder, and spirit away tongues in their praise. Among these sisters, Donna Chiara Margarita Cozzolani merits the highest praise. Chiara [her chosen name, meaning "clear"] in name but even more so in merit, and Margarita ["daisy"] for her unusual and excellent nobility of [musical] invention.

At a time when women's roles in the Catholic Church were extremely limited, this was extraordinary acknowledgment indeed of the power of female spirituality.

In the *Ecstasy of Saint Teresa* (1652), sculpted by **Gian Lorenzo Bernini**, the nun experiences both extreme pain from the sword of the angel and, through divine intervention, a great love of God.

Cozzolani's *Magnificat*

It is not surprising that feast days dedicated to the Virgin Mary were important occasions at St. Radegunda, celebrated with polyphonic singing. But Cozzolani must have felt a personal devotion to the Virgin. Among the many works she wrote in her honor are two settings of the Magnificat, or Canticle of Mary, the concluding and climactic part of the evening office of Vespers. Both are large-scale, polychoral settings for two choirs of four voices each, accompanied by organ continuo. One mystery surrounding settings like these, which feature soprano, alto, tenor, and bass parts, is who sang the lower voices. Evidence suggests that some nuns could sing the tenor part without difficulty, but that the bass part was either sung up an octave or simply sounded by the basso continuo instrument rather than sung (our recording combines both these options). What is clear is that men, even priests, did not sing polyphony with the nuns in their services.

We can imagine that the Magnificat text—the Virgin's song of praise, from the biblical Gospel of Luke, upon learning that she would bear the son of God—was particularly attractive to women. Cozzolani's setting (LG 11) is dramatic and mystical, intended to intensify the nuns' experience of the Virgin's Annunciation and to help them reach a heightened level of religious ecstasy. A similar effect can be

Cozzolani: *Magnificat*

Date: Published 1650

Genre: Selection from the Vespers service

Performed by: Cappella Artemisia, Candace Smith, director

What to Listen For

Melody	Lyrical, small-range duets; static choral lines.	**Form**	Refrains bring back several lines of text/music.
Rhythm/meter	Shifts between duple and triple meter.	**Expression**	Varied tempos; some sections move freely.
Harmony	Consonant; some dissonance in solo passages.	**Performing forces**	Two soprano soloists and two double choirs (SATB) with organ and strings.
Texture	Shifts between homorhythmic ensembles and two-voiced duets; some imitation.	**Text**	Luke 1:46–55. * = repeated text/music.

TEXT

TRANSLATION

0:00 Magnificat anima mea magnificat Dominum,*
et exsultavit spiritus meus in Deo salvatore meo,
quia respexit humilitatem ancillae suae.*
  anima mea magnificat Domino

My soul glorifies the Lord,*
and my spirit rejoices in God my Savior,
who looks on His servant in her lowliness.*
  my soul glorifies the Lord

1:43 Ecce enim ex hoc beatam me dicent omnes generationes,
quia fecit mihi magna,
qui potens est,
et sanctum nomen eius,
  anima mea magnificat

Henceforth all ages will call me blessed.
He has done great things for me,
He who is mighty,
and holy is His name.
  my soul glorifies the Lord

2:57 et misericordia eius in progenies et progenies*
timentibus eum.
Fecit potentiam in brachio suo,*
  quia fecit mihi magna

And His mercy is from age to age,*
on those who fear Him.
He puts forth His arm in strength*
  He has done great things for me

4:10 dispersit superbos mente cordis sui;
deposuit potentes de sede*
et exaltavit humiles;
esurientes implevit bonis*
  mihi magna fecit

and scatters the proud-hearted.
He casts the mighty from their thrones,*
and raises the lowly.
He fills the starving with good things,*
  He has done great things for me

5:11 et divites dimisit inanes.
Suscepit Israel puerum suum,*
recordatus misericordiae suae,
  magna mihi fecit

sends the rich away empty.
He protects Israel His servant,*
remembering His mercy,
  He has done great things for me

5:55 sicut locutus est ad patres nostros,*
  Abraham et semini eius in saecula.

the mercy promised to our fathers,*
  to Abraham and to his sons forever.

Doxology closing

7:16 Gloria Patri
  anima mea magnificat Dominum
et Filio
  anima mea magnificat Dominum

Glory be to the Father
  my soul glorifies the Lord
and to the Son
  my soul glorifies the Lord

	et in spiriti sancto.	and to the Holy Ghost.
	anima mea magnificat Dominum	*my soul glorifies the Lord*
8:09	Sicut erat in principio et nunc et simper et in secula saeculorum.	As it was in the beginning, now and ever shall be world without end.
	anima mea magnificat Dominum	*my soul glorifies the Lord*
8:42	Amen.	Amen.

seen in Bernini's dynamic sculpture *Ecstasy of St. Teresa* (illustration on p. 129), created around 1650, the same time as our *Magnificat*. Here, St. Teresa is resting on a cloud, confirming her divine experience. Dramatic gilded rays illuminate her, as she suffers both intense pleasure and pain at the hand of an angel who stabs her repeatedly with a golden spear. In Cozzolani's inspired work, virtuosic duets interrupt the larger choral forces that sing in homorhythm, and text and music are freely repeated in a highly expressive setting rich in word-painting that is at once spiritual and sensual, like the sculpture.

Several text lines recur as refrains, including the first, "My soul glorifies the Lord," and "He has done great things for me"; the latter often signals a shift from the free, rhapsodic motion to a lilting triple meter. These are lines that describe the personal experience of the Virgin Mary: through their repetition, the nuns would have had the opportunity to reflect on this all-too-rare female voice in Christian Scripture. The *Magnificat* closes with a prayer of praise to God called the **doxology**; its words may be familiar to you, as they are frequently sung in Christian services today.

Radegunda withdrawing to the monastery, from the eleventh-century manuscript *The Life of Saint Radegunda.*

Chiara Margarita Cozzolani (1602–c. 1676)

The youngest daughter of a wealthy Milanese merchant, Margarita Cozzolani entered the convent of St. Radegunda (see illustration above), taking the religious name Chiara and professing her final vows at age eighteen. One of her sisters and two of her aunts were also members of the convent; such networks of relatives in religious houses were common at the time. Soon Chiara took up an active role in music, serving as the director of one of the convent's two choirs and composing music. These talents were clearly encouraged: she published three collections of music, ranging from solo motets with accompaniment to large-scale Magnificat settings for double choir. Notable are her musical "dialogues" elucidating famous religious scenes, like that between Mary Magdalene and the angels at Christ's tomb on Easter morning. Her collection of 1650 contains a complete set of Vespers psalms for the major feasts of the year.

While some of Cozzolani's music is conservative in style, her larger works in particular mark her as one of the leading composers of the day. Later in her life, she served as abbess and prioress at St. Radegunda through years of conflict both within the convent (between rival choirs) and from outside, when religious authorities attempted to ban the performance of polyphony by the sisters, an order they blatantly disobeyed.

MAJOR WORKS: Several collections (1640 [now lost], 1642, 1648) that include motets for one to four voices with continuo and a four-voice mass • One collection of Vespers music (1650), including two *Magnificats* and dialogues for eight-voice choir as well as other motets, some accompanied by violins and continuo.

This well-dressed woman is probably a courtesan making music with her suitors. *Musical Entertainment,* by **Sebastiano Florigerio** (1500–c. 1545).

In Their Own Words

" Since I am no more held back by feminine weakness than by any allowance made for my sex, I fly in lightest leaves in devotion to make my bow."

—*Barbara Strozzi*

Barbara Strozzi and the Baroque Aria

Barbara Strozzi was certainly one of the more intriguing figures of her time. She gained recognition among her peers as both a composer of high-quality music and as a singer. Her performing world was small and intimate, focused in the exclusive academies of Venice and alongside aristocratic intellectuals and patrons of her art. Especially impressive is the fact that eight volumes of her music were published in her lifetime—an extraordinary feat for a woman. In fact, she published more arias than any male singer-composer of her time—possibly because sending her music out through print was her only way to "appear in public" while maintaining the reputation for modesty that was essential for women of her day.

Strozzi's secular arias focus on the theme of love, in particular the suffering of unfulfilled love. At times she treats this topic humorously, at times with much intensity and seriousness, but always with eloquence. Our selection, the lighthearted aria *Amor dormiglione* (*Sleepyhead, Cupid!*; LG 12)—an invocation to the God of Love—exemplifies her careful sensitivity to the text. Notice how the melody fires downward to depict Cupid's weapons of love (arrows). And when he doesn't awake easily, Strozzi writes a static melodic line to emphasize his laziness. Her arias, some of which include partial or full returns of the opening, foreshadow the **A-B-A** structure (called **da capo aria**) that soon became standard in opera.

Both Strozzi and Cozzolani engaged with musical traditions that had been defined and shaped by men; each found a way to reflect her experience as a woman in a male-dominated society as well as her personal creative spark. Strozzi's *Sleepyhead, Cupid!* is a clever song that allows a female singer to express coy engagement with love through a gender-neutral text (most song texts of the time are clearly

Barbara Strozzi (1619–c. 1677)

Strozzi is a unique figure in the early Baroque era. She was the adopted (and probably illegitimate) daughter of the Venetian poet and playwright Giulio Strozzi; her mother, Isabella Garzoni, was his servant. Giulio oversaw Barbara's education and introduction to the intellectual elite of Venice through an academy (not unlike the Florentine Camerata) where she performed as a singer, participant in debates, and hostess or mistress of ceremonies—all highly unusual, since such academies were generally open to men only.

It has been suggested that Strozzi was a courtesan, and while it's true that she possessed the relevant artistic skills—singing, playing the lute, and writing poetry—this remains

only a theory. Courtesans were a special social class in Venice that was not only tolerated but generally accepted; those considered *cortigiane oneste* (honest, or intellectual, courtesans), like Barbara Strozzi, were well educated and worldly. English traveler Thomas Coryat noted his astonishment in 1608 that there were some 20,000 courtesans in Venice! Strozzi's musical talents were praised by her contemporaries, one noting her "bold and graceful singing," and another comparing her voice to the harmonies of the spheres. Although Strozzi did not hold any official musical post (at court, in churches, or at the theater), she did publish many of her compositions.

MAJOR WORKS: Eight books of vocal music, including madrigals, arias, cantatas, and motets.

LISTENING GUIDE 12

🔊 2:16

Strozzi: *Amor dormiglione (Sleepyhead, Cupid!)*

Date: Published 1651

Genre: Da capo aria

Performed by: Musica Secreta

What to Listen For

Melody	Rising opening melody; lines are shaped to express the text.	**Texture**	Homophony (accompanied solo song).
		Form	Da capo aria (three parts: **A-B-A**).
Rhythm/ meter	Lilting triple meter; a brief switch to duple at beginning of the second section.	**Performing forces**	Solo soprano with harpsichord or bass lute.
Harmony	Consonant, with some chromaticism.	**Text**	Anonymous Italian poem.

TEXT	TRANSLATION
A section	
0:00 Amor, non dormir più!	Cupid, stop sleeping!
Sù, sù svegliati oh mai,	Get up, wake up now,
ché mentre dormi tu	for while you sleep
dormon le gioie mie, vegliano i guai!	my joys sleep too and my pains are awake!
Non esser, Amor dappoco!	Cupid, don't be a good-for-nothing!
Strali, strali, foco, foco!	Arrows, arrows, fire, fire!
Sù, sù non dormir più!	Get up, stop sleeping!
Amor, svegliati, su su!	Cupid, wake up, get up now!
B section	
1:01 Oh pigro, oh tardo,	O lazy, O idle one,
tu non hai senso,	you feel nothing,
Amor melenso,	foolish Cupid,
Amor codardo!	cowardly Cupid!
Ahi, quale io resto,	Alas, while I stay here
che nel mio ardore	consumed with ardor,
tu dorma Amore:	you are sleeping, Cupid:
mancava questo!	this is more than I can stand!
A section repeated	
1:37 Amor, non dormir più! . . .	Cupid, stop sleeping!

Examples of word-painting—rising line at the opening paints the idea of waking Cupid up:

A-mor, a - mor non dor-mir più, sù, sù, sù, sù,

Quick, descending line to depict "arrows" and "fire":

Stra - li,__ stra - li fo - co,__ fo - co,

In Their Own Words

66 So just, so small, yet in so sweet a note, / It seemed the music melted in the throat."

—*John Dryden*

from a male speaker's perspective). And in its combination of ritual text and innovative musical expression distinctive to her gender, Cozzolani's *Magnificat* is a striking example of the tension between individuality and tradition that has characterized Western sacred music for centuries.

CRITICAL THINKING

1. What role did women play in sacred and secular music in seventeenth-century Italy?

2. In what ways might the *Magnificat* text and Cozzolani's setting have been significant to seventeenth-century nuns?

3. How might the text and performance of *Sleepyhead, Cupid!* have resonated with male audiences who were accustomed to thinking of certain women singers as being courtesans?

YourTurn TO EXPLORE

Can you find examples of women musicians (performers, ensemble leaders/conductors, composers/arrangers/producers) working within a primarily male tradition, or men in a primarily female tradition? Are there aspects of their music-making that seem distinctive to their gender? If so, which ones? And how do they blend in with the prevailing gender? What can you find out about the people who have chosen this kind of "non-gender-conforming" musical path, and their perspective on their experiences?

24

Performing Grief: Purcell and Early Opera

"Opera is the delight of Princes." —Marco da Gagliano (Italian composer, 1582–1643)

KeyPoints

- The most important new genre of the Baroque era was **opera**, a large-scale music drama that combines poetry, acting, scenery, and costumes with singing and instrumental music.

- The principal components of opera include the orchestral **overture**, solo **arias** (lyrical songs) and **recitatives** (speechlike declamations of the text), and ensemble numbers, including **choruses**.

- The text of an opera is called a **libretto**. The earliest opera libretti were based on mythology, epic poetry, and ancient history.

- Henry Purcell wrote *Dido and Aeneas*, based on *The Aeneid*, a Roman epic by Virgil. The closing Lament of Dido is a powerful expression of grief that reflects contemporary ideals about womanhood.

Dramatists and musicians who developed the tradition of sung drama—what we now call opera—understood music's power to intensify events; their aim was not realistic depiction but "hyper-reality." Then as now, audiences knew that people don't sing to each other in real life. But characters in opera could convey strong emotions through music, making the experience of those emotions all the more compelling for the listener. The intense hyper-reality of sung drama has guaranteed its appeal and staying power for more than four centuries, and accounts for the use of music to enhance narrative multimedia (musical theater, film, video games) up to the present day.

The Components of Opera

An **opera** is a large-scale drama that is sung. It combines the resources of vocal and instrumental music—soloists, ensembles, chorus, orchestra, and sometimes ballet—with poetry and drama, acting and pantomime, scenery and costumes. To unify these diverse elements is a challenge that has attracted some of the most creative minds in the history of music. The plot and action are generally advanced through a kind of musical declamation, or speech, known as **recitative**. This vocal style is designed to imitate and emphasize the natural inflections of speech; its movement is shaped to the rhythm of the language.

Recitative

Recitative gives way from time to time to the **aria** (Italian for "air" or "tune"), which releases through melody the tension accumulated in the course of the action. The aria is a song, usually of a highly emotional nature. It is what audiences

Aria

Set design for a Baroque opera
based on the story of Dido and
Aeneas, by Italian set designer
Giuseppe Galli da Bibiena
(1696–1757).

wait for, what they cheer, what they remember. An aria, because of its tunefulness, can be effective even when sung out of context—for example, in a concert or on a recording. Arias can be "detached" in this way because they take place in "stop time"—the action is frozen and the character has the opportunity to dwell on a particular intense emotion. Words or groups of words, as well as musical phrases or even whole sections, are often repeated, as if the character were mulling them over in her or his mind. Once the aria ends, the action "un-freezes" and the drama returns to the "clock time" of recitative.

An opera may contain ensemble numbers— duets, trios, quartets, and so on—in which the characters pour out their respective feelings. The chorus may be used to back up the solo voices or may function independently. Sometimes it comments on the action, like the chorus of a Greek tragedy, and at other times it is integrated into the action.

The orchestra sets the appropriate mood for the different scenes. It also performs the **overture**, heard at the beginning of most operas, which may introduce melodies from the arias. Each act of the opera normally opens with an orchestral introduction, and between scenes we may find interludes, or **sinfonias**.

Libretto   The composer works with a librettist, who creates the characters and the story line, with its main threads and subplots. The **libretto**, the text or script of the opera, must be devised to give the composer an opportunity to write music for the diverse numbers—recitatives and arias, ensembles, choruses, interludes—that have become the traditional features of this art form.

Early Opera in Italy

An outgrowth of Renaissance theatrical traditions, early opera lent itself to the lavish spectacles and scenic displays that graced royal weddings and similar ceremonial occasions. A striking example of this tradition that is still performed and

Claudio Monteverdi   recorded today is *Orfeo* (1607), composed by Claudio Monteverdi, who even in his own time was recognized for having solidified early experiments with drama-through-music (as it was called) into a mature and powerful new genre.

Spread of opera   By the time of Monteverdi's last opera, *The Coronation of Poppea* (1642), the first public opera houses had opened in Venice; opera was moving out of the palace and becoming a public and widespread entertainment. The accompanying orchestra, a string group with wind or brass instruments occasionally added for variety in timbre, became standard as Italian-style opera spread throughout Europe.

By the turn of the eighteenth century, Italian opera had gained wide popularity in the rest of Western Europe. Only in France was the Italian genre rejected; here, composers set out to fashion a French national style, in keeping with their strong traditions of court ballet and classical tragedy.

Opera in England

In early seventeenth-century England, the **masque**, a type of entertainment that combined vocal and instrumental music with poetry and dance, became popular among the aristocracy. Later, in the period of the Commonwealth (1649–60), stage plays were forbidden because the Puritans regarded the theater as an invention of the devil. A play set to music, however, could be passed off as a concert, and this is the tradition behind one of the earliest English operas (and certainly the most famous), Henry Purcell's *Dido and Aeneas* (LG 13).

English painter **Thomas Jones** depicts Dido and Aeneas as lovers (1769).

Dido and Aeneas

Purcell's opera, *Dido and Aeneas,* is based on an episode in Virgil's *Aeneid*, the ancient Roman epic that traces the adventures of the hero Aeneas after the fall of Troy. Since his contemporary audiences knew this Virgil classic, librettist Nahum Tate could compress the plot and suggest rather than fill in the details. Aeneas and his men are shipwrecked at Carthage on the northern shore of Africa. Dido, the Carthaginian queen, falls in love with him, and he returns her affection. But Aeneas cannot forget that the gods have commanded him to continue his journey until he reaches Italy, since he is destined to be the founder of Rome. Much as he hates to hurt the queen, he knows that he must depart.

In the last act, the crew is ready to leave Carthage, although Aeneas has not yet told Dido of his imminent departure. Purcell begins the act with a sprightly tune in the style of a **hornpipe**, a dance form often associated with sailors, and characterized by a reversed dotted figure called a **Scotch snap** (short-long rhythm on the word "ne-ver"). This lively tune, introduced by the orchestra, is sung responsorially: one sailor sings the verse, and the chorus answers him. Underlying this festive mood, the growing chromaticism of the bass line foreshadows Dido's Lament.

Hornpipe

Henry Purcell (1659–1695)

Purcell's standing as a composer gave England a leading position in the world of Baroque music. The London-born composer's career began at the court of Charles II (r. 1660–85) and extended through the turbulent reign of James II (r. 1685–88)—both Stuart kings—and into the period of William and Mary (r. 1689–1702). At these courts, Purcell held various posts as singer, organist, and composer. He wrote masques and operas for several venues. Whether *Dido and Aeneas* was premiered at court or at the girls' boarding school where Purcell taught is unclear; we do know that the opera was performed in 1689 by his students at a school run by dancer Josias Priest. His incidental music for plays includes *Abdelazar (The Moor's Revenge)*, from which Benjamin Britten borrowed a dance as the basis for his *Young Person's Guide to the Orchestra* (see Chapter 11).

A truly international figure, Purcell wrote in many genres, assimilating the Italian operatic style along with the majesty of French music, all while adding his own lyrical gift for setting the English language to music.

MAJOR WORKS: Dramatic music, including *Dido and Aeneas* (1689), *The Fairy Queen* (1692), and incidental music for plays (including *Abdelazar*, 1695) • Sacred and secular vocal music • Instrumental music, including fantasias, suites, and overtures.

5:32

Purcell: *Dido and Aeneas*, Act III, Opening and Lament

Date: 1680s
Genre: Opera, English
Basis: Virgil's *Aeneid*

Act I, Opening, performed by: The Scholars Baroque Ensemble, David van Asch, director
Lament performed by: Lorraine Hunt Lieberman; Philharmonia Baroque Orchestra, Nicholas McGegan, director

Characters: Dido, queen of Carthage (soprano); Belinda, Dido's serving maid (soprano); Aeneas, adventuring hero (baritone); Sorceress, Spirit, Witches

Act III, Opening   1:32

	What to Listen For		
Melody	Jaunty, playful tune.	**Form**	Strophic form, with instruments, solo voice, then chorus.
Rhythm/ meter	Sprightly tempo, in triple meter; use of Scotch-snap dotted figures.	**Performing forces**	String orchestra, with solo voice and chorus.
Harmony	Major key, with chromatic foreshadowing of Lament.		

Opening of hornpipe as solo verse:

Come a - way,   fel - low   sai - lors, come a - way,

0:00 **Orchestral prelude**

0:32 **Solo verse** (first sailor):
Come away fellow sailors, come away,
Your anchors be weighing;
Time and tide will admit no delaying;
Take a boosey short leave of your nymphs on the shore,
And silence their mourning with vows of returning,
Tho' never intending to visit them more.

1:02 **Chorus:** repeats verse.

Recitative and Lament

	What to Listen For		
Melody	Recitative with half-step movement; more lyrical aria.	**Form**	Aria is in two sections, each repeated (**A-A-B-B**), over the ground bass.
Rhythm/ meter	Free recitative; slow aria in triple meter.	**Performing forces**	Baroque-period instruments with solo voice.
Harmony	Aria is based on a repeated chromatic ground bass.		

Recitative: "Thy hand, Belinda," sung by Dido (accompanied by basso continuo only)   0:57

0:00   Thy hand, Belinda; darkness shades me.
On thy bosom let me rest;
More I would, but Death invades me;
Death is now a welcome guest.

Aria: "When I am laid in earth," Dido's Lament

3:03

Basis: Ground bass, five-measure pattern in slow triple meter, descending chromatic scale, repeated eleven times:

	SECTION	GROUND BASS STATEMENT NO.
0:57 **Instrumental introduction.**		1
1:09 When I am laid in earth, may my wrongs create	A	2
no trouble in thy breast.		3
When I am laid . . .	A	4
no trouble . . .		5
2:17 Remember me, remember me, but ah, forget	B	6
my fate, remember me, but ah, forget my fate.		7
Remember me . . .	B	8
forget my fate . . .		9
Instrumental closing.		10
		11

🔊 **AnotherHearing** Our recording was performed using "historically informed" instruments and vocal techniques. Now compare this Baroque style with a jazz rendition by the Calefax Reed Quintet. What differences in musical detail, style, and timbre (tone color) do you note between the performances? Which do you prefer, and why?

Upon hearing of Aeneas's mission, a grief-stricken Dido decides her fate—death—in the moving recitative "Thy hand, Belinda," and the heartrending Lament that is the culminating point of the opera, "When I am laid in earth." In Virgil's poem, Dido mounts the funeral pyre, whose flames light the way for Aeneas's ships as they sail out of the harbor. Her Lament unfolds over a five-measure **ground bass**, a repeated phrase that descends along the chromatic scale, often symbolic of grief in Baroque music. The repetitions of the text and music encourage the listener to dwell in the timelessness of the emotions performed through this scene. The scene also provides a powerful model for female grief, one considered appropriate by Purcell's society; but keep in mind that this was a model created by men based on male notions of suitable female behavior. This is another feature of opera, in common with all popular multimedia: it provides a reflection of what the librettist and composer wished their society to think about human character and interaction.

Ground bass

CRITICAL THINKING

1. How was the distinction between "clock time" and "stop time" achieved in early opera? Why was this distinction important?
2. Which musical elements change in the course of Dido's recitative and Lament? Which stay the same? How do these aspects convey grief?

YourTurn TO EXPLORE

Consider an example of one of your favorite "hyper-real" forms of narrative/dramatic entertainment—science fiction/fantasy movie, TV show, video game. How is the more-than-real aspect conveyed? What role does music play in making emotions more intense? How does the music reinforce images and character or behavior?

Sounds Obstinate

Some musical ideas are so flexible and powerful that they show up over and over again both within and beyond the classical canon. The idea of unifying a composition with a repeating bass line—a *basso ostinato* (Italian for "obstinate")—is widespread across musical genres, and is a procedure that can easily be recognized. The practice flourished in the Renaissance era, in dances where instrumentalists improvised over a repeating bass line. By the Baroque era, it was a standard compositional procedure heard in vocal, keyboard, chamber, and orchestral music. The insistent bass line you heard in *Dido's Lament* is one such *basso ostinato*. This particular ground bass, featuring a descending chromatic line, is appropriately referred to as a *basso lamento*, and is used in similarly emotionally charged works as diverse as Bach's B-minor Mass (the *Crucifixus*) and Beethoven's Piano Variations in C minor.

Another excellent—and popular—example of a piece built on a repeating bass line is the *Canon in D* by Johann Pachelbel, a prolific German composer from a generation before Bach. (Interestingly, Pachelbel's son Charles become one of the first notable European composers to emigrate to the American colonies, where he figured prominently in the musical life of Charleston, South Carolina.) With the *Canon in D*, we can differentiate between the two uses of the word "canon" we described in Chapter 15: the composition is, in fact, a musical canon, in which the various lines played by the high strings strictly imitate one another at a fixed distance throughout (see p. 25 for a simpler example of

this) while the work is also in the canon, that is, it holds a firm place in the performance repertory. But the most obvious structural procedure, more readily heard than the imitative canon, is the slow-moving *basso ostinato* in the low strings. Remarkably, we hear this eight-note bass line (given below) twenty-eight times in the work, clearly audible under the lush variations played by the three violins in increasingly faster-moving lines. Chances are you will recognize this very popular work.

The use of a repeating bass pattern is very common in popular music as well. The same kind of repeating bass line found in Pachelbel's *Canon*—one which moves by fourths—can be found in songs like U2's first breakout hit "With or Without You" (1987), "Basket Case" by Green Day (1994), and "Graduation (Friends Forever)" by Vitamin C (2000). Coolio's rap "C U When You Get There" (1997) and, more recently, "Memories" by Maroon 5 (2019) both unfold over exactly the same harmonic progression used by Pachelbel almost 300 years earlier. You can hear a *basso lamento* in Led Zeppelin's "Stairway to Heaven" (1971), Bob Dylan's "A Simple Twist of Fate" (1975), and "Sorry Seems to Be the Hardest Word" by Elton John (1976); the bass line in this Elton John song is strikingly similar to what you heard in Purcell's lament aria.

Later we will consider a standard jazz form, the twelve-bar

blues, which works on a similar principle, employing repeated bass lines and chord progressions, on top of which melodies unfold (p. 368). See if you can identify other songs from your personal playlist that employ a *basso ostinato*.

Many Voices Expanded
- Bach, Crucifixus from B-Minor Mass
- Dylan, "Simple Twist of Fate"
- Maroon 5, "Memories"

The German composer Johann Pachelbel (1653–1706).

25

Musical Sermons:
Bach and the Lutheran Cantata

*"I wish to make German psalms for the people, that is to say sacred hymns,
so that the word of God may dwell among the people also by means of song."*

—Martin Luther

KeyPoints

- Lutheran musical worship is structured around congregational hymns, known as **chorales**, which are specific to each Sunday service.

- The **church cantatas** of Johann Sebastian Bach were mostly written for the Lutheran church service; they are multimovement works with solo arias, recitatives, and choruses, all with orchestral accompaniment.

- Bach's cantata *Wachet auf* (*Sleepers, Awake*) is based on a well-known Lutheran chorale tune.

One of the most important and lasting contributions that Martin Luther made to Western culture was the idea that musical worship belongs to the congregation. Both he and his fellow reformer John Calvin, as noted in Chapter 21, believed that the faithful should sing their praise collectively during the church service, rather than leaving song entirely to the priest and the choir. Unlike Calvin, however, Luther also believed that professional musicians—both singers and instrumentalists—had an important role in creating beautiful polyphony for the congregation to hear and reflect upon, much as the leader of the congregation played an important role in helping the faithful understand Scripture through sermons. As a sermon is an elaboration of a reading from the Bible, updating it for the congregation's contemporary concerns, the Lutheran cantata was an elaboration of the weekly hymn, allowing the congregation to understand the hymn from a new perspective.

Bach worked for many years at Leipzig's St. Thomas Church (on the right) and its famous choir school, seen on the left in this engraving from c. 1749.

The Lutheran Chorale and Cantata

Luther and his followers created weekly hymns (known as **chorales**) for their congregations to sing by composing (or sometimes recycling) simple and memorable melodies, and then writing German poetry in multiple stanzas that translated or interpreted passages in the Bible. Congregational singing of a specific chorale was (and still is) integrated into each weekly Lutheran service, along with the Gospel reading, prayers, and a sermon.

In these hymns, sung in unison by the congregation and in four-part harmony by the professional choir, the melody was in the soprano, where all could hear it

In Their Own Words

❝ As Cantor of the St. Thomas School . . . I shall set the boys a shining example . . . serve the school industriously . . . bring the music in both the principal churches of this town into good estate . . . faithfully instruct the boys not only in vocal but also in instrumental music . . . arrange the music so that it shall not last too long, and shall . . . not make an operatic impression, but rather incite the listeners to devotion."

—*J. S. Bach*

and join in the singing. In this way, the chorales greatly strengthened the trend toward clear-cut melody supported by chords (homophonic texture).

Arrangements of chorales gradually expanded, so that instead of using every stanza of the chorale the same way, musicians and poets began to substitute some inner stanzas with new poetry, further elaborating their message. The resulting elaboration-of-chorale, a sort of musical sermon on the original hymn, is what we now call the **Lutheran cantata**.

Bach and the Lutheran Cantata

Raised to serve Lutheran worship in his role as a professional musician, Johann Sebastian Bach was deeply familiar both with chorales and with the ways they could be elaborated. In his time, the cantata was an integral part of the church service, related, along with the sermon and prayers that followed it, to the Gospel reading for the day. Most Sundays of the church year required their own cantata, as did holidays and special occasions. Bach composed four or five such yearly cycles, from which only about two hundred works survive.

Bach's cantatas typically include five to eight movements, of which the first, last, and usually one middle movement are full-ensemble numbers—normally fashioned from the chorale tune—ranging from simple hymnlike settings to

Johann Sebastian Bach (1685–1750)

Bach is the culminating figure of the Baroque style and one of the giants in the history of music. Born in Eisenach, Germany, he was raised a Lutheran and followed the family vocation of organist. At the age of twenty-three, he was appointed to his first important position: court organist and chamber musician to the duke of Weimar. During his Weimar period (1708–17), Bach's fame as organ virtuoso spread, and he wrote many of his most important works for that instrument.

From 1717 to 1723, he served as composer at the court of the prince of Anhalt-Cöthen, where he produced suites, concertos, sonatas for various instruments, and a wealth of keyboard music. Bach's two marriages produced at least nineteen offspring, many of whom did not survive infancy; four of his sons became leading composers of the next generation.

Bach was thirty-eight when he was appointed to one of the most important music positions in Germany: cantor at St. Thomas Church in Leipzig. His duties were formidable (see quote above). He supervised the music for the city's four main churches, selected and trained their choristers, and wrote music for the daily services. He also served as director of the **collegium musicum**,

a group of university students and musicians that gave regular concerts (see p. 160). In the midst of all this activity, Bach managed to produce truly magnificent works during his twenty-seven years in Leipzig (1723–50).

Two hundred or so church cantatas, the *St. John* and *St. Matthew Passions,* and the epic *Mass in B Minor* form the centerpiece of Bach's religious music, constituting a personal document of spirituality. Best known in his lifetime as an organist, Bach wrote organ compositions in both improvisatory and strict forms. His most important keyboard works are *The Well-Tempered Clavier,* forty-eight preludes and fugues in two volumes, and his last masterwork, *The Art of Fugue.* His orchestral music includes four suites of dance movements and the often-performed *Brandenburg Concertos.* Bach raised existing forms to the highest level rather than originating new forms. His mastery of contrapuntal composition, especially fugal writing, has never been equaled.

MAJOR WORKS: Sacred vocal music (over 200 church cantatas, four Passions, and the *Mass in B Minor,* 1749) • Orchestral music (four suites) • Concertos (including six *Brandenburg Concertos*) • Solo sonatas and keyboard music (*The Well-Tempered Clavier, The Art of Fugue*) • Organ works (*Toccata and Fugue in D Minor,* "Little" Fugue in G Minor).

intricate fugues. Interspersed with the ensembles are solo or duet arias and recitatives, some of which may also retain the chorale melody or its text, or set new poetry that expands on the theme of the chorale.

In *The Parable of the Wise and Foolish Virgins*, by **Peter von Cornelius** (1763–1867), the wise virgins greet Christ, the bridegroom.

Bar form

Wachet auf (Sleepers, Awake)

Bach wrote his cantata *Wachet auf* (LG 14) in 1731, for the end of the church year. The reading of the Gospel for this church feast is the parable of the Wise and Foolish Virgins, in which the watchmen sound a call on the city wall above Jerusalem to the wise virgins to meet the arriving bridegroom (Christ). The biblical text (Matthew 25:1–3) clearly urges all Lutherans to prepare themselves spiritually for the second coming of Christ (see illustration at right).

Bach builds his "musical sermon" on a hymn by Philipp Nicolai (1599), using its tune in three of the cantata's seven movements. The chorale is in a standard three-part structure known as **bar form** (**A-A-B**), in which the first section (**A**) is repeated with new words, and the second section (**B**) is rounded off with the same closing phrase as the first. The first movement is a grand choral fantasia that features a majestic, marchlike motive signaling the arrival of Christ and an instrumental refrain that recurs between the vocal statements of the chorale. The fourth movement presents a unison chorale sung by the tenors against the watchman's memorable countermelody.

The last movement, for chorus and orchestra, celebrates in rich, full harmonies the union of Christ and his bride. Bach generally closed his cantatas with an unadorned, hymnlike setting that allowed the congregation to join in the singing. To familiarize yourself with the chorale tune, begin your listening with this last movement.

The whole cantata reveals Bach's deep-rooted faith and his ability to communicate a meaningful spiritual message. The tune would still be resonating in the ears of the congregation as they sang the unison hymn later in the service, thereby deepening their appreciation for the words of the day's sermon.

CRITICAL THINKING

1. How does Bach's cantata portray the biblical story of the Wise and Foolish Virgins?
2. How is polyphony used in contrasting ways in the first and fourth movements of the work?

YourTurn TO EXPLORE

Find recordings of a sacred song or hymn that has been reused or elaborated by musicians from different traditions. (African American spirituals might be a good resource. For example, *Motherless Child*; *Swing Low, Sweet Chariot*; or *Amazing Grace*.) How are different meanings of the song highlighted through different performances? Which ones do you think are more effective, and why?

LISTENING GUIDE 14   11:49

Bach: Cantata No. 140, *Wachet auf* (*Sleepers, Awake*), Nos. 1, 4, and 7

Date: 1731, performed in Leipzig

Basis: Chorale (three stanzas) by Philipp Nicolai, in movements 1, 4, and 7

Performed by: American Bach Soloists, Jeffrey Thomas, director

Overview: 1. **Chorale fantasia** (stanza 1), E-flat major
2. Tenor recitative (freely composed), C minor
3. Aria: Soprano/bass duet (freely composed), C minor
4. **Unison chorale** (stanza 2), E-flat major
5. Bass recitative (freely composed), E-flat to B-flat major
6. Aria: Soprano/bass duet (freely composed), B-flat major
7. **Chorale** (stanza 3), E-flat major

Chorale tune
(**A** section)

1. Chorale fantasia (chorus and orchestra)   6:06

What to Listen For			
Melody	Sopranos have slow-moving chorale melody; opening rising line = watchmen's motive; long melisma on "Alleluja."	**Texture**	Alternation between instrument groups; complex, imitative polyphony in lower voices.
Rhythm/ meter	Insistent dotted rhythm in orchestra, begun in ritornello 1.	**Performing forces**	Four-part choir (SATB), with strings, double reeds, horn, bassoon, organ, violino piccolo.
Harmony	Uplifting major key (E-flat).		
Form	Three-part bar form (**A-A-B**), based on chorale tune structure.	**Text**	Music depicts the text (watchmen, wake-up call), by Philipp Nicolai.

0:00   **Ritornello 1**, marchlike dotted rhythm, alternating between violins and oboes:

A section

0:29   Wachet auf, ruft uns die Stimme
der Wächter sehr hoch auf der Zinne,
auf der Zinne,
wach auf, du Stadt Jerusalem!

Awake! The voice of the
watchmen calls us from high
on the tower,
awake, town of Jerusalem!

1:32	**Ritornello 2.**	
	A section repeated (new text)	
2:00	Mitternacht heisst diese Stunde,	Midnight is this very hour;
	sie rufen uns mit hellem Munde:	they call to us with bright voices:
	wo seid ihr klugen Jungfrauen?	where are you, wise virgins?
3:04	**Ritornello 3.**	
	B section	
3:24	Wohl auf, der Bräut'gam kommt,	Take cheer, the bridegroom comes,
	steht auf, die Lampen nehmt!	arise, take up your lamps!
	Alleluja!	Alleluia!
	Macht euch bereit,	Prepare yourselves
	zu der Hochzeit,	for the wedding,
	ihr müsset ihm entgegengehn!	you must go forth to meet him.
5:32	**Ritornello 4.**	

4. Unison chorale

4:13

What to Listen For

Melody	Tenors sing chorale melody in unison, set against moving countermelody in strings.	**Form**	Three-part bar form (**A-A-B**), with instrumental ritornellos between vocal sections.
Harmony	Bright major key (E-flat).	**Texture**	Slow-moving vocal line; faster strings and "walking" bass line.

0:00	**Ritornello 1.**	
0:41	**A section**	
	Zion hört die Wächter singen,	Zion hears the watchmen singing,
	das Herz tut ihr vor Freuden springen,	for joy her very heart is springing,
	sie wachet und steht eilend auf.	she wakes and rises hastily.
1:11	**Ritornello 2.**	
1:50	**A section** (new text)	
	Ihr Freund kommt vom Himmel prächtig,	From resplendent heaven comes her friend,
	von Gnaden stark, von Wahrheit mächtig,	strong in grace, mighty in truth,
	ihr Licht wird hell, ihr Stern geht auf.	her light shines bright, her star ascends.
2:20	**Ritornello 3.**	
2:47	**B section**	
	Nun komm du werte Kron,	Now come, you worthy crown,
	Herr Jesu, Gottes Sohn.	Lord Jesus, God's own son.
	Hosiana!	Hosanna!
3:08	**Ritornello 4** (in minor).	
3:29	**B section** (continues)	
	Wir folgen all	We follow all
	zum Freudensaal	to the joyful hall
	und halten mit das Abendmahl.	and share the Lord's supper.

continued on next page

Chorale tune in tenors set against countermelody in strings:

7. Chorale

1:30

What to Listen For

Melody	Chorale prominent in soprano line; fanfare-like opening.	**Texture**	Homorhythmic; all parts move together.
Harmony	Inspirational major key (E-flat).	**Performing forces**	Four-part chorus (SATB) and orchestra.
Form	Three-part bar form (**A-A-B**).		

0:00   **A section**

Gloria sei dir gesungen
mit Menschen- und englischen Zungen,
mit Harfen und mit Zimbeln schön.

Glory be sung to you
with men's and angel's tongues,
with harps and beautiful cymbals.

0:24   **A section** repeated (new text)

Von zwölf Perlen sind die Pforten
an deiner Stadt, wir sind Konsorten
der Engel hoch um deinen Thron.

Of twelve pearls are the gates
of your city; we are consorts
of the angels high about your throne.

0:47   **B section**

Kein Aug hat je gespürt,
kein Ohr hat mehr gehört
solche Freude.
Des sind wir froh,
io, io,
ewig in dulci jubilo.

No eye has ever sensed,
no ear has ever heard
such a delight.
Of this we rejoice,
io, io,
forever in sweet joy.

26

Textures of Worship: Handel and the English Oratorio

"What the English like is something they can beat time to, something that hits them straight on the drum of the ear."

—*George Frideric Handel*

KeyPoints

- The **oratorio** is a large-scale dramatic genre with a sacred text performed by solo voices, chorus, and orchestra; it is not staged or costumed.

- Originally conceived to put forth the message of the Catholic Church, the oratorio bears many similarities to opera.

- George Frideric Handel built his career as a composer of Italian-style opera; later in life, he invented the English oratorio, combining elements of Italian and English musical style.

- Handel's oratorios (including *Messiah*) have remained popular ever since the composer's day.

Most of the music composed in Europe before the later 1700s enjoyed only a short arc of success: even the most highly esteemed works and composers fell into obscurity within one or two generations. George Frideric Handel's oratorios, and in particular *Messiah*, broke that trend: from their beginnings more than two and a half centuries ago, they have been performed continuously. Today, even small North American towns will feature a performance of *Messiah* every year as a staple of Christmastime celebrations; and larger urban centers often offer several performances, some incorporating audience sing-along during the most-loved choruses. The success of these works comes in part from their fitting the national mood during a time of British self-confidence, and in part from Handel's ingenuity in combining some of the most effective musical resources of his day as he invented an entirely new genre, the English oratorio. From their beginnings, Handel's oratorios have marked the meeting place of community worship with the grandeur and glory of power—political, sacred, and musical.

Saint Philip Neri (1515–1595) promoted lay singing in the oratory (prayer room) of the church. **Giandomenico Tiepolo** (1727–1804).

The Oratorio

The **oratorio**, one of the great Baroque sacred vocal genres, descended from the religious play-with-music of the Counter-Reformation. It took its name from the Italian word for "place of prayer," and early oratorios were sponsored by the Catholic Church in public meeting places as ways to convey its messages about faith to as wide an audience as possible. A large-scale musical work for solo voices, chorus, and orchestra, the oratorio was generally based on a biblical story and

147

George Frideric Handel (1685–1759)

If Bach represents the spirituality of the late Baroque, Handel embodies its worldliness. Born in the same year, the two giants of the age never met.

Handel was born in Halle, Germany, and attended the University of Halle. He then moved to Hamburg, where he played violin in the opera-house orchestra and absorbed the Italian operatic style popular at the time. In 1706, he traveled to Italy, where he composed his first sacred works and Italian operas. Six years later, he settled permanently in London, where his opera *Rinaldo* had conquered the English public the year before.

Handel's great opportunity came in 1720 with the founding of the Royal Academy of Music, launched for the purpose of presenting Italian opera. For the next eight years, he was active in producing and directing his operas as well as writing them. When the Italian style fell out of favor, he turned from opera to oratorio, quickly realizing the advantages offered by a genre that dispensed with costly foreign singers and lavish scenery. Among his greatest achievements in this new genre were *Messiah* and *Judas*

Maccabaeus. Shortly after his seventy-fourth birthday, Handel collapsed in the theater at the end of a performance of *Messiah* and died some days later. The nation he had served for half a century accorded him its highest honor: a burial at Westminster Abbey.

Handel's rhythm has the powerful drive of the late Baroque. His melodies, rich in expression, rise and fall in great majestic arches. And with his roots in the world of the theater, Handel knew how to use tone color for atmosphere and dramatic expression. His more than forty operas tell stories of heroes and adventurers in ingenious musical settings, with arias that run the gamut from brilliant virtuosic displays to poignant love songs. His most important instrumental works are the concertos and two memorable orchestral suites, the *Water Music* (1717) and *Music for the Royal Fireworks* (1749).

MAJOR WORKS: Over 40 Italian operas (including *Rinaldo* and *Julius Caesar*) • English oratorios (including *Israel in Egypt*, *Judas Maccabaeus*, and *Messiah*) • Other vocal music • Orchestral suites, including *Music for the Royal Fireworks* and *Water Music* • Keyboard and chamber music.

In Their Own Words

" My Lord, I should be sorry if I only entertained them; I wished to make them better."

—*Remark made by Handel after a performance of* Messiah

performed without scenery, costumes, or acting. The action was sometimes depicted with the help of a narrator, but in other ways oratorio was very much like opera but based on a religious theme—on purpose, since the Catholic Church wanted to propose oratorio as a more moral alternative to opera. Like operas, oratorios unfolded as a series of recitatives and arias, with duets, trios, and choruses.

Handel had become familiar with the Catholic oratorio during his musical study in Italy. After successfully becoming the leading producer of Italian opera in England, he decided to diversify his musical efforts. Handel invented the genre by combining elements of Italian opera (and Catholic oratorio) with a grand choral style that had been associated with the English monarchy. And unlike the Catholic oratorio, the text (called **libretto**, as in opera) was written by trusted poets rather than by religious leaders. Just as important, English oratorios were not sponsored officially by the church: they were an entrepreneurial venture by Handel and his collaborators, designed to turn a profit.

Handel's oratorios quickly became popular: not only was the music grand and inspiring while still being memorable and singable, but the religious stories about a "chosen people" (most Handel oratorios tell Old Testament stories) were very appealing to an English public who saw economic expansion into its colonies as an indication of divine blessing. By a few decades after Handel's death, oratorio performances featuring hundreds of singers and instrumentalists (see illustration opposite)—many times more than the composer would ever have envisioned—had become common. As the British Empire grew, and with it an increasing interest in choral singing throughout the English-speaking world, Handel's oratorios followed the empire's expansion.

Messiah

In the spring of 1742, the city of Dublin witnessed the premiere of what became one of the English-speaking world's best-loved works, Handel's *Messiah* (LG 15). The composer was reputed to have written down the oratorio in only twenty-four days, working as if possessed. The story circulated of his servant finding him, after the completion of the "Hallelujah Chorus," with tears in his eyes. "I did think I did see all Heaven before me, and the Great God Himself!" he reportedly said. Such stories about divine inspiration and the genius composer's ability to create in an almost superhuman fashion helped to build the reputation of *Messiah* and oratorios like it.

The libretto is a compilation of biblical verses from the Old and New Testaments, set in three parts. The first part (the Christmas section) relates the prophecy of the coming of Christ and his birth; the second (the Easter section), his suffering, death, and the spread of his doctrine; and the third, the redemption of the world through faith. The orchestration features mainly strings; oboes and bassoons strengthen the choral parts, and trumpets and drums are reserved for special numbers.

The lovely soprano aria "Rejoice greatly, O daughter of Zion" is in three-part, or **A-B-A′**, form. In this type of **da capo aria**, the composer usually did not write out the third part (**A′**), since it duplicated the first, allowing the star singer the opportunity to ornament or elaborate the third part on the fly, a crowd-pleasing device in both opera and oratorio. For "Rejoice greatly," though, Handel did write out the last section, varying it considerably from the first. This may have been partly because he liked having as much control as possible over the expressive shape of the music, rather than leaving too many choices up to his performers. It may also have had to do with the fact that some of the first English oratorio performers were less skilled (especially in improvisation) than their Italian operatic counterparts, so Handel may have thought it prudent to give his singer as detailed a set of instructions as possible.

At the beginning of this aria, violins introduce an energetic figure that will soon be taken up by the voice. Notable are the melismatic passages on the word "rejoice." Throughout, the instruments exchange motives with the voice and help provide an element of unity with the **ritornellos**, or instrumental refrains, that bring back certain passages.

The climax of *Messiah* comes at the close of the second part, the Easter section, with the familiar "Hallelujah Chorus." In this movement, we hear shifting textures in which the voices and text overlap and then come together to clearly declaim the text. Handel's extraordinary ability to combine tuneful melodies and intriguing textures with striking homorhythmic passages is most evident in this beloved chorus.

London's Westminster Abbey is packed for this Handel performance on the centenary of the composer's birth, as depicted by **Edward Edwards** (1738–1806).

Giovanni Battista Cipriani's (1727–1785) allegorical study for a Handel memorial reflects how revered the composer was after his death.

LISTENING GUIDE 15   ◀)) 7:48

Handel: *Messiah*, Nos. 18 and 44

Date: 1742
Genre: Oratorio, in three parts
Parts: I: Christmas section
            II: Easter section
            III: Redemption section

Performed by: Boston Baroque,
Martin Pearlman, conductor,
Karen Clift, soprano

Part I: Christmas Section / 18. Soprano aria, "Rejoice greatly"   4:15

What to Listen For		
Melody	Lyrical lines, with a long melisma on "rejoice"; slower second part begins in a minor key.	**Form** Three part (da capo, **A-B-A'**), with shortened last section; instrumental introduction (ritornello).

0:00	**Instrumental ritornello**	Vocal theme presented in violins in B-flat major.
	A section	
0:16	Rejoice greatly, O daughter of Zion shout, O daughter of Jerusalem, behold, thy King cometh unto thee.	Disjunct rising line, melismas on "rejoice"; melody exchanged between soprano and violin.
	Instrumental ritornello	Syncopated, choppy melody, ends in F major.
	B section	
1:30	He is the righteous Saviour and he shall speak peace unto the heathen.	Begins in G minor, slower and lyrical; modulates to B-flat major.
	A' section	
2:33	Rejoice greatly . . .	After an abridged ritornello, new melodic elaborations; longer melismas on "rejoice."

Extended melisma on "rejoice" from the **A'** section:

re-joice —— great-ly,

Part II: Easter Section / 44. "Hallelujah Chorus"   3:33

What to Listen For		
Texture	Varies from homorhythmic (all voices together) to imitative polyphony; fugal treatment, with overlapping voices.	**Performing forces** SATB chorus, with voices in alternation, accompanied by orchestra.
Expression	Varied dynamics for dramatic effect.	

0:00	**Short instrumental introduction**	
	Hallelujah!	Four voices, homorhythmic at the opening.
0:24	For the Lord God omnipotent reigneth.	Brief unison monophony, leading to imitation and overlapping of text; builds in complexity, imitative entries.
1:12	The kingdom of this world is become the Kingdom of our Lord and of His Christ;	Homorhythmic treatment, simple accompaniment.
1:29	and He shall reign for ever and ever.	Imitative polyphony, voices build from lowest to highest.
1:51	King of Kings and Lord of Lords. Hallelujah!	Women's voices introduce the text, punctuated by "Hallelujah"; closes in homorhythmic setting with trumpets and timpani.

Opening of chorus, in homorhythmic style:

CRITICAL THINKING

1. What are the contrasting ways Handel sets individual words to music in "Rejoice greatly"? in the "Hallelujah Chorus"?

2. What religious or inspirational story do you think might lend itself to a modern oratorio? Why?

Your Turn TO EXPLORE

Find a recording of a contemporary setting of a sacred text. How have the composer and performers chosen to use texture and other musical devices to bring out the spiritual aspects of the words that they, or their communities, find most important? Is the music designed to encourage participation by the community for which it has been designed, or is the expressive power left up to trained specialists?

27

Independent Study: Billings and the North American Sacred Tradition

"I don't think myself confined to any Rules for Composition laid down by any that went before me . . . in fact I think it best for every composer to be his own carver."

—William Billings

KeyPoints

- Colonists in New England took part in congregational hymn singing, which often involved a call-and-response practice called **lining out**.

- Some congregations later fostered choirs that developed more elaborate, notation-based singing traditions.

- By the end of the 1700s, a tradition of singing schools had developed in North America: William Billings's **anthem** *David's Lamentation* is an example of a work composed for congregational singing.

Even as we've come to rely more and more on sound recordings rather than live performance for our musical entertainment, the opportunities and resources for studying music have multiplied. Most towns have at least one community music school, hundreds of books are available to provide music lessons, and thousands of YouTube videos offer demonstrations (some more skillful than others) of performance on every imaginable instrument. Basic musical literacy in North America is comparatively high, thanks to a long tradition of both formal and informal music teaching (especially self-study).

From "Lining Out" to Singing Schools

The Calvinist-inspired Pilgrims in seventeenth-century New England used a system called **lining out** for their psalm singing in church: a leader sang each line of a psalm, and the congregation repeated it in turn. In communities that could not afford a psalm book for each church member, everyone could learn the melody and text this way, and could participate equally in the musical worship. The intent of lining out was to create monophonic, unison singing by the repeating congregation; more often than not, however, individuals modified the melody slightly when singing it back, to suit their interpretation of the text. This resulted in a **heterophonic** effect—many people singing slight variants of the same melody simultaneously.

Church leaders, unhappy with the rather "sloppy" musical effects of this oral tradition, also complained that the practice had discouraged congregants from

Heterophony

Inter*face*

Shape-Note Singing and Worship in North America

The Pilgrims who settled New England in the early decades of the 1600s were Calvinists for whom psalm singing was an identity-defining practice. The first book published in North America was a book of psalms—the *Bay Psalm Book* (1628)—designed for singing both in congregation and at home. The first edition did not include music notation, since the standard melodies were well known and the English poetic translations were designed to fit those melodies. By the time singing schools had taken hold in New England in the late 1700s, music literacy was widespread in the North American colonies. A booming musical print industry arose as a result, helping to keep the literacy level in the United States high from that point on.

Since the earliest days of Western notation, music had been taught with a system called **solfège**, in which syllables were used to memorize intervals between notes in a standard scale

pattern. The original system had six syllables, which were eventually expanded to seven in order to account for the full seven-note scale: *do–re–mi–fa–sol–la–ti–do* (see Chapter 3). However, teachers realized that it was possible to simplify the system and account for all seven notes by using only four syllables, *mi–fa–sol–la*; that method was the one used in the New England colonies. As the singing schools became more widespread, teachers in search of additional ways to improve solfège instruction came up with the

idea of changing the shape of the note head depending on the syllable. The result, what we now call **shape-note notation** (see example below), was invented around 1790 in Philadelphia and contributed to the explosion of musical worship in the young and expanding United States. Some communities still sing from shape notes today, following a tradition known as **Sacred Harp singing**. Search online for amateur performances of *David's Lamentation 268*, and consider how they differ from the LG recording.

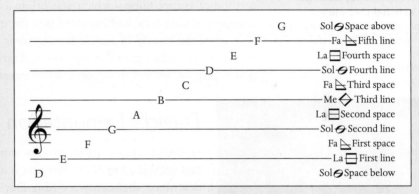

learning to read music, which they considered to be an important part of literacy for a good Christian. By the 1720s, leaders were encouraging people to read actual music notation rather than repeat a leader's melodies. While many congregations continued the practice of lining out, others sponsored "singing schools" that were designed to teach a congregation the basics of notation and theory. Along with these schools came the need for both printed instructional materials and local individuals able to lead them. Thus, the first opportunities arose for musicians born in North America to teach music at least semiprofessionally. And a growing musically literate public began to express an interest in singing music that was more complex than monophonic psalms, which meant that some choirs embraced polyphonic singing in church—a move considered scandalous by more conservative Puritan leaders. By the time of the Revolutionary War, some of the polyphonic repertory was composed by American composers—the most famous of whom was a friend of Paul Revere, William Billings.

In Their Own Words

❝ [My new compositions have] more than twenty times the power of the old slow tunes."

—*William Billings*

William Billings (1746–1800)

Billings, likely a self-taught musician, practiced a number of other trades, especially leather tanning; he also held some minor public posts in the city of Boston. He taught at singing schools in the Boston area for most of his life, and his musical publications quickly became popular partly because they rode the wave of the movement for independence from England: a number of his songs mixed sacred texts with political references. Billings had close connections to the radical elements of the independence movement in Boston: not only did Paul Revere engrave the frontispiece for the composer's *New England Psalm-Singer*, but one of the movement's foremost leaders, Samuel Adams, was a good friend. While Billings was less financially successful in his later years and died in poverty, he was viewed in his own lifetime and in the early years of the Republic as an iconic figure, embodying in his music the scrappy self-sufficiency of an emerging nation.

MAJOR WORKS: Over 340 works for use in singing schools and churches • Six primary collections: *The New England Psalm-Singer* (Boston, 1770); *The Singing Master's Assistant* (Boston, 1778); *Music in Miniature* (Boston, 1779); *The Psalm-Singer's Amusement* (Boston, 1781); *The Suffolk Harmony* (Boston, 1786); *The Continental Harmony* (Boston, 1794).

Billings and *The New England Psalm-Singer*

Billings's *New England Psalm-Singer* (1770) was a collection of his own compositions, a significant departure from the reliance on British arrangements previously published in the colonies. In the introduction to the book, Billings discussed the basics of music notation and theory (especially useful for singing schools) and his own method of composition—which was original and not bound by the rules of the European tradition he had inherited (see the quote that begins this chapter). This style consisted mostly of simple homophonic textures, often with the melody in the tenor line rather than the soprano, and an occasional simple passage of imitation to give the singers an opportunity to interact in a slightly more complex way.

An illustration by **Randolph Caldecott** (1846–1886) of parishioners enjoying singing in an early American church, for the 1882 edition of Washington Irving's *Old Christmas*.

David's Lamentation

One of Billings's most famous works is *David's Lamentation* (LG 16), first published in 1778. The text is a paraphrase of the biblical passage describing the sorrow of King David when he discovered that his son Absalom had been killed (2 Samuel 18:33). It is a poignant moment—Absalom had rebelled against his father, and yet David could not bring himself to punish him. This **anthem** was designed for sacred congregational singing; its text is a single stanza, though the second section is repeated, resulting in an **A-B-B** form. The first section features homophony in all voices; the second begins with a short solo by the bass before a return to the full ensemble in homophony; and then a quasi-imitative passage passes a short musical idea among voice pairs before a final homophonic close. There is enough variety in this short setting to make things interesting for each voice part, but not so much textural complexity that amateur singers would be overly challenged.

Billings's music helped to cement a nationwide commitment to musical literacy that made it possible for the North American music industry to find a steady market as it blossomed in the 1800s. We have him to thank, in part, for the institutional importance of music in our lives today, as well as for the model of musical self-reliance that we can find in every town and every corner of the Internet.

CRITICAL THINKING

1. How did lining out differ from the practice taught in the singing schools?
2. What are the most noteworthy features of Billings's career and music?

YourTurn **TO EXPLORE**

Consider how a person might learn to read music today. Look online for free sites that offer basic music-reading lessons, and choose a couple to compare. If you can already read music, consider the differences between online methods and the way you learned. Are there aspects of notation that you think they discuss more or less clearly? If you don't yet read music, try a couple of basic lessons from each site. How are the approaches similar and different, what makes them more or less helpful?

LISTENING GUIDE 16   🔊 1:48

Billings: *David's Lamentation*

Date: Published 1778   **Performed by:** Hilliard Ensemble,
Genre: Anthem   Paul Hillier, director

What to Listen For

Melody	Mostly stepwise, moving through various voices.	**Form**	A-B-B.
Rhythm/ meter	Duple meter, regular rhythmic patterns.	**Expression**	Simple declamation of spiritualism.
Harmony	Consonant.	**Performing forces**	SATB voices.
Texture	Homorhythmic, four-part chorus, with solos and duets.	**Text**	Paraphrase of 2 Samuel 18:33.

	TEXT	DESCRIPTION
0:00	David, the king, was grieved and moved,	Homorhythmic, four voices, mostly syllabic, a little text repetition.
0:09	He went to his chamber and wept;	
0:18	And as he went, he wept, and said:	Bass solo, monophonic, syllabic.
0:26	"O my son! O my son!	Homorhythmic, four voices.
0:36	Would to God I had died	Text repeated three times: tenor-bass duet, soprano-bass duet, four voices in homorhythm.
0:49	For thee, O Absalom, my son!"	Ending is homorhythmic.
1:01	And as he went . . .	Choir repeats text.

Opening of the soprano part, with shape-note notation (for easy music reading):

Da-vid, the king,   was griev-ed and mov-ed, He went to his cham-ber, his cham-ber, and wept;

Blending Worship Traditions in Colonial Latin America

Sixteenth-century Spanish settlers came to the New World in search of gold and other goods to take back to Europe; in the Americas, they were surprised to find complex societies with long-standing traditions, which included elaborate ceremonies that incorporated singing and musical instruments. We have found no evidence of music notation in the complex pictographs (image-based narratives) that native societies developed, and the Spaniards were not concerned with preserving what they considered "pagan" customs, so we have little idea of what indigenous American musical traditions sounded like before the Europeans arrived. Spaniards *were* concerned, however, with bringing Catholic religious practice to the conquered peoples, and as we have seen, Christian worship was closely tied with music.

Catholics in New Spain (as the European settlements were called) actively worked to assimilate the local peoples into their religious communities. The philosophy of the Jesuit religious order, the main Catholic teaching branch at the time, held that most beliefs could be reconciled with the message of their One True Church. And the reforms of the Council of Trent had stated that while prayers and songs for the church service needed to be in Latin, other devotional texts and songs could be in the local languages of the worshippers. Thus, the missionaries who came to spread the word of God to the American natives taught them plainchant in Latin, but also worked with them to develop worship songs in their native language that incorporated imagery from their own religious traditions, so that the local people could embrace the new religion at least partly on their own terms.

A few of these mixed-language and mixed-imagery devotional songs (**villancicos**) have survived: some were composed by Gaspar Fernandes

Aztec musicians performing on membranophones and idiophones. *Codex Florentine*, by **Friar Bernardino de Sahagun,** from *General History of Things in New Spain* (mid-sixteenth century).

(1566–1629), a native of Portugal who moved to Mexico to become choirmaster at the splendid Puebla Cathedral in the early 1600s. His duties there included teaching both chant and polyphony to the choirboys (children of Native Americans or of Spaniards who had married local women), and playing the organ. He also assembled a large manuscript collection of ritual, devotional, and secular music that was being used (and in part composed) in Mexico at the time.

The impressive façade of the Puebla Cathedral, noted for its mix of Renaissance and Baroque styles (completed 1690).

The villancico by Fernandes that we will hear uses the Nahuatl language of the indigenous Nahua people (in italic below) in alternation with Spanish—and the Spanish spelling may reflect the pronunciation of Nahua contemporaries of Fernandes. The text mixes traditional Christian nativity imagery (the mule and the ox next to the Christ child) alongside other images more typical of Aztec culture (pearls, gems, flowers). Although the manuscript only includes vocal lines, modern performances often incorporate the kinds of percussion instruments that are documented in both Aztec and Christian images from New Spain. Some scholars think that the rhythmic patterns of the song, unusual for European music of the time, are an attempt by Fernandes to convey the unique sonic flavor brought to musical worship by his Native American collaborators.

What to listen for:

- A short-long rhythm unusual for European music of this time, possibly derived from Aztec practices.
- Solo/ensemble refrain alternating with solo/duet verse.
- Varied instrumental accompaniment (including guitar, recorder, and percussion), elaborated by modern performers on the basis of images and accounts of the time (but not present in the original score).

A Nahua ceremonial Deer Dance mask.

Text	Translation	Performance
Tleycantimo choquiliya Mis prasedes, mi apisión. Aleloya.	Why now do you cry, my pleasures, my passion. Alleluia.	**Refrain**: Soloist alone, then five voices mostly in slightly staggered homophony with some imitation toward the end of phrases.
Dejalto el llando crecida, miral to el mulo y el buey. *Ximoyollali*, mi rey. *Tlein mitztolinia*, mi vida?	Stop your growing tears, look at the mule and the ox. Take comfort, my king. What disturbs you, my beloved?	**Verse, section 1**: Two solo voices alternate phrases.
Jesós de mi goraçón, no lloreis, mi pantasía.	Jesus of my heart, do not cry, my fantasy.	**Verse, section 2**: Homophonic duet, in a slower tempo.
No sé por qué deneis pena, tan lindo cara de rosa. *Nocpiholotzin*, niño hermosa, *nochalchiuh, naxoquena*.	I know not why you are pained, such beautiful rosy face, precious noble child, lovely child, my green jade, my lily.	**Verse, section 3**: Returns to the alternation between two solo voices.
Tleycantimo choquiliya Mis prasedes, mi apisión. Aleloya	Why now do you cry, my pleasures, my passion. Alleluia.	**Refrain**: Opening refrain returns.

28

Grace and Grandeur:
The Baroque Dance Suite

"To enjoy the effects of music fully, we must completely lose ourselves in it."
—Jean-Philippe Rameau (1683–1764)

KeyPoints

- In the Baroque era, instruments were greatly improved and featured in several large-scale genres, including the **suite** (a collection of dances).

- Dances in a suite, usually all in the same key, are in binary form (**A-A-B-B**) or ternary form (**A-B-A**).

- J. S. Bach wrote four suites for orchestra in the French style, made up of dances popular in his day.

Technology has always played a crucial role in the development of music. We have already encountered notational technologies (handwriting and print) that were essential to preserving and transmitting musical ideas. We now consider more closely the technologies of sound production: how musicians and craftspeople collaborated to imagine and manufacture increasingly sophisticated musical instruments.

Though humans have been involved in this creative practice since before recorded history, it was during the Baroque era that the Western tradition developed a remarkable focus on instruments and music written for them—a focus that eventually became the central feature of Western concert music in the following century. This flowering of instrumental music was encouraged by wealthy patrons who were eager to invest money and resources in magnificent displays. Since that time, elaborate instrumental music has often been used to convey grandeur on special occasions; most likely every time you have witnessed a grand celebration, it has been enhanced by graceful and powerful soundscapes made possible by the evolving technology of musical instruments.

Baroque Instruments

The seventeenth century saw a dramatic improvement in the construction of string instruments. Some of the finest violins ever built came from the northern Italian workshops of Stradivari, Guarneri, and Amati: to this day musicians seek them out, and pay millions of dollars for the best-made exemplars. The strings were made of gut rather than the steel used today. Gut, produced from animal intestines, yielded a softer and warmer sound. In general, the string instruments of the Baroque resemble their modern descendants except for certain details of construction. Playing techniques, though, have changed somewhat, especially bowing.

While woodwind instruments were used primarily for loud outdoor events through the 1600s, in the late Baroque composers prized such instruments increasingly for color as builders expanded their range and subtlety. The penetrating timbres of the recorder, flute, and oboe, all made of wood at the time, were especially effective in suggesting pastoral scenes, while the bassoon cast a somber tone.

The trumpet developed from an instrument used for military signals to one with a solo role in the orchestra. It was still a "natural instrument"—that is, without the valves that would enable it to play in all keys—demanding real virtuosity on the part of the player. Trumpets contributed a bright sonority to the orchestral palette, to which the French horns, also natural instruments, added a mellow sound reminiscent of the hunting horn. Timpani were occasionally added, furnishing a bass to the trumpets.

In recent years, a new drive for authenticity has made the sounds of eighteenth-century instruments familiar to us. Recorders and wooden flutes, restored violins with gut strings, and mellow-toned, valveless brass instruments are being played again, so that the Baroque orchestra has recovered not only its smaller scale but also its transparent tone quality.

Baroque instruments, including a natural trumpet, natural horn, and timpani, in the Bach House, in Eisenach, Germany.

The Baroque Suite

One of the most important instrumental genres of the Baroque was the **suite**, a group of short dances performed by the diverse array of instruments just described. It was a natural outgrowth of earlier traditions, which paired dances of contrasting tempos and character.

The suite's galaxy of dance types, providing contrasting moods but all in the same key, could include the German **allemande**, the French **courante**, the Spanish **sarabande**, and the English **jig** (**gigue**), as well as a **minuet**, **gavotte**, lively **bourrée** or **passepied**, or jaunty **hornpipe**. Some dances were of peasant origin, bringing a touch of earthiness to their more formal surroundings. The suite sometimes opened with an overture, and might include other brief pieces with descriptive titles reflecting their origin in choreographed theatrical dance.

Dance types

Each piece in the Baroque suite was set either in **binary** form, consisting of two sections of approximately equal length, each rounded off by a cadence and each repeated (**A-A-B-B**); or in **ternary** form (**A-B-A**). In binary form, the **A** part usually moves from the home key (tonic) to a contrasting key (dominant), while the **B** part makes the corresponding move back. The two sections often share closely related melodic material. The form is easy to hear because of the modulation and the full stop at the end of each part.

Binary and ternary form

The principle of combining dances into a suite could be applied to solo instrumental music (notably for harpsichord or solo violin) and to chamber ensembles, as well as to orchestral forces. It was an important precedent to the multimovement cycle that later became standard in Classical instrumental music.

Bach's Orchestral Suite No. 3

Bach conducting a performance with his Collegium Musicum in Leipzig.

Shortly after he arrived in Leipzig, J. S. Bach wrote a number of instrumental works meant for performance with the Collegium Musicum ensemble that he directed. This group of forty to fifty university students and professional musicians performed weekly concerts at Zimmerman's, a large coffeehouse in Leipzig with a hall that could accommodate some 150 audience members as well as an orchestra that included trumpets and timpani. A 1733 announcement from the coffeehouse noted the beginning of that year's series "with a fine concert. It will be maintained week by week, with a new clavicymbel [harpsichord] of a kind that has not been heard here before, and lovers of music as well as virtuosos are expected to be present."

Bach's four orchestral suites were among the repertory written for this group. The suites are in the French style: each opens with an overture, which is followed by a series of French dances that were popular across Europe. We will hear two movements from the Suite No. 3: the Air and the Gigue. The Air (popularly known as "Air on a G String") features a gloriously serene melody carried by the first violin, with a reduced orchestra (two violins, viola, and basso continuo with cello and harpsichord). Richly ornamented, the asymmetrical melody unfolds over a steady, even bass line. The suite closes with a highly spirited Gigue, which adds a festive complement of oboes, trumpets, and timpani. Both movements are in binary form, with each of the two sections repeated (LG 17).

Bach's performances at Zimmerman's were early examples of the instrumental concert tradition, and were very popular both with locals and with visitors to Leipzig. Almost three centuries after they were first performed, Bach's orchestral suites continue to be a concert staple and a favorite with lovers of instrumental music. We need to hear only a few measures to understand why—and they provide a perfect example of using technology (the latest instruments) for the most marvelous result possible.

The Zimmermann Coffeehouse in Leipzig, where Bach's Collegium Musicum gave weekly concerts.

CRITICAL THINKING

1. How would you describe the sound of Baroque-era instruments compared with modern ones?
2. How is the suite an international music genre?

YourTurn TO EXPLORE

Find a performance of a band playing a march—the marches by John Philip Sousa are a great example of the genre. How do the changing timbres of the various instrument combinations compare with the timbres of Bach's Air and Gigue? How does the structure of the march resemble and differ from the binary form of the dances from Bach's suite? Why do you think these similarities and differences exist?

Bach: Orchestral Suite No. 3, Air and Gigue

Date: 1731   **Performed by:** Freiburger Barockorchester

Genre: Dance suite for orchestra

Movements: Overture   Bourrée
              Air   **Gigue**
                     Gavotte I and II

Air   4:37

What to Listen For

Melody	The serene, aria-like line is played by the first violin.
Form	Two-part form, each section repeated (binary, **A-A-B-B**); the **B** section is longer than the **A** section.
Texture	Homophonic texture focused on the melody, accompanied by a "walking" bass line and some moving lines in the lower strings.
Expression	The graceful, singing melody, with expressive upward leaps and embellishments, unfolds in a slow tempo; the pace is marked by the moving basso continuo line (played by cello and harpsichord)

0:00   **A section**: rhapsodic and lyrical melody over a regularly moving cello line; strings only.

0:46   **A section** repeated.

1:31   **B section**: longer, with melodic phrases embellished and treated in sequence.

3:01   **B section** repeated.

Opening of the Air, the soaring solo violin melody accompanied by a "walking" bass in the continuo:

continued on next page

Gigue

2:47

What to Listen For

Rhythm/ Meter	Fast-paced compound (6/8) meter that feels like a propelling duple pattern.	**Texture**	Largely homophonic, with counterpoint created by the basso continuo line.
Harmony	Bright D major; moves to the dominant key (A major), then returns to the tonic; highly consonant.	**Performing Forces**	Festive sound with oboes, trumpets, and timpani added to the strings; alternation of ideas between strings and winds (with percussion).

0:00   **A section**: vigorous dance with continuous motion as the strings and oboes exchange musical phrases with the trumpets.

0:27   **A section** repeated.

0:53   **B section**: longer, with some development of musical ideas as the music modulates (returns) to the tonic key.

1:46   **B section** repeated.

Opening of the violin and trumpet melody, played in octaves:

🔊 **AnotherHearing**   Now that you have heard this dance performed by a small orchestra using "historically informed" instruments and techniques, listen to an arrangement for digital synthesizer by Herbert Waltl, a composer and producer active in the commercial music industry. How does the digital medium create contrast in ways different from the original "analog" ensemble version? Which do you prefer, and why?

29

Sounding Spring:
Vivaldi and the Baroque Concerto

"[His playing] terrified me . . . he came with his fingers within a mere grass-stalk's breadth of the bridge, so that the bow had no room——and this on all four strings with imitations and at incredible speed."

—A contemporary musician (describing Vivaldi's violin technique)

KeyPoints

- Baroque musicians developed the **concerto**, a genre that generally featured either a solo instrument or a small group of soloists set against a larger ensemble.

- First and last movements of concertos tended to follow a refrain-based structure known as **ritornello form**.

- Antonio Vivaldi, a virtuoso violinist, composed *The Four Seasons*, a well-loved set of solo violin concertos that exemplify **program music**.

How can sound mean something independently of words? Many of us today automatically refer to musical works as "songs," but as we know, the term is really only accurate when lyrics are involved. And one of the characteristics of the Western tradition is the complexity of its independent instrumental music. Separated from the need to follow the meanings and patterns of text, instrumental music can create meaning just through patterns of sound. However, even as they explored purely musical ways of fashioning "sound stories," composers frequently called on written language to help them, as well as their listeners, explore the possibilities for what music could mean. These explorations played out in especially interesting ways through a new genre: the concerto.

The Baroque Concerto

Contrast was as basic an element of Baroque music as unity. This twofold principle found expression in the **concerto**, an instrumental form based on the opposition between two dissimilar bodies of sound. The concerto contrasted one or more "featured" instruments with a larger orchestral ensemble, an arrangement that lent itself to experiments in sonority and virtuoso playing. A Baroque concerto usually consisted of three movements, in the sequence Allegro–Adagio–Allegro. The first and last movements tended to follow a loosely structured form based on the alternation between orchestral refrains and virtuosic outbursts by the

Antonio Vivaldi (1678–1741)

The son of a violinist, Vivaldi grew up in his native Venice. He was ordained in the church while in his twenties and became known as "the red priest," a reference to the color of his hair. For the greater part of his career, Vivaldi was *maestro de' concerti*, or music master, at the most important of the four music schools for which Venice was famous, the Conservatorio dell'Ospedale della Pietà. These schools were attached to charitable institutions established for the upbringing of orphaned children—mostly girls—and played a vital role in the musical life of Venetians. Much of Vivaldi's output was written for concerts at the school, which attracted visitors from all over Europe.

One of the most prolific composers of his era, Vivaldi also wrote, in addition to his many concertos, chamber music and operas as well as cantatas, an oratorio, and an extended setting of the *Gloria*, which is today one of his most performed works. His life came to a mysterious end: a contemporary Venetian account notes that the composer, who had once earned 50,000 ducats in his day (about $4 million today), died in poverty as a result of his extravagance.

MAJOR WORKS: Over 230 violin concertos, including *Le quattro stagioni* (*The Four Seasons*, c. 1725) • Other solo, double, triple, and orchestral concertos • Sinfonias • Vocal music, including operas and oratorios, Mass movements, and a *Magnificat*.

Ritornello form

soloist(s), which has taken on the Italian name for "refrain," **ritornello form**. This flexible form prepared the way for the more complex structures in the concerto of the Classical and Romantic periods.

The concerto was first developed in the Italian peninsula in the late 1600s, but quickly spread north and was eagerly embraced by performers and patrons alike. J. S. Bach took the concerto to a new and almost encyclopedic level in his six *Brandenburg Concertos*. But of all the composers in the Baroque concerto tradition, Antonio Vivaldi was the most famous and the most prolific.

A concert by the girls of one of Venice's famous *ospedali*, or orphanages, by **Gabriele Bella** (1730–1799). Vivaldi taught music at the most prestigious of these institutions.

Program Music: Vivaldi's *The Four Seasons*

Vivaldi is in fact best remembered for his more than 500 concertos, about 230 of which are for solo violin, some with descriptive titles. He was active during a period that was crucially important to a new style in which instruments were liberated from their earlier dependence on vocal music. His novel use of rapid scale passages, extended arpeggios, and contrasting registers contributed decisively to the development of violin style and technique. And he played a leading part in the history of the concerto, effectively exploiting the contrast in sonority between large and small groups of players.

Vivaldi's best-known work is *The Four Seasons*, a group of four solo violin concertos, each named for a season. We have observed the fondness for word-painting in Renaissance and Baroque vocal works, where the music is meant to portray the action and emotion described by the text. In *The Four Seasons*, Vivaldi applies this principle to instrumental music. While each concerto has an independent musical logic, it is also accompanied by a poem, describing the joys of that particular season. Each line of the poem is printed above a certain passage in the score; the music at that point mirrors graphically the action described. This literary link is called **program music**.

In the first movement of *Spring* (*La primavera*; LG 18), an Allegro in E major, both poem and music evoke the birds' joyous welcome to spring and the gentle murmur of streams, followed by thunder and lightning. The image of birdcalls takes shape in staccato notes, trills, and running scales; a storm is portrayed by agitated repeated notes answered by quickly ascending scales. Throughout, an orchestral ritornello (refrain) returns again and again (representing the general mood of spring) in alternation with the **episodes**, which often feature the solo violin. Ultimately, "the little birds take up again their melodious song" as we return to the home key. A florid passage for the violin soloist leads to the final ritornello.

In the second movement, a Largo in 3/4, Vivaldi evokes the poetic image of a goatherd who sleeps in a "pleasant, flowery meadow" with his faithful dog by his side. Over the bass line played by the violas, which sound an ostinato (repeated) rhythm, he writes, "The dog who barks." In the finale, an Allegro marked "Rustic Dance," we can visualize nymphs and shepherds cavorting in the fields as the music suggests the drone of bagpipes. Ritornellos and solo passages alternate in bringing the work to a happy conclusion.

Like Bach, Vivaldi was renowned in his day as a performer rather than a composer. Today, he is recognized both as the "father of the concerto," having established ritornello form as its basic procedure, and as a herald of musical Romanticism in his use of pictorial imagery. In his compositions, we encounter an early attempt to empower instrumental music to create independent meanings apart from words and beyond the enhancement of dance.

St. Cecilia, patroness of musicians, plays a Baroque violin in this painting by **Guido Reni** (1575–1642). Typically for this time, there is no chin rest; she plays the violin braced against her shoulder. Her grip on the bow also differs from that of modern players.

CRITICAL THINKING

1. How did composers achieve both unity and contrast in the concerto?
2. What musical techniques did Vivaldi employ in *Spring* to depict the imagery of that season?

YourTurn TO EXPLORE

With a classmate or two, find an example of instrumental music with a title that describes some place or mood or activity. What specific elements of the music do you think were designed to convey that image? Did you and your classmate come up with the same correspondences? What might account for similarities and differences in your interpretation? Can you think of ways that the composer or performers might have made the image even more compelling or clear?

Maestre Violinists of Venice

The cosmopolitan city of Venice was so rich in musical life in the seventeenth and eighteenth centuries that it was referred to as the "Republic of Music," and women musicians were uniquely part of this flourishing artistic culture. We have already met several remarkable Italian women musicians of this era: Chiara Margarita Cozzolani, a nun who dedicated her talents to sacred compositions intended for monasteries and convents like the one she entered in Milan; and Barbara Strozzi, who composed and performed music for an elite Venetian academy of male intellectuals, possibly as a courtesan (see Chapter 23). These two life paths, although very different, allowed women an education, especially in music, and some degree of dignity and independence in this otherwise highly patriarchal society. While music was not considered a suitable occupation for a well-brought-up woman, it was essential to the callings of the convent as well as to courtesan culture.

Young Venetian women of wealthy families had two options: either marriage or consignment to one of the city's many communities of nuns. For poor families—or unwed mothers—Venice provided another option: abandoning a child anonymously at one of the city's *ospedali,* or orphanages, where they would be raised and educated. Remarkably, institutions in this welfare system valued music training for the young women in their care, and four of Venice's *ospedali* were particularly famous for their level of music performances. We can consider here the careers of two women musicians who were trained in this system.

Anna Maria della Pietà (c. 1689–after 1750, originally called dal Violino as she had no known surname) was abandoned at the Ospedale della Pietà, where she thrived despite a strict lifestyle. Girls at the Pietà had very limited contact with the outside world. They had to attend Mass and Confession regularly, and be obedient and silent—casual talk was forbidden. The primary goal was to train the girls to be marriageable, and most did leave the Ospedale to marry. But this institution also hired excellent music teachers, among them Antonio Vivaldi, who became Anna Maria's tutor. She excelled in music, both in singing and playing the violin, and rapidly moved up in the school hierarchy, serving as a violin instructor and eventually as the *maestra de concerti* (the head of the orchestra). She never married but rather dedicated her entire career to music at the Pietà.

Anna Maria's playing attracted the attention of many visitors, in spite of the fact that she and other musicians at the Pietà performed behind wrought-iron grills in elevated choir lofts (see illustration). One German court councilor announced that she was brilliant as a concerto soloist, and that the orchestra was "as grand as any at the courts of Europe." Other visitors agreed, claiming she was unsurpassed as a violin virtuosa. So talented was Anna Maria that Vivaldi wrote at least twenty-eight concertos expressly for her; we know this because she had a lovely bound partbook bearing her name and including the solo parts for these works.

We can tell a different story of another musician trained at a famous Venetian institution. Maddalena Lombardini's (1745–1818) mother was intent that her daughter study music at the Ospedale dei Mendicanti, and after several auditions, the girl was accepted as a student at age seven. (By this time, the education provided by these institutions was in such demand that not all students were orphans.) Like Anna Maria, Maddalena excelled in her studies, so much so that she was eventually allowed to leave the Mendicanti for lessons in nearby Padua with the virtuoso violinist Giuseppe Tartini. At age twenty-one, she wished to pursue a performance career, but was not allowed to leave the ospedale

Female musicians at the Pietà were heard but not seen, performing behind a grill in the choir loft. Drawing by **Jan van Grevenbroek** (1731–1807).

Maddalena Sirmen's 1773 publication of Sonatas for Two Violins.

Virtuoso violinist Giuseppe Tartini (1692–1770), Maddalena's tutor.

permanently unless she was married. Thus she wed the violinist Ludovico Sirmen, and they embarked on a long and successful concert tour. Critics noted her distinguished talent: one claimed, "When she plays, her violin is transformed into the lyre of Orpheus, and she becomes the goddess of music."

But Maddalena's legacy extends beyond her performances: long overlooked in the Western canon, she has recently been recognized for her compositions, including her violin concertos and string quartets. She was fortunate that her compositions were not only published in her lifetime, but

also widely disseminated throughout Europe. Her string quartets appeared in 1769, the same year that Joseph Haydn issued his first set of quartets (we'll meet Haydn in Chapter 31). Maddalena's compositions show similar traits to those of the early Classical-era composers, offering a hint at the complex formal structures we will meet in the next unit of the book. Her concertos follow the traditional three-movement form we heard in Vivaldi's *Spring* Concerto. Listen to the first movement of her A Major Violin Concerto, noticing how she handles the ritornello procedure and the embellished solo episodes and

cadenza. How does her style compare to Vivaldi's?

Many Voices Expanded

- Maddalena Lombardini Sirmen, Violin Concerto in A Major, Op. 3, No. 3, I
- Maddalena Lombardini Sirmen, String Quartet No. 2 in B-flat Major, Andantino and Allegro
- Antonio Vivaldi, Violin Concerto in C Major, RV 581 (for the Feast of the Assumption), I
- Schola Pietatis Antonio Vivaldi (Vivaldi's Women), http://www.spav.co.uk/index.html

167

Vivaldi: *Spring*, from *The Four Seasons* (*La primavera*, from *Le quattro stagioni*), I

Date: Published 1725 (Op. 8, No. 1)

Genre: Programmatic concerto for solo violin, based on an Italian sonnet:

Collection: **No. 1:** *Spring (La primavera)*   No. 3: *Autumn (L'autunno)*
                  No. 2: *Summer (L'estate)*   No. 4: *Winter (L'inverno)*

Performed by: Brecon Baroque; Rachel Podger, solo violin and director

I. Allegro
Joyful spring has arrived,
the birds greet it with their cheerful song,
and the brooks in the gentle breezes
flow with a sweet murmur.

The sky is covered with a black mantle,
and thunder and lightning announce a storm.
When they fall silent, the little birds
take up again their melodious song.

II. Largo
And in the pleasant, flowery meadow,
to the gentle murmur of bushes and trees,
the goatherd sleeps, his faithful dog at his side.

III. Allegro (Rustic Dance)
To the festive sounds of a rustic bagpipe
nymphs and shepherds dance in their favorite spot
when spring appears in its brilliance.

I: Allegro, E major

What to Listen For

Melody	Flashy solo violin; fast scales and trills.
Form	Ritornello acts as a unifying theme; alternates with contrasting episodes.
Timbre	Distinctive sound of Baroque instruments.
Performing forces	Solo violin with string orchestra and basso continuo (keyboard).
Expression	Musical images from the poem (birds, brooks, breeze, storm).

Ritornello theme (2nd part):

	DESCRIPTION	PROGRAM
0:00	Ritornello 1, in E major, in two parts, the second part heard more often.	Spring
0:30	Episode 1; solo violin with birdlike trills and high running scales, accompanied by violins.	Birds
1:02	Ritornello 2.	Spring
1:09	Episode 2; whispering figures like water flowing, played by orchestra.	Murmuring brooks
1:31	Ritornello 3.	Spring
1:38	Episode 3 modulates; solo violin with repeated notes, fast ascending scales, accompanied by orchestra.	Thunder, lightning
2:03	Ritornello 4, in the relative minor (C-sharp).	Spring
2:12	Episode 4; trills and repeated notes in solo violin.	Birds
2:29	Ritornello 5, returns to E major; brief solo passage interrupts.	Spring
2:56	Closing tutti (whole ensemble).	

30

Process as Meaning: Bach and the Fugue

"He, who possessed the most profound knowledge of all the contrapuntal arts, understood how to make art subservient to beauty."

—*Carl Philipp Emanuel Bach (1714–1788), about his father, J. S. Bach*

KeyPoints

- The **organ** and **harpsichord** were the main keyboard instruments of the Baroque era.
- Keyboard players improvised and created free-form pieces called **preludes** or **toccatas**, followed by more structured works, such as **fugues**.
- *The Well-Tempered Clavier* and *The Art of Fugue* are J. S. Bach's most comprehensive collections of contrapuntal writing.
- Among Bach's many keyboard fugues, the "Little" Fugue in G Minor is one of his most popular.

Instrumental music, in several contemporary traditions, often includes a component of improvisation: musicians will elaborate counterpoint on the spot, drawing on established conventions as well as their own creative imagination. Without the distraction of words, the listener's ear can focus on the shape and interaction of musical lines: this interaction provides the music's expressive resources and meaning. Thus, while some counterpoint-based music can be understood as individual "pieces" (which are always played the same way), counterpoint is also a process. And just like today's rock and jazz stars, the great composers of the past frequently *improvised* their polyphonic processes, so that the composer-performer and listener were more equal participants in the unfolding of meaning through sound.

Keyboard Instruments in the Baroque Era

Keyboard instruments, which are inherently suited to polyphonic performance, have been featured in Western music since the Middle Ages; in the 1600s, however, instruments such as the **organ** and **harpsichord** reached a new level of refinement. These technological advances encouraged musicians to broaden their technique, and musicians' experiments likewise spurred instrument builders to new heights.

Organ and harpsichord

The harpsichord differs from the modern piano in two important ways. First, its strings are plucked by quills rather than struck with hammers, and its tone cannot be sustained like that of the piano, a product of the early Classical era. Second, the pressure of the fingers on the keys can produce subtle dynamic nuances but not the piano's extremes of loud and soft.

169

Johann Sebastian Bach performed the dedicatory recital on this organ in St. Boniface Church in Arnstadt, Germany, as an eighteen-year-old virtuoso.

German builders of the 1600s and 1700s created organs with various sets of pipes, each with a sharply contrasting tone color, so that the ear could pick out the separate lines of counterpoint. The organ's multiple keyboards made it possible to achieve terraced levels of soft and loud. J. S. Bach was famous for his ability to improvise at the organ or harpsichord—and his improvisations ranged from relatively free-form approaches with highly contrasting musical ideas and tempos (in what was often called a **toccata** or **prelude**) to a much more systematic working-out of a single musical thought (generally labeled fugue). Bach wrote out a number of his most successful improvisations, usually to serve as models for his students.

The toccata and prelude were designed to showcase the performer's dexterity and were often paired for contrast with more systematically organized forms—you may know Bach's famous *Toccata and Fugue in D Minor*, which was the opening music for Disney's 1940 film *Fantasia* and has been heard in many films since. We will focus on the more tightly structured form, the fugue, since it illustrates the Baroque ideal of systematic elaboration of short musical ideas.

The Fugue and Its Devices

A **fugue** is a contrapuntal composition in which a single theme pervades the entire fabric, entering in one voice (or instrumental line) and then in another. The fugue, then, is based on the principle of **imitation**. Its main theme, the **subject**, constitutes the unifying idea, the focal point of interest in the contrapuntal web.

We have already encountered the fugue or fugal style in *The Young Person's Guide to the Orchestra*, by Britten; in Handel's choruses in *Messiah*; and in the opening movement of Bach's cantata *Wachet auf*. Though a fugue may be written for a group of instruments or voices, as in these works, Bach was most renowned for writing—and improvising—fugues for a solo keyboard instrument.

The subject of the fugue is stated alone at the beginning in one of the voices—referred to by the range in which it sounds: soprano, alto, tenor, or bass. It is then

Subject and answer
Countersubject

imitated in another voice—this is the **answer**—while the first can continue with a **countersubject** (a different theme heard against the subject) or new material. When the subject has been presented in each voice once, the first section of the

Exposition
Episodes

fugue, the **exposition**, is at an end. From then on, the fugue alternates between sections that feature entrances of the subject and **episodes**—interludes (lacking the subject) that serve as areas of relaxation.

In **Josef Albers's** (1888–1976) *Fugue* (1925), the interlocking and parallel lines resemble the polyphonic textures of the fugue.

Contrapuntal devices

Contrapuntal writing is marked by a number of devices used since the earliest days of polyphony. A subject can be presented in longer time values, often twice as slow as the original, called **augmentation** (see box above), or in shorter time values that go by faster, called **diminution**. The pitches can be stated backward (starting from the last note and proceeding to the first), known as **retrograde**, or turned upside down (in mirror image), moving by the same intervals but in the opposite direction, a technique called **inversion**. Overlapping statements of the subject, called **stretto**, heighten the tension.

Bach's Keyboard Fugues

Bach worked his entire life to refine his fugal technique, combining mastery of craft with creativity and beauty. Although every fugue follows the same principle, with an exposition that presents the subject in at least two (and usually three or more) voices, and then an alternation between returns of the subject and contrasting musical ideas, no two fugues are alike in detail. Indeed, the process of combining predictable material with fresh ideas is at the core of musical composition, and Bach was a master. *The Well-Tempered Clavier*, a collection of forty-eight preludes and fugues issued in two volumes and demonstrating a new system for tuning keyboard instruments that's close to our contemporary equal-semitone norm, is a testament to his skill. Bach intended the collection as a teaching aid, with each individual prelude and fugue demonstrating a different set of expressive and technical challenges. Bach's last demonstration of contrapuntal mastery was *The Art of Fugue*, a collection of fugues and canons that systematically explores all the wizardry of fugal devices.

The Well-Tempered Clavier **and** *The Art of Fugue*

"Little" Fugue in G Minor

Bach's Fugue for Organ in G Minor (generally called "Little" to distinguish it from a longer fugue in the same key) has long been acknowledged as a great teaching example; it was copied by hand many times during his day by students and admirers, and was republished in multiple copies when Bach's music was "rediscovered" a century after his death. The organist is tasked with playing all four simultaneous musical lines, or voices (designated soprano, alto, tenor, and bass, according to their range). Three lines are played on the keyboard (or keyboards; many organs have more than one keyboard, each of which can be associated with different pipes and therefore timbres) and one line with feet on the pedalboard (which is also associated with a different set of pipes). Bach was known for his extraordinary pedal technique, and for his ability to teach his students to move their feet as nimbly on the pedalboard as their fingers did on the keyboard.

The opening of the subject is very distinctive, outlining a minor triad; the middle part repeats with a slight variation to help the listener recognize the melody within the multivoice texture; and the end picks up steam in a flow of sixteenth notes to propel the music forward.

Order of entries   As the exposition of this fugue begins, we hear the subject first in the top (soprano) voice, followed by the alto accompanied by the counter-subject (featuring a trill and continuous sixteenth notes). The two lower voices each announce the subject, the bass played on the pedals.

For the remainder of the fugue, Bach alternates modified returns of the subject with free material (episodes): he does not return to the subject in the original (tonic) key of G minor until the very end, after the longest episode of all. The final chord, a major triad, jolts us from the contemplative minor-key setting; this shifting from minor to major at the end was a common feature in Baroque keyboard music.

Since all of Bach's keyboard music was designed to teach prospective students to refine their technique, this work can be understood as a stimulating dexterity exercise for both fingers and brain. Bach would have expected his advanced students to go on to improvise such processes on their own, as they demonstrated their professional independence.

CRITICAL THINKING

1. How does Bach help you recognize the subject each time he introduces it? What are some of the ways he changes it?
2. In what ways does Bach create variety and contrast between the episode sections?

Your Turn TO EXPLORE

Seek out a recording or a live performance of an improvisation-oriented musician such as a rock guitarist or a jazz pianist. Listen for how the melody and harmony of each "standard tune" are first presented relatively straightforwardly, and then varied through several repetitions. How does the performer weave aspects of a recognizable melody through the improvised texture? Are there parts of the melody that are featured more prominently, and if so, why do you think this is?

LISTENING GUIDE 19   🔊 4:04

Bach: "Little" Fugue in G Minor, BWV 578

Date: 1703–07

Genre: Fugue for organ in four voices (SATB)

Performed by: E. Power Biggs, organ

What to Listen For

Melody	The subject is in three phrases, with the middle phrase repeated; the countersubject features a trill.
Harmony	Begins in a minor tonality; the subject appears in a major mode in the middle; the final cadence is on a major triad.

Texture	Four-part imitative polyphony, with a changing number of musical lines.
Form	Fugue in three parts: exposition, middle entries, closing section.
Performing forces	Solo organ.

EXPOSITION		MIDDLE ENTRIES		CLOSING SECTION	
0:00	Soprano (subject).	1:14	Episode, no subject.	3:40	Subject in the bass, in G minor.
0:18	Alto (answer; the soprano continues with the countersubject).	1:25	Subject starts in the tenor, then continues in soprano after a brief pause.	3:54	Final chords, ending with a G major triad.
0:35	Brief transition, no subject.	1:43	Episode, no subject.		
0:41	Tenor (subject; the alto has the countersubject).	1:52	Subject in the alto, in B-flat major.		
0:58	Bass (answer; the tenor has the countersubject); end of the subject is changed slightly.	2:08	Episode, no subject.		
		2:20	Subject in the bass, in B-flat major.		
		2:36	Episode, no subject.		
		2:54	Subject in soprano, in C minor.		
		3:10	Longest episode, no subject.		

Fugue subject, in three phrases:

Music in Words

Reviewing Baroque Style

You have now heard examples of a number of Baroque genres, both vocal and instrumental, that provide a frame of reference for other music from this era that you may encounter. Here are some things to listen for when you hear an unfamiliar Baroque work.

MELODY: Consider whether the melodic line is made up of short, regular ideas or long, asymmetrical phrases. Melodies can be built on diatonic scales but are sometimes colored by chromaticism and decorated with embellishments. What expressive elements do you hear in the melodic line?

RHYTHM/METER: Baroque instrumental music often features regular rhythmic motion. How does the work progress—with animated rhythms or a relaxed energy? Is the meter duple or triple? Simple or compound?

HARMONY: By this era, major-minor tonality is firmly established. Do you perceive the music as major (built on a major scale) or minor (darker sounding, built on a minor scale)? Consider how the concept of tonality (built around a central tonal center, or home base) functions here. Is the work largely consonant (based on agreeable-sounding combinations of notes) or dissonant (based on unstable notes in need of resolution)? Listen for moments that are more dissonant and unstable: what expressive purpose might they serve?

TEXTURE: Baroque music can be highly varied in its texture, depending on the circumstances of its composition and its function, and whether it is vocal or instrumental. Think about how the composer achieves contrast (thick vs. thin texture) and how many independent lines seem to happen at once.

TIMBRE: What instrument(s) are featured in the selection? Do they sound modern or more archaic? What qualities of tone color do you hear to support your answer?

DYNAMICS: Think about how the work exploits contrasts in volume. How do the performing forces contribute to the contrasts? Do changes in dynamics correlate with other expressive elements such as dissonance/consonance or texture?

FORM: Baroque music can be sectional, in simple two-part (binary) or three-part (ternary) forms. Larger works can, however, feature the same basic principles: repetition, contrast, and variation. What is the role of repetition here? of contrast (that is, new music)? What holds the piece together?

Listen and Respond

Let's see how you well you can apply what you have learned to a new musical example. Be sure to consult the listening suggestions above and also the style summary chart opposite. Compare this new work with Vivaldi's *La primavera*.

J. S. Bach, Concerto for Violin, BWV 1041, I

1. Create a simple listening outline for the piece. Think about melody, rhythm, harmony, texture, timbre, and form. How is the piece organized? Are there significant repeated sections?

2. How might you describe this work to a friend who is not in the class and not familiar with the terminology we've been developing? What general descriptions can you apply to the melody? harmony? texture? overall effect of the piece?

3. Now write a short paragraph describing the work as you might for a concert report assignment. Here you can demonstrate your understanding of the terms and concepts you have learned as well as your response to the work's expressive qualities. Refer back to Chapter 14 for ways to frame your perspective on the new work.

Style Summary for Baroque Music (c. 1600–1750)

Composers	Monteverdi, Cozzolani, Strozzi, Purcell, Vivaldi, Bach, Handel
Melody	Continuous melody with wide leaps, chromatic tones for emotional effect; speechlike melody in recitative
Rhythm/meter	Single rhythm predominant; steady, energetic pulse; freer in early Baroque vocal music
Harmony	Major-minor tonal system established; chromatic harmony used for expressive effect
Texture	Homophony and polyphony both common, often used in alternation or to provide contrasts; linear-horizontal dimension
Vocal genres	Opera, Mass, Magnificat, oratorio, cantata, anthem
Instrumental genres	Concerto, suite, sonata, prelude, fugue, dance music
Form	Binary and ternary forms predominant; ritornello (refrain) procedure in larger forms
Dynamics	Subtle dynamic nuances; *forte/piano* contrasts; echo effects
Timbre	Continuous tone color throughout a movement; penetrating sound of historical instruments
Instrumental forces	String orchestra, with added woodwinds; organ and harpsichord prevalent
Improvisation	Improvisation expected; harmonies realized from figured bass
Expression	Emotional exuberance and theatricality

Eighteenth-Century Classicism

"In truth, there is nothing like music to fill the moment with substance, whether it attune the quiet mind to reverence and worship, or whether it make the mobile senses dance in exultation."

—German poet Johann Wolfgang von Goethe (1749–1832)

OVERVIEW

1715
Louis XIV dies; reign of Louis XV begins.

1732
George Washington born.

1751
Benjamin Franklin's experiments with electri published.

1700　　1710　　1720　　1730　　1740　　1750

1732
Joseph Haydn born.

1741
Antonio Vivaldi dies.

Learning Objectives

By the end of Part 4, you will be able to

- recognize that the music has balanced melodic lines and phrases, accompanied by diatonic harmonies in major and minor.

- distinguish the regular rhythmic movement and clear duple or triple meters.

- perceive how the vertical, homophonic texture helps you focus on the melody.

- follow the unfolding of medium- and large-scale forms built around one or two main themes.

- identify some of the main vocal and instrumental genres and forms in the Classical era, as you become familiar with the most renowned composers of the period.

1775
American Revolutionary War begins.

1771
First edition of *Encyclopaedia Britannica*.

1785
Friedrich von Schiller writes "Ode to Joy."

1789
French Revolution begins.

1804
Napoleon crowned emperor of France.

1760   1770   1780   1790   1800   1810

1763
Child prodigy W. A. Mozart tours Europe.

1781
Haydn writes string quartets Op. 33.

1791
Mozart dies, leaving his *Requiem* incomplete.

1801
Ludwig van Beethoven writes his *Moonlight* Sonata.

Music as Order and Logic

"Music [is] the favorite passion of my soul."
—Thomas Jefferson (1743–1826)

Some artistic movements can easily be pinpointed in time: those whose leaders make strong statements about the need for radical change. Classicism is not such a movement; in fact, in some ways classicism is a constant concern in Western culture, since its roots are in the values of order and reason expressed by the ancient Greeks and Romans, who laid the foundations for the very notion of European identity. Ideals of classicism have repeatedly resurfaced through the centuries, and in some cases have coexisted with other stylistic concerns. For example, French artists and musicians in the early 1700s never thought of their own work as "baroque": they introduced the term to disparage others who didn't share their "classical" sensibility.

The later 1700s were a time when classical ideals were especially strong in Europe, combined with a philosophical and intellectual movement known as the **Enlightenment**, which stressed the centrality of reason in human experience. Artists and musicians strove to join the social push toward order and reason, developing works characterized by clarity and regularity of structure, and by an ideal of "natural simplicity." This tendency led to the development of an international musical style that was held up by subsequent generations as timeless, embodying the most perfect manifestations of musical logic. While previous styles had risen and fallen with fashion, the music of the Classical style was preserved and treasured even as later styles developed in contrast to its ideals— and this music continues to form the core of the Western concert tradition in the twenty-first century.

The Pantheon, in Rome (completed c. 126 CE), embodies the classical ideals of order and harmonious proportions.

Classicism and Enlightenment Culture

The Classical era in music encompasses the last half of the eighteenth century and the early decades of the nineteenth (c. 1750–1825). During this era, the rule of strong aristocratic sovereigns continued throughout Europe. Louis XV presided over extravagant celebrations in Versailles, and Frederick the Great ruled in Prussia, Maria Theresa in Austria, and Catherine the Great in Russia. In such societies, the ruling class enjoyed its power through hereditary right. At the same time, a new economic power was growing through the Industrial Revolution, which gathered momentum in the mid-eighteenth century through a series of important inventions—from James Watt's improved steam engine and James Hargreaves's spinning jenny in the 1760s to Eli Whitney's cotton gin in the 1790s. These decades saw significant advances in science—Benjamin Franklin harnessed electricity, Joseph Priestley discovered oxygen, and Edward Jenner perfected vaccination—and intellectual life, with the publication of the French *Encyclopédie* and the first edition of the *Encyclopaedia Britannica*. (See Interface, p. 180.)

The eighteenth century has been called the Age of Reason as well as the Enlightenment. Philosophers considered social and political issues in the light of reason and science, but they were also advocates for the rising middle class. The intellectual climate, then, was nourished by two opposing streams. While Classical art captured the exquisite refinement of a way of life that was drawing to a close, it also caught the first wave of a new social structure that would emerge with the revolutionary upheavals at the end of the century.

Just as eighteenth-century thinkers idealized the civilization of the Greeks and Romans, artists revered the unity and proportions of ancient architecture and fine arts. In this spirit, Thomas Jefferson patterned the nation's Capitol, the University of Virginia (see illustration above), and his home at Monticello after Greek and Roman temples. His example spurred on a classical revival in the United States, which made Ionic, Doric, and Corinthian columns indispensable features of public buildings well into the twentieth century.

By the 1760s, though, a Romantic point of view was emerging in literature. The French philosopher Jean-Jacques Rousseau, sometimes called the "father of Romanticism," produced some of his most significant writings in these years. One celebrated declaration, "Man is born free, and everywhere he is in chains," epitomizes the temper of the time. The first manifestation of the Romantic spirit in Germany was a literary movement known as *Sturm und Drang* (storm and stress). Two characteristic works appeared in the 1770s by the era's most significant young writers: *The Sorrows of Young Werther,* a novel by Johann Wolfgang von Goethe, and *The Robbers,* a play by Friedrich von Schiller. The famous poem "Ode to Joy," set by Beethoven in his Ninth Symphony, was Schiller's proclamation of universal brotherhood; and Goethe would become the favorite lyric poet of the Romantic composers.

By the end of the century, the old world of the aristocracy was beginning to give way to a new society of the people and to an era that produced some of the greatest Western artworks. Thus, backward-looking classicism itself contained the seeds of what would become the most significant and self-conscious progressive redefinition of European culture.

Thomas Jefferson's design for the Rotunda of the University of Virginia at Charlottesville, completed in 1826, reflects his admiration for classical architecture. Note the similarities of this building with the Roman Pantheon (opposite).

Romanticism in literature

Edited by Denis Diderot and with contributions from many specialists, the great French *Encyclopédie* (1751–72) sought to bring together knowledge from all over the world.

Classicism in Music

The Classical period in music is characterized best by the masters of the so-called Viennese School—Haydn, Mozart, Beethoven, and their successor Franz Schubert. These composers worked in an age of great musical experimentation and discovery, when musicians took on new challenges: first, to explore thoroughly the possibilities offered by the major-minor

Inter*face*

Science, Philosophy, and Music in the Age of Enlightenment

In a major intellectual and cultural shift, the eighteenth century looked toward the advancement of knowledge through reason and science. Among those who spearheaded change were the philosopher Voltaire and the physicist who developed the laws of gravity, Isaac Newton. These thinkers embraced a new philosophy that sought to understand all things according to nature and mathematics rather than religion. Scholars assiduously collected information to increase the overall body of knowledge, and society in general embraced a focus on learning. One result was the great French *Encyclopédie*, a thirty-five-volume reference source purporting to systematize all knowledge, written by the leading intellectuals of the day, including Voltaire and

A glass armonica from Boston, c. 1830.

Jean-Jacques Rousseau. Musicians took part in this effort to amass learning: Rousseau (also a composer) published a comprehensive dictionary of musical terms; Jean-Philippe Rameau wrote an important music theory treatise; and in 1776, the Englishman Charles Burney penned the first music history text (the ancestor of your textbook), which sought to record all knowledge about musicians and their works.

Some of the most celebrated technological achievements were connected to music: for example, "music boxes" with rotating cylinders and other mechanical means of plucking strings or striking metal plates when wound up. (Many of these musical machines were created by clock makers, who were making tremendous technological strides in miniaturizing time-keeping devices in the 1700s.) Some musical machines, known as automata, were made to resemble humans: a life-size human flute player played twelve separate melodies, and there's a famous automaton, now in the museum of Art and History in Neuchâtel, Switzerland, of a woman playing an organ, pressing the keys of the instrument with her fingers. While the "robotic" performer's bodily movements may seem less convincing to us in an age of sophisticated CGI animation, they were certainly among the most humanlike mechanical actions that had ever been seen at the time, and they demonstrated the power of human ingenuity.

Across the Atlantic, the statesman and scientist Benjamin Franklin was central to the American Enlightenment through his scientific experiments with electricity and his diverse inventions, including the lightning rod, bifocal glasses, the Franklin stove, and the glass armonica—a musical instrument made of tuned water glasses, for which both Mozart and Beethoven composed works. Franklin was a musician himself (he played harp and guitar), and he wrote a treatise on musical aesthetics, in which he espoused a philosophy of simplicity in melody and harmony.

We can easily relate the Enlightenment's goals of reasoned thought and simplicity to the music we are studying from this period. Both the individual musical elements—melody, rhythm, and harmony—and the overall structures are designed to embody a clarity, balance, and logic new to composition. This was truly intended as a "universally understandable" language of sound, and it is partly because of this quasi-scientific clarity that many still point to the music of the Classical era as the most straightforward pathway into understanding the musical logic of the European tradition.

An automaton of a mandolin player, built by P. Gaultier (eighteenth century).

system; and second, to perfect a large-scale form of instrumental music—known as sonata form—that exploited those possibilities to the fullest degree. Having found this ideal structure, composers then developed it into the solo and duo sonata, the trio and quartet (especially the string quartet), the concerto, and the symphony.

"Classicism" did not imply a strict adherence to traditional forms; as we will see, the composers of the Viennese School experimented boldly and ceaselessly with the materials at their disposal. And it should not surprise us to find that Romantic elements appear as well in the music of Haydn, Mozart, and Beethoven, especially in their late works. These composers dealt with musical challenges so brilliantly that their works have remained unsurpassed models for all who followed.

Elements of Classical Style

The music of the Viennese masters is notable for its elegant, lyrical melodies. Classical melodies "sing," even those intended for instruments. They are usually based on symmetrical four-bar phrases marked by clear-cut cadences, and they often move stepwise or by small leaps within a narrow range. Clarity is further provided by repetition and the frequent use of sequence (a pattern repeated at a higher or lower pitch). These devices make for balanced structures that are readily accessible to the listener.

The harmonies that sustain the melodies are equally clear. Chords are built from the seven tones of the major or minor scale (meaning they are diatonic) and therefore are firmly rooted in the key. The chords underline the balanced symmetry of phrases and cadences, and they form vertical columns of sound over which the melody unfolds freely, generally in a homophonic texture (a melody with accompanying harmony).

Much of the music is in one of the four basic meters—2/4, 3/4, 4/4, or 6/8—and moves at a steady tempo. If a piece or movement begins in a certain meter, it is apt to stay there until the end. Rhythm works closely with melody and harmony to make clear the symmetrical phrase-and-cadence structure of the piece. Well-defined sections establish the home (tonic) key, move to contrasting but closely related keys, and return to the home key. The result is the beautifully molded architectural forms of the Classical style, fulfilling the listener's need for both unity and variety.

Despite its aristocratic elegance, music of the Classical era absorbed a variety of folk and popular elements. This influence made itself felt not only in the German dances, minuets, and waltzes of the Viennese masters but also in their songs, symphonies, concertos, string quartets, and sonatas.

The minuet was one of the most popular dances in the eighteenth century. *The Minuet under an Oak Tree* (1787), by **François Louis Joseph Watteau** (1758–1823).

Detail of aristocratic performers in *The Concert*, Meissen porcelain from c. 1760.

The Patronage System

The culture of the eighteenth century thrived under the **patronage**, or sponsorship, of an aristocracy that viewed the arts as a necessary adornment of life. Music was part of the elaborate lifestyle of the nobility, and the center of musical life was the palace.

Portrait of French opera singer Marie Fel (c. 1753), by **Maurice Quentin de La Tour** (1704–1788).

The social events at court created a steady demand for new works from composers, who had to supply whatever their patrons wanted. Although musicians ranked little better than servants, their situation was not quite as depressing as it sounds. The patronage system actually gave musicians economic security and provided a social framework within which they could function. It offered important advantages to those who successfully adjusted to its requirements, as the career of Joseph Haydn clearly shows (see p. 187).

Opportunities for Women

While aristocratic women like Marie Antoinette, archduchess of Austria and wife of French king Louis XVI, continued their regular music studies, middle-class women also found a place as musicians under the patronage system. In Italy and France, professional female singers achieved prominence in opera and in court ballets. Others found a place within aristocratic circles as court instrumentalists and music teachers, offering private lessons to members of the nobility.

Two women in particular, both associated with Wolfgang Amadeus Mozart, stand out as impressive keyboard players of the late eighteenth century. His sister, Maria Anna Mozart (1751–1829; see illustration on p. 196), known as Nannerl, was an accomplished pianist who as a child toured widely with Wolfgang, performing concertos and four-hand piano works. Their father noted that Nannerl, at age twelve, played "so beautifully that everyone is talking about her and admiring her execution." A friend of Mozart's, the blind composer Maria Theresia von Paradis (1759–1824), was an excellent pianist and organist, renowned for her remarkable

Map of Europe, 1763–89, showing major musical centers.

musical memory, which retained some sixty different concertos that she prepared for an extended European tour. And later in this unit we will meet Marianne Martinez, another woman active in the Vienna orbit of Haydn and Mozart, in the context of considering musicians who were prominent at the time but are now overshadowed by the fame of a few (see Many Voices: Masters—and Non-Masters, p. 206).

The public prominence achieved by these women was unusual for the era. However, the many engravings and paintings of the time illustrating music-making scenes make it clear that women participated frequently in performances at home, in aristocratic salons, and at court. Ultimately, with the growth of the music trades, especially music printing and publishing, women found more professional opportunities open to them. And as more amateurs participated in music-making, women of the middle as well as upper classes found an outlet for their talents.

Performance Matters

FROM PALACE TO CONCERT HALL

At this time, musical performances were beginning to move from the palace to the concert hall. The rise of the public concert gave performers and composers a new venue (site) in which to perform their works. Haydn and Beethoven conducted their own symphonies at concerts, and Mozart and Beethoven played their own piano concertos. The public flocked to hear the latest works—unlike the majority of modern classical-music concertgoers, who are interested mainly in music of the past. The eagerness of eighteenth-century audiences for new music surely stimulated composers to greater productivity.

A public concert of a Haydn oratorio in the Festival Hall of the University of Vienna (1808), honoring the composer, by **Balthasar Wigand** (1771–1846).

Though great virtuoso performers continued to be highly prized, the clarity and simplicity of the Classical style made it increasingly accessible to the informed amateur—whether through performance or through careful listening. More and more instrumental music was described in terms of dialogue and communication—whether between performers or between the composer and the public. As the idea of communication through instrumental storytelling became ingrained, the notion of using that communication to build a deep and intimate connection between the uniquely inspired composer-genius and the receptive listener grew more appealing to musicians and their audiences. This too was an essential element in the emerging Romantic sensibility, as we will see in the work of Beethoven and in the public response to Mozart's late compositions.

CRITICAL THINKING

1. What were the primary characteristics of Classicism?
2. How are Classical ideals reflected in eighteenth-century music?

31

Musical Conversations: Haydn and Classical Chamber Music

"You listen to four sensible persons conversing, you profit from their discourse, and you get to know their several instruments."

—Johann Wolfgang von Goethe (writing about string quartets)

KeyPoints

- Form is the most important organizing element in **absolute music**, which has no specific pictorial or literary program.

- Musical ideas, or **themes**, are used as building blocks in a composition; these themes are made up of short melodic or rhythmic fragments known as **motives**.

- Themes can be expanded by varying the melody, rhythm, or harmony through **thematic development**; this usually happens in large-scale works.

- The Classical era is the golden age of **chamber music** (ensemble music for two to about ten performers, with one player per part). The **string quartet** (two violins, viola, and cello) was the most important chamber-music genre of the era.

- The finale of Joseph Haydn's *Joke* Quartet features a playful tune that recurs as a refrain in a **rondo** form.

You get together with some friends and begin a conversation on a topic of common interest. Members of your group will agree or disagree with each other, expand on others' perspectives, interrupt each other as things get more heated, all while keeping a friendly spirit going, with the goal of reaching a satisfactory conclusion. This is how eighteenth-century Europeans understood chamber music, and in particular the string quartet: the equal participation of various instruments was an essential aspect of a new sensibility. These were conversations without words, but they were just as purposeful, and just as structured, as real conversations might be. The way composers achieved this was through an emphasis on predictable musical forms, which would allow musicians and listeners alike to "follow the discussion" to its logical conclusion, and to profit, as Goethe's quote above suggests, from its artistic expression.

Expanding Musical Ideas

As noted in Chapter 6, a musical idea that is used as a building block in the construction of a composition is called a **theme**. Varying a theme's melodic outline, **Thematic development** rhythm, or harmony is considered **thematic development**. This is one of the most

A modern-day photograph of the Eszterháza Palace in Fertöd, Hungary, where Haydn was employed.

important techniques in composition and requires both imagination and craft on the part of the creator. In addition to its capacity for growth, a theme can be fragmented by dividing it into its constituent motives, a **motive** being its smallest melodic or rhythmic unit. A motive can grow into an expansive melody, or it can be treated in **sequence**—that is, repeated at a higher or lower level. Thematic development is generally too complex for short pieces, where repetition, a simple contrast between sections, and a modest expansion of material usually supply the necessary continuity. But thematic development is necessary in larger forms, where it provides clarity, coherence, and logic.

Motive and sequence

The development of thematic material—through extension, contraction, and repetition—occurs in music from all corners of the world (see Many Voices, p. 201). In considering the fugue by Bach, we have already seen that musical structure and logic can unfold through a partly planned, partly improvised process. Other traditions reflect this approach: in jazz, for example, musicians organize their improvised melodies within a highly structured, preestablished harmonic pattern, time frame, and melodic outline that is understood by all the performers.

The most prominent musicians of the Classical era were also excellent improvisers—both Mozart and Beethoven, for example, drew crowds when they improvised at the keyboard. However, the forms of the Classical style are composed-out and fixed: they indicate a fully worked-out rational argument, rather than a flexible process-in-motion like the one we encountered in Bach's fugue. Because this music is so dependent on the listener's expectation of recognizable structures, it's crucial for us to understand the conventions on which composers and listeners based musical meaning.

Classical Forms

Every musical work has a form; it is sometimes simple, other times complex. In **absolute music**, where there is no prescribed story or text to hold the music together, form is especially important. The story is the music itself, so its shape is of primary concern for the composer, the performer, and the listener. Most instrumental works of the Classical era—symphonies, sonatas, concertos, string quartets, and other types of chamber music—follow a sequence of sections or movements that is known as a **multimovement cycle**. We will briefly look at the

Absolute music

Multimovement cycle

Multimovement Cycle: General Scheme

Movement	Character/Tempo	Form	Examples
First	Long, dramatic Allegro	Sonata-allegro	Mozart, *Eine kleine Nachtmusik*, I Beethoven, Symphony No. 5, I
Second	Slow, lyrical Andante or Adagio	Theme and variations or **A-B-A**	Haydn, Symphony No. 94 (*Surprise*), II
Third **(optional)**	Dancelike Allegro or Allegretto	Minuet and trio (18th c.) Scherzo and trio (19th c.)	Mozart, *Eine kleine Nachtmusik*, III Beethoven, Symphony No. 5, III
Fourth **(last)**	Lively, spirited Allegro or Vivace	Sonata-allegro (or rondo or sonata-rondo)	Beethoven, Symphony No. 5, IV Haydn, *Joke* Quartet, IV

overall characteristics of that cycle, and then dwell in turn (in this and the following chapters) on the formal conventions of each movement.

The outline of the multimovement cycle above sums up the common practice of both the Classical and Romantic eras. It can help you build expectations and listening strategies, provided you remember that it is no more than a general scheme.

Each individual movement has an internal form that binds its different sections into one artistic whole. You have already learned two of the simplest forms: two-part, or binary (**A-B**), and three-part, or ternary (**A-B-A**). Rather than start with the customary form of the first movement of the cycle (sonata-allegro form), which is more intricate and will be the subject of a later chapter, we will begin with a less complex form, as exemplified by the last movement of a string quartet by Haydn.

This anonymous watercolor depicts a performance of a string quartet, the most influential chamber-music genre of the era.

The Fourth Movement

Many multimovement classical works close with a **rondo**—a lively movement with a lighthearted theme, leaving the listener with an upbeat impression of the work. Its distinguishing formal characteristic is the recurrence of a musical idea—the main theme, or **refrain**—in alternation with contrasting episodes, much like the ritornello procedure in Baroque concertos (see Chapter 29). In its simplest form, **A-B-A-C-A**, the rondo is an extension of three-part form; its symmetrical sections create a balanced architecture that is satisfying and easy to hear. You might think of it as a "now you hear it, now you don't" experience.

Chamber music, as we have seen, is music for a small ensemble—two to about ten players—with one player to a part. In this intimate genre, each instrument is expected to assert itself fully, but function as part of a team rather than as a soloist. The central position in Classical chamber music was held by the **string quartet**, which consists of two violins (a first and a second), a viola, and a cello. Other favored combinations were the duo sonata (violin and piano, or cello and piano); the piano trio (violin, cello, and piano); and the quintet, usually a combination of string or wind instruments, or a string quartet with solo instrument such as the piano or clarinet. (See chart in Chapter 11.) Because the string quartet was intended to be enjoyed by a small group of cultivated music lovers, composers did not need expansive gestures here. They could present their most private thoughts, and indeed, the final string quartets of Haydn, Mozart, and Beethoven contain some of their most profound music. Joseph Haydn, with his sixty-eight string quartets, played a central role in the evolution of this genre.

Statue of Grand Duke (later Emperor) Paul I of Russia (1754–1801), dedicatee of Haydn's Op. 33 string quartets.

The *Joke* Quartet

Haydn wrote most of his string quartets in sets of six, and his Op. 33 is no exception. He dedicated this set to the Grand Duke Paul of Russia, the son of Catherine the Great, after a visit to Vienna by the nobleman during which several Haydn quartets were the featured entertainment. Having already established the four-movement form in his earlier quartets, Haydn introduced several new elements here: each quartet has a lively scherzo in place of the traditional minuet dance movement; and he sometimes inverts the expected order of the middle movements, placing the dance movement second and a slow, expressive movement third (as in our selection).

Joseph Haydn (1732–1809)

Haydn was one of the most prolific composers of the Classical period. Born in the small Austrian village of Rohrau, he absorbed the folk songs and dances of his homeland. The beauty of his voice secured him a place as a choirboy at St. Stephen's Cathedral in Vienna.

In 1761, when he was twenty-nine, Haydn entered the service of the Esterházys, a family of enormously wealthy Hungarian princes famous for their patronage of the arts, with whom he remained for almost thirty years. The family palace of Eszterháza was one of the most splendid in Europe (see illustration, p. 185), and music played a central role in the constant round of festivities there. The musical establishment under Haydn's direction included an orchestra, an opera company, a marionette theater, and a chapel. His life exemplifies the patronage system at its best.

By the time Haydn reached middle age, his music had brought him much fame. After his prince's death, he made two visits to England in the 1790s, where he conducted his works with phenomenal success. He died in 1809, revered throughout Europe.

It was Haydn's historic role to help perfect the new instrumental music of the late eighteenth century, as well as expand the orchestra's size and resources through greater emphasis on the brass, clarinets (new to the orchestra), and percussion. His expressive harmony, structural logic, and endlessly varied moods embodied the mature Classical style.

MAJOR WORKS: Chamber music, including 68 string quartets (*Joke*, Op. 33, No. 2; *Emperor*, Op. 76, No. 3) • Over 100 symphonies (including the 6 *Paris* Symphonies, Nos. 82–87; and the 12 *London* Symphonies, Nos. 93–104) • Concertos for violin, cello, harpsichord, and trumpet • Sacred vocal music (Masses, motets, and two oratorios, including *The Creation*) • 14 operas • Keyboard music (including 40 sonatas).

Haydn: String Quartet in E-flat Major, Op. 33, No. 2 (*Joke*), IV

Date: 1781   **Performed by:** Kodály Quartet

Movements: I. Allegro moderato, sonata-allegro form
            II. Scherzo, scherzo and trio form
            III. Largo e sostenuto
            IV. Presto, rondo form

What to Listen For

Melody	Memorable melody in short, balanced phrases and with staccato notes.	**Form**	Simple rondo (**A-B-A-C-A** + coda), with a rounded binary main theme.
Rhythm/ meter	Lilting 6/8, dancelike, with pauses; very quick tempo with an abrupt slow section near the end.	**Expression**	Cheerful mood, with surprise pauses at the end.
Harmony	Major tonality (E-flat, with one episode in the subdominant of A-flat).	**Performing forces**	String quartet (two violins, viola, and cello).
Texture	Homophonic; violin 1 has the melody.		

IV: Presto

0:00   **A section** (rounded binary form, **a-a-ba-ba**)—opens with a jaunty rondo theme (**a**) in three short phrases (eight measures divided 2 + 2 + 4) and staccato, repeated:

0:15   Second part (**b**) has a more chromatic melody; a *crescendo* leads to a brief return of the main rondo theme (**a**); this part is repeated.

1:09   **B**—**episode** in a new key develops ideas from the **A** section; features *sforzando* emphases on the downbeats.

1:40   **A section**—return of the opening material without repeats (**a-ba**).

2:14   **C**—**episode** remains in the home key; features the violin in a high range; *pianissimo* section leads to long held notes.

2:47   **A section** returns with the opening eight measures.

2:55   **Coda**—sudden Adagio tempo, a final-sounding cadence, followed by a short pause, then the main theme; a longer pause, then a surprise ending.

We will hear the second quartet of the set, the *Joke*, specifically the clever fourth movement that gives the work its nickname. The movement opens with a catchy tune that is easily recognizable, the first element in a **rounded binary form** (expanded to include a brief return of the opening at the end of the second section; LG 20). Such symmetry often occurs in dance forms, like the minuet and trio (we will encounter rounded binary again in Chapter 33). After this refrain idea is established, the listener's goal is to focus on its return in between several developmental episodes. The first violin takes the lead in this conversation between refrain and episodes, with the other instruments adding support throughout. Haydn reveals his sense of humor in the playful treatment of the coda. Here, the main tune is cut short by a series of pauses leading to a whispered close. By spreading out the length of the pauses and slightly changing the musical phrases, he repeatedly tricks us into thinking that perhaps the work is over, and then makes us expect that it will continue when it *is* over.

As you listen to this movement, think about the kinds of expectations Haydn would like you, the listener, to have about this conversation—which is not only an interaction between four string-instrument-playing friends but also an interaction between the composer and you. These simultaneous conversations between equals—musicians and listeners—helped drive the popularity of the string quartet during the Classical era.

In Their Own Words

" I learned from Haydn how to write quartets. No one else can do everything—be flirtatious and be unsettling, move to laughter and move to tears—as well as Joseph Haydn."

—W. A. Mozart

CRITICAL THINKING

1. What are some ways composers unify their compositions?
2. How is this chamber work similar to the Baroque ritornello form heard in Vivaldi's concerto (Chapter 29)? How is it different?

YourTurn TO EXPLORE

Look for videos of performers from different chamber-music traditions—from the Classical era, but also jazz, country, rock, hip-hop, and maybe Indian or Chinese classical/traditional repertories. In what way do these performers appear to be "performing friendship" through their music-making? What differences are there in the interactions or conversations between performers and between performers and audience, in these various traditions?

32

The Ultimate Instrument: Haydn and the Symphony

"My Prince was always satisfied with my works. I not only had the encouragement of constant approval but as conductor of an orchestra I could make experiments, observe what produced an effect and what weakened it, and . . . improve, alter, make additions or omissions, and be as bold as I pleased."

—Joseph Haydn

KeyPoints

- The **symphony**, a genre designed to demonstrate the expressive capabilities of a full orchestra, arose as one of the principal instrumental traditions during the Classical era.

- The heart of the Classical orchestra (about thirty to forty players) was the strings, assisted by woodwinds, brass, and percussion.
- Joseph Haydn wrote over 100 symphonies; among these, his last 12—the so-called *London* Symphonies—are his masterpieces in the genre.

The palette of tone colors available to a symphony composer is remarkable. Even the most complex synthesizers cannot match the nuance of live instruments, especially when they are combined by the dozens into a carefully coordinated unit—the orchestra. It was during the Classical era that the notion of the orchestra as the "ultimate instrument" began to develop, and composers sought to realize their greatest expressive potential through this medium, which remains today (even as it has changed over the centuries) probably the most versatile and powerful musical resource of the Western tradition. While you can hear orchestral sounds (often electronically manipulated) in television and film, experiencing a symphony orchestra in person is so much more compelling than hearing it on a recording. Witnessing the sonic and physical coordination and interaction between dozens of musicians is something you owe to yourself, now that you have learned (through LG 1 in Chapter 11) how to distinguish between instrumental timbres in an orchestra.

The Classical Orchestra and Symphony

The Classical masters established the orchestra as we know it today: an ensemble of the four instrumental families. The heart of the orchestra was the string family.

Woodwinds provided varying colors and assisted the strings, often doubling them. The brass sustained the harmonies and contributed body to the sound, while the timpani supplied rhythmic life and vitality. In the 1700s, the orchestra numbered from thirty to forty players; thus, the volume of sound was still more appropriate for the salon than the concert hall. (We will hear a movement played on eighteenth-century period instruments.)

Classical composers created a dynamic style of orchestral writing in which all the instruments participated actively and each timbre could be heard. The interchange of themes between the various instrumental groups assumed the excitement of a witty conversation; in this, the **symphony**, which held the central place in Classical instrumental music, also resembled the string quartet.

Natural horns (without valves) and woodwinds are seen in this painting of a small orchestra performing in an eighteenth-century Venetian palace.

The symphony had its roots in the Italian opera **overture** of the early eighteenth century, an orchestral piece in three sections: fast-slow-fast. First played to introduce an opera, these three sections eventually became separate movements, to which the early German symphonists added a number of innovations. One was the use of a quick, aggressively rhythmic theme rising from low to high register with such speed that it became known as a "rocket theme." Equally important was the use of drawn-out *crescendos* (sometimes referred to as a "steamroller effect"), slowly gathering force as they built to a climax. Finally, composers added a dance movement, an elegant minuet. As we will see, composers exploited new formal procedures in the symphony; here we will consider one favorite approach to the second movement.

The Second Movement: Theme and Variations

The second is usually the slow movement of the multimovement cycle, offering a contrast to the first movement—usually a spirited Allegro—and characterized by lyrical, songful melodies. Typically, it is an Andante or Adagio in **A-B-A** or theme-and-variations form.

We have already noted that variation is an important procedure in music, but in one form—**theme and variations**—it is the ruling principle. Here, the theme is clearly stated at the outset and serves as the point of departure; it may be newly invented or borrowed (like the theme in Britten's *Young Person's Guide to the Orchestra*; see LG 1). The theme is likely to be a small two- or three-part idea, simple in character to allow room for elaboration. It is followed by a series of variations in which certain features of the original idea are retained while others are altered. Each variation sets forth the idea with some new modification—you might say in a new disguise—through which the listener glimpses something of the original theme.

Any musical element may be developed in the variation process. The melody may be varied by adding or omitting notes—a favorite procedure in jazz, where the solo player embellishes a popular tune with a series of decorative flourishes. Or it may be shifted to another key. The chords that accompany a melody may be replaced by

In Their Own Words

" Can you see the notes behave like waves? Up and down they go! Look, you can also see the mountains. You have to amuse yourself sometimes after being serious so long."

—*Joseph Haydn*

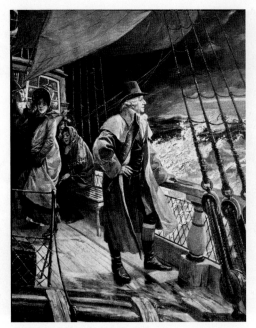

Haydn crossing the English Channel on his way to England in 1791.

The Main Hall of the Eszterháza Palace in Hungary, where the music master Haydn spent his summer months along with the court (eighteenth century).

others; the shape of the accompaniment may be changed; note lengths, meter, or tempo can also be altered through rhythmic variation, and the texture may be enriched by interweaving the melody with new themes or countermelodies.

Haydn's Symphony No. 94 (*Surprise*)

Joseph Haydn contributed well over 100 symphonies to the genre, establishing the four-movement structure and earning himself the nickname "Father of the Symphony." His masterworks in the genre include the six *Paris* Symphonies, commissioned by composer-conductor Joseph Boulogne, a musician of color whose compositions and contributions to French musical life have been largely overlooked in the classical music canon (see Many Voices: Masters—and Non-Masters, p. 206), and the last set of twelve—the so-called *London* Symphonies—commissioned for a concert series in London. This last set abounds in expressive effects, including syncopation, sudden *crescendos* and accents, dramatic contrasts of soft and loud, daring modulations, and an imaginative plan in which each family of instruments plays its own part.

The best-known of Haydn's symphonies, No. 94 in G major, is one of the twelve composed for London. The work is nicknamed *Surprise* because of a sudden *fortissimo* crashing chord in the slow movement, intended to startle a dozing audience. The first movement opens with a slow, reflective introduction, followed by a forceful Vivace assai (very fast) in sonata form. The abrupt changes from *piano* to *forte* impart a dramatic quality to the movement and foreshadow Beethoven's emotion-charged style.

The second movement, a theme and four variations, is a great favorite with audiences (LG 21). This memorable theme, with all the allure of a folk song, is set in two repeated sections (**A** and **B**) of eight measures each (a binary structure). After the opening **A** section is repeated *pianissimo*, it ends abruptly in a loud crash—the "surprise" chord. And the variations continue to display Haydn's workmanship and wit: with countermelodies (1), a dramatic shift to the minor (2), quick repeated notes (3), and a new triplet rhythm heard against offbeat chords (4).

The third movement is a rollicking minuet that leaves the elegant, courtly dance far behind in favor of a folklike romp. The finale, an energetic Allegro molto in sonata-allegro form, captures for its aristocratic listeners all the charm and humor of a traditional peasant dance. This work radiates the precise qualities that made the *London* Symphonies so successful—innocent, appealing melodies within a masterful treatment of forms.

As you listen to the way the melody is varied and to the contrasting timbres in the second movement, think about the notion of conversation that we explored in Chapter 31. What can Haydn "tell" you when he has so many more sonic resources at his disposal?

LISTENING GUIDE 21   🔊 6:11

Haydn: Symphony No. 94 in G Major (*Surprise*), II

Date: First performed in 1792

Movements: I. Adagio cantabile; Vivace assai; sonata-allegro form, G major
II. Andante: theme-and-variations form, C major
III. Menuetto: Allegro molto; minuet-and-trio form, G major
IV. Allegro molto; sonata-allegro form, G major

Performed by: Hanover Band,
Roy Goodman, conductor

What to Listen For

Melody	Folklike theme in two regular phrases, each repeated.	**Form**	Theme (in binary form) with four variations and coda.
Rhythm/ meter	Slow, walking tempo in duple meter; some prominent accents.	**Expression**	Simple yet witty, with a "surprise" interjection.
Harmony	Major tonality (C major); variation 2 is in C minor.	**Performing forces**	Eighteenth-century string, wind, and percussion instruments.
Texture	Largely homophonic, with an occasional countermelody.		

II: Andante

0:00   **Theme**—folklike melody in two parts, each repeated (binary).
A section—melody outlines a triad, played staccato in the strings:

A section repeated, *pianissimo*, with a *fortissimo* chord on the last beat.

0:33   **B** section—disjunct theme, ending in the style of **A:**

B section repeated, with flutes and oboes.

1:05   **Variation 1**—A begins with a loud chord, features a violin countermelody:

A repeated.

continued on next page

1:38   **B**, with a decorated violin line.

      B repeated.

2:09   **Variation 2**—A played *fortissimo*, in C minor (later shifts to a major key):

2:42   **A** repeated.

      Development of **A** (rather than **B**), with fast passages in strings; remains in minor.

      Solo violins lead into Variation 3.

3:17   **Variation 3**—A in a fast rhythm, heard in oboes:

      A repeated in violins, with a woodwind countermelody; low strings drop out.

3:49   **B** continues with violins and woodwinds alone.

      B repeated.

4:22   **Variation 4**—A heard in full orchestra, *fortissimo*, with accents heard on offbeats:

      A in violins in an uneven, dotted rhythm, with accompaniment playing offbeats.

4:55   **B** continues in uneven rhythms in strings.

      B repeated in a loud statement by the full orchestra.

5:26   Bridge to the coda; staccato pattern, followed by a sustained chord.

5:40   **Coda** returns to A melody, with varied harmony underneath; ends quietly in C major.

CRITICAL THINKING

1. What contributions did Haydn make to the genre of the symphony?

2. How can musical elements be modified to achieve variation? How is this different from using new musical elements to create contrast?

Your Turn TO EXPLORE

Look for (ideally video) recordings of large instrumental ensembles from several varied traditions—Western orchestras, but also (for example) gamelan ensembles from Indonesia, a Vietnamese Nha Nhac performance, a big-band jazz group. How does the range or variety of timbres differ from ensemble to ensemble? How is each similar to and different from a Western orchestra?

33

Expanding the Conversation: Mozart, Chamber Music, and Larger Forms

"People make a mistake who think that my art has come easily to me. Nobody has devoted so much time and thought to composition as I. There is not a famous master whose music I have not studied over and over."

—Wolfgang Amadeus Mozart

KeyPoints

- The first movement of the Classical multimovement cycle is usually in a fast tempo and in **sonata-allegro form**, with three main sections: **exposition**, **development**, and **recapitulation**.

- The third movement is a triple-meter pair of dances, usually a **minuet and trio**.

- Wolfgang Amadeus Mozart, a child prodigy who started to write music before the age of five, contributed to nearly all musical genres of the Classical era, including the symphony, sonata, concerto, chamber music, sacred music, and opera.

- One of Mozart's best-known chamber works is *Eine kleine Nachtmusik* (*A Little Night Music*), a **serenade** for strings.

All narrative and interactive genres—novels, plays, movies, video games—rely on a structural framework. Those engaging with the narrative learn to understand the conventions of the genre, and the creators engage in a "conversation" with the reader/spectator/player through fulfilling or challenging their expectations. Your enjoyment of such genres hinges on your willingness to learn the structural conventions and understand the subtlety with which the creators are manipulating them. Sonata-allegro form, which we begin exploring in this chapter, quickly became a favorite resource for instrumental composers, since the musical story it can tell is significantly more dynamic than the one available through simpler forms (like, for example, theme and variations). Comprehending its principles and being able to follow its unfolding are essential for a deeper understanding of all instrumental music from this period onward: the form opens up opportunities for a profound conversation between composers, performers, and listeners. And if the string quartet can be understood as a conversation between four close friends, other genres of chamber music reveal a more wide-ranging discussion among a more diverse cohort; we will examine one such expanded conversation composed by Mozart.

In Their Own Words

" Only when the form grows clear to you will the spirit become so too."

—Robert Schumann

Mozart's *Eine kleine Nachtmusik*

Two popular expanded chamber genres in Mozart's day were the **divertimento** and the **serenade**. Both are lighter genres that were performed in the evening or at social functions. Mozart wrote a large variety of social music of this sort, the most famous of which is *Eine kleine Nachtmusik* (1787), a serenade for strings whose title means literally *A Little Night Music*. The work was most likely written for a string quartet supported by a double bass and was meant for public entertainment, in outdoor performance. The four movements of the version we know (originally there were five) are compact, intimate, and beautifully proportioned.

The First Movement: Sonata-Allegro Form

The most highly organized and often the longest movement in the multimovement cycle is the opening one, which is usually in a fast tempo such as Allegro and is written in **sonata-allegro form** (also known as **sonata form**). This movement establishes a home (tonic) key, then moves, or **modulates,** to another key, and ultimately returns to the home key. We may therefore regard sonata-allegro form as a drama between two contrasting key areas. In most cases, each key area is associated with a theme, which has the potential for development. The themes are stated, or "exposed," in the first section; developed in the second; and restated, or "recapitulated," in the third.

(1) The opening section of sonata-allegro form—the **exposition**, or statement—generally presents the two opposing keys and their respective themes. (In some cases, a theme may consist of several related ideas, in which case we speak of a **theme group**.) The first theme establishes the home key, or tonic. A **bridge**, or transitional passage, leads to a second theme in a contrasting key; in other words, the function of the bridge is to modulate. After the second theme, a closing section, sometimes with a new closing theme, rounds off the exposition in the contrasting key. In eighteenth-century sonata-allegro form, the exposition is repeated.

(2) Conflict and action, the essence of drama, characterize the **development**. This section may wander through a series of foreign keys, building up tension against the inevitable return home. The frequent modulations contribute to a sense of activity and restlessness. Here, the composer reveals the potential of the themes by varying, expanding, or contracting them, breaking them into their component motives, or combining them with other motives or with new material. When the development has run its course, the tension lets up and a bridge passage leads back to the key of the tonic.

(3) The beginning of the third section, the **recapitulation**, or restatement, is the psychological climax of sonata-allegro form. The return of the first theme in the tonic satisfies the listener's need for unity. The recapitulation restates the first and second themes more or less in their original form, but with one important difference from the exposition: both themes now remain in the tonic, thereby asserting the dominance of the home key. The movement often ends with a **coda**, an extension of the closing idea that leads to the final cadence in the home key.

The features of sonata-allegro form, summed up in the chart opposite, are present in one shape or another in many movements, yet

Leopold Mozart with his two young children, Nannerl and Wolfgang, performing in Paris (1763–64), a watercolor by **Louis de Carmontelle** (1717–1806).

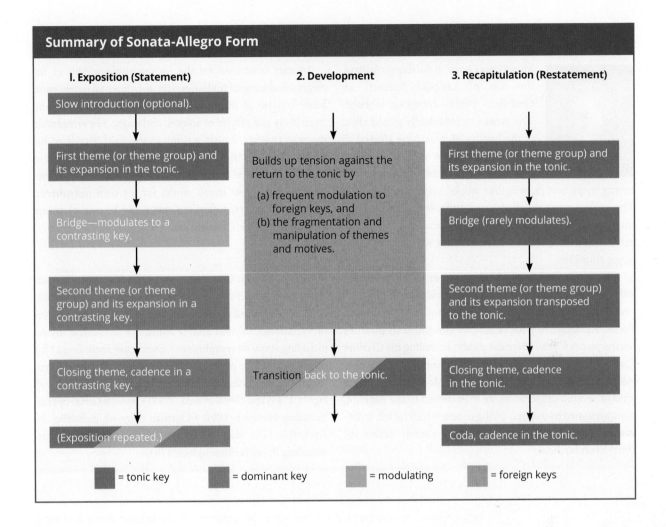

Summary of Sonata-Allegro Form

I. Exposition (Statement)	2. Development	3. Recapitulation (Restatement)
Slow introduction (optional).		
First theme (or theme group) and its expansion in the tonic.	Builds up tension against the return to the tonic by (a) frequent modulation to foreign keys, and (b) the fragmentation and manipulation of themes and motives.	First theme (or theme group) and its expansion in the tonic.
Bridge—modulates to a contrasting key.		Bridge (rarely modulates).
Second theme (or theme group) and its expansion in a contrasting key.		Second theme (or theme group) and its expansion transposed to the tonic.
Closing theme, cadence in a contrasting key.	Transition back to the tonic.	Closing theme, cadence in the tonic.
(Exposition repeated.)		Coda, cadence in the tonic.

■ = tonic key   ■ = dominant key   ■ = modulating   ■ = foreign keys

no two pieces are exactly alike. What might at first appear to be a fixed plan actually provides a supple framework for infinite variety in the hands of the composer.

Let's examine how Mozart deploys sonata-allegro form in the first movement of *Eine kleine Nachtmusik* (LG 22). The movement opens with a strong, marchlike theme that rapidly ascends to its peak (an example of a "rocket theme"), then turns downward at the same rate. Mozart balances this idea with an elegant descending second theme. The closing theme exudes a high energy level, moving the work into its short development; and the recapitulation brings back all the themes, ending with a vigorous coda.

The Third Movement: Minuet-and-Trio Form

In the Classical instrumental cycle, the third movement is almost invariably a **minuet and trio**. The minuet was originally a Baroque court dance whose dignified triple (3 / 4) meter embodied the ideal of an aristocratic age. Since dance music lends itself to symmetrical construction, you often find in a minuet a clear-cut structure based on phrases of four and eight measures. The tempo ranges from stately to lively and whimsical.

The movement's name results from the custom of presenting two different dances as a group, the first repeated after the second (resulting in **A-B-A**). The dance in the middle was originally arranged for only three instruments, hence the

Wolfgang Amadeus Mozart (1756–1791)

Mozart was born in Salzburg, Austria, the son of Leopold Mozart, an esteemed court composer-violinist. The most extraordinarily gifted child in the history of music, he started to compose before he was five; by age thirteen, he had written sonatas, concertos, symphonies, religious works, and several operas. The young artist rebelled against the social restrictions imposed by the patronage system, and at twenty-five established himself in Vienna as a struggling freelance musician.

Mozart reached the peak of his career in the late 1780s with his three comic operas (*The Marriage of Figaro, Don Giovanni,* and *Così fan tutte*) on librettos by Lorenzo da Ponte. Although in poor health, he continued to produce masterpieces for the Viennese public, including his Clarinet Concerto (he was one of the first to compose for this new instrument) and his final opera, *The Magic Flute*. With a kind of fevered desperation, he then turned to the *Requiem*, commissioned by a music-loving count, which he left unfinished. He died on December 4, 1791, shortly before his thirty-sixth birthday.

Mozart is revered for the inexhaustible wealth of his elegant and songful melodies. His instrumental music combines a sense of drama with contrasts of mood ranging from lively and playful to solemn and tragic. His symphonic masterpieces are the six written in the final decade of his life, and the last ten string quartets are some of the finest in the literature. One of the outstanding pianists of his time, Mozart also wrote many works for his own instrument. His piano concertos elevated this genre to one of prime importance in the Classical era.

MAJOR WORKS: Chamber music, including 23 string quartets • Divertimentos and serenades (*Eine kleine Nachtmusik,* K. 525) • Keyboard music, including 17 piano sonatas • Sets of variations (*Ah! vous dirai-je Maman*) • Orchestral music, including some 40 symphonies • Concertos, including 27 for piano, 5 for violin, others for solo wind instruments • Comic (*buffa*) operas, including *Le nozze di Figaro* (*The Marriage of Figaro,* 1786) and *Don Giovanni* (1787) • Serious (*seria*) operas, including *Idomeneo* (1791) • German *Singspiel*, including *Die Zauberflöte* (*The Magic Flute,* 1791) • Sacred choral music, including *Requiem* (incomplete, 1791).

A couple performing a minuet-quadrille, an eighteenth-century court dance.

name "trio," which persisted even after the customary setting for three had long been abandoned. At the end of the trio, you find the words **da capo** ("from the beginning"), signifying that the first section is to be played over again (as it was in the Baroque aria; see Chapter 23).

Each part of the minuet-trio-minuet in turn subdivides into two-part, or binary, form (see chart below). The second section of the minuet (**b**) or trio (**d**) may bring back the opening theme, making a rounded binary form. The composer indicates the repetition of the subsections within repeat signs (‖: :‖). However, when the minuet returns after the trio, it is customarily played straight through, without repeats (**a b**).

Minuet (**A**)	Trio (**B**)	Minuet (**A**)
‖:a:‖:b:‖	‖:c:‖:d:‖	a b

The minuet and trio that makes up the third movement of *Eine kleine Nachtmusik* is marked by regular four-bar phrases set in rounded binary form. The minuet opens brightly and decisively. The trio, with its polished, soaring melody, presents a lyrical contrast. The opening music then returns, satisfying the Classical desire for balance and symmetry.

While sonata-allegro and minuet-and-trio are different forms, they both rely on predictable principles of statement, contrast, and return that are at the core of the Classical style. Each movement of *Eine kleine Nachtmusik* provides a different perspective in a balanced, rational, yet inventive musical argument—the hallmark of Mozart's artistry.

CRITICAL THINKING

1. How does Mozart's serenade fit the model for multimovement instrumental works in this era?

2. How might musical structures from the Classical era be compared to a play, novel, movie, or video game?

Your Turn TO EXPLORE

Find video examples of dancing in contrasting traditions—for example, modern ballroom dance, country or square dancing, ballet, breakdancing or other hip-hop styles, Thai or Indian or Balinese classical dance, Native American ceremonial dance, or a TV dance program. Can you notice patterns of statement, repetition, contrast, and return in the music that accompanies the dance? How is the musical logic of those formal elements reflected in the dancers' movements?

LISTENING GUIDE 22   ◀)) 7:39

Mozart: *Eine kleine Nachtmusik* (*A Little Night Music*), K. 525, I and III

Date: 1787

Movements: **I. Allegro; sonata-allegro form, G major**
II. Romanza, Andante; sectional rondo form, C major
III. Allegretto; minuet-and-trio form, G major
IV. Allegro; sonata-rondo form, G major

Performed by: Moscow Virtuosi, Vladimir Spivakov, conductor

I: Allegro   5:30

What to Listen For

Melody	Marchlike; disjunct, ascending ("rocket") theme; then graceful descending tune.	**Form**	Sonata-allegro form in three sections: exposition-development-recapitulation.
Rhythm/ meter	Quick duple meter.	**Expression**	Sudden dynamic contrasts.
Harmony	Consonant, in G major (tonic key).	**Performing forces**	String quartet with double bass (or string orchestra).
Texture	Homophonic.		

Exposition

0:00   Theme 1—aggressive, ascending "rocket" theme, symmetrical phrasing, in G major:

Bridge, a modulating, transitional passage.

0:46   Theme 2—graceful, contrasting theme, less hurried, in the key of the dominant, D major:

continued on next page

0:58   Closing theme—insistent, repetitive, ends in D major.
        Repeat of the exposition.

Development

3:07   Short, begins in D major, manipulates theme 1 and closing theme; modulates, and prepares for the
        recapitulation in G major.

Recapitulation

3:40   Theme 1, in G major.

4:22   Theme 2, in G major.

4:34   Closing theme, in G major.

5:05   Coda—extends closing, in G major.

III: Allegretto   2:09

What to Listen For			
Melody	Decisive minuet melody in regular phrases; conjunct and expressive trio.	**Harmony**	Consonant, in G major (tonic key).
		Texture	Homophonic.
Rhythm/ meter	Strongly rhythmic dance, in triple meter.	**Form**	Two dances (minuet-trio), with the minuet returning; each dance is binary.

0:00   Minuet theme—in accented triple meter, decisive character, in two sections (eight measures each),
        both repeated:

0:44   Trio theme—more lyrical and connected, in two sections (8 + 12 measures), both repeated:

1:41   Minuet returns, without repeats.

North Indian Classical Music

We have seen how musical structures were expanded and developed in the Classical era, so that a single movement of a symphony or a concerto might take fifteen minutes or more to perform. Still, we can expect that its sections will be marked by predictable patterns of either repetition (or variation) or new material. Similar processes take place in the music of other cultures, although the end result is quite different. A case in point is North Indian classical music, a centuries-old performance tradition linked to Hinduism and its deities. This musical style is based not on entirely fixed musical works, but rather on long-standing traditional repertories of motives and themes elaborated by expert performers. Rather than featuring a key center, each semi-improvised elaboration introduces a **raga**, a series of pitches that also projects a particular mood and an association with a certain time of day.

We will hear *Raga Bhimpalasi*, performed by the venerable Indian musician Ravi Shankar (1920–2012), who plays a **sitar**, a long-necked plucked string instrument with metal strings and gourd resonators. He is often accompanied by a performer who plays a complex rhythmic cycle (**tala**, meaning "clap") with a small set of hand drums called **tabla**. A typical Indian classical piece can take up to several hours to play; our selection, however, is a mere twelve minutes. Indian audiences understand that *Raga Bhimpalasi* is performed in the afternoon—at the height of the day's heat—and it projects a mood of tenderness and longing.

The raga provides the pitches for the highly ornamented melody, and its tala

Composer and sitar player Ravi Shankar performing with tabla player Alla Rakha at the 1969 Woodstock Festival.

is an additive rhythmic cycle of fourteen; you can hear Shankar explain both the raga and tala in a brief demonstration at the beginning. Harmony is not really a part of this music, except for what's produced by the striking of strings that sound **drones** (sustained pitches). As in a sonata-allegro form, we can expect the work to play out in sections; but while there is a general outline to the overall structure, improvisation plays a key role throughout. As the performance progresses, the tempo gradually accelerates to an extended climax, with dazzling passagework on the sitar accompanied by animated rhythms on the tabla.

Indian musicians learn to play this music by apprenticing to master players, who pass their performance techniques down to the next generation via an oral tradition. Ravi Shankar taught his daughter Anoushka this way, and she has herself become a great sitar artist (see p. 38). Shankar in fact introduced Indian classical music to the Western world, inspiring a genre of "raga-rock" in the 1960s and 70s. He gave a memorable performance at the

original Woodstock Festival in August 1969, and the Beatles employed sitar on their recordings. Beatle George Harrison even studied sitar with Shankar and collaborated on projects with him, thus ensuring broad international visibility for the Indian master— a fortuitous example of the Eastern and Western worlds of music colliding.

Raga Bhimpalasi

What to listen for:

- Improvised melodic elaborations by the sitar on a series of pitches.
- Raga in its ascending and descending form.
- Complex rhythmic accompaniment on the tabla (2 + 4 + 4 + 4).

The introductory section (*alap*) is slow and unmetered, played by the sitar alone; the pitches of the raga are established in this improvisatory section. The second section (*gat*) begins with the entrance of the tabla, which sets up the rhythmic cycle (tala). With the third section (*jhala*), the tempo speeds up and the interplay between the instruments becomes more complex.

34

Conversation with a Leader: The Classical Concerto

"Give me the best instrument in Europe, but listeners who understand nothing or do not wish to understand and who do not feel with me in what I am playing, and all my pleasure is spoilt."

—Wolfgang Amadeus Mozart

KeyPoints

- The Classical concerto form has three movements, alternating fast-slow-fast.
- The first movement, the longest and most complex, is called **first-movement concerto form**.

- Mozart's Piano Concerto in G Major, K. 453—with its graceful melodies, brilliant piano passagework, and virtuosic **cadenzas** (improvised solo passages)—is a notable example of the genre.

If chamber music in the Classical period was designed to convey a musical conversation among equals, the Classical **concerto** was closer to a political rally—an inspiring leader helping to advance a larger group to a common purpose. While the genre continued to display some of the traits of the Baroque concerto, it was also influenced by the logic of the multimovement principle that governed other Classical genres such as the string quartet and symphony. In the concerto, composers relied on outstanding performers to provide the soloist's vitality, and sought to balance that energy with the complex collaboration of many unified voices.

Movements of the Classical Concerto

During the Baroque era, "concerto" could refer to a solo group and orchestra or to a solo instrument and orchestra. The Classical era shifted the emphasis to the latter combination, while keeping the fast-slow-fast pattern established by Vivaldi **Cadenza** for the three movements. One unique feature of the solo concerto is the **cadenza**, a virtuosic solo passage in the manner of an improvisation that comes toward the end of a movement. It creates a dramatic effect: the orchestra falls silent, and the soloist (for example, the pianist or violinist) launches into a free play of fantasy on one or more themes of the movement.

Engraving of a piano concerto performance (1777), with a woman soloist, by **Johann Rudolf Holzhalb** (1723–1806).

The first movement adapts the principles of the Baroque concerto's ritornello procedure (based on a recurring theme) to those of sonata-allegro form. **First-movement concerto form** is sometimes described as a sonata-allegro form with a double exposition: the movement opens with an orchestral exposition (or ritornello) in the tonic key, presenting several themes, followed by the soloist playing elaborated versions of these themes. The solo cadenza appears near the end of the movement, and a coda brings it to a close with a strong affirmation of the tonic key. We will examine how this form unfolds in one of Mozart's most beloved concertos.

Mozart and the Piano Concerto

Mozart played a crucial role in the development of the genre. His twenty-seven piano concertos, written primarily as display pieces for his own public performances, abound in the brilliant flourishes and elegant gestures characteristic of eighteenth-century music. Five of his most impressive were written in just one year, 1784; one of these, the Concerto in G Major, K. 453, Mozart wrote for his young student Babette (Barbara) von Ployer. Proud of his talented student, he invited the composer Giovanni Paisiello to the premiere performance, writing to his father, "I am fetching Paisiello in my carriage, as I want him to hear both my pupil and my compositions."

This work beautifully illustrates the richness of Mozart's creativity and his formal clarity. In the first movement (LG 23), the orchestral exposition sets up the main themes, after which the soloist weaves figurations around these melodies—including a new, lighthearted one as well—in its own exposition. A full-ensemble tutti leads to the development section, which makes virtuosic demands on the

Mozart: Piano Concerto in G Major, K. 453, I

Date: 1784

Movements: I. Allegro; first-movement concerto form, G major
II. Andante; first-movement concerto form, C major
III. Allegretto, Presto; theme-and-variations form, G major

Performed by: English Chamber Orchestra, Murray Perahia, piano and conductor

I: Allegro

What to Listen For

Melody	Lilting first theme; quiet and lyrical second theme; new, graceful piano theme in the second exposition.	**Texture**	Mostly homophonic.
		Form	First-movement concerto form, with orchestral and solo expositions, then development, recapitulation, and coda.
Rhythm/ meter	Lively, marchlike rhythm and tempo.		
Harmony	Major key; shifts to key of the dominant (D) in the piano exposition.	**Expression**	Elegant and refined, with decorative turns.
		Performing forces	Solo piano and orchestra (strings, flute, pairs of oboes, bassoons, and horns).

Orchestral exposition (ritornello), in G major

0:00   Theme 1—refined theme in violins, with woodwind figurations:

0:27   Transitional theme—forceful, in full orchestra.
1:01   Theme 2—gently undulating theme in violins, answered in woodwinds:

1:40   Closing theme—stated quietly in orchestra.

Solo exposition

2:10   Theme 1—piano enters with a sweep into the main theme, decorated, in G major; woodwind accompaniment; scales and arpeggio figurations in piano.
2:45   Transitional theme—orchestral ritornello; piano has a decorative part; modulates to key of the dominant.
3:11   Piano theme—introduced by piano alone in D major, then presented in woodwinds:

4:01   Theme 2—in piano, with string accompaniment.
4:55   Closing—decisive, in D major.

Development

5:16   Virtuosic piano part, with references to the piano theme, runs and arpeggios against woodwinds; various modulations, leading back to the tonic.

Recapitulation

6:34	Theme 1—returns in strings, with woodwind accompaniment; piano plays a decorated version of theme.
7:01	Transitional theme—forceful, in full orchestra.
7:32	Piano theme, solo, in G major, more decorated, with a light orchestral accompaniment.
8:23	Theme 2—in piano, then in woodwinds, now in G major.
9:28	Cadenza—solo piano, variations on earlier themes; ends on the dominant.
10:44	Closing—final ritornello, in G major.

soloist. This concerto, notable also for its graceful writing for woodwinds, is usually performed today with a cadenza that Mozart wrote for it. The lyrical slow movement is followed by an Allegretto in theme-and-variations form; Mozart was so fond of its charming, dancelike tune that he taught it to his pet starling, who consistently missed one note and got the rhythm wrong.

The interaction of a virtuoso soloist with a larger and more varied ensemble allowed Mozart and his contemporaries to expand the Classical ideal of musical conversation to embrace a strong conversation leader—a "heroic" figure in keeping with an emerging ideal that we will explore in the chapters to come.

CRITICAL THINKING

1. How is the Classical concerto like the Baroque concerto? How does it differ?

2. How is the virtuosic ability of the performer displayed in the Classical concerto?

Mozart's fortepiano (by Anton Walter, 1780), now in the Mozarteum in Salzburg, Austria. Notice how the colors of the white and black keys are the reverse of today's piano.

YourTurn TO EXPLORE

Seek out videos of performances from different traditions that feature a soloist-leader: concertos from the Western orchestral tradition, but also (for example) rock bands, large jazz ensembles, or gospel groups. In what ways does the soloist interact with the larger ensemble? What are the respective roles of soloist and ensemble?

Masters—and Non-Masters

Part 4 of this book focuses exclusively on the works of three "master" composers—Haydn, Mozart, and Beethoven. Indeed, these musicians' compositions have been understood as defining the canon of the "Classical style" even since their own lifetimes. But of course there were many other Europeans at the time whose music was highly valued, though their place in the canon was not enshrined by subsequent generations. We will here consider two musicians whom Haydn and Mozart recognized as worthy peers, but who have been excluded from the music canon at least to some extent because of their identity and social role.

Joseph Boulogne (Bologne), Chevalier de Saint-Georges (1745–1799), was a champion fencer as well as violinist, composer, and conductor. A native of the French Caribbean colony of Guadeloupe and illegitimate son of a French plantation owner and his enslaved Senegalese servant Nanon, Saint-Georges was educated in France, where he obtained his earliest musical training. He began his career as a violin soloist, performing with the newly formed Concert des Amateurs in his early twenties; shortly thereafter, he was named the director of this celebrated orchestra. He was further recognized by his nomination in 1776 as the director of the Paris Opéra; unfortunately, this appointment was blocked by several influential prima donnas who petitioned the Queen, writing that they found it degrading to have to "submit to the orders of a mulatto." He was then named the director of a private opera theater belonging to Madame de Montesson, wife of the Duke d'Orléans, at which he presented several of his own operas. He eventually founded another orchestra in Paris that achieved great success: Le Concert de la Loge olympique. As director of his ensemble, he commissioned and conducted the premiere of Joseph Haydn's six *Paris* Symphonies (nos. 82–87 of 1785–86, see p. 187).

In addition to operas, Saint-Georges wrote a number of string quartets, violin concertos and sonatas, several symphonies, and vocal music. Wolfgang Amadeus Mozart almost certainly heard him perform when visiting Paris at age 22, and one of the violin works Mozart wrote soon thereafter seems to draw on a distinct virtuosic sequence pioneered by Saint-George, in which the violin climbs to its highest register and then dives to the lowest.

On top of his successes as a performer, composer, and conductor, Saint-Georges had a distinguished military career, serving as colonel of a specially formed regiment of people of color in the 1790s, and standing as France's premier fencer; future US President John Adams, then ambassador to Paris, referred to him as "the most accomplished man in Europe in horse-riding, shooting, fencing, dancing and music." How could so fascinating and talented an individual have been excluded from our histories? Try listening to his three-movement Symphony No. 1 in G Major, Op. 11, or one of his string quartets, and

The composer and champion fencer Joseph Boulogne, Chevalier de Saint-Georges; engraving by American artist **Mather Brown** (1761–1831).

consider what similarities and differences you can hear between his approach and Haydn's or Mozart's.

Another extraordinary biracial musician, George Bridgetower (1778–1860), was recognized in his day as a superb violinist who performed alongside Haydn in the London Salomon concerts; Beethoven wrote a highly virtuosic violin sonata specifically to display Bridgetower's talents alongside his own, and they performed the work to great acclaim. Beethoven even initially dedicated the sonata to Bridgetower, but then changed the dedication to the more famous violinist Rodolphe Kreutzer (the work is now known as the *Kreutzer* Sonata), even though Kreutzer thought it was too difficult to play and never performed it. Does the absence of

Boulogne's works from the Classical canon and the omission of any recognition of Bridgetower's musical talents reflect insufficient quality, or might there be other reasons for their noninclusion?

Even geographically closer to the "Classical Masters," we can consider Marianne Martinez (also Marianne von Martinez, 1744–1812), an Austrian composer of Spanish descent who made her way as a single woman in the music world, both as a performer and a composer. Martinez was born into a family well connected with the imperial court, and as such, she was favored by the Empress Maria Theresa, for whom she performed frequently. Martinez's musical training was overseen by none other than Pietro Metastasio, the imperial poet and foremost librettist in Europe, who shared lodgings not only with the Martinez family but also with the young Haydn, who lived in the attic apartment and was Marianne's first voice and keyboard teacher. One of her early compositions, a Mass setting, was performed at the imperial Church of St. Michael on the feast day for the Archangel Michael, to the amazement of "all those who understand the art." Martinez's reputation as a composer extended internationally, and in 1773 she was elected unanimously to the Accademia Filarmonica in Bologna, the first woman to hold this honor since the founding of the esteemed music institution in 1666. Members of the academy lavished praise on her large-scale motet *Dixit Dominus,* written for the organization: they noted in admiration its "beauty, ingenuity, nobility of expression, and astonishing correctness."

Martinez maintained a more private presence than her male colleagues, premiering most of her compositions in the various salons of Vienna—including the one she hosted—rather than in a more public sphere. In the 1790s she established a concert series that attracted Vienna's leading musicians and composers, Haydn and Mozart among them. She also maintained a vocal studio where she trained some excellent singers. Martinez's output of compositions is extensive, including oratorios, Masses, and motets as well as works for solo voice, solo keyboard, and orchestra. The same questions arise: how can a composer, so admired in her day, have been erased from historical record until recently? Was it because the incomparable compositions of towering giants Haydn, Mozart, and Beethoven are more worthy of inclusion in the canon? Or was it because she was a woman, and did not have the public visibility and reputation-building fan base in following generations that the three canonic "Classical Masters" had? You can be the judge, after listening to her inspired Concerto for Cembalo (harpsichord) in G Major (or another of her compositions).

Many Voices Expanded

- Joseph Boulogne, String Quartet, Op. 14, No. 1 in D Major
- Marianne Martinez, Concerto for Cembalo in G major
- Marianne Martinez, Sonata for Cembalo in A Major, Adagio

Austrian composer and singer Marianne Martinez, painted by **Anton von Maron** (1733–1808).

35

Personalizing the Conversation: Beethoven and the Classical Sonata

"To play without passion is inexcusable." —Ludwig van Beethoven

KeyPoints

- Classical **sonatas** were written either for one solo instrument (usually the piano) or for duos (violin and piano, for example).

- Sonatas were sometimes designed for amateur performance in the home, but were also used by composer-performers as showpieces.

- The solo sonatas of Mozart and especially Ludwig van Beethoven are among the most significant in the keyboard literature.

- The *Moonlight* Sonata, perhaps Beethoven's best-known piano work, evokes the new Romantic style in its expressive manipulation of Classical conventions.

A young Beethoven performs for Mozart. Engraving from the German School (early nineteenth century).

Group conversations can be heated, but our most intense interactions with friends tend to be one on one: this is where we reveal most about ourselves, and build the deepest emotional connections. Similarly, while quartets and other chamber music highlighted the group-conversational possibilities of the Classical style, the sonata was designed for a more intimate expressive space. Featuring one or two performers, it either gave amateurs the opportunity for one-to-one musical interactions or allowed a skilled professional the opportunity to communicate directly with the listener. It was especially through the sonata that Ludwig van Beethoven developed a style that has been continuously valued as strikingly individual and meaningful from the time of his first performances. Beethoven's individuality, however, is evident because he developed it within a set of formal conventions against which he could "push"; if we do not understand these formal expectations, which his contemporaries had internalized, his intimate musical conversations with us cannot have the power and the passion that he envisioned.

The Sonata in the Classical Era

Haydn, Mozart, and their successors understood the term **sonata** as an instrumental work for one or two instruments, consisting of three or four contrasting movements.

The movements followed the basic order of the multimovement cycle that we have been exploring (see chart on p. 186).

In the Classical era, the sonata—for piano alone or for two instruments (violin or cello and piano)—became an important genre for amateurs in the home, as well as for composers like Mozart and Beethoven performing their own music at concerts. Beethoven's thirty-two piano sonatas, which span his entire compositional output, are among his most important works. The so-called *Moonlight* Sonata (LG 24) dates from his formative years but looks forward to the emotional expressiveness of the Romantic era.

Countess Giulietta Guicciardi, the dedicatee of the *Moonlight* Sonata.

Beethoven's *Moonlight* Sonata

Shortly after Beethoven's death, the *Moonlight* Sonata was given its title by German poet Ludwig Rellstab, who likened the work to the moonlit scenery along Lake Lucerne in Switzerland. (Note that in this case the "program music" aspect of the piece was added by a listener, rather than the composer.) When Beethoven composed the sonata in 1801 (early in his career), he was enamored of a young pupil, Countess Giulietta Guicciardi. The sonata is dedicated to her, but since this dedication seems to have been a last-minute decision, the work is probably not a programmatic statement of his love.

This work, one of a pair from Op. 27, breaks the formal molds—Beethoven called it a "fantasy sonata" (*Sonata quasi una fantasia*), although he retained the typical three-movement format. In the dreamy first movement, one of the most famous of all his

Ludwig van Beethoven (1770–1827)

Beethoven was born in Bonn, Germany. From age eleven, he supported his mother and two younger brothers by performing as an organist and harpsichordist. At twenty-two he moved to Vienna, where, although he was not attached to the court of a prince, the music-loving aristocrats helped him in various ways—by paying him handsomely for lessons or presenting him with gifts. He was also aided by the emergence of a middle-class public and the growth of concert life and music publishing.

When he was still in his twenties, Beethoven began to lose his hearing. His helplessness in the face of this affliction dealt a shattering blow to his pride: "How could I possibly admit an infirmity in the one sense that should have been more perfect in me than in others," he wrote to his brothers. Although he never regained his hearing and struggled with a sense of isolation, the remainder of his career was spent in ceaseless effort to achieve his artistic goals. He died at age fifty-six, famous and revered.

Beethoven is the supreme architect in music, a master in large-scale forms like the sonata and the symphony. His compositional activity fell into three periods. The first reflected the Classical elements he inherited from Haydn and Mozart. The middle period saw the appearance of characteristics more closely associated with the nineteenth century: strong dynamic contrasts, explosive accents, and longer movements. In his third period, Beethoven used more chromatic harmonies and developed a skeletal language from which all nonessentials were rigidly pared away. It was a language that transcended his time.

Beethoven's nine symphonies, five piano concertos and Violin Concerto, thirty-two piano sonatas, seventeen string quartets, opera *Fidelio*, and the *Missa solemnis* are indispensable to their respective repertories.

MAJOR WORKS: Orchestral music, including nine symphonies (the "Ode to Joy" is featured in Symphony No. 9), overtures • Concertos, including five for piano and one for violin • Chamber music, including string quartets, piano trios, sonatas for violin and cello, wind chamber music • 32 piano sonatas, including Op. 13 (*Pathétique*) and Op. 27, No. 2 (*Moonlight*) • Other piano music (*Für Elise*) • One opera (*Fidelio*, 1814) • Choral music, including *Missa solemnis* (1823) • Songs and one song cycle.

works, the melody sings continuously, moving through various keys and registers. A short contrasting idea intervenes between two statements of the melody. Although the form of this movement displays elements of development and recapitulation, it does not present the opposition of themes or keys typical of a first movement. Instead, it looks ahead to song forms favored by Romantic composers—indeed, it is almost a "song without words," a genre that arose in the generation following Beethoven.

The second movement is a gentle **scherzo** (quick-paced dance, a variant of the minuet) and trio set in a major key, providing necessary psychological relief

---

LISTENING GUIDE 24 5:45

Beethoven: Piano Sonata in C-sharp Minor, Op. 27, No. 2 (*Moonlight*), I

Date: 1801

Performed by: John O'Conor, piano

Movements: I. **Adagio sostenuto; modified song form, C-sharp minor**
II. Allegretto; scherzo and trio, D-flat major
III. Presto agitato; sonata-allegro form, C-sharp minor

I: Adagio sostenuto

What to Listen For			
Melody	Delicate, singing melody, moves slowly; heard in various ranges; then short ideas are passed between the hands.	**Texture**	Homophonic, with active accompaniment; then contrapuntal.
Rhythm/ meter	Continuous arpeggiated pattern of accompaniment under a slow duple melody.	**Form**	Modified song form; strophic with two strophes separated by a developmental section.
Harmony	Expressive minor key; modulations.	**Expression**	Ethereal mood; soft dynamic.

Introduction

0:00   Four-measure arpeggiated chords.

Strophe 1

0:23   Melody in the right hand (shaded), with a dotted figure on a repeated note, accompanied by left-hand arpeggios, C-sharp minor; four-measure phrases:

0:48   Melody in a new key, expands and modulates.
1:12   New idea in dialogue between the two hands.
1:51   Melody returns, in a higher range.

Middle section
2:14   Motivic development of the dialogue, exchanged between the hands over a pedal on the dominant (G-sharp):

Strophe 2
3:20   Returns to the opening melody and key center (C-sharp minor), followed by a short dialogue idea.

Coda
4:52   Closes with the melody stated in the bass on a repeated pitch (left hand).
        Resolution on a tonic cadence, with arpeggios and chords.

🔊 **AnotherHearing**   Now that you've heard this famous sonata movement played on a modern piano, listen to a performance by Malcolm Bilson on a fortepiano, the instrument played in Beethoven's time, and compare the subtle differences in timbre. Which do you find more effective, and why?

between the emotionally charged opening movement and the stormy finale. The full force of Beethoven's dramatic writing is reserved for this closing movement, which he set in a full-blown sonata-allegro form.

Although Beethoven himself was not particularly won over by this sonata —"Surely I have written better things," he argued—it was an immediate success with audiences and remains one of the most beloved works in the Classical repertory. This may be partly because of a perception that Beethoven's musical ideas are "breaking out" of the conventions of the genre, making the intimacy of his message even more compelling. But again, if we were not expecting a particular set of structural milestones in the first movement, Beethoven's choice to reject those milestones would not be nearly as powerful. His intimate musical message would reveal less about his passionate convictions.

CRITICAL THINKING

1. What are the types of sonata composed in the Classical era?
2. What is unusual about the form of Beethoven's *Moonlight* Sonata?

YourTurn TO EXPLORE

Find video examples of solo piano performances, and contrast them with the ensemble conversations you have examined in other explorations. How are the performer's behavior, the setting, and the interaction with the audience different? Contrast solo performances of similar repertory by amateurs and professionals: besides the skill of the performer, what other aspects of the performance (self-presentation, connection with others, expressive gestures, and so on) are different?

36

Disrupting the Conversation: Beethoven and the Symphony in Transition

"I carry my thoughts about with me for a long time . . . before writing them down. I change many things, discard others, and try again and again until I am satisfied. . . . I turn my ideas into tones that resound, roar, and rage until at last they stand before me in the form of notes."

—Ludwig van Beethoven

KeyPoints

- Beethoven's music is grounded in the Classical tradition but pushes its limits in a way that helped define the emerging Romantic sensibility.

- Beethoven's nine symphonies exemplify his experiments with Classical conventions. Best known is his Fifth, built on a famous four-note motive that permeates all four movements.

The Theater an der Wien in Vienna, where (in 1808) Beethoven presented a concert that included his Fifth and Sixth Symphonies.

Even during his own lifetime, Beethoven was hailed as a genius, and his influence on the orchestral tradition that followed can be felt to the present day. His ability to disrupt the elegant, balanced musical conversation of the Classical era is seen as evidence of supreme inspiration, the mark of an artist who will say what he needs to say regardless of the effect on the social order. Indeed, the presence of "Beethoven the hero" in the imagination of Western culture has extended far beyond the concert hall—even if you had not encountered the name of any composer considered so far, you likely had heard of Beethoven. Yet this composer was also working carefully to balance the formal expectations of the tradition within which he had been trained with "strategic disruptions." His unique approaches do not entail rejecting the conventions of Classical form: in fact, formal considerations are absolutely essential to the meaning and power of his music. This transitional place between convention and disruption is one major element that keeps Beethoven's music so compelling more than two centuries after it was written.

Beethoven's Symphonies

The symphony provided Beethoven with the ideal medium through which to address his public. His first two symphonies are closest in style to the two Classical masters who preceded him, but with his third, the *Eroica*, Beethoven began to expand the possibilities of the genre—the work was originally dedicated to Napoleon, and it was quickly interpreted as a personal narrative of individual heroism. The Fifth Symphony, which we consider here, is popularly viewed as a model of the genre. The finale of the Ninth, or *Choral*, Symphony, in which vocal soloists and chorus join the orchestra, is a setting of Friedrich von Schiller's "Ode to Joy," a ringing prophecy of the time when "all people will be brothers" (for more on the Ninth, see Interface, p. 214).

Beethoven's funeral procession in 1827, a watercolor by **Franz Stoeber** (1760–1834).

The Fifth Symphony

Perhaps the best-known of all symphonies, Beethoven's Symphony No. 5 can be heard not just as a standard four-movement cycle but as a unified whole that progresses from conflict and struggle to victorious ending. Now that we have examined individual movements in the cycle, we can tackle an entire symphony and consider both how it fits the parameters of the Classical cycle and how it pushes beyond them (LG 25).

The first movement, in a sonata-allegro form marked "Allegro con brio" (lively, with vigor), springs out of the rhythmic idea of "three shorts and a long" that dominates the entire symphony. This idea, perhaps the most commanding and recognizable gesture in the whole symphonic literature, is pursued with an almost terrifying single-mindedness in this dramatic movement. In an extended coda, the basic rhythm reveals a new fount of explosive energy. Beethoven described the motive as "Fate knocking at the door."

First movement

The second movement is a serene theme and variations, with two melodic ideas. Beethoven exploits his two themes with all the procedures of variation—changes in melodic outline, harmony, rhythm, tempo, dynamics, register, key, mode, and timbre. The familiar four-note rhythm (short-short-short-long) is sounded in the second theme, relating this movement to the first.

Second and third movements

Third in the cycle is the scherzo, which opens with a rocket theme introduced by cellos and double basses. After a gruff, humorous trio in C major, the scherzo returns in a modified version, followed by a transitional passage to the final movement, in which the timpani sounds the memorable four-note motive.

The monumental fourth movement bursts forth without pause, once again bringing back the unifying rhythmic motive. This unification makes the symphony an early example of **cyclical form**, in which a theme or musical idea from one movement returns in a later one. Here, Beethoven unleashes not only a new energy and passion but also new instruments not yet part of the standard orchestra: piccolo, contrabassoon, and trombones all expand the ensemble's range and intensity. This last movement, in sonata-allegro form with an extended coda, closes with the tonic chord proclaimed triumphantly by the orchestra again and again.

Fourth movement

Beethoven's career bridged the transition from the old society to the new. His commanding musical voice and an all-conquering will forged a link to the coming Romantic age.

Inter*face*

Beethoven and the Politics of Music

Composers have produced some of their most powerful music in response to the political climate in which they lived. This is especially true of Beethoven, who was born in Germany but adopted Austria as his homeland during a time of great tumult and change.

An advocate for democracy and the underprivileged in his youth, Beethoven watched with interest as the French general Napoleon Bonaparte rose to power after the French Revolution (1789–99). At first, he greatly admired Napoleon: his Third Symphony (*Eroica*) was originally called *Bonaparte*. But when the ruler declared himself emperor in 1804, Beethoven tore up the title page bearing the dedication. "So he too is nothing more than an ordinary man," the composer wrote.

Besides Austria, Beethoven also claimed a kinship with Great Britain—for the people and their democratic parliamentary system, and possibly also because the British were allies of Austria against the French in the Napoleonic Wars. Heartfelt nationalistic

sentiments found expression in his *Battle Symphony* (1813), also known as *Wellington's Victory*, celebrating the recent British victory over the Napoleonic army at the Battle of Vitoria, in Spain. The work (replete with muskets and cannons) is programmatic in its vivid retelling of the battle through fanfares and patriotic tunes associated with both the French and the British (*Rule, Britannia* and *God Save the King*). Today, *Wellington's Victory* is heard most frequently at Fourth of July celebrations in the United States to accompany fireworks and ceremonial pageantry—an interesting "translation" of Beethoven's anti-French sentiments into American patriotism.

One of Beethoven's most famous works is the last movement of his Symphony No. 9 (1822–24), which features a choral setting of Friedrich von Schiller's poem "Ode to Joy." The text is an expression of universal brotherhood inspired by the powerful social forces behind the French Revolution. This great symphony has become a rallying cry for widely divergent philosophies ever since. At one extreme,

the German dictator Adolf Hitler demanded that Beethoven's work be played for his birthday in 1941. At another, the last movement was selected to celebrate the fall of the Berlin Wall in 1989, and today it is played on official occasions of both the Council of Europe and the European Union. The ideology behind the "Ode to Joy" is valued outside Western culture as well: in 1971, it was named the national anthem of Rhodesia (now Zimbabwe) in Africa; in 1989, student protestors at China's Tiananmen Square chose it as their freedom statement; and each year, the symphony is performed in Japan with a colossal choir to ring in the New Year.

More recently Beethoven's music took on yet another political role: to help build a musical bridge between North and South Korea. After a 2008 concert by the New York Philharmonic in Pyongyang, North Korea, the orchestra performed two days later in Seoul, South Korea, ending with the uplifting strains of Beethoven's Symphony No. 5; earlier that week, the "Ode to Joy" was played at the swearing-in ceremony of South Korean president Lee Myung-Bak.

The year 2020 marked the 250th anniversary of the composer's birth. In celebration, a new project, "All Together, A Global Ode to Joy," masterminded by conductor Marin Alsop, adapted Beethoven's and Schiller's universal message to people on six continents, including texts in Zulu (Africa), in te reo Maori (New Zealand), and in a rap (in America, created by Wordsmith), among others. Thus, we see that Beethoven's music—and especially his inspiring *Ode to Joy* from Symphony No. 9—continues to transcend both temporal and cultural boundaries.

LEFT: German crowds at the fall of the Berlin Wall in November 1989. RIGHT: The emperor Napoleon in his coronation robe (c. 1804), as painted by **Baron François Simon Gerard** (1770–1837).

LISTENING GUIDE 25   🔊 31:34

Beethoven: Symphony No. 5 in C Minor, Op. 67

Date: 1807–8

Movements:
- I. Allegro con brio; sonata-allegro form, C minor
- II. Andante con moto; theme and variations (two themes), A-flat major
- III. Allegro; scherzo and trio, C minor
- IV. Allegro; sonata-allegro form, C major

Performed by: Cleveland Orchestra, George Szell, conductor

I: Allegro con brio   7:31

What to Listen For

Melody	Fiery four-note motive, the basis for thematic development; contrasting, lyrical second theme.
Rhythm/ meter	The four-note rhythmic idea (short-short-short-long) shapes the movement.
Harmony	C minor, with dramatic shifts between minor and major tonality.
Texture	Mostly homophonic.
Form	Concise sonata-allegro form, with an extended coda; repetition, sequence, and variation techniques.
Expression	Wide dynamic contrasts; forceful, energetic tempo.

Exposition

0:00   Theme 1—based on the famous four-note motive (short-short-short-long), in C minor:

0:06   Motive is expanded sequentially:

0:43   Expansion from four-note motive; horns modulate to the key of the second theme.

0:46   Theme 2—lyrical, in woodwinds, in E-flat major; heard against relentless rhythm of the four-note motive:

basic rhythm

1:07   Closing theme—rousing melody in a descending staccato passage, then the four-note motive.

1:26   Repeat of the exposition.

Development

2:54   The beginning of the development is announced by a horn call.

3:05   Manipulation of the four-note motive through a descending sequence:

continued on next page

3:16   Melodic variation, interval of a third filled in and inverted:

4:12   Expansion through repetition leads into the recapitulation; music is saturated with the four-note motive.

Recapitulation

4:18   Theme 1—explosive statement in C minor begins the recapitulation.
4:38   Brief oboe cadenza.
5:15   Theme 2—returns in C major, not in the expected key of C minor.
5:41   Closing theme.
5:58   **Coda**—extended treatment of the four-note motive; ends in C minor.

II: Andante con moto

10:01

What to Listen For

Melody	Two contrasting themes: first one is smooth; rising second theme is built on the four-note idea.	**Texture**	Mostly homophonic.
		Form	Variations, with two themes; varied rhythms, melodies, harmony (major and minor).
Rhythm/ meter	Flowing triple meter.		
Harmony	In a related key: A-flat major.	**Timbre**	Warm strings, brilliant woodwinds, powerful brass.

0:00   Theme 1—broad, flowing melody, heard in low strings:

0:52   Theme 2—upward-thrusting four-note (short-short-short-long) motive heard first in clarinets:

Brass fanfare follows.

Examples of variations on theme 1

1:57   Embellished with running 16th notes, low strings:

3:52   Embellished with faster (32nd) notes in violas and cellos.
5:04   Melody exchanged between woodwind instruments (fragments of theme 1):

6:36   Melody shifts to minor, played staccato (detached version of theme 1):

8:10   **Coda**—*Più mosso* (faster), in the bassoon.

III: Allegro, Scherzo   5:27

What to Listen For

Melody	Wide-ranging, ascending scherzo theme; more conjunct, quick trio theme.	**Form**	**A-B-A′** (scherzo-trio-scherzo); plus a link to the final movement.
Rhythm/ meter	Quick triple meter throughout; insistent focus on the four-note rhythm.	**Expression**	Wide-ranging dynamic contrasts; fast tempo.
Harmony	Dramatic C-minor scherzo; trio in C major.	**Timbre**	Themes in low strings; plucked (pizzicato) strings at the return of the scherzo; timpani in transition to the last movement.
Texture	Homophonic; some fugal treatment in the trio.		

0:00   **Scherzo theme**—a rising, rocket theme in low strings, sounds hushed and mysterious:

0:19   Rhythmic motive (from movement I) explodes in the horns, *fortissimo*:

1:59   **Trio theme**—in C major, in double basses, set fugally, played twice; contrasts with C-minor scherzo:

2:30   Trio theme is broken up and expanded through sequences.

3:29   **Scherzo** returns, with varied orchestration, including pizzicato strings.

4:46   Transition to the next movement, with timpani rhythm from the opening four-note motive:

Tension mounts, orchestra swells to the heroic opening of the fourth movement.

IV: Allegro (without pause from movement III)   8:32

What to Listen For

Melody	Triumphant theme outlining C major triad; energetic second theme.	**Form**	Sonata-allegro form, with a long coda; cyclic (return of material from earlier movements).
Rhythm/ meter	Very fast duple meter; four-note rhythmic idea.	**Expression**	Forceful dynamics; *fp* (*forte-piano*) effects; intense and spirited.
Harmony	C major; remains in major throughout.	**Performing forces**	Added instruments (piccolo, contrabassoon, trombones).
Texture	Mostly homophonic.		

---

continued on next page

Exposition

5:30 Theme 1—in C major, a powerful melody whose opening outlines a triumphant C major chord:

6:03 Lyrical transition theme in French horns, modulating from C to G major.
6:29 Theme 2—in G major, vigorous melody with rhythm from the four-note motive, in triplets:

6:55 Closing theme—featuring clarinet and violas, decisive.

Development

7:30 Much modulation and free rhythmic treatment; brings back the four-note motive (short-short-short-long) from the first movement.
9:04 Brief recurrence, like a whisper, of the scherzo.

Recapitulation

9:39 Theme 1—in C major; full orchestra, *fortissimo*.
10:43 Theme 2—in C major, played by strings.
11:10 Closing theme, played by woodwinds.
11:38 **Coda**—long extension; tension is resolved over and over again until the final, emphatic tonic.

CRITICAL THINKING

1. Why is Beethoven's music considered "transitional" to a new artistic perspective?

2. Which Romantic qualities are heard in Beethoven's Fifth Symphony? Which are Classical-era traits?

Your Turn TO EXPLORE

Find several references to Beethoven or his music (visual, literary, or sonic) in popular culture or commercial contexts. What is being said or shown or implied about the composer and his work? Can you determine how accurate or invented those claims or images might be? Why do you think those aspects of Beethoven are being highlighted? How is the mythology of Beethoven being used, and to whose advantage?

37

Making It Real:
Mozart and Classical Opera

"I like an aria to fit a singer as perfectly as a well-tailored suit of clothes."

—*Wolfgang Amadeus Mozart*

KeyPoints

- In the Classical era, two types of Italian opera prevailed: *opera seria* (serious opera) and *opera buffa* (comic opera).
- While serious opera continued a tradition of idealized characters and plots, comic opera aimed

at a more realistic depiction of human concerns and emotions.

- Mozart's *The Marriage of Figaro* combines elements of serious and comic opera in a powerful dramatic work that is performed all over the world.

Musical theater has never been, and never will be, about full-out realism: after all, people don't converse by singing. However, certain traditions of opera (just like certain traditions of film) have tried to convey realistic nuances in human interactions and emotions. And while some operas (and movies) reflect specific historical or cultural priorities (as does the 1939 film *Gone with the Wind*, for example, which draws on stereotypes that are now considered racist and romanticizes slave-owner culture), and thus may seem dated or old-fashioned to following generations, other works convey aspects of the human condition that easily cross boundaries of time and location. Mozart's comic operas fall in this latter category: more than two centuries after their premieres, they still rank high with modern producers and performers (sometimes with creative choices of staging, costumes, or casting) and always succeed with audiences. The characters are often not entirely "comic"— they are fleshed-out human beings, with contradictory emotions that shift and develop through the drama. The persuasive power of musical characterization is what makes Classical opera, especially in the hands of Mozart, truly the first "modern" tradition of musical theater.

In Their Own Words

" I should say that in opera the poetry must be the obedient daughter of music."

—*W. A. Mozart*

Classical Opera

Operas of the early eighteenth century accurately reflected the society from which they sprang. The prevalent form was *opera seria*: "serious," or tragic, Italian opera, a highly formalized genre inherited from the Baroque that consisted mainly of recitatives and arias specifically designed to display the virtuosity of star singers to the aristocracy. Its rigid conventions were shaped largely by the poet Pietro

Opera seria

Metastasio (1698–1782), whose librettos, featuring stories of royalty and heroes drawn from classical antiquity, were set again and again throughout the century.

Increasingly, however, audiences and artists moved toward a simpler style that reflected human emotions more realistically. One result was the comic opera that flourished in every country of Europe. Known in England as **ballad** (or dialogue)

Opera buffa **opera**, in Germany as *Singspiel*, in France as *opéra comique*, and in Italy as *opera buffa*, these lighter genres were initially seen merely as a less important counterpart to the more "socially elevated" serious tradition. Eventually, however, the support of a rising merchant class with an increasing disposable income helped bring the comic tradition into the limelight.

St. Michael's Square in Vienna, with the Burgtheater (center right), where Mozart's opera *The Marriage of Figaro* was first performed.

Unlike serious opera, which was almost invariably in Italian, comic opera was generally in the local language of the audience (the vernacular), although Italian *opera buffa* was popular throughout much of Europe. *Opera buffa* presented lively, down-to-earth plots rather than the remote concerns of gods and mythological heroes. It featured an exciting ensemble at the end of each act in which all the characters participated, instead of the succession of solo arias heard in the older style. And it abounded in farcical situations, humorous dialogue, and popular tunes. As the Age of Revolution approached, comic opera became an important social force whose lively wit delighted even the aristocrats it satirized. *Opera buffa* spread quickly, steadily expanding its scope until it culminated in the works of Mozart.

Mozart's *The Marriage of Figaro*

In an effort to make a good impression on his emperor, Joseph II, Mozart chose to collaborate with prominent librettist Lorenzo da Ponte, and the result was three comic operas that are beloved by audiences around the world: *Così fan tutte* (*Women Are Like That*), *Don Giovanni*, and the work we will hear, *The Marriage of Figaro* (*Le nozze di Figaro*). *Figaro* was their first effort, and it was a risky one: the play it was based on, by French author Pierre Caron de Beaumarchais (1732–1799), had been banned in Vienna because of its depiction of common people being oppressed by the nobility. But Mozart and da Ponte changed the story's emphasis from political intrigue to love hijinks, making social critique secondary to complex musical slapstick, and the production was a great success.

In the story, Figaro, servant and right-hand man to the powerful Count Almaviva, and his beloved Susanna, servant to the Countess, are about to marry; but Susanna is being harassed by the Count, a notorious womanizer. Da Ponte retained Beaumarchais's premise that the Count wishes to claim his "right of first night" with Susanna—the semi-fictional right of a nobleman to sleep with the spouse of a servant on her wedding night—but made the Count somewhat more sympathetic by having him want Susanna to fall in love with him first. In the play, Figaro's anger is directed at the wrongful power of the Count, while in the opera he's more jealous of Susanna, afraid she might really fall for the Count. The opera could thus be played with knowing laughter and socially safe references to women's betrayal of men.

The Countess in turn is jealous of the Count. And adding to the two couples' woes (which will all be resolved at the end) is the character of Cherubino, a teenage boy who falls in love with every woman he sees, and with whom both Susanna and the Countess are clearly enchanted (resulting in further jealousy from Figaro and the Count). While the play's Cherubino is a younger version of the Count and represents the sins of the nobility, in *Figaro* he is an entirely appealing figure, often at the center of the most complicated comic situations.

When we first meet Cherubino, he's in Susanna's room, singing an aria to the Countess about his lovesick state: "I don't know what I am, what I'm doing; first I seem to be burning, then freezing; every woman makes me change color" (LG 26). Mozart wrote the role (sometimes called a **trouser role**) for a mezzo-soprano who dresses as a man, to convey the character of a teenager whose voice has not yet changed. The aria is followed by recitative, the rapid-fire, talky kind of singing accompanied by simple harmonies whose main function is to advance the plot—similar to spoken dialogue in a Broadway musical.

Now the action moves quickly. The Count arrives to arrange a tryst with Susanna, and Cherubino hides behind a large armchair. The music master Basilio, who delights in uncovering other people's secrets, comes looking for the Count, who also tries to hide behind the chair. Cherubino stealthily slips onto the chair and Susanna covers him with a throw. Basilio, who knows the Count is hiding, slyly provokes him to step forward by suggesting that Cherubino is wooing the Countess. In the trio that follows ("Cosa sento!"), Susanna is anxious to get both men to leave, the Count is angry but also tries to soothe and seduce her, and the devious Basilio is enjoying himself. At one point the Count flings off the throw to reveal the sheepish boy, and the trio resumes even more intensely.

Mozart's ability to match the demands of a dramatic situation with musical forms is fully evident in this trio, which resembles sonata form in its presentation, development, and recapitulation of themes. His extraordinary skill in conveying emotional realism, in both solo and ensemble numbers, is what makes his characters so believable and compelling. In *Figaro* and other comic operas, Mozart holds a mirror up to society and points out the contradictions inherent in separating people based on class and gender. This is another reason why his operas still speak so strongly to modern audiences: they can easily be understood to contain messages about social unfairness and the rights of individuals, ideas that appeal to enlightened audiences everywhere.

"The Count discovers the Page." Detail of an illustration from Beaumarchais's comedy *Le mariage de Figaro*. The engraving (c. 1784) is after **Jacques Philippe Joseph de Saint-Quentin**.

LISTENING GUIDE 26   **10:41**

Mozart: *The Marriage of Figaro*, Act I, excerpts

Date: 1786

Genre: *Opera buffa*

Librettist: Lorenzo da Ponte

Basis: Play by Pierre Caron de Beaumarchais

Performed by: Patrizia Ciofi (soprano; Susanna), Simon Keenlyside (baritone; Count), Angelika Kirchschlager (mezzo-soprano; Cherubino), Kobie van Rensburg (tenor; Basilio); Concerto Köln; René Jacobs, conductor

continued on next page

Aria (Cherubino)

2:51

What to Listen For

Melody	A descending scale pattern (**A**) with quick rhythms then becomes more passionate and lyrical (**B**); after a repeat of the opening scale pattern, a transition leads to a more intense emotional build (**C**), which is repeated and varied with a final flourish.	**Performing forces**	Mezzo-soprano voice supported by a small orchestra—mostly strings, with horns, bassoon, and clarinets adding variety and timbral contrast.
Form	**A-B-A-C-C′** (the final **C** is abridged).	**Expression**	Breathless, intense, and almost obsessive in repetition—reflecting the whirlwind passion of a lovestruck teenager.

A—quick rhythms (in E-flat):

Non so   più co - sa son, co - sa   fac - cio,

B—more lyrical (in B-flat):

A—return (in E-flat).

So   lo ai   no - mi d'a-mor di di - let - to,

C—begins quietly, then builds and modulates:

Par - lo d'a - mor ve - glian - do.

0:00	**A**	Non so più cosa son, cosa faccio,	I don't know what I am, what I'm doing;
		or di foco, ora sono di ghiaccio,	first I seem to be burning, then freezing;
		ogni donna cangiar di colore,	every woman makes me change color,
		ogni donna mi fa palpitar.	every woman I see makes me shake.
0:17	**B**	Solo ai nomi d'amor, di diletto,	Just the words "love" and "pleasure"
		mi si turba, mi s'altera il petto,	bring confusion; my breast swells in terror,
		e a parlare mi sforza d'amore	yet I am compelled to speak of love
		un desio ch'io non posso spiegar.	by a force which I cannot explain.
0:44	**A**	Non so più cosa son . . .	I don't know what I am . . .
1:03	**C**	Parlo d'amor vegliando,	I speak of love while waking,
		parlo d'amor sognando,	I speak of love while dreaming,
		all'acqua, all'ombra, ai monti,	to the water, to shadows, to mountains,
		ai fiori, all'erbe, ai fonti,	to the flowers, the grass, and the fountains,
		all'eco, all'aria, ai venti,	to the echo, to the air, to the winds
		che il suon de'vani accenti,	which carry the idle words
		portano via con se.	away with them.
1:37	**C′**	Parlo d'amor . . .	I speak of love . . .
		E se non ho chi m'oda,	And if there is no one to listen,
		parlo d'amor con me!	I'll speak of love to myself!

(Seeing the Count in the distance, Cherubino hides behind the chair.)

Recitative (Susanna, Count, Basilio)   3:43

What to Listen For

Melody	In a rapid, syllabic style without a distinct melodic shape; focus is on the text.
Performing forces	Three characters in turn—Susanna (soprano), the Count (baritone), and Basilio (tenor)—accompanied in our performance by a reproduction of a piano from Mozart's day (fortepiano) and a cello.
Expression	Occasional pauses and slight musical emphases at key words in the story, but otherwise the musical expression is secondary to the dialogue and the action that's building between the characters.

0:00   Susanna quickly hides Cherubino behind a big armchair in her room as the Count arrives . . .

0:07   The Count starts putting his moves on Susanna; she tries to shoo him away, but he presses and insists . . .

1:17   We hear Basilio offstage; the Count hides behind the armchair; Cherubino quickly scoots to the front, and Susanna covers him with a cloth . . .

1:39   Basilio enters ("Susanna, God keep you in health. Have you by any chance seen the Count?") and begins hinting broadly about the Count's love for her (he probably knows the Count is hiding somewhere nearby) and eventually about Cherubino's love for the Countess. Susanna denies everything and tries to get him to shut up and leave, but he keeps at it ("Tell that boy not to look at the Countess like that, because everyone's saying . . .").

3:38   The Count can't take it anymore, and jumps out from behind the armchair ("*What* is everyone saying?!?"). Basilio is delighted that he's flushed him out ("oh goody"), and we go straight into the trio.

Terzetto (Trio; Count, Basilio, Susanna)   4:07

What to Listen For

Melody	The Count tends to grandiose and pompous statements, Susanna is alternatively anxious and angry, and Basilio is devious and mealy-mouthed.
Form	Through-composed, with short sections repeated, modified, and rearranged for dramatic development.
Texture	Three voices in various overlapping combinations, with both imitative and contrasting ideas; mostly polyphonic, with moments of melody-plus-accompaniment homophony.
Expression	Orchestral instruments reinforce the characters' emotional roller coaster and their almost slapstick comedic-dramatic interactions as they struggle to hide or reveal their secrets.

The Count—angry:

Basilio and the Count—comforting

Susanna, who has fainted:

continued on next page

Basilio—gossiping, to the (slowed down) tune of Cherubino's aria:

Ah, del pag - gio, quel che ho det - to, e - ra so - lo un mio so - spet - to.

Count

0:00 Cosa sento! Tosto andate,   I heard it all! Go at once,
      e scacciate il seduttor!   throw the seducer out!

Basilio

In mal punto son qui giunto;   I have come at an unfortunate moment;
perdonate, o mio signor.   forgive me, o my lord.

Susanna

Che ruina! me meschina!   What a catastrophe! I am ruined!
Son' oppressa dal dolor!   Pain grips my heart!

Count

Tosta andate, andate . . .   Go at once, go . . .

Basilio

In mal punto . . .   I have come . . .

Susanna

Che ruina!   What a catastrophe!

Basilio

. . . son qui giunto;   . . . at an unfortunate moment;

Count

. . . e scacciate il seduttor.   . . . and throw the seducer out.

Basilio

. . . perdonate, o mio signor.   . . . forgive me, o my lord.

Susanna

Me meschina!   I am ruined!
Me meschina!   I am ruined!
Son' oppressa dal dolor.   Pain grips my heart.

Basilio, Count (*supporting Susanna*)

Ah! già svien la poverina!   Ah! The poor girl's fainted!
Come, oh Dio! le batte il cor.   Oh God, how her heart is beating.

Basilio

Pian, pianin, su questo seggio—   Gently, gently onto the chair—
(taking her to the chair)

Susanna (*coming to*)

Dove sono? Cosa veggio?   Where am I? What's this I see?
Che insolenza! andate fuor.   What insolence! Leave this room.

Basilio, Count

Siamo qui per aiutarvi, . . .   We're here to help you, . . .

Basilio

. . . è sicuro il vostro onor.   . . . your virtue is safe.

Count

. . . non turbarti, o mio tesor.   . . . do not worry, sweetheart.

Basilio

Ah, del paggio, quel che ho detto,   What I was saying about the page
era solo un mio sospetto.   was only my own suspicion.

Susanna

E un'insidia, una perfidia,   It was a nasty insinuation,
non credete all'impostor.   do not believe the liar.

Count

1:54   Parta, parta il damerino, . . .   The young skirt-chaser must go, . . .

Susanna, Basilio

Poverino!   Poor boy!

Count

. . . parta, parta il damerino.   . . . the young skirt-chaser must go.

Susanna, Basilio

Poverino!   Poor boy!

Count (*sarcastically*)

Poverino! poverino!   Poor boy! Poor boy!
ma da me sorpreso ancor!   But I caught him yet again!

Susanna

Come?   How?

Basilio

Che?   What?

Susanna

Che?   What?

Basilio

Come?   How?

Susanna, Basilio

Come? che?   How? What?

Count

2:11   Da tua cugina,   At your cousin's house
l'uscio jer trovai rinchiuso,   I found the door shut yesterday.
picchio, m'apre Barbarina   I knocked and Barbarina opened it
paurosa fuor dell'uso.   much more timidly than usual.
Io, dal muso insospettito,   My suspicions aroused by her expression,
guardo, cerco in ogni sito,   I had a good look around,
ed alzando pian, pianino,   and very gently lifting
il tappeto al tavolino,   the cloth upon the table,
vedo il paggio.   I found the page.

(*Imitating his own action with the dress over the chair, he reveals the page.*)

continued on next page

Ah, cosa veggio?	Ah, what do I see?

Susanna

Ah! crude stelle!	Ah! wicked fate!

Basilio

Ah! meglio ancora!	Ah! better still!

Count

2:55 Onestissima signora, . . .	Most virtuous lady, . . .

Susanna

Accader non può di peggio.	Nothing worse could happen!

Count

. . . or capisco come va!	. . . now I see what's happening!

Susanna

Giusti Dei, che mai sarà!	Merciful heaven, whatever will happen?

Basilio

Così fan tutte . . .	They're all the same . . .

Susanna

Giusti Dei! che mai sarà	Merciful heaven! Whatever will happen?
Accader non può di peggio,	Nothing worse could happen!
ah no! ah no!	ah no! ah no!

Basilio

. . . le belle,	. . . the fair sex,
non c'è alcuna novità,	there's nothing new about it,
così fan tutte.	they're all the same.

Count

Or capisco come va,	Now I see what's happening,
onestissima signora!	most virtuous lady!
or capisco, ecc.	Now I see, etc.

Basilio

Ah, del paggio, quel che ho detto,	What I was saying about the page
era solo un mio sospetto.	was only my own suspicion.

Susanna

Accader non può di peggio, ecc.	Nothing worse could happen, etc.

Count

Onestissima signora, ecc.	Most virtuous lady, etc.

Basilio

Così fan tutte, ecc.	They're all the same, etc.

CRITICAL THINKING

1. What are the prevailing types of opera in the Classical era, and how do these differ from one another?
2. How does Mozart convey the emotions of each character? Explain how credible you find the characters.
3. In what ways does *The Marriage of Figaro* mirror issues of modern-day society?

YourTurn TO EXPLORE

The Marriage of Figaro has been produced countless times. Find productions of this opera that emphasize a particular aspect of the design, characters, or plot. (One example that you might seek out is a 1990 production by Peter Sellars, reset in New York City's Trump Tower, stressing elements of political commentary and the "decay of the upper classes.") How do the singers' vocal qualities, their interaction with each other and the orchestra, and staging choices create different dramatic nuances?

38

Mourning a Hero:
Mozart and the Requiem

"I am writing a Requiem for myself."

—W. A. Mozart? (as quoted after his death in a contemporary newspaper)

KeyPoints

- Classical composers continued the tradition of writing worship music for their communities.
- Sacred music genres of the later 1700s included the **oratorio**, **Mass**, and **Requiem Mass**.

- Mozart's *Requiem*, left unfinished at the composer's death, exemplifies the grand style of Catholic music in Vienna.

The stereotype of a great artist dying tragically young is nowhere more evident than in the popular image of Mozart, whose passing at age thirty-five was understood even by his contemporaries as a huge loss. The fact that during his final illness Mozart was working on a powerful memorial work—music to accompany a funeral Mass—has compounded the opportunity to view his last composing moments as symbolic of the tragedy of his premature death. Yet while his *Requiem* has been recognized as a deeply moving work from its first performances, it can also provide us with a cautionary tale about mythologies of genius.

From shortly after his death came accounts of a mysterious stranger knocking on Mozart's door with a commission for a Mass that the composer understood as a premonition, along with rumors of Mozart believing himself poisoned rather than diseased in his final days. But his own letters in the months preceding his death show him in a cheerful mood, and he was working on a number of other projects alongside the *Requiem* during his last few weeks. Ultimately, myths surrounding a remarkable composer's early death continue to shape our culture's notions of creative genius (think of more recent musicians who died prematurely, like Jimi Hendrix, Janis Joplin, Selena, Prince, or Notorious B.I.G.).

Sacred Music in the Classical Era

Requiem

In this era, the principal genres of sacred choral music were the Mass, the Requiem Mass, and the oratorio. A **Mass**, you will recall, is a musical setting of the most solemn service of the Roman Catholic Church; a **Requiem** is a musical setting of the Mass for the Dead. The **oratorio,** of which Handel's *Messiah* is a prime example, is generally focused on a biblical story. All these genres were originally intended to be performed in church, although by the nineteenth century they would find a much larger audience in the concert hall. We will look at the Classical sacred tradition through one of the era's most beloved masterpieces, Mozart's *Requiem*.

Mozart's *Requiem*

Mozart's last large-scale composition was quickly hailed as one of the masterpieces of the Classical era. The composer left only sketches for the later movements of this work, which were eventually completed by his favorite pupil, Franz Xaver Süssmayr. We can, however, attribute to Mozart himself the dramatic *Dies irae* ("Day of Wrath"), a vision of Judgment Day. The text for this movement, a rhymed Latin poem by a thirteenth-century friar, is designed to emphasize the terrible power of divine intervention, beginning with the words "Day of wrath, day that will dissolve the world into burning coals, as David bore witness with the Sibyl" (LG 27).

The score calls for four soloists (soprano, alto, tenor, bass) and four-part chorus, accompanied by an orchestra that includes basset horns (alto-range clarinets) and bassoons. The extended use of low wind and brass timbres was a relative novelty in the later 1700s, and its effect is stunning even today. The power of Mozart's *Dies irae* unfurls against headlong running notes and shattering accents. On the words *Quantus tremor est futurus* ("How great a tremor there will be"), the wavering lines paint the text vividly. An abrupt cadence leads to the *Tuba mirum* ("A trumpet with an astonishing sound"), featuring a memorable trombone solo and bass singer who together summon souls before the throne of God. The other soloists enter one by one: first the tenor, who sings a slower Andante on *Mors stupebit et natura* ("Death will be stunned, as will Nature"), followed by the alto and soprano, all four ending in a solo quartet.

The final chorus, *Rex tremendae majestatis!* ("King of tremendous majesty"), fiercely projects the sense of the words. Dotted rhythms and syncopated chords in the orchestra impart an overwhelming urgency, leading up to the final plea—*Salva me, fons pietatis!* ("Save me, fount of piety")—which is sung softly.

A relative recounted that on December 4, 1791, as the composer lay feverishly weak on his bed, several professional singers sang through the completed portions of the *Requiem* with Mozart on the alto line. At the *Lacrimosa* ("Weeping") verse, he put the music aside and wept—and then he died that same night. It is likely that stories like this one were embellished by those who wanted to highlight the almost supernatural expressive palette of the work, and to raise Mozart's reputation to an even more remarkable level after his death.

And remarkable it is. Over the centuries since its composition, the expressive power of the *Requiem* has been widely recognized by audiences from many cultures. This moving work was chosen for the funeral of President John F. Kennedy, who was assassinated in 1963; and in 2002, on the one-year anniversary of the September 11 attack on the World Trade Center in New York, a rolling performance of Mozart's *Requiem* was given in all corners of the globe (in Europe, Asia, Central America, and the United States), each beginning at 8:46 a.m., the time of the first attack. Mozart could never have imagined how much his work would ultimately mean to the world.

Nineteenth-century portrait of Mozart composing his *Requiem* on his deathbed, by **William James Grant** (1829–1866).

St. Stephen's Cathedral in Vienna, where Mozart was offered the post of Kapellmeister shortly before he died.

CRITICAL THINKING

1. How does Mozart use various vocal and instrumental textures and timbres to convey the changing emotions of the "Day of Judgment" prayer?
2. What similarities and differences are there between this sacred choral work and the two Baroque sacred works we've considered (Bach's cantata and Handel's oratorio)?

Your Turn TO EXPLORE

Find examples of music designed to pay tribute to or memorialize tragic events (for example the 9/11 terrorist attacks, the AIDS epidemic, war or natural disasters). Is the music meant to soothe pain or rekindle grief, or for yet other purposes—and how do the composers make musical choices to achieve those purposes?

LISTENING GUIDE 27   🔊 6:29

Mozart: *Dies irae*, from *Requiem*

Date: 1791

Genre: Requiem Mass

Performed by: Boston Baroque, Martin Pearlman, conductor

What to Listen For

Melody	Dramatic choral opening, then operatic solo verses; final verse has choral outcry.	**Expression**	Mood shifts from fear (loud, accented) to wonderment to a quiet plea for salvation.
Rhythm/ meter	Forceful, accented duple meter; closing has strong dotted-rhythmic idea.	**Performing forces**	Chorus, solo voices, and orchestra; choral opening and closing; verses 3–7 focus on solo voices.
Harmony	Alternation between minor (opening and closing) and major; some harsh combinations.	**Timbre**	Trumpets and timpani prominent; bass voice and trombone duet in verse 3.
Texture	Largely homophonic.	**Text**	Rhymed Latin poem with eight three-line verses; clear text declamation with some word-painting.
Form	Set in eight verses, each treated with different performing forces.		

VERSE	TEXT	TRANSLATION	DESCRIPTION
0:00 **1.**	Dies irae, dies illa Solvet saeclum in favilla: Teste David cum Sibylla.	Day of wrath, day that will dissolve the world into burning coals, as David bore witness with the Sibyl.	Full chorus and orchestra; dramatic homophonic setting; clear text declamation.
0:13 **2.**	Quantus tremor est futurus, Quando judex est venturus, Cuncta stricte discussurus!	How great a tremor there will be, when the judge is to come briskly shattering every [grave].	Chorus and orchestra; more polyphonic texture. Verses 1 and 2 repeated.
1:47 **3.**	Tuba mirum spargens sonum Per sepulchra regionum, Coget omnes ante thronum.	A trumpet with an astonishing sound through the tombs of the region drives all [men] before the throne.	Trombone solo, echoed by bass solo; trombone continues with countermelody; homophonic orchestral accompaniment.

2:36	**4.**	Mors stupebit et natura, Cum resurget creatura, Iudicanti responsura.	Death will be stunned, as will Nature, when arises [man] the creature responding to the One judging.	Tenor solo, with homophonic orchestral accompaniment.
2:51	**5.**	Liber scriptus proferetur, In quo totum continetur, Unde mundus judicetur.	The written book will be brought forth, in which the whole [record of evidence] is contained whence the world is to be judged.	Tenor solo continues.
3:15	**6.**	Iudex ergo cum sedebit, Quidquid latet apparebit, Nil inultum remanebit.	Therefore when the Judge shall sit, whatever lay hidden will appear; nothing unavenged will remain.	Alto solo with orchestra.
3:30	**7.**	Quid sum miser tunc dicturus? Quem patronum rogaturus? Cum vix justus sit securus?	What am I the wretch then to say? what patron I to beseech? when scarcely the just [man] will be secure.	Soprano solo with orchestra. Last line repeated by all soloists.
4:37	**8.**	Rex tremendae majestatis! Qui salvandos salvas gratis! Salve me, fons pietatis!	King of tremendous majesty, who saves those to be saved, save me, fount of piety!	Dramatic full chorus setting.

Verse 1 opening; full chorus with clearly declaimed text:

Verse 3 duet, with trombone and bass solo:

Music in Words

Reviewing Eighteenth-Century Classical Style

You have now heard examples of instrumental and vocal Classical-era genres that will provide a frame of reference for other eighteenth-century music you may encounter. Here are some suggestions for things to listen for when you have the opportunity to hear an unfamiliar work from the Classical period.

MELODY: Consider whether the melodic lines are made up of short, regular ideas or long, asymmetrical phrases. Melodies can be built on diatonic or chromatic scales. Which do you hear in this work? What expressive elements do you hear in the melodic lines?

RHYTHM/METER: Classical-era instrumental music often features regular rhythms and meters. How does this work progress in time? What meter do you perceive?

HARMONY: By now, major-minor tonality is firmly established. Do you perceive the harmony in this selection as primarily major (built on a major scale) or minor (darker sounding, built on a minor scale)?

Is the work largely consonant (based on agreeable-sounding combinations of notes) or dissonant (based on unstable notes in need of resolution)? Listen for moments that are more dissonant and unstable: what expressive purpose might they serve?

TEXTURE How do the various instruments work together? Is the texture more vertical (homophonic) or linear, with independent lines (polyphonic)? Does the texture change as the work progresses?

FORM: Larger works can feature the basic formal principles of repetition, contrast, and variation. What is the role of repetition in the work? of contrast (that is, new music)? of variation? What holds the piece together?

PERFORMING FORCES: Which instruments perform this work? Does one instrument dominate, or does the focus shift from one instrument to another? Describe the roles of the various instruments.

Listen and Respond

Let's see how you well you can apply what you have learned to a new musical example. Be sure to consult the listening suggestions above and also the style summary chart opposite. Compare this new work with the chamber music and symphony movements we heard.

Mozart: Symphony No. 40 in G Minor, III

1. Create a simple listening outline for the piece. Think about melody, rhythm and meter, harmony, texture, performing forces, and form. How is the piece organized? Are there major repeated sections?

2. How might you describe this work to a friend who is not in the class and not familiar with the terminology we've been developing? What general descriptions can you apply to the melody? rhythm and meter? harmony? texture? overall effect of the piece?

3. Now write a short paragraph describing the movement as you might for a concert report assignment. Here you can demonstrate your understanding of the terms and concepts you have learned as well as your response to the work's expressive qualities. Refer back to Chapter 14 for ways to frame your perspective on the movement.

Style Summary for Classical-Era Music (c. 1750–1825)

Composers	Haydn, Mozart, Beethoven
Melody	Lyrical melody in balanced, symmetrical phrases and with regular cadences; diatonic, with few wide leaps
Rhythm/meter	Clear rhythmically, with regularly recurring accents; dance rhythms favored
Harmony	Diatonic harmony favored; tonic-dominant relationships expanded, become the basis for large-scale forms
Texture	Homophonic textures; chordal-vertical perspective
Vocal genres	Opera, Mass, Requiem Mass, oratorio
Instrumental genres	Symphony, concerto, solo sonata, string quartet, other chamber-music genres
Form	Ternary forms predominant; sonata-allegro form developed; absolute forms preferred
Dynamics	Continuously changing dynamics through *crescendo* and *decrescendo*
Timbre	Changing tone colors between sections of works
Performing forces	String orchestra, with woodwinds and some brass and timpani; thirty-to-forty-member orchestra; piano becomes prominent
Virtuosity	Improvisation largely limited to cadenzas in concertos
Expression	Emotional balance and restraint

The Nineteenth Century

"Music can express everything. For describing scenes of nature it has ideal colors and lines, neither exact nor yet too minute, but which are all the more vaguely and delightfully poetical."

—French novelist Aurore Dupin, Baroness Dudevant, best known by her pen name, George Sand (1804–1876)

OVERVIEW

1803
Louisiana Purchase

1813
Jane Austen's *Pride and Prejudice* published.

1815
Napoleon defeated at Waterloo.

1845
Annexation of Texas into the US.

1810   1820   1830   1840   1850

1815
Franz Schubert writes *Elf-King* in Vienna.

1838
Frédéric Chopin composes his Op. 40 Polonaises.

1840
Adolphe Sax develops the saxophone.

1841
Fanny Hensel begins composing *The Year* while in Italy.

1851
Premiere of Giuseppe Verdi's *Rigoletto* in Veni...

Learning Objectives

By the end of Part 5, you will be able to

- distinguish the era's wide-ranging melodies, which often feature chromatic inflections, moving with variety and flexibility of rhythm.

- recognize increasingly chromatic harmonies and expanded concepts of tonality as well as changing textures within a composition.

- identify large-scale forms that are built around one or two main themes, and are often programmatic, with literary or pictorial associations.

- distinguish new instruments added to the orchestra, which provide more variety in tone colors and dynamic possibilities.

- identify some of the main vocal and instrumental genres, as well as some of the most influential composers, of the Romantic era.

1859
Charles Darwin's *Origin of Species* published.

1861
American Civil War begins.

1862
Victor Hugo's *Les misérables* published.

1877
Thomas Edison invents the cylinder phonograph.

1860   1870   1880   1890   1900

1854
Stephen Foster's *Jeanie with the Light Brown Hair* published in New York.

1870
First performance of Richard Wagner's *Die Walküre* in Munich.

1883
Johannes Brahms's Symphony No. 3 has its premiere in Vienna.

1875
Edvard Grieg writes incidental music for Ibsen's play *Peer Gynt*.

1899
Scott Joplin's *Maple Leaf Rag* registered for copyright.

5

Music as Passion and Individualism

"Music, of all the liberal arts, has the greatest influence over the passions."

—Napoleon Bonaparte (1769–1821)

If the time frame of Classicism is hard to pin down, Romanticism is one of the artistic trends for which beginnings can be most readily identified, since it was a self-conscious break from the ideals of the Enlightenment. The artistic movement really comes into its own through music in the early decades of the 1800s. Indeed, it is a musician—Ludwig van Beethoven—who is often identified as the first great creative Romantic, and whose influence looms to the present day as an embodiment of passionate individual expression. Many of the common tenets of Romanticism are still very much with us: the artist struggling against rather than working within society and convention; the need for art to unsettle rather than soothe; the belief that works display their creator's distinctive originality and self-expression.

The spirit of the French Revolution is captured in *Liberty Leading the People,* by **Eugène Delacroix** (1798–1863).

An Age of Revolutions

The Romantic era grew out of the social and political upheavals that followed the French Revolution in the last decade of the 1700s. The revolution signaled the transfer of power from a hereditary landholding aristocracy to the middle class. This change, firmly rooted in urban commerce and industry, emerged from the Industrial Revolution, which brought millions of people from the country into the cities. The new society, based on free enterprise, celebrated the individual as never before. The slogan of the French Revolution—"Liberty, Equality, Fraternity"—inspired hopes and visions to which artists responded with zeal. Sympathy for the oppressed; interest in peasants, workers, and children; and faith in humankind and its destiny all formed part of the increasingly democratic character of the Romantic period, and inspired a series of revolutions and rebellions that gradually led to the modern political landscape of Europe.

Romantic Writers and Artists

Romantic poets and artists rebelled against the conventional concerns of their Classical predecessors and were drawn instead to the fanciful, the picturesque, and the passionate. These men and women emphasized intense emotional expression and were highly aware of themselves as individuals apart from all others. "I am different from all the men I have seen," proclaimed philosopher Jean-Jacques Rousseau. "If I am not better, at least I am different." In Germany, a group of young writers created a new kind of lyric poetry that culminated in the art of Heinrich Heine, who became a favorite poet of Romantic composers. A similar movement in France was led by Victor Hugo, the country's greatest prose writer. In England, the revolt against the formalism of the Classical age produced an outpouring of emotional lyric poetry that reached its peak in the works of Lord Byron, Percy Shelley, and John Keats.

The French conquest of Algeria, in northern Africa, inspired **Eugène Delacroix** to paint an exotic harem: *The Women of Algiers* (1834).

The newly won freedom of the artist proved to be a mixed blessing. Confronted by a world indifferent to artistic and cultural values, artists felt more and more cut off from society. A new type emerged: the bohemian, a rejected dreamer who starved in an attic and shocked the establishment through peculiar dress and behavior. Eternal longing, regret for the lost happiness of childhood, an indefinable discontent that gnawed at the soul—these were the ingredients of the Romantic mood. Yet the artist's pessimism was based in reality. It became apparent that the high hopes fostered by the French Revolution were not to be realized overnight. Despite the brave slogans, all people were not yet equal or free. The short-lived optimism gave way to doubt and disenchantment, a state of mind that was reflected in the arts and in literature.

The nineteenth-century novel found one of its great themes in the conflict between the individual and society. Hugo dedicated *Les misérables* "to the unhappy ones of the earth." His novel's hero, Jean Valjean, is among the era's memorable discontented (well known from the 1985 musical and 2012 film of the same name). Some writers sought escape by glamorizing the past, as Walter Scott did in *Ivanhoe* and Alexandre Dumas *père* in *The Three Musketeers*. A longing for far-off lands inspired the exotic scenes that glow on the canvases of Jean-Auguste Dominique Ingres and Eugène Delacroix. The Romantic world was one of "strangeness and wonder": the eerie landscape we meet in Samuel Taylor Coleridge's poem *Kubla Khan*, the isolation we feel in Nathaniel Hawthorne's novel *The Scarlet Letter*, and the supernatural atmosphere we encounter in Edgar Allan Poe's poem *The Raven*.

Sympathy for the oppressed underscored the dramatic character of the Romantic movement. **Honoré Daumier** (1808–1879), *The Burden*.

Romanticism in Music

The Industrial Revolution brought with it the means to create more affordable and responsive musical instruments, as well as the technical improvements that strongly influenced the sound of Romantic music (see Interface, p. 267).

The rallying cry of the French people, as depicted in a 1993 performance in Madrid of the stirring musical *Les misérables*. The show is adapted from Victor Hugo's 1862 novel of the same name.

In Their Own Words

“ Our sweetest songs are those that tell of saddest thoughts.”

—*Percy Bysshe Shelley*

An engraving for Edgar Allan Poe's *The Raven* (1845), published in a poetry collection illustrated by **Charles Joseph Staniland** (1838–1916).

As music moved from palace and church to the public concert hall, orchestras increased in size. Naturally, this directly influenced the sound. New instruments such as the piccolo, English horn, tuba, and contrabassoon added varied timbres and extended the high and low ranges of the orchestra (see table opposite). The dynamic range also expanded—sweeping contrasts of very loud (*fff*) and very soft (*ppp*) lent new drama to the music of the Romantics. And as orchestral music developed, so did the technique of writing for instruments. **Orchestration** became an art in itself. Composers now had a palette as broad as those of painters, and they used it to create mood and atmosphere and to evoke profound emotional responses. With all these developments, it was no longer feasible to direct an orchestra from the keyboard or the first violin desk, as had been the tradition in the eighteenth century, and thus a central figure—the conductor—was needed to guide the performance.

In order to communicate their intentions as precisely as possible, composers developed a vocabulary of highly expressive terms. Among the directions frequently encountered in nineteenth-century scores are *dolce* (sweet), *cantabile* (songful), *dolente* (sorrowful), *maestoso* (majestic), *gioioso* (joyous), and *con amore* (with love, tenderly). A new interest in folklore and a rising tide of nationalism inspired composers to make increased use of the folk songs and dances from their native lands. As a result, a number of national styles—Hungarian, Polish, Russian, Bohemian, Scandinavian, and eventually American—flourished, greatly enriching the melodic, harmonic, and rhythmic language of music.

The exotic attracted composers as well as artists and writers. Russian, German, and French composers turned for inspiration to the warmth and color of Italy and Spain and to the glamour of Asia and the Far East. French and Italian opera composers also drew on exotic themes, notably Giuseppe Verdi in *Aida*, set in Egypt; and Giacomo Puccini in the Japanese-inspired *Madame Butterfly* (Chapter 50).

Romantic Style Traits

Above all, nineteenth-century musicians tried to make their instruments "sing." Melody was marked by a lyricism that gave it an immediate appeal, and it is no accident that themes from Romantic symphonies and concertos have been transformed

The Romantic Orchestra

Berlioz's Orchestra (*Symphonie fantastique*, 1830)	Brahms's Orchestra (Symphony No. 3, 1883)	Tchaikovsky's Orchestra (*The Nutcracker*, 1892)
STRINGS	**STRINGS**	**STRINGS**
Violins 1	Violins 1	Violins 1
Violins 2	Violins 2	Violins 2
Violas	Violas	Violas
Cellos	Cellos	Cellos
Double basses	Double basses	Double basses
2 harps		2 harps
WOODWINDS	**WOODWINDS**	**WOODWINDS**
2 flutes (1 on piccolo)	2 flutes	2 flutes and piccolo
2 oboes	2 oboes	2 oboes, 1 English horn
2 clarinets (1 on E-flat clarinet)	2 clarinets	2 clarinets, bass clarinet
English horn	2 bassoons, contrabassoon	2 bassoons
4 bassoons		
BRASS	**BRASS**	**BRASS**
4 French horns	4 French horns	4 French horns
2 cornets, 2 trumpets	2 trumpets	2 trumpets
3 trombones (1 bass trombone)	3 trombones	2 trombones, bass trombone
2 ophicleides		Tuba
PERCUSSION	**PERCUSSION**	**PERCUSSION**
Timpani	Timpani	Timpani
Cymbals		Cymbals, gong, triangle
Snare drum		Tambourine, castanets
Bass drum		Bass drum
Tubular bells (chimes)		Tubular bells (chimes)
		Keyboard
		Celesta
		Other special effects (including toy instruments)

into popular songs, and that tunes by composers such as Frédéric Chopin, Verdi, and Peter Ilyich Tchaikovsky have enjoyed an enduring popularity with the public.

Composers employed combinations of pitches that were more chromatic and dissonant than those of their predecessors, allowing for emotionally charged and highly expressive harmony. They expanded the instrumental forms they had inherited from the Classical masters to give their ideas more time to play out. A symphony by Haydn or Mozart takes about twenty minutes to perform; one by Johannes Brahms lasts at least twice that long. Where Haydn wrote more than a hundred symphonies and Mozart more than forty, Franz Schubert (following the example of Beethoven) wrote nine, and Brahms four.

Romantic harmony and form

New orchestral forms emerged as well, including the one-movement symphonic poem, the choral symphony, and works for solo voice with orchestra. In many of these works, we can see how music in the nineteenth century drew steadily closer to the other arts. Even in their purely orchestral music, Romantic composers

This watercolor (English School, nineteenth century) shows the Royal Pavilion at Brighton, England, with its Islamic domes and minarets reflecting the nineteenth-century fascination with Eastern culture. Designed by **John Nash** (1752–1835).

captured with remarkable vividness the emotional atmosphere that surrounded poetry and painting.

Nineteenth-century music was linked to dreams and passions—to profound meditations on life and death, human destiny, God and nature, pride in one's country, desire for freedom, the political struggles of the age, and the ultimate triumph of good over evil. These intellectual and emotional associations brought music into a commanding position as a link between the artist's most personal thoughts and the realities of the outside world.

Performance Matters

THE MUSICIAN IN SOCIETY

Virtuoso violinist Niccolò Paganini, painted in 1832 by **Eugène Delacroix**.

The newly democratic societies liberated composers and performers. Musical life now reached the general populace, since performances took place in the public concert hall as well as in the salons of the aristocracy. Where eighteenth-century musicians had belonged to a glorified servant class and relied on aristocratic patronage and the favor of royal courts, nineteenth-century musicians, supported by the new middle class, met their audience as equals; they could make a living in their profession. Indeed, as solo performers began to dominate the concert hall, whether as pianists, violinists (Niccolò Paganini, at left), or conductors (Franz Liszt, both pianist *and* conductor; see opposite), they became "stars" who were idolized by the public.

Although composition remained largely a man's province, a few women broke away from tradition and overcame social stereotypes to become successful composers. Among them are Clara Wieck Schumann, a talented performer and composer of piano, vocal, and chamber music, and Fanny Mendelssohn Hensel, known for her songs and piano music and also for the salon concerts she hosted in her home (see Chapter 42). We will see too that women exerted significant influence as patrons of music or through their friendships with composers. Novelist George Sand played a key role in Chopin's career (see Chapter 41), as did Princess Carolyne Sayn-Wittgenstein in Liszt's. Nedezhda von Meck is remembered as the mysterious woman who supported Tchaikovsky in the early years of his career and made it financially possible for him to compose (see Chapter 49). These activities highlight the crucial, but largely private, contributions of women to music in this era.

With the creation of a lucrative musical market for both the home and the concert hall, debates arose about the relationship between art and commerce. While some composers (such as songwriter Stephen Foster, Chapter 40) were exploited by the growing publishing industry, others (such as opera composer Giuseppe Verdi, Chapter 46) were savvy businessmen and helped to establish economic models that benefit musicians to this day.

The Hungarian pianist and composer Franz Liszt conducting one of his oratorios in Budapest.

In the later 1800s, distinctions widened between "light music" for entertainment and "art music" for serious listening, a separation that gradually led to categories of "popular" and "classical" music in the century to come. So paradoxically, while access to music became much more democratic, there arose a distinction between "highbrow" and "lowbrow" in musical repertories. But this only happened later in the century: the early and middle Romantic period was a time of expansion for all aspects of music, and musicians became more important to the imagination of society than they had ever been before.

CRITICAL THINKING

1. What are the principal ideas of Romanticism? How are these reflected in art and literature?
2. How did changing roles of musicians in society affect the development of Romantic music?

A Paris salon concert, from the series *Soirées parisiennes,* by **Henri de Montaut** (1825–1890?).

39

Musical Reading: Schubert, Schumann, and the Early Romantic Lied

"Out of my great sorrows I make my little songs." —Heinrich Heine

KeyPoints

- Typical Romantic song structures include **strophic** and **through-composed** forms; some songs fall between the two, into a **modified strophic** form.

- The German **art song**, or **Lied**—for solo voice and piano—was a favored Romantic genre. Composers also wrote **song cycles** that unified a group of songs by poems or theme.

- The poetry of the Lied projects themes of love and nature; favored poets were Johann Wolfgang von Goethe and Heinrich Heine.

- Franz Schubert wrote more than 600 Lieder and two masterful song cycles. *Elf-King* (*Erlkönig*), a through-composed Lied based on a Danish legend related in a dramatic poem by Goethe, is one of his most famous songs.

- Robert Schumann wrote over 200 Lieder, many inspired by his fiancée, pianist and composer Clara Wieck. These include *A Poet's Love* (*Dichterliebe*), a song cycle set to the poetry of Heine.

The immense appeal of the Romantic art song was due in part to the increased popularity and availability of the piano. A lithograph by **Achille Devéria** (1800–1857), *In the Salon.*

If a song is meaningful to us, we may have a tendency to identify the words as carrying that meaning. But those words are sung, not spoken, and if someone were to read them, we would likely not find the effect nearly as compelling. This is the power and paradox of song: it may be easy to focus on the text, yet the music carries the subtle intensity. Some songs rely on simple musical elements, highlighting the predominance of the voice; others employ greater complexity of melody, texture, and timbre, providing multiple resources for the expression of emotion. Within the music you listen to on a regular basis, you can probably identify a wide range of approaches to the interaction between text and music. Becoming aware of these different approaches will increase your understanding of the expressive potential of song.

The Lied

Though songs have existed throughout the ages, the **art song** as we know it today was a product of the Romantic era. The **Lied** (plural, **Lieder**), as the new genre was called, is a German-texted solo song, generally with piano accompaniment. Prominent composers in this tradition were Franz Schubert, Robert Schumann, and Johannes Brahms, as well as Fanny Mendelssohn Hensel and Clara Wieck Schumann.

In some repertories, the words for a song are newly written; in others, composers choose preexisting poetry for their musical settings. Composers of the Lied were especially dedicated to the latter option, often releasing "competing" musical settings from the outpouring of poetry that marked German Romanticism. Johann Wolfgang von Goethe (1749–1832) and Heinrich Heine (1797–1856) were the two leading figures among a group of poets who, like Wordsworth, Byron, Shelley, and Keats in England, favored short, personal, "lyric" poems. Overall, Romantic poems range from tender sentiment to dramatic balladry; common themes are love, longing, and the beauty of nature. Some composers, like Schubert and Schumann, wrote groups of Lieder that were unified by a narrative thread or descriptive theme, known as **song cycles**.

Schubert (walking at left) on an outing in the Austrian countryside with his friends (known as Schubertians), painted by one of them (also at left), **Leopold Kupelwieser** (1796–1862).

Another circumstance that made the art song popular was the emergence of the piano as the preferred household instrument of the nineteenth century. Voice and piano together infused the short lyric form with feeling and made it suitable for amateurs and artists alike, in both the home and the concert hall.

Types of Song Structure

In the nineteenth century, two main song structures prevailed. One was **strophic** form, in which the same melody is repeated with every stanza, or strophe, of the poem; hymns, carols, and most folk and popular songs are strophic. This form sets up a general atmosphere that accommodates all the stanzas, all sung to the same tune.

The other song type, **through-composed**, proceeds from beginning to end without repetitions of whole sections. Here the music follows the story line, changing according to the text. This makes it possible for the composer to mirror every shade of meaning in the words.

There is also an intermediate type that combines features of the other two. The same melody may be repeated for two or three stanzas, with new material introduced when the poem requires it. This is considered a **modified strophic** form, similar to what we heard in the lovely first movement of Beethoven's *Moonlight* Sonata.

In Their Own Words

" [With a good poem] you immediately get a good idea; melodies pour in so that it is a real joy. With a bad poem you can't get anywhere; you torment yourself over it, and nothing comes of it but boring rubbish."

—*Franz Schubert*

Schubert and the Lied

Franz Schubert was a young songwriting prodigy who composed more than six hundred Lieder in his short life. Although some of his songs (like *Elf-King*, examined below) were performed in concert settings, most of his career was built on intimate musical performances in friends' and sponsors' homes, for which Schubert would write not only Lieder but also dances and chamber works. His gift for melodic writing and the subtle interactions he created between vocal part and accompaniment have made his Lieder a staple of the art-song repertory for both amateurs and professionals to the present day.

Franz Schubert (1797–1828)

Schubert was born in Vienna and educated at the Imperial Chapel, where he sang in the choir that later became the famous Vienna Boys' Choir. Although his father hoped he would pursue a career in teaching, Schubert fell in with a small group of writers, artists, and fellow musicians who organized a series of concerts, called Schubertiads, where the young composer's newest works could be heard. One of his friends claimed that "everything he touched turned to song."

He wrote *Elf-King*, along with many other great songs, when he was still a teenager (see Many Voices: Folk Song, Popular Song, Art Song, p. 250). This work won him swift public recognition; still, he had difficulty finding a publisher for his instrumental works, and he was often pressed for money, selling his music for much less than it was worth. His later works, including the song cycle *Winter's Journey*, sound a somber lyricism that parallels his struggle with life, made worse by being afflicted with syphilis. Schubert's dying wish, at age thirty-one, was to be buried near the master he worshipped—Beethoven; his wish was granted.

Schubert's music marks the confluence of the Classical and Romantic eras. His symphonies and chamber music are Classical in their clear forms. In his songs, though, he was wholly the Romantic, writing beautiful melodies that match the tone of the poetry he set. To his earlier masterpieces he added, in the final year of his life, a group of profound works that includes the String Quintet in C Major, three piano sonatas, and thirteen of his finest songs.

MAJOR WORKS: More than 600 Lieder, including *Erlkönig* (*Elf-King*, 1815), *Die Forelle* (*The Trout*, 1817), and the song cycles *Die schöne Müllerin* (*The Lovely Maid of the Mill*, 1823) and *Winterreise* (*Winter's Journey*, 1827) • Nine symphonies, including the *Unfinished* (No. 8, 1822) • Chamber music, including quintets, string quartets, piano trios • Piano sonatas • Seven Masses • Other choral music • Operas and incidental music.

Elf-King (Erlkönig)

This masterpiece of Schubert's youth (LG 28) captures the Romantic "strangeness and wonder" of the poem, a celebrated ballad by Goethe, in which a father and his sick child are riding through a forest on a windy night. *Elf-King* is based on a legend that whoever is touched by the king of the elves must die.

The eerie atmosphere of the poem is first established by the piano. Galloping triplets are heard against a rumbling figure in the bass. This motive, perhaps suggesting a horse's pounding hooves (or maybe a child's fast heartbeat?), pervades the song, helping to unify it. The poem's four characters—the narrator, father, child, and seductive elf—are all sung by one soloist but vividly differentiated through changes in the melody, register, harmony, rhythm, and accompaniment.

The legend of *The Elf-King* (c. 1860), as portrayed by **Moritz von Schwind** (1804–1871), a good friend of Schubert's.

The child's terror is suggested by clashing dissonance and a high vocal range. The father calms his son's fears with a more rounded vocal line, sung in a low register. And the Elf-King cajoles the child in suavely melodious phrases set in a major key.

The song is through-composed; Schubert chose to avoid stanza-based repetition, instead changing the accompaniment for each stanza of Goethe's poem, shaping his music to follow the action of the story with a steady rise in tension—and pitch—that builds almost to the end. The work of an eighteen-year-old, *Elf-King* was a milestone in the history of musical Romanticism: Schubert chose it as his first work to be published (though he had written many other songs), and it quickly became one of the most popular songs of the nineteenth century.

LISTENING GUIDE 28   4:00

Schubert: *Elf-King (Erlkönig)*

Date: 1815
Genre: Lied

Performed by: Thomas Quasthoff, baritone;
Charles Spencer, piano

What to Listen For

Melody	Wide-ranging; each character sings in a different range.
	   Narrator: middle register, minor key.
	   Father: low register, minor key.
	   Son: high register, minor key.
	   Elf-King: middle register, major key.

Rhythm/ meter	Almost constant triplets in the piano; duple meter; more lilting feel for Elf-King.
Harmony	Shifts from minor to major (for Elf-King); dissonance projects the boy's terror.
Form	Through-composed.
Expression	Fast, with a mood of urgency in the accompaniment and dramatic dialogue.
Performing forces	Solo voice and piano.
Text	Narrative poem in eight stanzas by Johann Wolfgang von Goethe.

0:00   Piano introduction—minor key and rapid repeated octaves in triplets set the mood, simulating horse's hooves:

TEXT   TRANSLATION

Narrator (minor key, middle range)

0:23   Wer reitet so spät durch Nacht und Wind?   Who rides so late through night and wind?
       Es ist der Vater mit seinem Kind;   It is the father with his child;
       Er hat den Knaben wohl in dem Arm,   he has the boy close in his arm,
       Er fasst ihn sicher, er hält ihn warm.   he holds him safely, he keeps him warm.

Father (low range)

       "Mein Sohn, was birgst du so bang dein Gesicht?"   "My son, why do you hide your face in fear?"

Son (high range)

       "Siehst, Vater, du den Erlkönig nicht?   "Father, don't you see the Elf-King?
       Den Erlenkönig mit Kron' und Schweif?"   The Elf-King with his crown and train?"

Father (low range)

       "Mein Sohn, es ist ein Nebelstreif."   "My son, it is a streak of mist."

Elf-King (major key, melodic)

1:29   "Du liebes Kind, komm, geh mit mir!   "You dear child, come with me!
       Gar schöne Spiele spiel' ich mit dir;   I'll play very lovely games with you.
       Manch' bunte Blumen sind an dem Strand;   There are lots of colorful flowers by the shore;
       Meine Mutter hat manch' gülden Gewand."   my mother has some golden robes."

Son (high range, frightened)

1:51   "Mein Vater, mein Vater, und hörest du nicht,   "My father, my father, don't you hear
       Was Erlenkönig mir leise verspricht?"   the Elf-King whispering promises to me?"

continued on next page

Father (low range, calming)

"Sei ruhig, bleibe ruhig, mein Kind;   "Be still, stay calm, my child;
In dürren Blättern säuselt der Wind."   it's the wind rustling in the dry leaves."

Elf-King (major key, cajoling)

2:13   "Willst, feiner Knabe, du mit mir geh'n?   "My fine lad, do you want to come with me?
Meine Töchter sollen dich warten schön;   My daughters will take care of you;
Meine Töchter führen den nächtlichen Reih'n   my daughters lead the nightly dance,
Und wiegen und tanzen und singen dich ein."   and they'll rock and dance and sing you to sleep."

Son (high range, dissonant outcry)

2:31   "Mein Vater, mein Vater, und siehst du nicht dort,   "My father, my father, don't you see
Erlkönigs Töchter am düstern Ort?"   the Elf-King's daughters over there in the shadows?"

Father (low range, reassuring)

"Mein Sohn, mein Sohn, ich seh' es genau,   "My son, my son, I see it clearly,
Es scheinen die alten Weiden so grau."   it's the gray sheen of the old willows."

Elf-King (loving, then insistent)

3:00   "Ich liebe dich, mich reizt deine schöne Gestalt,   "I love you, your beautiful form delights me!
Und bist du nicht willig, so brauch' ich Gewalt."   And if you're not willing, then I'll use force."

Son (high range, terrified)

3:12   "Mein Vater, mein Vater, jetzt fasst er mich an!   "My father, my father, now he's touching me!
Erlkönig hat mir ein Leids gethan!"   The Elf-King has done me harm!"

Narrator (middle register, speechlike)

3:26   Dem Vater grausets, er reitet geschwind,   The father shudders, he rides swiftly,
Er hält in Armen das ächzende Kind,   he holds the moaning child in his arms;
Erreicht den Hof mit Müh und Noth: with effort and urgency he reaches the courtyard:
In seinen Armen das Kind war todt.   in his arms the child was dead.

Melody of son's dissonant outcry on
"My father, my father":

AnotherHearing   You just heard a performance of the original Schubert score by a male singer, Thomas Quasthoff, accompanied by piano. Now compare that recording with the song as arranged and performed by the renowned a cappella group The Swingle Singers. How does the vocal ensemble create the character contrasts between the narrator, the child, the Elf-King, and the father? In what ways is this different from the characterizations in the Quasthoff performance? What other differences do you note between the recordings? Which do you prefer, and why?

In Their Own Words

❝ The singing voice is hardly sufficient in itself; it cannot carry the whole task of interpretation unaided. . . . the finer shadings of the poem must be represented as well—provided that the melody does not suffer in the process."

—*Robert Schumann*

Schumann and the Song Cycle

"Music is to me the perfect expression of the soul."

The turbulence of early German Romanticism, its fantasy and subjective emotion, found its voice in Robert Schumann. Like Schubert, Schumann showed his lyric gifts in his songs, many of which appear in unified song cycles with texts from a single poet.

A Poet's Love (Dichterliebe)

Schumann wrote his great cycle *A Poet's Love*, sixteen songs to poems by Heinrich Heine, in 1840. Though the texts come from the same poetry collection, they tell

Robert Schumann (1810–1856)

Schumann was born in Zwickau, Germany, and studied law at the University of Leipzig and at Heidelberg. But he soon surrendered to his passion for music—it was his ambition to become a pianist and to study with Friedrich Wieck, one of the foremost teachers of his day. When an injury to his right hand dashed his dream of being a pianist, Schumann turned his efforts to composition. While still in his twenties, he created many of his most important piano works. Meanwhile, his literary talent found expression through a publication he established, *Neue Zeitschrift für Musik* (*The New Journal of Music*); this soon became the leading journal of music criticism in Europe.

Throughout the 1830s, Robert carried on an intense courtship with the gifted pianist and composer Clara Wieck, daughter of his former teacher. Friedrich, who viewed his daughter as his supreme achievement, refused to allow them to marry; but they did finally, in 1840, when Clara was twenty-one and Robert thirty. The two settled in Leipzig, pursuing their careers side by side. Clara furthered her husband's music as the foremost interpreter of his piano works, but her devotion could not ward off Robert's increasing withdrawal from the world and auditory hallucinations. After he threw himself into the Rhine River, Clara was forced to place him in an asylum, where his psychotic behavior gave way to advanced dementia, the result of syphilis. He died in 1856, at the age of forty-six.

Schumann's music is imbued with impassioned melodies, novel changes of harmonies, and driving rhythms that reveal him as a true Romantic. His four symphonies exude a lyric freshness and Romantic approach to harmony. He often attached literary meanings to his piano music and was fond of cycles of short pieces connected by a literary theme or musical motto. In his songs, he stands alongside Schubert. Just as Schubert had an affinity for the poetry of Goethe, Schumann favored the texts of Heine, whose poems make up his song cycle *A Poet's Love* (*Dichterliebe*).

MAJOR WORKS: More than 200 Lieder, some in song cycles, including *Dichterliebe* (*A Poet's Love*, 1840) • Orchestral music, including four symphonies and a piano concerto • Chamber music, including string quartets, piano trios, a piano quintet, and a piano quartet • Piano music, including sonatas and numerous miniatures • One opera • Choral music • Incidental music.

no real story; rather, they follow a psychological progression that spirals downward from the freshness of love through a growing disappointment to complete despair.

We will consider the first song in the cycle, *In the Lovely Month of May* (LG 29), which consists of two strophes (verses, or stanzas). The piano's introduction to the first strophe sets a wistful rather than joyous mood, and the song proceeds to evoke the fragility of a new love—through its harmonic meandering between two key centers and by its lack of a final resolution. We are left suspended at the end, knowing there is much more to this story in the songs that follow.

There is lovely text-painting at the end of the first verse, as the melody rises to a climax on "did love rise up." The piano's introduction, interlude, and postlude frame the two text strophes and provide a circular shape to the song. We might wonder if this Lied is really about a new relationship, or rather expresses the longing and desire of a lost or unrequited love.

Both Schubert and Schumann created a unity of expression between text and music (and voice and piano) that enhanced the words of the poems they chose, giving them meanings beyond what their poets had envisioned. This is the nature of song, and the reason why we still thrill at its power.

Schumann at age forty with his wife, the renowned pianist-composer Clara Wieck Schumann (1819–1896).

CRITICAL THINKING

1. What are the respective roles of the singer and pianist in a Lied?
2. What is Romantic about these two songs of Schubert and Schumann?

YourTurn TO EXPLORE

Consider a couple of your favorite songs. Are they strophic, through-composed, or modified strophic? Why do you think the songwriters have chosen those particular forms? Do they differentiate the stanzas? How are instruments used to reinforce musical repetitions and to help underline key moments?

LISTENING GUIDE 29   1:38

Schumann: *In the Lovely Month of May,*
from *A Poet's Love (Dichterliebe)*

Date: 1840
Genre: Lied, from a song cycle

Performed by: Werner Gura, tenor;
Jan Schultsz, piano

What to Listen For			
Melody	Winding melodic line, set syllabically; both verses rise to a climax.	**Form**	Strophic (two verses); with a piano prelude, interlude, and postlude.
Rhythm/ meter	Piano part moves somewhat freely in rising lines.	**Expression**	Melancholic mood portrays unrequited love.
Harmony	Meandering, with a lack of resolution to the tonic.	**Performing forces**	Solo voice and piano.
		Text	Heinrich Heine poem, with text-painting in the music.

	TEXT	TRANSLATION
0:00	**Piano introduction**	
	Strophe 1	
0:13	Im wunderschönen Monat Mai	In the lovely month of May,
	als alle Knospen sprangen,	as all the buds were blossoming,
	da ist in meinem Herzen	then in my heart
	die Liebe aufgegangen.	did love rise up.

0:45   **Piano interlude**

Strophe 2

0:52   Im wunderschönen Monat Mai   In the lovely month of May,
       als alle Vögel sangen,   as all the birds were singing,
       da hab ich ihr gestanden   then did I confess to her
       mein Sehnen und Verlangen.   my longing and desire.

1:18   **Piano postlude**, ending on a dissonance with no final resolution of the harmony.

Opening of vocal line:

Im wun - der-schö-nen Mo - nat Mai,

Folk Song, Popular Song, Art Song

Erlkönig (Elf-King) was the first song Schubert published, and it helped him launch his successful career. However, the author of the ballad, renowned playwright, novelist, and poet Johann Wolfgang von Goethe (1749–1832), was not impressed with the young composer's dramatic setting, possibly because it did not convey the "folk song" character that the poet wanted to evoke. Goethe himself was not a musician, so he relied on collaborators to set his poetic ballads as songs: and one of his favorites was his friend, renowned actress, singer, and composer Corona Schröter (1751–1802), who had sung her own folk song–style setting of Erlkönig when she and Goethe premiered the ballad in 1782, almost a quarter century before Schubert created his version.

Why was folk song so important in the transition between Classical and Romantic ideals? Proponents of classicism in art and music focused on clarity, regularity, and balance as reflections of the universal order that scientists were also seeking in the eighteenth-century Enlightenment. By the late 1700s, however, the idea of universal order was being confronted by the principle of individual freedom, and the Enlightenment trust in modern science and rationality was being challenged by creative individuals—poets, artists, musicians—who sought inspiration in forces beyond the rational: the chaotic sublime, rather than the orderly beautiful. Folklore was a powerful resource for these proponents of *Sturm und Drang*—storm and stress—and folk songs became increasingly appealing for their ability

Portrait of composer and singer Corona Schröter, by **Anton Graff** (1736–1813).

to evoke a shadowy past that could speak deep truth to the present.

English poets, musicians, and publishers flooded the market with folktales and folk songs that could be part of family entertainments for a rising middle class in the late 1700s. At the height of his popularity with the English public, Haydn was commissioned by London publisher William Napier to set Scottish folk songs for voice and piano, with optional violin—he wrote 150 between 1792 and 1795, and arranged more than 400 overall. A selection of these was translated into

Portrait of Johann Wolfgang von Goethe, by **Joseph Karl Stieler** (1781–1858).

German and republished in Vienna a few years later. Haydn's settings are strophic (one melody for multiple stanzas) and extremely accessible for amateur performance: they were very popular with both English and German music lovers for recreational use in their own homes.

Especially in the German-speaking lands, poets were inspired by the concept of folktale and folk song to write new ballads and other multistanza poems intended to continue the spirit of "the folk" through simple language, intense imagery, and tales of myths and supernatural beings. Goethe was probably the most famous German poet who adopted and expanded the "storm and stress" principle within the emerging Romantic sensibility, writing ballads designed to resemble folksong texts: in Corona Schröter he found a skilled musical collaborator.

Born into a musical family, Schröter had the good fortune to be one of the first young women to study voice at a new coeducational singing school established by opera composer Johann Adam Hiller. Though women were discouraged from singing in public, a German newspaper asked the question in 1798, "Why should girls be excluded from singing? Are not the best voices found among persons of the opposite sex, who moreover are not subjected to the male change of voice?"

Like Haydn's folk-song arrangements, Schröter's 1782 setting of *Erlkönig* consists of a simple melody with chordal piano accompaniment, each of the ballad's eight stanzas designed to be sung to that same melody—a strophic approach very different from Schubert's later through-composed drama. When Schröter later published a collection of her folk song–like settings, one reviewer noted that, while she had little training in composition, her works should not be disdained, but rather heard performed by Schröter herself "to discern precisely what was in them."

Erlkönig quickly became Goethe's most famous and popular ballad, and many musicians after Schröter tried their own hand at settings of the poem in the emerging Romantic German art-song (*Lied*) tradition. While the most renowned of these today is the Schubert setting you have heard, it's worthwhile to listen to Schröter's version in comparison because it was, after all, the poet's "approved" setting!

Many Voices Expanded
- Haydn "Scottish Songs"
- Settings of *Erlkönig* by Schröter, Carl Friedrich Zelter (1797), Carl Loewe (1818)

Young women singing at home, in *The Folk Song*, by **Silvestro Lega** (1826–1895).

40

Marketing Music:
Foster and Early "Popular" Song

"Weep no more my lady,
Oh! Weep no more today;
We will sing one song for the old Kentucky home,
For the old Kentucky home far away."

—Stephen Foster

KeyPoints

- Nineteenth-century songwriters in the United States combined elements of European art song and opera with other traditions to create commercially successful "popular" music.

- Songs often were popularized through **minstrel shows**, which were racially charged theatrical variety shows.

- The minstrel and **parlor songs** of Stephen Foster (including *Jeanie with the Light Brown Hair*) were very successful during his lifetime and remain so today.

What makes a song successful? Some melodies have become so beloved and familiar that we no longer associate them with an individual composer—for example, "Happy Birthday," which you probably have sung countless times without compensating a copyright holder. This is one meaning of "popular"—we think of "Happy Birthday" as belonging to "the people." Another meaning connects to the idea of success: some music has brought great financial profit, partly because it has been carefully marketed. These two meanings of "popular" intersect in the songs of Stephen Foster, whose music has long saturated North American culture. Foster helped build a powerful musical industry in the nineteenth-century United States, while earning very little profit from the skyrocketing sales of his sheet music. The accessibility of his songs laid the foundation for the enormous international influence of North American musical culture in the following century.

Music in Early North America: Cultivated and Vernacular

European immigrants to the Americas brought with them cultivated repertories such as operas, chamber music, and symphonies. Along with this imported "high art," they also began to develop traditions of lighter music—for dancing, singing at home, and public events such as parades. These traditions were thought of as vernacular, more connected to new notions of "American popular identity." However, there was not yet a clear split between "classical" and "popular" music in the nineteenth century; the various traditions were mutually influential, and audiences would often encounter them in the same spaces and even performed by the same ensembles.

Stephen Foster, Parlor Song, and Minstrelsy

The songs of Stephen Foster exemplify the intersection between the vernacular American spirit and the European art tradition. Foster was familiar with the Italian operas that were popular among the upper classes, and was also aware of the great financial success of nostalgic "folk songs" that helped second- and third-generation Anglo immigrants fantasize about an ideal Old Country their grandparents had left. He blended the two traditions in his **parlor songs**, which are often sweet, sentimental, and nostalgic; we will consider one, *Jeanie with the Light Brown Hair*. Though many of Foster's songs were designed for amateur performance in the parlor (a reception or gathering place) of a middle-class home, several became popular through a very prominent and uniquely North American nineteenth-century musical tradition: the minstrel show.

Posters advertising minstrel shows often used images of performers both in blackface costume (below) and in more formal poses (above), perhaps to reassure audiences of the "proper" nature of the show.

Minstrelsy is jarring for modern audiences to face because of its explicit racist stereotypes: the shows featured white performers in blackface, acting out idealized "scenes from the plantation" that were vastly different from the realities of enslaved people's lives. Minstrelsy is one of the first traditions that revealed white Americans' fascination with—and misunderstanding of—African Americans, and because of its widespread popularity in the 1800s, it shaped stereotyping of African American culture well into the twentieth century—for example, several US college alma mater songs originally arose out of white students' amateur minstrel performances.

Stephen Foster's *Lula Is Gone* was one of his most successful parlor songs; it was included in this collection of *Parlor Gems* from 1900.

Two well-known examples of Foster's songs written for or incorporated into minstrel shows are *Camptown Races*, in which a slave sings of his happy time betting on horses, and *Old Folks at Home* ("Way down upon the Swanee River"): you may have encountered these songs in school, with texts altered to remove the original parodies of Black speech. While Foster himself was ostensibly sympathetic toward the abolitionist cause and claimed that he wanted his "plantation songs" to inspire compassion for the plight of enslaved Blacks, ultimately he earned most of his income from these problematic minstrel songs rather than from his parlor songs.

A Song by Foster

Jeanie with the Light Brown Hair (LG 30) was written in 1853–54, just after the composer separated from his wife. In his sketchbook, the original title was not "Jeanie" but "Jennie," from Jane Denny McDowell's name. The

Stephen Foster (1826–1864)

Foster grew up outside Pittsburgh, where he spent much of his life, and attended Jefferson College (now Washington & Jefferson College). Rather than completing his degree, he moved to Cincinnati, where he wrote his first hit song, *Oh! Susanna*. Many of Foster's early songs were for the blackface minstrel shows that were popular during this era. From 1847 on, he was under contract with the Christy Minstrels, who specialized in performing blackface shows. For them, he wrote some of his most enduring songs, including *Camptown Races* and *Old Folks at Home*. Later he turned to ballads and parlor songs, like *Jeanie with the Light Brown Hair*. These songs, evoking themes of lost youth and happiness, reflect his desire to write more serious music. Although Foster did not spend much time in the South, it is thought that *My Old Kentucky Home*, today the state song of Kentucky, was inspired by Harriet Beecher Stowe's antislavery novel *Uncle Tom's Cabin*.

Foster was perhaps the first American to make a living as a professional songwriter, but composers in this era made little profit from their publications. After he and his wife separated, Foster moved to New York, where he wrote his famous song *Beautiful Dreamer*, conceived in the style of an Italian air. He died there at age thirty-seven, a penniless alcoholic, victim to a fall in a cheap New York hotel room. Today, Foster's songs are much better known than he is.

The title page to *Jeanie with the Light Brown Hair* (1854).

tone is bittersweet, wishing for days gone by, and draws on the then-popular tradition of Anglo-Irish folk song. The song, like most of Foster's, is strophic and set for solo voice and piano, thereby meeting the growing need for parlor music appropriate for amateurs. The brief cadenza before the return of the opening music marks a moment of free interpretation for the performer. Though we might be tempted to read this as a personal narrative expressing Foster's own nostalgia, we must also keep in mind that Foster was not a singer and would have expected the song to be performed primarily by amateurs in their homes, each of whom would bring her or his own interpretation of the object of the melancholy "dreaming."

Unlike some other Foster songs, *Jeanie* was not a huge success during his lifetime. However, it reached millions nearly a century later when, in 1941, a dispute broke out over licensing fees charged by companies that owned the rights to newly composed music, and some radio broadcasters chose to air older music that would cost them less to play. Thus, economic considerations once again helped to make this song even more "popular."

CRITICAL THINKING

1. How did ideas about "high" and "low" culture come together in nineteenth-century North American music?
2. What makes the lyrics and music of Stephen Foster "popular" today?

Your Turn TO EXPLORE

What can you find out about the economic networks that support musicians or bands? How do you suppose the musicians' creative choices (country, rap, folk-rock) have influenced their commercial distribution? Do you think technologies have influenced these creative choices, and if so, how?

Foster: *Jeanie with the Light Brown Hair*

Date: 1854

Genre: Parlor song

Performed by: Wolodymyr Smishkewych, tenor; Yonit Lea Kosovske, piano

---

What to Listen For

Melody	Wavelike (descending, then ascending); syllabic setting.	**Texture**	Homophonic.
Rhythm/ meter	Moderate tempo in a broad quadruple meter.	**Form**	Strophic, in **A-A'-B-A″** song form.
		Performing forces	Tenor and piano.
Harmony	Major key, simple block- and broken-chord accompaniment.	**Text**	Strophic poem by Foster (verse 1 only).

0:00   **Piano introduction**

0:12   **Verse**

I dream of Jeanie with the light brown hair,   **A section**
Borne, like a vapor, on the summer air!
I see her tripping where the bright streams play,   **A′ section** (varied)
Happy as the daisies that dance on her way.
Many were the wild notes her merry voice would pour,   **B section**
Many were the blithe birds that warbled them o'er;   Ascending cadenza on "Oh!"
Oh! I dream of Jeanie with the light brown hair,   **A″ section** ends the song.
Floating like a vapor, on the soft summer air.

1:13   **Piano postlude**

Opening of verse, with descending melodic line:

I dream of Jea - nie with the light brown_ hair,

B section, with wavelike line:

Ma - ny were the wild notes her mer - ry voice would pour.

41

Fire and Fury at the Keyboard: Chopin and Romantic Piano Music

"To be a great composer, one needs an enormous amount of knowledge, which . . . one does not acquire from listening only to other people's works, but even more from listening to one's own."

—Frédéric Chopin

KeyPoints

- Technical improvements to the nineteenth-century piano led to the development of the modern concert grand piano.

- Polish composer Frédéric Chopin dedicated his entire compositional output to the piano; he is said to have originated the modern piano style.

- Chopin's works include **études** (highly virtuosic study pieces), meditative nocturnes, preludes,

and dances (including Polish **mazurkas** and **polonaises**), as well as sonatas and concertos for piano. His music calls for the use of **rubato**, or "robbed time."

- The *Revolutionary* Étude (Op. 10, No. 12) is one of Chopin's most popular works; its highly emotional quality has been linked to the composer's distress over his native Poland's war with Russia.

Of all musical instruments, the piano is the most central to the Western musical tradition. From the nineteenth century onward, the instrument was increasingly hailed as equally suited to amateurs and professionals, to the home and to the concert hall. Before the arrival of recorded sound, families and communities alike gathered around the piano to make and hear music. Learning to play has long been a staple of refined education, and you may have taken at least a few lessons yourself. One of the most valued aspects of the piano is its suitability for polyphonic and homophonic textures, whether on its own or as accompaniment to voices or instruments. It can also create a variety of dynamic and resonant effects. Today the piano is still considered the most expressive instrument available to most musicians, and we owe this to the skilled individuals who refined the technologies of construction and performance in the early nineteenth century.

The Nineteenth-Century Piano

The rise in popularity of the piano helped shape the musical culture of the Romantic era. It proved especially attractive to amateurs because melody and harmony could be performed on one instrument, as they couldn't on strings or

Idealized depiction of virtuoso pianist Chopin at the piano, by **Lionello Balestrieri** (1872–1958).

In Their Own Words

❝ The pianoforte is the most important of all musical instruments; its invention was to music what the invention of printing was to poetry."

—*George Bernard Shaw*

winds. The piano thus played a crucial role in the taste and experience of the new mass public.

Hardly less important was the rise of the virtuoso pianist. At first, the performer was also the composer; Mozart and Beethoven introduced their own piano concertos to the public. With the developing concert industry, however, a class of virtuoso performers arose whose only function was to dazzle audiences by playing music composed by others.

The nineteenth century saw a series of crucial technical improvements that led to the development of the modern concert grand, mandated by Romantic composers' quest for greater power and dynamic range. Piano manufacturing eventually moved from the craft shop to the factory, allowing a huge increase in production at a significantly reduced cost. A standardized instrument was developed that had a metal frame supporting increased string tension, as well as an improved mechanical action and extended range of notes—from five octaves to seven or more. At the Paris Exhibition of 1867, two American manufacturers took the top awards, among them Steinway, maker of some of today's finest pianos. By the early twentieth century, the piano had become a universal fixture in the homes of middle-class and upper-class families.

Portrait of George Sand (Aurore Dupin, Baroness Dudevant, 1804–1876), famous novelist and Chopin's lover.

The Short Lyric Piano Piece

With its ability to project melodious and dramatic moods within a compact form, the short lyric piano piece, or **character piece**, was the equivalent to the song. Composers adopted new and sometimes fanciful terms for such works. Some titles—"Prelude," "Intermezzo" (interlude), "Impromptu" (on the spur of the moment), and "Nocturne" (a night piece), for example—suggest free, almost improvisational

Frédéric Chopin (1810–1849)

Chopin was born outside Warsaw to a French father and a Polish mother. He studied at the Conservatory of Warsaw, but in 1831 left for Paris, where he spent the remainder of his career. Paris in the 1830s was the center of the new Romanticism, and the circle in which Chopin moved included the most famous composers, writers, and artists in France.

Through the virtuoso pianist Franz Liszt, Chopin met the novelist George Sand, with whom he had a long relationship. He spent his summers at Sand's estate in Nohant, where she entertained prominent artists and writers. These were productive years for the composer, although his health grew progressively worse and his relationship with Sand ran its course from love to conflict, jealousy, and hostility. He died of tuberculosis in Paris at the age of thirty-nine.

Chopin's works, central to the pianist's repertory, include four epic ballades, the thoroughly Romantic Sonatas in B-flat Minor and B Minor, and two piano concertos. The nocturnes are melancholic and meditative. The preludes are visionary fragments, and in the études, which crown the literature of the study piece, Chopin's piano technique is transformed into poetry. The mazurkas, derived from a Polish peasant dance, evoke the idealized landscape of his youth, and the polonaises revive the stately processional dance in which Poland's nobles hailed their kings.

MAJOR WORKS: Two piano concertos • Piano music, including four ballades, three sonatas, preludes, études, mazurkas, polonaises, scherzos, waltzes, impromptus, and nocturnes • Chamber music, all with piano • Songs.

forms. Many composers produced keyboard versions of dances like the Polish mazurka and polonaise and the Viennese waltz, as well as the lively scherzo. They sometimes chose more descriptive titles for character pieces that depict a mood or scene, such as "Wild Hunt," "The Little Bell," and "Forest Murmurs" (all by Franz Liszt).

Nineteenth-century composers who refined the short piano piece—Schubert, Chopin, Liszt, Felix Mendelssohn, Fanny Mendelssohn Hensel, Robert and Clara Schumann, and Brahms—showed inexhaustible ingenuity in exploring the technical resources of the instrument and its potential for expression.

Étude, Op. 10, No. 12 (*Revolutionary*), by Chopin

Chopin's music, rooted in the heart of Romanticism, made this era the piano's golden age. His style was entirely his own—there is no mistaking it for any other—and he remains one of the most original artists of the nineteenth century. His entire creative life revolved around the piano, and he is credited with originating the modern piano style. Chopin's music calls for the use of **rubato**, or "robbed time," in which certain liberties are taken by the performer without upsetting the basic pulse. He taught his students that the left hand should remain steady while the right-hand melody might hesitate a little here and hurry forward there. We will hear one of the composer's most popular works—the so-called *Revolutionary* Étude (LG 31). Note that the mood and propulsion of this particular piece may make any rubato more difficult to hear.

Chopin composed his first set of études—twelve virtuoso showpieces—between 1829 and 1832, while on a European tour: first to Vienna, where he stayed for eight months, and then on to Paris, where he remained for the rest of his life. Just one week after his arrival in Vienna, he learned of the disastrous Polish uprising in Warsaw against Russian domination. The homesick musician wanted to return home, but was advised by family and friends to stay away. In Paris salons, where he was already famous as a composer and pianist, he met the virtuoso pianist Franz Liszt, to whom he dedicated his étude collection.

November Uprising in Warsaw 1830 was the event that inspired Chopin's *Revolutionary* Étude; painting by **Georg Benedikt Wunder** (1786–1858).

Chopin's études, generally regarded as the finest of the genre, explore a wide range of technical problems for the pianist; but far more than practice studies, they are established works for the concert repertory—albeit not for every pianist. The German critic Ludwig Rellstab found them highly difficult, noting that "those who have distorted fingers may put them right by practicing these studies, but those who have not should not play them . . . without having a surgeon at hand."

The last étude in the set, dubbed the *Revolutionary,* is believed to have been inspired by the composer's strong feelings for his homeland and for the Polish cause. The work is a stormy outpouring of emotions, from beginning to end: while the left hand races through dazzling sixteenth-note figurations, the right hand delivers an impassioned dotted-rhythm melody that develops increasing rhythmic complexities. The brooding, C minor key contributes to the feeling of conflict throughout; the coda suggests resolution, but then a torrential downpour of notes drives the piece toward its forceful final C-major chords.

When Poland was finally defeated, Chopin wrote: "All this has caused me so much pain." Schumann praised the expressive depth of Chopin's music, suggesting he was a "poet." And to this day, his music is revisited around the world by pianists of all abilities, each finding a unique way to revitalize the composer's extraordinary connection with this most technologically versatile of instruments.

CRITICAL THINKING

1. How does the *Revolutionary* Étude evoke the unrest in Chopin's native Poland?
2. Why is Chopin considered "the poet of the piano"?

Your Turn TO EXPLORE

Compare videos of different keyboard players, ideally performing the same Chopin piece. Try to find a work that's more lyrical than our étude, perhaps a nocturne or mazurka, and listen closely for any rubato. Do the performers choose the same tempo, both overall and at specific "rubato" moments? How do different performers' choices reveal different notions of expressiveness? How do pianists' physical movements create different ideas of "singing through the piano"?

Chopin: Étude, Op. 10, No. 12 (*Revolutionary*)

Date: c. 1831
Genre: Étude for solo piano

Performed by: Murray Perahia, piano

What to Listen For

Melody	Minor-key, dotted-rhythm melody, accented and in octaves.
Rhythm/ meter	Duple meter, with steady, virtuosic 16th-note figurations in the left hand and a dotted-rhythm melody that explores triplets, syncopations, and cross-rhythms.
Harmony	Dark minor key, with many chromatic inflections; an abrupt C major closing chord.

Texture	Homophonic, with prominent melody over constant running 16th notes.
Form	Modified strophic form (**A-A′**), with variations, and coda.
Expression	Fiery and emotional; wide-ranging figurations performed at a rapid-fire pace, with large dynamic contrasts and a haunting theme; the tension is briefly released in a subdued (*sotto voce*) coda before a powerful closing.

0:00 **Introduction**
Dramatic chords, followed by rushing, descending passages.

0:13 **A section** (marked *Allegro con fuoco*, with fire)
Dotted-figure theme in C minor, played in octaves, above constantly swirling 16th notes.

0:32 Main theme returns, played much more softly.

1:00 Accented descending chords, played *fortissimo*, with swirling figurations in the left hand.

1:21 **A′ section**
Main theme returns in a dotted-triplet pattern; rhythm grows increasingly complex.

1:47 The accented descending chords return.

2:10 **Coda** (marked *sotto voce*, or softly)
Quiet chords, gently ascending, are followed by a sudden *fortissimo*, rushing passage, marked *appassionato*, closing with strong chords, the last one in C major.

42

Musical Diaries: Hensel and Programmatic Piano Music

"I have called my piano pieces after the names of my favorite haunts . . . they will form a delightful souvenir, a kind of second diary."

—*Fanny Mendelssohn Hensel*

KeyPoints

- While women in the nineteenth century were discouraged from composing by social convention, they played an essential role as patrons, sponsors, and teachers, as well as coordinating musical activity in the home.

- Fanny Mendelssohn Hensel, sister of Felix Mendelssohn and an important sponsor of his music, was also a talented pianist and composer, known today for her Lieder and piano music, including the autobiographical cycle *The Year* (*Das Jahr*).

In telling our story about the musical past, we've been focusing on composers, largely because written-down compositions constitute the most precise evidence we have of musical activity before the invention of sound recording at the end of the 1800s. But other types of individuals have been essential to music from even before the beginnings of notation: for example, performers have brought written compositions to life, teachers have passed on both performance skills and compositional savvy, and patrons have provided musicians with career-promoting opportunities. Social assumptions about women long discouraged them from composing (and limited their public performances), yet they were crucial teachers and sponsors of music from the earliest days of the European tradition. Considering these roles is important, since it can help us remember that composition and performance are only two aspects of musical activity, and that teaching—and active sponsorship—are still just as crucial to the success of both new and established musical works.

Women and Music in Nineteenth-Century Society

In this era, women made great strides in establishing careers as professional musicians and public advocates for musical innovation. This path was now possible through

German artist **Ludwig Richter** (1803–1884) portrays a typical family music-making scene in his woodcut *Hausmusik* (1851).

261

*Inter*face

Music, Gender, and Domesticity

A young woman enjoys the solitary diversion of the piano in *A Sonata of Beethoven*, painted by **Alfred Edward Emslie** (1848–1918).

In the nineteenth century, young women in Europe and in America alike were expected to have certain accomplishments, and primary among these was music. Though Fanny Mendelssohn Hensel received excellent music training—equivalent to that of her famous brother, composer Felix Mendelssohn—she was strongly advised by both her father and brother to exhibit these skills only in the private world of the parlor, where friends gathered for informal conversation and entertainment, rather than in a public venue, and to focus her life entirely on home and family. Such was the burden of upper-class women: societal expectations were rigid, and few challenged these attitudes.

If you have read Jane Austen's novel *Pride and Prejudice* (or seen one of the several film adaptations), you may recall Mr. Darcy's high standard for the women of his day: "A woman must have a thorough knowledge of music, singing, drawing, dancing, and the modern languages." Notice that music comes first; indeed, in this and other Austen novels, women are frequently called upon to play the piano, sometimes accompanying themselves while singing. The purpose of this demonstration is not only for the entertainment of family and friends; an accomplished performance by a woman of marriageable age could attract—and seduce—a possible suitor at home, all within the bounds of socially acceptable behavior.

In *Pride and Prejudice*, Mary Bennet is devoted to practicing her music skills in an effort to compensate for her less-than-beautiful appearance. The scenes presented here mirrored Austen's own life; according to one family memoir, Jane "began her day with music," choosing to practice before breakfast, in solitude. Beyond the written word, the image of the young woman at the keyboard is strongly reinforced by artists, whose scenes of domestic music-making, ranging from the Baroque era (see the Vermeer painting on p. 124) through the nineteenth century (see Emslie painting at left), confirm not only the importance of music in the lives of women, but also the increasing popularity of the piano and the secure place it won in middle- and upper-class homes.

Miss Elizabeth Bennet plays the pianoforte for Mr. Darcy and a friend, from an 1895 edition of Jane Austen's *Pride and Prejudice* (originally published 1813), illustrated by **Charles Edmond Brock** (1870–1938).

the broadening of educational opportunities: in public conservatories, women could receive training as singers, instrumentalists, and even composers. Likewise, the rise of the piano as the favored chamber instrument, both solo and with voice or other instruments, provided women of the middle and upper classes with a performance outlet that was socially acceptable. Indeed, as music for the home grew in importance with the mass-marketing of instruments and sheet music, such music-making was increasingly associated with female social graces. This made instruction on the piano and other amateur-friendly instruments more and more desirable; and women often became piano teachers as well as students.

Although composition remained largely a man's province, some women broke away from tradition and overcame social stereotypes to become successful composers. Among them were Fanny Mendelssohn Hensel, known for her songs, piano music, and chamber works; and Clara Wieck Schumann, a talented performer and composer of piano, vocal, and chamber music (see p. 247). Both, however, were only tentatively encouraged by their male relatives. Women also exerted a significant influence as patrons of music or through their friendship with composers. We noted earlier that novelist George Sand enabled Chopin to focus on his creative work during their sometimes stormy relationship. Several women of the upper class, including Fanny Hensel, presided over musical salons where composers could gather to perform and discuss their music.

Hensel's programmatic piano work *September: At the River* captures the motion of a flowing river while evoking the scenery it passes.

Fanny Mendelssohn Hensel and the Piano Miniature

The music of Fanny Hensel has been neglected until recent years, when she was lifted from the shadow of her famous brother to reveal her genuine talents. Well educated in music and recognized in her lifetime as a gifted composer, she remained reluctant to make her compositions public. Her story enhances our modern-day understanding of the challenges faced by women musicians in the Romantic era.

A Piano Cycle: *The Year* (*Das Jahr*)

Hensel's cycle of piano works entitled *The Year* shows her at the pinnacle of her artistry. This set of twelve pieces, each named for a month of the year, and one postlude was once thought to be a kind of travel diary, documenting her yearlong trip to Italy in 1839–40. But with the discovery in 1989 of a lost manuscript in her hand, missing for nearly 150 years, scholars have found a deeper meaning in the works. Each miniature piece is prefaced by a poetic epigram and a painting by her husband, Wilhelm Hensel, and is written on different-colored paper. The poems and artwork seem to suggest the passage of time or the seasons of one's life, perhaps her own. The cycle is unified through recurring motives, tonal schemes, and references to the works of other composers, including her brother Felix.

We will consider the character piece entitled *September: At the River* (LG 32), which is accompanied by a drawing of a barefooted woman by the stream and several poetic lines from Goethe: "Flow, flow, dear river, / Never will I be happy." This melancholic idea is captured in the haunting, meandering melody, sounded below a stream of notes signifying the flowing river. The piece takes us on a daring journey through distant key centers, unfolding in a typical three-part form of

In Their Own Words

" I want to admit how terribly uppity I've been and announce that six 4-part Lieder . . . are coming out next. . . . My choir has enjoyed singing them . . . and I've made every effort to make them as good as possible."

—*Fanny Mendelssohn Hensel*

Fanny Mendelssohn Hensel (1805–1847)

Fanny Mendelssohn was born into a highly cultured family (her grandfather, Moses Mendelssohn, was a leading Jewish scholar and philosopher). She was especially close to her younger brother Felix, a renowned composer and conductor.

Raised in Berlin, Fanny learned piano from her mother and studied theory and composition with the well-known composer Carl Friedrich Zelter. Because of her gender, however, she was actively discouraged from pursuing music as a career. Her father cautioned her to focus on "the only calling for a young woman—that of a housewife." In 1829, Fanny married the court artist Wilhelm Hensel. She remained active during the following years as a composer, pianist, and participant in the regular salon concerts held each Sunday at the Mendelssohn residence, which she eventually organized. She died suddenly of a stroke on May 13, 1847, while preparing to conduct a cantata written by her brother. Having lost his dearest companion, Felix died just six months later.

Although she wrote several large-scale works, including a piano trio and a string quartet, Hensel's output was dominated by Lieder, choral part songs, and piano music, notably *The Year*, a set of twelve character pieces. Most of her compositions were intended for performance at the family's Sunday musical gatherings. Her solo vocal music is highly lyrical, and her choice of Romantic poets and complex piano writing place her in the mainstream of the Lieder tradition. Her piano music reflects a strong interest in Bach's contrapuntal procedures.

MAJOR WORKS: Instrumental music, including an orchestral overture, a string quartet, and a piano trio • Over 125 piano works: sonatas, preludes and fugues, and character pieces, including *Das Jahr* (*The Year*, 1841) • Vocal music, including four cantatas and part songs for chorus, and over 250 Lieder.

statement-departure-return, framed by a brief introduction and coda. *The Year* was never published in its entirety in her lifetime; indeed, only *September* was included in Fanny's collection of piano works and without its literary and visual details. The musical and extramusical links in this set make it a significant large-scale venture for the composer, who reached a new level of achievement that even her brother had not yet attained in his piano works.

CRITICAL THINKING

1. Why was the piano considered such an important domestic instrument?
2. What difficulties did a woman composer face in this era? What other important roles did women play in music, and why?

Your Turn TO EXPLORE

In contemporary society, are certain musical styles, genres, and/or instruments associated more with women than with men, or vice versa? If so, why? How do different ideals of gender in your community play out in the way music is performed, created, or supported?

3:02

Hensel: *September: At the River,* from *The Year (Das Jahr)*

Date: 1841

Genre: Character piece, from a programmatic cycle of 12

Performed by: Sarah Rothenberg, piano

What to Listen For

Melody	Slow-paced melody in piano's middle range, set against fast-moving, churning notes; much chromaticism.
Rhythm/ meter	Lilting 6/8 meter; constant running 16th notes; some rubato.
Harmony	Begins and ends in B minor; modulates through various distant keys in the middle; very chromatic.

Texture	Polyphonic, with slow-moving melodies accompanied by fast-moving lines and chords.
Form	Ternary (**A-B-A′**), with a short introduction and coda.
Expression	Free push and pull of the beat (rubato); *crescendo* and *decrescendo* in dynamics; movement evokes the flow of the river.

Introduction

0:00   Gentle, flowing 16th notes, punctuated by chords and octaves; slows down before the next section.

A section

0:12   Wistful, slow-moving melody in the middle register, in B minor, accompanied by constantly flowing fast notes and bass chords (melody notes are circled):

More movement in the main melody; grows chromatic and modulates; slows into next section, growing louder.

B section

1:23   Melody moves more quickly, in a new key, with more emphasis under a churning accompaniment. Grows louder and more chromatic, with high-range octaves exchanging a three-note idea with the main melody; builds in a swirling *crescendo.*

A′ section

1:56   Returns to the main melody, in B minor, but with more chromaticism; octave chords make a long descent to the tonic.

Coda

2:38   Introduction returns; fast-moving notes with chords; dies away *pianissimo.*

43

Personal Soundtracks:
Berlioz and the Program Symphony

"The painter turns a poem into a painting; the musician sets a picture to music."

—Robert Schumann

KeyPoints

- Many Romantic composers cultivated **program music**—instrumental music with a literary or pictorial association supplied by the composer—over **absolute music**.

- Hector Berlioz's *Symphonie fantastique* is a five-movement **program symphony** unified by a recurring theme (*idée fixe*) that represents the composer's beloved.

Shakespeare's tragedy *King Lear* inspired not only composers but Romantic-era painters, including **William Dyce** (1806–1864): *King Lear and the Fool in the Storm* (c. 1851).

As we walk through campus wearing our headphones or earbuds, we might think of the music we listen to as a personal soundtrack, a musical accompaniment to our everyday life. Of course, when we choose our playlists, we pick from favorite songs we have purchased, rather than creating our own soundscapes from scratch. In an era before recording technology, those who wanted a soundtrack for their lives had to compose it themselves. One extraordinary example comes from the work of Hector Berlioz, who combined his musical creativity with the idea of personal storytelling and raised program music to a new level.

Romantic Program Music

Music often evokes specific ideas or visual images. Sometimes these are the products of the listener's imagination, but other times they are intended by the composer. Schumann's quote above aptly suggests how a composer might think when creating such a work. The genre that evokes images and ideas became known as **program music**, instrumental music with literary or pictorial associations. The program is supplied by the composer, either in the title or in an explanatory note. A title such as *King Lear* (by Berlioz), for example, suggests specific characters and events, while *Pièces fugitives* (*Fleeting Pieces*, by Clara Schumann) merely labels the mood or character of the work. Program music is distinguished from **absolute**, or

Inter*face*

Musical Instruments and New Technologies

Two instruments invented by Belgian inventor Adolphe Sax: the bass saxhorn (1855) and the tenor valve trombone (1863).

By the early nineteenth century, the Industrial Revolution was affecting virtually every aspect of daily life, including music-making. The increased availability of raw materials, improvements in the production of metal alloys, and the ability to cast metal parts with machines powered by steam engines made refinements possible in all types of instruments. The piano, as the preferred household instrument, acquired a new key action that made it easier to repeat a single note quickly, and a cast-iron frame that allowed for heavier strings. This new frame lent both stability of pitch (the old wooden frame was prone to warping) and the potential for much louder dynamics. Piano maker Nannette Streicher (1769–1833)—a talented musician as well as successful businesswoman in Vienna—expanded the instrument's range and developed a stronger key action that was favored by Beethoven.

In 1812, Streicher's factory added a concert hall next to the showroom that soon became a hub of Viennese musical life. Eventually, the American firms of Chickering (in Boston) and Steinway (in New York) took the lead in the development of the modern grand piano.

Although the violin had undergone improvements in the Baroque era (see p. 158), it reached its modern form in the nineteenth century with a secure chin rest and a newly designed bow with which players could achieve more playing power. Harpists and timpanists could change pitches more quickly with their new foot pedals, developed from mechanical automata devices (see p. 180). While trumpets and horns had previously been limited to the pitches available on a natural instrument (the overtone series), new technology offered the possibility of valves—both rotary and piston—that diverted the air flow to longer and shorter segments of tubing, thereby increasing the pitch range to the full chromatic scale.

One of the first valved instruments was the *cornet à pistons*, a mellow and agile brass instrument that was promptly adopted into military bands. Hector Berlioz pronounced it vulgar at first, but soon realized its potential, adding two to his large orchestra for an 1833 performance of the *Symphonie fantastique*. (Listen for them in the *March to the Scaffold*.) Woodwind instruments gained increased flexibility with the advent of new key mechanisms.

Bavarian inventor Theobold Boehm (1794–1881) provided flutists with the means to cover sound holes their fingers could not reach, and he eventually developed a metal flute that replaced the standard wooden model. Similar innovations carried over to other instruments, such as the clarinet, oboe, and bassoon.

This period of technological innovation also encouraged inventors to dream up newfangled instruments. Around the midcentury, Belgian inventor Adophe Sax developed the saxophone, along with various saxhorns, some with bells. The saxophone has never been fully established as an orchestral instrument (although French composers like Maurice Ravel gave it a fleeting chance to be heard), yet it found a solid niche in military bands and, from the early twentieth century, in jazz. What is clear is that modern concert bands, jazz bands, and orchestras would be quite different today without the sweeping changes and developing technologies of the nineteenth-century industrial world.

The Chickering piano, made in Boston, was a focal point for entertainment in many nineteenth-century homes.

Listeners flee Berlioz's bombastic orchestra in this satirical engraving from 1846.

Berlioz's *idée fixe* was inspired by the Shakespearean actress Harriet Smithson (1800–1854).

pure, **music**, which consists of musical patterns that are designed without intended literary or pictorial meanings, like Beethoven's Fifth Symphony.

Program music was especially important during the nineteenth century, when musicians became sharply conscious of the connection between their art and the world around them. Adding a programmatic title brought music closer to poetry and painting, and helped composers relate their own work to the moral and political issues of their time. The passion for program music was so strong that it invaded even the most revered form of absolute music, the symphony. We will consider Berlioz's monumental program symphony, the *Symphonie fantastique*.

Berlioz and the *Symphonie fantastique*

"To render my works properly requires a combination of extreme precision and irresistible verve, a regulated vehemence, a dreamy tenderness, and an almost morbid melancholy."

The flamboyance of Victor Hugo's poetry and the dramatic intensity of Eugène Delacroix's painting found their musical counterpart in the works of Hector Berlioz, whose music is intense, bold, and passionate. He was the first great proponent of musical Romanticism in France.

Berlioz wrote his best-known program symphony when he was twenty-seven, basing its story on his personal life. His score describes "a young musician of morbid sensibility and ardent imagination, in . . . lovesick despair, [who] has poisoned himself with opium. The drug, too weak to kill, plunges him into a heavy sleep accompanied by strange visions. . . . The beloved one herself becomes for him a melody, a recurrent theme that haunts him everywhere."

The symphony's recurrent theme, called an ***idée fixe*** (fixed idea), acts as a musical thread unifying the five diverse movements, though its appearances are varied in harmony, rhythm, meter, tempo, dynamics, register, and instrumental color. This type of unification, called **thematic transformation**, serves the huge, expansive form of Berlioz's symphony. These transformations take on literary as well as musical significance, as the following description by Berlioz shows.

The Program

I. *Reveries, Passions*. "[The musician] remembers the weariness of soul, the indefinable yearning he knew before meeting his beloved. Then, the volcanic love with which she at once inspired him, his delirious suffering . . . his religious consolation." The Allegro section introduces a soaring melody, the fixed idea.

II. *A Ball*. "Amid the tumult and excitement of a brilliant ball he glimpses the loved one again." This dance movement is in ternary (three-part) form. In the middle section, the fixed idea reappears in waltz time.

III. *Scene in the Fields*. "On a summer evening in the country he hears two shepherds piping. The pastoral duet, the quiet surroundings . . . all unite to fill his heart with a long-absent feeling of calm. But she appears again [*idée fixe*]. His heart contracts. Painful forebodings fill his soul." The composer said that his aim in this pastoral movement was to establish a mood of "sorrowful loneliness."

Hector Berlioz (1803–1869)

Berlioz was born in southern France. His father, a well-to-do physician, expected the boy to follow in his footsteps, but the Romantic revolution was brewing in Paris, and Berlioz, under the spell of such artists as Victor Hugo and Eugène Delacroix, followed his dream to study music. He became a huge fan of Beethoven and of Shakespeare, to whose plays he was introduced by a visiting English troupe. Berlioz fell madly in love with an actress in this troupe, Harriet Smithson: "I became obsessed by an intense, overpowering sense of sadness," he wrote. "I could not sleep, I could not work, and I spent my time wandering aimlessly about Paris and its environs."

In 1830, Berlioz won the coveted Prix de Rome, which gave him an opportunity to work in Italy. That same year, he composed the *Symphonie fantastique*, his most celebrated work. After returning from Rome, he began a hectic courtship of Harriet Smithson, whom he married, only to realize it was Shakespeare he had loved rather than Harriet.

Berlioz's works, showing the favorite literary influences of the Romantic period, draw on Goethe, Lord Byron, and especially Shakespeare, the source for his overture *King Lear,* his opera *Béatrice et Bénédict,* and his dramatic symphony *Romeo and Juliet.* It was in the domain of orchestration that Berlioz's genius asserted itself most fully. His scores, calling for the largest orchestra that had ever been used, abound in novel effects and discoveries, revealing him as one of the boldest innovators of the nineteenth century.

MAJOR WORKS: Orchestral music, including overtures (*King Lear*) and program symphonies (*Symphonie fantastique* and *Romeo et Juliette*) • Choral music, including a Requiem Mass • Three operas, including *Les Troyens* (*The Trojans*) • Nine works for solo voice and orchestra • Writings about music, including an orchestration treatise.

IV. *March to the Scaffold.* "He dreams that he has killed his beloved, that he has been condemned to die and is being led to the scaffold. . . . At the very end the fixed idea reappears for an instant, like a last thought of love interrupted by the fall of the blade."

V. *Dream of a Witches' Sabbath.* "He sees himself at a witches' sabbath surrounded by a host of fearsome spirits who have gathered for his funeral. Unearthly sounds, groans, shrieks of laughter. The melody of his beloved is heard, but it has lost its noble and reserved character. It has become a vulgar tune, trivial and grotesque. It is she who comes to the infernal orgy. A howl of joy greets her arrival. She joins the diabolical dance. Bells toll for the dead. A burlesque of the *Dies irae.* Dance of the witches. The dance and the *Dies irae* combined."

The last two movements are perfect examples of the Romantic era's preoccupation with the grotesque and the supernatural (LG 33). In the fourth, a diabolical

Francisco Goya (1746–1828) anticipated the passionate intensity of Berlioz's music in this painting of the *Witches' Sabbath,* c. 1819–23.

march in minor, the theme of the beloved appears at the end presented by the clarinet, and is cut off by a grim *fortissimo* chord. In this vivid portrayal of the story, we clearly hear the final blow of the guillotine blade, the head rolling, and the resounding cheers of the crowd.

In the final movement, Berlioz sounds an infernal spirit that nourished a century of satanic operas, ballets, and symphonic poems. The mood is heightened by the introduction of the traditional religious chant *Dies irae* ("Day of Wrath") from the ancient Mass for the Dead, scored for the bassoons and tubas.

This composition is an extraordinary example of the Romantic desire to reflect the intensity of personal experience through music, but it also opens up the essential paradox of program music: if you heard the *March to the Scaffold* without knowing its title or its descriptive program, would you understand the story it's supposed to tell? Can the music convey meaning without the story?

CRITICAL THINKING

1. What musical effects did Berlioz use to "paint" the image of a march to the scaffold?
2. What is Romantic about the program and music of *Symphonie fantastique*?

LISTENING GUIDE 33   ◀)) 14:22

Berlioz: *Symphonie fantastique*, IV and V

Date: 1830

Genre: Program symphony with five movements

Program: A lovesick artist in an opium trance is haunted by a vision of his beloved, which becomes an *idée fixe* (fixed idea).

Performed by: Baltimore Symphony, David Zinman, conductor

 ◀)) *Idée fixe*

Movements: I. *Reveries, Passions*: Largo; Allegro agitato e appassionato assai (lively, agitated, and impassioned)
II. *A Ball*: Valse, Allegro non troppo
III. *Scene in the Fields*: Adagio
IV. *March to the Scaffold*: Allegretto non troppo
V. *Dream of a Witches' Sabbath*: Larghetto, Allegro assai

IV. *March to the Scaffold*   4:37

What to Listen For			
Melody	Two main march themes (**A** and **B**), both strongly accented.	**Expression**	Diabolical mood; sudden dynamic changes, idea of the beloved at the end as a clarinet solo, then a sudden chord (beheading).
Rhythm/ meter	Duple-meter march.		
Harmony	Set in the minor mode.	**Timbre**	Prominent timpani; instruments in unusual ranges.
Form	Sonata-like, with two themes introduced, developed, then recapped.		

0:00   Opening motive: muted horns, timpani, and pizzicato low strings;
forecasts syncopated rhythm of a march (theme **B**):

0:24   Theme **A**—an energetic, downward minor scale in low strings, then violins (with bassoon countermelody):

1:31   Theme **B**—diabolical march tune, played by brass and woodwinds:

1:56   Developmental section:

Theme **B**—in brass, accompanied by strings and woodwinds.

Theme **A**—soft, with pizzicato strings.

Theme **B**—brass, with woodwinds added.

Theme **A**—soft, pizzicato strings, then loud in brass.

3:02   Theme **A**—full orchestra statement in original form, then inverted (now an ascending scale).

4:05   Fixed idea in clarinet ("a last thought of love"), marked "as sweetly and passionately as possible," followed by a
loud chord that cuts off the melody ("the fall of the blade"):

Pizzicato bass notes, possibly intended to depict the fall of the head, are followed by loud, triumphant chords
that close the movement.

V. *Dream of a Witches' Sabbath*

9:45

What to Listen For

Melody	Opening chromatic scales, then the transformed theme of the beloved; *Dies irae* (chant for the dead).	**Texture**	Some polyphony, where two melodies are combined.
Rhythm/ meter	Slow and eerie, then Allegro in a quick 6/8.	**Expression**	Nightmarish mood evoked by unusual instrumental effects.
Harmony	Much dissonance and chromaticism.	**Timbre**	Muted strings, squawky woodwinds, bells and brass with the chant melody.

0:00   Larghetto—very soft muted strings evoke a diabolical atmosphere; chromatic scales in the strings, low brass,
and high woodwinds depict "unearthly sounds, groans, shrieks of laughter."

1:27   Allegro—high clarinet sounds the fixed idea in a transformed version with trills and grace notes
("a vulgar tune, trivial and grotesque"):

continued on next page

1:35   Orchestral *fortissimo* signals a "howl of joy" at the beloved's arrival.

1:46   Fixed idea continues in woodwinds, with bassoons in a grotesque accompanying figure.

2:53   "Bells toll for the dead."

A dance tune is forecast by its opening motive in the violas, followed by foreboding sounds in the low brass:

3:19   Chant tune *Dies irae* sounded in bassoons and tubas, first slow, then twice as fast in the brass:

3:49   "Burlesque of the *Dies irae*" in strings and woodwinds in an altered rhythm; alternates with brass and bells.

5:08   "Dance of the Witches" ("Ronde du Sabbat")—begins in the low strings, then builds in a fugal setting:

The dance dies out, followed by strange sounds in the low strings with a fragment of *Dies irae*; builds to *fortissimo*.

7:56   "The dance and the *Dies irae* combined"; strings play the dance tune with wood of bows alternating with loud brass statements of *Dies irae*; builds to a final cadence.

🔊 **AnotherHearing** On our recording, this excerpt was performed in the orchestral version envisioned by Berlioz. Now compare our primary recording with an arrangement for concert band, performed by the US Navy Band, which features only wind, brass, and percussion instruments (no strings). Can you tell which instruments are playing the parts that are played by the string instruments in Berlioz's orchestral version? What differences in timbre (tone color) do you note between the recordings? Which do you prefer, and why?

YourTurn TO EXPLORE

What excerpts from your favorite music might you use to tell a story about yourself and your emotional life? List the songs or pieces. How might you want to modify the music (its tempo, instrumentation, texture, etc.) to convey your emotions more precisely? How would you try to make sure a listener would understand your story accurately?

44

Sounding Literature: Orchestral Program Music by Mendelssohn and Grieg

"I dipped into the rich treasures of native folk song and sought to create a national art out of this hitherto unexploited expression of the folk soul of Norway."

—Edvard Grieg

KeyPoints

- Prominent types of Romantic program music include the **concert overture**, **incidental music** to a play, and the **symphonic poem** (a one-movement work).
- Felix Mendelssohn drew on his passion for Shakespeare's plays in writing a concert overture that he felt encapsulated the story and expressive qualities of *A Midsummer Night's Dream*.

- Political unrest throughout Europe stimulated schools of nationalistic composers in Russia, Scandinavia, Spain, England, and Bohemia.
- Edvard Grieg looked to the folklore of his native Norway in many of his works. His incidental music for *Peer Gynt* was written to accompany a play by Henrik Ibsen about this folk legend, then was excerpted into an independent suite.

One of the most important roles that music plays in all human societies is building community cohesion. Since the nineteenth century, the notion of community has been strongly tied to the concept of nationality: a distinctive culture and heritage shared by people who live in a common territory. But although individuals are associated with a nation by birth or immigration, they can choose whether or not—and how—to highlight that association through their music. Literary references are also a powerful way to express shared heritage, whether national or cross-cultural, and the nineteenth century saw increasing interest in the linking of instrumental music and literature. In this chapter, we will explore two contrasting orchestral approaches to such linking: Felix Mendelssohn's *A Midsummer Night's Dream* and Edvard Grieg's *Peer Gynt*.

Varieties of Orchestral Program Music

One type of program music came out of the opera house, where the overture, a rousing orchestral piece in one movement, served as an introduction to an opera (or a play). Some operatic overtures became popular as separate concert pieces, which in turn pointed the way to a new type of **overture** not associated with opera: a single-movement concert piece for orchestra that might evoke a land- or seascape, or embody a patriotic or literary idea, like Tchaikovsky's *Romeo and Juliet*.

Program overture

Another type of program music, **incidental music**, usually consists of an overture and a series of pieces performed between the acts of a play and

Incidental music

273

Oberon, Titania, and Puck, with dancing fairies, from Shakespeare's play *A Midsummer Night's Dream*; illustration by **William Blake** (1757–1827).

during important scenes. The most successful pieces of incidental music were arranged into suites (such as Felix Mendelssohn's *A Midsummer Night's Dream*), which we will consider below. This use of music to enhance spoken drama was influential in the development of musical accompaniment to silent film at the very end of the 1800s, and in the tradition of film soundtracks after the 1920s.

Eventually, composers felt the need for a large orchestral form that would serve the Romantic era as the symphony had served the Classical. Franz Liszt created the **symphonic poem**, the nineteenth century's most original contribution to large forms. A symphonic poem is program music for orchestra in one movement, with contrasting sections that develop a poetic idea (like Debussy's *Prelude to "The Afternoon of a Faun,"* Chapter 51), suggest a scene, or create a mood. It differs from the concert overture, which usually retains a traditional Classical form, by having a much freer structure. The symphonic poem (also called **tone poem**) gave composers the flexibility they needed for a big single-movement work. It became the most common type of orchestral program music through the second half of the century.

A Midsummer Night's Dream

In his mid-teens, Felix Mendelssohn read Shakespeare's *A Midsummer Night's Dream*, probably in a new German edition published in 1825, after which he wrote to his sister Fanny that he would soon begin to "dream the Midsummer Night's Dream." By early August 1826, the talented seventeen-year-old had completed a concert overture based on the play, and he premiered a piano duet version with his sister at a salon concert at their home. In the following months, he orchestrated the overture, which received its first public performance in February 1827. The playwright George Bernard Shaw claimed that the musical world had been astonished by its "musical style at once fascinating, original, and perfectly new."

Shakespeare's comedy   As you may know (perhaps you have read the play), there are four groups of characters in Shakespeare's comedy: a courtly pair in Athens (Theseus and Hippolyta), four young Athenians, the fairies (including King Oberon and Queen Titania), and the clownish tradesmen. The action focuses on pairs of lovers from these groups, and transformations brought on by the mischievous Puck, mistaken identities, and a magical potion.

Mendelssohn's overture captures the spirit and delightful intrigue of the play (LG 34). Four quiet chords in the woodwinds and horns open the portals to the magical realm of the fairy king and queen, setting up a "once upon a time" atmosphere. The scurrying fairy dance in the enchanted woods near Athens appears as the first theme, in a minor key, played softly and quickly by the violins. An energetic transition, representing the royal court in Athens where the play takes place, leads to the lovers' theme, a lyrical and singing melody. Third is the noisy dance of the clowns, played *fortissimo* in an energetic rhythm with wide leaps to

Felix Mendelssohn (1809–1847)

Mendelssohn, born in Hamburg, Germany, was the grandson of a famous Jewish philosopher, Moses Mendelssohn (his family converted to Protestantism when Felix was still a child). When he was two, his family moved to Berlin, where their home became a meeting place for Berlin intellectuals, their garden house the scene of memorable concerts. Here, an orchestra under the direction of the seventeen-year-old Felix performed his Overture to *A Midsummer Night's Dream* for a captivated audience. Felix was not the only musician in the household, as we have seen: his sister Fanny (Chapter 42) was a gifted pianist and composer as well—in fact, some of her works were published under her brother's name.

Felix's education was thorough and well rounded. He worshipped the music of Bach, Mozart, and Beethoven: in 1829, he organized a performance of Bach's *St. Matthew Passion* (neglected since the death of its composer in 1750) that proved to be a turning point in the nineteenth-century revival of Bach's choral music.

Mendelssohn excelled in a number of roles—as pianist, conductor, organizer of music festivals, and educator. At twenty-six, he was named conductor of the Gewandhaus Orchestra in Leipzig and went on to transform the orchestra into the finest in Europe. Later he founded the Conservatory of Leipzig, which raised the standards considerably for the training of musicians. His life was shattered, though, in 1847 by the death of his sister Fanny, to whom he was devoted. This blow, along with his very demanding musical career, may have brought on the stroke from which he died at age thirty-eight.

Mendelssohn composed with a speed and facility comparable to Mozart or Schubert, and was dedicated to preserving the tradition of Classical forms in an age that was turning away from them.

MAJOR WORKS: Orchestral music, including five symphonies, concert overtures (*A Midsummer Night's Dream*, 1842), two piano concertos, a violin concerto • Dramatic music, including one opera and incidental music for plays • Choral music, including two oratorios (*Elijah*, 1846) • Chamber music, including string quartets and quintets • Keyboard music, including *Songs without Words* and transcriptions of music by Bach, Handel, Mozart, and Beethoven.

LISTENING GUIDE 34   11:26

Mendelssohn: Overture to *A Midsummer Night's Dream*

Date: 1826; incidental music in 1842

Genre: Concert overture

Performed by: Cleveland Orchestra, George Szell, conductor

What to Listen For

Melody	Light, dancelike first theme; lyrical second theme; and rowdy third theme.	**Form**	Sonata-allegro, with three themes and an extended coda.
Rhythm/ meter	Fast duple meter; energetic throughout.	**Performing forces**	Orchestra, with pairs of woodwinds and brass.
Harmony	E major, with a shift to the minor.	**Expression**	Descriptive of the characters and plot in Shakespeare's play.
Texture	Airy and largely homophonic.		

PROGRAM	DESCRIPTION
Introduction	
0:00 The realm of the fairies	Four long chords in the winds.

continued on next page

Exposition

0:23   Dance of the fairies   Theme 1, soft, lively theme played staccato by the violins, in a minor key:

1:05   The royal court at Athens   Transitional theme, descending, then ascending, now loud and energetic:

2:07   The young lovers   Theme 2, lyrical and expressive; descending, chromatic melody in the violins, which builds to a *fortississimo*:

2:58   The clowns' dance   Theme 3, rhythmic and disjunct, with a wide leap sounding like a donkey's hee-haw:

3:19   The royal hunting party   Closing theme, fanfare in the brass.

Development

3:43   Fairies' dance   Theme 1 is developed and exchanged between the strings in imitation; loud brass interruptions:

5:30   Slows to a closing-sounding cadence.
5:53   Realm of the fairies   The four long chords of the introduction return.

Recapitulation

6:18   Fairies' dance   Theme 1 returns, played lightly and staccato.
7:00   Lovers' theme   Theme 2 returns.
7:51   Clowns' theme   Theme 3 returns and is extended.
8:48   Royal court and hunting themes   Transitional theme, then a hunting fanfare as the closing.

Coda

9:19   Fairies' dance   Theme 1 returns briefly.
10:06 Royal court theme, now slower:

10:59 Realm of the fairies   Four closing chords, as in the opening.

underscore its boisterous character; this represents the tradesmen, who perform a play within the play. The last four notes suggest the braying "hee-haw" of the donkey's head magically bestowed by Puck on Bottom the weaver. A fanfare-like closing theme in the brass suggests the approach of the royal hunting party from Athens. All these ideas are introduced in the first section, developed in the middle section, and restated in the last section—in short, presented through a sonata-allegro form.

A coda concludes the work on a note of quiet farewell. As the composer explained, "After everything has been satisfactorily settled and the principal players have joyfully left the stage, the elves follow them, bless the house, and disappear with the dawn. So ends the play, and my overture too."

Some years later, in 1842, King Frederick William IV of Prussia decided on a production of Shakespeare's comedy at his royal theater and suggested to Mendelssohn that he write incidental music for the play. The resulting music included the now famous "Wedding March."

Musical Nationalism

"I grew up in a quiet spot and was saturated from earliest childhood with the wonderful beauty of Russian popular song. I am therefore passionately devoted to every expression of the Russian spirit. In short, I am a Russian through and through!" —Peter Ilyich Tchaikovsky

In nineteenth-century Europe, political conditions so encouraged the growth of nationalism that it became a decisive force within the Romantic movement. The pride of conquering nations and the struggle for freedom of suppressed ones gave rise to strong emotions that inspired the works of many creative artists.

Romantic composers expressed their nationalism in a variety of ways. Some based their music on the songs and dances of their people, others wrote dramatic works based on folklore or peasant life—for example, the Russian fairy-tale operas and ballets of Tchaikovsky. And some wrote symphonic poems and operas celebrating the exploits of a national hero, a historic event, or the scenic beauty of their country: Bedřich Smetana's *The Moldau* is a popular tone poem depicting the river that was the lifeblood of the emerging state of Bohemia.

In associating music with the love of homeland, composers sought to give expression to the hopes of millions of people. The political implications were not lost on the authorities. Some of Giuseppe Verdi's operas, for example, had to be altered again and again to suit the censor (his plots often portrayed rulers as unjust or suggested "dangerous" ideas). During the Second World War, the Nazis outlawed the playing of Chopin's polonaises in Warsaw and Smetana's descriptive symphonic poems in Prague because of the powerful symbolism behind these works.

Several regions throughout Europe gave rise to a national voice through music. In particular, the Russian school produced a circle of young musicians called "The Mighty Five" (or "The Mighty Handful"), whose members sought to free themselves from the older sounds of the German symphony, French ballet, and Italian opera and express a true Russian spirit. England and Spain produced nationalistic composers as well whose music was intended to echo the souls of their countries (see map on p. 278).

In Their Own Words

❝ The art of music above all other arts is the expression of the soul of a nation. The composer must love the tunes of his country and they must become an integral part of him."

—*Ralph Vaughan Williams*

Schools of Musical Nationalism in Europe

ENGLAND
Edward Elgar (1857–1934)
Pomp and Circumstance March
Ralph Vaughan Williams (1872–1958)
Fantasia on a Theme by Thomas Tallis

SCANDINAVIA
Edvard Grieg (1843–1907)
Peer Gynt
Jean Sibelius (1865–1957)
Finlandia

RUSSIA
Alexander Borodin (1833–1887)
Prince Igor
Modest Musorgsky (1839–1881)
Pictures at an Exhibition
Nikolai Rimsky-Korsakov (1844–1908)
Sheherazade
Peter Ilyich Tchaikovsky (1840–1893)
Nutcracker, 1812 Overture

SPAIN
Isaac Albéniz (1860–1909)
Iberia
Manuel de Falla (1876–1946)
The Three-Cornered Hat

CZECH REPUBLIC
Bedřich Smetana (1824–1884)
My Country (Moldau)
Antonín Dvořák (1841–1904)
Slavonic Dances

A Scandinavian Nationalist: Edvard Grieg

Among nationalist composers of the nineteenth century, the Norwegian master Edvard Grieg stands out for his ability to capture the essence of his country's folklore and dance through music. It was his goal to create an art that was accessible to all the public.

Peer Gynt, Suite No. 1

Henrik Ibsen's play *Peer Gynt,* based on a Norwegian folk tale, premiered in Christiana, Norway, in 1876. Like most folk tales, the story presents a strong moral

Edvard Grieg (1843–1907)

Born in Bergen, Norway, Grieg attended the famous Leipzig Conservatory in Germany, where he fell under the spell of Felix Mendelssohn and Robert Schumann. After returning to Norway, Grieg worked to promote Scandinavian music through an academy he helped found. Though he tried his hand at larger musical forms—the symphony and the sonata—he felt more at home with smaller-scale works, including songs, for which he had a lyric gift. He also wrote many piano works, including arrangements of Norwegian folk tunes. His growing stature brought him a stipend from the Norwegian government that allowed him to focus on composition and an invitation to collaborate with the famous playwright Henrik Ibsen on his play *Peer Gynt*. By the 1880s, Grieg was truly an international figure, having brought much visibility to his homeland through music. He died suddenly in 1907, just as he was to embark on a concert tour to England.

Grieg's music is notable for its lyricism and for his nationalistic use of folk music and dances, leading the way for early twentieth-century composers like Béla Bartók (see Chapter 64). His well-crafted piano miniatures are among his best works, as is his popular Piano Concerto in A Minor, which was admired and performed by virtuoso Franz Liszt and is often played today.

MAJOR WORKS: Orchestral works, including incidental music and suites (*Peer Gynt*, Nos. 1 and 2), overtures, symphonic dances • Piano music, including a concerto, a sonata, many small-scale pieces and dances • Chamber music, including violin sonatas, a string quartet • Songs.

message. Peer is an idle and boastful youth; his mother Åse reprimands him for his laziness, which caused him to lose his bride-to-be, Ingrid, to another. At her wedding, however, Peer abducts Ingrid, only to abandon her later. He runs away to a forest, where he seduces a young girl who turns out to be a daughter of the Mountain King, ruler of the trolls. When her sisters find out she is pregnant, they vow to avenge her, but Peer manages to escape them. Now an outlaw, he builds a cottage in the woods, where Solveig, a girl he once loved, comes to live with him. Life seems safe for a while, but when Peer's mother dies, he sets off on a series of fantastical adventures; on the shores of North Africa, he cavorts with the Arabian girl Anitra, who performs a sultry dance for him. Peer finally returns home many years later to find Solveig, now a middle-aged woman, still faithful to him.

At Ibsen's invitation, Grieg composed some twenty-two pieces, including preludes and dances, as incidental music for the play. Not altogether happy with the result, he later extracted eight of the movements and combined them—in a different order—into two orchestral suites, of four movements each.

Two of the most endearing and popular pieces—*Morning Mood* and *In the Hall of the Mountain King* (LG 35)—are from Grieg's first suite, which also includes *Åse's Death* and *Anitra's Dance*. *Morning Mood*, an atmospheric depiction of the sunrise, opens the suite. It features a lyrical theme that is passed between instruments, building to a long climax. Grieg wrote that he imagined "the sun breaking through the clouds at the first *forte*."

In the Hall of the Mountain King was conceived as grotesque ballet music—a march for the wild troll daughters of the Mountain King. The girls taunt and

The King of the Trolls, from Ibsen's *Peer Gynt* as illustrated by **Arthur Rackham** (1867–1939).

LISTENING GUIDE 35   🔊 6:21

Grieg: *Peer Gynt*, Suite No. 1 (Op. 46), excerpts

Date: 1875–76 (play); 1888 (suite)

Genre: Incidental music to a play by Henrik Ibsen

Movements: *Morning Mood*
             Åse's Death
             Anitra's Dance
             In the Hall of the Mountain King

Performed by: New York Philharmonic, Leonard Bernstein, conductor

---

What to Listen For

MORNING MOOD

Melody	Dreamy melody in an inverted arch shape, with decorative grace notes.
Rhythm/meter	Lilting 6/8 meter.
Harmony	E major, with many harmonic inflections; static chords.
Texture	Homophonic.
Form	Three-part (**A-B-A′**) plus coda.
Expression	Grows to a loud climax; swells in dynamics, then dies away.
Performing forces	Pastoral instruments (flute, oboe, horn) are prominent.

IN THE HALL OF THE MOUNTAIN KING

Melody	Ghostly melody in two phrases, with a rising accented line.
Rhythm/meter	Duple-meter march; short, staccato notes and offbeat accents.
Harmony	B minor.
Texture	Homophonic.
Form	A single theme repeated over and over; closing coda.
Expression	Huge *crescendo* and *accelerando* to a dramatic ending.
Performing forces	Pizzicato strings and staccato woodwind effects; offbeats in brass and percussion.

Morning Mood
                                                        3:50

A section

0:00   A flowing melody is exchanged between flute and oboe, with sustained string chords; builds in a *crescendo*:

0:49   Full orchestral statement, marked *forte*; continues to build, then dies down; cello motive leads to a new *crescendo*.

B section

1:29   Reaches a climax, then cellos alternate with higher strings in sudden dynamic changes; builds in a *crescendo*, then *decrescendo*; a brief shift to the minor.

A′ section

1:59   French horn has the main theme, accompanied by wavering woodwinds.

2:12   Louder statement in low strings and woodwinds.

2:32   Horn introduces a slower statement of the theme in violins, answered by clarinet.

Coda

2:45   A quiet mood, with trills in woodwinds; solo French horn.

3:17   Flute has the theme, slowing, then bassoon; tranquil chords in strings; closing chords in full orchestra with a soft timpani roll.

In the Hall of the Mountain King
2:31

0:00   An eerie theme is heard six times, played softly in low pizzicato strings and bassoons:

0:55   Theme continues in violins, answered by woodwinds, with strong offbeat accents.

1:11   Pizzicato theme moves to a higher range in violins, grows louder and a little faster; answered by oboes and clarinets.

1:26   Louder statement accompanied by a bowed-string spinning figure.

1:40   Full orchestra at *fortissimo*, with strong accents.

1:52   Brass is prominent as the music speeds up and is more accented.

Coda

2:12   Sudden chords, alternating with running passages; a timpani roll leads to the final chord.

threaten Peer for seducing one of them, with the insistent theme growing louder and faster as they chase him. The crashing final chords signify the collapse of the mountain on top of the trolls.

Though they share the common orchestral language of the nineteenth century, these strikingly expressive works, like other examples of program music, draw on the unique imagery of Shakespeare's play and Norwegian folk traditions. Can you "hear" the imagery that Mendelssohn and Grieg meant to convey?

CRITICAL THINKING

1. What are the various genres of program music that developed in the nineteenth century, and how do they differ from each other?

2. How did Mendelssohn use contrasting musical resources to convey the dramatic effect of Shakespeare's play?

3. What are some ways that nationalism is reflected in nineteenth-century music?

Your Turn TO EXPLORE

What kinds of musical repertories do you think best represent the communities with which you identify? Are those communities shaped by regional or ethnic identity, and does their music reflect those identities? If you are a fan of a particular musician or group, what characteristics do your fellow fans share, and how does the music reinforce those common elements?

45

Absolutely Classic: Brahms and the Nineteenth-Century Symphony

"It is not hard to compose, but it is wonderfully hard to let the superfluous notes fall under the table."

—Johannes Brahms

KeyPoints

- Composers continued writing instrumental music without a program (**absolute music**) throughout the nineteenth century, including symphonies, concertos, and chamber music.
- Romantic symphonies were characterized by lyrical themes, colorful harmonies, expanded proportions, and larger orchestras featuring new instruments.
- German composer Johannes Brahms continued the Classical traditions of the Viennese masters in his four symphonies. His Third Symphony is Classical in structure but Romantic in tone.

Music may not be a truly universal language, but it is certainly more flexible in meaning than any communication based on words. Sound can seem to dig deeper into our emotions than the logic of words—and this aspect of music made it especially appealing to the Romantics, as we have seen. Yet many thought that program music, linking sound to a narrative or an image, was a step backward from the potential of music to express things beyond words. These were (and are) the proponents of **absolute music**: music without a program, relying entirely on structures of sound for its expressive power. This repertory continues to dominate in orchestral concerts, since audiences enjoy the opportunity for individual interpretation that is opened up when music is not explicitly linked to anything else. And indeed, in most Western traditions, even when a voice is ostensibly the primary focus of a song, there is often an instrumental break in which the expressive potential of music is allowed to float freely and expand the listener's experience.

Absolute Music in the Romantic Era

In addition to new programmatic genres such as the symphonic poem and program symphony, Romantic composers continued writing in the multimovement genres established in the Classical era, which included the symphony, the concerto, and chamber music (string quartets and quintets, piano trios and quartets). As we have seen, the most important organizing element in absolute music is form, since there is no prescribed story or extramusical literary program provided by the composer. Though the basic components of the three- or four-movement cycle covered in Chapters 31–36 were retained, nineteenth-century composers did not always follow the "traditional rules."

Form and Expression in the Romantic Symphony

In the course of its development beyond the Classical-period tradition of Haydn, Mozart, and Beethoven, the symphony gained weight and importance. Nineteenth-century composers found the symphony a suitable framework for their lyrical ("singing") themes, harmonic experiments, and individual expressions. By the Romantic era, music had moved from palace to public concert hall, the orchestra had vastly increased in size (see chart on p. 239) and the symphonic structure was growing steadily longer and more expansive.

The first movement, the most dramatic of the Romantic symphony, generally retains the basic elements of sonata-allegro form. It might have a drawn-out, slow introduction, and it often features a long and expressive development section. The second movement, often in a loose three-part form, may retain its slow and lyrical nature but can also range in mood from whimsical and playful to tragic and passionate. Third in the cycle is a strongly rhythmic dance or scherzo, with overtones of humor, surprise, caprice, or folk dance. The fourth and final movement has a dimension and character designed to balance the first. Often it also follows sonata-allegro form and may close the symphony on a note of triumph or pathos.

The nineteenth-century orchestra offered the composer new instruments and a larger ensemble. Engraving of an orchestral concert (including military bands) at the Covent Garden Theatre, London, 1846.

Johannes Brahms (1833–1897)

Born in Hamburg, Germany, Brahms gave his first performance on piano at age ten. He soon developed what would be a lifelong affection for folk music, collecting songs and folk sayings throughout his life. Brahms had the good fortune to study with Robert Schumann at Düsseldorf, who recognized in his pupil a future leader of the circle dedicated to absolute music. Robert and his wife Clara took the young musician into their home, and their friendship opened up new horizons for him.

The death of Brahms's mother in 1865 inspired him to write his *German Requiem,* with biblical texts that he selected himself, in her memory (see Chapter 48). He ultimately settled in Vienna, where, at age forty, he began writing his great symphonic works. During these years, he became enormously successful, the acknowledged heir of the Viennese masters. Robert Schumann had died of syphilis in 1856, and Brahms had tenderly supported Clara through the ordeal of his mental collapse. Forty years later, Clara's declining health gave rise to his *Four Serious Songs.* Her death deeply affected the composer, already ill with cancer. He died ten months later and was buried in Vienna, near Beethoven and Schubert.

Brahms's four symphonies are unsurpassed in the late Romantic period for their breadth of conception and design. In his two piano concertos and violin concerto, the solo instrument is integrated into a full-scale symphonic structure. Brahms gorgeously captured the intimacy of chamber-music style, and is an important figure in piano music as well. As a songwriter, he stands in the direct succession from Schubert and Schumann, with about two hundred solo songs.

MAJOR WORKS: Orchestral music, including four symphonies, variations, overtures • Four concertos (two for piano, one for violin, one double concerto for violin and cello • Chamber music, including piano trios and quartets • Duo sonatas • Piano music, including sonatas, character pieces, dances, variations • Choral music, including *Ein deutsches Requiem* (*German Requiem*, 1868) and part songs • Lieder, including *Wiegenlied* (*Lullaby*).

LISTENING GUIDE 36 6:20

Brahms: Symphony No. 3 in F Major, III

Date: 1883

Genre: Symphony

Movements: I. Allegro con brio; sonata-allegro, F major
II. Andante; modified sonata form, C major

Performed by: Cleveland Orchestra, George Szell, conductor

III. Poco allegretto; A-B-A′ form, C minor
IV. Allegro; sonata-allegro; F major

III: Poco allegretto

What to Listen For

Melody	Lyrical, melancholic melody with waltz-like feeling; arched, regular phrases.	**Harmony**	Alternates minor-major-minor keys; chromatic in middle section.
Rhythm/ meter	Moderate triple meter; rhythmic complexity with three-against-two patterns (contrasting rhythms sounded together) and syncopation.	**Form**	Three-part structure (**A-B-A′**).
		Expression	Arched dynamics and subtle rubato.
		Timbre	Woodwinds featured in middle section; French horns bring a return to **A**.

0:00   **A section**—yearning cello melody, accompanied by rustling string figures; symmetrical phrasing:

0:27   Violins repeat the cello theme, extending the range and dynamics.

0:52   Theme 2, played by violins, "leans" over the bar line above a moving cello line; violins and cellos in duet.

1:27   Return of opening theme in flutes and oboes, with broader accompaniment.

1:57   **B section**—a connected three-note figure in woodwinds, in A-flat major, accompanied by offbeat 16th notes in the cellos:

3:27   Woodwinds hint at a return to the main theme, accompanied by sustained strings.

3:46   **A′ section**—French horns announce the opening theme in C minor, with richer orchestration.

4:14   Oboes take up the haunting melody as the accompaniment builds.

4:41   Theme 2, now heard in the clarinets and bassoons.

5:17   Violins and cellos take up the main theme, played in octaves for greater intensity; generally thicker and more contrapuntal accompaniment.

5:44   **Brief coda**—reminiscent of **B** section; the last chord is punctuated by pizzicato strings.

 AnotherHearing On our recording, this movement from Brahms's Third Symphony was performed by an orchestra as specified by Brahms. Now compare the style and timbres with a recording by the Peter Lehel Quartet, which draws on the principal melody of the movement for an elaboration in jazz style. How does the expressive quality of the opening of this recording compare to the orchestral version? What changes in instrumentation, timbre, and expressive quality do you hear after about a minute and a half? Which of these recordings do you prefer, and why?

Brahms's Symphony No. 3 in F Major

Brahms's study and personal library in Vienna, in a nineteenth-century painting.

Johannes Brahms was a traditionalist; his aim was to show that new and important things could still be said in the tradition of the Classical masters. The Third Symphony, written in 1883 when he was fifty years old, is the shortest of his four symphonies and the most Romantic in tone. In form, however, the work looks back to the Classical structures of the eighteenth century. The first movement, a conventional sonata-allegro, opens with a dramatic figure: a three-note motive (F–A-flat–F) that could be related to the composer's personal motto, "Frei aber froh" ("Free but happy," perhaps referring to his bachelorhood). This idea permeates the entire symphony. The slow movement, a haunting Andante in sonata-allegro form, evokes the peacefulness of nature with its simple, hymnlike theme in the woodwinds.

Rather than following with a scherzo, Brahms wrote a melancholy waltz in C minor, set in ternary form (LG 36). The opening theme, a poignant cello melody, is heard throughout this impassioned orchestral "song without words," accompanied by restless string figures. First the violins, then the woodwinds take up the melody, whose arched rise and fall suggests a huge orchestral sigh. The middle section, now in a major key, presents two themes set against an expressive, chromatic accompaniment. The return of the opening theme is newly orchestrated, then closes with an emotional statement by the violins and cellos playing in octaves. A short coda brings back the mood of the middle section, closing with two soft pizzicato chords. The finale, a dramatic sonata-allegro, features concise themes and abrupt changes of mood. Throughout, the listener is challenged by shifting moods, timbres, and melodies that affirm the technical command and the creative invention of a great Romantic master.

Later generations of orchestral composers have often tried to find a middle way between fully absolute and explicitly programmatic music. Certainly, however, the appeal of Classical forms continues to the present day, thanks in no small measure to their revitalization through the music of Brahms and his followers.

CRITICAL THINKING

1. What remains "Classical" about the treatment of absolute music in the Romantic era? What is "Romantic" about these structures?
2. How would you describe the expressive devices (melody and harmony, for example) of the Romantic symphony in comparison with those of the Classical symphony?

YourTurn TO EXPLORE

Choose a pop song that includes one or more extended instrumental passages, and focus on the sections when the voice is silent. What do the instruments express beyond the meaning of the words? What specific elements (melody, harmony, timbre) does the composer employ to emphasize those wordless meanings? How do those meanings influence the overall effect of the song?

Multimedia Hits:
Verdi and Italian Romantic Opera

"The box office is the proper thermometer of success." —*Giuseppe Verdi*

KeyPoints

- Romantic opera developed distinct national styles in Italy, Germany, and France, and women singers excelled in all styles.

- Both **opera seria** (serious opera) and **opera buffa** (comic opera) were favored in Italy; they marked the peak of the **bel canto** (beautiful singing) style.

- Giuseppe Verdi is best known for his operas, which embody the spirit of Romantic drama and passion. His *Rigoletto*, based on a play by Victor Hugo, is one of the most performed operas today.

A portrait of Swedish soprano Jenny Lind (1820–1887).

Music is an essential component of contemporary multimedia, whether films, television shows, or video games. Hit songs are often associated with them—and so it was from the beginning of what we might call commercially successful multimedia, which arose in the Italian theatrical tradition in the 1800s. Before the age of recording, catchy excerpts from operas were marketed in arrangements, whether for the home (piano four-hands, voice and guitar) or for public places (wind-band medleys). This allowed the music to saturate its culture, becoming popular in both the economic and the social sense. In the process, it became connected to the social aspirations of its audiences, providing emotional reinforcement to political messages—another important role played by music to this day.

Women and Nineteenth-Century Opera

Successful multimedia has always relied on the draw of star performers, and this was true of the Italian musical-theatrical tradition—opera—from its early days. By the time of Mozart, fashion had shifted from the castrati toward the more "natural" voices of female sopranos, and from that point on, women opera singers were among the most prominent performers of their day, in demand throughout Europe and the Americas. One international star was Jenny Lind, famous for her roles in operas by the Italians Gaetano Donizetti and Vincenzo Bellini, among others. A concert artist as well, Lind made her American debut in 1850 in a tour managed with immense hoopla by circus impresario P. T. Barnum. During her tour, Lind, known as the "Swedish Nightingale," sang both Italian operatic excerpts and American parlor ballads, emphasizing the flexible boundary between art and popular music in nineteenth-century North America.

One of the most celebrated Italian singing stars, Giuseppina Strepponi, helped to launch the career of Giuseppe Verdi, who later became her husband. While

Milan's famous opera house La Scala (c. 1850), where some of Verdi's operas premiered.

Strepponi's own singing career faded as Verdi's career rose, she continued to provide suggestions and artistic support—underlining the important role many women played not only as singers and composers, but also as teammates to their musical partners.

Verdi and Italian Opera

"Success is impossible for me if I cannot write as my heart dictates!"

Italy in the nineteenth century still recognized the opposing genres of *opera seria* (serious opera) and *opera buffa* (the Italian version of comic opera), legacies of an earlier period. One of the most important composers of this era was Gioachino Rossini (1792–1868), whose masterpieces include *Il barbiere di Siviglia* (*The Barber of Seville*, 1816) and *Guillaume Tell* (*William Tell*, 1829). These operas marked the high point of a **bel canto** (beautiful singing) style, characterized by florid melodic lines delivered by voices of great agility and purity of tone.

Verdi was the consummate master of nineteenth-century Italian opera. In his case, time, place, and personality were happily merged. He inherited a rich musical tradition, his capacity for growth was matched by extraordinary energy, and he was granted a long life in which to engage fully his creative gifts. He also came into his professional peak at a time when music publishers were helping to build markets for composers who were willing to work closely with them on licensing and other commercial ventures.

Verdi's music was adopted by those who supported political independence for Italy, which was then largely under Austrian rule. The intensity of his compositions and the potential for some of the stories to be read as calls for liberation made him a figurehead for the Italian unification movement—though Verdi himself was only mildly political: he agreed to serve in the senate of newly unified Italy, but retired after only one term. The combination of appealing melodies, intense dramatic situations, and savvy marketing by his publisher Ricordi made Verdi's music a national soundtrack for the new Italian spirit. Every town in Italy,

In Their Own Words

❝ It seems to me that the best material I have yet put to music is *Rigoletto*. It has the most powerful situations, it has variety, vitality, pathos; all the dramatic developments result from the frivolous, licentious character of the Duke. Hence Rigoletto's fears, Gilda's passion, etc., which give rise to many dramatic situations, including the scene of the quartet.❞

—Giuseppe Verdi

Giuseppe Verdi (1813–1901)

Born in a small town in northern Italy, Verdi got off to an early start by writing operas for Milan's La Scala opera house. After the tragic deaths of his daughter, baby son, and young wife in 1838–40, the distraught composer wrote no music for months. Then one night he met the director of La Scala, who insisted he take home a libretto about Nebuchadnezzar, king of Babylon. Verdi returned to work, and the resulting opera, *Nabucco,* launched him on a spectacular career.

Italy at the time was liberating itself from Austrian Hapsburg rule, and Verdi identified himself with the national cause. His works took on special meaning for his compatriots; the chorus of exiled Jews from *Nabucco* became an Italian patriotic song that is still sung today. In 1848, Verdi began an association with soprano Giuseppina Strepponi, whom he later married, and proceeded to produce one masterpiece after another. At seventy-three, he completed *Otello,* his greatest lyric tragedy. And in 1893, on the threshold of eighty, he astonished the world with *Falstaff* (a comic opera based on *The Merry Wives of Windsor*). In all, he wrote twenty-eight operas.

Verdi's favorite literary source was Shakespeare, whose plays inspired *Macbeth, Otello,* and *Falstaff. La traviata* is based on *La dame aux camellias* by Alexandre Dumas, and *Il trovatore* on a fanciful Spanish play. *Aida,* a monumental work commissioned in 1870 by the ruler of Egypt to mark the opening of the Suez Canal, premiered in Cairo. On his death, Verdi left his fortune to a home for aged musicians (Casa Verdi) that he founded in Milan and that still exists today.

MAJOR WORKS: 28 operas, including *Macbeth* (1847), *Rigoletto* (1851), *Il trovatore* (*The Troubadour,* 1853), *La traviata* (*The Lost One,* 1853), *Un ballo in maschera* (*The Masked Ball,* 1859), *Don Carlos* (1867), *Aida* (1871), *Otello* (1887), and *Falstaff* (1893) • Vocal music, including a *Requiem* Mass.

no matter how small, has a street bearing Verdi's name, and his operas are still the most frequently performed around the world.

Rigoletto

Engraving from the cover of the score to Verdi's opera *Rigoletto.* On the right, Rigoletto and his daughter Gilda watch as the Duke woos Maddalena inside the tavern.

The epitome of Romantic drama and passion, Verdi's music for *Rigoletto* communicates each dramatic situation with profound emotion. A play by Victor Hugo, an acknowledged leader of French Romanticism, was Verdi's source of inspiration.

The setting is a Renaissance-era ducal court in northern Italy. The plot revolves around lechery, deceit, and treachery. At a ball in the Duke's palace, the hunchbacked jester Rigoletto taunts a nobleman, whose wife is the object of the Duke's wandering eye, while another nobleman places a curse on the Duke for compromising his daughter's honor and on Rigoletto for making a joke of it. Unbeknownst to Rigoletto, his daughter Gilda will be the Duke's next conquest, despite the fact that the jester has kept her in seclusion. Through complicated trickery involving the Duke and some conspirators, Gilda is carried off from Rigoletto's house. The jester then plots his revenge—to kill the Duke—with the assassin Sparafucile and his sister Maddalena. In the last act, Maddalena lures the Duke to a lonely tavern where Rigoletto forces Gilda to watch through a window as the man she loves woos Maddalena.

RIGOLETTO
del Maestro Verdi.

In Act III, the Duke sings the best known of Verdi's tunes, "La donna è mobile" ("Woman is fickle"), a simple but rousing song accompanied by a guitarlike orchestral strumming (LG 37). The orchestra previews the catchy melody, which is heard numerous times in a strophic setting that brings back the opening text as a refrain.

The quartet that follows shortly is a masterpiece of operatic ensemble writing, as Verdi himself noted ("In Their Own Words," p. 287). Each character presents a different point of view: the Duke woos Maddalena in a lovely bel canto–style melody; Maddalena answers with a laughing line in short notes; Gilda, watching from outside, is heartbroken as she laments her lost love; and Rigoletto swears vengeance for his beloved daughter.

The jester arranges to send Gilda away, dressed as a man, but she deceives her father, allowing herself to be stabbed by Sparafucile, as a sacrifice for the unworthy man she loves. In the closing scene, Rigoletto is about to dispose of the sack containing what he believes is the Duke's body ("All'onda! All'onda!" ["Into the water!"]) when he hears the voice of the Duke from afar, singing "La donna è mobile" yet again. Horrified, Rigoletto opens the bag to find Gilda inside, dying as she confesses her guilt: "V'ho ingannato . . . l'amai troppo" ("I deceived you . . . I loved him too much"). Rigoletto recalls the curse one last time, as Gilda dies in his arms.

These show-stopping numbers, along with the heartbreaking closing scene, ensured the immediate success of *Rigoletto*. It remains one of the most performed operas of the international repertory—and every Italian singer can belt out "La donna è mobile." Verdi's music is simultaneously great art and powerful pop.

Rigoletto's costume for a production at the Paris Opera on February 27, 1885.

CRITICAL THINKING

1. How does the drama in the quartet from *Rigoletto* work differently from an ensemble scene in a spoken play?
2. Why was opera a good vehicle for nationalism?

YourTurn TO EXPLORE

Identify a song or instrumental track made popular through films, TV, or video games. Search online to determine how the music has been circulated or "remixed" outside the film/show/video itself. How well does the music work in a new context—does its expressive quality change without the framework of the original story?

LISTENING GUIDE 37   🔊 8:13

Verdi: *Rigoletto*, Act III, excerpts

First performance: 1851, Venice

Librettist: Francesco Maria Piave

Basis: *Le roi s'amuse*, a play by Victor Hugo

Major characters: The Duke of Mantua (tenor)
Rigoletto, the Duke's jester, a hunchback (baritone)
Gilda, Rigoletto's daughter (soprano)
Sparafucile, an assassin (bass)
Maddalena, Sparafucile's sister (contralto)

Performed by: Roberto Alagna (Duke),
Renato Bruson (Rigoletto),
Andrea Rost (Gilda),
Mariana Pentcheva (Maddalena);
Orchestra del Teatro alla Scala,
Riccardo Muti, conductor

continued on next page

What to Listen For

ARIA		QUARTET	
Melody	Soaring tenor line, with accented notes.	**Melody**	Dialogue between characters; then a simpler, square melody, "Bella figlia."
Rhythm/ meter	Lilting triple-meter, "oom-pah-pah" accompaniment; some rubato.	**Rhythm/ meter**	Allegro, with agitated movement.
Form	Two strophes, framed by an orchestral ritornello that unifies the aria.	**Expression**	Each character reveals his/her emotion.
Expression	Stirring music, with broadly contrasting dynamics.	**Performing forces**	Quartet (Duke, Maddalena, Gilda, Rigoletto).

Aria: "La donna è mobile" (Duke)   2:43

0:00   Orchestral ritornello previews the Duke's solo; opening melody of aria:

(The Duke, in a simple cavalry officer's uniform, sings in the inn; Sparafucile, Gilda, and Rigoletto listen outside.)

Duke

0:12	La donna è mobile	Woman is fickle
	qual piuma al vento,	like a feather in the wind,
	muta d'accento,	she changes her words
	e di pensiero.	and her thoughts.
	sempre un amabile	Always lovable,
	leggiadro viso,	and a lovely face,
	in pianto o in riso,	weeping or laughing,
	è menzognero.	is lying.
	La donna è mobile, etc.	Woman is fickle, etc.
1:01	*Orchestral ritornello*	
1:11	È sempre misero	The man's always wretched
	chi a le s'affida,	who believes in her,
	chi lei confida	who recklessly entrusts
	mal cauto il core!	his heart to her!
	pur mai non sentesi	And yet one who never
	felice appieno	drinks love on that breast
	chi su quel seno	never feels
	non liba amore!	entirely happy!
	La donna è mobile, etc.	Woman is fickle, etc.

(Sparafucile comes back in with a bottle of wine and two glasses, which he sets on the table; then he strikes the ceiling twice with the hilt of his long sword. At this signal, a laughing young woman in Gypsy dress leaps down the stairs: the Duke runs to embrace her, but she escapes him. Meanwhile Sparafucile has gone into the street, where he speaks softly to Rigoletto.)

Quartet (first part): "Un dì" (Duke, Maddalena, Gilda, Rigoletto)   5:29

Duke

2:44	Un dì, se ben rammentomi,	One day, if I remember right,
	o bella, t'incontrai . . .	I met you, O beauty . . .

Mi piacque di te chiedere,	I was pleased to ask about you,
e intesi che qui stai.	and I learned that you live here.
Or sappi, che d'allora	Know, then, that since that time
sol te quest'alma adora!	my soul adores only you!

Gilda

Iniquo!	Villain!

Maddalena

Ah, ah! . . . e vent'altre appresso	Ha, ha! . . . And perhaps now
le scorda forse adesso?	twenty others are forgotten?
Ha un'aria il signorino	The young gentleman looks like
da vero libertino . . .	a true libertine . . .

Duke (*starting to embrace her*)

Sí . . . un mostro son . . .	Yes . . . I'm a monster . . .

Gilda

Ah padre mio!	Ah, Father!

Maddalena

Lasciatemi, stordito.	Let me go, foolish man!

Duke

Ih che fracasso!	Ah, what a fuss!

Maddalena

Stia saggio.	Be good.

Duke

E tu sii docile,	And you, be yielding,
non fare tanto chiasso.	don't make so much noise.
Ogni saggezza chiudesi	All wisdom concludes
nel gaudio e nell'amore.	in pleasure and in love.

(*He takes her hand, vowing his love for her. Outside, Rigoletto reveals the unfaithful lover to Gilda as the dialogue continues, leading to the famous quartet below.*)

Quartet (second part): "Bella figlia"

Overall form: **A-B-A'-C** plus coda

How characters interact in the ensemble and how they fit into the musical structure:

Opening melody of "Bella figlia," sung by the Duke:

continued on next page

	Duke		**Section**
4:15	Bella figlia dell'amore,	Beautiful daughter of love,	**A**
	schiavo son de' vezzi tuoi;	I am the slave of your charms;	
	con un detto sol tu puoi	with a single word you can	
	le mie pene consolar.	console my sufferings.	
	Vieni, e senti del mio core	Come, and feel the quick beating	
	il frequente palpitar . . .	of my heart . . .	
	Con un detto sol tuo puoi	With a single word you can	
	le mie pene consolar.	console my sufferings.	

(Many text lines repeated.)

Maddalena

5:19	Ah! ah! rido ben di core,	Ha! Ha! I laugh heartily,	**B**
	chè tai baie costan poco.	for such tales cost little.	

Gilda

	Ah! cosí parlar d'amore . . .	Ah! To speak thus of love . . .	

Maddalena

	Quanto valga il vostro gioco,	Believe me, I can judge	
	mel credete, sò apprezzar.	how much your game is worth.	

Gilda

	. . . a me pur l'infame ho udito!	. . . I too have heard the villain so!	

Rigoletto (to Gilda)

	Taci, il piangere non vale.	Hush, weeping is of no avail.	

Gilda

	Infelice cor tradito,	Unhappy, betrayed heart,	
	per angoscia non scoppiar. No, no!	do not burst with anguish. Ah, no!	

Maddalena

	Son avvezza, bel signore,	I'm accustomed, handsome sir,	
	ad un simile scherzare.	to similar joking.	
	Mio bel signor!	My handsome sir!	

Duke

6:01	Bella figlia dell'amore, etc.	Beautiful daughter of love, etc.	**A′**
	Vieni!	Come!	

Rigoletto

	Ch'ei mentiva sei sicura.	You are sure that he was lying.	
	Taci, e mia sarà la cura	Hush, and I will take care	
	la vendetta d'affrettar.	to hasten vengeance.	
	sì, pronta fia, sarà fatale,	Yes, it will be swift and fatal,	
	io saprollo fulminar.	I will know how to strike him down.	
	taci, taci . . .	Hush, hush . . .	

All characters

(Repeated text from above.)   **C**

7:27	**Coda**, featuring all characters.		**Coda**

47

Total Art: Wagner and German Romantic Opera

"The whole [Ring] will then become—out with it! I am not ashamed to say so—the greatest work of poetry ever written."

—*Richard Wagner*

KeyPoints

- In Germany, the genre *Singspiel* (light, comic drama with spoken dialogue) gave way to more serious works, including Richard Wagner's **music dramas**, which integrated music, poetry, drama, and spectacle.

- Wagner's music dramas are not sectional (with arias, ensembles, and the like) but are continuous, unified by **leitmotifs**—recurring themes—that represent a person, place, or idea. His most famous work is the four-opera cycle *The Ring of the Nibelung*.

Through Hollywood blockbusters, we have become accustomed to being told by the movie soundtrack when a character is in danger from an evildoer or monster, or when we should start crying. Films and TV shows have also taught us to associate musical ideas with specific characters, so that we can be made aware that someone on screen is thinking about an absent character through the appearance of that character's music in the soundtrack. We owe this supremely effective resource to the work of Richard Wagner, who established the idea that multimedia can convey multiple meanings at once: words may be telling us one thing, and the music may be adding something else that is more subtle. Contemporary composers have repeatedly credited Wagner's concept of "leitmotif," which we will explore in this chapter, with opening up opportunities to create powerful musical reinforcement in film, TV, and computer gaming.

In Their Own Words

" True drama can be conceived only as resulting from the collective impulse of all the arts to communicate in the most immediate way with a collective public. . . . Thus the art of tone . . . will realize in the collective artwork its richest potential. . . . For in its isolation music has formed itself an organ capable of the most immeasurable expression—the orchestra."

—*Richard Wagner*

Wagner and German Musical Theater

Nineteenth-century Germany had no long-established opera tradition, as Italy and France did. The immediate predecessor of German Romantic opera was the *Singspiel*, a light or comic drama with spoken dialogue like Mozart's *The Magic Flute* (*Die Zauberflöte*). One element that characterized German musical theater of the early 1800s was **melodrama**: scenes with spoken dialogue or minimal singing, but striking orchestral accompaniment to intensify the dramatic effect of the words.

The greatest figure in German opera, and one of the most significant in the history of the Romantic era, was Richard Wagner. Historians often divide the period into before and after Wagner. The course of post-Romantic music is unimaginable without the impact of this complex and fascinating figure. We will consider his

Richard Wagner at Home in Bayreuth, a painting by **W. Beckmann**, 1882. Wagner's wife Cosima is on the left and her father, Franz Liszt, on the right.

music drama *Die Walküre* (*The Valkyrie,* which includes the famous *Ride of the Valkyries*), part of his cycle *The Ring of the Nibelung.*

The Ring of the Nibelung

Wagner did away with the concept of separate arias, duets, ensembles, choruses, and ballets, developing an "endless melody" that was molded to the natural inflections of the German language, more melodious than the traditional recitative but freer and more flexible than the traditional aria. He conceived of opera as a **total artwork** (in German, *Gesamtkunstwerk*) in which the arts of music, poetry, drama, and visual spectacle were fused together, each element created and controlled by his creative genius: a **music drama**.

The orchestra became its focal point and unifying element, fashioned out of concise themes—the **leitmotifs**, or "leading motives," that recur throughout a work, undergoing variation and development like the themes and motives of a symphony. The leitmotifs carry specific meanings, suggesting in a few notes a person, an emotion, an idea, an object. Through a process of continual transformation, they trace the course of the drama, the changes in the characters, their experiences and memories, and their thoughts and hidden desires.

Richard Wagner (1813–1883)

Wagner was born in Leipzig, Germany. After studying briefly at the University of Leipzig, he gained practical experience conducting in provincial theaters. At twenty-three, he married the actress Minna Planer, and began to produce his first operas. He wrote the librettos himself, as he did for all his later works, unifying music and drama more than anyone had before.

Wagner's early opera *Rienzi* won a huge success in Dresden. With his next three works, *The Flying Dutchman, Tannhäuser,* and *Lohengrin,* Wagner chose subjects derived from medieval German epics. In them, he displayed a profound feeling for nature, employed the supernatural as an element of the drama, and glorified the German land and people. In 1849, after a failed revolution in Dresden, Wagner fled to Switzerland, where he set forth his theories of the music drama, the name he gave his complete integration of theater and music. He proceeded to put theory into practice in the cycle of four music dramas called *The Ring of the Nibelung,* and two more—*Tristan and Isolde* and *Die Meistersinger von Nürnberg.*

Wagner soon won the support and admiration of the young monarch Ludwig II of Bavaria, who commissioned

him to complete the *Ring* and helped him build a theater to present his music dramas, which ultimately became the Festival Theater at Bayreuth. And the composer (now separated from Minna) found a woman he considered his equal in will and courage—Cosima, the daughter of his old friend Franz Liszt (see illustration above). She left her husband and children in order to join him.

The Wagnerian gospel spread across Europe as a new art-religion. The *Ring* cycle was completed in 1874 and presented to worshipful audiences at the first Bayreuth Festival two years later. Wagner's final work was *Parsifal,* based on the legend of the Holy Grail.

MAJOR WORKS: 13 operas (music dramas), including *Rienzi* (1842), *Der fliegende Holländer* (*The Flying Dutchman,* 1843), *Tannhäuser* (1845), *Lohengrin* (1850), *Tristan und Isolde* (1865), *Die Meistersinger von Nürnberg* (*The Mastersingers of Nuremberg,* 1868), and *Parsifal* (1882) • Cycle of music dramas: *Der Ring des Nibelung* (*The Ring of the Nibelung*), consisting of *Das Rheingold* (*The Rhine Gold,* 1869), *Die Walküre* (*The Valkyrie,* 1870), *Siegfried* (1876), and *Götterdämmerung* (*The Twilight of the Gods,* 1876) • Orchestral music • Piano music • Vocal and choral music • Writings: *Art and Revolution; The Art Work of the Future.*

Wagner based his musical language on chromatic harmony, which he pushed to its then furthest limits. Chromatic dissonance gives his music its restless, intensely emotional quality. Never before had unstable pitch combinations been used so eloquently to portray states of the soul.

The story of *The Ring of the Nibelung* centers on the treasure of gold that lies hidden in the depths of the Rhine River, guarded by three Rhine Maidens. Alberich the Nibelung, who comes from a hideous race of dwarfs who inhabit the dark regions below the earth, tries to make love to the maidens. When they repulse him, he steals the treasure and makes it into a ring that will bring unlimited power to its owner. Wotan, father of the gods (for whom Wednesday, or Wotan's Day, is named), tricks Alberich out of the ring, whereupon the dwarf pronounces a terrible curse: may the ring destroy the peace of mind of all who gain possession of it, may it bring them misfortune and death.

Thus begins the cycle of four dramas that ends only when the curse-bearing ring is returned to the Rhine Maidens. Gods and heroes, mortals and Nibelungs, intermingle freely in this tale of betrayed love, broken promises, magic spells, and general corruption brought on by the lust for power. Wagner freely adapted the story from the myths of the Norse sagas and the legends associated with a medieval German epic poem, the *Nibelungenlied*. (Norse mythology and Wagner's *Ring* were also the inspiration for J. R. R. Tolkien's epic *Lord of the Rings* and for the three movies based on that literary work, as well as for many role-playing games.)

A Valkyrie on her winged horse, in a design (c. 1876) by **Carl Emil Doepler** (1824–1905).

Die Walküre (The Valkyrie)

Die Walküre, the second work in the cycle, revolves around the lovers (who are twin brother and sister, unbeknownst to them) Siegmund and Sieglinde, the offspring of Wotan by a mortal. Their love is not only incestuous but also adulterous, for she has been forced into a loveless marriage with the grim chieftain Hunding, who challenges Siegmund to battle. The second act opens with a scene between Wotan and Brünnhilde, one of his nine daughters, called Valkyries. The Valkyries' perpetual task is to circle the battlefield on their winged horses and swoop down to gather up the fallen heroes, whom they bear away to the great hall of Valhalla, where they will sit forever feasting with the gods. At the insistence of Fricka, goddess of marriage and Wotan's wife, Wotan acknowledges that Siegmund has violated the holiest law of the universe and sadly realizes that he must die in combat with Hunding. Brünnhilde decides to disobey her father's command to let Hunding win the duel by shielding Siegmund. But Wotan appears and holds out his spear, upon which Siegmund's sword is shattered. Hunding then buries his own spear in Siegmund's breast. Wotan, overcome by his son's death, turns a ferocious look upon Hunding, who falls dead. Then the god hurries off in pursuit of the daughter who dared to defy his command.

Act III opens with the famous *Ride of the Valkyries*, a vivid orchestral picture of the nine warrior maidens on their way from the battlefield back to Valhalla, carrying fallen heroes slung across the saddles of their winged horses (LG 38). This prelude features some of Wagner's most brilliant scoring. The rustling strings and woodwinds give way to the memorable "Ride" theme (familiar from movie soundtracks and even commercials), which is sounded repeatedly by a huge and varied brass section through a dense orchestral texture that builds to several climaxes beneath the warriors' voices.

Brünnhilde is the last Valkyrie to arrive, carrying Sieglinde and several fragments of Siegmund's sword. Sieglinde wants to die, but Brünnhilde tells her she

Ride of the Valkyries

Arthur Rackham's drawing portrays Brünnhilde asleep in a ring of fire.

must live to bear his son, who will become the world's mightiest hero. Brünnhilde remains to face her father's wrath. Her punishment is severe: she is to be deprived of her godhood, Wotan tells her, to become a mortal. He will put her to sleep on a rock, and she will fall prey to the first mortal who finds her. Brünnhilde begs him to soften her punishment: let him at least surround the rock with flames so that only a fearless hero will be able to penetrate the wall of fire. Wotan relents and grants her request. He kisses her on both eyes, which close at once. Striking the rock three times, he invokes Loge, the god of Fire. Flames spring up around the rock, and the "magic fire" leitmotif is heard, followed by the "magic sleep" and "slumber" motives. "Whosoever fears the tip of my spear shall never pass through the fire," he sings, as the orchestra announces the theme of Siegfried, the fearless, yet-unborn son of Sieglinde who in the third music drama will force his way through the flames and awaken Brünnhilde with a kiss.

Although the action in this final scene is fairly static, Wagner brings together several strands of meaning through the interaction of the leitmotifs, even introducing us to a character (Siegfried) who has not even been born. Wotan does not name Siegfried, but the striking brass motive names him through music, and prepares us to meet him on the following night (Wagner conceived the *Ring* to be performed on four consecutive evenings). Contemporary film composers such as John Williams also have used this foreshadowing device (in the *Star Wars* films, for example; see Chapter 71), introducing early in the film subtle musical references that prepare us for a full "reveal" later on.

LISTENING GUIDE 38   5:51

Wagner: *Die Walküre* (*The Valkyrie*), Act III, Opening and Finale

Date: 1856; first performed 1870, in Munich

Genre: Music drama: second in a cycle of four (*The Ring of the Nibelung*)

Characters: Wotan, father of the gods (bass-baritone)
Brünnhilde, his favorite daughter (soprano)
Valkyries, the nine daughters of Wotan

Performed by: Theo Adam, bass; Staatskapelle Dresden, Marek Janoski, conductor

Act III, scene 1: *Ride of the Valkyries*   1:17

What to Listen For			
Melody	Swirling strings and woodwinds, then famous "Ride" leitmotif ascends, repeated many times.	**Expression**	Excited mood; great dynamic contrasts; evokes battle cries and flying warriors.
Rhythm/ meter	Lively dotted rhythm in 9/8 for the "Ride" leitmotif.	**Performing forces**	Huge orchestra featuring brass (including eight French horns, bass trumpet, various-sized trombones, Wagner tubas, and contrabass tuba); woodwinds (piccolos, English horn, and bass clarinet); large percussion section (cymbals, triangle, glockenspiel, gong); and strings (including six harps).
Harmony	Leitmotif heard in both minor and major.		
Texture	Polyphonic, combines main theme and swirling idea.		

0:00   Orchestral prelude, marked *Lebhaft* (Lively), in 9/8 meter.
       Rushing string figure alternates with fast wavering in woodwinds, then—

0:08   insistent dotted figure begins in horns and low strings.
       Swirling string and woodwind lines, accompanied by dotted figure.

0:22   "Ride" motive, heard first in a minor key in the horns:

0:34   "Ride" motive is now heard in a major key in the trumpets.
       Four-note dotted motive exchanged between low and high brass instruments, heard above swirling idea.

1:04   "Ride" motive played *fortissimo*, as curtain opens.

       (Four Valkyries, in full armor, have settled on the highest peak above a cave.)

Act III, closing of scene 3: Wotan and Brünnhilde   4:34

What to Listen For		
Melody	Three recurring themes (leitmotifs); endless melody; forceful descending trombone melody.	
Rhythm/ meter	Broad, duple meter; majestic.	
Harmony	Rich, chromatic harmony.	
Texture	Continuous orchestral sound.	

Expression	Melodies signify magic fire, magic sleep, slumber, Siegfried; dramatic invocation of Loge, god of Fire; long closing, *ff* to *ppp*.
Performing forces	Bass (Wotan) with orchestra; focus on trombones (calling Loge); woodwinds and French horns (in "magic fire" music); harps (in "magic sleep" music) and brass (Siegfried theme).

(Wotan clasps Brünnhilde's head in his hands. He kisses her long on the eyes. She sinks back with closed eyes, unconscious in his arms. He gently bears her to a low mossy mound . . . and lays her upon it. He looks upon her and closes her helmet; his eyes rest on the form of the sleeper, whom he covers with the great shield of the Valkyrie. He turns slowly away, then again turns around with a sorrowful look.)

(He strides with solemn decision to the middle of the stage and directs the point of his spear toward a large rock.)

0:00   A forceful trombone passage precedes Wotan's invocation of Loge, god of Fire:

Wotan's evocation of Loge:

Lo - ge, hör'!   Lau - sche hie-her!

Wotan

0:08   Loge, hör'! Lausche hieher!   Loge, listen! Harken here!
       Wie zuerst ich dich fand, als feurige Gluth,   As I found you first, a fiery blaze,
       wie dann einst du mir schwandest,   as once you vanished from me,
       als schweifende Lohe;   a random fire;
       wie ich dich band, bann' ich dich heut'!   as I allied with you, so today I conjure you!
       Herauf, wabernde Lohe,   Arise, magic flame,
       umlod're mir feurig den Fels!   girdle the rock with fire for me!

continued on next page

(He strikes the rock thrice with his spear.)
Loge! Loge! Hieher!   Loge! Loge! Come here!

(A flash of flames issues from the rock, which swells to an ever-brightening fiery glow. Bright shooting flames surround Wotan. With his spear he directs the sea of fire to encircle the rock; it presently spreads toward the background, where it encloses the mountain in flames.)

1:03   "Magic fire" music, heard in full orchestra:

1:40   "Magic sleep" motive, evoked in a descending chromatic line in woodwinds:

1:53   "Slumber" motive, heard in woodwinds:

                              Wotan (singing to "Siegfried" motive)

2:03   Wer meines Speeres Spitze fürchtet,   Whosoever fears the tip of my spear
        durchreite das Feuer nie!   shall never pass through the fire!

(He stretches out the spear as a spell. He gazes sadly on Brünnhilde. Slowly he turns to depart. He turns his head again and looks back. He disappears through the fire.)

2:34   Brass in *fortissimo* announce the "Siegfried" motive; long orchestral closing:

CRITICAL THINKING

1. What innovations did Wagner bring to the world of opera?
2. In what ways do leitmotifs contribute to the shaping of drama?

YourTurn TO EXPLORE

Consider an instance of epic-scale multimedia—the *Star Wars* or *Lord of the Rings* movie cycles, or an MMORPG like World of Warcraft or RuneScape. Can you identify leitmotifs associated with situations, characters, key objects? Do they evolve along with the characters as the drama progresses, and if so, how? How do you think the use of leitmotifs helps shape the dramatic or gaming experience?

48

Embracing Death: Brahms and the Requiem

"I speak through my music. The only thing is that a poor musician such as myself would like to believe that he was better than his music."

—*Johannes Brahms*

KeyPoints

- Choral music grew in popularity during the Romantic era and provided an artistic outlet for the middle classes.

- Favored genres in the nineteenth century include **part songs** (unaccompanied secular songs for three or four voice parts), the oratorio, the Mass, and the **Requiem Mass**.

- Brahms's *German Requiem*, set to biblical texts chosen by the composer, is a masterpiece of the Romantic choral repertory.

We often turn to music for comfort in times of trouble. "When all hope is gone," sings Elton John, "sad songs say so much." Many also seek spiritual sustenance in music—and these two strands combine in the **Requiem**, or Mass for the Dead, a genre long cultivated by musicians in the Western tradition. Although the Catholic Church specifies certain texts and prayers for the Requiem Mass, composers have often customized these for their own spiritual tendencies and expressive goals. Several musicians of the nineteenth century wrote unique Requiems. Johannes Brahms, in particular, chose texts that were purposefully detached from specific religious practice, trying for a message that would comfort grieving listeners regardless of their faith. In this chapter, we examine a work that Brahms called *A German Requiem* (though he considered calling it "A Requiem for People")—both as representative of the Romantic-era choral repertory and as an early example of successful interfaith music.

Romantic Choral Music

The nineteenth century witnessed a spreading of the democratic ideal and an enormous expansion of the audience for music. This climate was uniquely favorable to choral singing, a group activity enjoyed by increasing numbers of amateur music lovers that played an important role in the musical life of the Romantic era.

Choral music offered people an ideal outlet f or their artistic energies. Although the repertory centered on the great choral heritage of the past, a vast literature of secular choral pieces also appeared. These works, settings for chorus of lyric poems in a variety of moods and styles, were known as **part songs**—that is, songs with three or four voice parts. Most of them were short melodious works, easy enough

Part songs

In the nineteenth century, enormous choral and orchestral forces were a common sight, as in this engraving of the opening concert at St. Martin's Hall, London, in 1850.

for amateurs. They gave pleasure both to the singers and to their listeners, and played an important role in developing the new audience of the nineteenth century.

Large-scale choral works

Among the large-scale genres of choral music in the nineteenth century were the Mass, the Requiem Mass, and the oratorio. Though all three were originally intended to be performed in church, by the nineteenth century they had found a wider audience in the concert hall. This is certainly the case with Brahms's *Requiem*, which is far removed from the traditions of the Catholic Church that gave birth to the genre.

Brahms's *German Requiem*

A German Requiem was rooted in the Protestant tradition into which Brahms was born. Its aim was to console the living and lead them to a serene acceptance of death as an inevitable part of life, hence its gentle lyricism. Brahms chose his text from the Old and New Testaments: from the Psalms, Proverbs, Isaiah, and Ecclesiastes as well as from the writings of Paul, Matthew, Peter, and John, and the book of Revelation. He was not religious in the conventional sense, nor was he affiliated with any particular church. He was moved to compose his *Requiem* by the deaths first of his teacher and friend Robert Schumann, then of his mother, whom he idolized; but the piece transcends personal emotions and endures as a song of mourning for all humanity. Brahms wrote to his dear friend Clara Schumann, sending her two slow movements he had completed of the Requiem, expressing his hope that "a German text of this sort will please you as much as the usual Latin one" and that he would have "enough courage and zest" to complete the work.

Written for soloists, four-part chorus, and orchestra, *A German Requiem* is in seven movements arranged in a formation resembling an arch: there are connections between the first and last movements, between the second and sixth, and between the third and fifth. That leaves the fourth movement, the widely sung chorus "How lovely is Thy dwelling place," as the centerpiece.

This movement is based on a verse from Psalm 84 (LG 39). The first two lines of the psalm are heard three times, separated by two contrasting sections that present the other lines. The form, therefore, is **A-B-A′-C-A′**. The first two sections move largely in quarter notes, but the third section (**C**) moves more quickly.

This vigorous rhythm better suits the line "die loben dich immerdar" (that praise Thee evermore), with much expansion on "immerdar." With the final reappearance of the **A** section, the slower tempo returns. Marked *piano* and *dolce* (soft and sweet), this passage serves as a coda that brings the piece to its gentle and serene close.

Brahms's approach to the Requiem is especially unusual in that he chooses to comfort the living rather than dwell on the fate of the dead: he omits the intense references to religious judgment (for example, the Dies irae) found in the Catholic Requiem Mass. Perhaps because of its focus on divine compassion outside of a specific sectarian message, his *German Requiem* was quickly embraced across Europe among many communities of faith. It is still among the best-known and most frequently performed of Brahms's works, sought after in large part for its power to console those of us who are left contemplating how to continue after loved ones have passed.

Brahms turned to Clara Schumann, widow of his teacher Robert Schumann, for support in writing his Requiem.

CRITICAL THINKING

1. How, and why, did choral music undergo a revival in the nineteenth century?
2. How would you describe Brahms's view of death, based on his Requiem? How does the music portray these feelings?

Your Turn TO EXPLORE

Find an example of a musical work designed to reflect on a tragic event and/or offer comfort or hope to those who have witnessed it. If words are incorporated, where are they from, and what kind of imagery do they evoke? How is music used to reinforce particular words or bring out specific meanings? What instrumental (and vocal) forces are used, and why do you think that particular instrumentation was chosen? What musical (as opposed to word-related) elements might be intended to express the intensity of sorrow, or foster the lightness of hope?

Brahms: *A German Requiem*, IV

Date: 1868

Genre: Protestant Requiem, in seven movements

Performed by: Arnold Schoenberg Choir, Vienna Philharmonic; Nikolaus Harnoncourt, director

IV: Mässig bewegt (at a moderate tempo)

What to Listen For

Melody	Lyrical, wavelike choral melody that returns, rondo-like, to unify the form.
Rhythm/ meter	Slow, waltz-like triple meter; more accented motion in middle section.
Harmony	Changes between major and minor keys to follow the text.

Form	Rondo-like, with the main theme returning to unify the movement.
Expression	Emotional expressions of loss and acceptance of death through text-painting and harmonic shifts.
Text	Based on Psalm 84 (in the Protestant Bible; 83 in the Vulgate, or Latin Bible).

Opening melody—clarinets and flutes begin with inverted first phrase of the chorus:

0:00	**Orchestral introduction.**		
0:08	Wie lieblich sind deine Wohnun- gen, Herr Zebaoth!	How lovely is Thy dwelling place, O Lord of Hosts!	**A**—a flowing, arched melody in an SATB homophonic setting (in E-flat major); text is repeated in the tenors; then in the other voices.
1:27	Meine Seele verlanget und sehnet sich nach den Vorhöfen des Herrn;	My soul longs and even faints for the courts of the Lord;	**B**—shift to the minor mode, builds fugally from lowest to highest voices;
2:04	mein Leib und Seele freuen sich in dem lebendigen Gott.	my flesh and soul rejoice in the living God.	sudden accents on first beat of measures, with plucked strings; climax on "lebendigen."
2:49	Wie lieblich . . . Wohl denen, die in deinem Hause wohnen,	How lovely . . . Blessed are they that live in Thy house,	**A′**—opening returns in E-flat major, with new text and varied melody.
3:55	die loben dich immerdar!	that praise Thee evermore!	**C**—martial quality, faster movement; voices declaim polyphonically.
4:51	Wie lieblich . . .	How lovely . . .	**A′**—coda-like return of opening material; soft orchestral closing.

49

Poetry in Motion:
Tchaikovsky and the Ballet

"Dance is the hidden language of the soul." —Martha Graham

KeyPoints

- **Ballet** became an independent dramatic form in the eighteenth and nineteenth centuries, particularly in France and Russia.

- The ballets of Russian composer Peter Ilyich Tchaikovsky—*Swan Lake, Sleeping Beauty*, and *The Nutcracker*—remain central to the repertory today.

Out of movement, dance weaves an enchantment all its own. We watch with amazement as dancers synchronize their actions to the music, performing pirouettes and intricate footwork with the utmost grace, and leaps that seem to triumph over the laws of gravity. A special glamour attaches to the great dancers—Mikhail Baryshnikov, Fred Astaire, Martha Graham, Isadora Duncan, Lil Buck, and their peers—yet theirs is an art based on an inhumanly demanding discipline. Their bodies are their instruments, which they must keep in excellent shape in order to perform the gymnastics required of them. They create moments of elusive beauty, made possible only by total control of their muscles. It is this combination of physical and emotional factors, blended with the expressive resources of music, that marks the distinctive power of choreographed dance.

A French court dancer from the era of Louis XIV.

The Ballet

Beginning in the Renaissance, the choreographed dance known as **ballet** was central to lavish festivals and theatrical entertainments presented at the courts of kings and dukes. Royal weddings and other celebrations were accompanied by spectacles with scenery, costumes, and staged dancing known as *intermedio* in Italy, **masque** in England, and *ballet de cour* in France. Louis XIV himself took part in one, as the Sun King. Elaborate ballets were also featured in the operas by French composers.

The eighteenth century saw the rise of ballet as an independent art form. French ballet was preeminent in the early nineteenth century, then Russian ballet came into its own—helped along considerably by the arrival in 1847 of French-born Marius Petipa, the great choreographer at St. Petersburg. Petipa created the dances for more than a hundred works, invented the structure of the classic *pas de deux* (dance for two), and brought the art of staging ballets to unprecedented heights.

Tchaikovsky and *The Nutcracker*

A traditional Russian nutcracker—a toy soldier who comes alive in Tchaikovsky's ballet.

The giant of Russian ballet in the later nineteenth century was Peter Ilyich Tchaikovsky, who also composed well-loved works in other instrumental genres. Tchaikovsky belonged to a generation that saw its truths crumbling and found none to replace them; his music typifies the end-of-the-century mood of pessimism that engulfed the late Romantic movement.

Tchaikovsky had a natural affinity for the theater. His three ballets—*Swan Lake*, *The Sleeping Beauty*, and *The Nutcracker*, all choreographed by Petipa— were quickly established as basic works of the Russian repertory. We will hear excerpts from the popular ballet that's performed every Christmas all over the world, *The Nutcracker*.

Act I takes place at a Christmas party during which two children, Clara and Fritz, receive a nutcracker from their godfather. After the children have gone to bed, Clara returns to gaze at her gift, falls asleep, and begins to dream. First she is terrified to see mice scampering around the tree. Then the dolls she has received come alive and fight a battle with the mice, which reaches a climax in the combat between the Nutcracker and the Mouse King. Clara helps her beloved Nutcracker by throwing a slipper at the Mouse King, who is vanquished. The Nutcracker then becomes a handsome Prince, who sweeps Clara away with him.

Act II finds them in Confiturembourg, the land of sweets, ruled by the Sugar Plum Fairy (LG 40). The Prince presents Clara to his family, and a celebration follows, with a series of dances that reveal all the attractions of this magic realm. The dances are accompanied by colorful instruments; Tchaikovsky wrote to his

Peter Ilyich Tchaikovsky (1840–1893)

The son of a Russian government official, Tchaikovsky entered the newly founded Conservatory of St. Petersburg at the age of twenty-three. He was immediately recommended by Anton Rubinstein, director of the school, for a teaching post in the new Moscow Conservatory, and his twelve years in Moscow saw the production of some of his most successful works.

Extremely sensitive by nature, Tchaikovsky was subject to attacks of depression. The social stigma associated with being a homosexual may have led him to marry a student at the conservatory, but they soon separated. Good fortune followed when in 1877 Nadezhda von Meck, the wealthy widow of an industrialist, sent Tchaikovsky money to go abroad, and launched him on the most productive period of his career. Bound by the rigid conventions of her time and class, von Meck had to be certain that her enthusiasm was for the artist, not the man; hence she stipulated that she never meet the recipient of her patronage.

Tchaikovsky was the first Russian whose music appealed to Western tastes—it was performed in Vienna, Berlin, and Paris—and in 1891 he was invited to participate in the inaugural concert of Carnegie Hall in New York. Two years later, he conducted his *Pathétique* Symphony in St. Petersburg, where the work met with a lukewarm reception. He died within several weeks, at the age of fifty-three, and the tragic tone of his last work led to rumors that he had committed suicide. More likely he contracted cholera from tainted water.

Although Tchaikovsky declared, "I am Russian through and through!" he also came under the spell of Italian opera, French ballet, and German symphony and song. These he joined to the strain of folk melody that was his heritage as a Russian, imposing on this mixture his sharply defined personality.

MAJOR WORKS: Eight operas, including *Eugene Onegin* (1878) • Three ballets: *Swan Lake* (1877), *The Sleeping Beauty* (1890), and *The Nutcracker* (1892) • Orchestral music, including seven symphonies (one unfinished), three piano concertos, a violin concerto, symphonic poems (*Romeo and Juliet*, 1880), and overtures (*1812 Overture*, 1880) • Chamber and keyboard music • Choral music • Songs.

publisher that he had discovered a new one in Paris, "something between a piano and a glockenspiel, with a divinely beautiful tone, and I want to introduce it into the ballet." The instrument was the **celesta**, whose timbre perfectly suits the Sugar Plum Fairy's dance. In the *Trepak* (Russian Dance, featuring the famous Cossack squat kick; see illustration opposite), the orchestral sound is enlivened by a tambourine. Other exotic dances follow, from Arabia and China, climaxing with the *Waltz of the Flowers*.

Celesta

This engaging work conjures up everything we have come to associate with the Romantic ballet. It is an example of the way music has been combined with movement in the Western tradition to tell stories that are both more precise than instrumental program music and more subtle and nuanced than opera and song.

CRITICAL THINKING

1. How does Tchaikovsky use instruments to portray characters in his dances?
2. How does *The Nutcracker* embrace and depart from musical nationalism and exoticism?

Your Turn TO EXPLORE

Find two videos of dancers from separate traditions (for example, classical ballet, modern dance, tap, jazz and/or Broadway dance, hip-hop)—some extraordinary performers you might look for are Rudolf Nureyev, Savion Glover, Bob Fosse, Katherine Dunham, Lil Buck, Michael Jackson. Note how the dancer varies and repeats movements, the variety of melodic ideas in the music, and the way the music and movement are synchronized. Do you think the dancer is conveying a story through their moves, and if so, how would you describe it? If not, what do you think the dancer is conveying?

LISTENING GUIDE 40 🔊 2:56

Tchaikovsky: *The Nutcracker*, Two Dances

Date: 1892

Genre: Ballet (from which an orchestral suite was made)

Basis: E. T. A. Hoffmann story, expanded by Alexandre Dumas *père*

Choreographer: Marius Petipa

Performed by: Philadelphia Orchestra, Eugene Ormandy, conductor

Sequence of dances: *March*
Dance of the Sugar Plum Fairy
Trepak
Arab Dance

Chinese Dance
Dance of the Toy Flutes
Waltz of the Flowers

Dance of the Sugar Plum Fairy: Andante non troppo

1:44

What to Listen For			
Melody	Staccato melody, somewhat chromatic.	**Expression**	Quiet, magical mood.
Rhythm/ meter	Bouncy duple meter.	**Performing forces**	Bell-like timbre of celesta, accompanied by bass clarinet and pizzicato strings.
Form	Three-part (**A-B-A**).		

continued on next page

A section

0:00   Short introduction (four measures) of pizzicato strings.

0:08   Main theme introduced by celesta, staccato in a high range (in dialogue with bass clarinet):

B section

0:39   Brief section with arched lines in woodwinds and celesta, answered by strings.

A section

1:11   Solo celesta leads back to the main theme, accompanied by staccato strings. Closes with a loud pizzicato chord.

Trepak (Russian Dance): Tempo di trepak, molto vivace (very lively)   1:12

What to Listen For			
Melody	Short, staccato melody, descending, with *sforzandos* (accents).	**Form**	Three-part (**A-B-A**).
Rhythm/ meter	Lively peasant dance, heavy accents; *accelerando* (getting faster).	**Expression**	Vivacious mood; builds to a frenzy at the end.
Texture	Homophonic; denser texture in **B** section.	**Performing forces**	Tambourine featured with strings and woodwinds; trumpet fanfare.

A section

0:00   Lively dance tune in strings, repeated in full orchestra:

B section

0:27   Brief diversion in the same rhythmic style, melody in the low strings.

A section

0:47   Return of the dance tune; quickens at the end, with trumpet fanfare and syncopations.

Mikhail Baryshnikov as the Nutcracker Prince, who fights the Mouse King, in an American Ballet Theatre production of *The Nutcracker*.

50

Exotic Allure: Puccini and the Italian Verismo Tradition

"It may be a good thing to copy reality; but to invent reality is much, much better."

—*Giuseppe Verdi*

KeyPoints

- At the turn of the twentieth century, there arose an important movement called **post-Romanticism**, which reflected an expansion and intensification of late Romantic trends, especially in Germany, Austria, and Italy.

- Italian composer Giacomo Puccini wrote some of the best-loved operas of all time, including *Madame Butterfly*, which combines two end-of-the-century trends: **verismo** (realism) and **exoticism** (Japanese culture and music).

The intensity that musical accompaniment brings to words can generate meanings that surpass those of the poetry or lyrics being set. This is why musical multimedia always produces an effect that is at least a little unreal, or even "hyper-real." However, realism is also an effective artistic choice: a way to make a message more powerful because the characters delivering it are recognizable to an audience. And a way to spice up realism is to mix it with elements of a foreign or fantastic setting, so that familiar perspectives are filtered through unfamiliar contexts. This tactic is what makes many science fiction and fantasy movies and video games so compelling; and we can see it too in the exotic realism that characterizes post-Romantic musical trends at the turn of the twentieth century.

La Japonaise (1876), by **Claude Monet** (1840–1926), depicting the nineteenth-century Paris fad for all things Japanese.

Post-Romanticism

The late Romantic ideals were carried into the **post-Romantic** era through the Italian operatic tradition—in particular, by Giacomo Puccini—and by German composers such as Richard Strauss (1864–1949) and Gustav Mahler (1860–1911), both notable for inspired orchestral writing infused with sensuous lyricism. Mahler, like many of his contemporaries, also had a strong fascination with Eastern culture. So did Puccini: his enduring opera *Madame Butterfly* radiates an **exoticism** that was gaining popularity in the arts at the time (see p. 309).

Puccini and Verismo Opera

"God touched me with His little finger and said, 'Write for the theater, only for the theater.' And I obeyed the supreme command."

Giacomo Puccini was the main voice among a group of opera composers associated with a movement known as **verismo**, or realism. The advocates of this trend tried to bring into the theater the naturalness of writers such as Émile Zola and Henrik Ibsen. Instead of choosing historical or mythological themes, they picked subjects from everyday life and treated them in down-to-earth fashion. The most famous verismo operas include Puccini's *La bohème* (*Bohemian Life*, 1896) and *Tosca* (1900), and Ruggero Leoncavallo's *Pagliacci* (*The Clowns*, 1892). Although it was a short-lived movement, verismo had counterparts in Germany and France, and arguably was influential in the rising multimedia tradition of film. And it produced some of the best-loved works in the operatic repertory.

Madame Butterfly

Puccini's style emphasizes soaring melodies and rich orchestral timbres and colors, as well as elements borrowed from Wagner, notably leitmotifs (recurring melodies). His style is thoroughly accessible, yet his operas are complex mechanisms built from many different influences.

Puccini's inspiration for *Madame Butterfly* came in 1900 during a visit to London, where he attended a performance of David Belasco's play of the same name. Like his other operas, this one tells the story of a tragic-heroic female protagonist, a young geisha named Cio-Cio-San (Madame Butterfly) from Nagasaki

Giacomo Puccini (1858–1924)

Puccini was born in Lucca, Italy, the son of a church organist. He entered the conservatory in Milan in 1880, and thirteen years later had his first operatic success with *Manon Lescaut*. His partners were librettists Luigi Illica and Giuseppe Giacosa, both of whom also collaborated with him on the three most successful operas of the early twentieth century: *La bohème*, *Tosca*, and *Madame Butterfly*.

Puccini's travels to oversee the international premieres of several of his works were demanding. In 1903, a serious car crash left him bedridden for six months, and in 1908 an extramarital affair caused a public scandal. "I am always falling in love," he once declared. "When I no longer am, make my funeral." In 1910, *The Girl of the Golden West* received its world premiere at the Metropolitan Opera in New York; this was followed by a trio of three one-act works that included *Gianni Schicchi*, one of his best-loved masterpieces.

Puccini's last opera, *Turandot*, is based on a Chinese fairy tale about a beautiful but cruel princess. Struggling with cancer, Puccini died in 1924 before finishing the final scene. His friend Franco Alfano completed the opera, using Puccini's sketches. The first performance took place in 1926 at La Scala, and was conducted by Arturo Toscanini, Puccini's greatest interpreter. The opera ended as Puccini had left it, without the final scene—Toscanini laid down his baton after the Lament over the death of one of the main characters, turned to the audience, and said in a choking voice, "Here ends the master's work."

MAJOR WORKS: 12 operas, including *Manon Lescaut* (1893), *La bohème* (1896), *Tosca* (1900), *Madame Butterfly* (1904), *La fanciulla del west* (*The Girl of the Golden West*, 1910), *Gianni Schicchi* (1918), and *Turandot* (1926) • Choral works • Solo songs • Orchestral, chamber, and solo piano works.

The geisha Cio-Cio San and her maid Suzuki, in a print by **Leopoldo Metlicovitz** (1868–1944).

who renounces her profession and religion in order to marry an American naval officer called Pinkerton. (A **geisha** is most closely equivalent to a courtesan in Western culture; these women were highly trained in the arts of classical music, poetry, and dancing, and were easily recognizable by their black, laquered hair, distinctive makeup, and ornate silk kimono.) Butterfly and Pinkerton are married in a house promised to the couple by the marriage broker, and Pinkerton departs soon thereafter. When he returns several years later—with a new American wife in tow—he learns that Butterfly has given birth to their son and decides to take the child back with him to America. Butterfly accepts his decision with dignity, but rather than return to her life as a geisha, she commits suicide (the samurai warrior's ritual *seppuku,* also known as *hara-kiri).*

Geisha

Madame Butterfly marks a turn-of-the-century interest in exoticism. The entire score is tinged with Japanese color: traditional Japanese melodies are juxtaposed with **pentatonic** and **whole-tone** passages, and you can hear instrument combinations evoking the timbres of a *gagaku* orchestra (with harp, flute, piccolo, and bells). Simple moments in the score—a single, unaccompanied melody, for example—have their visual equivalent in the clear lines of Japanese prints. Another exotic touch comes in the opening of Act I, where Puccini makes a brief reference to *The Star-Spangled Banner.*

Exoticism

Our selection is from Act II, which takes place three years after the marriage (LG 41). Butterfly has heard nothing from her husband, leading her maid Suzuki to doubt that Pinkerton will ever return. She is quickly rebuked, however, in Butterfly's aria "Un bel dì" ("One beautiful day"), in which the young bride pictures their happy reunion and recalls Pinkerton's promise to return "when the robins build their nests." This aria is one of the most memorable in all opera. At first, Butterfly sings with a distant, ethereal quality, accompanied by solo violin, while she dreams of Pinkerton's return. The intensity rises when she imagines seeing his ship in the harbor. Her speechlike melody peaks on the word "morire" ("die"), as she explains how she will playfully hide from him at first in order not to die from happiness at their reunion. The emotional level builds—along with the dynamics—and her final soaring line climaxes on "l'aspetto" ("I wait for him"), with the orchestra now playing the heartrending music at *fff.*

While Butterfly may be an idealized rather than a believable character by today's standards, her naivety and vulnerability make her a beloved heroine. Puccini's ability to combine realistic references to Japanese culture with memorable melodies of the bel canto tradition of his predecessor Verdi, along with his own unique orchestral language, cemented his position in the operatic repertory. After him, the Italian tradition lost its predominance, and indeed opera gradually became displaced in the popular imagination by other musical-theatrical traditions and eventually by film—which took on the values of multimedia intensity and hyper-reality that draw us to the movies in droves.

CRITICAL THINKING

1. How does Puccini evoke exoticism in *Madame Butterfly*?
2. Do you find the character of Butterfly realistic? Explain why or why not.

YourTurn TO EXPLORE

Find an example of contemporary music (for example, a popular song) that is intended to evoke an exotic quality. What is that quality, and how is it reflected in the music—melody, choice of instruments, unusual rhythms, and so on? Why do you think the musicians have chosen this exotic topic? How might it reflect our society's understanding (stereotypes?) of the culture that is being depicted?

LISTENING GUIDE 41 4:35

Puccini: *Madame Butterfly,* "Un bel dì"

Date: 1904

Librettists: Giuseppe Giacosa and Luigi Illica

Basis: Play by David Belasco, from a short story by John Luther Long, derived from Pierre Loti's tale *Madame Chrysanthème*

Setting: Nagasaki, Japan, at the beginning of the twentieth century

Principal characters: Cio-Cio-San, or Madame Butterfly (soprano)
Suzuki, her maid (mezzo-soprano)
B. F. Pinkerton, lieutenant in the US Navy (tenor)
Sharpless, US consul at Nagasaki (baritone)
Goro, marriage broker (tenor)
Prince Yamadori (tenor)
Kate Pinkerton, American wife of Pinkerton (mezzo-soprano)

Performed by:
Miriam Gauci, soprano;
Czecho-Slovak Radio
Symphony Orchestra,
Alexander Rahbari, conductor

What to Listen For

Melody	Soaring line, alternating with speechlike section; reaches several climaxes.
Rhythm/meter	Slow and dreamy, then more agitated rhythmically.
Harmony	Rich accompaniment; some unison writing.

Expression	Dreamlike, then passionate and emotional; rising dynamic lines.
Performing forces	Sparse accompaniment at the opening by a solo violin.

Opening, ethereal vocal line:

Final climactic moment on "l'aspetto" ("I wait for him"):

TEXT	TRANSLATION
0:00	Un bel dì, vedremo	One lovely day we'll see

0:00   Un bel dì, vedremo
        levarsi un fil di fumo
        sull'estremo confin del mare.
        E poi la nave appare—
        poi la nave bianca entra nel porto,
        romba il suo saluto.
        Vedi? E venuto!
        Io non gli scendo incontro. Io no.
        Mi metto là sul ciglio del colle
        e aspetto gran tempo e non mi pesa,
        la lunga attesa.
        E uscito dalla folla cittadina
        un uomo, un picciol punto
        s'avvia per la collina.

2:14   Chi sarà? Chi sarà?
        E come sarà giunto
        che dirà? Che dirà?
        Chiamerà Butterfly dalla lontana.
        Io senza dar risposta me ne starò nascosta
        un po' per celia
        e un po' per non morire al primo incontro,
        ed egli alquanto in pena chiamerà:
        piccina mogliettina olezzo di verbena,
        i nomi che mi dava al suo venire
        tutto questo avverrà, te lo prometto.
        Tienti la tua paura,
        io con sicura fede l'aspetto.

One lovely day we'll see
a thread of smoke rise
at the distant edge of the sea.
And then the ship appears—
then the white ship enters the harbor,
thunders its salute.
You see? He's come!
I don't go down to meet him. Not I.
I place myself at the brow of the hill
and wait a long time, but the long
wait doesn't oppress me.
And coming out of the city's crowd
a man, a tiny speck
starts toward the hill.

Who will it be? Who?
And when he arrives
what will he say? What?
He'll call Butterfly from the distance.
I'll stay hidden, partly to tease him
and partly not to die
at our first meeting,
and a little worried he'll call
little wife, verbena blossom,
the names he gave me when he came here.
All this will happen, I promise you.
Keep your fear to yourself,
with certain faith I wait for him.

Chinese Opera

Musical theater has been one of the leading forms of entertainment in China for centuries, and Beijing (or Peking) opera is perhaps the most prestigious of the many regional styles. Beijing opera is a blend of music, mime, and dance, with

The costumes in Beijing opera are often colorful and elaborate.

stylized gestures and movements as well as colorful costumes and masks. Its repertory is large, with many works based on novels about the country's political and military struggles.

After flourishing in the early 1900s, both in China and internationally, the genre suffered during the decade-long period known as the Cultural Revolution, a movement begun by the chairman of the Communist Party, Mao Zedong, in 1966 to purge China of a class-structured society. No person or institution was safe during this decade of social upheaval; anyone "elitist" or influenced by the capitalist West was considered an enemy. Operas that did not present communist themes were considered subversive and therefore banned. They were replaced by eight approved "model plays" that fostered the ideals of communism: one of these was *The Story* (or *Legend*) *of the Red Lantern*.

This drama concerns communist underground activities during the Japanese occupation of China in 1939. We saw that the libretto for Verdi's *Rigoletto* was based on a contemporaneous play by Victor Hugo; *The Story of the Red Lantern* likewise draws on a contemporary (1958) novel, *There Will be Followers of Revolution*, by Qian Daoyuan. And as Verdi's operas, written during a time of political turmoil in Italy, became rallying cries in the nationalistic movement for his country's liberation from oppressive

regimes, so too was this Chinese opera written as a political manifesto against the Japanese occupation of China in the 1920s and 30s.

The protagonist Li Tiemei learns from her adoptive grandmother of the sacrifices her parents made during the communist revolution, and of the work of Li Yuhu, who then took up the cause of the communist martyrs and was taken prisoner. Li Tiemei vows that she will follow the example of her father, determined "to do such a thing and to be such a person." Her anger toward the Japanese enemy grows increasingly intense as the opera progresses.

Dramatic works of all genres and cultures rely on powerful human passions to engage the audience. The title character of *Rigoletto* is an ambiguous one, only partly sympathetic: bitter and revengeful toward his noble employer, the Duke, desperately possessive of his only child, the jester lets his emotions bring about his downfall through the death of his beloved daughter. The death of her parents is the starting point for Li Tiemei's quest; she too demonstrates extreme anger and hatred toward her enemies, but her determination to carry on the work of her father makes her a more likable character. Unlike Western operas, there is no tale of romance in *The Story of the Red Lantern*; rather, it presents an ideological family—not blood-related—drawn together by revolutionary martyrs.

The so-called model plays were heard often on the radio and seen in stage and film versions (including a widely circulated 1963 film). Indeed, this was a political art form well known to all the Chinese people. Beijing opera enjoyed a revival after the "lost decade" of the Cultural Revolution and remains a popular form of entertainment today; new works are being premiered, and traditional works updated, for modern audiences in China and abroad.

You will hear that the singing styles and accompanying instruments are vastly different in the Western and Chinese operatic traditions; this is the result of differing aesthetics of vocal timbre as well as divergent conceptions of melodic and harmonic movement. But both styles rely on acting, particular gestures, and other body movements (as well as a focused use of instruments) to communicate the story behind the words being sung. Our selection, "To be such a person," is for a soprano soloist accompanied by traditional Chinese instruments, including the erhu, an ethereal-sounding bowed-string instrument; the yang qin, a kind of hammered dulcimer; and the pipa, a plucked lute (see photo below). The opera is sung in Mandarin, one of the main Chinese languages.

What to listen for:

- Singing lines in the erhu.
- Hammering, repeated notes on the yang qin.
- Percussive plucking on the pipa.
- The penetrating vocal timbre.

After an instrumental introduction, the voice begins, singing melismatically, wavering between pitches and with a wide vocal vibrato. The instruments drop out occasionally, then rejoin the voice, weaving heterophonic lines around the melody and punctuating the voice with percussive sounds rather than harmony. The vocal range and pace of the song pick up several times, reaching a loud climax near the end, when Li Tiemei resolves to carry on the work of her father.

The Story of the Red Lantern

"To be such a person" text:

My grandma told me the tale of the red light,
She used few words but expressed them deeply.
Why should my father and uncle dare to take risks?
All for the sake of saving China and saving the poor
As well as defeating Japanese invaders.
Encouraged by what they have been doing,
I am determined to follow their example,
To do such a thing and to be such a person.

I am seventeen years old this year,
Old enough to share my father's burdens.
If my father is carrying a load weighing one thousand jin
    [about 1,100 pounds]
I should carry eight hundred for him.

A young Chinese woman in traditional dress plays the pipa, a plucked-string instrument.

Mythical Impressions: Program Music at the End of the Nineteenth Century

"For we desire above all—nuance,
Not color but half-shades!
Ah! nuance alone unites
Dream with dream and flute with horn."

—Paul Verlaine (1844–1896)

KeyPoints

- **Impressionism** in music is characterized by modal and exotic scales (chromatic, whole tone, and pentatonic), unresolved dissonances, tone combinations such as ninth chords, subtle orchestral color, and free-flowing rhythm, all generally cast in small-scale programmatic forms.

- The most important French Impressionist composer was Claude Debussy. His orchestral work *Prelude to "The Afternoon of a Faun"* was inspired by a Symbolist poem, and later choreographed by the great Russian dancer Vaslav Nijinsky.
- Debussy and his contemporaries were highly influenced by non-Western and traditional music styles heard at the Paris World Exhibition of 1889.

There is something about mythological characters that speaks both to essential human nature and to the mystery of the supernatural. They can serve as a resource for a musician, poet, or painter to pull us out of the ordinary, give us a glimpse into the possible. Mythological themes have been especially prominent in Western multimedia, from the sung plays of ancient Greece to contemporary film and role-playing games. A striking example is provided by one of the most famous works of the later 1800s, Claude Debussy's *Prelude to "The Afternoon of a Faun,"* which we will examine in this chapter. Looking backward to ancient mythology and forward to new sound worlds and expressions, it reflects the subtle perspectives of several creative minds through words, sounds, and movement.

Symbolism and Impressionism in Paris

In the 1860s, breaking with what they considered the static grandiosity of contemporary art, Impressionist painters tried to capture on canvas the freshness of their first impressions and the continuous change in the appearance of their subjects through varied treatment of light and color. A hazy painting by Claude Monet,

Impression: Sunrise, exhibited in 1874, was rebuffed by the academic salons of Paris (see illustration below), and **Impressionism** quickly became a term of derision. However, Monet's luminous painting style was eagerly embraced by Parisian artists such as Edgar Degas and Auguste Renoir. We will see how composers like Debussy tried to emulate the use of color and iridescence that characterize this new style.

A parallel development in poetry was similarly influential to French composers: the Symbolist movement sought to evoke poetic images through suggestion rather than description, through symbol rather than statement. This literary revolt against tradition gained prominence in the works of French writers Stéphane Mallarmé and Paul Verlaine, both of whom were strongly influenced by the American poet Edgar Allan Poe. Through their experiments in free verse forms, the Symbolists were able to achieve in language an abstract quality that had once belonged to music alone.

Translating Impressions into Sound

This music scene is typical of the everyday activities captured by Impressionists. *Young Girls at the Piano* (1892), by **Pierre-Auguste Renoir** (1841–1919).

Inspired by the Impressionist and Symbolist movements, a number of French composers of the later 1800s also attempted to break from tradition in order to experiment with greater subtlety and expressive ambiguity. The major-minor system, as we saw, is based on the pull of the active tones to the tonic, or rest tone. Impressionist composers regarded this as a formula that had become too obvious. In their works, we don't hear the triumphal final cadence of the Classical-Romantic period, in which the dominant chord is resolved to the tonic chord with the greatest possible emphasis. Instead, more subtle harmonic relationships come into play. Rather than viewing dissonance as a momentary disturbance, composers began to use dissonance as a goal in itself, freeing it from the need to resolve. They taught their listeners to accept tone combinations that had formerly been regarded as inadmissible, just as the Impressionist painters taught people to see colors in sky, grass, and water they had never seen there before. Composers made use of the entire spectrum of notes in the chromatic scale, and also explored the whole-tone scale and others derived from various non-Western musics.

The Impressionists took painting out of the studio and into the open air; their subject was light. **Claude Monet**, *Impression: Sunrise.*

Freed from a strong tonal center and rigid harmonic guidelines, composers experimented with new tone combinations such as the **ninth chord**, a set of five notes in which the interval between the lowest and highest tones is a ninth. The effect was one of hovering between tonalities, creating elusive effects that evoke the misty outlines of Impressionist painting.

These floating harmonies demanded the most subtle colors, and here composers learned new techniques of blending timbres from their counterparts in art. Painters juxtaposed brush strokes of pure color on the canvas, leaving it to

Interface

Music, World Colonization, and the Exotic

In 1889, France hosted a fair called the Paris World Exhibition, to mark the centenary of the French Revolution. The fair highlighted technological achievements, including the newly invented Edison phonograph—a huge attraction—and the Eiffel Tower, constructed specially for this event. In addition to displaying triumphs of human ingenuity, the exhibition was highly political, reflecting imperialist and nationalist trends throughout Europe.

France's colonial empire was immense at this time, including territories in northern and western Africa, parts of the Middle East, and Indochina, which today takes in Vietnam and Cambodia. The French sought to affirm their position as a world power by showcasing these far-reaching colonies and their cultures. Accordingly, spectators were treated to displays of antiphonal singing from sub-Saharan Gabon, belly dancers and whirling dervishes from the Middle East, dancers from Cambodia, and Annamite (Vietnamese) theatrical productions—all in an effort to upstage the great

The Central Dome at the 1889 Paris Exhibition, as depicted by **Louis Béroud** (1852–1930).

British Empire, whose vast imperial holdings had been represented just three years earlier at a London Colonial Exhibition. The Dutch for their part showcased their wealthy East Indian colonies with a gamelan orchestra and dancers from Java, the most populated island of modern-day Indonesia.

With the spread of nationalism across Europe, countries were eager to offer their native repertories of both classical and folk music. The French were introduced to contemporary Russian composers in concerts conducted by composer Nicolai Rimsky-Korsakov, while Spanish national styles, including flamenco and Gypsy dance music, quickly became favorites. This international soundscape captured the ears of musicians, who responded with their own "exotic" music. It was here that French composers Claude Debussy and Maurice Ravel first heard the unique sound of the Javanese gamelan (an ensemble made up of gongs, chimes, and drums; see p. 424). Debussy later raved to a friend about "the Javanese music able to express every nuance of meaning, even unmentionable shades, and which makes our tonic and dominant seem like empty phantoms for the use of unwise infants." He attempted to capture something of this sound world—its pentatonic scale, unfamiliar timbre, and texture—in compositions like the famous symphonic poem *La mer* (*The Sea*, 1905), the piano work *Pagodas* (from *Estampes*, 1903), and several piano preludes. We will see that twentieth-century composers, including the bold American innovator John Cage (Chapter 65), continued to explore the unique timbre of the gamelan.

This photogravure of a *Cambodian Dancer* (1911), by the French artist **Auguste Rodin** (1840–1917), reflects the artistic interest in exotic subjects.

Composers were also charmed by the folk and popular musics they heard at the fair. Debussy sought to recreate the rhythms of Spanish Gypsy and flamenco dancers in his piano music (*The Interrupted Serenade* and *Evening in Granada*). Ravel's roots in the Basque region of France (where the Pyrénées separate France and Spain) brought him even closer to Spanish folk traditions, which he emulated in his hypnotic *Boléro*, the *Spanish Rhapsody*, and the violin work *Tzigane* (*Gypsy*, 1924). But Ravel too looked to faraway cultures he first experienced at the fair, evoking Middle Eastern folk tales (from *Arabian Nights*) and Persian music in his orchestral song cycle *Sheherazade* (1903). What began as an exhibition of world power and national pride among industrialized nations thus had far-reaching effects; music, appropriated to deliver a political message, was also opening eyes and ears to the wonder of the exotic.

Claude Debussy (1862–1918)

The most important French composer of the late nineteenth–early twentieth century, Debussy was born near Paris and entered the Paris Conservatory when he was eleven. Within a few years, he was shocking his professors with bizarre harmonies that defied the rules. He was only twenty-two when his cantata *The Prodigal Son* won the coveted Prix de Rome. By this time, he had already realized his future style.

The 1890s, the most productive decade of Debussy's career, culminated in the opera *Pelléas and Mélisande*, based on the Symbolist drama by the Belgian poet Maurice Maeterlinck. At first, *Pelléas* was attacked as being decadent and lacking in melody and form, but this opera made Debussy famous. His energies sapped by the ravages of cancer, Debussy died in March 1918, during the bombardment of Paris.

Like artist Claude Monet and writer Paul Verlaine, Debussy considered art to be a sensuous experience. "French music," he believed, "is clearness, elegance, simple and natural declamation . . . aiming first of all to give plea-

sure." His fame rests on a comparatively small output; *Pelléas and Mélisande* is viewed by many as his greatest achievement. Among his orchestral compositions, the *Prelude to "The Afternoon of a Faun"* became a favorite with the public early on, as did *The Sea*.

Many of his piano pieces demonstrate an interest in non-Western scales and instruments (he regarded sonata-allegro form as an outmoded formula), which he first heard at the Paris Exhibition in 1889 (see Interface opposite). Debussy also helped establish the French song (*mélodie*) as a national art form. His settings of the French Symbolist poets Verlaine and Mallarmé are exquisite and refined.

MAJOR WORKS: Orchestral music, including *Prélude à "L'après midi d'un faune"* (*Prelude to "The Afternoon of a Faun,"* 1894), *Nocturnes* (1899), *La mer* (*The Sea*, 1905) • Dramatic works, including the opera *Pelléas et Mélisande* (1902) and a ballet • Chamber music, including a string quartet and various sonatas • Piano music, including two books of preludes (1909–10, 1912–13) • Songs, choral music, and cantatas.

the eye of the viewer to do the mixing. Debussy similarly replaced the lush, full sonority of the Romantic orchestra with veiled sounds: flutes and clarinets in their dark, velvety registers, violins in their lustrous upper range, trumpets and horns discreetly muted; and over the whole, a shimmering gossamer of harp, celesta, triangle, glockenspiel, muffled drum, and brushed cymbal. One instrumental color flows into another close by, as from oboe to clarinet to flute, in the same way that Impressionist painting moves from one color to another in the spectrum, from yellow to green to blue.

Debussy's *Prelude to "The Afternoon of a Faun"*

Debussy's best-known orchestral work draws its program from a pastoral poem by Symbolist writer Stéphane Mallarmé describing the faun, a mythological forest creature that is half man, half goat, and symbolizes raw sensuality. Debussy intended his music to be a series of "backdrops" that would illustrate the faun and his actions. We can thus consider this work a coming together of visual Impressionism and textual Symbolism through sound (LG 42).

The work follows the familiar pattern of statement-departure-return (**A-B-A′**), yet the progression is fluid and rhapsodic, with a relaxed, free-flowing rhythm. We first hear a flute solo in the lower register. The melody glides along the chromatic scale, narrow in range and languorous. Glissandos on the harp usher in a brief dialogue in the horns, a mixture of colors never heard before.

In Their Own Words

❝ The century of aeroplanes deserves its own music. Since there are no precedents, I must create anew."

—*Claude Debussy*

Debussy: *Prelude to "The Afternoon of a Faun"* *(Prélude à "L'après-midi d'un faune")*

Date: 1894

Genre: One-movement programmatic symphonic poem

Performed by: New Philharmonia Orchestra, Pierre Boulez, conductor

---

What to Listen For

Melody	Lyrical, sinuous melody; chromatic at opening and closing.	**Texture**	Homophonic; light and airy.	
Rhythm/ meter	Free-flowing rhythms; sense of floating; lacks pulse; middle section is more animated.	**Form**	Loose **A-B-A'** structure.	
		Expression	Evocative mood; sensual.	
		Timbre	Subtle colors, especially in the woodwinds.	
Harmony	Use of "blue" chords, with lowered thirds.	**Performing forces**	Strings (with two harps), woodwinds, French horns, and antique cymbals.	

Opening of poem, by Stéphane Mallarmé:

Ces nymphes, je les veux perpétuer.
 Si clair
Leur incarnat léger, qu'il voltige dans l'air
Assoupi de sommeils touffus.
 Aimai-je un rêve?

These nymphs I would perpetuate.
 So light
their gossamer embodiment, floating on the air
inert with heavy slumber.
 Was it a dream I loved?

A section

0:00 Opening chromatic melody in flute; passes from one instrument to another, accompanied by muted strings and a vague sense of pulse:

p doux et expressif

B section

2:48 Clarinet introduces a more animated idea, answered by a rhythmic figure in cellos.

3:16 New theme with livelier rhythm in solo oboe, builds in a *crescendo*:

doux et expressif

4:34 Contrasting theme in woodwinds, then strings, with syncopated rhythms, builds to a climax:

p *expressif et très soutenu* *mf* *p*

A' section

6:22 Abridged return, in a varied setting.

Next, a more decisive motive emerges, marked *en animant* (growing lively). This is followed by a third theme, an impassioned melody that carries the piece to an emotional climax. The first theme then returns in an altered guise. At the close, antique cymbals (small disks of brass whose rims are struck together gently and allowed to vibrate) play *pianissimo*. "Blue" chords (with lowered thirds and sevenths) are heard by the muted horns and violins, sounding infinitely remote. The work dissolves into silence, leaving us, and the faun, in a dreamlike state.

Debussy's symphonic poem was widely performed (as far away as Boston in 1902), but it gained even more prominence when it was choreographed by the great Russian dancer Vaslav Nijinsky (about whom we will learn more in Chapter 56). Nijinsky himself danced the role of the faun (see illustration at right), and his sensuous cavorting among the nymphs caused a scandal in Paris: this choreography is often viewed as a turning point in modern ballet. Nijinsky's choreography helped make Debussy's work all the more successful, but it also introduced a problem: to what extent does the meaning added by a dancer/choreographer shape the interpretation of a musical work? Does a storytelling choreography go against the subtlety and vagueness of Debussy's Symbolist/Impressionist approach?

The great Russian dancer Vaslav Nijinsky in the ballet version of *The Afternoon of a Faun*. Design by **Léon Bakst** (1866–1924).

CRITICAL THINKING

1. How did composers translate the literary devices of Symbolism and the innovative use of color in Impressionist painting into sound?
2. How did non-Western musical ideas affect Debussy and his contemporaries?

Your Turn TO EXPLORE

Pick a movie, TV show, or video game that includes music and draws on mythology. How are specific elements like timbre, melody, and harmony used to reinforce certain characters or dramatic moments? How do you think those musical choices contribute to the simultaneously real and unreal qualities of mythology?

52

Nationalism Crosses the Ocean: Dvořák and Late Romanticism in the USA

"When I wrote this quartet in the Czech community of Spillville in 1893, I wanted to write something for once that was very melodious and straightforward, and dear Papa Haydn kept appearing before my eyes, and that is why it all turned out so simply. And it's good that it did."

—Antonín Dvořák, writing about his American *String Quartet*

KeyPoints

- European immigrant composers looked to both Native American and African American musics in their efforts to establish a national American school.
- One of these composers was Antonín Dvořák, who, while teaching music in New York City, challenged American composers to embrace the "folk songs" of America.

- Dvořák's *New World* Symphony and String Quartet, Op. 96 (dubbed *American*), both written while he was in the United States, draw on scales typical of African American spirituals as well as his native Central European folk music.

Musical nationalism in the nineteenth century was often described as a way to hold a composer's regional traditions—the distinctive folk melodies of his or her "people," for example—equal in expressive power to the acknowledged great tradition of German art music. But the question of how to express national identity in music was more complex in a nation like the United States, composed of immigrants from various European regions, descendants of slaves shipped from Africa, and members of Native American tribes. In the 1890s, a famous European "nationalist" composer, Antonín Dvořák, became the figurehead for intense debate about the definition of American music. And more than a century later, discussions about the nature and future of concert music in the United States still regularly evoke his name.

Music in a Nation of Immigrants

European immigrants who populated the United States in multiple waves maintained their languages (German, Swedish, Czech) and continued to perform or write music in the traditions of their native lands (see Chapter 34). There were also efforts to create music that would rival the "high culture" institutions of Europe. But what would be the defining characteristics of a musical language in a nation of diverse peoples, rather than one composed of families grounded in the land for many generations? A number of musicians of European descent chose Indian themes, though these were based on stereotypical notions of Native American music rather than an accurate understanding. Others drew on African American traditions; German immigrant composer Henry Schoenefeld suggested in 1890 that the "American school will be based upon the Negro melodies of the South, as the Russians have founded the Russian school by looking to the Slav melodies." Still others argued for an international style, often couched in terms of "universality"; but their models were based on German or Anglo-American traditions. The cultural racism that had defined citizenship around white identity within the US Constitution was still shaping a definition of "universal" that excluded nonwhites.

St. Wenceslaus Church in Spillville, Iowa, where Dvořák spent the summer of 1893.

Into this ongoing debate stepped Antonín Dvořák, recruited in 1892 by Jeannette Thurber, founder of the National Conservatory of America, to be the conservatory's director. Dvořák had become well known both as a practitioner of German absolute music and as a champion of musical nationalism in his native Prague. As he prepared to take his post, he told a London newspaper, "America will have to reflect the influence of the great German composers, just as all countries do." But once in New York, when he listened to his African American composition students—most notably Harry T. Burleigh—perform spirituals from their communities, he was struck by the music's expressive potential. His symphony titled *From the New World,* written the following year, was, he said, grounded in "the spirit of Negro and Indian melodies."

In the summer of 1893, Dvořák traveled with his family to Spillville, Iowa, home to a community of Bohemian immigrants. From there he wrote to a friend: "You probably know that the children arrived safely in America. As soon as they got here, we left New York for Spillville for our summer holidays. It's a Czech settlement. There are Czech church services and a school—so it seems as if we were in [Bohemia]." Dvořák felt at ease in Spillville, as he indicated in a later letter: "I liked to be among these people and they all liked me as well, especially the elderly citizens, who were pleased when I played 'O God, we bow before Thee' or 'A thousand times we greet Thee' for them on the church organ." In Spillville, he wrote an entire string quartet in just a few days, and it was premiered shortly after the *New World* Symphony the following January. It quickly became known as the "Negro Quartet" (now it's called the *American* Quartet) because critics felt that it borrowed ideas from African American traditions. But is that really the case?

Dvořák's *American* String Quartet

The melodies Dvořák chose for his quartet make significant use of the five-note **pentatonic scale**, rather than a seven-note major or minor scale. Pentatonic scales do occur frequently in African American spirituals, but they are also characteristic of folk traditions of Bohemia and central Europe in general; so the composer may have had either an American or a Czech association in mind. The first movement,

Pentatonic scale

Antonín Dvořák (1841–1904)

Dvořák was born in Bohemia (now part of the Czech Republic). At sixteen, he moved to nearby Prague, where he secured a position playing viola in the Czech National Theater under the baton of Bedřich Smetana, a notable Czech nationalist composer. In 1874, he resigned his orchestra post to devote himself to composing, in which he was much encouraged by Johannes Brahms. Later, he took up a position as professor of composition at the Conservatory of Prague, where he was able to exert an important influence on the musical life of his country.

In 1891, Jeannette Thurber, who ran the National Conservatory of Music in New York City, invited Dvořák to become its director. His stay in the United States was highly productive, resulting in, among other works, his *New World* Symphony, which drew inspiration from African American spirituals. During his time in the United States, Dvořák challenged American composers to embrace "the beautiful and varied themes" that are "the folk songs of America." Several of his students did just so,

including Harry T. Burleigh, who published a landmark collection of spirituals arranged as art music. After three years in New York, Dvořák returned to his beloved Bohemia and spent his remaining years in Prague. He died at sixty-three, revered throughout his native land as a national artist.

Dvořák's great gift for melody, love of native folk tunes, and solid craftsmanship enabled him to shape musical ideas into large forms notable for their clarity. His operas, many based on Czech themes, are the most strongly national of his country. His symphonies reflect a mastery of Classical procedures, and the Cello Concerto is a crowning achievement in that instrument's repertory.

MAJOR WORKS: Orchestral music, including nine symphonies (No. 9, *From the New World*, 1893), symphonic poems, other symphonic works (*Slavonic Dances*, 1878/87) • Concertos, including one for cello • Vocal music, including 14 operas • Choral music (including a *Requiem*, 1890) • Chamber music (*American* String Quartet) • Songs • Keyboard music, including dances and character pieces.

DR. DVORAK INSTRUCTING AN AMERICAN COMPOSER.

Cartoon of Dvořák instructing a student at the National Conservatory in New York City.

unusually, is almost entirely homophonic: the primary melodies presented by one string instrument, with unobtrusive accompaniment in the other three. The effect is thus "melodious and straightforward," as Dvořák described it. Yet the movement is very much part of the tradition that had passed from Haydn (see the quote at the beginning of the chapter) through Beethoven, Schubert, and Brahms, following a clear sonata-allegro form (LG 43). Its key of F major, long associated with the countryside, contributes to the wistfulness of the folk-infused pentatonic melodies.

Is this quartet about American nationalism via African American empowerment, or is it a nostalgic fantasy of blissful Bohemian isolation in remote cornfields? Absolute music allows for many interpretations. And it is perhaps appropriate that this striking musical contribution to conversations about national identity in the United States should have been conceived within an immigrant community that had chosen not to integrate into the US mainstream, one that likely saw itself as Bohemian at least as much as American.

CRITICAL THINKING

1. How do the first and second themes of this movement provide opportunity for contrasting emotions?

2. What might be the benefits and drawbacks of thinking of this quartet as "American music"?

YourTurn TO EXPLORE

While we have focused on Dvořák's interest in African American spirituals, he and his contemporaries also mentioned Native American / "Indian" traditions as possible resources for an American national style. Seek out works by composers who composed using Native American themes in the so-called "Indianist" tradition around the time of Dvořák (for example, Amy Beach, Arthur Farwell, or Edward MacDowell, all of whom were Euro-American), and compare them to more recent works by Native American composers that draw on their own heritage, such as Dawn Avery, Louis Ballard, Brent Michael Davids, and Jerod Tate. How is the "Indian-inspired art music" around Dvořák's time different from the more recent works by Native Americans that is grounded in Native American tradition? How do both repertories relate to Dvořák's approach?

LISTENING GUIDE 43   9:38

Dvořák: String Quartet in F Major, Op. 96 (American), I

Date: 1893   **Performed by:** Pavel Haas Quartet

Genre: String quartet

Movements: I. Allegro ma non troppo; sonata-allegro form, F major

II. Lento; sectional form (**A-A-B-B-C-C-A′**), D minor

III. Molto vivace; scherzo and trio, F major/minor

IV. Finale: Vivace ma non troppo; sonata-rondo form, F major

What to Listen For

Melody	First theme is arpeggiated and pentatonic; second theme, more stepwise with ornaments, also uses the pentatonic scale.	Harmony	The pentatonic scale is ambiguous—between major and minor; the main key areas are related by thirds rather than fifths (F major / A major in the exposition, F major / A-flat major / F major in the recapitulation).
Rhythm/ meter	Rhythmic drive in quick-paced 4/4 meter; some syncopation in themes.		
Texture	Mostly homophonic; melody is passed from instrument to instrument as the others provide accompaniment; moments of imitation.	**Form**	Sonata-allegro form, with a long transition between the first and second themes and an extended development.
		Expression	Engaging, folklike melodies; evocative mood.

continued on next page

Exposition

0:00 Theme 1, in F major and based on the pentatonic scale, is played by the viola, then by the first violin; accompanied by oscillating thirds and arpeggios in the cello.

First violin with theme:

0:24 Transition begins with repetitions of the final notes of theme 1; after an elaboration of short motives from theme 1, the music modulates to A minor.

0:54 Short rhythmic motives are passed back and forth; dramatic contrasts in dynamics.

1:39 Theme 2, in A major, is played by the first violin, ornamented; other instruments provide slow, quiet chords.

Development

2:25: Snatches of theme 1 and rhythmic motives from the transition are passed back and forth between instruments.

4:05 Theme 2 returns in varied and expanded form, again with the first violin most prominent.

4:53 Theme 1 again, with variations on the opening section in a dialogue between instruments.

6:12 *Fugato* section: all four instruments play short motives in imitation, with the solo first violin fading out at the end.

Recapitulation

6:48 Theme 1 in F major, first played by the viola then by the first violin.

7:12 A new cello solo in A-flat major begins the transition.

8:26 Theme 2, back in F major, now alternates between the first violin in a low range and the cello in its highest range.

9:02 **Coda**—short, based on motives from the transition.

53

Jubilees and Jubilation: The African American Spiritual Tradition

"In the Negro melodies of America I discover all that is needed for a great and noble school of music."

—*Antonín Dvořák*

KeyPoints

- In the early 1800s, Americans of all backgrounds came together in **camp meetings** to sing songs of worship.

- In their own meetings, enslaved Blacks and freedmen developed a semi-improvised tradition of sacred songs known as **spirituals**.

- Spirituals such as *Swing Low, Sweet Chariot* were popularized by choral groups from African American colleges in the late 1800s and were arranged as art songs in the early 1900s. They have served as the basis for other elaborations ever since.

From the United States' earliest decades, immigrants from all lands (including the involuntary immigrants brought to North America through slavery) have intersected here, sharing their cultures and musical practices. While in some cases racial and ethnic segregation were obstacles to musicians' performing together, in others they were a starting point for musical exchange. The mixtures of traditions that characterize the American musical landscape today have direct parallels in past centuries, especially in the rise of sacred songs known as spirituals.

Spirituals and the Jubilee Tradition

At the turn of the 1800s, a Christian movement known as the Second Great Awakening was sweeping the United States. In **camp meetings,** lasting days or even weeks, African Americans (freedmen, freedwomen, and enslaved Blacks) and European Americans alike gathered to sing hymns of praise to popular or folk tunes of the times. Blacks also brought the tradition of the **ring shout**, developed by the enslaved people from African traditions into an extended call and response that built to a religious fervor. White church leaders noted that some in their community were modifying their own worship after witnessing these inspirational practices.

In separate camp meetings organized by enslaved Blacks, the tradition of the spiritual crystallized as both a way of worship and a subversive political endeavor,

Camp meeting

Ring shout

A nineteenth-century depiction of a camp meeting during the Second Great Awakening (c. 1830).

with coded messages about earthly escape concealed in texts that promised heavenly deliverance. Spirituals offered enslaved people both a sense of community and solidarity through the monophonic singing (often with some heterophonic elaboration) of their shared musical ideas. White Northerners who first documented this oral tradition around the time of the Civil War were struck by the "foreignness" of the spirituals, which tended to be full of rhythmic and melodic traits that did not fit European norms.

Spirituals gained a broader cultural presence immediately after the Civil War, when a group of students at Fisk University (a newly established college for Black freedmen in Nashville, Tennessee) formed the Fisk Jubilee Singers, to raise funds for the institution. And this they did: the singers toured with great success throughout the northern United States and even Europe in the 1870s, eventually raising the amazing-for-the-time sum of $150,000, enough to construct a major building and endow the college's future. The choir built a repertory of sacred European choral masterworks, but it was the arrangements of spirituals from the singers' own tradition that most astounded audiences. When the original cohort disbanded after a few years, the university reconstituted the Fisk Jubilee Singers as a smaller ensemble, and they continued performing even as the popularity of the choral spiritual faded at the end of the 1800s. The group continues as a jewel of Fisk University to this day.

A nineteenth-century poster advertising a tour by the Fisk Jubilee Singers.

Spirituals and the Art-Song Tradition

In 1893, on the coattails of the European craze for "jubilee" spirituals, and in the context of his own experiments with creating a "national style" for music in the United States (see Chapter 52),

Czech composer Antonín Dvořák made the claim that opens this chapter. Not many white American composers agreed, since Black traditions were still widely considered inferior. But as noted in the last chapter, some African Americans took up Dvořák's challenge and began to create arrangements of spirituals for solo voice and piano. Perhaps the most influential was Harry T. Burleigh, who not only sang for and worked with Dvořák during the years the Czech composer taught in the United States, but also became editor for an important international music publisher. Burleigh's many voice-and-piano settings of spirituals, first published in the 1910s, were quickly adopted as concert staples by Black and white singers alike.

One of the earliest recording technologies was the wax cylinder, pioneered by Thomas Edison in the 1870s.

The trend toward "art-song" arrangements of spirituals overlapped with one of the most important cultural movements of the early twentieth century: the **Harlem Renaissance**, an attempt by African American artists and philosophers to claim a "high culture" space for their people, in order to counteract the systemic racism and marginalization they suffered in America. (See Chapter 60 for more on the Harlem Renaissance.) Presenting spirituals as art songs positioned the Black tradition alongside the European American as a valid aspect of American art.

Swing Low, Sweet Chariot

One of the most famous of spirituals reflects the intersection between Native American, African American, and European American peoples in the American West. *Swing Low, Sweet Chariot* may or may not have been created by Wallace Willis, an enslaved man who worked at a Choctaw boarding school in what is now southeastern Oklahoma; but it was from Willis and his wife Minerva that the school's director, Reverend Alexander Reid, heard the spiritual, maybe as early as the 1840s. Decades later, Reid attended a performance of the Fisk Jubilee Singers and suggested that they add *Swing Low* and other spirituals he and his wife had heard from Willis to their repertory. So, ironically, this iconic song was introduced to the African American ensemble that made it most famous by a white man who had first heard it at a Native American school.

The spiritual *Swing Low, Sweet Chariot* as interpreted by folk artist **Margaret Ramsey** (1932–2011).

Swing Low became one of the favorites of the Fisk Singers, who recorded it several times in the first decade of the 1900s

LISTENING GUIDE 44   ◀)) 4:25

Spiritual: *Swing Low, Sweet Chariot*

Date: Composed before 1850, arrangement from 1909

Performed by: Fisk Jubilee Quartet

What to Listen For

Melody	"Gapped" pentatonic, limited range, paired open and closed phrases.	**Form**	Strophic, with first stanza as a chorus.
Rhythm/ meter	Duple meter, with some triplets; flowing, with flexible syncopations.	**Expression**	Straightforward delivery of lyrics and repetitive harmonization.
Harmony	Simple and mostly diatonic.	**Text**	Elaboration of II Kings 2, 11.
Texture	Homophonic, with clear lead singer.	**Performing forces**	TTBB male quartet.

Fisk arrangement

0:00 *Swing low, sweet chariot,*   Tenor 1 alone.
      Coming for to carry me home,   TTBB.
      Swing low, sweet chariot,   Tenor 1 with words, others humming.
      Coming for to carry me home.   TTBB.

0:23 I'm sometimes up, and I'm sometimes down
      (Coming for to carry me home),
      But still my soul feels heavenly bound
      (Coming for to carry me home).   Alternation of soloist with humming and TTBB response.
      Chorus

0:46 If you get there before I do
      (Coming for to carry me home),
      Tell all my friends I'm coming too
      (Coming for to carry me home).
      Chorus

1:35 I never shall forget that day
      (Coming for to carry me home),
      When Jesus washed my sins away
      (Coming for to carry me home).
      Chorus

2:26 I looked over Jordan, and what did I see?
      (Coming for to carry me home),
      A band of angels coming after me,
      (Coming for to carry me home).

3:18 *Chorus sung twice more.*

Beginning of chorus:

Swing low,   sweet char - i - ot,   Com-ing for to car-ry me   home,

◀)) **AnotherHearing** Compare the male quartet version of this spiritual (by the Fisk Jubilee Quartet) with the art-song arrangement for voice and piano by Harry T. Burleigh (sung by Karen Parks). What qualities change the traditional spiritual into art music? Which delivery do you find more powerful, and why?

(we will hear a recording the Fisk Jubilee Quartet made in 1909; LG 44). The spiritual was also arranged as an art song by several African American composers, including Burleigh in 1917. In many arrangements and reworkings, it has since become a staple of American musical culture.

The text of the spiritual is loosely based on a passage from the biblical Second Book of Kings, in which the prophet Elijah is taken up to Heaven in a whirlwind and a chariot of fire. The melody uses a five-note (**pentatonic**) scale, and features several repetitions of both music and text. The Fisk recording provides harmonies that are in keeping with the Euro-American sacred choral tradition and sustain the melody as unobtrusive accompaniment. The piano part in Burleigh's arrangement establishes a more complex and blues-related harmony, and a more polyphonically independent interaction between voice and instrument. Burleigh also chooses to modify one of the notes of the melody the second time the text is sung, perhaps imitating the blue-note bending of pitch characteristic of the African American singing tradition.

With its origins in the Indian country of the West, transmission by white Americans to the most celebrated African American vocal ensemble of the day, reconfiguration by Black composers and singers into art song, and subsequent spread throughout the American musical landscape, *Swing Low, Sweet Chariot* is a striking example of the cultural mixture and renewal that characterize the vernacular music of the United States. Many of our most loved "traditional" songs have histories that are as complex as the country and the peoples that have created them, and some have also moved into the concert repertory, as examples of American art song.

CRITICAL THINKING

1. How did the Fisk Jubilee Singers contribute to the spread of the spiritual?
2. What are some differences between the Fisk and Burleigh arrangements of *Swing Low, Sweet Chariot*?

YourTurn TO EXPLORE

Find two or three separate arrangements of a song from a folk tradition—like *Amazing Grace, Greensleeves,* or *Yankee Doodle*. How does each arrangement create a balance between the simple folk melody and the additional musical resources—is the arrangement homophonic or polyphonic? Is the original melody modified in any way, and if so, how? In what way do you think each arrangement is faithful to the traditional melody, or to the cultural tradition from which it is derived? Which one do you think is most musically expressive, and why?

54

A Good Beat: American Vernacular Music at the Close of an Era

"Ragtime is the American Creation and the Marvel of Musicians in all Civilized Countries."

—*John Stark (Scott Joplin's publisher)*

KeyPoints

- The great bandmaster and composer John Philip Sousa fostered the American wind-band tradition, an outgrowth of the British military band.
- **Ragtime** was an African American piano style characterized by syncopated rhythms and sectional forms, made famous by Scott Joplin, the "King of Ragtime."

- Joplin's *Maple Leaf Rag* is made up of four repeated **strains** in a form that resembles the marches of Sousa, whose band often played arrangements of Joplin's rags.
- The **piano roll** was an early form of musical playback technology.

The US Marine Band, with its director, John Philip Sousa, playing cornet (in right front) in the inaugural parade for President Grover Cleveland (1885).

We often show appreciation for music by saying it has "a good beat"—we like it because it makes us want to move to it. Musicians have been putting bodies into joyful motion from before recorded history, and our music-inspired movements help us come together on a wide variety of social occasions—such as marching and dancing. Although these may seem like separate endeavors, they both rely on music to structure their regular patterns of moving, and in late nineteenth-century America those patterns overlapped and reinforced each other in two very popular traditions: the ragtime piano dance and the wind-band march. These two traditions were supported by the development of new technologies in both instrument-making and recording.

John Philip Sousa and the Band Tradition

In addition to parlor ballads (like those of Stephen Foster) and spirituals, nineteenth-century America's vernacular traditions also encompassed music for brass bands. An outgrowth of the British military band, wind groups thrived throughout the United States, beginning with the regimental bands that played during the Revolutionary War (1775–83). The most famous eighteenth-century band was the US Marine Band, originally just a small group of woodwinds, French horns, and percussion. By the Civil War era (1861–65), both Northern and Southern regiments marched to the sound of bands that included brass instruments as well as woodwinds, thanks to the pioneering efforts of such designers as the Belgian Adolphe Sax (inventor of the saxophone and several brass instruments; see p. 267). After the war, many bands reorganized as concert and dance ensembles. Such was the case with the Union Army group under the direction of virtuoso cornet player and bandmaster Patrick S. Gilmore (1829–1892), who wrote the lyrics for the rousing *When Johnny Comes Marching Home* to welcome back soldiers from North and South alike.

Patrick S. Gilmore

America's most famous bandmaster was John Philip Sousa (1854–1932), who conducted the US Marine Band from 1880 to 1892, after which he formed his own group. Known as the "March King," Sousa wrote over 130 marches for band, along with dance music and operettas. He toured North America and Europe extensively with his group, delighting audiences with his *Semper Fidelis* (1888), *Washington Post* (1889), and the ever-popular *Stars and Stripes Forever* (1897), as well as arrangements of ragtime, the newest rage in dance music. Sousa's fame spread further through hundreds of thousands of sheet-music copies of his marches and, early in the new century, through the new mass-marketing of recordings: he created, nearly single-handedly, a national music for America that continues to resonate in its concert halls, on its streets, in its sports stadiums, and in the hearts of its people.

Washington Post

Scott Joplin and Ragtime

While bands were sought after to accompany social dancing, often it was more practical to just hire a piano player (since you could count on a piano being present in every social hall and almost every living room, as sound systems are today). In the last decades of the 1800s, a style developed primarily among African American performers that took Euro-American traditions and modified them through rhythmic and melodic variation. It was called **ragtime**, and it became a vital precursor of jazz. Scott Joplin, known as the "King of Ragtime," was one of the first Black Americans to gain widespread visibility as a composer.

The popular Turkey Trot was danced to ragtime; the woman wears a feathered headdress typical of the early 1900s.

Joplin is best remembered today for his piano "rags," which reflect his preoccupation with classical forms. They combine balanced phrasing and key structures with highly syncopated melodies. And like earlier dance forms, they are built in clear-cut sections, their patterns of repetition reminiscent of those heard in Sousa marches.

The *Maple Leaf Rag,* probably the best-known rag ever composed, is typical in its regular, sectional form (LG 45). Quite simply, the dance presents four sixteen-measure sections, called **strains**, in a moderate duple meter; each strain is repeated before the next one begins. As in most rags, the listener's interest is focused throughout on the syncopated rhythms of the melodies, played by the right hand, which are supported by a steady, duple-rhythm accompaniment in the left hand. Joplin's sophisticated piano rags brought him worldwide recognition.

This performance of the *Maple Leaf Rag* is also noteworthy because it is the first example we have encountered so far of music played by its own composer, rather than by more modern performers. This is achieved not through a sound recording but rather by a **piano roll**, a long strip of paper with holes punched in it, designed to be recorded and played back in a mechanically enhanced **player piano**. As Joplin played the rag, the player piano punched holes in the roll that corresponded to the notes he played as well as to their length and dynamics. You could then purchase a copy of the roll to recreate Joplin's performance on a similar machine.

Scott Joplin (1868–1917)

Joplin was born in Texarkana, Texas, to a musical family. His father, a former enslaved man, played violin, and his mother sang and played banjo. He began musical instruction on the guitar and bugle and quickly showed such a gift that he was given free piano lessons. He left home when he was only fourteen and traveled throughout the Mississippi Valley, playing in honky-tonks and piano bars and arriving in 1885 in St. Louis, the center of a growing ragtime movement.

Joplin helped ragtime gain public notice when he and a small orchestra he had formed performed at the 1893 World Exposition in Chicago. Around this time, he also sought more formal musical training at the George R. Smith College in Sedalia, Missouri. It was at a club in Sedalia that Joplin, surrounded by a circle of Black entertainers, introduced his *Maple Leaf Rag*. Fame came to the composer in 1899 when the sheet music of the piece sold a million copies. Financial security came as well: he insisted on receiving royalties rather than a flat payment for this and other ragtime pieces. He eventually moved to New York, where he was active as a teacher, composer, and performer.

Joplin strove to elevate ragtime from a purely improvised style to a more serious art form that could stand on a level with European art music. Realizing that he must lead the way in this merger of styles, he began work on his opera *Treemonisha*, which he finished in 1911. But the opera was not well received, and Joplin fell into a severe depression from which he never fully recovered; he died in New York City on April 1, 1917. *Treemonisha* remained unknown until its successful revival in 1972 by the Houston Grand Opera. In 1976, nearly sixty years after his death, Joplin was posthumously awarded a Pulitzer Prize for his masterpiece.

MAJOR WORKS: Stage works, including two operas (*Treemonisha,* 1911) • Piano rags, including *Maple Leaf Rag* (1899) and *Pine Apple Rag* (1908) • Piano music • Songs.

Title page of *Maple Leaf Rag* (1899).

Only because some player pianos and piano rolls have survived the ever-changing process that makes most technologies obsolete, we can hear Joplin's own rendition of his signature rag.

Some in Joplin's day were not enthusiastic about the emerging recording technologies. Sousa himself, though he benefited economically from the sales of recordings of his band, warned that reliance on recordings would not only take their livelihood away from musicians by reducing demand for live performances, but also create a population of Americans who could not play music for themselves. Every time we download a music file because it has a good beat that we can dance to—especially if we obtain it for free—we help to confirm Sousa's worst fears.

CRITICAL THINKING

1. Why were bands and Sousa in particular so important to the musical culture of the United States?
2. How is piano-roll technology similar to and different from modern MP3 recordings?

YourTurn TO EXPLORE

Seek out examples of phonograph recordings online. Try to find a couple of different examples—78 rpm discs, 45 rpm, 33 1/3 rpm (or even older cylinder technologies). How are these playback technologies similar and different? What do you think of the sound quality—is the noise level distracting, can you ignore it to focus on the music? Why do you think each of these formats was considered groundbreaking in its day? Now compare these with a digital recording from a streaming service of your choice. How is this technology similar to and different from the earlier recording formats? What advantages and disadvantages does each format provide?

LISTENING GUIDE 45   🔊 3:21

Joplin: *Maple Leaf Rag*

Date: Published 1899
Genre: Piano rag

Performed by: Scott Joplin, piano

What to Listen For

Melody	Catchy, syncopated, disjunct melodies.
Rhythm/ meter	Marchlike duple meter; syncopated in right hand, steady beat in left hand.
Harmony	Major key; shifts to a new key in **C** section (the trio); decorative rolled chords.
Texture	Homophonic; chordal accompaniment to the melody.
Form	Dance made up of four sections (strains), each 16 measures and repeated: **A-A-B-B-A-C-C-D-D**.
Performing forces	Joplin plays on a 1910 Steinway piano roll.

0:00   **A**, strain 1—syncopated, middle-range ascending melody, in A-flat major; accompanied by a steady bass; begins with an upbeat in bass; Joplin adds ornamental flourishes in left hand:

0:22   **A**—strain 1 repeated.

0:44   **B**, strain 2—similar syncopated pattern in melody; begins in a higher range and descends; steady bass accompaniment; in A-flat major:

1:06   **B**—strain 2 repeated.

1:28   **A**—return to strain 1.

1:50   **C**, strain 3, also called the trio—in D-flat major; more static melody; new rhythmic pattern with right hand playing on downbeats; bass accompaniment is more disjunct:

2:12   **C**—strain 3 repeated.

2:34   **D**, strain 4—returns to A-flat major, with a contrasting theme; its syncopated pattern is related to strain 1:

2:56   **D**—strain 4 repeated.

Music in Words

Reviewing Romantic Style

You have now heard examples of Romantic-era genres, both instrumental and vocal, that provide a frame of reference for other nineteenth-century music that you will encounter beyond your course. Here are some suggestions for things to listen for when you have the opportunity to hear an unfamiliar work from the Romantic period.

MELODY: Consider whether the melodic lines are made up of short, regular ideas or long, expansive phrases. Melodies can be built on diatonic or chromatic scales. Which do you hear in this work? What expressive elements do you hear in the melodic lines?

RHYTHM/METER: Romantic-era music can have a regular metric flow or complex rhythms with offbeat accents. What kind of rhythmic treatment and meter do you hear in this work? What dance elements do you perceive?

HARMONY: Tonality is often clouded by chromaticism and dissonance, but there is also always a strong sense of a central tonal center, or home base. Listen for moments that are more dissonant and unstable: what expressive purpose might they serve? How

does the composer use instrumentation or dynamics to highlight the return of the consonant (stable) moments as a contrast to the dissonant (unstable) ones?

TEXTURE: How do the various instruments work together? Is the texture more homophonic (vertical) or polyphonic (with independent lines)? Does the texture change as the work progresses, and if so, how? What expressive purpose might these changing textures serve?

FORM: Romantic-era works feature the basic formal principles of repetition, contrast, and variation. What is the role of repetition in this work? of contrast (that is, new music)? What holds the selection together, or helps it make sense to the listener?

PERFORMING FORCES AND TIMBRE: Which instruments are most prominent here? Do you hear a blend of instrumental colors, or does a single tone color predominate? How does the timbral effect change as the work progresses?

DYNAMICS: How do the dynamics influence the emotional expression of the work?

Listen and Respond

Let's see how you well you can apply what you have learned to a new musical example. Be sure to consult the listening suggestions above and also the style summary chart. Compare this new work with other symphonic works we have heard from the Romantic era.

Tchaikovsky: Final Waltz, from *The Nutcracker*

1. Create a simple listening outline for the piece. Think about melody, rhythm and meter, harmony, texture, performing forces, and form. What Romantic traits do you hear? What new instruments are featured? How is the piece organized? Are there major repeated sections? contrasting sections?

2. How might you describe this waltz to a friend who is not in the class and not familiar with the terminology we've been developing? What general descriptions can you apply to the melody? harmony? texture? overall effect of the piece?

3. Now write a short paragraph describing the work as you might for a concert report assignment. Here you can demonstrate your understanding of the terms and concepts you have learned as well as your response to the work's expressive qualities. Refer back to Chapter 14 for ways to frame your perspective.

Style Summary for Romantic-Era Music (c. 1820–1900)

Composers	Schubert, R. Schumann, Foster, Chopin, Hensel, Berlioz, Mendelssohn, Grieg, Brahms, Verdi, Wagner, Tchaikovsky, Puccini, Debussy, Dvořák, Sousa, Joplin
Melody	Expansive, singing melodies; wide-ranging with many chromatic inflections and dramatic leaps
Rhythm/meter	Much rhythmic diversity and use of rubato
Harmony	Increasing chromaticism and dissonance; expanded concepts of tonality become the basis for large-scale forms
Texture	Homophonic (early Romantic); increasingly polyphonic in later years
Vocal genres	Lied (solo), song cycle, Mass, Requiem Mass, opera, spiritual
Instrumental genres	Symphony, symphonic poem, program symphony, incidental music, concert overture, character piece, concerto, string quartet, dance music, ballet, march, rag
Form	Expanded forms; miniature and narrative programmatic forms
Dynamics	Continuously changing dynamics through *crescendo* and *decrescendo*
Timbre	Continual change and blend of instrumental colors; experiments with new instruments
Performing forces	Large orchestra, with new instruments (English horn, tuba, valved brass, piccolo); piano is a prominent solo instrument
Virtuosity	Rise of virtuoso solo performers
Expression	Emotionally charged and personal; exoticism explored

Twentieth-Century Modernism

"So long as the human spirit thrives on this planet, music in some living form will accompany and sustain it and give it expressive meaning."

—American composer Aaron Copland (1900–1990)

OVERVIEW

1905
Albert Einstein introduces his theory of relativity.

1919
18th Amendment (Prohibition) passes.

1914
First World War begins (US enters in 1917).

1920
19th Amendment (women's suffrage) passes.

1905   1910   1915   1920   1925

1913
Igor Stravinsky's ballet *The Rite of Spring* shocks Paris.

1922
Alban Berg composes his opera *Wozzeck*.

1924
George Gershwin writes *Rhapsody in Blue*.

Learning Objectives

By the end of Part 6, you will be able to

- distinguish the era's wide-ranging, disjunct melodies—sometimes influenced by folk music and jazz—accompanied by dissonant harmonies that often move away from tonality.

- discern the complexity of rhythm, with much syncopation and changing meters, and the polyphonic textures in which lines move linearly.

- recognize the crisp, lean orchestral sound, with unusual instrument combinations

and some instruments playing in extreme ranges.

- perceive the broad dynamic range and high levels of virtuosity that help provide new means of expression.

- identify the era's tightly structured forms, some of which derive from earlier eras.

- become familiar with some of the most influential composers of the Modernist era.

1929
Great Depression begins.

1933
WPA (Works Progress Administration) offers jobs to Harlem Renaissance writers and artists.

1939
Second World War begins (US enters in 1941).

1945
First nuclear weapon tested.

1930   1935   1940   1945   1950

1936
Billie Holiday records *Billie's Blues*.

1939
Film *La noche de los Mayas*, score by Silvestre Revueltas, celebrates Mayan culture.

1945
Collaboration between Aaron Copland and Martha Graham results in ballet *Appalachian Spring*.

6

Making Music Modern

"The entire history of modern music may be said to be a history of the gradual pull-away from the German musical tradition of the past century."

—*Aaron Copland*

Modernisms

Much of the twentieth century was characterized by artists' self-conscious attempts to make their art "modern," not only expressing their own creative visions but suggesting progressive directions for others to follow. This led to purposeful departures from tradition, which have been labeled with a variety of "isms"— Expressionism, Futurism, Fauvism, serialism, Neo-Classicism, and so on. What these "isms" all have in common is a concern with "making art new." However, the particular strategies through which individuals tried to make music modern were often quite different from one another. This is why it can be useful to think of multiple musical modernisms, each serving a different creative purpose. We will examine several of them in the chapters to come.

Most modernists did share a wish to reject nineteenth-century models and a suspicion of popular or mass culture. The twentieth century, however, was also a time when sound recording made vernacular traditions ever more prominent, and modernist musicians often grappled with this powerful cultural phenomenon—sometimes rejecting it, other times integrating some aspects of popular music and culture into their search for the new.

LEFT: The powerful abstraction of African sculpture strongly influenced European art.

RIGHT: **Henri Rousseau** (1844–1910) found his subject matter in distant places. *The Sleeping Gypsy* (1897).

Early Modernist Art

Just as European and American societies saw great changes in the era from 1890 to 1940, the arts witnessed a profound upheaval. A first wave of modernist attitudes took hold just before the First World War (1914–18), when European arts tried to break away from overrefinement and capture the spontaneity and freedom from inhibition that was associated with "primitive" life (though artists often had an idealized notion of "exotic" cultures outside Europe; see the Rousseau illustration opposite). Likewise, some composers turned to what they perceived as the revitalizing energy of non-Western rhythm, seeking fresh concepts in the musics of Africa, Asia, and eastern Europe.

In the years surrounding the war, two influential arts movements arose: **Futurism**, whose manifesto of 1909 declared an alienation from established institutions and a focus on the dynamism of twentieth-century life; and **Dadaism**, founded in Switzerland in 1916. The Dadaists, mainly writers and artists who reacted to the horrors of the war's bloodbath, rejected the concept of art as something to be reverently admired. To make their point, they produced works of absolute absurdity. They also reacted against the excessive complexity of Western art by trying to recapture the simplicity of a child's worldview. Following their example, the French composer Erik Satie (1866–1925) wrote music in a simple, "everyday" style.

The Dada group, with artists like Marcel Duchamp, merged into the school of **Surrealism**, which included Salvador Dali and Joan Miró (see p. 340), both of whom explored the world of dreams. Other styles of modern art included **Cubism**, the Paris-based style of painting in geometric patterns embodied in the works of Pablo Picasso, Georges Braque, and Juan Gris (see p. 346); and **Expressionism**, which made a significant impact on music of the early twentieth century (as we will see in Chapter 55). The new styles in both art and music that flourished after the war are often referred to as **avant-garde**, a French term originally used to describe the part of an army that charged first into battle. Artists who identify as avant-garde distinguish themselves from traditional high culture and from mass-market taste, seeking to explore true creativity by breaking from social and artistic conventions, sometimes radically.

TOP: In *Girl Running on a Balcony* (1912), Futurist painter **Giacomo Balla** (1871–1958) experiments with how art can portray movement.

BOTTOM: **Pablo Picasso**'s use of vibrant colors and bold overlapping shapes in *Mandolin and Guitar* (1924) looks beyond Cubism toward the surrealist school.

Musical Markets in the United States

We have seen how musicians in the young United States often blended high-art music with more vernacular styles in search of commercial success. This emphasis on the marketplace helped to create a set of distinctly American musical traditions and contributed to the international spread of those traditions in the twentieth century.

Throughout the United States, minstrel shows (see Chapter 40) expanded into the tradition of **vaudeville**, which combined all kinds of comedic theatrical and musical acts, many written by immigrant composers and often satirizing new

Spanish artist **Joan Miró** (1893–1983) explores the Surrealist world of dreams through the distortion of shapes. *Dutch Interior I.*

immigrants in ways similar to the portrayal of African Americans in minstrelsy. New York City (especially the thoroughfare called Broadway) became the most vibrant center for vaudeville, and by the turn of the twentieth century it was the most prolific center of music publishing as well. The popular music written in the following decades, along with its writers and publishers, is known as **Tin Pan Alley**, the nickname for the street in Manhattan where publishers had their business. Perhaps the most successful Tin Pan Alley composer was Irving Berlin, whose first hit song, *Alexander's Ragtime Band* (1912), helped catapult the ragtime craze worldwide; he followed this with such timeless songs as *White Christmas* and *Easter Parade,* among many others.

In 1917, the United States officially entered the First World War, an act that spurred the composition of patriotic songs, marches, and love ballads. Songwriter George M. Cohan's inspirational *Over There* (see below), announcing that "the Yanks are coming," resounded across oceans and eventually won him the Congressional Gold Medal. The war facilitated the dissemination of American music abroad, in part through the efforts of James Reese Europe (1881–1919), an African American musician and army bandleader who introduced ragtime and early jazz styles to France. Upon his return home in 1919, Europe declared that he was "more firmly convinced than ever that Negros should write Negro music. We have our own racial feeling and if we try to copy whites, we will make bad copies."

Between Two Wars: Music in the Great Depression

America came out of the "Great War" a changed country. The next decade, known as the Roaring Twenties, witnessed the growth of radio—in 1920, a Detroit station aired the first news broadcast—and film, with the advent of the "talkies." The 1920s were relatively prosperous and brought many social changes, including the Eighteenth Amendment (Prohibition), which banned the manufacture and sale of alcohol; the ratification of the Nineteenth Amendment, granting women the right to vote; the Harlem Renaissance (see Chapter 60), celebrating African American literary and artistic culture; and the Jazz Age, which spread the ballroom culture across the United States (the seductive tango and the "kicky" Charleston were all the rage), as well as "flapper" fashions for women that discarded Victorian modes of dress in favor of shapeless straight shifts that stopped at the knees.

In 1929, the booming world economy suffered a catastrophic setback with the Wall Street crash, and the country settled into a decade-long Great Depression, the most serious

LEFT: The cover to the sheet music of George M. Cohan's famous First World War song *Over There* (1917).

RIGHT: A vaudeville show from 1917. Watercolor by **Charles Demuth** (1883–1935).

economic collapse in the history of the United States. Tin Pan Alley faded, though the jazz club scene, as well as films and Broadway musical theater, allowed a brief escape from the difficulties of the era. Among the popular entertainments from the Depression was George Gershwin's musical *Girl Crazy* (1930), featuring the very popular *I Got Rhythm*. Big-band jazz (swing) dominated popular music, promoted by the dance craze, radio, and live concerts. One of the most well-known bands was the Duke Ellington Orchestra, and we will hear their signature tune, *Take the A Train*, in Chapter 59.

The big-band phenomenon continued through the Second World War (1939–45), during which time many musicians toured with the USO (United Service Organizations), performing for the soldiers serving their country. By now, radio had reached into most corners of the world; American troops abroad listened to Armed Forces Radio. Once again, songwriters capitalized on the patriotic spirit with such tunes as *Boogie Woogie Bugle Boy (of Company B)* and Irving Berlin's *God Bless America,* sung by singer Kate Smith in a famous and moving 1938 radio broadcast (photo below).

Otto Dix (1891–1969) captures the energy of the Charleston dance craze in *Metropolis* (1928).

As Europeans rejected their own Romantic past, American modernist composers saw the opportunity to take the lead in defining the future in the new "American century." The cultural diversity of North America provided a wealth of resources to inspire modernist musicians, and their different backgrounds and goals—both creative and social-political—resulted in a variety of styles (some incorporating folk music, blues, and jazz) that we will explore. Like previous movements, modernism was both a reaction against the past and a distillation of it; the movement transformed a culture and allowed for endless experimentation.

Features of Early Musical Modernism

"To study music, we must learn the rules. To create music, we must break them."   —Nadia Boulanger

With Europe on the brink of entering the Second World War, Kate Smith's 1938 radio broadcast of *God Bless America* stirred strong nationalist sentiments at home.

The New Rhythmic Complexity

Twentieth-century music enriched the standard patterns of duple, triple, and quadruple meter by exploring the possibilities of nonsymmetrical patterns based on odd numbers: five, seven, eleven, or thirteen beats to the measure. In nineteenth-century music, a single meter customarily prevailed through an entire movement or section. Now the metrical flow might shift constantly (**changing meter**), even with each measure. Formerly, one rhythmic pattern was used at a time. Now some composers turned to **polyrhythm**, the simultaneous use of several patterns. As a result of these innovations, Western music achieved something of the complexity and suppleness of Asian and African rhythms. This revitalization of rhythm is one of the major achievements of early twentieth-century music.

Composers also enlivened their music with materials drawn from popular styles. Ragtime, with its elaborate syncopations, traveled across the Atlantic to Europe. The rhythmic freedom of jazz captured the ears of a great many composers, who strove to achieve something of the spontaneity of that popular style.

The infinite looping and interlacing of colorful circles in *Endless Rhythm* (1934) by **Robert Delauney** (1885–1941) is suggestive of the new rhythmic energy of the modernist movement.

Irregular lines and sudden leaps, comparable to those found in early modernist melodies, characterize this wintery vista from Arches National Park in Utah.

The New Melody and Harmony

Nineteenth-century melody is fundamentally vocal in character: composers tried to make the instruments sing. In contrast, early twentieth-century melody is conceived in relation to instruments rather than the voice, abounding in wide leaps and dissonant intervals. Composers greatly expanded our notion of what a melody is, rejecting the neatly balanced phrase repetitions of earlier music and creating tunes and patterns that would have been inconceivable before the early 1900s.

No single factor sets off early twentieth-century music from that of the past more decisively than the new conceptions of harmony. The triads of traditional harmony gave way to stacked chords with more and more notes added, eventually forming highly dissonant chords of six or seven notes; these created multiple streams of harmony, or **polyharmony**. The new sounds burst the confines of traditional tonality and called for new means of organization, extending or replacing the major-minor system. The most significant changes to harmonic organization came in the work of Arnold Schoenberg and his followers, who advocated for the elimination of tonal centers altogether (what is generally described as **atonality**; see Chapter 55) and developed an entirely new and extremely influential principle known as **serialism**, or **twelve-tone composition** (Chapter 58).

Orchestration

The rich sonorities of nineteenth-century orchestration gave way to a leaner, brighter sound, played by a smaller orchestra. Instrumental color was used not so much for atmosphere as for bringing out the form and the lines of counterpoint. The string section, with its warm tone, lost its traditional role as the heart of the orchestra; attention was focused on the more penetrating winds. The emphasis on rhythm brought the percussion group into greater prominence, and the piano, which in the Romantic era was preeminently a solo instrument, found a place in the orchestral ensemble.

Modernist musical culture was above all individualistic: in seeking out the new, composers tried to distinguish their work not just from the past but from other competing visions of the musical future. Musicians belonging to the high-art tradition were also keenly conscious of the growing presence of mass culture, and grappled with the extent to which vernacular styles could coexist with (or be assimilated into) their creative visions. And even as they rejected many facets of Romanticism, modernists shared concerns about national identity and artistic independence that had been founded by that revolutionary and deeply influential nineteenth-century movement.

Performance Matters

MODERNIST GESTURES

As modernist composers pushed the boundaries of harmony, timbre, and form, they also provided increasingly specific instructions to performers to ensure that their modern vision would be accurately conveyed. Metronome markings and other interpretive and technical instructions, which had become increasingly common during the nineteenth century, became an essential component of composers' instructions on musical scores. New timbres required specific unusual actions by performers, whether with the wooden part of the bow rather than the hairs (*col legno*), unconventional fingerings on wind instruments, or generally more harsh and percussive ways of articulating sound. Composers now wanted a crisp and dispassionate clarity of sound that they perceived as the path to the future, often drawing their inspiration from the technological innovations of the early twentieth century (automobiles, airplanes, electric motors—and even machine guns).

Early twentieth-century performers were sometimes caught between preserving the traditions of their nineteenth-century counterparts and embracing the ideal sounds for a new century. There came to be a division between musicians specializing in avant-garde performing approaches designed to take advantage of new sound ideals and musicians who continued to focus on the glorious orchestral soundscapes of the Romantic era. It is in this era that musicians begin to record their performances, first on wax cylinders, then on vinyl, and eventually on magnetic tape: we thus have precious records of how musicians from the early twentieth century balanced nineteenth-century traditions with newer interpretive ideas.

Intersecting lines and bold blocks of color mirror modernist orchestration in this work: *Composition in Red, Yellow, and Blue* (1937–42), by **Piet Mondrian** (1872–1944).

In Their Own Words

" We look for new sonorities, new intervals, new forms. Where it will lead, I don't know. I don't want to know. It would be like knowing the date of my death."

—*Pierre Boulez*

CRITICAL THINKING

1. How did the United States move past domination by European music in the nineteenth century toward its own musical voice in the early twentieth?

2. What are some of the most important features of musical modernism?

55

Anything Goes: Schoenberg and Musical Expressionism

"I personally hate to be called a revolutionist, which I am not. What I did was neither revolution nor anarchy."

—*Arnold Schoenberg*

KeyPoints

- Austrian composer Arnold Schoenberg was highly influential in the movement called **Expressionism**. He believed in making music new by freeing dissonance from having to resolve to consonance, and eventually rejected tonality altogether (**atonality**).

- Schoenberg's song cycle *Pierrot lunaire*, from his atonal-Expressionist period, incorporates **Sprechstimme** (speechlike melody) and **Klangfarbenmelodie** (tone-color melody).

Arnold Schoenberg's Expressionist painting *The Red Gaze* (1910) is highly reminiscent of Edvard Munch's *The Scream*.

Creativity involves finding a balance between innovation and tradition. Even a seemingly novel creation—for example, the iPad—depends on decades of experiments and earlier products that establish a context within which something can be defined as groundbreaking. Throughout the Western tradition, artists have sought to redefine the new, and this was especially true for those who embraced the concept of modernism in the early 1900s. Some ways of making music new were perceived as more radical than others, and even today listeners react strongly to the expansion of musical parameters that took place at that time. But musicians whose experiments are still considered extreme did not necessarily consider their music revolutionary (see the epigraph above); rather, they believed they were taking the appropriate next steps in what they thought of as music's evolution into the present and future.

The Emancipation of Dissonance

Throughout the history of music, as listeners became increasingly tolerant of unfamiliar sounds, one factor remained constant: a clear distinction was drawn between dissonance (the element of tension) and consonance (the element of rest). Consonance was the norm, dissonance the temporary disturbance. In many twentieth-century works, however, tension became the norm. A dissonance could serve even as the chord of resolution in a final cadence, provided it was less dissonant than the chord that came before; in relation to the greater dissonance, it was judged to be consonant. Twentieth-century composers emancipated dissonance by freeing it from the obligation to resolve to consonance. Their music taught listeners to accept tone combinations whose like had never been heard before.

Arnold Schoenberg (1874–1951)

Schoenberg was born in Vienna into a lower-class Jewish family. Largely self-taught, he took lessons in counterpoint with a young composer, Alexander von Zemlinsky. Through Zemlinsky, he was introduced to the advanced musical circles of Vienna, which at that time were under the spell of Wagner's operas.

Schoenberg became active as a teacher himself, and soon gathered about him a band of students that included Alban Berg and Anton Webern. With each new work, he moved closer to taking as bold a step as any composer ever has—the rejection of tonality. Military service in the First World War was followed by a compositional silence of eight years (1915–23), during which he evolved a set of structural procedures to replace tonality. His "method of composing with twelve tones" firmly established him as a leader of contemporary musical thought.

Schoenberg taught composition in Berlin until Hitler came to power in 1933. He emigrated to America and joined the faculty of the University of Southern California, then was appointed professor of composition at the University of California, Los Angeles. He became an American citizen in 1940, taught until his retirement at the age of seventy, and continued his musical activities until his death seven years later.

Schoenberg's early works exemplify post-Wagnerian Romanticism; they still used key signatures and remained within the boundaries of tonality. In his second period, the atonal-Expressionist, he abolished the distinction between consonance and dissonance and any sense of a home key. In his third style period, Schoenberg exploited the twelve-tone method, and in the last (American) phase of his career carried the twelve-tone technique to further stages of refinement. Several of the late works present the twelve-tone method in a manner markedly more accessible than earlier pieces, often with tonal implications, as in the cantata *A Survivor from Warsaw*.

MAJOR WORKS: Orchestral music, including *Five Pieces for Orchestra*, *Variations for Orchestra*, and two concertos • Operas • Choral music, including the cantata *A Survivor from Warsaw* (1947) • Chamber music, including four string quartets, string sextet *Verklärte Nacht* (*Transfigured Night*, 1899), and *Pierrot lunaire* (1912) • Piano music.

Schoenberg and Atonality

While French artists explored radiant impressions of the outer world through Impressionism, their German counterparts preferred digging down to the depths of the psyche. As with Impressionism (Chapter 51), the impulse for the Expressionist movement came from painting. Artists such as Edvard Munch (famous for *The Scream*) influenced Arnold Schoenberg and his disciples Alban Berg and Anton Webern (as well as writers like Franz Kafka), just as the Impressionist painters influenced Debussy.

The musical language of Expressionism favored hyper-expressive harmonies, extraordinarily wide leaps in the melody, and the use of instruments in their extreme registers. Expressionist music soon reached the boundaries of what was possible within the major-minor system. Inevitably, it had to push beyond. Schoenberg eventually advocated doing away with tonality altogether by giving the twelve tones of the chromatic scale equal importance—creating what is commonly known as **atonal** music, or music rejecting the framework of key. Consonance, according to Schoenberg, was no longer relevant to his expressive needs: he started writing music that moved from one level of dissonance to another, functioning always at maximum tension, without areas of relaxation. Schoenberg developed his atonal-Expressionist style for a number of years, before moving on to a more systematic "twelve-tone" method (to be discussed in Chapter 58). One work in which he explored the atonal style most thoroughly was the song cycle *Pierrot lunaire*, composed in 1912.

In Their Own Words

❝ Whether one calls oneself conservative or revolutionary, whether one composes in a conventional or progressive manner, whether one tries to imitate old styles or is destined to express new ideas . . . one must be convinced of the infallibility of one's own fantasy and one must believe in one's own inspiration."

—*Arnold Schoenberg*

Spanish painter **Juan Gris**'s *Pierrot with a Guitar* (1919), roughly contemporary with Schoenberg's song cycle, is one of many such renderings of this character.

Pierrot lunaire

Schoenberg chose the texts for his song cycle from an 1884 collection of poems by Belgian writer Albert Giraud, a disciple of the French Symbolists. Giraud's Pierrot was a poet-rascal-clown (connected to a long tradition of improvised theater) whose chalk-white face, passing abruptly from laughter to tears, enlivened every puppet show and pantomime in Europe. The poems were liberally spiced with elements of the macabre and the bizarre that suited the end-of-century taste for decadence; with their abrupt changes of mood from guilt and depression to atonement and playfulness, they fired Schoenberg's imagination. He picked twenty-one texts (in German translation), arranged them in three groups of seven, and set them for a female vocalist and a chamber ensemble of five players on eight instruments: piano, flute/piccolo, clarinet/bass clarinet, violin/viola, and cello. No song in the cycle uses the same combination of instruments.

One of the composer's goals was to bring spoken word and music as close together as possible; he achieved this aim through ***Sprechstimme*** (speechlike melody), a new style in which the vocal melody is spoken rather than sung. The result is a weird but strangely effective vocal line. Schoenberg also experimented with what he called ***Klangfarbenmelodie*** (tone-color melody), where each note of a melody is played by a different instrument, creating a shifting effect that evokes the moonbeams mentioned in the text.

Each poem is a **rondeau,** a fifteenth-century verse form in which the opening lines of the poem return as a refrain in the middle and at the end (see the Machaut example in Chapter 18). We will focus on No. 18 from the cycle, *The Moonfleck* (*Der Mondfleck*; LG 46). Pierrot, out to have fun, is disturbed by a white spot—a patch of moonlight—on the collar of his jet-black jacket. He rubs and rubs but can't get rid of it. The piano introduces a three-voice fugue, while the other instruments unfold devices such as strict canons in diminution (smaller note values) and retrograde (backward). Schoenberg was obviously fascinated by such constructions, which recall the wizardry of the Renaissance and Baroque contrapuntists.

The combination of atonality, *Sprechstimme*, and *Klangfarbenmelodie* in this work shocked many in Schoenberg's audience. Others found his experiments with sound entirely appropriate not only for Giraud's poems but to contemporary fascinations with the unconscious and the uncanny; they eagerly subscribed to the series of private concerts Schoenberg offered. Avant-garde music that pushes the boundaries of convention may not be to everyone's taste, but there have always been listeners who have been intrigued by the inventiveness of modern composers.

CRITICAL THINKING

1. How did Schoenberg and his fellow Expressionists emancipate dissonance?
2. What are the most innovative aspects of *Pierrot lunaire*?

Your Turn TO EXPLORE

Seek out recordings of musicians who are currently attempting to expand the parameters of musical expression. How are they "making music new"? Which elements of the Western tradition (or other traditions) are they keeping, and which are they rejecting? What is their rationale for doing this? Who are their audiences, and how do their audiences respond to this new music?

LISTENING GUIDE 46   🔊 0:51

Schoenberg: *Pierrot lunaire*, Part III, No. 18

Date: 1912

Genre: Song cycle (21 songs, 7 each in three parts)

Performed by: Lucy Shelton, soprano; Da Capo Chamber Players, Oliver Knussen, conductor

Part I: Pierrot, a sad clown figure, is obsessed with the moon, having drunk moonwine; his loves, fantasies, and frenzies are exposed.

Part II: He becomes ridden with guilt and wants to make atonement.

Part III: He climbs from the depths of depression to a more playful mood, but with fleeting thoughts of guilt; then he becomes sober.

18. The Moonfleck (Der Mondfleck)

What to Listen For			
Melody	Disjunct line, quasi-speechlike (*Sprechstimme*).	**Form**	Rondeau text with poetic/musical refrain (shown in italics below).
Rhythm/ meter	Very fast, sounds free-flowing.	**Timbre**	Pointillistic, with flickering instrumental effects (*Klangfarbenmelodie*).
Harmony	Harshly dissonant.	**Performing forces**	Voice with five instruments (piccolo, clarinet, violin, cello, piano).
Texture	Complex counterpoint with canonic (strict imitative) treatment.	**Text**	Poem in rondeau form, from Albert Giraud's *Pierrot lunaire*.

TEXT

0:00 *Einen weissen Fleck des hellen Mondes*
      Auf dem Rücken seines schwarzen Rockes.
      So spaziert Pierrot im lauen Abend,
      Aufzusuchen Glück und Abenteuer.

      Plötzlich stört ihn was an seinem Anzug,
      Er besieht sich rings und findet richtig—

0:23 *Einen weissen Fleck des hellen Mondes*
      Auf dem Rücken seines schwarzen Rockes.

      Warte! denkt er: das ist so ein Gipsfleck!
      Wischt und wischt, doch—bringt ihn
          nicht herunter!
      Und so geht er, giftgeschwollen, weiter,
      Reibt und reibt bis an den frühen Morgen—
      Einen weissen Fleck des hellen Mondes.

TRANSLATION

With a fleck of white from
the bright moon on the back of his black jacket.
Pierrot strolls about in the
mild evening seeking his fortune and adventure.

Suddenly something strikes
him as wrong, he checks his
clothes and sure enough finds

a fleck of white from the
bright moon on the back of his black jacket.

Damn! he thinks: that's a
spot of plaster! Wipes and
wipes, but—he can't get it off.
And so goes on his way,
his pleasure poisoned, rubs
and rubs till the early morning—
a fleck of white from the bright moon.

Opening of vocal line:

56

Calculated Shock: Stravinsky and Modernist Multimedia

"I hold that it was a mistake to consider me a revolutionary. If one only need break habit in order to be labeled a revolutionary, then every artist who has something to say and who in order to say it steps outside the bounds of established convention could be considered revolutionary."

—Igor Stravinsky

KeyPoints

- Modernist approaches to art, music, and dance were combined by the Ballets Russes in Paris, under the leadership of impresario Serge Diaghilev.

- Russian composer Igor Stravinsky revitalized rhythm by increasing its complexity—using, for example, **polyrhythms** and **changing meters**.

- Stravinsky's early works, including his ballets *The Firebird*, *Petrushka*, and *The Rite of Spring*, are strongly nationalistic; the last evokes rites of ancient Russia through new instrumental combinations and the percussive use of dissonance, as well as polyrhythmic and polytonal writing.

Dance plays an important role in every human society, whether social, expressive, or religious. Although it was a ritual part of early Christianity, this religious function faded out during the Middle Ages. Much Western music has been designed for dancing, whether simple social types or more elaborate choreographies that tell a story. Much multimedia today involves dance (music videos are perhaps the most striking example), which helps to emphasize important aspects of the music and also provides complementary meanings.

The Rite of Spring: Collaborative Multimedia

Serge Diaghilev

The art of ballet was significantly revitalized with the career of the impresario Serge Diaghilev (1872–1929), whose Paris-based dance company, the Ballets Russes, opened up a new chapter in the cultural life of Europe. He surrounded his dancers—the greatest were Vaslav Nijinsky and Tamara Karsavina—with productions worthy of their talents. He invited artists such as Picasso and Braque to paint the scenery, and commissioned the three ballets—*The Firebird*, *Petrushka*, and *The Rite of Spring*—that catapulted Russian composer Igor Stravinsky to fame.

The Rite of Spring was designed as a fully integrated modernist multimedia spectacle, with an innovative choreography by Vaslav Nijinsky (whose provocative way with Debussy's music had helped build "buzz" for the Ballets Russes), Russian folk costumes, and experimental stage designs by renowned artist Nicholas Roerich. Nijinsky's choreography was considered as groundbreaking as Stravinsky's music: it involved dancers creating jerky and irregular movements with individual limbs, jumping up and down in place, and forming rotating geometric patterns onstage (see illustrations at right and on p. 350).

Audience members at the premiere, held on May 29, 1913, at the swanky Parisian Théâtre des Champs-Élysées, had been primed for a work that would push the envelope of dance and music. And reaction to the ballet was immediate that first night: mild protests as soon as the initial dissonant notes sounded soon turned to an uproar. Cries of "Shut up!" were heard around the theater from both supporters and detractors, and one critic barked obscenities at the elegantly dressed ladies who found the work offensive: finally the dancers couldn't hear the music, and the show had to be interrupted. When the dust settled, the reactions ranged from "magnifique" to "abominable."

Yet several more performances were given that season, none of which were greeted with such a hullabaloo. And there is some evidence that the management of the Ballets Russes "seeded" some of the individuals who disrupted the premiere, trying to ensure press coverage. While Stravinsky was publicly incensed with the disrespect that had been shown his music, he must have been aware of its shocking and unsettling quality. The very fact that the work was received negatively by traditionalists made him the darling of the avant-garde, providing crucial support for his rise to prominence as a modernist composer.

Valentine Hugo's (1887–1968) sketches of the *Sacrificial Dance* from the ballet *The Rite of Spring*, choreographed by Nijinsky.

Musical Innovation

For more than half a century, Stravinsky reflected several main currents in twentieth-century music. First through his ballets, he was a leader in the revitalization of rhythm in European art music. He is also considered one of the great orchestrators, his music's sonority marked by a polished brightness and a clear texture. *The Rite of Spring*, subtitled "Scenes of Pagan Russia," not only embodies the cult of primitivism that so startled its first-night audience, but also sets forth a new musical language characterized by the percussive use of dissonance, as well as polyrhythms and polytonality.

Though later modernist principles would call for more bare-bones ensembles, here the size of the orchestra is monumental. Stravinsky often uses the full force of the brass and percussion to create a barbaric, primeval sound and gives the strings percussive material such as pizzicato and successive down-bow strokes. The overall impact of the orchestration is harsh and loud, with constantly changing colors. Some melodies quote Russian folk songs, and the remaining melodic material, often heard in short fragments, uses limited ranges and extended repetition in

Igor Stravinsky (1882–1971)

Born in Russia, Stravinsky grew up in a musical environment and studied composition with Nikolai Rimsky-Korsakov. His music attracted the attention of impresario Serge Diaghilev, who commissioned him to write a series of ballets (*The Firebird, Petrushka, The Rite of Spring*) that launched the young composer to fame. The premiere of *The Rite of Spring* in 1913 was one of the most scandalous in music history. Just a year later, however, when presented at a symphony concert, it was received with enthusiasm and deemed a masterpiece. When war broke out in 1914, Stravinsky took refuge first in Switzerland and then in France. With the onset of the Second World War, he decided to settle his family in Los Angeles; he became an American citizen in 1945. His later concert tours around the world made him the most celebrated figure in twentieth-century music. He died in New York in 1971.

Stravinsky's musical style evolved throughout his career, from the post-Impressionism of *The Firebird* and the primitivism of *The Rite of Spring* to the controlled Classicism of his mature style (*Symphony of Psalms*), and finally to the twelve-tone method of his late works (*Agon*). In his ballets, which are strongly nationalistic, Stravinsky invigorated rhythm, creating a sense of furious and powerful movement. His lustrous orchestrations are so clear that, as Diaghilev remarked, "one can see through [them] with one's ears."

MAJOR WORKS: Orchestral music, including *Symphonies of Wind Instruments* (1920) and *Symphony in Three Movements* (1945) • Ballets, including *L'oiseau de feu* (*The Firebird*, 1910), *Petrushka* (1911), *Le sacre du printemps* (*The Rite of Spring*, 1913), *Agon* (1957) • Operas, including *Oedipus Rex* (1927) • Other theater works, including *L'histoire du soldat* (*The Soldier's Tale*, 1918) • Choral music, including *Symphony of Psalms* (1930) and *Threni: Lamentations of the Prophet Jeremiah* (1958) • Chamber music • Piano music • Songs.

a folk song–like manner. Similarly, within each scene, he minimizes harmonic changes through the use of ostinatos, pedal points, and melodic repetition.

The most innovative and influential element of *The Rite of Spring* is the energetic interaction between rhythm and meter. In some scenes, a steady pulse is set up, only to serve as a backdrop for unpredictable accents or melodic entrances. In other passages, the concept of a regular metric pulse is totally abandoned as downbeats occur seemingly at random. With this ballet, Stravinsky freed Western music from the traditional constraints of metric regularity.

The *Introduction*'s writhing bassoon melody, played in its uppermost range, depicts the awakening of the Earth in spring (LG 47). The *Dance of the Youths and Maidens* then erupts with a series of violent chords, with unpredictable accents that veil any clear sense of meter. These dissonant chords alternate with folklike melodies, as the music builds to a loud, densely textured climax. We get a brief respite in the *Game of Abduction*, as another folk melody is introduced; but the level of activity quickly becomes chaotic, replete with seemingly random accents. The primitive atmosphere continues to the culminating *Sacrificial Dance* that closes Part II, during which the young girl—the "chosen one"—dances herself to death in a frenzy.

Stravinsky capitalized on the scandal-success of *The Rite of Spring* by having the work performed only orchestrally, detaching it from its original multimedia project. Indeed, he (deceptively) began to claim that the music had always been the driving reason behind the project: that choreography and staging had been afterthoughts. Today, *The Rite* stands as one of the

The Kirov Ballet performs "The Glorification of the Chosen One" from Stravinsky's *Rite of Spring,* with costumes and choreography reconstructed from the original production.

landmarks in twentieth-century symphonic literature. But it never would have come about had it not been for the Ballets Russes and the opportunity the group gave Stravinsky to collaborate on pathbreaking multimedia.

CRITICAL THINKING

1. What elements made *The Rite of Spring* shocking to its first audiences? Do you think it is still shocking today?
2. How did different media contribute to the expressive effect of *The Rite of Spring*?

YourTurn TO EXPLORE

Consider the music videos for one of your favorite songs, or any video of music you consider especially meaningful that adds a story line (not just images of musicians playing). How does the dancing or story line help bring out specific elements of the music? Are there aspects of the music/song that you think are obscured or made less effective by the addition of the video/dancing? How might you change the video track to bring out different aspects of the music, perhaps ones that you would find more significant?

LISTENING GUIDE 47 4:34

Stravinsky: *The Rite of Spring (Le sacre du printemps)*, Part I, excerpts

Date: 1913

Genre: Ballet (often performed as a concert piece for orchestra)

Basis: Scenes of pagan Russia

Scenario: Nicholas Roerich and Igor Stravinsky

Choreography: Vaslav Nijinsky

Performed by: Philharmonia Orchestra, Esa-Pekka Salonen, conductor

Sections: Part I: *Adoration of the Earth*
    Introduction
    Dance of the Youths and Maidens
    Game of Abduction
    Spring Rounds
    Games of the Rival Tribes
    Procession of the Sage
    Dance of the Earth

Part II: *The Sacrifice*
    Introduction
    Mystic Circle of the Adolescents
    Glorification of the Chosen One
    Evocation of the Ancestors
    Ritual Action of the Ancestors
    Sacrificial Dance

Introduction (closing measures)   0:30

What to Listen For			
Melody	Disjunct, floating, folk-song melody.	**Expression**	Haunting mood, represents awakening of the earth; very slow tempo (*Lento*).
Rhythm/ meter	Free shifting meter; the four-note pizzicato idea establishes a duple pulse.	**Timbre**	High-range bassoon with solo clarinets, pizzicato strings.

continued on next page

0:00   Folk tune played by the bassoon, from the opening:

0:12   Pizzicato rhythmic figure in violins:

0:19   Clarinet flourish, followed by a sustained string chord.
0:22   Violin figure returns to establish the meter for the next section.

Dance of the Youths and Maidens   2:47

What to Listen For

Melody	Russian folk-song melodies alternate with nonmelodic sound blocks.	**Form**	Sectional, with opening section recurring several times (**A-B-A′-C-A-D-E-F-G-A″-F′**).
Rhythm/ meter	Basic duple pulse with irregular accents; constant eighth-note motion.	**Expression**	Forceful, with high energy and changing dynamics.
Harmony	Dissonant chord (polytonal) repeated over and over; sound blocks.	**Timbre**	Changing instrumental colors throughout.
Texture	Dense, complex polyphony.	**Performing forces**	Huge orchestra with expanded brass, woodwind, and percussion sections.

0:30   Strings play harsh, percussive chords (**A**), reinforced by eight horns, with unpredictable accents:

0:37   English horn (**B**) plays the pizzicato motive from the *Introduction*.
0:42   Brief return of the opening accented chords (**A′**).
0:45   Motives combine with new ideas (**C**). Strings continue their chords; English horn repeats its four-note motive; loud brass interruptions and a descending melodic fragment.
1:02   Return of opening accented chords (**A**).
1:10   Bassoon plays syncopated folk melody (**D**), over accented string chords:

1:38   Steady eighth-note pulse (**E**); four-note motive alternates between the English horn and trumpet; scurrying motives in the winds and strings, and sustained trills.
1:50   Four-note motive (English horn, then violins) and sustained trills; low string instruments hit the strings with the wood of their bows (*col legno*).

1:58   French horn and flute introduce a folklike melody (**F**); texture thickens with activity:

2:16   Flutes repeat the theme (from **F**).

2:29   New melody (**G**) appears in trumpets with parallel chords:

2:42   Texture is abruptly reduced; accents of the opening section (**A″**) return; frenetic activity continues.

2:50   Melody (**F′**) in piccolo, then in flutes and strings; unpredictable accents, scurrying activity, and an expanding texture lead to the climax.

Game of Abduction   1:17

What to Listen For			
Melody	Scurrying melodic figures and horn calls, brief folk tune.	**Texture**	Dense, with shifting activity.
Rhythm/ meter	Fast tempo, meter not established; unpredictable accents.	**Expression**	Frenetic and primitive mood.
		Timbre	Quickly shifting instrumental colors.
Harmony	Harshly dissonant, crashing chords.		

3:16   Sustained chords, hurrying string sounds, and syncopated accents.

3:20   Woodwinds and piccolo trumpet introduce a folk theme; texture is dense, with constantly changing activity and timbres:

3:29   Horns introduce a new motive, alternating the interval of a fourth:

3:48   New thematic idea, in a homorhythmic texture and changing meters:

3:56   Horn motive returns.

4:07   Timpani and full orchestra alternate strong beats; irregular accents.

4:24   A series of loud chords and a sustained trill end the movement.

57

Still Sacred: Religious Music in the Twentieth Century

"The Church knew what the Psalmist knew: Music praises God.
Music is well or better able to praise Him than the building of the church
and all its decoration; it is the Church's greatest ornament."

—Igor Stravinsky

KeyPoints

- Talented French artists and composers have long competed for a special prize, the Prix de Rome, that allows them the opportunity to live in Rome and explore their creativity.

- Lili Boulanger, the first woman to win the prize, combined Impressionist ideas with the emerging modernist approach to dissonance. Her sister

Nadia was a highly respected teacher as well as a composer.

- Boulanger's *Psalm 24* is an example of modernist sacred music written from the perspective of personal devotion rather than commissioned by a religious institution.

Religious institutions provided the primary employment and sponsorship for the Western musical tradition for centuries. From the 1800s, as secular music became more and more prominent, many musicians still continued to play and write for their worship communities and draw on religious themes, for works not necessarily designed to be performed in church but rather meant to convey their own spiritual convictions. Spiritual topics inspired expressive sounds even before the development of notation; it's not surprising that they have continued to do so into the modernist era and beyond.

Post-Impressionism, Lili Boulanger, and the Prix de Rome

Many composers of the early twentieth century fell under the spell of Impressionist music by Debussy and his followers; the influence of such post-Impressionist trends can be heard not only in France (in the music of Maurice Ravel, for example), but across Europe and in the United States. At the same time, however, new currents led to radical changes in music composition that assaulted the ears of listeners, as we saw in the previous two chapters. In France, composers could be found representing both camps; among the innovators in the developing French school was Lili Boulanger, who embraced not only Impressionism but an innovative harmonic language as well. Like several notable musicians before her, she was singled out for her talent in the prestigious French competition known as the Prix de Rome (Rome prize).

The coveted Prix de Rome, extending back as far as the seventeenth century, was open to young artists and musicians under the age of thirty; the winner received a monetary award and a three-year grant to study at the Villa Medici in Rome. Some of France's most renowned composers were awarded the prize, including Hector Berlioz, Georges Bizet, Claude Debussy, and, once women were allowed to enter (from 1903), Lili Boulanger. The prize meant instant fame for the winners, and it launched the careers of many great French artists and musicians. The recognition for Boulanger, though, the first woman to win, was bittersweet, as the celebrity status and hectic schedule associated with her position took a toll on her already fragile health.

Psalm 24

Boulanger's setting of *Psalm 24* (LG 48), written in 1916, is one of three choral works she set to Psalm texts; these are largely recognized as some of her finest compositions. *Psalm 24* is the briefest of the three, but powerfully majestic, featuring forces typical for French sacred music. The dramatic introduction, a fanfare for brass, harp, organ, and timpani, sets a commanding tone, after which the tenors and basses sing the first three verses, punctuated with accented instrumental

Lili Boulanger (seated) with her sister Nadia, a famous music pedagogue.

Lili Boulanger (1893–1918)

Parisian composer Lili Boulanger, younger sister of the famous pedagogue Nadia Boulanger and the daughter of two musicians, showed an early affinity for music, but her training was hampered by chronic illness that resulted in her untimely death at the age of twenty-four. Her immune system had been damaged from having bronchial pneumonia at age two, and she suffered painful bouts of Crohn's disease throughout her short life. A precocious child, Lili learned to sing and play violin, cello, harp, and piano through private instruction, and she sat in on classes at the Paris Conservatory with her sister when her health permitted.

Both sisters set their sights on winning the famous Prix de Rome competition for composition, which their father had won in 1835. Nadia took second prize in 1908 (after almost being eliminated for writing an instrumental, rather than choral, fugue), and Lili, after withdrawing from the 1912 competition because of ill health, won first prize in 1913 for her cantata *Faust et Hélène*. She received a contract with the Ricordi music-publishing house, but her illness prevented her from fulfilling the three-year term in Rome, and the onset of the First World War directed her energies

away from composition and toward an organization she founded that attempted to keep musicians in contact with their families during the war.

Although Boulanger focused on choral and chamber music, she was under contract to write two operas as well, and completed part of one, *La Princesse Maleine*, on a libretto by the well-known writer Maurice Maeterlinck. In 1917, she underwent an appendectomy that doctors hoped would relieve her pain, but she soon weakened. Her final composition, a poignant *Pie Jesu*, was dictated from her deathbed to her devoted sister Nadia. Lili's choral music—both secular and sacred—is among her most distinguished work, and her moving Psalm settings reflect the strength of her Catholicism. Her music is lyrical, with innovative harmonies and complex counterpoint.

MAJOR WORKS: An unfinished opera, *La Princesse Maleine* • Sacred and secular choral works, including settings of Psalms 24, 129, and 130 • Songs for voice and orchestra, including the song cycle *Clarières dans le ciel* (voice and piano/orchestra, 1915) and *Pie Jesu* (soprano, string quartet, and organ, 1918) • Cantata *Faust et Hélène* (1913) • Piano and chamber music.

LISTENING GUIDE 48 3:25

Boulanger: *Psalm 24*

Date: 1916
Genre: Choral Psalm setting

Performed by: Chorale Elisabeth Brasseur,
Orchestre Lamoureux, Igor Markevitch, conductor

What to Listen For

Melody	Lyrical, small-ranging, and conjunct.	**Form**	Three-part (**A-B-A**).
Rhythm/ meter	Triple meter; highly accented in the opening and closing.	**Expression**	Dramatic, martial tone, with an ethereal middle section.
Harmony	Vague harmonic direction.	**Performing forces**	Tenor solo, SATB chorus, brass, harp, organ, timpani.
Texture	Largely chordal, homophonic; parallel lines evoke Impressionism.	**Text**	Psalm 24 (English version from the New Revised Standard Bible).

0:00   **Introduction:** Short brass fanfare, sets dramatic tone.

0:06   1. La terre appartient à l'Éternel, et tout ce qui s'y trouve,
la terre habitable et ceux qui l'habitent.
The earth is the Lord's, and all that is in it;
the world and those who live in it.

       2. Car Il l'a fondée sur les mers,
et l'a établie sur les fleuves.
For He has founded it on the seas,
and established it on the rivers.

       3. Qui est-ce qui montera à la montagne de l'Éternel,
et qui est-ce qui demeurera au lieu de sa sainteté?
Who shall ascend the hill of the Lord,
and who shall stand in His holy place?

Tenors and basses only, highly accented.
Voices alternate with fanfare in brass
and organ.

0:45   4. Ce sera l'homme qui a les mains pures, et le coeur net,
dont l'âme n'est point portée à la fausseté
et qui ne jure point pour tromper.
Those who have clean hands and pure hearts,
who do not lift up their souls to what is false
and who do not swear falsely.

Men's voices and organ; more serene.

1:12   5. Il recevra la bénédiction de l'Éternel
et la justice de Dieu son sauveur.
They will receive the blessing from the Lord,
and vindication from the God of their salvation.

Tenor solo, with harp; ecstatic mood.

1:37   6. Telle est la génération de ceux qui Le cherchent,
qui cherchent Ta face en Jacob.
Such is the company of those who seek Him,
who seek the face of the God of Jacob.

Chantlike chorus; mystical mood.

2:03   7. Portes, Élevez vos têtes, portes éternelles,
haussez-vous, et le Roi de gloire entrera.
Lift up your heads, O gates, and be lifted up,
O ancient doors! That the King of Glory may come in.

Full chorus, martial and triumphant.

       8. Qui est ce Roi de gloire? C'est l'Éternel fort
et puissant dans les combats.

> *Who is the King of Glory? He is the Eternal King of Glory,*
> *strong and mighty in battle.*

9. Portes, élevez vos têtes,
   élevez-vous aussi, portes éternelles;
   et le Roi de gloire entrera.
   Lift up your heads, O gates, and be lifted up, O ancient doors!
   That the King of Glory may come in.

2:53   10. Qui est ce Roi de gloire? C'est l'Éternel des armées,
   c'est Lui qui est le Roi de gloire, Éternel.
   Who is the King of Glory? The Lord of Hosts,
   He is the King of Glory.

Tempo picks up, piece closes on a *fortissimo* chord.

exchanges. The fourth verse, with men and organ alone, is calmer, projecting a Debussy-like air. The tranquility continues with a rapturous tenor solo, which promises the benediction, and an ethereal, chantlike delivery of the sixth verse by unison men with harp. The last verses return to a triumphal tone, with full chorus and instruments, marching to a resplendent close—hardly the music one expects from a frail, dying woman. Her death silenced a highly individual voice, one of the most promising of the early twentieth century.

The French text of *Psalm 24* would have been incompatible with the Latin-only rule governing the services of the Catholic Church until 1963. Like many of her contemporaries, Boulanger composed sacred music that was not specifically designed for traditional worship: the *Psalm* is an expression of her personal devotion rather than a strictly functional religious work. This approach has become more common in the last century, as composers and musicians have responded to the increasingly flexible relationship between individual spirituality and the multitude of religious traditions that intersect in the modern world.

In Their Own Words

66 To be a composer and not a musician is a tragedy; it is to have genius and not talent."

—*Nadia Boulanger*

CRITICAL THINKING

1. Why was the Prix de Rome important in French musical culture? What were the features of the competition?
2. How do the musical elements of *Psalm 24* reflect different aspects of turn-of-the-twentieth-century styles, as well as older traditions?

Your Turn TO EXPLORE

Find one or more musical works that set a spiritual or sacred text *not* connected with a specific religious service, or that are meant to reflect an individual or a community's connection with the divine using newly chosen words rather than a standard prayer text. For example, you might look at Christian rock, hip-hop affiliated with the Five Percenter Nation, or the Jewish Renewal movement. What are the musical resources (melody, harmony, instrumentation) that are used to convey those words? Are they the same resources that might be chosen for secular music, or are they different in some way? Where is this music performed, and by whom? How do the musical features, text setting, and context in which these works are performed compare with the Boulanger *Psalm*, and with other sacred examples you have encountered before, whether through this course or in your personal experience?

58

War Is Hell:
Berg and Expressionist Opera

"Boredom . . . is the last thing one should experience in the theater." —Alban Berg

KeyPoints

- Arnold Schoenberg and his students Alban Berg and Anton Webern became known as a **Second Viennese School**, of modernist composition, in the first half of the 1900s.

- Berg's music is rooted in the post-Romantic tradition, but he also drew on the **twelve-tone method** devised by his teacher.

- Berg's most famous work is *Wozzeck*, an Expressionist opera based on a play about a disturbed man who moves between reality and hallucination in a society that has turned its back on him.

Art is sometimes designed to evoke ideal beauty, or to create a place of inspiration beyond the everyday. But other times the artist's goal is to shine a light on social problems and raise questions about inequality and the oppression of disenfranchised people. "Protest music" may be simple and easily performed as a resource to rally large groups in support of a cause, but it can also be extremely complex and experimental. Especially during the first half of the twentieth century, several composers combined social advocacy with their cutting-edge exploration of new musical techniques. Probably the most striking example comes from the theatrical work of Alban Berg, who was the most commercially successful Expressionist composer, finding a compelling path midway between the lushness of late Romanticism and the disconcerting atonality of his teacher Arnold Schoenberg.

The Second Viennese School and the Twelve-Tone Method

Having accepted the necessity of moving beyond the existing tonal system, Schoenberg sought a unifying principle that would take its place. He found this in a strict technique, worked out by the early 1920s, that he called "the method of composing with twelve tones"—that is, with the twelve chromatic pitches, each one carrying equal weight. Any composition that uses Schoenberg's **twelve-tone method**, also **Serialism, tone row** known as **serialism**, is based on a particular arrangement of the twelve tones called a **tone row**. The composer can arrange the pitches in any order, and once the row is established, it becomes the basis for all the piece's themes, harmonies, and musical patterns.

Schoenberg provided flexibility and variety in this seemingly confining system through alternative forms of the tone row. A **transposed row** keeps the same order of intervals but begins on a different pitch. In **inversion,** the movement of the notes is in the opposite direction—up instead of down, and vice versa—so that the row appears upside down. **Retrograde** is an arrangement of the pitches in reverse order, so that the row comes out backward, and **retrograde inversion** turns the row upside down *and* backward. (The same techniques were used in the Baroque fugue; see diagram on p. 171.)

Schoenberg's pioneering efforts in the breakdown of the traditional tonal system and his development of the twelve-tone method revolutionized musical composition. His innovations were taken further by his most gifted students, Alban Berg and Anton Webern. These three composers are often referred to as the **Second Viennese School** (the first being the school of Haydn, Mozart, and Beethoven).

Alban Berg and *Wozzeck*

Berg brought great lyrical imagination to the abstract procedures of the Schoenbergian technique. In his operas, he was drawn to Expressionist themes focusing on human foibles and depravity, and on characters who were utterly powerless to control the world around them.

Berg's style was rooted in German Romanticism—the world of Brahms and Wagner, and especially the late-Romantic soundscapes of Gustav Mahler (1860–1911). The Romantic streak in his temperament tied him to this heritage even after he had adopted the twelve-tone method. Berg was a musical dramatist: for him, music was bound up with character and action, mood and atmosphere. Yet, like his teacher, he also leaned toward the formal patterns of the past—fugue and passacaglia, variations, sonata, and suite.

Berg's opera *Wozzeck* was inspired by an early Romantic play by German writer Georg Büchner that was based on gruesome, real-life events. In the title character of Wozzeck, a common soldier, Büchner created an archetype of the "insulted and injured" inhabitants of the earth.

Wozzeck is the victim of his sadistic Captain and the coldly scientific Doctor, who uses the soldier for his experiments— to which he submits because he needs the money. (Wozzeck is given to hallucinations; the Doctor is bent on proving his theory that mental disorder is related to diet.) The action centers on Wozzeck's unhappy love for Marie, by whom he has an illegitimate son. Marie, however, is infatuated with the handsome Drum Major. Wozzeck slowly comes to the conclusion that she has been unfaithful to him. Ultimately he cuts her throat, then, driven back to the death scene by guilt and

Expressionist painter **Wassily Kandinsky** (1886–1944) defied notions of beauty in order to define the artist's inner self. *Improvisation 33* (1913).

The crazed Wozzeck stabs Marie in Act III of Berg's opera, in this 1952 production at the Théâter des Champs-Élysées, Paris.

remorse, he drowns himself. The story ends when Marie's child hears of the death of his mother, a traumatic event that implicitly begins the cycle of social alienation all over again.

Berg's libretto organized the play into three acts, each containing five scenes that are linked by brief orchestral interludes. Harmonically, the greater part of the opera is cast in an atonal-Expressionist idiom. Berg anticipates certain twelve-tone procedures, and generally organizes each scene and interlude as a systematic study on a particular musical idea. He also looks back to the tonal tradition, writing a number of passages in major and minor keys and using leitmotifs in the Wagnerian manner. Throughout, we hear moments of passionate lyricism that alternate with speechlike vocal lines (*Sprechstimme*).

In the next-to-last scene of the opera (LG 49), Wozzeck returns to the path near the pond where he has killed Marie and stumbles against her body. He asks, "Marie, what's that red cord around your neck?" He finds the knife with which he committed the murder, throws it into the pond, and, driven by his delusions, follows it into the water. His last words as he drowns are "I am washing myself in blood—the water is blood . . . blood!" The Doctor appears, followed by the Captain. We see the haunted scene through their eyes as they both ignore Wozzeck's drowning groans and respond to a general sense of dread.

The final scene opens with a symphonic interlude in D minor, a passionate lament for the life and death of Wozzeck that shows how richly Berg's music was influenced by the final vestiges of Romanticism. The scene takes place in the morning in front of Marie's house, where children are playing. Marie's son rides a hobbyhorse. Other children rush in with news of the murder, but the little boy does not understand—or at least appears not to. The children run off as he

Alban Berg (1885–1935)

Berg was born in Vienna into a well-to-do family and grew up in an environment that fostered his artistic interests. At nineteen, he began studying with Arnold Schoenberg, an exacting master and mentor who shaped his outlook on art.

At the outbreak of war in 1914, Berg was called up for military service despite his uncertain health (he suffered from asthma and a nerve ailment). After the war, with the premiere of his opera *Wozzeck* at the Berlin State Opera in 1925, Berg rose from obscurity to international fame. During his mature years, he was active as a teacher and also wrote about music, propagandizing tirelessly on behalf of Schoenberg and his school. But with the coming to power of Hitler, the works of the twelve-tone composers were banned in Germany as alien to the spirit of the Third Reich.

Exhausted and ailing after the completion of his Violin Concerto, Berg went to the country for a short rest before resuming work on his second opera, *Lulu*. An insect bite

brought on an abscess, then infection, and finally blood poisoning on his return to Vienna. He died on Christmas Eve that year, seven weeks before his fifty-first birthday.

Besides *Wozzeck*, Berg's most widely known composition is the *Lyric Suite*, an instrumental work in six movements, the first and last of which strictly follow the twelve-tone method. Berg spent the last seven years of his life working on *Lulu*, which is based on a single twelve-tone row. The opera remained unfinished at his death until the orchestration was completed by the Austrian composer Friedrich Cerha, and now *Lulu* has taken its place alongside *Wozzeck* as one of the more challenging and effective works of the modern lyric theater. Berg is probably the most widely admired master of the twelve-tone school. His premature death robbed contemporary music of a major figure.

MAJOR WORKS: Two operas: *Wozzeck* (1917–22) and *Lulu* (unfinished, 1935) • Orchestral music, including *Three Orchestral Pieces*, Op. 6 (1915), and the Violin Concerto (1935) • Chamber music, including *Lyric Suite* (1926) • Piano music • Songs.

continues to ride and sing. Then, noticing that he has been left alone, he calls "Hop, hop" and rides off after them on his hobbyhorse. This final scene—with the curtain closing on an empty stage—is utterly heartbreaking.

Wozzeck envelops the listener in a hallucinated world that could only have come from the avant-garde movements in central Europe in the 1920s. But its characters reach out beyond time and place to become eternal symbols of the human condition, and especially of the struggle of disenfranchised people—poor, mentally ill, and war-torn—within societies that turn their back on them.

In Their Own Words

" When I decided to write an opera, my only intentions . . . were to give the theater what belongs to the theater. . . . The music was to be so formed as consciously to fulfill its duty of serving the action at every moment."

—*Alban Berg*

CRITICAL THINKING

1. What are the essential principles of the twelve-tone method of composition?
2. How does Berg's Expressionism in *Wozzeck* relate to early Romantic ideals?

YourTurn TO EXPLORE

Find examples of musical works designed to bring attention to social problems or to protest against established political situations—protest songs against war or oppression, music associated with "pride" movements, and the like. If there are words, how does the music reinforce the meaning and impact of the words? What musical style and specific elements of melody, harmony, and instrumentation have the composer and/or performers chosen, and how do those musical elements represent opposition? What can you find out about the effect that those works have had on the political struggle or social debate with which they are associated?

LISTENING GUIDE 49   🔊 9:55

Berg: *Wozzeck*, Act III: scene 4, Interlude, scene 5

Date: 1917–22; premiered 1925

Genre: Opera, in three acts

Basis: Expressionist play by Georg Büchner

Characters: Wozzeck, a soldier (baritone)
Marie, his common-law wife (soprano)
Marie and Wozzeck's son (treble)
Captain (tenor)
Doctor (bass)
Drum Major (tenor)

Performed by: Walter Berry (Wozzeck), Albert Weikenmeier (Captain), Karl Donch (Doctor); Paris National Opera Orchestra and Children's Chorus, Pierre Boulez, conductor

Act III, scene 4: By the pond

What to Listen For

Melody	Use of *Sprechstimme* (speechlike melody); disjunct line.	**Expression**	Intensely emotional vocal line, supported by dissonance and surging dynamics.
Rhythm/ meter	Movement alternates between metric and free-flowing.	**Timbre**	Eerie mood created by a celeste and unusual instrument combinations; colorful orchestral effects.
Harmony	Both tonal and atonal language; dissonant and chromatic.		

continued on next page

Wozzeck

0:00	Das Messer? Wo ist das Messer? Ich hab's dagelassen. Näher, noch näher. Mir graut's . . . da regt sich was. Still! Alles still und tot.	The knife? Where is the knife? I left it there. Around here somewhere. I'm terrified . . . something's moving. Silence. Everything silent and dead.

(shouting)

	Mörder! Mörder!	Murderer! Murderer!

(whispering again)

	Ha! Da ruft's. Nein, ich selbst.	Ah! Someone called. No, it was only me.

(Still looking, he staggers a few steps farther and stumbles against the corpse.)

0:54	Marie! Marie! Was hast du für eine rote Schnur um den Hals? Hast dir das rote Halsband verdient, wie die Ohrringlein, mit deiner Sünde! Was hängen dir die schwarzen Haare so wild? Mörder! Mörder! Sie werden nach mir suchen. Das Messer verrät mich!	Marie! Marie! What's that red cord around your neck? Was the red necklace payment for your sins, like the earrings? Why's your dark hair so wild about you? Murderer! Murderer! They will come and look for me. The knife will betray me!

(looks for it in a frenzy)

	Da, da ist's.	Here! Here it is!

(at the pond)

	So! Da hinunter!	There! Sink to the bottom!

(throws knife into the pond)

	Es taucht ins dunkle Wasser wie ein Stein.	It plunges into the dark water like a stone.

(The moon appears, blood-red, from behind the clouds. Wozzeck looks up.)

2:03	Aber der Mond verrät mich, der Mond ist blutig. Will denn die ganze Welt es ausplaudern! Das Messer, es liegt zu weit vorn, sie finden's beim Baden oder wenn sie nach Muscheln tauchen.	But the moon will betray me: the moon is bloodstained. Is the whole world going to incriminate me? The knife is too near the edge: they'll find it when they're swimming or diving for mussels.

(wades into the pond)

	Ich find's nicht. Aber ich muss mich waschen. Ich bin blutig. Da ein Fleck— und noch einer. Weh! Weh! Ich wasche mich mit Blut— das Wasser ist Blut . . . Blut . . .	I can't find it. But I must wash myself. There's blood on me. There's a spot here— and another. Oh, God! I am washing myself in blood— the water is blood . . . blood . . .

(drowns)

Wozzeck's last words before drowning, accompanied by very soft ascending chromatic scales in strings:

(The Doctor appears, followed by the Captain.)

Captain

3:12	Halt!	Wait!

Doctor *(stops)*

	Hören Sie? Dort!	Can you hear? There!

Captain *(stops as well)*

Jesus! Das war ein Ton!	Jesus! What a ghastly sound!

Doctor *(pointing to the pond)*

Ja, dort!	Yes, there!

Captain

Es ist das Wasser im Teich. Das Wasser ruft. Es ist schon lange niemand ertrunken. Kommen Sie, Doktor! Es ist nicht gut zu hören.	It's the water in the pond. The water is calling. It's been a long time since anyone drowned. Come away, Doctor. It's not good for us to be hearing it.

(tries to drag the Doctor away)

Doctor *(resisting and continuing to listen)*

3:50	Das stöhnt, als stürbe ein Mensch. Da ertrinkt Jemand!	There's a groan, as though someone were dying. Somebody's drowning!

Captain

Unheimlich! Der Mond rot, und die Nebel grau. Hören Sie? . . . Jetzt wieder das Ächzen.	It's eerie! The moon is red, and the mist is gray. Can you hear? . . . That moaning again.

Doctor

Stiller, . . . jetzt ganz still.	It's getting quieter . . . now it's stopped altogether.

Captain

Kommen Sie! Kommen Sie schnell!	Come! Come quickly!

(He rushes off, pulling the Doctor along with him.)

Orchestral interlude in D minor

3:45

What to Listen For			
Rhythm/ meter	Very slow tempo.	**Harmony**	Lush, chromatic chords; a dissonant climax.
		Timbre	Strings, then brass, woodwinds, and timpani in a forceful climax.

0:00   Strings with rich chromatic chords; very slow (*Adagio*), builds to a loud climax in brass and woodwinds with timpani.

Act III, scene 5: Children playing in front of Marie's house

1:26

What to Listen For			
Melody	"Off-key" children's song, then speechlike lines; disjunct, "jumping" melody from Marie's son.	**Harmony**	Sweetly dissonant.
		Expression	Quietly surreal closing, powerfully emotional.
Rhythm	Lilting 12/8 meter, then pulse is more obscured.	**Timbre**	Children's voices accompanied by colorful orchestra

continued on next page

Melody of children's song, distorted:

Children

0:00 Ringel, Ringel, Rosenkranz, Ringelreih'n
Ringel, Ringel, Rosenkranz, Ring . . .

Ring-a-ring-a-roses,
A pocket full of . . .

(Their song and game are interrupted by other children bursting in.)

One of the newcomers

Du, Käthe! Die Marie!

Hey, Katie! Have you heard about Marie?

Second child

Was is?

What's happened?

First child

Weisst' es nit? Sie sind schon Alle 'naus.

Don't you know? They've all gone out there.

Third child *(to Marie's little boy)*

Du! Dein' Mutter ist tot!

Hey! Your mother's dead!

Marie's son *(still riding)*

Hopp, hopp! Hopp, hopp! Hopp, hopp!

Hop, hop! Hop, hop! Hop, hop!

Second child

Wo ist sie denn?

Where is she, then?

First child

Drauss' liegt sie, am Weg, neben dem Teich.

She's lying out there, on the path near the pond.

Third child

Kommt, anschaun!

Come and have a look!

(All the children run off.)

Marie's son *(continuing to ride)*

Hopp, hopp! Hopp, hopp! Hopp, hopp!

Hop, hop! Hop, hop! Hop, hop!

(He hesitates for a moment and then rides after the other children.)

Child on hobbyhorse, with *pianissimo* accompaniment:

59

American Intersections: Jazz and Blues Traditions

"All riddles are blues,
And all blues are sad,
And I'm only mentioning
Some blues I've had."

—Maya Angelou (1928–2014)

KeyPoints

- The roots of **jazz** lie in African traditions, Western popular and art music, and African American ceremonial and work songs.

- **Blues**, a genre based on three-line stanzas set to a repeating harmonic pattern, was an essential factor in the rise of jazz.

- Louis Armstrong (trumpet player, singer) was associated with **New Orleans–style jazz**, characterized by a small ensemble improvising simultaneously.

- Armstrong's groundbreaking improvisatory style was a huge influence on jazz musicians, including singer Billie Holiday.

- The 1930s saw the advent of the **Swing** (or **big-band**) **era** and the brilliantly composed jazz of Duke Ellington.

- By the late 1940s, big-band jazz gave way to smaller group styles, including **bebop**, **cool jazz**, and **West Coast jazz**; Latin American music also influenced later jazz styles.

Some call jazz the "American classical music," and there's no question that the tradition has been associated with the United States for more than a century. Primary antecedents of jazz were West African musical traditions brought to this continent by slaves and developed (sometimes in secret) to both maintain continuity with a lost homeland and provide a creative distraction from hard labor. But jazz was also heavily influenced by Euro-American vernacular traditions, partly through the tradition of minstrelsy (see Chapter 40), and music from the Americas. Jazz bands played for the popular dances (such as ragtime) that swept the country from the 1890s into the 1940s. As the century wore on, many musicians attempted fruitful cross-pollinations between jazz and blues, another tradition rooted in Black culture, as well as between jazz and Euro-American cultivated music (as we will see in the case of George Gershwin). Jazz has since taken many forms, and it remains one of the most vibrant and powerful musical traditions of our day, evolving along with the multifaceted culture of the United States.

In Their Own Words

66 It don't mean a thing if it ain't got that swing."

—*Duke Ellington*

Painter **Romare Bearden** (1911–1988) captures the spirit of jazz performance in his colorful collage *Empress of the Blues* (1974).

Roots of Jazz and Blues

Many enslaved Africans who were brought to the Americas came from cultures that relied on call-and-response singing and favored distinctive vocal inflections, and for whom dancing was an integral part of musical expression. Their descendants shaped this heritage into distinctive North American Black vocal and movement traditions of the nineteenth century: **work songs** (communal songs that synchronized the rhythm of work), **ring shouts** (religious rituals that involved moving counterclockwise in a circle while praying, singing, and clapping hands), and **spirituals** (see Chapter 53). The art of storytelling through music and praise singing (glorifying deities or royalty) were other African traditions that were incorporated into the rich African American repertories.

In the years after the Civil War, a new style of music arose in the South, especially in the Mississippi Delta: country, or rural, blues, originally performed by a male singer and, by the turn of the century, accompanied by a steel-string guitar. This music voiced the difficulties of everyday life. A blues text typically consisted of a three-line stanza whose first two lines were identical. The vocal lines featured melodic

Blue notes

"pitch bending," or **blue notes**, sung over standard harmonic progressions (**chord changes**)—usually twelve (or occasionally sixteen) bars in length. Among the greatest blues singers were Charlie Patton (c. 1891–1934), Bessie Smith (1894–1937), and, more recently, B. B. King ("King of the Blues," 1925–2015). Blues style derives from the work songs of Southern Blacks, but may also owe some elements to the folk songs of poor Euro-Americans in the Southern Appalachians—one example of the complexity of identifying purely African American musical traditions.

Sheet-music cover for the popular foxtrot *La jazzbandette* (1921), published in Paris.

New Orleans Jazz

Blues was an essential factor in the development of the **New Orleans jazz** tradition. This city, which had long facilitated interaction across races and cultures, was where jazz gained momentum through the fusion of ragtime (see Chapter 54) and blues with other traditional styles—spirituals, work songs, and ring shouts, but also Caribbean and Euro-American styles. There, in Congo Square, enslaved people met in the pre–Civil War era to dance to the accompaniment of drums, gourds, mouth harps, and banjos. Their music featured a strong underlying pulse with syncopations and polyrhythm. Melodies incorporated African-derived techniques such as rhythmic interjections, vocal glides, and percussive sounds made with the tongue and throat, and were often set in a musical scale with the lowered third, fifth, or seventh of a major scale (blue notes).

New Orleans ensembles depended on the players' improvisation to create a polyphonic texture. One of the greats of New Orleans–style jazz was trumpet player and singer Louis "Satchmo" Armstrong (1901–1971), a brilliant improviser who transformed jazz into a solo art that presented improvised fantasias on chord changes. Armstrong's instrumental-like approach to singing (**scat-singing**), his distinctive inflections, and his improvisatory style were highly influential to jazz vocalists, including Billie Holiday, one of the leading singers in jazz history.

Billie Holiday, with jazz trumpeter Louis Armstrong in the 1947 film *New Orleans*.

The Jazz Singer Billie Holiday

Holiday had a unique talent that was immediately recognized by other musicians. "You never heard singing so slow, so lazy, with such a drawl," one bandleader reminisced. Although she had never received formal vocal training, she had a remarkable sense of pitch and a flawless delivery—a style she learned from listening to her two idols, Bessie Smith and Louis Armstrong. We will hear a song that Holiday wrote and recorded in 1936, *Billie's Blues* (LG 50), and performed regularly throughout her career. It's a twelve-bar blues, with a short introduction and six choruses. A **chorus** is a single statement of a melodic-harmonic pattern, like in a twelve-bar blues or thirty-two-bar popular song—some of which are instrumental. The first verse (chorus 2) is a typical three-line strophe, but as the work progresses, the form becomes freer. In the vocal choruses, Holiday demonstrates her masterful rhythmic flexibility and talent for jazz embellishments (scoops and dips on notes). In this performance, we hear Artie Shaw's creative clarinet improvisations and Bunny Berigan's earthy, "gutbucket" trumpet playing (displaying an unrestrained, raspy quality of tone).

Billie Holiday (1915–1959)

Known as Lady Day, Holiday was born in Philadelphia and grew up in Baltimore. In 1928, with barely any formal education, she moved to New York, where she probably worked as a prostitute. Around 1930, Holiday began singing at clubs in Brooklyn and Harlem, and was discovered three years later by a talent scout who arranged for her to record with the white clarinetist Benny Goodman. This first break earned her $35.

By 1935, Holiday was recording with some of the best jazz musicians of her day. As her popularity increased, she was featured with several prominent big bands—making her one of the first Black singers to break the color barrier and sing in public with a white orchestra. She recorded her most famous song in 1939—*Strange Fruit*, about a Southern lynching. With its horrible images of Blacks dangling from trees, the song resonated with Blacks and whites alike and became a powerful social commentary on Black identity and equality.

By the 1940s, Holiday's life had deteriorated, the result of alcohol and drug abuse, and relationships with abusive men. She was jailed on drug charges in 1947. Her health—and her voice—suffered because of her addictions, although she still made a number of memorable recordings. She died of cirrhosis of the liver in 1959, at the age of forty-four.

SELECTED RECORDINGS: *God Bless the Child* and *Billie's Blues*, both on the album *Lady Day: The Best of Billie Holiday; Fine & Mellow* and *Strange Fruit*, on the album *Strange Fruit*.

LISTENING GUIDE 50

🔊 3:38

Holiday: *Billie's Blues*

Date: Recorded 1936
Genre: 12-bar blues

Performed by: Billie Holiday, vocal; Bunny Berigan, trumpet; Artie Shaw, clarinet; Joe Bushkin, piano; Dick McDonough, guitar; Pete Peterson, bass; Cozy Cole, drums

What to Listen For

Melody	Syncopated melodies with pitch inflections; free improvisations.
Rhythm/ meter	Slow tempo, 4/4 meter; steady rhythmic accompaniment under more-complex, flexible solo lines.
Harmony	Repeated harmonic progressions for each chorus (I–IV–I–V–I).
Texture	Polyphonic, with countermelodies against a solo voice or instrument.

Form	12-bar blues (introduction and six choruses; choruses 2, 3, 6 are vocal).
Expression	Laid-back feeling, different moods in the solos.
Performing forces	Holiday, vocal, with trumpet, clarinet, piano, guitar, string bass, and drums.
Text	Chorus 2 is a typical blues text; the others are more free.

0:00   **Introduction** (4 bars)—bass and piano.

0:07   **Chorus 1**—ensemble (12 bars).

0:32   **Chorus 2**—vocal (12 bars):   Lord, I love my man . . .
              [repeated text line]
              But when he mistreats me . . .

Opening of first vocal chorus, showing syncopated line, with upward slide at the end:

0:56   **Chorus 3**—vocal (12 bars):   My man wouldn' gimme . . .
              [new text without repeated lines]

1:21   **Chorus 4**—solo clarinet improvisation (12 bars).

1:45   **Chorus 5**—solo trumpet improvisation (12 bars).

2:11   **Chorus 6**—vocal (12 bars): Some men like me . . .
              [new text without repeated lines]

Holiday's song exemplifies the intersection between jazz and blues, and also the continuing connection between jazz and dance, since the regular musical phrases and repeating structure are perfectly suited to the popular dances of the time. Most jazz of the first half of the 1900s was performed in dance clubs, and patrons would be as likely to dance to Holiday's song as they would be to listen.

Duke Ellington and the Swing Era

"Somehow I suspect that if Shakespeare were alive today, he might be a jazz fan himself."

In the 1930s and 40s, early jazz gave way to the **Swing**, or **big-band**, era. Bands needed arranged and composed music—that is, written down, rather than improvised—and one musician who played a major role in its development was Edward Kennedy "Duke" Ellington, whose group first went on the road in 1932 and remained popular until his death. His unique big-band style of jazz won over a wide audience, both Black and white, who danced away their cares in clubs and hotel ballrooms across the country.

In 1939, Ellington began a collaboration with Billy Strayhorn (1915–1967), a classically trained pianist who served as an arranger and composer for the band; together they achieved an unparalleled success with their suites, tone poems, ballets, and even sacred music. Ellington and Strayhorn collaborated for many years, each man's work so complementary to the other that, in many cases, their individual efforts are difficult to determine. One of the few works solidly credited to Strayhorn, however, is *Take the A Train* (first recorded in 1941; LG 51), and it epitomizes the swing style. (The A train refers to one of the subway lines that run through Manhattan to Harlem.)

Although some have said that Duke Ellington's true instrument was his band, he was an exceptionally gifted pianist.

Take the A Train

Ellington's orchestral palette was much richer than that of the New Orleans band. It included two trumpets, one cornet, three trombones, four saxophones (some of the players doubling on clarinet), two string basses, guitar, drums, vibraphone,

Edward Kennedy ("Duke") Ellington (1899–1974)

Ellington was born in Washington, D.C., and began to study piano at age seven. By the 1920s, he was playing in New York jazz clubs—including Harlem's Cotton Club—with his group The Washingtonians. He soon reached a leading position in the jazz world with his renowned orchestra, which toured the United States and Europe in the 1930s and 40s.

Ellington was a highly talented pianist, but he rarely played extended solos with his group; rather, he was a facilitator and accompanist who shared rhythmic and melodic ideas with the entire ensemble. Largely a self-taught musician, Ellington learned how to orchestrate for his ensemble through experimentation, trying new effects with different timbres and voicings. Indeed, some consider the entire jazz orchestra to be his instrument.

His recordings feature his compositions and arrangements, along with those by collaborator Billy Strayhorn.

A concern for structure resulted in works with complex forms not usually associated with jazz. Among his most famous compositions are *Black and Tan Fantasy* (1927), *Mood Indigo* (1930), *Sophisticated Lady* (1933), *Ko-Ko* (1940), and *Black, Brown and Beige* (1943); his most famous recording is *Take the A Train*. He also scored music for film, including Otto Preminger's *Anatomy of a Murder* (in which he also acted, 1959). Today Ellington is remembered as a composer who brought the jazz art to new heights; as an arranger who served as a teacher and model to several generations of musicians; and as a major artistic figure in the Harlem Renaissance (see Chapter 60).

SELECTED RECORDINGS: *Best of the Duke Ellington Centennial Edition* (1999, available for download), which includes *Black and Tan Fantasy, East St. Louis Toodle-O, Take the A Train,* and *Sophisticated Lady.*

Dizzy Gillespie, a major figure in the development of bebop and modern jazz, playing his custom-made trumpet, with raised bell.

and piano. This piece is a **thirty-two-bar song form**, with four phrases (**A-A-B-A**) of eight measures each; each **A-A-B-A** iteration makes a chorus. The introduction features Ellington on piano, with a syncopated chromatic motive; this is followed by three choruses. In the first chorus, the saxophones present the memorable tune, answered by muted trumpets and trombones in call and response. The second chorus stars band member Ray Nance on muted trumpet, with an underlying conversation in the reeds. Nance's masterful improvisation, complete with bent notes, **shakes** (shaking the lips to fluctuate between pitches), and glissandos, has been imitated by trumpet players everywhere. An energetic four-measure interlude that feels like triple meter suddenly intervenes, followed by the third chorus—another trumpet solo (this one open, or unmuted). The coda is a big-band signature closing: it repeats the opening eight bars of the piece twice, each time more softly.

Like many jazz tunes, *Take the A Train* was built on the chord changes of an earlier song, but it is enhanced with playful tunes, complex harmonies, and rich orchestration. Its lush, composed-out style is quite different from the more sparse and apparently spontaneous approach we hear in Holiday's song, but both demonstrate the combination of preplanned road map and in-the-moment elaboration that defines jazz as a tradition.

Bebop, Cool, Latin Jazz

By the end of the 1940s, musicians were rebelling against big-band jazz and developing new styles. **Bebop** (also known as **bop**) was an invented word mimicking the two-note trademark motive of this new style of fast tempos and complex harmonies. Trumpeter Dizzy Gillespie, saxophonist Charlie Parker, and pianist Thelonious Monk were among the leaders of the bebop movement in the 1940s. Over the next two decades, the term "bebop" came to include a number of sub-styles such as cool jazz, West Coast jazz, hard bop, and soul jazz. Trumpeter Miles Davis was the principal exponent of **cool jazz**, a laid-back style characterized by dense harmonies, lowered levels of volume, moderate tempos, and a new lyricism. **West Coast jazz** was a small-group, cool-jazz style featuring mixed timbres (one instrument for each color, often without piano) and contrapuntal improvisations. Among the important West Coast ensembles that sprang up in the 1950s were the Dave Brubeck Quartet (with Paul Desmond on saxophone) and the Gerry Mulligan Quartet (with Chet Baker on trumpet). Since the 1970s, jazz has branched out in more directions than this short overview can name.

In Their Own Words

❝ Bop is mad, wild, frantic, crazy . . . and not to be dug unless you've seen dark days, too."

—*Langston Hughes*

Latin American music has always been highly influential in the development of jazz, chiefly its dance rhythms and percussion instruments (for example, conga drum, bongos, and cowbells). In the 1930s and 40s, bandleaders such as Xavier Cugat brought Latin dance music—especially the rumba—into the mainstream. Duke Ellington's band recorded two hit Latin numbers: *Caravan* (1937, featuring Puerto Rican trombonist Juan Tizol) and *Conga Brava* (1940). Latin elements were integral to the bebop style of the late 1940s, and the next decades saw a strong Brazilian, as well as Cuban, influence on jazz. We will see that these influences were significant in musical theater as well, particularly in the shows of Leonard Bernstein (Chapter 66).

In the last century, many strands of jazz have developed, and there are controversies about whether some of them can legitimately be labeled jazz. There is no question, however, that jazz is among the most vibrant and original North American contributions to the modern musical landscape.

CRITICAL THINKING

1. What were some of the traditions that led to the development of jazz?
2. How does New Orleans–style jazz differ from big-band jazz? How do later jazz styles differ from big-band jazz?

YourTurn TO EXPLORE

Find an example of a jazz performance by one of the renowned singers of the twentieth century (like Ella Fitzgerald or Louis Armstrong) or a more recent jazz singer. How does the singer's delivery of syncopation and blue notes and other elaborations compare with the one taken by Holiday in *Billie's Blues*? How do the instrumentalists interact with the singer? How do any extended instrumental solos compare with the ones on our recording? If you find a video recording, what is the venue for the performance (concert hall, dance club?), and how is the performer interacting with the audience (and what is the audience response)? How does this performance compare with those in other repertories we've been exploring?

LISTENING GUIDE 51

 2:54

Strayhorn: *Take the A Train*

Date: Recorded February 15, 1941
Genre: Big-band jazz

Performed by: Duke Ellington Orchestra; Duke Ellington, director

---

What to Listen For

Melody	Disjunct, syncopated themes with call-and-response exchanges between instruments.
Rhythm/meter	Broad quadruple meter, at a moderate tempo; syncopated rhythms, short riffs (repeated phrases).
Harmony	Complex, advanced harmonies; chromatic; modulates to another key.
Form	32-bar song form (**A-A-B-A**) for each of three choruses, with introduction and coda.
Expression	Animated movement with special jazz effects (bent notes, shakes, glissandos).
Timbre	Big-band sound, with reed, brass, and percussion sections.
Performing forces	Jazz big band (trumpets, trombones, saxophones, piano, guitar, bass, drums); soloists: Duke Ellington (piano), Ray Nance (trumpet).

0:00   **Introduction**—four measures in the piano (Ellington), with a syncopated, chromatic motive.

Chorus 1 (A-A-B-A)

0:06   **A**—unison saxophones state the disjunct melody, in the key of C, with interjections from muted trumpets and trombones (eight bars), against a steady rhythm accompaniment:

0:17   **A**—repeated (eight bars).

0:28   **B**—contrasting episode in saxophones; syncopated melody with low brass and rhythm section.

0:39   **A**—saxophones restate main melody with a new rhythmic figure from the brass; rippling piano figures.

continued on next page

0:50   **Chorus 2 (A-A-B-A)**
Ray Nance on muted trumpet, accompanied by saxophones and rhythm section;
trumpet solo in the second phrase, with bent pitches:

1:35   **Interlude**—four measures, sustained accents as though in triple rather than quadruple meter.

1:41   **Chorus 3 (A-A-B-A)**
A—saxophones play a version of main theme (four measures), followed by unmuted trumpet solo (Nance).

1:52   A—trumpet solo continues, with sustained chords in saxophones.

2:04   B—trumpet solo with countermelodies in saxophones and trombones; closes with a fanfare without rhythm accompaniment; punctuated by a cymbal crash.

2:14   A—original theme played by saxophones in a new key (E-flat); brass interjects, alternating with muted and open notes.

2:26   **Coda**—two repetitions of **A** (eight bars each), first *mezzo piano*, then softer, with a final closing saxophone riff.

🔊 **AnotherHearing** Compare the recording you heard of the Duke Ellington Orchestra with a more recent, extended one by the Lincoln Center Jazz Orchestra, featuring Wynton Marsalis on trumpet. Can you hear the 32-bar song form in this performance? How does the improvisation by the pianist and Marsalis compare with what you heard in the Ellington performance? Which version do you prefer, and why?

60

Modern America: Still and Musical Modernism in the United States

"What are the qualities which must be inherent in the person who aspires to write music? First, and most important, is the ability to induce the flow of inspiration, that indefinable element which transforms lifeless intervals into throbbing, vital, and heartwarming music."

—*William Grant Still*

KeyPoints

- American composers of the early twentieth century sought to define a unique tradition of American modernism.

- The **Harlem Renaissance** was a cultural movement in the 1920s and 30s that highlighted African American contributions to the country's cultural heritage.

- African American composer William Grant Still broke numerous racial barriers in the art-music tradition. His Suite for Violin and Piano looks to three Black visual artists for inspiration.

How can or should music reflect the identity of a composer? Romanticism introduced the ideal of autobiographical expression by the creative individual, and nationalism added the question of group identity, leaving artists to struggle with striking a balance between those two mandates. The 1920s and 30s were a time when African American artists in many media banded together to identify creative outlets for Blacks that would both pay tribute to their heritage and recognize individual excellence regardless of race or ethnicity. One of the most prominent and successful musicians who joined this effort, William Grant Still, is now regarded as a pioneer both in the search for a modern American sound and in opening a wider range of musical opportunities for African Americans.

In Their Own Words

66 Life is for the living,
Death is for the dead,
Let life be like music,
And death a note unsaid."

—*Langston Hughes*

The Harlem Renaissance

In the early 1900s, economic opportunity brought increasing numbers of African Americans to New York City, and specifically to the northern part of Manhattan called Harlem. By the beginning of the economic boom of the 1920s, a contemporary poet referred to Harlem proudly as "not merely a Negro colony or community, [but] a city within a city, the greatest Negro city in the world."

Inter*face*

Identity and the Arts in the Harlem Renaissance

African American poet **Langston Hughes** (1902–1967) was an important Harlem Renaissance figure.

You may know that the French term "renaissance" describes a rebirth or renewal of something from the past. The cultural movement known as the Harlem Renaissance, sometimes referred to as "the New Negro movement," was a literary, artistic, and sociological movement that highlighted African American intellectual life in the 1920s and 30s. It was a renewal of sorts in that African Americans looked to their historical and ethnic roots; centered in the predominantly Black area of New York City known as Harlem, the movement was sparked in part by the craze for jazz that was sweeping the country. Among the artists associated with it was sculptor Richmond Barthé, whose portrayals of Blacks—field workers, historical figures, victims of racial violence, and African dancers—emphasized their individuality and physicality.

The most important literary figure was Langston Hughes, a highly innovative African American poet whose works, depicting the struggles of working-class Blacks, radiated with Black pride. A frequent visitor to the Harlem jazz clubs, Hughes wrote verse that imitated the rhythms and flow of jazz, thus creating a new kind of jazz poetry. His first collection, *The Weary Blues* (1926), included his most famous poem, "The Negro Speaks of Rivers," dedicated to W. E. B. DuBois, founder of the National Association for the Advancement of Colored People (NAACP), comparing the spirit of his people to the rivers of the world.

Another literary figure central to this movement was Zora Neale Hurston (see right), whose creative efforts explored what it meant to be Black and female in a male-dominated society. Her essay "How It Feels to Be Colored Me" reveals a woman strengthened by the hardships she has endured. Yet Hurston rejected "the sobbing school of Negrohood" that promoted self-pride. She claimed to transcend her race: "I belong to no race nor time. I am the eternal feminine with its string of beads." Her famous essay colorfully describes moments when she feels racial differences, such as when she attends a jazz club with a white friend who does not experience the sense of the "jungle beyond" that she feels from the music.

Most jazz musicians, including Duke Ellington and Billie Holiday, gained early recognition performing in such famous Harlem jazz clubs as the Apollo Theater and the Cotton Club. A prolific composer as well, Ellington considered his works to be "tone parallels" to the lives of Blacks. Like Hurston, African American musicians uniformly rejected the stereotyped images of Blacks that had been popular in minstrel shows, and they worked to break down the long-standing prejudice against Black musicians and artists. Among these crusaders was composer William Grant Still, whose creative efforts merge art and traditional musical genres: he held the view that "the Negro artist is important in American society because he demonstrates that achievement is possible in our democracy."

African American author and folklorist Zora Neale Hurston beats a traditional Haitian drum (1937).

Building on a growing sense of a new Black cultural identity, a book of essays called *The New Negro* was published in 1925, edited by philosopher Alain Locke, a Harvard graduate who became the first African American Rhodes scholar. Locke and the other authors of *The New Negro* encouraged their fellow Black artists to look to Africa for inspiration on how to shape their American future, and the essays spoke about racial equality and pride in Black cultural heritage. The ideas from the essays in *The New Negro* are credited with sparking the so-called **Harlem Renaissance** (see Interface opposite).

Still's Suite for Violin and Piano

In choosing the genre of the suite, which had long been part of the European dance and programmatic tradition, Still was able to use an established genre (one that reflected the modernist neo-Classical trend) and also to evoke images that he felt exemplified the artistic efforts of Black America in a progressive way. He based each movement on an artwork by a different African American artist. The spirited first movement was inspired by the sculpture *African Dancer* by Richmond Barthé, a noted Harlem Renaissance artist. The second movement evokes the expressive mood of a drawing of an African American mother and child by Sargent Johnson, one of the first Californian Black artists to achieve fame. And the rhythmically charged closing movement shares the impish humor of *Gamin* by Augusta Savage, the most prominent African American woman artist of her day. Her sculpture captures the confident image of a street-smart kid in Harlem ("gamin" suggests a street urchin).

The movements of the suite all employ modal harmonies and melodies featuring lowered thirds and sevenths, typical of the blues. Throughout his career,

William Grant Still (1895–1978)

Still grew up in Little Rock, Arkansas. His parents, both educators, encouraged his early music studies on violin. He left college to work as a professional musician in Memphis and then New York, earning a reputation as an arranger for radio and musical theater, while continuing his classical music studies with French-born composer Edgard Varèse. Still deliberately moved away from the avant-garde, however, to find his original voice in the music of his cultural heritage.

His first symphony, the *Afro-American*, was premiered in 1931 by the Rochester Philharmonic Orchestra: the first symphony by an African American composer to be performed by a major American orchestra. The symphony brought him numerous commissions from major orchestras, including the New York Philharmonic. In 1934, he won a Guggenheim Fellowship and moved to Los Angeles, where he wrote film and television scores. An opera, *Troubled Island*, was produced by New York's City Opera in 1949, marking another first for a Black composer. Still was recognized with many honorary degrees during his last years, and contributed to theme music for such popular TV series as *Gunsmoke* and *Perry Mason*. He remained in Los Angeles until his death in 1978. In his music, Still looked to writers and artists of the Harlem Renaissance for inspiration, including the renowned poet Langston Hughes, whose libretto he set for *Troubled Island*, on the struggles of the Haitian people.

MAJOR WORKS: Orchestral music, including four symphonies (No. 1, *Afro-American* Symphony, 1930) • Orchestral suites • Film scores • Stage works, including four ballets (*La Guiablesse*, 1927; *Sahdji*, 1930) • Eight operas, including *Troubled Island* (1937–49) • Chamber music, including Suite for Violin and Piano (1943) • Vocal music, including *Songs of Separation* (1949) and spiritual arrangements • Piano music • Choral music.

Still: Suite for Violin and Piano, III

Date: 1943

Genre: Suite for violin and piano

Performed by: Lynn Chang, violin;
Vivian Taylor, piano

Movements: I. Majestically and vigorously (based on Richmond's Barthé's *African Dancer*)
    II. Slowly and expressively (based on Sargent Johnson's *Mother and Child*)
    III. Rhythmically and humorously (based on Augusta Savage's *Gamin*)

III: Rhythmically and humorously

What to Listen For

Melody	Bluesy, short, syncopated ideas, with flatted third and seventh scale tones; ideas exchanged between violin and piano.
Rhythm/meter	Quick 2/4 meter; rhythmic and highly syncopated, with chords played on the offbeats.
Harmony	Modal, with blues chords; stride bass; ostinatos.
Texture	Mostly homophonic.
Form	Sectional form, with four- and eight-measure ideas; the opening returns frequently.
Timbre	Violin trills, glissandos, and double stops.
Expression	Playful and humorous; evokes image of cocky street kid depicted by sculpture.

0:00   Four-measure introduction in piano, with ostinato bass and offbeat chords.

0:05   Violin enters with a syncopated line, a four-measure idea in fragments, with stride-piano accompaniment:

0:26   Rising line to a new syncopated violin idea, accompanied by a syncopated, more active piano part.

0:35   Low-range, repeated-note idea in violin, against a moving piano line.

0:45   Piano takes over low-range melody, with violin playing double stops.

0:56   Opening motive returns, varied, in violin; piano is more syncopated.

1:06   Humorous repeated-note exchange between piano and violin.

1:17   Opening motive returns in violin, includes glissando and more active piano accompaniment.

1:27   Repeated-note idea is developed in violin.

1:38   Recapitulation of opening, including the brief piano introduction.

1:59   **Coda**, with rising violin line, then triumphant double-stop chords and glissando to the last chord.

Still favored blues as source material for his music, explaining that "they, unlike spirituals, do not exhibit the influence of Caucasian music." The last movement of the suite (LG 52) zips along with a flashy and syncopated violin line accompanied by an insistent bass that resembles the jazz piano style known as **stride**.

Sometimes called "Harlem stride piano," this style evolved from ragtime and features a regular pulse with chords on the offbeats. The movement unfolds in sections, sometimes engaging the piano and violin in a call-and-response exchange, but it keeps returning to the opening exuberant idea, varied with ornamentation and dazzling glissandos in the violin.

Not all members of the concert-music establishment embraced blues and jazz as compositional resources. And while the Harlem Renaissance was a powerful cultural moment for the growth of Black cultural prestige, its supporters were more interested in fostering musical traditions that they understood as more thoroughly African American—blues, jazz, and spirituals—than in encouraging the development of modernist art music. Today there are still too few African Americans involved in shaping the idea of an American art-music tradition; though as the twenty-first century progresses, a lively interaction of musical styles and repertories is helping to bring a wider range of voices into that dialogue.

Sculptor **Augusta Savage** (1892–1962) was an activist for African Americans in the arts.

CRITICAL THINKING

1. How does the music of William Grant Still fit the ideals of the Harlem Renaissance?

2. Why would the proponents of the Harlem Renaissance have been more interested in jazz and blues than in modernist art music?

YourTurn TO EXPLORE

Seek out works by African American art-music composers of the twentieth and twenty-first centuries. (Three examples are Will Marion Cook, Undine Smith Moore, and Olly Wilson; how might you go about finding more?) How have these individuals chosen to incorporate their heritage into their compositions? Are their approaches to racial/ethnic heritage different from Still's, or from the way European or Euro-American composers have used their own heritage as inspiration?

61

Jazz Gets Classical: Gershwin's Modern Experiment

"Jazz has contributed an enduring value to America in the sense that it has expressed ourselves."

—George Gershwin

KeyPoints

- George Gershwin built international fame through his **Tin Pan Alley** songs, musical theater productions, and "jazzy" compositional and performance style.

- Seeking to unite elements of jazz and the European concert tradition, Gershwin composed several hybrid works, including his very popular *Rhapsody in Blue*.

In Their Own Words

❝ My *Rhapsody in Blue* represents what I have been striving for since my earliest composition. I wanted to show that jazz is an idiom not to be limited to a mere song and chorus. . . . Jazz is not merely a dance; it comprises bigger themes and purposes. It may have the quality of an epic."

—George Gershwin

Throughout our survey so far, we have seen how music is an essentially collaborative art, and this is nowhere more true than in the multifaceted tradition of jazz, which is defined primarily around performers adding their distinctive interpretations to a preexisting musical framework. Some songs have become jazz "standards," attracting performers because of their memorable melodies and harmonic structures, and resulting in hundreds or even thousands of creative reworkings. Among the most talented composer of such tunes was George Gershwin, one of several musicians of the mid-1900s (both African American and Euro-American) who attempted to bring the jazz tradition forward not only as a booming commercial enterprise but also as a distinctive kind of cultivated music. Gershwin's all-too-short life was dedicated to the proposition that jazz could be as expressive an art form as any European-derived tradition; his "cultivated jazz" compositions were not only creatively outstanding but also financially successful and influential on other musicians. Yet Gershwin was criticized both for "whitewashing" an African American tradition and for introducing commercial music into the lofty halls of art—joining a long, still-continuing line of artists who have been accused of "selling out" the purity of a musical heritage.

From Song Plugging to the Concert Hall

Gershwin first broke into the music business as a "song plugger" who demonstrated and sold sheet music on New York's **Tin Pan Alley**. From the early years of that

George Gershwin (1898–1937)

Gershwin grew up in Manhattan, where he worked for a Tin Pan Alley publisher, playing and singing new releases for customers. "This is American music," he told one of his teachers. "This is the kind of music I want to write." He had his first big hit in 1920, with the song *Swanee,* recorded by Al Jolson.

During the 1920s, Gershwin won international acclaim with *Rhapsody in Blue,* premiered in 1924 by the Paul Whiteman Orchestra. This was followed by his *Concerto in F* and the tone poem *An American in Paris.* He also had a string of hit musicals, beginning with *Lady, Be Good* (1924), his first collaboration with his brother Ira, who wrote many of his song lyrics. Gershwin wrote enduring film scores, including *Shall We Dance* (featuring the song *They Can't Take That Away from Me*), starring Fred Astaire and Ginger Rogers. His folk opera *Porgy and Bess* is perhaps his masterpiece. He died of a brain tumor in 1937, at not quite thirty-nine.

In his music, Gershwin achieves an appealing rhythmic vitality through the use of syncopation, blue notes, and an "oom-pah" accompaniment typical of jazz piano style. His harmonic language extends from diatonic to very chromatic, with sudden shifts in tonality. His melodies range from declamatory to highly lyrical, and his forms are typical blues and song structures. No master has achieved this union of styles—popular and classical, vernacular and art—more successfully than Gershwin.

MAJOR WORKS: Orchestral works, including *Rhapsody in Blue* (1924, for piano and jazz band), *Concerto in F* (1925), and *An American in Paris* (1928) • Piano music • More than 30 stage works, including *Strike Up the Band* (1927), *Girl Crazy* (1930), *Of Thee I Sing* (1931), and *Porgy and Bess* (1935) • Songs for films, including *Shall We Dance* (1937) • Other songs (such as *Swanee,* *'S Wonderful, Embraceable You, The Man I Love*).

industry, songwriters had capitalized on the rising fashion for ragtime and then jazz styles. Many of the most popular songs printed, performed onstage, and eventually recorded and broadcast made some reference to ragtime or jazz, though the songs themselves followed structural and melodic conventions similar to the Anglo-American parlor ballads of Foster (Chapter 40) and other nineteenth-century songwriters.

Gershwin, a talented pianist, became familiar with a variety of techniques developed by African American jazz performers, and gained renown for his ability to play songs in a particularly effective and jazzy way—and this afforded opportunities to him as a white musician that Black musicians could not enjoy in the 1920s. As Gershwin began writing his own Broadway/Tin Pan Alley songs, he incorporated syncopations and harmonic variations that closely resembled improvised jazz. As a result, his songs became among the most commercially and artistically successful in the entire Tin Pan Alley repertory (and many remain beloved jazz standards).

Not content with his commercial success, and also inspired by the goals of the Harlem Renaissance (p. 374), Gershwin joined those who sought to expand jazz into the cultivated sphere. A number of his instrumental works were both groundbreaking and much loved from their premiere—most notably the *Rhapsody in Blue,* which Gershwin performed at a concert entitled "An Experiment in Modern Music," held at New York City's Aeolian Hall on Lincoln's birthday, February 12, in 1924.

Cover for the jazz-band version of *Rhapsody in Blue* (1924).

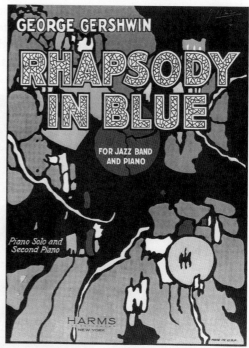

"An Experiment in Modern Music"

The concert was the brainchild of bandleader Paul Whiteman (1890–1967), whose big-band orchestra had become extremely popular in the early 1920s for its carefully planned and coordinated ensemble sound—quite different from the jubilant chaos of small-group jazz improvisation of the kind we heard in Chapter 59. Whiteman was among the leading advocates for the status of jazz as an uniquely American art music, and he enlisted Gershwin to write a new work—which Whiteman hyped as "a jazz concerto"—to provide the finale of a concert that would demonstrate the cultivated status of jazz. Whiteman's "Experiment" concert was attended by prominent critics and composers, and Gershwin's *Rhapsody* was immediately hailed as the highlight.

Rhapsody in Blue: Tunes Collaboratively Developed

As Gershwin's success rose in the years following the *Rhapsody*, his accounts of its creation became legendary: he told of having envisioned the work "on the train, with its steely rhythms, its rattlety-bang... I suddenly heard, even saw on paper, the complete construction of the *Rhapsody*, from beginning to end." This image of inspired creativity is firmly in keeping with the ideals of individual genius we have seen associated with nineteenth-century heroic composers.

But the *Rhapsody* was a collaborative endeavor from the start: not only was it created specifically for the Whiteman Orchestra, it was also strongly influenced by the person responsible for the unique Whiteman sound: Ferde Grofé (1892–1972), principal arranger for the ensemble. As Gershwin hurriedly sketched out the melodies and harmonies of the *Rhapsody* over the span of about three weeks in January 1924, he passed those sketches on to Grofé, who expertly adapted the musical ideas to the Whiteman soundscape. There is still extensive debate about how much Grofé added—did he just assign Gershwin's notes to specific instruments, or did he tweak the music to tailor-fit the ensemble he knew so well, as had been his custom?

Paul Whiteman and his jazz-band orchestra, who premiered *Rhapsody in Blue*, in the 1920s.

The *Rhapsody* is based on six musical ideas—five themes and a short motive—elaborated using different jazz performing conventions of the time, with the piano having the lion's share of the elaboration: like Mozart with his own concertos, Gershwin gave himself the platform to demonstrate his creativity in a semi-composed, semi-improvised framework. In some ways the work is very like a piano concerto—dialogue between the soloist and the larger ensemble, recurring stable and recognizable themes alternating with more fanciful and unpredictable virtuosity. In terms of overall form, however, it also evokes the kind of dance-hall medley that Gershwin would have associated with jazz performances of his Tin Pan Alley hits.

LISTENING GUIDE 53   🔊 **16:12**

Gershwin: *Rhapsody in Blue*

Date: Premiered 1924;
reorchestrated by Ferde Grofé 1926, 1942

Genre: Concerto-like, a one-movement "rhapsody"

Performed by: Philippe Entremont, piano;
Philadelphia Orchestra, Eugene Ormandy, conductor

What to Listen For

Melody	Bluesy stepwise tunes alternate with more jagged and forceful disjunct ideas.
Rhythm/ meter	Duple meter; extensive syncopation and rubato, especially in the solo piano cadenzas.
Harmony	Consonant and tonal overall, incorporating the blues scale.
Texture	Homophony alternates with nonimitative polyphony; solo piano alternates with orchestra.

Form	Recurring themes and motives, some similarities to Baroque ritornello form.
Expression	Draws on ragtime, blues, and jazz conventions to create a lively dialogue between piano and orchestra.
Performing forces	Piano and jazz band, complemented with a full orchestra.

0:00   The opening clarinet solo, characterized by a unique glissando into the high range, leads into the *ritornello* theme:

0:07   *Ritornello* theme: bluesy, syncopated melody; clarinet answered by low brass.

0:35   *Stride* theme: chromatic, repeated notes heard first in the brass:

continued on next page

0:47   *Ritornello* theme featuring a solo "wah-wah" muted trumpet, answered by the piano's *tag* motive:

1:01   *Ritornello* theme in full orchestra.

1:09   Piano solo builds on themes/motives introduced to this point, free and cadenza-like.

1:52   *Ritornello* theme in piano alternates with low woodwinds.

2:16   Piano solo builds again on themes/motives, with free tempo shifts.

3:09   *Ritornello* theme in full orchestra.

3:44   New: the broad *train* theme, led by trumpets in octaves and featuring flutter-tonguing (player's tongue flutters while blowing into the instrument):

4:29   *Stride* theme returns in full orchestra.

4:55   Tempo slows, solo clarinet is answered by a wah-wah trumpet.

5:18   New: the *shuffle* theme in full orchestra, played *marcato* (marked, or stressed):

6:17   Piano solo builds on the *stride* theme, horns join with a countermelody.

7:58   *Ritornello* theme in piano is followed by the *tag* motive.

8:10   *Ritornello* theme heard quietly in oboes and bassoons, piano and strings support it with clear downbeats.

8:35   Extended piano solo focusing on the *shuffle* theme.

10:50   New: expansive *love* theme in strings and winds, with a chromatic countertheme first in brass, then piano:

12:33   Extended piano solo elaborates on the *love* theme, with virtuoso passagework.

14:21   Brass joins piano in varying the *love* theme, building to . . .

15:15   *Stride* theme in full orchestra.

15:46   *Ritornello* theme in full orchestra, piano answers with the *tag* motive.

🔊 **AnotherHearing** The symphonic performance you just heard is by far the most performed setting of *Rhapsody in Blue*. Now listen to a recent recording of the original 1924 jazz-band version featuring, through the marvels of modern technology, Gershwin himself on piano, recorded in 1925 on a piano roll, accompanied by the Columbia Jazz Band, directed by Michael Tilson Thomas. Note differences you hear in texture, instrumentation, and overall interpretation. Which version do you prefer, and why?

In order to make the *Rhapsody* more marketable through the sale of sheet music, Grofé subsequently arranged it for theater orchestra and eventually for full symphony orchestra, which is the version most commonly performed today (LG 53). As Grofé moved further away from the original Whiteman scoring, the *Rhapsody* became more polished in sound quality; while Gershwin's melodic and harmonic ideas remained, the scrappy dance-band timbre was left behind.

After the success of his *Rhapsody*, Gershwin traveled to Paris to broaden his knowledge of the European art tradition, but was turned away by renowned teacher Nadia Boulanger (see p. 355), who was concerned that classical training would have a negative effect on his jazz-influenced style. During his brief stay in France, Gershwin wrote *An American in Paris*, another of his most successful orchestral-jazz works; it was later (1951) choreographed in a film featuring dance stars Gene Kelly and Leslie Caron.

The question of whether the *Rhapsody in Blue* truly is jazz has been debated from the day it was premiered. Since there have been many different arrangements and reinterpretations beyond the official Grofé scores, we might better ask whether a given performance (or arrangement) is in keeping with one of the several strands of music-making that have been described as jazz over the last century.

CRITICAL THINKING

1. How did Gershwin contribute to different musical traditions of the early 1900s?
2. In what ways does *Rhapsody in Blue* resemble a concerto? What elements of the work correspond to other genres or styles?

YourTurn TO EXPLORE

Find a recording of a Tin Pan Alley song by Gershwin (*I Got Rhythm, 'S Wonderful, But Not for Me, The Man I Love,* or another) and compare it with the recording of *Billie's Blues*. What musical similarities do you hear (in blue notes, syncopation, other melodic or rhythmic elements), and what differences? Do you think it's legitimate to think of Gershwin's compositions as jazz? Why or why not? Why might it matter whether this is jazz, and to whom?

62

Sounds American: Ives, Copland, and Musical Nationalism

"I no longer feel the need of seeking out conscious Americanism. Because we live here and work here, we can be certain that when our music is mature it will also be American in quality."

—Aaron Copland

KeyPoints

- Several modernist composers in the United States attempted to craft a musical style that would reflect a truly American sound.
- Charles Ives drew on the music of his New England childhood—hymns, songs, marches—which he set using **polytonality** and **polyrhythms**.

- Aaron Copland used the early American song *Simple Gifts* in his famous ballet *Appalachian Spring*, commissioned by the great choreographer/dancer Martha Graham.

In Their Own Words

❝ Beauty in music is too often confused with something that lets the ear lie back in an easy chair. . . . Analytical and impersonal tests will show that when a new or unfamiliar work is accepted as beautiful on its first hearing, its fundamental quality is one that tends to put the mind to sleep."

—Charles Ives

Patriotism has been an essential part of national identity since democracies began to replace authoritarian states in the late 1700s. As a nation founded explicitly on ideals of democracy, the United States has rightly fostered pride in the principles that distinguish it from other countries. But as a nation of immigrants with diverse cultural heritages, part of a large continent that can also legitimately claim the label "America," we have also struggled to define the shifting nature of American identity (understood as a quality that all US citizens have in common). Music has always played a part in that definition, and some of the most compelling American sounds have emerged from attempts to integrate vernacular musical traditions with styles that are designed to evoke transcendent artistic expression.

Ives and New England Modernism

We have explored the vital roles that nonconcert traditions—especially parlor songs, brass band marches, and worship songs—played in North American musical life of the late 1800s. One New England musician born into this rich environment was Charles Ives. Since his father was a Civil War bandmaster, Ives was thoroughly steeped in the vernacular heritage of his country. His compositional voice, however, followed very modernist tendencies, making him one of the more innovative, and misunderstood, composers of the early twentieth century.

Ives's tonal imagery was taken from music of his childhood—hymns, patriotic songs, marches, parlor ballads, and fiddling songs. Growing up in a small

Connecticut town, he was accustomed to hearing the pungent clash of dissonance when two bands in a parade, each playing a different tune in a different key, came close together. He was familiar with the effect of quarter tones (an interval half the size of a half step) when fiddlers at country dances veered a bit off pitch. And as an adult, he remembered the sound of the wheezy harmonium (a reed organ) accompanying church hymns, both sung and played out of tune. All these dissonances, Ives realized, were not exceptions but rather the norm of American musical life. They naturally led him to such concepts as polytonality, polyharmony, and polyrhythm.

Country Band March

Ives took bold steps in his *Country Band March* (LG 54), an early work written around 1903, just after he graduated from Yale. Here he set his compositional path for the future by using well-known musical quotations—from children's songs, patriotic tunes, hymns,

American Gothic, by **Grant Wood** (1891–1942), is an example of regionalism, celebrating rural life in the United States.

Charles Ives (1874–1954)

Ives was born in Danbury, Connecticut, the son of a US Army bandleader in the Civil War. At thirteen he held a job as church organist, and at twenty he entered Yale, where he studied composition with Horatio Parker. Ives's talent for music was evident at Yale, yet he decided against a professional life in music, suspecting that society would not pay him for the kind of music he wanted to compose. He was right.

Ives entered the business world in 1899, and two decades later he was head of the largest insurance agency in the country. He composed at night, on weekends, and during vacations, concerned only to set down the sounds he heard in his head. As the conductors and performers he tried to interest in his compositions pronounced them unplayable, he hired a few musicians to play his works so he could hear them. When well-meaning friends suggested that he try to write music people would like, he could only respond, "I can't do it—I hear something else!"

Ives's double life as a business executive by day and composer by night finally took its toll. In 1918, when he was forty-four, he suffered a physical breakdown that left his heart damaged. Although he lived almost forty years longer, he produced very little music in those years.

When Ives recovered, he privately printed his Piano Sonata No. 2 (*Concord*) and *Essays Before a Sonata*, a kind of elaborate program note that formulated his views on life

and art. These were followed by the *114 Songs*. The three volumes, distributed free to libraries, music critics, and whoever else asked for them, gained Ives the support of other experimental composers who were also struggling to make their way in an indifferent music world. Beginning with a performance in 1939 of his *Concord* Sonata in New York City, Ives was finally discovered by the general public and proclaimed as the "grand old man" of American music. In 1947, his Third Symphony won a Pulitzer Prize. At age seventy-three, Ives found himself famous. He died in New York City at the age of seventy-nine.

The central position in Ives's orchestral music is held by the four symphonies. Among his other orchestral works are *Three Places in New England, The Unanswered Question,* and *A Symphony: New England Holidays* (a cycle of four symphonic poems). The Piano Sonata No. 2—"Concord, Mass., 1840–1860"—which occupied him from 1909 to 1915, reflects various aspects of New England culture. Ives was a master songwriter as well, penning over 100 songs, with familiar tunes—patriotic, religious, or popular—tinged with bittersweet harmonies.

MAJOR WORKS: Orchestral music, including four symphonies, *Three Places in New England* (1914), *The Unanswered Question* (1908), and *A Symphony: New England Holidays* (1913) • Chamber music, including string quartets and violin sonatas • Piano music, including sonatas (No. 2, *Concord*, 1915) • Choral music • Many songs.

LISTENING GUIDE 54   🔊 4:20

Ives: *Country Band March*

Date: c. 1903

Genre: March, arranged for wind band

Performed by: United States Marine Band, Timothy W. Foley, director

What to Listen For

Melody	Forceful march theme, over which many well-known tunes occur; main march returns throughout.
Rhythm/ meter	Mostly duple, but with syncopation and triplets that disguise the meter.
Harmony	Harshly dissonant, polytonal.
Form	Sectional (**A-B-A-B′-A′**).

Expression	Humorous; the realism of amateur bands; nostalgic American tunes.
Performing forces	Large wind ensemble, including woodwinds (piccolo, flutes, oboes, clarinets, bassoons, saxophones), brass (cornets, trumpets, French horns, trombones, baritones, tubas), and percussion (drums, cymbals, bells, triangle, xylophone).

A section

0:00 Short introduction, with a chromatic descending line in the full ensemble, syncopated and shifting meters; a repeated-note transition.

0:11 Main march tune in a regular duple meter, with on-beat and offbeat accents:

0:27 Fleeting reference to *London Bridge* in trumpets and oboe.

0:33 Slower passage in woodwinds and saxophones, followed by repeated-note transition.

0:45 *Arkansas Traveler* tune heard in trumpets and cornets, slightly offset rhythmically:

0:55 *Semper Fidelis* march by Sousa (trio), as cornet solo:

Battle Cry of Freedom heard simultaneously (followed by four-note hint of *Yankee Doodle*):

B section

1:05 Lyrical oboe solo, followed by *Marching Through Georgia* in flute and piccolos:

1:28 Clear statement of *London Bridge*:

1:44 *My Old Kentucky Home*, in slow triplets:

A section repeated

1:51   Introduction.

2:03   March tune.

2:38   *Arkansas Traveler*, then *Semper Fidelis / Battle Cry of Freedom*; hint of *Yankee Doodle*.

B′ section, with a new closing section

2:58   Oboe solo leads to new material.

3:05   Rhythmic, syncopated idea.

A′ section, with variations

3:19   March tune in a new key, with harsh "wrong note" dissonance in brass.

3:29   *British Grenadiers* march:

3:42   Brief transition, leads to return of the march theme.

and even a march by John Philip Sousa (see Chapter 54). The main march theme we hear is most likely by Ives himself, but he weaves into it a highly complex mesh of other tunes, creating all manner of chaos. We hear polytonality and polyrhythms as tunes collide and overlap. The songs cited are nostalgic ones for Ives, from his Protestant New England upbringing, but we also catch the playful side of the composer—who simulates the realism of an amateur band's performance skills by having musicians play out of tune, make bad entrances, miscount, and hit wrong notes. You will recognize some of the tunes: *London Bridge* and *Yankee Doodle*; *My Old Kentucky Home* (by Stephen Foster); and the Sousa march *Semper Fidelis*. The work is not actually in a march form, but is rather a five-part sectional form that brings back the opening march theme in various guises.

Ives is now considered especially visionary and progressive for having embraced vernacular (including commercial) music in his work. But most of his contemporaries in the art-music sphere considered commercial music inadequate as a resource for artistic development. Rural folk traditions were thought to be more closely linked to the American spirit, and the composer who most successfully transformed these traditions into a national sound was Aaron Copland.

Yankee Doodle

In Their Own Words

❝ Stand up and take your dissonance like a man."

—*Charles Ives*

Copland and the American Orchestral Soundscape

Copland is one of America's greatest twentieth-century composers. Few have been able to capture the spirit of this country so successfully—his well-crafted and classically proportioned works have an immediate appeal. His ballet suites are quintessentially American in their portrayal of rural life (*Appalachian Spring)* and the Far West (*Rodeo* and *Billy the Kid).*

Copland came self-consciously to an American sound: born in New York of Jewish immigrant parents, he trained in Europe with proponents of early twentieth-century modernism, then returned to the United States during the Great Depression of the 1930s and espoused the ideal that art should "serve the

Aaron Copland (1900–1990)

Copland was born in Brooklyn, New York, and during his early twenties studied in Paris with the famous teacher Nadia Boulanger (p. 355). After his return from Paris, he wrote works in jazz and neo-Classical styles, but at the same time realized that a new public for contemporary music was being created by the radio and phonograph and film scores: "It made no sense to ignore them and to continue writing as if they did not exist."

The 1930s and 40s saw the creation of works that established Copland's popularity. *El Salón México* is an orchestral piece based on Mexican melodies and rhythms. His three well-known ballets—*Billy the Kid, Rodeo,* and *Appalachian Spring*—continue to delight international audiences. Among his film scores are two on novels by John Steinbeck and director William Wyler's *The Heiress,* which brought him an Academy Award. He wrote two important works during

wartime: *A Lincoln Portrait,* for speaker and chorus, with texts drawn from Lincoln's speeches, and the Third Symphony. Despite his evident nationalism, Copland was investigated in the 1950s as a supporter of the Communist Party, and in 1953 he was removed from the inaugural ceremonies for President Eisenhower as a result of his leftist politics. In the 1960s, Copland demonstrated that he could also handle twelve-tone techniques when he wrote his powerful *Connotations for Orchestra.*

MAJOR WORKS: Orchestral music, including three symphonies, a piano concerto, *El Salón México* (1936), *A Lincoln Portrait* (1942), *Fanfare for the Common Man* (1942) • Ballets, including *Billy the Kid* (1938), *Rodeo* (1942), and *Appalachian Spring* (1944) • Operas, including *The Tender Land* (1954) • Film scores, including *Of Mice and Men* (1939), *Our Town* (1940), *The Red Pony* (1948), and *The Heiress* (1948) • Piano music • Chamber music • Choral music • Songs.

Martha Graham dancing in the ballet *Appalachian Spring.*

American people" during times of economic and social struggle. His new American modernist style was designed to have wide appeal and be "useful" in a variety of contexts (radio, film, theater). In keeping with this ideal, Copland wrote incidental music for plays and scores for significant films that spoke to the American condition during the Depression, such as *Of Mice and Men* (1939) and *Our Town* (1940).

Though Copland admired jazz and incorporated it in his early works, his American style was rooted primarily in Appalachian and other Anglo-American folk melodies (as well as Mexican folk melodies). He also cited Stravinsky's startling approach to rhythm and orchestration as a basic influence. Like Stravinsky's early ballets, some of Copland's most successful compositions involved a collaboration with prominent dancers and choreographers, who were also seeking to establish a genuinely American tradition of modern dance.

Appalachian Spring

Among Copland's ballets, *Appalachian Spring* is perhaps his best known, written in collaboration with the celebrated choreographer Martha Graham (1894–1991), who also danced the lead. Copland noted that when he wrote the music, he took into account Graham's unique choreographic style: "She's unquestionably very American: there's something prim and restrained, simple yet strong, about her, which one tends to think of as American." The ballet portrays "a

Members of the Protestant Shaker sect in a dance. Lithograph by **Nathaniel Currier** (1813–1888).

pioneer celebration in spring around a newly built farmhouse in the Pennsylvania hills in the early part of the nineteenth century. The bride-to-be and the young farmer-husband enact the emotions, joyful and apprehensive, their new partnership invites." The ballet, which premiered in 1944 in Washington, D.C., was given new life in Copland's popular 1945 orchestral suite, set in seven sections.

The opening section of the suite introduces the characters in the ballet with a serene, ascending motive that evokes the first hint of daybreak over the vast horizon (LG 55). In the most famous part of the work, we hear the well-known early American song *Simple Gifts* ("'Tis the gift to be simple"), a tune associated with the Shaker religious sect, known for rituals that included spinning around and dancing. This simple, folklike tune is designed to provide a quintessential American sound; Copland sets it in a clear-cut theme and variations, with a colorful orchestration tinged with gentle dissonance. The flowing tune takes on several guises, shaded by changing timbres, keys, and tempos.

Copland's music was quickly embraced as a truly American orchestral sound. It continues to be widely heard at events (or even in commercials!) that aim to emphasize national pride, as well as incorporated (and imitated) in movie scenes that illustrate the grandeur of the West. The America that his music envisions is a rural one, connected to the land and its traditions; it is also mostly an Anglo America, since the Appalachian tunes he employs have their roots in Anglo-Celtic folk music. Copland's goal was to create an inclusive soundscape for the United States; and his music, like Sousa's, is still a powerful presence in the cultural life of the nation.

In Their Own Words

" To be great, art . . . must belong to the country in which it flourishes, not be a pale copy of some art form perfected by another culture and another people."

—*Martha Graham*

CRITICAL THINKING

1. What elements make the music of Ives so experimental and modernist? What older traditions does he draw on?

2. What qualities in Copland's music have been understood as particularly American? What other kinds of American sounds and identities are not part of his music, and why might this matter?

Copland: *Appalachian Spring*, excerpts

Date: 1945

Genre: Ballet suite in seven sections

Performed by: New York Philharmonic, Leonard Bernstein, conductor

What to Listen For

SECTION 1		SECTION 7	
Melody	Rising motive quietly unfolds, outlining a triad.	**Melody**	Theme with four phrases (**a-a′-b-a″**); later variations use only parts of the tune.
Rhythm/ meter	Very slow, tranquil; changing meter is imperceptible.	**Rhythm/ meter**	Flowing duple meter, then tune in augmentation (slower).
Harmony	Overlapping of chords (polychordal) produces a gentle dissonance.	**Harmony**	Moves between various keys.
Texture	Individual instruments are featured.	**Form**	Theme and five variations, on a traditional Shaker song.
Expression	Introduces the characters; evokes a broad landscape at daybreak.	**Timbre**	Each variation changes tone colors; individual instruments are featured.
		Expression	Calm and flowing; majestic closing.

Section I: Very slowly   2:42

0:00   Low strings on a sustained pitch; solo clarinet, then flute with a rising motive:

0:16   Violin and flutes alternate the rising figure; harp punctuates; other instruments enter, creating dissonance.

0:52   Violin in high range, with more movement; the rising figure is heard in various instruments.

1:25   Solos in various woodwinds and trumpet.

1:54   Solo oboe, then bassoon; descending motive.

2:31   Clarinet with closing triad, over sustained harmony.

Section 7: Theme (*Simple Gifts*) and five variations   3:03

Theme

0:00   Solo clarinet with tune in four phrases (**a-a′-b-a″**), accompanied by harp (playing harmonics) and flute:

0:28   Brief transition.

Variation 1

0:34   Oboe and bassoon present the tune; grows dissonant, with *sforzando* on third phrase played by all woodwinds.

0:56   Short, rhythmic transition.

Variation 2

0:59   Tune in violas in augmentation (steady rhythmic accompaniment continues); violins (in octaves) enter in second phrase, in canon with the violas (dissonance on the last note is marked with arrow):

1:35   Transition.

Variation 3

1:45   Trumpets and trombones, with swirling strings; loud brass section; then quieter in woodwinds.

Variation 4

2:10   Woodwinds with a slower version of the tune.

Variation 5

2:30   Full orchestra with majestic, homophonic statement; somewhat dissonant; *fortissimo,* then dies out.

Your Turn TO EXPLORE

Identify two musical works (songs or any other genre) that you consider to be purposefully American: not only the text, but the music as well. What elements of each work project its American identity? What kind of America does each suggest—what kinds of individuals or attitudes or backgrounds does it include, and what kinds does it leave out? What parallels and contradictions can you find between the two different versions of "musical American-ness"?

Forgetting and Rediscovering J. S. Bach and Florence Price

The story of a great composer being forgotten and then rediscovered is a powerful narrative. It suggests that musicians may not be fully appreciated in their lifetimes, but that later generations are finally able to understand their inherent genius. Such a story has been told about Johann Sebastian Bach, and recently it is being told about African American composer Florence Price (1887–1953), whose music is now entering the contemporary canon after being "rediscovered." These two musicians' situations raise similar questions about how canons are created—and just as importantly, *who* creates them.

The story of Felix Mendelssohn "rediscovering" the music of Bach nearly a century after his death and bringing about the "Bach Revival" has become one of the central tales of the Western canon (see p. 275). The reality is more complex: Bach's music had never been "lost" but had rather been continuously valued, especially as a resource for high-level teaching, thanks to the efforts and success of several of his sons, who became more internationally prominent musicians than their father had been. The link to Mendelssohn may have been established by Sara Levy (1761–1854), a prominent Jewish cultural influencer in late eighteenth-century Berlin who studied keyboard with Bach's eldest son. Levy became highly skilled on the harpsichord and piano, and collected a substantial number of Bach's handwritten musical scores to perform and study with friends and professional musicians at social events at her home. Levy helped to create a consensus about the value of preserving these repertories as "classics," a shift in perspective from a previous assumption that musical novelty was ideal. About fifteen years after she donated her collection to a prominent musical institution, her grand-nephew Felix Mendelssohn (whose musical education Levy had fostered) led a performance of Bach's *Saint Matthew Passion* with that very institution, kicking off the "Bach Revival"—without Levy's collecting and encouragement, Mendelssohn's performance in 1829 might never have taken place. In 1850, the Bach Society (Gesellschaft) was formed to publish the complete works of J. S. Bach; among the founders and editorial board members were two prominent composers: Robert Schumann and Johannes Brahms.

A native of Arkansas, Florence Price trained at the New England Conservatory (one of few that would accept African American students at the time) at the end of the nineteenth century. She later moved to Chicago, where she became involved with a vibrant community of African American artists, musicians, and writers—a group active from the mid-1930s to the 1950s that became known as the Chicago Black Renaissance, in parallel with the artistic movement that had flourished earlier in Harlem (see p. 374). Price's prizewinning First Symphony, one of dozens of works in many genres that she composed, was premiered at a special concert offered by the Chicago

African American composer Florence Price at work, from the University of Arkansas archives.

Symphony Orchestra at the Chicago World's Fair of 1933. From that point on Price was likely the most widely known African American composer until her death two decades later.

Then (according to the most common version of the story), Price's music faded from public view—until in 2009 a large collection of her handwritten scores was found in an abandoned house that had formerly belonged to the Price family, and when that collection came to the University of Arkansas, Price's music was brought out into the open again and began to be performed and recognized for its inherent value.

In reality, Price's music (especially her songs and her piano and organ compositions) continued to be performed regularly—especially at historically Black colleges and universities, and among the community of African Americans in Chicago who continued in the tradition of the Chicago Renaissance, several of them worthy composers and performers in their own right. After Price's daughter donated a collection of her papers to the University of Arkansas in the mid-1970s, African American scholars began to write systematically about Price's music and to document her creativity and influence. But white mainstream musicians and critics had moved on.

As Price's daughter attempted to continue having her mother's works performed after her death, she encountered a genre-related bias many women musicians have faced through the ages: Price's songs were popular, but nobody wanted to consider her a

"serious" enough composer to program her orchestral or chamber works. The composer herself explained that "I have two handicaps—those of sex and race. I am a woman; and I have some Negro blood in my veins." While J. S. Bach had his heritage preserved by male heirs who were professional musicians and well "tapped in" to the growing canon-establishing trends, Price's daughter was not a musician, and as a Black woman she encountered layered biases against her own perspective as well as her mother's. Price's songs remained in African American musicians' repertoire throughout the twentieth century; her more "ambitious" orchestral music had to await mainstream "rediscovery" in the twenty-first.

Price explained that her Symphony No. 1 in E Minor was "intended to be Negroid in character and expression." Rather than quoting or adapting existing folk tunes, she drew on characteristics of African American music, including pentatonic scales, call and response, altered or "blue" notes, and highly syncopated rhythms. You can hear this novel treatment of the European symphonic genre in the third movement, a Juba dance, which simulates the African American dance style once practiced on plantations and featuring highly syncopated patting and slapping rhythms. Price claims she did not wish to present African American music in a traditional way, but rather as a "not-too-deliberate attempt to picture a cross-section of present-day Negro life and thought with its heritage of that which is past."

"JUBA," AT VAUXHALL GARDENS.

Master Juba (alias William Henry Lane), known in the United States as "King of all Dancers," toured London in 1848.

Many Voices Expanded
- Florence Price, Symphony No. 1 in E Minor, III (*Juba Dance*)
- Price: *Mississippi River Suite*
- Price: *Dances in the Canebreaks* (solo piano)

63

Also American: Revueltas and Mexican Musical Modernism

"From an early age I learned to love [the music of] Bach and Beethoven. . . . I can tolerate some of the classics and even some of my own works, but I prefer the music of my people that is heard in the provinces."

—*Silvestre Revueltas*

KeyPoints

- The music of Mexican composer Silvestre Revueltas is expressively nationalistic, with folkloric rhythms and melodies set in a dissonant framework.

- Revueltas celebrated the heritage of the ancient Mayan empire in his film score for *La noche de los Mayas* (*The Night of the Mayas*).

- Revueltas and other American modernists were influenced by the **mariachi** ensemble, a vernacular Mexican tradition.

Mexican painter **Diego Rivera** (1886–1957) glorified his native culture and people. *Flower Festival* (1925) depicts a working man burdened by a huge basket of calla lilies.

Latin American musical repertories have long been important to Anglo-American audiences and musicians, especially in the areas close to the southern US border: the culture and history of the United States and Mexico have been intertwined since well before the two countries came into their modern borders. Like their counterparts in the United States, other American musicians have worked to reconcile their connection to European traditions with crafting a uniquely American sound. And like Copland and Still, they have realized their nationalist approach largely through reference to vernacular traditions.

Musical Traditions of Mexico

The modern musical traditions of Mexico are rich and varied, embracing the indigenous Amerindian cultures as well as Hispanic culture. Mexico's ties to Spain began in 1519, when Spanish soldiers colonized the territory, and continued until 1821, when the country achieved its independence.

By the late nineteenth century, the goal of creating a nationally distinctive style lured musicians and artists alike to Amerindian and mestizo cultures. (Mestizos are people of mixed Spanish and Amerindian ancestry; today they are the majority in Latin American countries.) The Mexican Revolution of 1910 further changed the artistic life of the country, conjuring strong feelings of patriotism.

In the post-revolutionary period, sometimes called the "Aztec Renaissance," composers tried to evoke or suggest, rather than recreate, the character of this native music for a modern age. The works of Carlos Chávez (1899–1978), including seven symphonies and two Aztec ballets, are rich in Amerindian flavor. Chávez and Silvestre Revueltas were two of the most decisive influences on Mexican musical culture.

Carlos Chávez

Silvestre Revueltas: "Mestizo Realist"

Revueltas is considered a representative of "mestizo realism," a nationalist modernist movement that drew on elements of Mexico's traditional culture. His music is highly flavored with folk elements, including **mariachi-band** traditions.

La noche de los Mayas

After composing several orchestral and chamber works, Revueltas contributed scores to Mexican films. Most prominent is the one for *La noche de los Mayas* (*The Night of the Mayas*), a 1939 film by prolific Mexican director Chano Urueta that was billed as a "Mexican tragedy." Set at the time when European colonizers first came to the Americas, it celebrates the heritage of the native Maya empire. The arrival of a white explorer sets up a story of conflicting cultures and a tragic love triangle. As was often the case in his compositions, Revueltas mostly evoked the musical soundscape of his country's traditions rather than using actual folk melodies.

After Revueltas's death, composer and director José Yves Limantour arranged excerpts from the full soundtrack into a four-movement suite that was premiered

In Their Own Words

> There is in me a particular interpretation of nature. Everything is rhythm. . . . Everybody understands or feels it. . . . My rhythms are dynamic, sensual, vital; I think in images that meet in melodic lines, always moving dynamically."
>
> —*Silvestre Revueltas*

Silvestre Revueltas (1899–1940)

Born in the mountain state of Durango, Revueltas was a child prodigy on violin and later studied composition at the Conservatorio Nacional de Música in Mexico City. He continued his studies in the United States until 1929, when he was called home by his friend Carlos Chávez to serve as assistant conductor of the Orquesta Sinfónica de Mexico.

With the onset of the Spanish Civil War in the late 1930s, the intensely political Revueltas went to Spain, where he participated in the cultural activities of the Loyalist government. Upon his return home in late 1937, he produced a series of masterworks, including his best-known orchestral piece, *Sensemayá*, inspired by the verses of Afro-Cuban poet Nicolás Guillén (another anti-Fascist), which imitate onomatopoetically the sounds and rhythm of Afro-Cuban music and speak against colonial imperialism. In 1939, Revueltas wrote

the film score for *La noche de los Mayas* (*The Night of the Mayas*), which projects a modern primitivism not unlike Stravinsky's *Rite of Spring*. The composer died at age forty of alcohol-induced pneumonia.

Revueltas's love for Mexican provincial music is immediately obvious, voiced through lyrical, direct melodies that are driven by such rhythmic techniques as polyrhythms and ostinatos. Despite a modern harmonic language rich in dissonance and chromaticism, Revueltas's music is deeply emotional and Romantic in its inspiration. His skillful handling of the orchestral palette evokes the traditional orchestras of Mexico.

MAJOR WORKS: Orchestral music, including *Sensemayá* (1938) • Seven film scores, including *La noche de los Mayas* (*The Night of the Mayas*, 1939) • Chamber music, including *Homenaje a Federico García Lorca* (*Homage to Federico García Lorca*, 1937) • Two ballets • Songs, including seven *Canciones* (1938, on texts by García Lorca).

Musicians perform for an ancient Maya festival in this reproduction of a ninth-century fresco detail from Bonampak, Chaipas, Mexico.

Platform for dancers in front of the ancient Maya pyramid of Kukulcan, Yucatán.

in 1961. The expanded percussion section of this work is especially striking: various Latin American instruments derived from the intersection of native, African, and European cultures—bongos, congas, tom-toms, rattles, guiro (a notched or grooved gourd), caracol (conch shell), and tumkul (a kind of log drum)—are featured prominently alongside the established timpani, bass drum, snare drum, and xylophone from the European orchestral tradition.

The second movement, "Noche de jaranas" ("Night of Revelry," LG 56), is taken from the early part of the film, where the newcomers—the white men—are welcomed by the Mayas into their festivities. It is labeled "Tempo di *son*," suggesting a popular Latin American dance genre based on a mixture of indigenous, African, and Spanish traditions. Unlike in a traditional *son*, which shifts between simple triple (3/4) and duple compound (6/8) meter, the meter of this work is irregular—alternating 6/8 meter with 5/8, in patterns that are not entirely predictable. Revueltas thus evokes the spirit of the *son* while experimenting with rhythmic energy and tension much the same way Stravinsky did in *The Rite of Spring*. Violins playing in parallel thirds, answered by the brass section, bring to mind the traditional style of the mariachi ensemble (see p. 398). The form of the movement resembles a classical rondo, featuring the return of distinctive melodic snippets and contrasts in melody, harmony, and timbre; at the end, Revueltas thins out the texture and fades the dynamics as if to depict revelers wandering away from their celebration but still dancing drunkenly. The mood of the movement is both playful and sarcastic.

By collaborating with film writers and producers, Revueltas was not only engaging in what was considered one of the most innovative multimedia traditions of the time, but also celebrating his national heritage through a distinctively modernist American soundscape.

CRITICAL THINKING

1. How did Revueltas merge vernacular and art-music traditions?
2. What elements are distinctive in mariachi music, and how did composers emulate these in their compositions?

Your Turn TO EXPLORE

Find examples of music associated with Mexico (for example, mariachi ensembles), and compare it with music associated with South America (for example, Brazilian samba, Argentinian tango, or Chilean Andean traditions). What are the similarities and differences (in instrumentation, vocal quality, the use of solo voices versus ensembles, how featured voices or instruments are backed up by other voices/instruments, characteristic rhythmic patterns)?

Revueltas: "Noche de jaranas" ("Night of Revelry"), from *La noche de los Mayas* (*The Night of the Mayas*)

Date: Film score, 1939; suite arrangement, 1961

Genre: Suite from film score

Movements:
  I. "Noche de los Mayas"
  II. "Noche de jaranas"
  III. "Noche de Yucatán"
  IV. "Noche de encantamiento" ("Night of Enchantment")

Performed by: Los Angeles Philharmonic, Esa-Pekka Salonen, conductor

II: "Noche de Jaranas"

What to Listen For

Melody	Short snippets of tune passed around the ensemble; a contrasting flowing melody in the central section.
Rhythm/ meter	Highly syncopated; alternation between compound (6/8) and irregular (5/8, 10/8) meters.
Harmony	Tonal, with expanded chromaticism and unusual harmonic shifts.
Texture	Homophony alternating with nonimitative polyphony.
Form	Rondo-like.
Expression	Combines elements of a symphonic scherzo with Latin American *son* dance music.
Performing forces	Full orchestra with piano and Latin American percussion instruments.

0:00 **A section**—strings play the main rondo theme in thirds, accompanied by Latin American percussion, alternating irregularly between 5/8 and 6/8 meter:

0:28 Piccolos join the ensemble.

0:45 Full orchestra, different timbres in dialogue with short melodic snippets; harmony is more unstable and unpredictable.

2:28 **B section**—a new metric pattern, 3 + 3 + 2 (8/8 meter), in trumpet and xylophone:

A slower, rising melodic idea in the French horns, then trumpets:

2:59 Quiet variant of the rhythmic idea in flutes and strings.

3:15 **A′**—modified return of the rondo theme, *forte*.

3:49 **B′**—Suddenly *pianissimo*, 8/8 meter returns in horns, with expanded orchestral reinforcement.

4:20 **C section**—dynamic builds to *fff* in the most regular meter up to this point, 6/8; powerful melody in the brass and strings, with a cross-rhythm in the accompaniment:

4:36 **A″**—a short transition in the low brass and percussion leads to the return of the opening rondo (5/8–6/8) theme; dynamics fade as if the ensemble were disappearing into the distance.

Musical Traditions in Mexico

s Mexico began nurturing its own artistic traditions, based not only on the country's Hispanic culture but also on its rich indigenous Amerindian cultures, composer Carlos Chávez took a leadership role in this new musical movement. Paralleling the example of artists like Diego Rivera and José Orozco, who had already begun a nationalist school of painting, Chávez instigated a government-sponsored program to develop a national voice in music. His efforts caught the attention of Aaron Copland, who accepted Chávez's invitation to visit Mexico City in 1932; there, he was immediately captivated by the country's traditional music, noting that "Mexico possesses a very strong folk art . . . which provides the artist with rich source material." This cultural interaction resulted in Copland's delightful orchestral work *El Salón México,* subtitled "A Popular Type Dance Hall in Mexico City" and including at least four Mexican folk songs. Chávez premiered his friend's work in 1937 with the Mexico City Orchestra to great success. While in Mexico, Copland also befriended Silvestre Revueltas, whose colorful orchestral poems, he claimed, conjured up "the bustling life of a typical Mexican fiesta." Copland noted that Revueltas's music was derived from the "everyday side of Mexican life," and that he composed "organically tunes which are almost indistinguishable from the original folk material itself."

One strong voice of the growing Mexican nationalism was the mariachi ensemble. This group originated in the mid-nineteenth century near Guadalajara, as a string orchestra with both bowed and plucked instruments: violins, guitars (including a large acoustic bass guitar known as the guitarrón), and vihuelas (a kind of folk guitar). By the 1930s, the group as heard by Copland had taken on a distinctly urban sound, adding trumpets and other instruments. The mariachi ensembles we hear today were standardized during the 1950s. Modern players often wear the costumes of the charros—Mexican cowboys with wide-brimmed sombreros—or other, more regional dress. The band includes a melody group, with violins and trumpets, and a rhythm section of vihuelas, guitar, guitarrón, and occasionally harp. Their repertory is largely dances,

The Mariachi Regio Internacional (playing violins, trumpets, guitarrón, and guitar) in Plaza Garibaldi, Mexico City.

many set in triple meter but with shifting meters and strong accents.

We can hear this folk style in *El Cihualteco*, a famous dance piece in the mariachi tradition. The dance type *son* (with shifting meters) stands at the heart of the mariachi repertory, and this one is associated with the Spanish flamenco-style dance known as *zapateado*, characterized by strongly syncopated rhythms against which dancers stamp their boots into the floor. Our selection falls into the standard verse-chorus structure, with witty four-line verses alternating with the chorus ("Ay, sí, sí; ay, no, no"). The melodic lines are often played in thirds, making the sound consonant, and the shifting accents give a sense of restlessness and unpredictability to the dance.

Muralist **José Clemente Orozco** (1883–1949) captures the spirit of the revolutionary movement in *Zapatistas* (1931).

El Cihualteco (The Man from Cihuatlán)

What to listen for:
- Strongly syncopated rhythms.
- Verse-chorus, alternating with instrumental interludes.
- Trumpets and violins playing the melody in parallel thirds.

	Text	Translation
Verse 1 (sung twice)	Arriba de Cihuatlán le nombran "la água escondida" donde se van a bañar Cihualtecas de mi vida.	Above Cihuatlán they call it "hidden waters," where the dear Cihualtecan girls go to bathe.
Chorus	Ay, sí, sí; ay, no, no. Ay, sí, sí; ay, no, no. Ay, sí; ay, no. Ay, sí; ay, no. De veras sí, de veras no. Lo que te dije se te olvidó y al cabo sí, y al cabo no.	Ay, yes, yes; ay, no, no. Ay, yes, yes; ay, no, no. Ay, yes; ay, no. Ay, yes; ay, no. Surely yes; surely no. You forgot what I told you and finally yes, and finally no.
Verse 2 (sung twice)	Cihualteco de mi vida, dime quién te bautizó. ¿Quién te puse "Cihualteco" para que te cante yo?	Dear Cihualteco, tell me who baptized you. Who named you "El Cihualteco" so that I can sing to you?
Chorus repeated (text slightly changed).		

Classic Rethinking: Bartók and the Neo-Classical Turn

"Folk songs bind the nation, bind all nations and all people with one spirit, one happiness, one paradise."

—Leos Janáček

KeyPoints

- Twentieth-century composers used more authentic folk and traditional elements in their nationalistic music than nineteenth-century composers did.

- Hungarian composer Béla Bartók collected traditional songs and dances from his native land and incorporated elements from them into his compositions.

- Bartók's music displays new scales and rhythmic ideas and a modern, polytonal harmonic language, all set in **Neo-Classical** forms. In his programmatic *Concerto for Orchestra*, the whole ensemble is the "soloist."

Increased access to recording technology and mass distribution of music through the Internet now make musical traditions across the planet available to us at the click of a mouse. In the last few decades, a "world music" recording industry has exposed contemporary listeners to more and more musical variety—often combining different traditions and modifying them to suit what producers think will appeal to a particular audience. So while the music that we hear may feature more elements from disparate cultures, sometimes the combination of those elements masks the uniqueness of each regional style. It's worthwhile to consider how musical characteristics meaningful in a particular cultural context may change meaning when taken outside of that context. Sometimes new musical meanings can arise from the integration of traditional and folk music into experimental art music, as a number of modern composers have found.

Neo-Classicism

One way of rejecting the nineteenth century was to return to even earlier eras. Instead of revering Beethoven and Wagner, as the Romantics had done, composers began to emulate the great musicians of the eighteenth century and the detached, objective style often associated with their music. **Neo-Classical** composers turned away from the symphonic poem and the Romantic attempt to bring music closer to poetry and painting. They preferred absolute to program music, and they focused attention on craftsmanship and balance, an affirmation of the Classical virtues of objectivity and control but also of twentieth-century ideals of progress through science. These composers revived a number of older forms such as toccata, fugue, concerto grosso, and suite, while retaining the traditional symphony, sonata, and concerto. They valued the formal above the expressive; accordingly, the new Classicism, like the old, strove for purity of line and proportion.

Modernist Nationalism

Twentieth-century nationalism differed from its nineteenth-century counterpart in one important respect: composers approached traditional music with a scientific spirit, prizing the ancient tunes precisely because they departed from the conventional mold. By this time, the phonograph had been invented. The new students of folklore (**ethnomusicologists**, who study music in its cultural and global context) took recording equipment into the field to preserve the songs exactly as the village folk sang them. And composers who were inspired by these folk elements tried to retain the original flavor of the songs and dances in their works.

Modernist painter **Anton Romako** (1832–1889) captures an image of rural life in Eastern Europe, in *Hungarian Farm* (c. 1877).

Many of the Romantic-era national schools (see Chapter 44) continued into the twentieth century. The modern English school, for example, is best represented by Benjamin Britten (1913–1976), whose operas include *Peter Grimes* (1945), about an English fishing village, and *Billy Budd* (1951), based on a Herman Melville story; we heard his *Young Person's Guide to the Orchestra* in Chapter 11. The Russian school continued with two important figures: Sergei Prokofiev (1891–1953), known for his symphonies, operas, and piano concertos, as well as the popular, narrated *Peter and the Wolf*; and Dmitri Shostakovich (1906–1975), whose symphonies and operas established his international reputation during the era of the Soviet Union (1917–91). And Hungarian nationalism is strongly evoked by another leading composer: Béla Bartók.

Bartók and the Eastern European Tradition

Béla Bartók reconciled the traditional songs of his native Hungary with the main currents of European music, thus creating an entirely personal language. His search for authentic folk music led him to collect, with his colleague Zoltán Kodály (1882–1967), more than 2,000 songs and dances representing various Eastern European cultures. In the characteristic rhythmic and melodic features of these folk traditions, Bartók found distinctive raw material for his neo-Classical style.

Concerto for Orchestra

Bartók rejected the late Romantic orchestral sound in favor of a palette of colors all his own. His orchestration ranges from brilliant mixtures to threads of pure color that bring out the intertwining melody lines. In the summer of 1943, two years before his death, Bartók was commissioned to write the *Concerto for Orchestra*, a work in five movements that treats "the single orchestral instruments in a concertante or soloistic manner." Here, the virtuoso is the entire orchestra.

We will hear the fourth movement, *Interrupted Intermezzo*, which opens with a plaintive tune in the oboe and flute; its pentatonic structure evokes a Hungarian folk song (LG 57). The nonsymmetrical rhythm, alternating between 2/4 and 5/8 meter, gives the movement an unpredictable charm. Then a memorable broad theme is heard in the strings, but the mood is disrupted by a harsh clarinet melody borrowed from Shostakovich's Symphony No. 7, a musical portrayal of the Nazi

In Their Own Words

> To handle [a] folk tune is one of the most difficult tasks. . . . We must penetrate it, feel it, and bring out its sharp contours."
>
> —*Béla Bartók*

Béla Bartók (1881–1945)

A native Hungarian, Bartók studied at the Royal Academy in Budapest. His interest in the nationalist movement and folklore led him to realize that what passed for Hungarian in the eyes of the world was really music of the Roma, or Gypsies. With his fellow composer Zoltán Kodály, he toured the remote villages of the country, determined to collect the native songs before they died out forever.

The alliance between the Hungarian government and Nazi Germany on the eve of the Second World War spurred him to move to New York City in 1940. Suffering from leukemia in his final years, he received a series of commissions for works that rank among his finest. He died in New York at the age of sixty-four.

Bartók discovered that Eastern European traditional music was based on ancient modes, unfamiliar scales, and nonsymmetrical rhythms. His study of this music brought him to new concepts of melody, harmony, and rhythm—his harmony can be bitingly dissonant, and polytonality abounds in his work. He is also one of the great rhythmic innovators of modern times. Like Stravinsky, Bartók used pounding, stabbing rhythms, syncopation, changing meters, and repeated patterns (ostinatos). His linear textures are brilliant examples of modern dissonant counterpoint. But despite the newness of his musical language, he adhered to the logic and beauty of Classical form.

A virtuoso pianist himself, Bartók was a master of modern piano writing, and his six string quartets are among the finest in the twentieth century. He is best known to the public for the major works of his last period: the *Music for Strings, Percussion, and Celesta*, regarded by many as his masterpiece; and the *Concerto for Orchestra*, a favorite with American audiences.

MAJOR WORKS: Orchestral music, including *Music for Strings, Percussion, and Celesta* (1936) and *Concerto for Orchestra* (1943) • Concertos (two for violin; three for piano) • Stage works, including an opera (*Bluebeard's Castle*, 1918) and two ballets • Chamber music, including six string quartets, sonatas, duos • Piano music, including *Mikrokosmos* (six books, 1926–39) • Choral music • Folk-song arrangements for solo voice and for choir.

---

invasion of Russia in 1942. Bartók made an autobiographical statement in this movement: "The artist declares his love for his native land in a serenade, which is suddenly interrupted in a crude and violent manner; he is seized by rough, booted men who even break his instrument." The two opening themes eventually return in a sentimental declaration of the composer's love for his homeland.

In gathering material from Eastern European folk music, Bartók was going "back to his roots" and seeking to express an authentic and distinctive Hungarian sensibility. Much of our encounters with folk music nowadays are with cultures that are different from our own. And musicians often borrow freely from distant cultures, integrating foreign instruments or musical ideas for their intriguing or exotic sound qualities, not necessarily to convey a distant tradition accurately.

Béla Bartók recording a folk song during his travels to Transylvania, in Eastern Europe.

CRITICAL THINKING

1. What are some of the main characteristics of neo-Classicism?
2. How does Bartók evoke nationalistic ideas in his music?

Your Turn TO EXPLORE

Find recordings of Western musicians who have incorporated instruments or melodies from a non-Western tradition into their compositions and performances; compare them with recordings of those instruments or melodies by ensembles from the original culture. What musical elements have the Western musicians adopted from the other culture, and which elements have they maintained from Western tradition? Why do you think they have made those choices? Which versions do you find more compelling? Does hearing the original version change your perception of the "blended" version?

LISTENING GUIDE 57 4:20

Bartók: *Interrupted Intermezzo,* from *Concerto for Orchestra*

Date: 1943

Genre: Orchestral concerto

Movements: 1. Introduction, Allegro non troppo / Allegro vivace; sonata-allegro form
2. *Game of Pairs,* Allegretto scherzando; **A-B-A′ form**
3. Elegia, Andante non troppo; in three episodes
4. ***Interrupted Intermezzo,* Allegretto; rondo-like form**
5. Pesante / Presto; sonata-allegro form

Performed by: Los Angeles Philharmonic, Esa-Pekka Salonen, conductor

4: *Interrupted Intermezzo,* Allegretto

What to Listen For			
Melody	Three contrasting themes: folklike and pentatonic (**A**); broad and lyrical (**B**); harsh descending line in clarinet (**C**).	**Form**	Rondo-like structure (**A-B-A′-C-B′-A″**).
Rhythm/ meter	Shifting meters (2/4, 5/8, 3/4, 5/8) and irregular rhythms.	**Expression**	Nostalgic and sentimental; violent interruption at the idea of Nazi invasion.
Harmony	Polytonal and atonal harmonies; dissonant.	**Timbre**	Solo woodwinds are featured (oboe, clarinet, flute); darkly colored (violas).

0:00   Dramatic four-note introduction, unison in strings.

0:05   **A section**—plaintive, folklike tune, played by oboe in a changing meter with asymmetrical rhythms:

Theme is heard in flute and clarinets; dialogue continues in woodwinds and French horn.

1:00   **B section**—sweeping lyrical melody in violas, in shifting meter:

Violins take up lyrical theme an octave higher, with a countermelody in violas; marked "Calmo" (calm).

1:44   **A′ section**—dissonant woodwinds lead to a varied statement of opening theme; more chromatic.

2:04   **C section**—tempo picks up; clarinet introduces a new theme (from a Shostakovich symphony):

2:17   Dissonant punctuations in brass and woodwinds.

2:31   Theme is parodied in violins.

2:44   Theme is introduced by tubas in its original form, then heard in inversion in strings:

2:57   **B′ section**—flowing **B section** theme returns in muted strings.

3:31   **A″ section**—woodwinds play fragments of opening theme; flute cadenza; leads into a gentle closing.

Music in Words

Reviewing Modernist Style

The examples of early twentieth-century music featured in Part 6 provide a frame of reference for other modernist-era compositions you may encounter beyond your course. Here are some suggestions for things to listen for when you hear an unfamiliar work from this period.

MELODY: How many important melodic ideas can you identify? Are they lyrical and singable, or wide-ranging with leaps? What expressive elements do you hear in the melodic lines?

RHYTHM/METER: Is the meter clear throughout? Do you perceive elements that might be associated with dance? How does the composer maintain the energy throughout the work?

HARMONY: In this era, tonality is often clouded by chromaticism and dissonance, but there is often a strong sense of a tonal center, or home base. Listen for moments that are more dissonant and unstable; what expressive purpose might they serve?

TEXTURE: How do the various instruments work together? Is the texture more vertical (homophonic), or does it feature independent lines (polyphonic)? Does the texture change as the work progresses, and if so, how?

FORM: Most compositions are built on the basic formal principles of repetition, contrast, and variation. What is the role of repetition in the work? of contrast (that is, new music)? What holds the selection together, or helps it make sense to the listener?

PERFORMING FORCES AND TIMBRE: Some modernist-era works require an orchestra with new instruments and timbres; unlike in earlier periods, the string section may not always be the center of the ensemble. What timbres strike you as new or unusual? Do you hear a blend of instrumental colors, or do individual tone colors stand out?

Listen and Respond

Let's see how you well you can apply what you have learned to a new musical example. Be sure to consult the listening suggestions above and also the style summary chart. Compare this new work with other symphonic works we have heard from the modernist era.

Revueltas, *Homage to Federico García Lorca,* III (*Son*)

1. Create a simple listening outline for the piece. Think about melody, rhythm and meter, levels of dissonance, texture, performing forces, and form. Do you hear repeated sections? What modernist elements do you hear in this work?

2. How might you describe this work to a friend who is not in the class and not familiar with the terminology we've been developing? What general descriptions can you apply to the melody? rhythm? harmony? texture? overall effect of the piece?

3. Write a short paragraph describing the work as you might for a concert report assignment. Here you can demonstrate your understanding of the terms and concepts you have learned as well as your response to the piece's expressive qualities. Refer back to Chapter 14 for ways to frame your perspective.

Style Summary for Modernist-Era Music (c. 1900–1940)

Composers	Schoenberg, Stravinsky, Boulanger, Berg, Holiday, Ellington, Still, Gershwin, Ives, Copland, Revueltas, Bartók
Melody	Melodies conceived instrumentally; disjunct, wide-ranging lines; elements from folk and traditional music
Rhythm/meter	Changing meter, polyrhythms, much syncopation; influence of jazz styles
Harmony	Atonality, polychords and polyharmony; use of tone rows (serialism); extremes in dissonance
Texture	Contrapuntal; linear movement
Vocal genres	Motet, opera, solo song with chamber ensemble
Instrumental genres	Neo-Classical genres (symphony, concerto, suite), ballet suites, film music; jazz band and wind band music
Form	Succinct, tight forms; revival of older forms
Dynamics	Wide-ranging dynamics for expressive purposes
Timbre	Bright, lean sound; winds and percussion favored; quickly shifting instrumental colors
Performing forces	Smaller orchestra, including piano; diverse percussion instruments; unusual combinations of instruments
Virtuosity	New challenges for vocalists and instrumentalists
Expression	Dramatic and emotional, often with high energy

Postmodernism: The Mid-Twentieth Century and Beyond

"A nice blend of prediction and surprise seems to be at the heart of the best art."

—American composer and electronic music pioneer Wendy Carlos (b. 1939)

OVERVIEW

1949
Communists under Mao assume power in China.

1958
First mass-produced stereo recordings made.

1963
President John F. Kennedy assassinated.

1968
Martin Luther King Jr. assassinated.

1977
Home computers enter mass market.

1950   1955   1960   1965   1970   1975

1949
John Cage's *Sonatas and Interludes*, for prepared piano, introduced.

1957
Leonard Bernstein's *West Side Story* opens on Broadway.

1956
Chuck Berry records *Roll Over Beethoven*.

1965
George Crumb writes madrigals on texts by García Lorca.

1970
Steve Reich studies African drumming in Ghana.

Learning Objectives

By the end of Part 7, you will be able to

- recognize mixtures of consonant and dissonant harmonies, as well as repetitive melodic fragments reaching toward longer gestures.

- perceive eclectic and idiosyncratic approaches to expression and style.

- follow experimental techniques that expand the timbral capabilities of instruments and voices.

- recognize the influence of electronic technology as well as popular and non-Western music styles.

- realize the wide variety in forms and procedures, including anti-rationalism, improvisation, and chance.

- identify some of the underlying cultural, social, and political issues that have inspired composers of the postmodern era.

2001
Terrorists attack the World Trade Center and Pentagon.

2008
Barack Obama elected first African American president.

2007
Apple introduces the iPhone.

1991
Soviet Union dissolved.

1985   1990   1995   2000   2005   2010   2020

1977
John Williams writes score for the first *Star Wars* movie.

1992
Philip Glass's First Symphony pays homage to Bowie's album *Low*.

2005
John Adams's opera *Doctor Atomic* premieres in San Francisco.

1985
John Tavener composes hymns for the Greek Orthodox church.

2014
Malala Yousafzai wins Nobel Peace Prize.

7

Beyond Modernism?

"From Schoenberg I learned that tradition is a home we must love and forgo."

—Lukas Foss

The Postmodern Turn

No one agrees on how to define **postmodernism**, and perhaps, as with modernism, it makes more sense to talk about several different departures from tradition, as mid-twentieth-century artists strove to find new means of expression beyond the principles of modernism. With the increasing social turmoil that followed the Second World War, the arts passed through a period of violent experimentation with new media, new materials, and new techniques. Artists introduced popular elements into their work; emphasized combinative techniques like collage, pastiche, or quotation; and revived traditional and classical elements. Their ideas continue to open broad possibilities for artistic expression: all art—highbrow or lowbrow—is considered to have equal potential for greatness.

Art, Film, Literature

In architecture, for example, the trend is away from sleek, glass skyscrapers and toward a more neo-eclectic look. While modernist designer Mies van der Rohe believed that "less is more," Robert Venturi, a leader in the postmodern movement in architecture, countered with "less is a bore," suggesting that buildings were more interesting if they had some decorative elements. One stunning example is Frank Gehry's design for the Walt Disney Concert Hall in Los Angeles, the interpretation of which has ranged from a blossoming flower to a sailing ship (see photo at left).

A trend away from objective painting led to **abstract expressionism** in the United States during the 1950s and 60s. In the canvases of painters such as Robert Motherwell (see illustration opposite) and Jackson Pollock, space, mass, and color were freed from the need to imitate objects in the real world.

The Walt Disney Concert Hall in Los Angeles, designed by Canadian-American artist **Frank Gehry** (b. 1929) and completed in 2003, is considered a masterpiece of postmodern architecture.

LEFT: *XX* (1985), a collage by **Robert Motherwell** (1915–1991), features the score for a song by Mozart on abstract blocks of color.

RIGHT: *Three Standing Forms* (1964), by English sculptor **Barbara Hepworth** (1903–1975), is an abstraction representing the relationship between nature and humankind.

TOP: **Andy Warhol**'s iconic pop-art image of *Beethoven* (1987).

BOTTOM: *The London Mastaba,* a monumental floating art installation of colorful stacked barrels that evokes an ancient Egyptian tomb, was the last project completed by **Christo** (1935–2000).

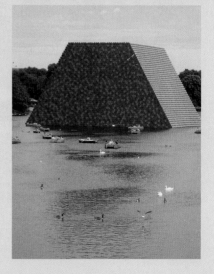

The urge toward abstraction was felt equally in sculpture, as is evident in the work of such artists as Henry Moore and Barbara Hepworth (above). At the same time, however, a new kind of realism appeared in the art of Jasper Johns, Robert Rauschenberg, and others, who owed some of their inspiration to the Dadaists of four decades earlier. Rauschenberg's aim, as he put it, was to work in the "gap between life and art." This trend culminated in **pop art**, which drew its themes from modern urban life: machines, advertisements, comic strips, movies, commercial photography, and familiar objects connected with everyday living. A similar aim motivated Andy Warhol's pop-art paintings (right) and the comic-strip art of Roy Lichtenstein.

Other subcategories of postmodern art include **new classicism**, **minimalism**, and performance and multimedia art. Artists have explored ecological and natural issues through environmental art, or **earthworks**, which advocates an approach akin to that of minimalism (spare and simple). Bulgarian artists Christo and his wife Jeanne-Claude (both used only their first names) exploited installation art as a new way to view old landscapes and to draw attention to form by concealing it. Their projects included wrapping Paris's Pont Neuf Bridge (1985) and the Reichstag government building in Berlin (1995) in fabric; one of their largest installations, called *The Gates* (2005), placed 7,503 gates with orange-colored fabric over the paths of New York's Central Park.

Postmodernist art embraces a pluralistic attitude toward gender, sexual orientation, and ethnicity. One creative artist whose expression is distinctively feminist is Judy Chicago, best known for *The Dinner Party* (1979), a triangular table with thirty-nine place settings that pay tribute to important women throughout history. African American artist Faith Ringgold creates "storybook" quilts, narrative paintings with quilted borders; some of these make up a *Jazz Series*, depicting Black musicians in the context of life in the 1920s and 30s (see p. 410).

Artists have featured recognizable images in their work, sometimes employing the technique of collage or quotation from a literary, musical, or visual source. Jasper Johns's work incorporated

TOP: African American artist **Faith Ringgold** (b. 1930) celebrates jazz in *Groovin High* (1986), with couples dancing at the Savoy Ballroom in Harlem.

MIDDLE: *The Logo* from *Holocaust Project: From Darkness into Light* (stained glass, 1992), by **Judy Chicago** (b. 1939), explores issues relating to the human condition.

BOTTOM: A hyperkinetic scene of urban life, from **Godfrey Reggio**'s film *Koyaanisqatsi* (1982), for which Philip Glass wrote the minimalist musical score.

common symbols—flags, numbers, letters. He wrote that using the flag "took care of a great deal for me because I didn't have to design it," allowing him to focus on the makeup of the work as a whole. Such techniques enabled artists to take something familiar and make it unique—just as Ives did in *Country Band March* (Chapter 62).

Postmodern ideas were easily extended to the medium of film, beginning with the "new wave" movement of the 1950s and 60s, epitomized in the films of Jean-Luc Godard (*Breathless*, 1960), Federico Fellini (*La Strada*, 1954; 8½, 1963), and Michelangelo Antonioni (*Blowup*, 1966; *The Passenger*, 1975). More recent directors who explore postmodernism include Jane Campion (*Two Friends*, 1986; a saga of two schoolgirls that is arranged in reverse order) and Quentin Tarantino, in the *Kill Bill* films (2003–04)—which pay homage to the Italian spaghetti western, Kung Fu movies, and other familiar stereotypes—and the genre-bending *Inglourious Basterds* (2009). Visual collage is used in Godfrey Reggio's non-narrative *Koyaanisqatsi* (1982; left) and *Powaqqatsi* (1988), both of which set soundtracks by minimalist composer Philip Glass (Chapter 69).

Among the postmodern novelists you might know are J. D. Salinger, whose *Catcher in the Rye* (1951) focuses on timeless themes of teenage angst and identity; Joseph Heller, whose wartime satire *Catch-22* (1961) contributed a term (its title) to the English language; Colombian author Gabriel García Márquez, whose *One Hundred Years of Solitude* explores the fluidity of time; and Canadian author Margaret Atwood, whose dystopian novel *The Handmaid's Tale* (1985; retold in a 2017 TV series) deals with the subjugation of women and how they gain independence. The works of Kurt Vonnegut, a classic novelist on many required reading lists (*Cat's Cradle*, 1963; *Slaughterhouse Five*, 1969), create a chaotic, fictional universe. Many recent authors have explored their identities through their writings, among them African American writer Toni Morrison (*The Bluest Eye*, 1970; *Beloved*, 1987), and Chinese American Amy Tan (*The Joy Luck Club*, 1989). Even J. K. Rowling's Harry Potter books spin out postmodern themes that establish the mythic Harry among our contemporary superheroes.

Music in a Postmodern World

The definition of postmodernism in music is even more elusive than it is in other art forms. But we can start with a breaking away from the modernist stance that mass media is incompatible with art. Like Warhol and fellow proponents of pop art, mid-twentieth-century musicians could not ignore the cultural saturation of technology, especially as recordings became more readily available in the 1950s, both LP (long-playing 33-rpm) and 45-rpm records. Many consumers purchased hi-fis (high-fidelity music systems) as well as the newly invented television for their homes. TV shows like *Your Hit Parade* (1950–59) and Dick Clark's *American Bandstand* (1952–89; see below) introduced the newest acts to the public, and the earliest early rock-and-roll performers. The boom of FM radio in the 1970s made listeners' choices increasingly vast and complex, and musical mass media took a further jump forward with the launch of MTV in 1981. In the past decade, the Internet has added yet another unfathomable resource to our musical landscape: many of us can't imagine living without the teeming media buffet that is YouTube, launched in 2005.

It was also in the prosperous 1950s that some of our most enduring musicals were first produced, including Alan Jan Lerner and Frederick Loewe's *My Fair Lady,* Richard Rodgers and Oscar Hammerstein's *The Sound of Music,* and Leonard Bernstein's *West Side Story,* which we will examine in Chapter 66. Musical theater and film have gone hand in hand since the invention of synchronized sound, and for much of the late twentieth century, movies were an essential source of musical pleasure. Now video games have added a more customized touch to the multi-media experience.

While some composers continued the path set out by Schoenberg toward ever stricter organization in music, others looked toward freer forms and procedures. The anti-rational element in art—leaning on intuition, chance, and improvisation—was favored by composers like John Cage, who wrote **chance**, or   **Chance music**

Teens dancing on Dick Clark's *American Bandstand* in 1961; some are dancing the Twist, popularized by Chubby Checker.

LEFT: Folk-song writer-singer Pete Seeger, famous for his protest songs, accompanies himself on banjo in an outdoor concert in New York City.

RIGHT: The legendary guitarist-singer Jimi Hendrix at the Woodstock Festival (1969).

aleatoric, **music** that left decisions determining overall shape to the performer or to chance (Chapter 65). In music as in the visual arts, the distinctions between elite and popular are shrinking: we will hear, for example, how composer Philip Glass repurposed small borrowings from David Bowie's album *Heroes* in his symphony of the same name (Chapter 69), and how film and video game scores rely extensively on the conventions of art music (Chapter 71). And the globalization of society has hugely impacted musical composition, opening composers up to a vast world of non-Western music, as in the works of John Cage, Steve Reich, and George Crumb.

Music as Protest

Political issues, a concern for musicians since the Middle Ages, have been especially so since the mid-1900s. The "Red scare" of communism during the 1950s and early 60s saw the blacklisting of many creative Americans—among them composers Aaron Copland (who wrote the very American *Appalachian Spring*) and Leonard Bernstein (*West Side Story*), clarinetist Artie Shaw (whom we heard performing with Billie Holiday in Chapter 59), and folksinger Pete Seeger (above), as well as writers Langston Hughes and W. E. B. DuBois. Even the physicist J. Robert Oppenheimer, the "father of the atomic bomb" and subject of the John Adams opera *Doctor Atomic*, was not exempt (Chapter 73).

Protest songs are a long-standing American tradition, and the last decades of the twentieth century provided causes worthy of musicians' creativity. Bob Dylan's voice was clearly heard with landmark protest songs (*Blowin' in the Wind* and *The Times They Are a-Changin'*; see opposite) during the 1960s civil rights movement, and Pete Seeger's *If I Had a Hammer* became, along with *We Shall Overcome*, an anthem for civil rights causes.

America's involvement in the Vietnam War supplied more ammunition for musical protests, like those performed at the 1969 Woodstock Festival, a seminal event for such artists as guitarist Jimi Hendrix (see above). New musical styles that developed in the 1980s—punk rock and rap, in particular—protested strongly against discrimination, poverty, corruption, and government policies (Public

Enemy's *Don't Believe the Hype,* 1988), while some pop singers, like Michael Jackson, worked to end a disastrous famine in Africa (*We Are the World,* 1985).

The intense drug culture and sexual revolution of the 1960s was reflected in songs of rock groups (including the Rolling Stones) and in the antiwar musical *Hair* (1967, revived 2008). Musical feminism took varied forms as well, from the folksy protest songs of Joan Baez to the "in-your-face" songs of the Dixie Chicks. Other significant social causes include protecting the environment and grappling with the atrocities of war, notably the Holocaust (the subject of Steven Spielberg's 1993 film *Schindler's List,* with a soundtrack by John Williams). Wars in Iraq and Afghanistan fueled a revival of musical commentaries, as have recent political campaigns. Barack Obama's 2008 campaign for the presidency attracted the talents of Black Eyed Peas' member will.i.am, who wrote the now famous collage-style video *Yes We Can.*

Bob Dylan performing *The Times They Are a-Changin'* in London, 1965.

New Technologies

Probably the most important development that affected music during the mid-twentieth century was the refinement of recording and playback technologies, which heralded the advent of electronic music. Two trends emerged simultaneously in the late 1940s and early 50s. *Musique concrète,* based in Paris, relied on sounds made by any natural source, including musical instruments, that were recorded onto magnetic tape and then manipulated by various means. *Elektronische Musik,* originating in Cologne, Germany, and explored by Karlheinz Stockhausen among others, used only electronically produced sounds. By the 1960s, compact and affordable synthesizers suited for mass production were being developed by Robert Moog and Donald Buchla, but it was a recording called *Switched-On Bach,* made in 1968 by Walter Carlos (a transgender musician now known as Wendy Carlos), that catapulted the synthesizer and the genre of electronic music to instant fame. The Moog synthesizer was quickly adopted by musicians for a variety of commercial purposes, including film scores for Stanley Kubrick's *A Clockwork Orange* (1971) and *The Shining* (1980).

In 1983, the Yamaha DX7, one of the best-selling synthesizers of all time, was unveiled. That same year saw the official adoption of a standardized protocol known as the Musical Instrument Digital Interface (MIDI), which allowed composers to record data such as pitch, duration, and volume on the computer for playback on one or more synthesizers. By the mid-1980s, digital-sampling synthesizers, capable of recreating a realistic-sounding grand piano, trumpet, violin, bird call, car crash, or any other sound that can be sampled, was accessible to the average musician. With the affordability of digital synthesizers and personal computers, and their ability to communicate with one another, the digital revolution took the world of electronic music by storm.

Much of the music we hear today as movie and TV soundtracks is electronically generated, although some effects resemble the sounds of conventional instruments so closely that we are not always aware of the new technology. Popular-music groups have been "electrified" for years, but now most of them regularly feature synthesizers and samplers that both simulate conventional rock band instruments and produce altogether new sounds; electronic resources like

In Their Own Words

" The synthesizer world opens the door to musical infinity."

—*Jazz guitarist John McLaughlin*

German musicians Tassilo Ippenberger (right) and Thomas Benedix, of the techno group Pan-Pot, in their Berlin studio (2015).

In Their Own Words

❝ It will be the task of the future to somehow synthesize the sheer diversity of our present resources into a more organic and well-ordered procedure."

—*George Crumb*

autotune help them manipulate vocal and instrumental pitch either in the studio or in performance.

Collage, a major genre of art, has also found a place in music: composer Lukas Foss (1922–2009) juxtaposed or overlapped fragments of Bach, Handel, and Scarlatti in his *Baroque Variations*, just as John Lennon created a sound collage of special effects and vocals in *Revolution 9* (*The Beatles*, 1968). And the device of quotation has proved its significance to popular as well as art music, since the entire tradition of hip-hop hinges on the creative sampling and layering of musical excerpts in ways the composer feels are artistically striking and/or culturally significant. All these techniques and many more make up the palette of the modern composer. We will listen for the individuality of each musical voice as we try to comprehend the expressive and eclectic language of today's music.

Performance Matters

POSTMODERN PROLIFERATION

The increasing interconnection of global musical traditions through radio, television, and the Internet has given musicians in the late twentieth and twenty-first centuries more and more performance options. Where musicians previously learned techniques directly from a master specialist, now recordings can provide almost endless opportunities for study and emulation. Recordings, which are usually manipulated in the studio to merge the best sections of several takes, have also set a new bar of performing perfection for musicians: audiences have come to expect the same kind of flawless sound live that they hear through their headphones, and many feel that has put unsustainable pressure on performers, giving them less freedom to take expressive risks.

Recording technology has also expanded the possibilities for musical virtuosity, as musicians have continued to work with manufacturers to redefine the nature of musical instruments (physical, electrically amplified, or digital). The changing economics of sound recording—shellac, vinyl, plastic, digital—has proved to be both a challenge and an opportunity for musicians to complement the centuries-old practices of earning income through public concertizing and private entertainment.

International exchanges in the global economy of the last half century have also inspired composers to integrate instruments and techniques from other cultures into the Western orchestral families. And the lines between commercial and "art" traditions, drawn fairly clearly in the 1800s, are now blurring again—creating a kaleidoscopic timbre-palette of resources for musicians across overlapping styles.

CRITICAL THINKING

1. What makes postmodernism so difficult to define?
2. What are some of the most significant musical developments of the late twentieth century?

Music Technology

As early as 1955, composers set out to see how the computer could enhance the creative process of composition. Could the machine possibly compose by itself? Composer, record producer, and multimedia artist Brian Eno showed that it could in a way; he coined the term "generative music" for his compositions in which the computer grows "little seeds" that produce ever-changing music, thereby introducing the idea of chance music to audiences. Other composers have sought out ways for musicians and computers to interact in live performances.

One of the most creative minds in the world of music technology is Tod Machover, described by the *Los Angeles Times* as "America's most wired composer." Machover's explorations into interactivity—between the audience and at-home listeners as well as between performers and computers—and his outreach to popular culture have made him a leader in the contemporary music scene. The composer admits that the 1967 release of the Beatles' *Sgt. Pepper's Lonely Hearts Club Band* album piqued his interest in manipulating sounds and creating entirely new ones. Now a professor at the Massachusetts Institute of Technology (MIT), he heads up the Media Lab there, where the popular video games *Guitar Hero* and *Rock Band* were developed by two of his students, Alex Rigopulos and Eran Egozy. In his effort to be inclusive in the music-making process, Machover oversaw the development of a program called Hyperscore, which allows anyone, even children, to compose music using just lines and colors; *Toy Symphony* (2003), which provided children with appealing high-tech "music toys," was one result. "Technology has paved the way for almost anyone to hit the right notes," he claims.

Machover also developed the technology of "hyperinstruments," using the computer to expand the expressive ability of traditional instruments. His work for hypercello *Begin Again Again . . .* was written for the virtuoso Yo-Yo Ma and, in keeping with the postmodern idea of quotation, pays homage in its opening theme to the Sarabande from J. S. Bach's Cello Suite No. 2. Throughout, the cellist is in control of an array of devices that both produce and transform sound through the angle and pressure of the bow. This piece is so crazily virtuosic that the composer asked Yo-Yo Ma after one rehearsal, "Is there any hair left on your bow?"

Machover's interest in popular culture, another postmodern hallmark, extends to others of his compositions. And his sci-fi operas are just as wired. *VALIS* (1987; acronym for Vast Active Living Intelligent System), based on

Composer Tod Machover experiments with the hypercello in his lab at MIT.

the popular novel by Philip Dick and written for the tenth anniversary of the postmodern Pompidou Center in Paris, closes with a pounding rock finale, evoking the music that was formative to Machover; and *Death and the Powers* (2010) not only features a high-tech chorus of dancing robots, but also relies on over forty computers to run the production and 140 speakers to create an ultramodern sound world.

Machover's hyperpiano concerto titled *Jeux Deux* was written in 2005 for the Boston Pops Orchestra and features an augmented percussion section. The work's title plays off Debussy's masterpiece *Jeux* (*Games*), a dance piece that begins with a tennis match in which the ball goes missing. Machover notes that *Jeux* was a "spiritual antecedent" to *Jeux Deux*, which builds on two matches (it translates loosely as "two-person game"): one between the piano soloist and the orchestra (as in most concertos) and another between the human and the hyperpiano, which can do amazing nonhuman things. The pianist plays an electronic piano (a Yamaha Disklavier Grand), which is augmented by software that analyzes what the soloist is playing and signals the computer to trigger a sequence of notes or multiply and speed up notes to exceed what any human hand can do—at times, it sounds as if ghosts are playing along on the keyboard. The work is traditional in its three-section, fast-slow-fast structure, but the movements are played without pause.

Listen to the third movement, *Buoyant and Precise*, and note how it starts off with a spritely tune that seems straightforward enough until it hiccups with rhythmic displacements,

Tod Machover rehearses *Philadelphia Voices* with members of the Philadelphia Orchestra and several youth choirs.

building in dense, dissonant polyphony. Machover's groundbreaking musical technologies are as fun as they are innovative: a *Boston Globe* reviewer found the playful *Jeux Deux* to be "a wild, lovely, and utterly modern collision of art and science."

One of Machover's more recent projects involves a series of collaborative "City Symphonies" in which he creates a sonic portrait of a city and its residents. He's done this for several cities in Europe as well as in Canada and the United States. His *Philadelphia Voices* was premiered in 2018 with the Philadelphia Orchestra and several choirs (see photo above); in this work, residents contributed samplings of cityscapes, vocalizations, and texts to the music, giving voice to the diverse

communities of Philadelphia, with a goal of celebrating the birthplace of American democracy.

Many Voices Expanded

- Machover, *Begin Again Again*, for hypercello, *Introduction*
- Machover, Hyperpiano concerto *Jeux Deux*, III (*Buoyant and Precise*)
- Videos about *Philadelphia Voices* at https://citysymphonies.media.mit.edu/audiovideo

New Sound Palettes: Mid-Twentieth-Century American Experimentalists

"I thought I could never compose socially important music. Only if I could invent something new, then would I be useful to society."

—John Cage

KeyPoints

- Contemporary music often calls for innovative and highly virtuosic instrumental or vocal effects that challenge performers to new technical levels.
- Composer John Cage used a specially modified **prepared piano** to simulate the sound of the **Javanese gamelan**, an ensemble of metallic

percussion instruments played in Indonesia (on the islands of Java and Bali, in particular).

- In his four books of madrigals, which treat the voice as a virtuosic instrument, composer George Crumb set texts by the Spanish poet Federico García Lorca.

Since the beginning of recorded history, musicians have been expanding their sound-production resources—by inventing new scales and harmonies, developing increasingly complex and versatile instruments, and training their bodies to sing and play in experimental ways. In order to do so, they have reached out to other cultures for inspiration, but also taken advantage of the inventiveness of their fellow musicians. The mid-twentieth century was an especially fertile time for musical expansion in North America, and we will hear examples by two composers who shaped such expansion: John Cage and George Crumb.

Early Experiments

Two earlier American composers in particular helped shape the pioneering genius of John Cage. One, Henry Cowell (1897–1965), was drawn toward a variety of non-Western musics. His studies of the musics of Japan, India, and Iran led him to combine Asian instruments with traditional Western ensembles. Cowell also experimented with non-Western scales, which he harmonized with Western chords. **Tone clusters** Several of his innovations involved the piano; these include **tone clusters** (groups of adjacent notes played with the fist, palm, or forearm) and the plucking of the piano strings directly with the fingers. This novel approach to the piano helped to inspire Cage's idea of the "prepared piano," which we will encounter below.

Microtones The most serious proponent of microtonal technique was Harry Partch (1901–1974), who developed a scale of forty-three **microtones** to the octave in the 1920s and adapted Indian and African instruments to fit this tuning. Among his original instruments are cloud-chamber bowls (made of glass), cone gongs (made of metal), and gourd trees. Partch used such instruments to create melody and varying timbre, rather than harmony.

The Music of John Cage

Cage represents the type of eternally questing artist who no sooner solves one problem than presses forward to another. His works explored new sounds and concepts that challenged the very notion of what makes up music. Probably his most important contribution, and one that shaped many strands of music in the second half of the twentieth century, was the idea of **chance**, or **aleatoric**, **music**. His experimental compositions and writings defined him as a leader in the postwar avant-garde scene.

Sonatas and Interludes

Sonatas and Interludes represents Cage's crowning achievement for the **prepared piano**, approximating the subtle sounds of the Javanese gamelan and preserving the effect of music floating above time. There are sixteen sonatas in this set, ordered in four groups of four, and separated by interludes (LG 58). Cage provides

In Their Own Words

" Once in Amsterdam, a Dutch musician said to me, 'It must be very difficult for you in America to write music, for you are so far away from the centers of tradition.' I had to say, 'It must be very difficult for you in Europe to write music, for you are so close to the centers of tradition.'"

—*John Cage*

John Cage (1912–1992)

Born in Los Angeles, Cage exhibited an early interest in non-Western scales, which he learned from his mentor, Henry Cowell. He soon realized that the traditional division between consonance and dissonance had given way to a new opposition between music and noise, as a result of which the boundaries of the one were extended to include more of the other.

In 1938, Cage invented what he called the "prepared piano," in which various foreign substances were inserted at crucial points in the strings of a grand piano. From this instrument came a myriad of sounds whose overall effect resembled that of a Javanese gamelan. Cage wrote a number of works for the prepared piano, notably the set of *Sonatas and Interludes*. His interest in indeterminacy, or chance, resulted in works in which performers make choices by throwing dice.

Cage maintained an intense interest in exploring the role of silence, which led to a composition entitled *4'33"*, without any musical content at all, consisting of four minutes and thirty-three seconds of "silence." The piece was

first "performed" by the pianist David Tudor in 1952. He came onstage, placed a score on the piano rack, sat quietly for the duration of the piece, then closed the keyboard lid and walked off the stage. Cage viewed *4'33"* as one of the most radical statements he had made against the traditions of Western music, one that raised profound questions. What is music, and what is noise? And what does silence contribute to music? In any case, *4'33"*, which can be performed by anyone on any instrument, always makes us more aware of our surroundings.

MAJOR WORKS: Orchestral music • Piano music, including *Music of Changes* (1951) • Prepared-piano works, including *Bacchanale* (1940) and *Sonatas and Interludes* (1946–48) • Percussion works, including *First, Second, Third Construction* (1938, 1940, 1941) • Vocal works, including *Aria* (1958) • Electronic music, including *Fontana Mix* (1958), *Cartridge Music* (1960), and *HPSCHD* (for harpsichord and tapes, 1969) • Indeterminate works, including *4'33"* (for any instrument, 1952) • Writings, including *Silence* (1961), *Notations* (1969), *Themes and Variations* (1982), and *I–VI* (1990).

LISTENING GUIDE 58   🔊 1:23

Cage: *Sonata V, from Sonatas and Interludes*

Date: 1946–48 (first performed 1949)

Performed by: Joshua Pierce, piano

Overall structure: 16 sonatas, in four groups of 4, each group separated by an interlude

---

What to Listen For

Melody	Irregular phrases, with a small-range and undulating chromatic line; second section is more disjunct.	**Texture**	The focus is on linear movement.
		Form	Binary structure (**A-A-B-B**).
Rhythm/ meter	Regular movement at first, then changing rhythmic flow, seemingly without a clear meter.	**Expression**	Evokes ethereal, otherworldly sounds.
		Timbre	Piano produces percussive effects, both pitched and nonpitched; varied tone quality and pitches.
Harmony	Minimal sense of harmony; dissonant ending.		

0:00   **A section**—18 measures, grouped in irregular phrases (4 + 5 + 4 + 5).

Opening of sonata, with regular rhythmic movement and two-voice texture:

(una corda pedal)

An irregular sense of meter develops.

0:12   Upper line is sustained over a moving lower line (in last 9 measures).

0:20   **A section** repeated.

0:38   **B section**—22½ measures, in irregular phrases (4 + 5 + 4 + 5 + 4½).

Rests break the music into sections.

0:46   Quicker tempo, lines are more disjunct and accented.

Second half of **B section**, with more disjunct lines and accents:

0:55   Sustained dissonance at the closing.

1:00   **B section** repeated.

detailed instructions at the beginning of the score, indicating that forty-five of the piano's eighty-eight keys should be prepared by inserting nails, bolts, nuts, screws, and bits of rubber, wood, or leather between the strings. The effect is varied, depending on the material inserted, its position, and whether the soft pedal is depressed. Some strings produce a nonpitched, percussive thump, while others produce tones whose pitch and timbre are altered. This music is not concerned with the simultaneous sounding of pitches (harmony) but rather with timbral effects and the rhythmic grouping of sounds.

Sonata V is short but highly structured; its overall shape is binary (a prevalent form in the Baroque and Classical eras), with each section repeated (**A-A-B-B**). The sonority of the prepared piano is almost ethereal. Here and elsewhere, Cage's music for prepared piano is made of wholly original sounds that delight the ears and, as intended by the composer, "set the soul in operation."

George Crumb and Avant-Garde Virtuosity

John Cage's prepared-piano works call for screws, nails, and other materials to be inserted between the strings.

Avant-garde musical styles call for a new breed of instrumentalists and vocalists, and a new arsenal of unusual techniques, to cope with the music's performance demands. The music of George Crumb, for example, draws from art-music traditions, folk themes, and non-Western sounds. Crumb displays a real talent for turning ordinary instruments, including the voice, into the extraordinary. His imaginative music resounds with extramusical and symbolic content that infuses it with a deep meaning waiting to be unlocked.

Caballito negro (Little Black Horse)

Caballito negro (LG 59) is the last of three songs in Crumb's second book of madrigals. All three are set to poetry by Federico García Lorca, and are scored for soprano with metallic percussion instruments and a flute or piccolo. The piccolo player uses a technique called **flutter-tonguing**: quickly moving the tongue as though "rolling an R" while blowing into the instrument. In *Caballito negro*, a hair-raising image of death, Crumb extracts only the two refrains from the poem, alternating between them: "Little black horse, where are you taking your dead rider? Little cold horse. What a scent of knife-blossom!" Most phrases end with a downward

In Their Own Words

❝ I think composers are everything they've ever experienced, everything they've ever read, all the music they've heard. . . . I think there's a lot of music that has a darker side and maybe some of this music influenced me."

—*George Crumb*

George Crumb (b. 1929)

Crumb studied at Mason College of Fine Arts in Charleston, West Virginia, and earned graduate degrees at the University of Illinois and University of Michigan. He taught composition in Colorado and New York before he was appointed to the University of Pennsylvania, where he remained until he retired in 1999. Crumb has shown a special affinity for the poetry of Federico García Lorca, the great poet killed by the Fascists during the Spanish Civil War. Among his works based on García Lorca's poetry is the song cycle *Ancient Voices of Children*, which abounds in unusual effects. He also set García Lorca's poetry in his four books of madrigals, in which he explores *Sprechstimme* (spoken melody), quarter tones, and a "white" tone (without vibrato) for the voice.

Crumb's music is focused on creating new sonorities as well as exploring theatrical concepts. In *Echoes of Time and the River*, for which he won a Pulitzer Prize in 1968,

performers whisper and shout as they move around the stage. His music is charged with emotion, which derives from a highly developed sense of the dramatic. And his use of contemporary techniques for expressive ends is extremely effective with audiences.

MAJOR WORKS: Orchestral music, including *Echoes of Time and the River* (1967) • Vocal music set to García Lorca poetry, including four books of madrigals (1965–69) and *Ancient Voices of Children* (1970) • *Spanish Songbook* series (2009–12) and American Songbook series (2001–10), both for solo voice and amplified instruments • Chamber music, including *Black Angels* (for electric string quartet, 1970), *Lux aeterna* (*Eternal Light*, for voice and chamber ensemble with sitar, 1971), and *Vox balaenae* (*The Voice of the Whale*, for amplified instruments, 1971) • Music for amplified piano, including two volumes of *Makrokosmos* (1972–73), *Music for a Summer Evening* (1974), *Zeitgeist* (1988), and *Otherworldly Resonances* (two pianos, 2003) • Other piano music.

Many composers set the poetry of Spanish poet Federico García Lorca, shown here at age twenty.

melodic line, on ominous words. The rhythmic treatment might remind you of the galloping horse in Schubert's equally chilling *Elf-King* (Chapter 39), and the vocalist is even asked to whinny like a horse.

Both Cage and Crumb rely on the extraordinary creativity of others for their works to be successful, whether through the artistic ability to shape unconventional sounds expressively, or the technical nuance to make beautiful phrases from highly complex scores. And this necessity of collaboration between composer and performer is one of the characteristic (and most wonderful) aspects of music, especially in an age of specialization and experimentation.

CRITICAL THINKING

1. What kinds of new techniques have modern musicians needed to learn in order to perform avant-garde music?
2. Compare Crumb's idea of madrigal with the Farmer song in Chapter 19. What is similar, and what is different?

Your Turn TO EXPLORE

Choose an instrument that you find interesting (the human voice can count!), and try to find examples of musicians pushing the technical possibilities of that instrument. What kinds of extended techniques can you discover? Do they have a significant expressive potential, and if so, how? Do you think those techniques could find a place in your favorite repertories? Can you envision other techniques that might be musically expressive?

LISTENING GUIDE 59

🔊 1:32

Crumb: *Caballito negro* (*Little Black Horse*)

Date: 1965

Genre: Song, from *Madrigals*, Book II

Performed by: Tony Arnold, soprano; Rachel Rudich, piccolo; David Colson, percussion

---

What to Listen For

Melody	Highly disjunct; extended techniques (flutter-tonguing, glissandos, whispering).
Rhythm/ meter	Regular pulsations, no firm sense of meter.
Harmony	Atonal.
Form	Three-part (**A-B-A′**).

Expression	Grimly playful; very animated.
Timbre	Bright, hard, metallic quality.
Performing forces	Soprano voice, piccolo, percussion (marimba, glockenspiel, antique cymbals).
Text	Text by Federico García Lorca.

	TEXT	TRANSLATION
0:00	Caballito negro.	Little black horse.
	¿Dónde llevas tu jenete muerto?	Where are you taking your dead rider?
0:30	Caballito frío.	Little cold horse.
	¡Qué perfume de flor de cuchillo!	What a scent of knife-blossom!
0:55	Caballito negro . . .	Little black horse . . .
	Caballito frío . . .	Little cold horse . . .
	Caballito negro . . .	Little black horse . . .

Opening of song, with pounding rhythm in piccolo and percussion, disjunct vocal line, and flutter-tonguing in piccolo:

Return of opening line, with the vocalist neighing like a horse:

Javanese Gamelan

L isteners at the 1889 Paris World Exhibition were captivated with the spectacle of Javanese dance and the accompanying orchestra called gamelan. French composer Camille Saint-Saëns observed that it was "a dream music which had truly hypnotized some people." From that time on, many composers have looked to the music of Southeast Asia and Oceania for inspiration in their own works. American West Coast musicians in particular had the opportunity to experience the gamelan on their own turf: in California, Santa Barbara–based composer-ethnomusicologist Henry Eichheim (1870–1942) brought Indonesian instruments back from his travels in the 1920s and also adopted elements of Balinese music in his work. Beginning in 1940, touring

Javanese ensembles traveled up the coast from Los Angeles. These events caught the attention of experimental composers Henry Cowell, who taught a class on "Music of the World's Peoples" at the New School for Social Research in New York, and Lou Harrison (1917–2003), who wrote a number of works for Javanese-style instruments. John Cage, a devotee of Cowell and Harrison, was certainly not blind to these influences, and he too undertook a study of Asian cultures. The prepared-piano technique Cage devised owes a significant debt to gamelan music, in both texture and timbre, although the sounds are achieved in quite a different way.

The gamelan, an orchestra of metallic percussion found on the Indonesian islands of Java, Bali, and Sunda, is comprised of melodic-percussive

instruments, each with its own function. The music is generally performed from memory, passed on through oral tradition from master musician to apprentice. It is only in recent years that a notational method has been devised. Gamelan music is often heard in ritual ceremonies, including court performances (there are four princely courts in central Java alone), and in *wayang*, or shadow-puppet theater.

The performance of a shadow-puppet play would normally begin in the early evening with an overture and continue until dawn. A master puppeteer operates the puppets from behind a screen, narrates and sings the songs, and signals the gamelan—here, soft and loud metallophones (tuned metal bars struck with a mallet), gongs of various sizes, wooden xylophones, and drums—when to play. Our

Indonesian gamelan musicians accompanying a shadow-puppet play on Java Island.

selection is an overture (called *Patalon*) to a shadow-puppet play. Like many Javanese dramas, the story comes from the great Hindu epic *Ramayana*, the story of King Rama, whose wife Sinta is kidnapped by an evil king named Rahwana. (Java today is predominantly Islamic, although Hindu and Buddhist beliefs are also important to the culture.) In this play, the evil king's brother is cast out of the kingdom for suggesting that Rahwana return Sinta to her husband.

In Javanese music, the interaction of the melodic movement with a cyclical rhythmic structure determines the form of the work. Here, the melody is based on the pentatonic scale (notes 1, 2, 3, 5, 6, or C, D, E, G, A). The work unfolds in sections, with the drum marking the transition between sections. The first, including an introduction, is slow and stately—the melody can be heard in the highest-pitched metallophone, which sounds each note of the pentatonic pattern twice. When the singer enters, he elaborates on the melody in quite a different way from the instruments, but both singer and instruments converge on accented notes. At dramatic moments in the text, the accents can jolt the listener. A fast-paced and excited closing section signals the entrance of the dancers and puppet characters.

Wayang: Patalon

What to listen for:

- Pentatonic (five-note) melodic patterns.
- Rhythmic cycles that develop in complex polyrhythms.
- Sectional alternations between loud and soft instruments.

Javanese shadow-drama puppets of King Rama, hero of the Hindu epic *Ramayana*, and his wife Sinta (left), who is kidnapped and later recovered.

A slow introduction features the high-sounding metallophone outlining the melodic pattern; the voice soon enters, elaborating on the main melody, which is punctuated by gongs.

A drum cues the transition to the next (faster) section; a loud-style section follows, featuring the first four notes of the melody and the gong playing on most main notes.

A transition leads to a soft-style section, featuring quieter instruments and the voice (with dramatic accents and leaps); the dynamic level grows, with loud instruments; recording fades out.

66

Staged Sentiment: Bernstein and American Musical Theater

"The hills are alive with the sound of music."

—Oscar Hammerstein

KeyPoints

- The roots of American musical theater lie both in vaudeville shows and in European operetta.
- **Musicals** feature romantic plots (some taken from novels), sometimes serious subject matter, comic moments, appealing melodies, and large ensembles and dance numbers; the dialogue is mostly spoken.
- The "golden age" of the American musical, the early to mid-1900s, was characterized by composer-lyricist teams (George and Ira Gershwin, Lerner and Loewe, Rodgers and Hammerstein).
- Leonard Bernstein, a versatile conductor and composer, wrote the music for *West Side Story*, which transports the Romeo and Juliet story into New York City and its gang warfare.

American musical theater is, like jazz, a tradition that is both rooted in the United States and tremendously influential and popular throughout the world. From the beginning, composers and lyricists of the **musical** (as it's most commonly known) have sought to make their themes current and vital, relevant to the concerns of their society. One such theme is urban life and especially urban violence, and one powerful treatment of that theme was understood as pathbreaking from the start and continues to influence theatrical multimedia today: *West Side Story*, a collaboration between composer Leonard Bernstein, lyricist Stephen Sondheim, and choreographer Jerome Robbins—three of the most talented artists of the mid-twentieth century.

Musical Theater in North America

Although theatrical productions were banned in most of the earliest North American colonies on religious and moral grounds, by the early nineteenth century immigrant musicians were helping to build a tradition of musical theater in North America. In the mid-1800s, New York became the cultural center of the country. In midtown Manhattan, the heart of the theater district, theaters lined the wide street called Broadway. Here and throughout the country, minstrel shows were giving way to vaudeville; these productions still featured some blackface, but more and more the characters were taken from new immigrant populations from Italy, Eastern Europe, and Asia. Some musical routines were parodies of the "funny way" the immigrants talked and behaved, yet often the actors themselves were immigrants, and the music could be sentimental and nostalgic as well as humorous—continuing a tradition established by Stephen Foster in an earlier generation (see Chapter 40). The vaudeville tradition expanded in New York into the variety show, which continued to offer musical and theatrical sketches, now often strung together by a loose topical theme.

Natalie Wood and Richard Beymer, in the balcony scene from the 1961 movie version of Bernstein's *West Side Story.*

The American musical theater of today developed both from the variety show and from the operetta tradition of late nineteenth-century European composers such as Johann Strauss Jr. and the team of W. S. Gilbert and Arthur Sullivan (*The Pirates of Penzance*, 1879; *The Mikado*, 1885). The genre was revamped to suit American tastes, both by immigrant composers like Victor Herbert (*Babes in Toyland*, 1903) and by "locals" like Will Marion Cook, an African American composer whose *Clorindy, or The Origin of the Cakewalk* (1898) was both the first Black production to play a major Broadway theater and the first musical to incorporate ragtime melodies and rhythms. By the 1920s, talented creative teams such as George and Ira Gershwin (*Lady, Be Good*, 1924) and Oscar Hammerstein and Jerome Kern (*Show Boat*, 1927) had ushered in what many consider the golden age of the American musical. In the ensuing decades, the musical established itself as America's unique contribution to world theater.

While plots for early musicals were often sentimental and contrived, this changed when composers looked to sophisticated literary sources (*Show Boat*, for example, is based on the Edna Ferber novel). In the 1940s, interest grew in adding more serious dramatic elements (for example, in the Richard Rodgers and Oscar Hammerstein productions *Oklahoma!* 1943; *South Pacific*, 1949; *The King and I*, 1951; *The Sound of Music*, 1959). Noted composers of musicals in more recent decades include Stephen Sondheim (*Sweeney Todd*, 1979; *Into the Woods*, 1988), who lifted the genre to new levels of sophistication; Andrew Lloyd Webber (*Cats*, 1981; *Phantom of the Opera*, 1986), who combined song and dance with dazzling scenic effects; and Claude-Michel Schönberg (*Les Misérables*, 1987) and Lin-Manuel Miranda (*Hamilton*, 2015), both of whom brought history alive with memorable songs. Jonathan Larson's hit show *Rent* (1996) is a modern rock opera based on Puccini's opera *La bohème*, and the Broadway hit *Wicked* (2003) derives from the classic book *The Wonderful Wizard of Oz* (1900, made into a movie with Judy Garland in 1939). Dance has taken precedence over story line in musicals like *Billy Elliot* (2005, with music by Elton John), and plays a striking role in *West Side Story.*

Leonard Bernstein and *West Side Story*

Composer-conductor Leonard Bernstein dedicated his life to promoting concert music to the general public, through his accessible compositions and his far-reaching educational efforts. Bernstein was deeply influenced both by Gershwin's successes in expanding the jazz idiom and by Copland's ability to create soundscapes that could quickly be recognized as reflecting American ideals. His most enduring project was a collaboration with several outstanding creative minds of the mid-1900s, which brought the culturally profound story of Shakespeare's *Romeo and Juliet* into the violent gang world of New York.

Bernstein, along with lyricist Stephen Sondheim and playwright Arthur Laurents, had first intended to replace Shakespeare's warring families with Jewish and Catholic families living in the tenements of Manhattan's Lower East Side. As the project developed, choreographer Jerome Robbins joined the team and suggested shifting

In Their Own Words

" This will be our reply to violence: to make music more intensely, more beautifully, more devotedly than ever before."

—*Leonard Bernstein*

Inter*face*

Music as Literature

Have you considered where composers find inspiration for their story-based compositions? Some make up their own stories—a case in point is Russian composer Sergei Prokofiev, who in *Peter and the Wolf* created a modern children's folktale. It should be no surprise that great literature has spawned countless operas, ballets, and programmatic orchestral works, as well as Broadway musicals. Some composers rely on the classics, as Purcell did for *Dido and Aeneas* (taken from Virgil's *Aeneid*), while others are inspired by new literary trends: Debussy's *Prelude to "The Afternoon of a Faun"* evokes a contemporaneous Symbolist poem of the same name. Verdi wrote operas on Shakespeare's tragedies *Macbeth* and *Othello,* as well as the comedy *Falstaff* (based on a Shakespeare character). Broadway musicals generally offered lighter fare, but composers and lyricists still occasionally looked to great writers (notably Shakespeare) for good stories—beginning with *The Boys from Syracuse* (1938), based on *A Comedy of Errors,* and Cole Porter's *Kiss Me, Kate* (1948), an updating of *The Taming of the Shrew.* These musicals enhanced familiar comedic plots with all the showy trappings of the golden era of Broadway: memorable tunes, spectacular chorus and dance sequences, and colorful costumes and sets, all with a feel-good story that ends happily.

The idea of a musical as tragedy was unheard of until Leonard Bernstein and Stephen Sondheim tested the waters with *West Side Story,* an updated version of Shakespeare's *Romeo and Juliet.* They wanted to tell a modern story not far removed from the opposing Capulets and Montagues. But was the public ready for a show that replaced the glamour and romantic clichés of the genre with the gritty reality of New York's street life? Critics and audiences alike were stunned by the electrifying dance sequences, choreographed by Jerome Robbins, and the violent onstage deaths of three of the show's lead characters, and *West Side Story* was immediately recognized as a bold step forward in musical theater. Then, as today, the familiarity of this tragic story of young love makes the show all the more compelling.

Modern composers of dramatic music continue to look to familiar literature—both comic and tragic—as a means to engage their audiences while pressing their eyes and ears to ever new sights and sounds. You might enjoy one of the modern operas based on famous books you may have read: for example, *Frankenstein* (1990), by Libby Larsen, on Mary Shelley's landmark horror novel; *Little Women* (1998), by Mark Adamo, on the popular Louisa May Alcott's tale; *The Handmaid's Tale* (2000), by Poul Ruders, on the dystopian novel by Margaret Atwood; *Alice in Wonderland* (2007), by Unsuk Chin, an adaption of the fantasy novels by Lewis Carroll; or *Moby Dick* (2010) by Jake Heggie, on the long-revered novel by Herman Melville, to name a few. Some contemporary musicals also look back to the classics. Surely *West Side Story* forged a path for one

Artists, like composers, found inspiration in Shakespeare's tale of star-crossed lovers. *The Last Farewell of Romeo and Juliet* (1832), by **Francesco Hayez** (1791–1882).

of the most intense and violent dramas that will ever grace the musical theater stage: the smash-hit show *Les Misérables,* by Claude-Michel Schönberg and Alain Boublil and based on Victor Hugo's great novel, a show that resounds even louder and to a broader public through its spectacular 2012 film adaptation. And who would have thought that the monumental biography of one of America's "Founding Fathers"—*Alexander Hamilton* by Ron Chernow (2004)—would spawn the hugely popular hip-hop–inspired musical *Hamilton* (2015), by Lin-Manuel Miranda.

Leonard Bernstein (1918–1990)

As a composer, conductor, educator, pianist, and television personality, Bernstein enjoyed a spectacular career. He was born in Lawrence, Massachusetts, entered Harvard at seventeen, attended the prestigious Curtis Institute of Music in Philadelphia, and then became a disciple of conductor Serge Koussevitzky. At twenty-five, he was appointed assistant conductor of the New York Philharmonic. When a guest conductor was suddenly taken ill, Bernstein took over a Sunday afternoon concert that was broadcast coast to coast, and led a stunning performance. Overnight he became famous. Fifteen years later, he was himself named director of the New York Philharmonic, the first American-born conductor to occupy the post.

As a composer, Bernstein straddled the worlds of serious and popular music. He explored his Jewish background in his Third Symphony (*Kaddish*) and also tried his hand at serial composition. But he was rooted in tonality, as he demonstrated in his choral masterwork *Chichester Psalms*. Bernstein's feeling for the urban scene, specifically that of New York City, is vividly projected in his theater music. In *On the Town, Wonderful Town*, and *West Side Story*, he created a sophisticated kind of musical theater that explodes with movement, energy, and sentiment. His harmonies are spicily dissonant, his jazzy rhythms have great vitality, and his melodies soar.

MAJOR WORKS: Orchestral music, including three symphonies (*Kaddish*, 1963) • Choral works, including *Chichester Psalms* (1965) • Operas, including *A Quiet Place* (1983) • Musicals, including *On the Town* (1944), *Wonderful Town* (1953), *Candide* (1956), and *West Side Story* (1957) • Other dramatic stage works, including the ballet *Fancy Free* (1944), the film score *On the Waterfront* (1954), and a staged *Mass* (1971) • Chamber and instrumental music • Solo vocal music.

the location to the West Side, turning the families into juvenile gangs, a topic that was saturating the news in the mid 1950s: the result was two gangs called the Jets and the Sharks (a Puerto Rican group). Robbins was especially eager to depict the setting's "gritty realism," and encouraged Bernstein to incorporate not only elements of jazz and early rock and roll, but also Latin American music like the mambo, an Afro-Cuban dance with a fast, syncopated beat that was extremely popular at the time.

This story of star-crossed lovers unfolds in scenes of great tenderness, with memorable songs such as *Maria, Tonight*, and *Somewhere* alternating with electrifying dance sequences choreographed by Robbins. We will first hear *Mambo* (LG 60), part of the dance scene where Tony (former member of the Jets) meets Maria (related to the Sharks). To a lively Latin beat, the bongos and cowbells keep

Rival gangs (the Sharks and the Jets) dance in a 2007 production of *West Side Story*, performed in Paris.

up a frenetic pulse under the shouts of the gang members and the jazzy riffs of the woodwinds and brass.

The *Tonight* Ensemble is set later the same day, after a fire-escape version of Shakespeare's famous balcony scene, where Tony and Maria first sing their love duet. As darkness falls, the two gangs anxiously await the expected fight, each vowing to cut the other down to size. Underneath the gang music, an ominous three-note ostinato is heard throughout. Tony sings the lyrical ballad *Tonight* over an animated Latin rhythmic accompaniment. The gang music returns briefly, after which Maria and later Tony repeat their love song, their voices soaring above the complex dialogue in an exciting climax to the first act.

West Side Story was an instant audience success, and more than sixty years later remains a powerful work of musical theater, which has claimed its place in North American culture not only through the remarkable 1961 film adaptation, but also as a favorite of school and college theatrical groups. Yet it has also caused controversy, both because of the focus on violence and gangs (and essentially sympathetic treatment of the gang members) and for what some have considered a stereotypical portrayal of Latino characters. Certainly, however, it was a groundbreaking multimedia work, as well as a landmark in our society's continuing struggle with artistic depictions of violence.

LISTENING GUIDE 60   🔊 5:26

Bernstein: *West Side Story*, excerpts

Date: 1957

Genre: Musical theater

Characters: Maria, Puerto Rican sister of Bernardo
Tony, former member of the Jets
Anita, Puerto Rican girlfriend of Bernardo
Riff, leader of the Jets
Bernardo, leader of the Puerto Rican Sharks

Performed by: Carol Lawrence (Maria), Chita Rivera (Anita), Larry Kert (Tony), Mickey Calin (Riff), Ken LeRoy (Bernardo); Max Goberman, music director

Act I: The Dance at the Gym, *Mambo*   1:48

What to Listen For

Melody	Disjunct, syncopated riffs (short ideas).	**Expression**	Frenetic Latin dance with excited voices and hand clapping.
Rhythm/ meter	Fast-paced Afro-Cuban dance; highly rhythmic with much syncopation.	**Timbre**	Brass and Latin rhythm instruments (bongo drums, cowbells) featured.
Harmony	Spicily dissonant.		
Texture	Dense and polyphonic.		

0:00   Percussion introduction, eight bars, with bongos and cowbells; very fast and syncopated.
0:07   Brass, with accented chords; Sharks shout "Mambo!" followed by a quieter string line, accompanied by snare-drum rolls; accented brass chords return; Sharks shout "Mambo!" again.
0:28   High dissonant woodwinds in dialogue with rhythmic brass.

0:33   Trumpets play a riff over ***fff*** chords:

Woodwinds and brass alternate in a highly polyphonic texture.

1:00   Rocking two-note woodwind line above syncopated low brass:

1:13   Solo trumpet enters in a high range above a complex rhythmic accompaniment:

Complex *fortissimo* polyphony until the climax; rhythm slows as music dies away at the close.

Act I: *Tonight* Ensemble

3:38

What to Listen For			
Melody	Speechlike exchanges; soaring love duet.	**Texture**	Complex and polyphonic.
Rhythm/ meter	Fast, accented, and rhythmic dialogue; ominous three-note ostinato; duple-meter love song in regular phrases, with gentle, offbeat accompaniment.	**Form**	32-bar popular-song form (8-bar sections, **A-A′-B-A″**, starting at 1:26).
		Expression	Breathless gang dialogue.
Harmony	Some unison singing; tonal but modulating.	**Performing forces**	Men's chorus as gangs; Maria (soprano) and Tony (tenor), with orchestra.

Setting: The neighborhood, 6:00–9:00 p.m. Riff and the Jets, Bernardo and the Sharks, Anita, Maria, and Tony all wait expectantly for the coming of night.

0:00   Short, rhythmic orchestral introduction featuring brass and percussion, based on a three-note ostinato:

Gangs sing in alternation.

0:07   **Riff and the Jets**
The Jets are gonna have their day tonight.

Riff and the Jets
The Puerto Ricans grumble: "Fair fight."
But if they start a rumble,
We'll rumble 'em right.

0:29   **Riff and the Jets**
We're gonna cut 'em down to size tonight.

Bernardo and the Sharks
The Sharks are gonna have their way tonight.

Bernardo and the Sharks
We're gonna hand 'em a surprise tonight.

Bernardo and the Sharks
We said, "O.K., no rumpus, no tricks."
But just in case they jump us,
We're ready to mix. Tonight!

All
0:43   We're gonna rock it tonight,
We're gonna jazz it up and have us a ball!
They're gonna get it tonight;
The more they turn it on, the harder they'll fall!

Unison chorus, more emphatic and accented; with accented brass interjections.

continued on next page

Riff and the Jets
Well, they began it!

Bernardo and the Sharks
Well, they began it!

All
And we're the ones to stop 'em once and for all,
Tonight!

Anita

1:09   Anita's gonna get her kicks tonight.
We'll have our private little mix tonight.
He'll walk in hot and tired, so what?
Don't matter if he's tired,
As long as he's hot. Tonight!

Opening melody now in uneven triplet rhythm,
sung sexily:

Tony

1:26   Tonight, tonight,
Won't be just any night,
Tonight there will be no morning star.

A section (8 bars):

Tonight, tonight,
I'll see my love tonight,
And for us, stars will stop where they are.

A′ section (8 bars); higher range, more emotional.

1:52   Today the minutes seem like hours,
The hours go so slowly,
And still the sky is light . . .
Oh moon, grow bright,
And make this endless day endless night!

B section (8 bars); strings in canon with voice.

A″ section (8 bars); reaches climax, then cuts off.

2:15

Instrumental interlude.

Riff (to Tony)
I'm counting on you to be there tonight.
When Diesel wins it fair and square tonight.
That Puerto Rican punk'll go down,
And when he's hollered "Uncle,"
We'll tear up the town!

Return to opening idea, sung more vehemently.

Ensemble finale

Maria sings *Tonight* in a high range, against simultaneous dialogue and interjections over the same syncopated dance
rhythm that accompanied Tony's solo; dramatic climax on last ensemble statement of "Tonight!"

Maria (warmly)

2:41   [A] Tonight, tonight

Won't be just any night,

Tonight there will be no morning star,

Riff: So I can count on you, boy?
Tony (abstractedly): All right.
Riff: We're gonna have us a ball.
Tony: All right.
Riff: Womb to tomb!
Tony: Sperm to worm!
Riff: I'll see you there about eight.
Tony: Tonight . . .

[**A'**] Tonight, tonight,
I'll see my love tonight,

And for us, stars will stop
Where they are.

Jets: We're gonna jazz it tonight!
Sharks: We're gonna rock it tonight!

Anita
Tonight, tonight, late tonight,
We're gonna mix it tonight.

Sharks
They're gonna get it tonight!
They began it, they began it.

Tony and Maria

3:07   [**B**] Today the minutes seem like hours,

Anita

Anita's gonna have her day,
Anita's gonna have her day,
Bernardo's gonna have his way tonight, tonight,
Tonight, this very night,
We're gonna rock it tonight.

The hours go so slowly,

Sharks   They began it . . .

And still the sky is light.

Jets

Tonight! They began it,
And we're the ones to stop 'em once and for all!
The Jets are gonna have their way,
The Jets are gonna have their day,
We're gonna rock it tonight. Tonight!

[**A''**] Oh moon, grow bright,

Sharks

They began it,
We'll stop 'em once and for all.
The Sharks are gonna have their way,
The Sharks are gonna have their day,
We're gonna rock it tonight, tonight!

And make this endless day endless night,
Tonight!

🔊 **AnotherHearing**   Now that you have heard the original cast recording from *West Side Story*, listen to a more recent recording of the *Mambo,* with added instruments, and of the *Tonight* Ensemble, in which the Puerto Rican gang—the Sharks—sing in their native Spanish. Describe how these change your perception of the dance scene and the two rival New York City gangs. Which performance do you prefer, and why?

CRITICAL THINKING

1. How did the tradition of North American musical theater change through the 1900s?
2. In what ways was *West Side Story* significant? What issues of race and ethnicity does it raise?

YourTurn TO EXPLORE

Choose a musical or multimedia work that addresses violence explicitly. What attitude do the performers project toward that violence, and what do you think they want listeners to understand about it? How does sound—rather than just the meaning of words—contribute to the performers' message about violence? Do you think that message is legitimate? What problems do you see with either its style or its substance?

67

Less Is More:
Reich and Minimalist Music

"The sounds that surrounded Americans from 1950 through 1980—jazz and rock and roll—cannot be ignored. They can be refined, filtered, rejected, or accepted in part, but they can't be ignored, or you're an ostrich: you're ill-informed."

—Steve Reich

KeyPoints

- Throughout the 1950s, the twelve-tone method gained prestige because of its perceived "scientific" nature.

- Some composers who rejected twelve-tone methods but did not find older tonal approaches satisfying developed **process music** and a style eventually called **minimalism**.

- Minimalist works rely on consonant musical elements repeated and gradually changed over extended time frames: an example is American composer Steve Reich's *Electric Counterpoint*, for multiple guitars.

Trinity (1965), by **Judy Chicago**, illustrates the clean lines and simplicity of minimalist art.

We may value a piece of music because it has a "good tune." Composers often try to come up with one, or some melodic element that will hook the listener and make their work memorable, and all of us have experienced an "earworm"—a melody that burrows into our brain and won't go away. Our idea of what makes a good tune, however, is shaped by both our cultural and our historical circumstances: Josquin, Mozart, and Billie Holiday built their hooks in drastically different ways. And musicians have sometimes attempted to redefine the possibilities of how music can grab us, as Schoenberg and Stravinsky did. This search for new hooks continues into the present, with one noteworthy approach coming from the tradition of process music and minimalism.

From Twelve-Tone to Process and Phase

The twelve-tone compositional approach of Schoenberg and his students became widespread in the 1940s and 50s: musicians valued not only the new expressive avenues it provided but also its very nature. At a time when Western society equated science with progress, the scientific rigor of serial music lent it a prestige in both European and American institutions. Some composers continued writing in tonal styles that were tuneful in pre-modernist terms, but their music was often characterized as backward-looking by those who argued for novelty.

Within modernist musical institutions, however, some became dissatisfied with serial music's implicit lack of a harmonic center, and decided to develop an approach that would treat stable harmonies in an entirely new way. The result was **process music**: a composer chooses a very simple and harmonically clear musical idea—one or two chords, or a few notes forming a consonant snippet—and repeats it over and over again, gradually changing or elaborating it. The goal was to make the musical unfolding transparent to a listener: as one of the pioneers of this method, Steve Reich, described it, "To facilitate closely detailed listening, a musical process should happen extremely gradually . . . so slowly and gradually that listening to it resembles watching the minute hand on a watch—you can perceive it moving after you stay with it a little while."

Process music

One way Reich and other experimental composers—such as Terry Riley (b. 1935) and LaMonte Young (b. 1935)—developed process music in the early 1960s was by using technology. They would record a musical idea on a loop of magnetic tape (a technology developed during the Second World War and made increasingly cost-effective through the 1950s) and play several copies of that loop simultaneously, slowly changing the tape speeds in order to combine the loops in various ways; this process was known as **phase music**. Some of Reich's early phase works were created entirely on tape, but he later experimented with having live musicians replicate the process, playing the same music and gradually speeding up or slowing down so that they would go "in and out of phase."

Phase music

Steve Reich (b. 1936)

Reich, born in New York City, was most influenced in his early musical thinking by hearing Stravinsky's *Rite of Spring* and the music of Bach as a fourteen-year-old. After playing the drums in several bands during his college years (he has also cited jazz as an essential influence), he studied modernist composition at the Juilliard School (in New York) and Mills College (in California) in the 1950s. But when one of his teachers advised him, "If you want to write tonal music, why don't you write tonal music?" he took it as a challenge to go in a new direction. Reich worked with several pioneers of process music (especially Terry Riley and Philip Glass) in San Francisco and later New York in the 1960s, holding day jobs as a taxi driver and furniture mover before his reputation eventually began to allow him to live on commissions and income from recordings and concerts.

After studying Ewe drumming in West Africa in 1970, Reich returned to the States, where he also soaked up influences from Balinese gamelan ensembles based in California, and formed Steve Reich and Musicians, the primary group that has interpreted his works. Another important cultural influence for Reich has been his Judaism: one of his prominent choral works is a setting of Hebrew psalms (*Tehillim*) that takes Jewish cantillation (chant) formulas as the inspiration for repeating and layering vocal lines. *Different Trains* (for string quartet and recorded voice) reflects on both his personal experience and that of European Jews at the time of Nazi Germany; it was awarded the Classical Music Grammy in 1990 and has been called by one critic "the only adequate musical response to the Holocaust." Reich is acknowledged by many innovative composers, including members of the rock band King Crimson, as one of the most influential musicians of the twentieth and early twenty-first centuries.

MAJOR WORKS: Tape music: *It's Gonna Rain* (1965) and *Come Out* (1966) • *Piano Phase* and *Violin Phase* (1967) • *Drumming*, for pitched and unpitched percussion (1970–71) • *Music for 18 Musicians* (1976) • *Tehillim*, for voices and ensemble (1981) • *Electric Counterpoint*, for guitars and tape (1987) • *Different Trains*, for string quartet and tape (1988) • *WTC 9/11*, for string quartet and tape (2010) • *Radio Rewrite* (reworked from two Radiohead songs, for small ensemble, 2012) • Orchestral music, including *Music for Ensemble and Orchestra* (2018).

African Influence

Reich's thinking shifted in 1970 when he encountered a musical tradition of West Africa: the percussion ensembles of the Ewe people of Togo, Benin, and Ghana. Ewe drummers had developed a performance style involving **polyrhythm**, in which each musician plays a unique rhythm pattern continuously. While each pattern starts at a different point, they all interlock under the leadership of a master player in the group. (For a parallel African tradition, see Many Voices on p. 438.)

Polyrhythm

After a month of listening and playing with drummers in Ghana, Reich was struck by the similarities between the Ewe style and his ideas about phase and process music. On his return to the United States, he was eager to incorporate what he had learned in West Africa, but in his own way:

> The least interesting form of influence, to my mind, is that of imitating the sound of some non-Western music. . . . Alternately, one can create a music with one's own sound that is constructed in light of one's knowledge of non-Western structures. . . . One can study the rhythmic structure of non-Western music and let that study lead one where it will while continuing to use the instruments, scales and any other sound one has grown up with. This brings about the interesting situation of the non-Western influence being there in thinking, but not in sound.
>
> This is a more genuine and interesting form of influence . . . the influence of non-Western musical structures on the thinking of a Western composer is likely to produce something genuinely new.

In Their Own Words

" It became clear to me after Ghana that I was going to use my own instruments, not theirs. . . . What one learns from African (or Balinese) music is how it's put together, how to organize sound."

—*Steve Reich*

The structural complexities in Ewe music also led Reich to think about process music differently, eventually concluding that "as the texture gets more filled up, as it gets richer, it becomes less possible and less necessary to follow the process." This more developed process-influenced style has come to be called **minimalism**.

Minimalism

Electric Counterpoint

One of Reich's new directions took him to a series of works he called "counterpoint." The last of these, *Electric Counterpoint* (1987) for twelve guitars, is the most nuanced and complex (LG 61). The work is traditionally performed by one live guitarist playing along with up to fourteen tracks he or she has prerecorded—this is how Pat Metheny, the renowned jazz guitarist for whom Reich wrote *Electric Counterpoint*, premiered the work—but it can also be played by an ensemble of live guitarists. The work is in three movements (labeled "fast"–"slow"–"fast" and thus harking back to the overall structure of the Baroque concerto), of which we will consider the third. In the repetitive nature of the initial musical idea, we can hear process elements of Reich's earlier style—the device of canon, another Baroque feature. Ambiguity and complexity are introduced by the layering of instruments in different ranges, and by small shifts in the musical patterns; eventually the ambiguity is resolved as the instrumental layers peel off.

Guitarist Pat Metheny working in a recording studio (2012).

Electric Counterpoint reveals a very different treatment of harmony from the goal-oriented tonality of the pre-modernist period. On the other hand, the consonant nature of the work distinguishes it from the modernist goal of emancipating dissonance. This is why process/phase works have sometimes been seen as the beginning of a postmodern trend, though again, the definition of postmodernism in music is elusive. The hook of music like *Electric Counterpoint* depends less on the initial musical idea, which is not especially memorable, and more on the way that idea is gradually combined with itself to reveal its layered possibilities—the essence of counterpoint since the beginning of the Western polyphonic tradition.

Reich: *Electric Counterpoint*, III

Date: 1987

Genre: Chamber work for guitars and tape

Performed by: Pat Metheny, guitar

What to Listen For

Melody	Short melodic ideas repeated as an ostinato.
Rhythm/ meter	3/2 meter; 12 "pulse-units" also presented as 6/4 and 12/8; regular rhythms with varying patterns and accents in syncopation.
Harmony	Diatonic, mostly static with some subtle shifts; predominant chords are C major, B minor, E minor.

Texture	Highly polyphonic, with canons.
Form	Through-composed.
Expression	An almost trancelike effect from the gradual addition and combination of regular patterns; striking moments created by subtle changes.
Performing forces	Live guitarist playing with 12 prerecorded tracks (2 bass guitars and 10 guitars).

0:00   Five guitars enter in turn with repetitions of the same short musical idea in canon.

0:43   Bass guitars play a shortened musical pattern that gradually builds to a complete melody at 0:58; it then repeats this melody.

1:06   Three-chord strumming pattern begins in one guitar track, slowly building to a three-track canon.

2:17   Harmony in the strumming tracks changes, then changes back and forth regularly between the original and new strumming harmony.

3:20   Bass guitar patterns and strumming tracks gradually fade out; the original pattern moves higher and higher in pitch until it suddenly stops at 4:21.

Example of changing meter:

CRITICAL THINKING

1. What are some of the main characteristics of process and phase music, and how did it differ from the twelve-tone tradition it rejected?

2. How did non-Western music influence Reich's minimalist style?

YourTurn TO EXPLORE

Find examples of polyrhythm in different musical traditions, such as those in sub-Saharan Africa (Ewe drumming, the "thumb piano" called mbira), those connected to the diaspora of African people throughout the world (Afro-Cuban music, jazz), Carnatic music of southern India, gamelan music of Indonesia. How are the rhythmic patterns similar to and different from the rhythms we have studied so far? What do you find distinctive about the melody, and how does it connect to the layered rhythms? What parallels can you find between the polyrhythmic tradition you are exploring and *Electric Counterpoint*?

East African Drumming

Since the era of late nineteenth-century European colonization known as the New Imperialism—and the 1889 Paris World Exhibition, where musicians and nonmusicians alike first experienced music and dance from cultures across the globe—an aura of mystery has surrounded the little-known regions of sub-Saharan Africa. Although French composers like Camille Saint-Saëns and Maurice Ravel were charmed by the music of Arab northern Africa, music of the sub-Saharan colonies was viewed as "primitive" for its lack of melodic and harmonic content. This "primitivism" soon took hold in the arts world, however, influencing early twentieth-century artists and musicians toward non-Western ideals of abstraction—among them painter Henri Rousseau, who was attracted to exotic cultures (p. 346), and Igor Stravinsky, whose *Rite of Spring* drew on pagan themes to reach new heights of rhythmic complexity (Chapter 56).

From the early twentieth century, composers have continued to look beyond Western musical ideas and constructs; some, like John Cage and Steve Reich, introduced Asian and African elements in their own works. Reich claims that when he first saw notated music from Ghana, in West Africa, he realized it was composed of repeating patterns that were superimposed on each other. "That was a real eye-opener," he said. "I thought it would be best if I went there and played it

myself." These patterns became part of Reich's phase technique. Upon his return from Ghana, he wrote *Drumming,* a large-scale percussion ensemble work for tuned bongos, marimba, and glockenspiel as well as voice; the use of all-tuned instruments lends interest not only to the dense polyrhythms but also to the short, repeated melodic patterns.

We will investigate here the music of another African nation: Uganda, a land-locked country in East Africa, bordering Kenya and Lake Victoria. The Ugandan people—representing many different cultures—have felt influences from the Arab world, from Indonesia, and also from their British colonizers. The modern Republic of Uganda was formerly subdivided into a number of powerful kingdoms, each with its own court and ruler. We will

hear music from one of these courts, performed by a royal drum (entenga) ensemble of six musicians playing fifteen drums. Four musicians play on twelve melody drums that are graduated in size and tuned to the pitches of a pentatonic scale, while the other two accompany on three unpitched drums (see chart opposite; note that they are sharing drums). The melody drums, called drum chimes, are conical in shape with cowhide skins laced tightly over both ends; their folk-song melodies are played with long, curved beaters.

Our example, *Ensiriba ya munange Katego,* tells the story of a sub-chief named Kangawo, who wears a leopard-skin headband for good luck. One night his precious headband disappears, and he feels so unprotected without his charm that he falls ill and

Members of the royal entenga drum chime ensemble of Uganda.

A pair of tuned drums, or drum chimes (c. 1910), from Uganda.

dies. In the performance, the players of the melody drums enter one after another, first striking the sides of their drums. One plays a melody pattern, which is then doubled an octave lower by another player. Then the other melody players enter in turn, playing new patterns. Once the melodic ideas are established, the large bass drums enter, punctuating the complex, polyrhythmic fabric with strong strokes. When the players move their sticks to the middle of the drumhead, the volume increases and the individual melodies can be heard more clearly. Although the royal entenga group disbanded in the 1960s, there is now an effort to revive the music

and the performance tradition, led by one of the last living members of the ensemble. This music is transmitted by oral tradition: an apprentice musician learns the repertory and technique by sitting beside an accomplished drummer, and so maintaining a vestige of Uganda's rich cultural past.

Ensiriba ya munange Katego

What to listen for:
- Pentatonic, gapped melodies in interlocking patterns.
- Developing complex polyrhythmic structures, with interlocking rhythmic patterns.

Players begin to establish rhythmic patterns by striking the sides of their drums, making a clicking sound.

The drum-chime players move one at a time to the drumheads, introducing several melodic ideas; the lower-pitched drum player moves to the drumhead, adding depth of sound.

The texture thins as lower-pitched drums drop out; one melodic pattern is heard above the others.

One drummer moves his sticks to the side of the drum (clicking), as the tempo slows to the end.

68

Rolling Beethoven Over: Roots and Reworkings of Rock

"You know my temperature's risin', / The juke box's blowin' a fuse, My heart's beatin' rhythm, / My soul keeps singin' the blues— Roll over, Beethoven, / Tell Tchaikovsky the news."

—*Chuck Berry*

KeyPoints

- The rise of **rock and roll** in the 1950s is one of the most significant phenomena in twentieth-century music.

- Rock had its origins in **rhythm and blues**, country-western, pop, and gospel; early rock crossed racial lines, featuring white and Black performers.

- Chuck Berry was one of the most significant contributors to the development of early rock and roll; one of his iconic songs is *Roll Over Beethoven*.

- Early rock-and-roll songs have been reinterpreted (in a **cover**) by many performers in the ensuing decades, demonstrating the flexibility and dynamic nature of the tradition.

Our historical survey has focused on music that has been considered in some way extraordinary and has therefore had a lasting cultural effect over time. As we draw closer to the present day, the explosion of musical traditions (and the rise in mass-market distribution) makes it more difficult to do justice to the variety of music that has been significant to the last few generations. We have chosen to focus this chapter on rock because of its prominence in the sphere of commercial music, touching briefly on its intersections with some other American traditions—each of which would deserve chapters (indeed books) of their own. And we dwell on a song that explicitly reflects on the overlap between commercial and art music—a song that embodied rock before the tradition had that name and has continued to reflect rock's changing landscape.

The Many Voices of Rock

The rise of **rock and roll** (and its offspring **rock**) is the most important music phenomenon of the second half of the twentieth century. Economically, rock has been the driving force behind a multibillion-dollar music industry; socially, it has had a far-reaching impact on fashion, language, politics, and religion; musically, it has influenced virtually every other style—classical, jazz, country-western, rap, Tejano, and contemporary global pop are just a few examples. Examining rock's development in the last half century can help us see how music adapts both to a mass market and to the cultural priorities of each new generation.

Rhythm and Blues

Rock and roll, which first emerged in the 1950s, was born of a union of African American rhythm and blues with country-western. **Rhythm and blues** (R&B), a genre of dance music with roots in swing jazz as well as blues singing, was popular from the late 1940s through the early 60s, and evolved into the R&B tradition that continues strong today. It is a predominantly vocal genre—solo singer accompanied by a small group often including piano, guitar (acoustic or electric), acoustic bass, drums, and tenor saxophone—with harmonies and structure drawn from the twelve-bar blues and thirty-two-bar pop song forms (Chapter 59). As the name implies, the style is characterized by a strong, driving rhythm, usually in a quadruple meter, with an emphasis on the second and fourth beats of the measure, or the **backbeat**. Almost all the great early rhythm-and-blues performers—Louis Jordan, Ruth Brown, Bo Diddley, and Big Joe Turner among them—were African Americans.

In the mid-1950s, the term "rock and roll" was coined to describe a form of rhythm and blues that crossed racial lines, incorporating elements of rural Anglo-American music. White singers like Bill Haley (*Rock Around the Clock*, with the Comets, 1954), Elvis Presley (*Heartbreak Hotel* and *Hound Dog*, both 1956), and Jerry Lee Lewis (*Great Balls of Fire*, 1957) combined "hillbilly" country music with the sounds of rhythm and blues. This style, sometimes known as **rockabilly**, featured twelve-bar blues progressions and "boogie" rhythms (in triplet patterns) while incorporating singing and guitar-picking techniques common in country music. At the same time, African Americans like Chuck Berry (*Maybelline*, 1955), Fats Domino (*Blueberry Hill*, 1956), and Little Richard (*Tutti Frutti*, 1955–56) caught the attention of a white audience.

Two rock-and-roll icons: Chuck Berry (top) and Elvis Presley (bottom).

Chuck Berry and *Roll Over Beethoven*

Charles Edward Anderson ("Chuck") Berry (1926–2017) had been playing blues guitar and singing to supplement his beautician's income in Saint Louis, Missouri, for some years when he started experimenting with blending styles in the early 1950s. Berry imitated the smooth vocal quality of big-band jazz singer Nat King Cole when playing blues songs, and also mixed African American blues with Anglo-American country songs in his performance sets. One of the major recording producers of the time, Leonard Chess of Chess Records, fostered this mixed country-blues style to great success. Berry's first hit, *Maybelline*, sold more than a million copies and rose to prominence not only on the R&B chart that tracked primarily sales to African American audiences (where it hit #1), but also on the broader-market "Best Sellers in Stores" chart, which meant that it was becoming a big hit with white audiences as well.

Berry's second major hit (1956) was a song about music—specifically about how the new style (which Berry still called rhythm and blues but which many of his fans called rock and roll) was about to displace older ones. Berry said that *Roll Over Beethoven* was written in part as a complaint to his sister, who played classical music on the family piano when he wanted to play popular hits instead. The song advises Beethoven to "roll over" (presumably in his grave) "and tell Tchaikovsky the news" (presumably that there's a new style threatening their popularity); the rest of the lyrics are a joyful celebration of the new "rockin' rhythm record" music that makes the singer's girl "dance like a spinnin' top."

In Berry's original release (on Chess Records, #1626; you can find it on Spotify, YouTube, and elsewhere), *Roll Over Beethoven* is in strophic, twelve-bar-blues form (the same formal and harmonic pattern as *Billie's Blues*, p. 376), though the text isn't structured **A-A-B** within each verse. Like Holiday's song, *Roll Over Beethoven* has both vocal and instrumental verses, nine choruses of the blues form in all: an opening instrumental twelve-bar section that starts with a short motive (**riff**) by Berry on electric guitar; four vocal verses, each with different text; another twelve-bar instrumental section in which Berry is the featured improviser; and three more vocal verses, the last of which consists mostly of repetitions of the title phrase.

In Their Own Words

❝ It used to be called boogie-woogie, it used to be called blues, it used to be called rhythm and blues . . . it's called rock now."

—*Chuck Berry*

Like many of the songs that helped early rock and roll dominate the charts, this one is a celebration of movement and dancing and rebellion; and when *Rolling Stone* magazine placed it on its list of "500 Greatest Songs of All Time" in 2004, they characterized it as "the ultimate rock & roll call to arms, declaring a new era."

As American teenagers came together across racial and ethnic communities to dance and celebrate the new dynamic soundscapes of rock and roll, musicians and marketers alike scrambled to meet the demand and reap the economic rewards. New markets were quickly formed by recording companies eager for sales and broadcasters hungry for advertising revenue. From the early 1960s onward, there arose many subtypes and spin-offs of rock; doing justice to them would require a separate book.

Rolling Past Berry

Musicians have adapted favorite compositions since the earliest notated traditions in the West. We have encountered a jazz rendition of a Purcell opera aria (p. 139), and virtuoso nineteenth-century performers such as Liszt built their fan base through stunning elaborations of melodies by earlier composers. In particular, since its first boom with Stephen Foster and his generation of songwriters in the 1800s, the commercial music tradition has relied on multiple performers conveying their individual versions of hit tunes—sometimes "authorized," sometimes **Cover**   not. Jazz drew its lifeblood from this practice, known as **covering** a song. Covers were also essential to the spread of early rock and roll, sometimes in controversial ways: for example, while Elvis Presley's cover of *Hound Dog* made him and the song famous, the co-creator of the song, Willie Mae "Big Mama" Thornton, was long ignored and drew little financial benefit from her original recording.

One of the most prominent groups that covered *Roll Over Beethoven* was the Beatles, who sought to establish their rock-and-roll legitimacy by performing Berry's songs in Britain before they took America by storm in 1964. The Beatles' version is structurally identical to Berry's (same number and order of verses, same placement of instrumental sections, same featured electric guitar), yet its sound-scape is more polished, moving away from gritty blues singing toward the post-production studio sound that characterized rock in the 1960s and 70s.

The chart below compares Berry's original song with two especially creative covers. An early cover by Carl Perkins (from 1957; on Spotify and elsewhere) demonstrates the differences between the "rockabilly" style (which incorporated country-western and bluegrass elements into rhythm and blues) and Berry's pioneering rock and roll. Perkins slows down the tempo, shortens the instrumental intro to six bars, and makes a characteristic rockabilly instrument—the honky-tonk piano—prominent in the texture, reinforced by the swinging rhythms that shaped R&B's distinctive sound. He switches Berry's first two verses, then immediately arrives at the repetitions of "Roll over Beethoven" that Berry had left for last. Perkins's recording leaves out several verses from the original text, emphasizing instrumental elaboration and repetitions of the title phrase.

The most inventive cover of the song is probably the one the British band Electric Light Orchestra (ELO) recorded in 1973 (for their album *Electric Light Orchestra II*, also on Spotify), which beautifully exemplifies the expansion of rock and roll into the elaborate "art rock" or "album rock" style of the 1970s. This version begins with a series of quiet chords played by the synthesizer, followed by the

Three Versions of Roll Over Beethoven

Label	Artists	Timing / form	Style / distinctive features
Chess, 1956	Chuck Berry, vocal and electric guitar; unnamed performers on drums, bass guitar, piano.	2:23 12-bar intro followed by nine strophic verses in 12-bar blues form (fifth verse is instrumental).	Rough, grainy-bluesy vocals by Berry; distinctive early electric-guitar sound in the signature opening riff. Bass guitar, drums, and piano provide a steady rhythmic background characteristic of R&B. Guitar is prominent at beginning and during instrumental verse but otherwise secondary to the voice.
Sun, 1957	Carl Perkins, vocal and electric guitar; James Wilson, piano; Clayton Perkins, bass guitar; W. S. Holland, drums.	2:51 6-bar intro followed by nine verses in 12-bar blues form (in a different verse order from Berry's): two verses are instrumental, two sets of verses are repeated.	Nasal, "twangy" vocals by Perkins, in a slower pace than Berry's; swinging rhythms and prominent honky-tonk piano (common in rockabilly). Instrumental elaboration and dialogue between guitar, piano, and voice.
Harvest, 1973	Jeff Lynne (lead vocal, electric guitar) and Richard Tandy (backup vocals, keyboards) leading the seven-member Electric Light Orchestra; instruments include violins, cellos, electric guitars and bass, drums, synthesizer.	8:09 Synthesizer intro leads to Beethoven motive in the strings and then to 12-bar blues form; verses start in same order as Berry version, but then blues form breaks down into free "conversation" between strings (Beethoven), guitar/bass/drums (Berry verses), and synthesizer.	Dense and elaborate "art rock/album rock" textures bring together Berry's guitar style, elements of honkytonk, string timbres associated with Beethoven's symphony, and synthesized sounds.

The Electric Light Orchestra performing in 1978.

memorable short-short-short-long motive from Beethoven's Fifth Symphony (played by a violin and two cellos). This leads directly into the guitar riff from the opening of Berry's recording. While ELO keep Berry's order for the first two verses, they add a honky-tonk piano (perhaps paying tribute to Perkins?), skip the third verse, and then break entirely from the blues progression with a dramatic set of synthesizer chords that move down scalewise. Again we hear a snippet of Beethoven's music, this time the horn call from the development section of the first movement (p. 215). The recording continues to combine Beethoven's musical ideas (mostly in the strings and synthesizer) with Berry's stanzas (voice, guitar, bass, drums), as if the two styles were in dialogue. If you listen to this version, notice who "wins" in the end.

ELO was one of the groups most dedicated to drawing out the potential complexities in rock in the 1970s. Their cover seems to redirect the rejection of classical music inherent in Berry's song into a statement about the opportunities for combining contrasting traditions. This is one of the most dynamic and inventive aspects of covers in rock (as well as jazz, blues, and country) music: songs can be reclaimed to meet the changing needs of artists and their audiences.

CRITICAL THINKING

1. From which diverse musical styles did rock originate?
2. How did Chuck Berry provide a significant contribution to the emergent rock-and-roll style?
3. What kinds of changes can we see in the rock tradition by listening for differences between cover songs?

YourTurn TO EXPLORE

Find another song from the early rock-and-roll years that has been covered repeatedly (you might look for *Don't Be Cruel* or *Heartbreak Hotel* by Elvis Presley, *Yesterday* or *Eleanor Rigby* by the Beatles—available on Spotify or YouTube), and compare at least two or three covers with the original song. What have the covering performers changed, and what have they kept? Can you find out something about the group and their fan base that might help explain why they made those changes? Which version or versions do you find most compelling, and why?

69

Returning with Interest: Bowie, Glass, and Postmodern Elaboration

"You never knew with David [Bowie]. He was a master unto himself."

—Philip Glass

KeyPoints

- Musicians often pay homage to earlier composers or elaborate on their ideas.
- David Bowie was one of the most inventive singer-composers of the late twentieth and early twenty-first centuries, working in a variety of rock and pop

styles and experimenting with collaborators from several traditions.

- Philip Glass, a prominent contemporary composer, drew from one of Bowie's most influential albums in crafting his Fourth Symphony, subtitled *Heroes*.

The ability to control creative content is both artistically and financially crucial to an artist's success. Laws concerning copyright and the unauthorized use of other artists' materials have become increasingly strict in the last century. It was not always so: in earlier times, using material by another musician in one's work was considered a tribute to a skilled predecessor. This was true especially if, in the words of a contemporary of J. S. Bach, you "returned with interest": that is, if the material was integrated so that it presented a new creative perspective. Contemporary musicians often borrow each other's ideas, and the boundaries between art and commercial music have repeatedly been crossed in search of inspiration. We will consider one remarkable example that links two of the most successful performer-composers of the last few decades, David Bowie and Philip Glass.

David Bowie (1947–2016) singing at a Toronto nightclub, March 1987.

David Bowie, Creative Chameleon

From his start as a folk-rocker in the late 1960s to his astounding jazz–rock–hip-hop fusion album *Blackstar* released shortly before his death in January 2016, Bowie reinvented his artistic persona and musical style multiple times. One of the most significant shifts resulted from contact in the mid-1970s with minimalist musicians (see Chapter 67) in New York City—part of a broader phenomenon often described as "Downtown music," which experimented with commercial styles as well as music from around the world.

445

In Their Own Words

" Soon after its composition [David Bowie] began using the *Heroes* symphony for his walk-in music for some of his concerts. . . . there's a version [in his archive] in which he superimposed his voice singing *Heroes* on to the symphonic recording. . . . It would be amazing to find it."

—*Philip Glass*

Bowie collaborated with renowned sound producer Brian Eno on a series of groundbreaking albums (*Low* and *Heroes*, 1977; *Lodger*, 1979). The second of these albums, *Heroes*, reveals that Bowie was influenced not only by Eno's ideas of electronic "ambient" music (with a static soundscape rather than clear melodies or form) but also by the works of such minimalist composers as Steve Reich (Chapter 67) and John Adams (Chapter 73). *Heroes* was a great success both critically and financially; and the title song, one of Bowie's signature tunes, was taken up by many other artists over the years (including Prince, who sang it as a tribute to Bowie in one of his own last concerts).

Heroes: from Album to "Symphonic Ballet"

One of the musicians who found the Bowie/Eno experiments particularly expressive was Philip Glass, a leader of the "Downtown NYC" creative group and leading exponent of minimalist composition. Building on the phase experiments of Reich and others, Glass developed a consonant, repetition-based style that appealed to a wide audience in the 1980s and 90s and made him perhaps the most commercially successful composer of art music in the United States today.

Glass and Bowie had met and become good friends in the 1970s, and when it came to writing his first symphony, Glass turned to the music of Bowie and Eno for ideas. The resulting work (1992) subtly incorporated large sections of musical material from the entire *Low* album. In his fourth symphony, subtitled *Heroes*, Glass focused more on small borrowings from Bowie/Eno, and expanded the

Philip Glass (b. 1937)

Although Glass is often associated with the minimalist movement, he rejects that term, preferring to call himself a composer of "music with repetitive structures" and even a "classicist" because of his close study of composers such as Bach, Mozart, and Schubert. Glass studied flute as a young man, and then piano and composition at the Juilliard School of Music in New York in the early 1960s, where Steve Reich was a fellow student. Shortly after graduating, he studied with Nadia Boulanger in Paris (1964–66). There he was strongly influenced by new-wave cinema and, through collaborating with Indian musicians Ravi Shankar and Alla Rakha on a film score, Indian additive rhythms (see p. 201). Returning to New York at the end of the 1960s, he encountered the phase music of Steve Reich and joined with that composer and others in creating an experimental tradition of "radical consonant" music in downtown New York City.

In 1971, the composer founded the Philip Glass Ensemble, with which he still performs on electronic keyboard instruments. The first of the three operas in his "Portrait Trilogy," *Einstein on the Beach*, premiered in both France and the United States in 1976, to enthusiastic response; the *Washington Post* called it "one of the seminal artworks of the century." Many commissions followed for both multimedia and instrumental works, making Glass one of the best-known composers of modern times. He has become renowned for his collaborations with artists in many media (from theater to film, visual art, and sound) and many traditions (non-Western, commercial-rock, jazz, concert music).

MAJOR WORKS: Operas, including *Einstein on the Beach* (1976), *Satyagraha* (1979), *Akhenaten* (1983), *The Perfect American* (on a book about Walt Disney, 2012), *Circus Days and Nights* (2021) • A song cycle, *Songs from Liquid Days* (1986) on texts by songwriters such as David Byrne and Paul Simon • Film scores, including *Koyaanisqatsi*, *Powaqqatsi*, *Naqoyqatsi* • Much chamber music, several concertos and 12 symphonies (1992–2019), 3 based on Bowie albums: No. 1 on *Low*; No. 4 on *Heroes*; No. 12, on lyrics of *Lodger*.

collaboration further to include modern dancer and choreographer Twyla Tharpe (b. 1941). In the composer's own words, "I set *Heroes* as a six-movement work, each movement based on a theme from [the album] *Heroes*, with an overall dramatic structure that would be suitable for dance. The result is a symphonic ballet—a transformation of the original themes combined with new material of my own and presented in a new dramatic form."

While Glass's *Heroes* was indeed premiered to choreography by Tharpe, it has since been performed and recorded as a six-movement symphony. Each movement takes as a starting point one of the songs or instrumental tracks from the album: we will hear the first (LG 62), which is based on the title track of Bowie's album. For those who have heard this song, there are a few clearly recognizable musical elements in Glass's movement—for example, the alternation of two chords a third apart, a motive with two adjacent repeating notes, and a distinct rhythmic pattern from the song's refrain. The final effect, however, entirely reflects Glass's own musical voice: musical ideas are repeated in both short and longer units, with much interplay between contrasting orchestral timbres.

The Philip Glass Ensemble performing in the Netherlands for the Lowlands Festival (2016).

Responding to Glass's symphony, Bowie said:

> Hearing this material is a bit like being introduced to a brother or sister that you've been told you had, and you weren't really aware of their existence. And when you do meet them, obviously the very familiarity of the family features registers, but there's a whole life and all these things have grown up without your knowledge. . . . It was as though Philip had fed into my voice . . . but somehow had arrived, I feel, a lot nearer to the gut feeling of what I was trying to do.

Though not all musical "returning with interest" may be as well received and amicable as the *Heroes* collaboration between Bowie and Glass (and Tharpe), there are abundant examples of successful crossover between traditions and media in contemporary music. Musical culture has been and continues to be dynamic as we move further into the twenty-first century; no matter how traditions and genres evolve, there will always be musicians prepared to push their boundaries, joining forces to challenge and delight audiences around the world.

CRITICAL THINKING

1. How was Bowie's interaction with other musicians crucial to his success in *Heroes*? What new collaborative aspects did Glass introduce?
2. In what ways is Glass's approach to minimalist composition similar to Reich's in *Electric Counterpoint*, and in what ways is it different?

Your Turn TO EXPLORE

Find a musical work that borrows significantly from earlier models, whether through digital sampling or reuse of melody, harmony, lyrics, and so on. Are there repertories or styles that rely more on borrowing than others? Why do you think the musicians have chosen to use specific ideas? What new elements are added to the borrowed material, and for what expressive goals? Do you think the result successfully "returns with interest"?

Glass: Symphony No. 4 (*Heroes*), I

Date: 1996

Genre: "Symphonic ballet" in six movements

    1. Heroes　　　　　　　　4. Sons of the Silent Age
    2. Abdulmajid　　　　　　　5. Neuköln
    3. Sense of Doubt　　　　　　6. V2 Schneider

Performed by: Bournemouth Symphony, Marin Alsop, conductor

1: Heroes

What to Listen For

Melody	Short motives repeated and combined.
Rhythm/ meter	Moderate quadruple meter, regular use of syncopation, triplets, four-note arpeggios.
Harmony	E-flat major; some passages introduce chromaticism.
Texture	Increasingly layered polyphony, with homophony at the opening and close.
Form	A motive is varied through layering and repetition, with a contrasting opening and close.
Expression	Musical ideas develop slowly through extended repetition and layering; they reflect on motives of the song's melody.
Performing forces	Orchestra, with an expanded percussion section.

0:00　Clarinets, bassoons, and horns softly introduce a two-note motive, punctuated by pizzicato strings and brass:

0:33　Change of timbre and mood as flutes and oboes enter; melodic, with syncopated rhythms in horns and strings, glockenspiel on the second beat.

0:48　Winds in octaves present a descending-third motive from the opening of the song:

    Motive is inverted, expanded, and repeated; a syncopated accompaniment continues with cross-rhythms between brass and strings:

1:34　Flutes, oboes, and brass play triplets; strings continue with syncopation; the song motive shifts to the brass.

2:37　The brass now take on syncopation, triplets shift to the strings; a new scalewise melody in the winds, first descending stepwise then gradually rising in waves:

3:54　The song motive returns again in the brass as the descending/ascending melody continues in winds; strings now shift to repeated sixteenth-note arpeggios.

4:40　Repeat of previous section.

5:26　Repeat of previous section.

6:23　Modified return of the opening two-note motive and clarinet-bassoon-horn timbre, punctuated by arpeggios in flutes and harp.

70

Neo-Romantic Evocations: Higdon and Program Music into the Twenty-First Century

"Music written now reflects now. . . . People are into variety . . . even in their concert experiences. . . . Many folks want a mix of musics. And many young composers are picking up on this."

—Jennifer Higdon

KeyPoints

- Some recent compositional trends speak to audiences alienated by highly intellectual modernist music.
- **Neo-Romanticism** favors the lush harmonic language of the late Romantic era: the music is mostly tonal, chromatic, and highly virtuosic, with innovative timbral combinations.
- Neo-Romantic works often feature programmatic elements connected with a personal story, as in Jennifer Higdon's tone poem *blue cathedral*.

One trend in recent concert music, labeled neo-Romanticism, is represented by composers who embrace aspects of nineteenth-century orchestral sound. Among those aspects is program music, which as we saw in earlier chapters was very important to Romantic composers, from both a personal and a nationalist perspective. This importance has endured to the present, as musicians continue to draw on their biographical and cultural experiences as sources for expression. The example we will examine, by Jennifer Higdon, aims to modernize the nineteenth-century orchestral tradition. It also shows an influence of non-Western cultures that has lasted beyond John Cage, and that reflects the never-ending search for new ways to expand and renew the tradition of concert music for the twenty-first century.

A New Romanticism?

We have traced several different approaches to making music new in the early twentieth century—and indeed, the multiple facets of modernism were very important to artists and their audiences. But the style that had developed in the 1800s never really went away; great works by renowned composers such as Beethoven, Brahms, Verdi, and Wagner were performed in concert halls and opera houses even

In Their Own Words

❝ Can music reflect colors and can colors be reflected in music? . . . I often picture colors as if I were spreading them on a canvas, except I do so with melodies and harmonies, and through the peculiar sounds of the instruments themselves."

—*Jennifer Higdon*

as the modernists were proposing new alternatives. Some early twentieth-century composers continued to update the Romantic style, building on the luxuriant orchestral tradition as well as the chamber genres that had been constantly evolving since the generation of Haydn and Mozart. One of the most prominent exponents of this continued commitment to Romantic ideals was American composer Samuel Barber (1910–1981), whose elegiac and well-loved *Adagio for Strings* (1936) is suffused with the feeling and grand gestures of the nineteenth century, and whose songs continue the multinational tradition of setting intense poetry to sweeping and beautiful melodies.

The music of Barber and others who upheld key elements of Romanticism was dismissed as regressive and antiquated by those who considered modernism the only legitimate artistic pathway into the twentieth century. The advent of postmodern styles, however, induced composers to look again to the past for inspiration—sometimes with an ironic or detached perspective (often the case with quotation music; recall Bartók's use of Shostakovich's tune in the *Concerto for Orchestra*), but sometimes with respect and perhaps even a touch of nostalgia for the expressive power of the Romantic style. In the last quarter of the twentieth century and into the twenty-first, orchestral repertories have been revitalized by this reclaiming of nineteenth-century harmonic and melodic language in a new context, one that takes into account the complexities of a postmodern world—an approach commonly known as **neo-Romanticism**.

Jennifer Higdon and *blue cathedral*

Hailed by one critic as a "savvy, sensitive composer . . . with a generous dash of spirit," Jennifer Higdon is one of the most widely performed of living American composers. Her music is richly neo-Romantic, displaying an innovative sound palette that has been described as "very American." We will consider her orchestral

Jennifer Higdon (b. 1962)

Born in Brooklyn, New York, Higdon pursued music studies at Bowling Green State University and then completed graduate degrees in composition at the University of Pennsylvania, where she studied with George Crumb (see Chapter 65). She claims that "the sheer number of Beatles tunes I listened to helped me to realize the ability of music to communicate." Higdon has been recognized with prestigious awards: she received the Pulitzer Prize in 2010 for her Violin Concerto and two Grammys in 2018, including one for her Violin Concerto. Since 1994, she has taught composition at the Curtis Institute of Music in Philadelphia.

Higdon's extensive output spans most genres, including orchestral music and compositions for her own instrument, the flute. Her "American" sound harks back to that of Aaron Copland, on which she imposes her own highly colorful timbral palette as well as dense textures and wide-ranging dynamics. Some works, like *blue cathedral*, exude a rich lyricism and shimmering beauty, while others, like *Fanfare Ritmico* and the Percussion Concerto, are more propulsive. Her rooting in tonality as well as the familiar quality in her music help mark her as a neo-Romantic.

MAJOR WORKS: Orchestral music, including *Fanfare Ritmico* (2000), *blue cathedral* (2000), *Concerto for Orchestra* (2002) • Concertos for oboe (2005), percussion (2007), violin (2008), low brass (2017), tuba (2017), and viola (2018) • Works for wind groups, including soprano saxophone concerto (with wind ensemble, 2009) • Chamber music, including *Amazing Grace* (for string quartet, 2002) • Choral works, including *Southern Grace* (1998) • Vocal works, including *Dooryard Bloom* (for baritone and orchestra, 2004) • Operas, including *Cold Mountain* (2015, based on novel by Charles Frazier).

work *blue cathedral* (LG 63), which is already garnering status as a classic.

Written in 2000 to commemorate the 75th anniversary of the Curtis Institute of Music in Philadelphia, *blue cathedral* is an orchestral tone poem with a subtext of personal grief over the untimely death from skin cancer of the composer's younger brother, Andrew Blue Higdon. The composer explains that she was contemplating the remarkable journey of life. The title incorporates her brother's name, and she also provides evocative imagery to help us understand the broader goals of her composition:

> Blue . . . like the sky. Where all possibilities soar. Cathedrals . . . a place of thought, growth, spiritual expression . . . serving as a symbolic doorway into and out of this world. I found myself imagining a journey through a glass cathedral in the sky. . . . The listener would float down the aisle, moving slowly at first and then progressing at a quicker pace, rising toward an immense ceiling which would open to the sky. . . . I wanted to create the sensation of contemplation and quiet peace at the beginning, moving toward the feeling of celebration and ecstatic expansion of the soul, all the while singing along with that heavenly music.

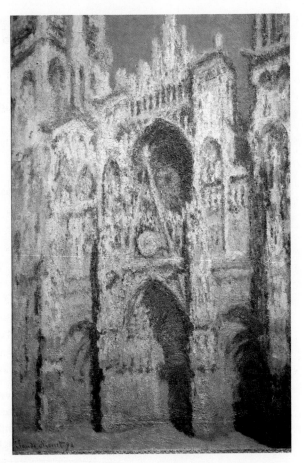

Higdon's *blue cathedral* evokes colorful Impressionist images like *Cathedral of Rouen: Full Sunlight, Blue Harmony and Gold* (1894), by **Claude Monet**.

The tone poem opens to shimmering, bell-like timbres (known as tintinnabulation) sounded over softly muted strings. An intimate dialogue ensues between an ethereal solo flute (the composer's instrument) and solo clarinet (her brother's instrument). Throughout, there is a sense of continual expansion and ascent as the work builds toward several stirring climaxes. The open string sonority is "very American" in its evocation of Aaron Copland's characteristic orchestral sound, while plaintive solos are heard from darker instruments, like the English horn, viola, and cello (Higdon notes that she is "hyper-aware of color"). Near the end, more soothing colors appear, in the guise of pitched crystal glasses (a finger is run around the rims) and the chiming of some fifty Chinese reflex balls, played by most of the orchestra's musicians—a borrowing from Asian soundscapes. *blue cathedral* closes in the same contemplative mood as at the beginning.

In her use of characteristic tone colors and biographical elements, Higdon maintains the tradition of program music that spurred nineteenth-century composers to such imaginative heights. Her approach, popular with modern audiences, has helped to keep the tradition of concert music vital and relevant to our day. This composition stands today as Higdon's most performed work.

Two Chinese reflex balls, like those used in the performance of *blue cathedral*.

CRITICAL THINKING

1. What are the qualities that make a musical work neo-Romantic?
2. How does Higdon evoke non-Western timbres in *blue cathedral*?

LISTENING GUIDE 63   12:19

Higdon: *blue cathedral*

Date: 2000

Genre: Orchestral tone poem

Performed by: Atlantic Symphony,
Robert Spano, conductor

What to Listen For

Melody	Languorous, lyrical lines; ascending ideas.
Rhythm/ meter	Mostly in 5/4 with a veiled sense of bar lines; some shifting meters.
Harmony	Prominent use of major triads but with no strong sense of key center.
Texture	Homophonic, focuses on individual lines and duets.
Form	Sectional, with a rondo-like structure.

Expression	Transcendent mood; includes several climaxes.
Timbre	Juxtaposes instrument families: metallic percussion, solo woodwinds, dark instruments, brass chorales.
Performing forces	Large orchestra with many percussion instruments (crotales, celesta, marimba, vibraphone, bell tree, chimes, triangle, tuned glasses, Chinese reflex balls).

A section

0:00   Gentle, bell-like tintinnabulation, then muted lower strings, with a two-note descending motive.

0:47   Solo flute with a rising line, accompanied by muted string chords; no sense of pulse.

1:14   Solo clarinet answers, with harp and string accompaniment.

1:30   Duet between flute and clarinet in overlapping high-register lines:

2:18   Violin solo joins with ascending lines; builds to a large *crescendo* into the next section.

B section

3:07   Wavering horn chords alternate with open high strings; more rhythmic and syncopated:

Builds to a loud climax as strings ascend, punctuated by brass.

4:12   *Fortissimo* climax, then fades quickly.

4:23   **A section** returns briefly; a falling motive in strings.

C section

4:50   A sustained pitch and rhythmic percussion chords introduce solo instruments;
plaintive English horn is accompanied by harmonics on harp and percussion in open fifths:

Other solo instruments enter one at a time (viola, piccolo, cello, oboe, bassoon) over now-syncopated
accompaniment; crotales (antique cymbals) add a bell-like timbre.

6:13   Builds to a gentle climax, with syncopated chords continuing.

6:30   Violins and violas pass the theme between them in dialogue; the texture grows complex with imitation
as the orchestration expands.

7:26   Quicker tempo, with focus on percussion and strings.

8:00   Shifting meters, with a lyrical melody floating across the bar lines; strings play in thirds, accompanied
by swirling woodwinds; rhythmic excitement builds:

9:02   Broad, "flying" theme in full orchestra, in a slower tempo:

9:35   Return to the opening flute-clarinet duet (**A**), accompanied by quiet, wavering strings; English horn enters and
"the clarinet continues on in the upward progressing journey."

10:26   String musicians play Chinese reflex balls, and brass musicians play tuned crystal glasses.

11:25   Prepared piano, with screws inserted in strings, sounds like chimes as the opening tintinnabulation returns.

YourTurn TO EXPLORE

Find a recent instrumental work that has an evocative title and/or a specific program.
What musical elements does the composer use to convey that title or program? How
does the availability of increasingly diverse musical styles in the twenty-first century
give contemporary musicians more expressive options? What kinds of musical colors and devices might you choose to describe your emotional response to something that deeply concerns you today?

71

Underscoring Meaning: Music for Film

"So much of what we do is ephemeral and quickly forgotten . . . so it's gratifying to have something you have done linger in people's memories."

—*John Williams*

KeyPoints

- A film's music sets the mood and helps establish the characters and a sense of place and time.

- There are two principal types of music in a film: **underscoring** and **source music**.

- The film music of John Williams uses full orchestral resources and **leitmotifs** (recurring themes) associated with characters or situations.

- Chinese composer Tan Dun has blended Asian and Western musical resources in his works, especially the soundtrack to the film *Crouching Tiger, Hidden Dragon*.

In Their Own Words

  A film is a composition and the musical composer is an integral part of the design."

—*H. G. Wells*

Multimedia has often been a powerful way to express emotion, as we have seen with opera and ballet: several creative individuals collaborating on a total effect can produce extraordinary results. We can see this perhaps most clearly in contemporary multimedia—film, television, and video games. Dramatic musical resources pioneered onstage have been transformed for the screen so successfully that their emotional effects can stay with us for years. We will look at the work of one of the most prominent film composers of our day: John Williams, who has shaped decades of blockbuster movies with his imaginative soundtracks.

Sound and Film

Music has played an indispensable role in creating some of the most memorable moments in film history. The opening of *2001: A Space Odyssey* (1968), the Paris montage from *Casablanca* (1942), and the shower scene in *Psycho* (1960) are all accompanied by music that has become an integral part of American culture. A composer's choices of style, instrumentation, and emotional quality are critical in fulfilling the director's vision. Even the absence of music in a scene or an entire movie (as in Alfred Hitchcock's *Lifeboat,* 1944) can contribute to the overall tone of the film.

Most Hollywood films use music to reflect the emotions of a given scene. John Williams, for example, guides us at the end of *E.T.: The Extra-Terrestrial* (1982) from sorrow at the apparent death of E.T. through joy at his recovery, excitement at the chase scene, and sadness at his final farewell. Howard Shore's scores to *The Lord of the Rings* trilogy help establish the dark, brooding mood surrounding

Frodo's quest, but also bring out the contrasting moments of humor and tenderness.

Composers can create irony by supplying music that contradicts what is being shown, a technique called "running counter to the action." Perhaps the best-known musical/visual contradiction is the chilling climactic scene of Francis Ford Coppola's *The Godfather* (1972). While filmgoers hear Bach organ music played during a baptism, they watch the systematic murders of Michael Corleone's enemies being brutally carried out. A number of action films since the 1990s, including Quentin Tarantino's *Pulp Fiction* (1994) and *Kill Bill, Vol. 1* and *Vol. 2* (2003–04), contain scenes of graphic violence accompanied by lighthearted rock music. This jarring contrast produces a sense of dark comedy and raises questions about the superficial treatment of violence in today's media.

Music can help create a sense of place and time, as do the bagpipes in *Braveheart* (1995) and the guitar in *Brokeback Mountain* (2005). The instruments do not have to be authentic but can merely suggest a time period. In *Avatar* (2009), a small choir sings in "Na'vi"—a language developed exclusively for the movie—in keeping with the film's setting in a future utopia.

There are two main types of music in a film. **Underscoring**, which is what most people think of as film music, occurs when music comes from an unseen source, often an invisible orchestra. Music that functions as part of the drama itself is referred to as **source music**. For example, someone may turn on a radio, or a character may be inspired to sing. In *Rear Window* (1954), director Alfred Hitchcock employs only source music, which emanates from the various apartments on the main character's block. In *Boyz n the Hood* (1991), source music of classical, jazz, Motown, and rap helps define the figures of the story.

John Williams composed the score for Steven Spielberg's 1982 blockbuster *E.T.: The Extra-Terrestrial.*

John Williams: *Star Wars* and Beyond

It would be difficult to overestimate the importance of composer John Williams to film music. His mastery of the techniques of **leitmotif** (a theme associated with a particular character) has defined the concept for our century; in *Jaws* (1975), for example, a scary two-note oscillating motive warns the audience of the shark's presence when the characters onscreen are oblivious to the danger, greatly intensifying the dramatic effect. Williams is often credited with the revival of the grand symphonic film score, writing unforgettable themes set in an accessible, neo-Romantic idiom. In keeping with postmodernist trends, he looked back to the familiar clichés and emotional appeal of older films. He also contributed to the 1980s hunger for sequels in movies like *Star Wars, Superman, Raiders of the Lost Ark,* and *Jurassic Park*.

The soundtrack to George Lucas's *Star Wars* has been called the greatest multi-film score ever written. Several factors support this claim, including the unity Williams (perhaps inspired by Wagner's *Ring* cycle) achieves through multiple leitmotifs that return in the sequels and prequels. Each motive in the *Star Wars* series—the opening fanfare (which becomes Luke Skywalker's theme), the "force" theme associated with the Jedi and Obi-Wan Kenobi, Yoda's gentle melody, Princess Leia's Romantic tune—supports the general nature of that character. Yet

Leitmotif

John Williams (b. 1932)

A native of Long Island, New York, Williams moved to Los Angeles as a youth, where he studied at UCLA. He then attended New York's Juilliard School, after which he worked as a jazz pianist. He began composing for television in the 1950s, and shifted to the big screen in the 1960s, when he wrote a series of scores for disaster films like *Jaws*. By the end of the 1970s, Williams had established himself as Hollywood's foremost composer, with three blockbusters to his name: *Star Wars*, *Close Encounters of the Third Kind*, and *Superman*. During the 1980s, he scored such box-office hits as the two *Star Wars* sequels, the *Indiana Jones* trilogy, and *E.T.*, and in the 1990s, *Home Alone*, *Jurassic Park*, and *Schindler's List*, among many others. More recent scores include those to the first three *Harry Potter* films. In addition to this amazing lineup, Williams has written classical works, including fanfares for the Olympics and inauguration music for President Barack Obama (*Air and Simple Gifts*). He also served as the director of the Boston Pops Orchestra from 1980 to 1993.

Williams's film music explores the Wagnerian ideas of extended chromatic harmony and the use of leitmotifs—themes that represent a person, object, or idea—throughout a work. His writing is highly lyrical, providing us with eminently memorable themes that capture our imagination.

MAJOR WORKS: Orchestral works, including *Winter Games Fanfare* (1989), *Summon the Heroes* (1996), and concertos for various solo instruments • Chamber music, including *Air and Simple Gifts* (2009) • More than 90 film scores, including *Jaws* (1975), *Close Encounters of the Third Kind* (1977), *Star Wars* (1977, 1980, 1983, 1999, 2001, 2004, 2015, 2017, 2018, 2019), *Superman* (1978), *Indiana Jones movies* (1981, 1984, 1989, 2008, 2022), *E.T.: The Extra-Terrestrial* (1982), *Jurassic Park* (1993), *Schindler's List* (1993), *Harry Potter* films (2001, 2002, 2004), *War Horse* (2011), *Lincoln* (2012) • Television series and themes, including *Gilligan's Island* (1957–60).

these motives can also be transformed to reflect totally different events. The theme for Luke Skywalker can sound sad or distorted when he is in trouble, triumphant when he is victorious. One of the finest musical moments occurs in *The Return of the Jedi* (1983): at the death of Darth Vader, his once terrifying theme is transformed into a gentle tune played by the woodwinds and harp.

Luke Skywalker and Darth Vader duel with light sabers in *The Empire Strikes Back*.

LISTENING GUIDE 64   🔊 **3:02**

Williams: *Imperial March,* from *The Empire Strikes Back*

Date: 1980

Genre: Film score

Performed by: Skywalker Symphony,
John Williams, conductor

What to Listen For

Melody	Accented, disjunct melody; two-measure phrases.
Rhythm/ meter	Quadruple meter, with repeated rhythmic ostinatos.
Harmony	G minor theme, with some chromaticism.

Form	Theme and variations.
Expression	Menacing and marchlike.
Performing forces	Full orchestra; brass is featured.

0:00   Introduction—rhythmic ostinato accompaniment sets the ominous mood; stuttering pattern, with repeated notes in horns, strings, and timpani.

0:09   Main theme is introduced by trumpets and other brass, in G minor, with stuttering accompaniment underneath:

12-measure statement (4 + 4, then last 4 repeated).

0:37   Accompaniment pattern; then other brass instruments join; fanfare builds in a *crescendo.*

0:46   New ostinato pattern: each downbeat is answered by a busy three-note motive in flutes, then strings.

1:04   Theme is varied in horns, played softly with an elongated note at the end of each two-measure phrase; new busy accompaniment is heard underneath.

1:37   Returns to opening stuttering accompaniment, then rises a whole step.

1:47   Theme in trumpets, returns to G minor, with full orchestra playing ostinato accompaniment.

2:14   Theme in horns, with full orchestra playing *fortissimo.*

2:33   Stuttering accompaniment passage, leads to a coda.

2:42   Coda—a varied brass statement of the theme grows dissonant; whirling strings lead to a final full orchestral statement of the ostinato.

Darth Vader, the character whose rise and fall spans all six *Star Wars* movies to date, does not have a distinguishable theme until *The Empire Strikes Back* (1980, now designated episode V owing to the prequels); his ominous-sounding theme, the *Imperial March* (LG 64), is first heard when he makes his appearance here, and its various motives are associated with this character throughout the rest of the films (in the prequels, they foreshadow who will become Darth Vader). The march begins with an incessant stuttering rhythmic accompaniment that sets the mood for the powerful brass melody, which recurs in various guises. The minor tonality contributes to the dark character of the march, as do the occasional chromaticism and low-instrument timbres. A middle section introduces a lighter, more disjunct ostinato that accompanies an unpredictable French horn statement of the theme in which some phrase endings are elongated. This uncertainty gives way to the commanding opening music and theme statement, and the march finishes with a *fortissimo* pounding of the ostinato. The *Imperial March* has made its determined

Soundtracks of Play

We have seen that throughout the Western tradition, musicians have helped to shape entertainment technology; and, as we learned in Chapter 18, mathematical-logical skills often go hand in

Ge Wang, cofounder of the software startup Smule, turned an iPhone into an instrument called an ocarina, which he plays here at the Macworld Expo 2009 in San Francisco.

hand with musical ability (training in one tends to reinforce strengths in the other). It's therefore not surprising that music plays an important role in gaming—not just in soundtracks to enhance the gaming experience (as they do in films) but also in games and apps for portable devices that are tied to music-making.

In 2005, the game *Guitar Hero* (and related multiplayer spin-offs like *Rock Band*)—designed by students of Tod Machover at MIT Media Lab (p. 416)—became a worldwide sensation: one or more specially designed controllers synchronized the player's actions as closely as possible with a soundtrack featuring musical hits of the time. Though that game faded away after a few years, other sound-related games have since been developed, and some of the most interesting come from a company called Smule. The company's cofounder and creative director, Ge Wang, is a composer and computer scientist (and professor at Stanford University) who has also directed "laptop orchestras" that mix technology with creative sound generation.

Smule specializes in creating apps for portable devices (primarily iOS) that are designed for sharing music across the Internet: players can upload their music to the "cloud" and not only listen to other contributions but combine them with their own, allowing for long-distance polyphonic interchanges. The first app developed by Smule, Ocarina (followed by Ocarina 2) enjoyed

very positive critical reception. This is yet another technologically enhanced spin on the opportunity for friendship through sound, and this one can forge worldwide connections, since language differences won't get in the way. Other music-related apps (SoundCloud, for example, which allows you to comment on as well as share musical compositions) also take advantage of the astounding reach of social networking.

Video games have long employed source music to help give more satisfying feedback to a player's actions (think of the sounds that characters make when a button is pressed to make them jump, or the fanfare you hear at the end of a level, or sounds that accompany significant moves in puzzle games) and underscoring to add intensity and meaning to the flow of action in a role-playing game. But underscoring in games is slightly different from that in films: the player's choices open up a much more dynamic set of musical options, so the composer needs to be able to create shorter musical tracks that can be combined in flexible ways. This means that no two players will hear exactly the same combination of underscoring and source music within a well-crafted game; and in a way, each player contributes uniquely, through his or her choices, to the sonic aspect of the gaming experience. Might we consider this a sort of performance, or even composition?

Among the most respected composers of video game music is Japanese native Nobuo Uematsu (b. 1959), best known for his highly successful *Final Fantasy* series in the 1990s. A self-taught pianist, he has also written for anime and other types of film and played in a rock band. For the last two decades, Uematsu has presented live orchestrations of his music in sold-out concerts throughout the world. His musical influences range from British and American rock of the 1970s to traditional music (Japanese but also Celtic), jazz, and late Tchaikovsky.

One of the best known compositions by Uematsu is "Aerith's Theme," from *Final Fantasy VII* (1997). Aerith was one of the three original playable characters in the game; unusually, she dies, and this may have contributed to players' extraordinary emotional investment in her character and theme (or leitmotif). This theme not only prepares the player for the story of the game when it's heard during the starting sequence, but also reinforces their emotional engagement when elements of the theme return during the flow of play.

Several twenty-first-century video-game composers have built on Uematsu's sophisticated style, combining complex orchestral textures (sometimes live, sometimes synthesized) with rhythmic aspects of rock and jazz. Los Angeles–based Sarah Schachner, for example, has created lush soundscapes interspersed with distorted folk and electronic timbres for multiple games in the popular series *Assassin's Creed* (2017–present) and *Call of Duty: Modern Warfare* (which

garnered her the Hollywood Music and Media Award for best original video game score of 2019). Schachner describes her approach to composing *Call of Duty*: "I wrote two-and-a-half hours of music. . . . You need creative endurance. You're not just writing whatever you want; it has to serve a very specific need and purpose in the game. It has to do a million things. It's very technical."

Whether escorting us through gameplay or thrilling us in the concert hall, video game music has clearly become established as an essential facet of contemporary art. Composers now readily work in multimedia styles that are effective from PlayStation to TV to movie theater, the same way their predecessors linked the concert hall with the opera and ballet stage. And as

technology continues to offer us new ways to integrate sound into our daily experience, composers will keep finding new ways to shape our emotions through music.

Many Voices Expanded
- Uematsu, "Aerith's Theme," from *Final Fantasy VII*
- Schachner, "Modern Warfare Main Theme," from *Call of Duty: Modern Warfare*

Los Angeles–based composer Sarah Schachner at her Moog composition station.

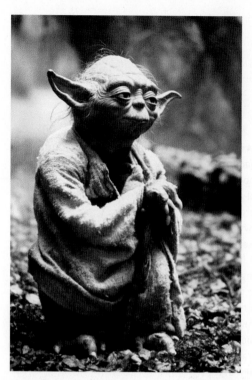

The Jedi master Yoda, who trains Luke Skywalker to fight against the Galactic Empire in *The Empire Strikes Back*.

way into the public consciousness, heard often at sporting events between rival teams, in covers by rock bands, and as a favorite ringtone.

Tan Dun: Blending East and West

Like John Williams, Tan Dun is both a critically recognized composer of art music and an award-winning writer of film scores. In 2000, he won an Academy Award and a Grammy for the score to *Crouching Tiger, Hidden Dragon,* a martial-arts fantasy directed by Ang Lee and featuring stunning visual and action sequences. In the score, Tan Dun creates a fascinating postmodern blend of Asian and Western musical traditions, including both avant-garde and popular elements, and employing instruments with both Chinese and European roots. The well-known Chinese American cellist Yo-Yo Ma (see p. 40) is featured throughout, the cello combined with the contrasting timbre of the **erhu**, a Chinese two-string bowed instrument (see below). The cello's lush melodic material includes slides and ornaments typical of the vocal style heard in Beijing Opera (see Many Voices: Chinese Opera, p. 312).

Based on a series of novels by Wang Du Lu, *Crouching Tiger, Hidden Dragon* involves two sets of star-crossed lovers caught up in a complex story of obligation and revenge, mysteries and miracles, moral codes and gender expectations. Our selection, *Farewell* (LG 65), combines two melodies that represent the lovers Jen Lu and the bandit king Lo, played by the cello and erhu and accompanied by a Western string orchestra with Chinese percussion instruments. The principal (cello) melody's two phrases are heard repeatedly against the ostinato lament of the erhu. Entering at the cadence of the cello's first phrase, the erhu countermelody also has two phrases that overlap and encircle the cello's line. You will hear that each entrance of the erhu begins with the same three pitches (A–C–D), which are central to much of the film's thematic material. The cello closes with a two-note motive associated with the powerful sword known as the Green Destiny, which reappears in the 2016 Netflix sequel *Crouching Tiger, Hidden Dragon: Sword of Destiny*. The composer reworked his film score into the *Crouching Tiger Concerto*, set in six movements linked with cadenzas for the solo instrument, either cello or erhu. The concerto adds more traditional instruments, evoking the sounds heard along the ancient trade route known as the Silk Road, linking the Far East to central Asia and Europe. In this free mixture of Western harmony, avant-garde techniques, and traditional Chinese sounds, Tan Dun creates an appealing new soundscape.

A woman plays the erhu, a traditional Chinese two-string violin.

The history of film music is now over a century old. During this time, the medium has attracted many of the world's best-known composers, including many we have met: Aaron

Tan Dun (b. 1957)

Born in Hunan Province in China, Tan Dun grew up during the Cultural Revolution (1966–76). When he was sent to work in the rice fields, he joined a musical group there and learned to play traditional instruments. Eventually he was able to study music at the Central Conservatory of Beijing; after hearing Beethoven's Fifth Symphony for the first time, he was inspired to join the "new wave" of Chinese musicians who were exploring Western music. When his music was banned in China, he left for New York and pursued a doctorate in composition at Columbia University. There, he discovered avant-garde composers like John Cage and Steve Reich and continued his efforts to blend disparate musical styles and cultures.

Among Tan Dun's extensive output are several operas that merge East and West: these include *Marco Polo*, which mixes Western avant-garde techniques with the vocal style of Beijing Opera; and *The First Emperor*, which relates the story of the first ruler of unified China (246–221 BCE). His monumental orchestral work *Symphony 1997 (Heaven, Earth, Mankind)* was composed for the ceremony marking the return of Hong Kong to China. This work, along with several of his concertos, focus on the natural elements of

Chinese philosophy (wood, water, fire, earth, and metal), and employ instruments made of these materials. His interest in multimedia is evinced not only in his acclaimed film music, but in his *Internet Symphony No. 1 (Eroica)*, commissioned by Google/YouTube for the first collaborative online orchestra. His recent work *Prayer and Blessing*, set to a poignant text by Chinese philosopher Laozi (c. 600–500 BCE), responds to the COVID-19 crisis: it can be performed with varying instrumentation, together or remotely, virtually or live, demonstrating that the power of music is both in its message and its flexibility. His three award-winning scores for the *wuxia* films, about martial arts heroes, form the basis for his *Martial Arts Trilogy*, in which he sought to present a music drama, retelling the story from the films.

MAJOR WORKS: 5 operas, including *Marco Polo* (1995) and *The First Emperor* (2006) • Orchestral music, including *Symphony 1997 (Heaven, Earth, Mankind)*, *Internet Symphony No. 1 (Eroica)* (2009), *Martial Arts Trilogy* (2010), *Crouching Tiger* Concerto (for cello or erhu, 2000–01), as well as concertos for various instruments (piano, viola, pipa, water-paper-stone percussion) • Chamber works, including *Prayer and Blessing* (varied instrumentation, 2020) • Film soundtracks, including *Crouching Tiger, Hidden Dragon* (2000), *Hero* (2002), *The Banquet* (2006).

Copland, George Gershwin, William Grant Still, Duke Ellington, Leonard Bernstein, Silvestre Revueltas, Steve Reich, and Philip Glass. The Hollywood industry also supported a number of soundtrack specialists, who, in addition to John Williams, include Max Steiner (*Gone with the Wind*, 1939), Miklós Rózsa (*Ben-Hur*, 1959), Bernard Herrmann (*Vertigo*, 1958; *Psycho*, 1960), Elmer Bernstein (*To Kill a Mockingbird*, 1962; *Ghostbusters*, 1984), and Hans Zimmer (*The Lion King*, 1994; *The Dark Night Rises*, 2012; Netflix's *The Crown*, 2016; *Dune*, 2021). In recent years, several women composers have received recognition for their film scores, including Rachel Portman (*Emma*, 1996; *Belle*, 2013) and Hildur Guðnadóttir (*Joker*, 2020). While each composer brought an individual sound to art, three general tendencies can be observed: the incorporation of the principles established by Wagner's music dramas; the assimilation of ever-changing trends in popular music; and the constant search for fresh, new sounds, including resources from across the globe. After one hundred years, film music remains a strong, vibrant medium and an integral part of filmmaking.

Zhang Ziyi as Jen Lu, who steals the magical jade sword, in *Crouching Tiger, Hidden Dragon.*

LISTENING GUIDE 65 2:25

Tan Dun: *Farewell, from Crouching Tiger, Hidden Dragon*

Date: 2000

Genre: Film score

Based on: Book by Wang Du Lu

Performed by: Yo-Yo Ma, cello; Ma Xiao Hui, erhu; Shanghai Symphony Orchestra, Tan Dun, conductor

What to Listen For

Melody	Singing cello line and lyrical erhu countermelody; expressive rising-fifth interval begins the main theme and is heard frequently throughout.
Rhythm/ meter	Duple-meter melody accompanied by irregular pulses in Chinese hand drum.
Harmony	Consonant accompaniment.
Texture	Mostly linear, with two main lines.

Form	Theme and variations; a two-phrase melody is varied in pitch, range, and dynamics.
Expression	Lush string timbres and varied dynamics; accelerating movement in accompaniment.
Performing forces	Cello (played by Yo-Yo Ma) and erhu (Chinese fiddle), accompanied by hand drum and Western orchestra.

0:00   Love theme played by cello, with interval of a rising fifth (pitches D–A): theme heard in two phrases, accompanied by sustained strings and hand drum. Higher-pitched erhu improvises an expressive countermelody against cello line; it also begins with a rising line (pitches A–C–D).

0:34   Variation 1—duet continues between cello and erhu, with differing pitches; drum accompaniment.

1:05   Variation 2—duet is closer to original statement; more expressive and louder, with quicker drum accompaniment.

1:38   Two varied statements of the second phrase, with quickening drum part.

2:07   A wavering between two pitches at the closing.

CRITICAL THINKING

1 How does the music for films contribute to their stories?

2. How has John Williams influenced film music?

3. How does Tan Dun bring two distinct musical styles and sound worlds together?

YourTurn TO EXPLORE

Choose a favorite film and watch it several times, paying attention to the use of sound. Which types of music discussed in this chapter are employed? Are there particular moments when you think sound and music are used most effectively? Can you identify moments where you feel the music is not effective for the dramatic purpose? How might a different choice at those points work better?

72

Icons in Sound: Tavener and Postmodern Orthodoxy

"I hope that my music resembles 'icons in sound,' insofar as I see music as a 'window of sound' onto the divine world."

—*John Tavener*

KeyPoints

- Alongside the concert tradition, composers have continued to write expressive music for their religious communities.
- Like the Western Christian tradition, the Greek Orthodox tradition has roots in Jewish practice, but it developed in significantly different ways over the centuries.

- English composer John Tavener's music employs concepts and specific traits of Orthodox ritual to convey a spiritual intensity that is designed to transcend individual religions.

We have seen that while religion was probably the most important concern of Western society before about 1800, in the century that followed, Europeans embraced secular music and also concert performances of sacred works (as with Boulanger's *Psalm 24*). The arts (especially music) themselves could even be felt to satisfy the human desire for experience that is "beyond this world." Musicians were thus given more and more opportunities to work in secular contexts, and as a consequence much of the repertory we encounter today has a nonsacred purpose. Still, composers have never stopped focusing on spiritual goals. We will examine one distinguished example, John Tavener, whose deeply meaningful works are a spiritual response to an increasingly secular world.

Frank Stella's (b. 1936) minimalist sculpture *The Chapel of the Holy Ghost* radiates a mystical spiritualism.

Spiritual Minimalism

Tavener was a prominent exponent of a branch of minimalism often referred to as **spiritual**, or **holy, minimalism**. Developed mostly by European composers, this is a nonpulsed music inspired by religious beliefs and expressed in deceptively simple—and seemingly endless—chains of modal or tonal progressions. Representatives of this deeply meditative music include the Polish composer Henryk Górecki (1933–2010), whose Symphony No. 3 (for soprano and orchestra, 1976) features modern sound masses couched in a slow-moving, tonal language; and Estonian Arvo Pärt (b. 1935), whose works (*Kanon Pokajanen*, 1997; *Berlin Mass*, 1992) combine the fervent mysticism of Russian Orthodox rituals with elements of Eastern European folk music and Gregorian chant. John Tavener's style infuses elements of neo-Romanticism with a devout spiritualism.

Tavener and Greek Orthodoxy

Born and raised in the Presbyterian tradition, Tavener evinced an interest from an early age in Christian mysticism. When he encountered the Greek Orthodox branch of Christianity, he was so moved by its spiritual message that he converted to that faith, undertook a systematic study of Greek Orthodox plainchant, and set about creating music for its services.

Although the Greek Orthodox and Western Christian chant traditions stem from the same Jewish roots over two thousand years ago, they developed in significantly different ways. This was in large part because the Eastern Christian Church separated from the Western in 1054 and then spread into Asia and Eastern Europe. The two churches differed in ritual practices: for example, Latin was the language of worship throughout the Western church, while the Eastern church developed rituals in the local languages (most prominently Greek). The melodic formulas of Greek Orthodox chant were also closely tied to the scales and modes of local Greek and Byzantine tradition, which include intervals smaller than half steps (**microtones**) and rhythms that differ sharply from Western notions of duple and triple regularity.

Tavener's sacred music draws not just on Greek Orthodox chant but on the patterns of repetition that Orthodox ritual implies, aiming toward a mystical effect of timelessness. Beyond his settings of Orthodox texts, his instrumental compositions tend to refer directly to imagery or beliefs central to Orthodox Christianity—

John Tavener (1944–2013)

Born in London, Tavener was quickly identified as a piano prodigy. From the age of sixteen he was active as a church organist, and he continued his education in keyboard and composition at London's Royal Academy of Music. His early successes (the cantata *The Whale*, 1968; *A Celtic Requiem*, 1969) showed the modernist influences of Stravinsky and Olivier Messiaen and received wider attention by being recorded on the Beatles' Apple Records label. His growing fame led to commissions for theatrical music, but after converting to Greek Orthodoxy in the mid-1970s, Tavener refocused his attention on mystical texts and topics.

After a decade dedicated almost entirely to choral music, his *Protecting Veil* for cello and orchestra expanded his style into instrumental genres, resulting in a series of instrumental works likewise concerned with Orthodox imagery. One of his shorter sacred works, *Song for Athene* (1994), was heard by millions at the close of the funeral ser-

vice for Princess Diana on September 6, 1997; its text, "Alleluia. May flights of angels sing thee to thy rest," is taken from Shakespeare's *Hamlet* and from the Orthodox Vigil Service. In more recent years, Tavener sought to combine the spiritual messages of many faiths into large-scale religious works: the most monumental is *The Veil of the Temple* (2004), for four choirs, several orchestras and soloist, and an overall duration of at least seven hours. Tavener was elevated to the British knighthood in 2000.

MAJOR WORKS: Settings of Greek Orthodox rite (*The Liturgy of Saint John Chrysostom*, 1977; *The Vigil Service*, 1984) • Choral works on broader sacred themes (*Resurrection*, 1989; *The Apocalypse*, 1993; *The Beautiful Names*, 2007) and shorter anthems (*The Lamb*, 1982, to a poem by William Blake) • Instrumental compositions based on images from Orthodox Christianity (*The Protecting Veil*, 1987; *The Last Sleep of the Virgin*, 1991; *Theophany*, 1993) • Dramatic works on sacred themes (*Mary of Egypt*, 1991; *The Play of Krishna*, 2012).

especially the idea of the icon, or key image that represents an aspect of the divine (the Protecting Veil of the Mother of God, for example, which inspired Tavener to write a work for cello and orchestra with that name).

A Hymn to the Mother of God

We will examine Tavener's *Hymn to the Mother of God*, scored for two six-voice choirs (LG 66). This hymn is from a service that is celebrated several times during the Greek Orthodox liturgical year, most notably on Sunday in Great Lent (a period of fasting before Easter); the text is attributed to Saint John Damascene, who lived in the eighth century. It's one of the most beloved of the hymns celebrating Mary as Mother of God, a central tenet of the Greek Orthodox as well as the Catholic faith.

Characteristic of Tavener's choral works is the presence of **drones** (continuous pitches held while other musical lines interweave, occasionally providing moments of intense dissonance within the slow-moving counterpoint) and harmonies based on Greek Orthodox modes that avoid the progressions of major/minor harmony and create an almost static effect. The use of short repeating musical ideas recalls organum and also the procedures of minimalism. You may hear some similarities with two other sacred compositions dedicated to Mary we have encountered—the organum *Gaude Maria virgo* from the 1200s and Josquin's motet *Ave Maria . . . virgo serena* from the late 1400s. This stylistic link is purposeful, since Tavener specifically looked to medieval and Renaissance polyphony for his choral writing. Like the Josquin motet, this hymn alternates homophonic with polyphonic passages.

As he continued in his quest for spiritual creativity, Tavener began to understand that "no single religion could be exclusive. . . . All religions are in the transcendent way inwardly united beneath their outward form." With this perspective, he began to incorporate sacred texts from several traditions into his vocal works (for example, he included a part for a pow-wow drum in *Hymn of Dawn*, a "mystical love song inspired by texts from the American Indians, Saint John's Gospel, the Sufis and the Hindus"). Still, the composer remained resolute in letting his own Orthodox sensibility govern his musical choices: spiritual identity served as a touchstone of his creative success.

This Greek Orthodox icon portrays Mary as the well of life; from the Basilica of St. George in Madaba, Jordan.

CRITICAL THINKING

1. How did Tavener achieve his musical connection with Greek Orthodox Christianity?
2. What are some similarities and differences between *A Hymn to the Mother of God* and the examples of medieval and Renaissance polyphony we have encountered?

YourTurn TO EXPLORE

Seek out recordings of works in the spiritual minimalism tradition that borrow from Greek Orthodox and/or Russian Orthodox sacred music. Note musical details such as instrumentation, melody, harmony, texture. How do these works resemble and differ from the examples from Western Christian traditions we have examined, or sacred music from your own experience (Christian or otherwise)?

LISTENING GUIDE 66   ◀)) 2:36

Tavener: *A Hymn to the Mother of God*

Date: 1985

Genre: Hymn

Performed by: Choir of St. John's College, Cambridge; Christopher Robinson, conductor

---

What to Listen For

Melody	Stepwise and very narrow range; clear syllabic text setting.	**Texture**	Homorhythmic and parallel motion in each choir; polyphony is achieved through rhythmically displaced canon between the two choirs.
Rhythm/ meter	Free rhythm, varying groups of rhythmic patterns; unmetered.	**Form**	A-B-A′.
Harmony	Diatonic and modal, parallel triads and other third-related "stacked" intervals; contrasting and slightly more chromatic harmonies in second section.	**Expression**	Mystical and almost chantlike.
		Performing forces	Twelve voices in two choirs, each SAA-TBB.
		Text	Greek Orthodox hymn, attributed to St. John Damascene.

Section A

0:00 In You, O Woman full of Grace,
The angelic choirs and the human race,
All creation rejoices!

First choir enters with parallel triadic intervals and drones; second choir follows slightly after with the same notes (a rhythmic canon at the dotted-half note), creating almost an "echo effect"; starts softly and builds to very loud.

0:45

Combined choirs end on an F major triad, a striking consonance after the dense weaving and overlapping dissonances; pause.

Section B

0:55 O sanctified Temple,
Mystical Paradise, and glory of Virgins.

Harmony shifts to an A-flat major triad; first choir is again followed by second choir singing same notes at the same time difference; slightly more chromatic; dynamics soft throughout.

1:25

Again choirs "meet" on a consonant triad, this time E-flat major; again a pause.

Section A′

1:36 In You, O Woman full of Grace,
All creation rejoices.

2:09 All praise be to You!

Begins the same way as the opening; builds more quickly to loud, original phrase is shortened; choirs join on a B-flat major triad. Melodic high point is reached on "All," and dynamics increase until the choirs join again on an F major triad. Tavener adds a long pause into the score at the end.

Beginning of soprano line in each choir:

73

Reality Shows: Adams and Contemporary Opera

"Whenever serious art loses track of its roots in the vernacular, then it begins to atrophy."

—John Adams

KeyPoints

- Operatic composers sometimes choose historical topics, seeking to convey emotional truths through semi-fictional accounts of past events.

- American composer John Adams's eclectic approach combines elements of minimalism with traits of neo-Romanticism, forging a **post-minimalist** style in his opera *Doctor Atomic*.

Verdi once said that in musical theater, "it may be a good thing to copy reality; but to invent reality is much, much better." And operatic composers and librettists—like directors and their teams in film—have often sought deeper truths in stories based in fiction rather than fact. History, however, has also regularly been present in opera, since the actions of significant individuals have long fascinated us. In recent years, several composers have taken recent historical events as the basis for operatic treatment. Operas are not documentaries, though: much of the content of a "historical opera" is based on the creativity of librettist and composer, rather than on documented dialogue between real-life individuals. The goal of these works is to evoke the intensity and complexity of the time and the emotions felt by the historical actors, rather than to provide a factually accurate account. One noteworthy example is *Doctor Atomic*, a collaboration between composer John Adams and provocative playwright-director Peter Sellars.

John Adams and Post-Minimalism

Minimalism has exerted a great influence on a variety of composers. Perhaps the most versatile of these post-minimalists is John Adams, whose works have gained wide appeal in large part because of their combination of accessible melodies and harmonies with intense, deeply expressive contemporary devices. Adams infuses the minimalist style with traits of neo-Romanticism, illustrated in his stirring opera *Doctor Atomic*.

John Adams (b. 1947)

Adams was educated at Harvard University, where he was steeped in serialism. In his dorm room, though, he preferred to listen to rock: "I was much inspired by certain albums that appeared to me to have a fabulous unity to them, like . . . *Abbey Road* and *Dark Side of the Moon*." In 1972, he drove his VW Beetle cross-country to San Francisco, where he began teaching at the San Francisco Conservatory of Music, and quickly became an advocate for contemporary music in the Bay Area.

Adams first gained notice with two hypnotic minimalist works—*Phrygian Gates* (for piano) and *Shaker Loops* (for string septet)—then earned a national reputation with *Harmonium* (1980–81) and *Harmonielehre* (1984–85, which pays homage to Arnold Schoenberg), both written for the San Francisco Symphony. He attracted much attention with his opera *Nixon in China*, on the historic visit of President Nixon in November 1972. The works that followed show an increasing awareness of the sumptuous orchestration and expressive harmonies of neo-Romanticism, including his next opera, *The Death of Klinghoffer*, based on the 1985 hijacking of a cruise liner by Palestinian terrorists. *El Niño*, a Nativity oratorio modeled on Handel's *Messiah*, has texts culled from English, Spanish, and Latin sources. Both these recent stage works were collaborations with stage director Peter Sellars.

Adams won a Pulitzer Prize for *On the Transmigration of Souls*, commissioned to mark the first anniversary of September 11, 2001, setting texts based on victims' names. His opera *Doctor Atomic* may be his most dramatic work yet. His recent piano concerto, *Must the Devil Have All the Good Tunes?*, commissioned by the Los Angeles Philharmonic, takes its title from a phrase attributed to the early Protestant reformer Martin Luther.

MAJOR WORKS: Stage works, including *Nixon in China* (1987), *The Death of Klinghoffer* (1991), *El Niño* (2000), and *Doctor Atomic* (2005) • Orchestral works, including *Short Ride in a Fast Machine* (1986), *Tromba lontana* (1986), *City Noir* (2009), *Doctor Atomic* Symphony (2007, drawn from the opera), and *Must the Devil Have All the Good Tunes?* (piano concerto, 2019) • Chamber music, including *Phrygian Gates* (1977), *Shaker Loops* (1978), and *Chamber Symphony* (1992) • Vocal works, including *On the Transmigration of Souls* (In Memory of September 11, 2001—for chorus, children's chorus, and orchestra, 2002) • Tape and electronic works.

Doctor Atomic

Gerald Finley as physicist J. Robert Oppenheimer in the San Francisco Opera production of *Doctor Atomic*.

For his third opera, Adams chose as his subject the awe-inspiring creation of the atomic bomb by a team of scientists, headed by physicist J. Robert Oppenheimer, working at the Los Alamos Laboratory in New Mexico. Peter Sellars's fascinating libretto is based on the memoirs of the project's scientists and some declassified government documents, as well as the poetry of John Donne, Charles Baudelaire, and the sacred Hindu scripture *Bhagavad Gita* (*Song of God*), the last three all literary texts well known to Oppenheimer. Adams's rich and dark score is complex texturally, as are his very human and well-developed characters.

The opera focuses on the last days and hours before the first atomic test on July 16, 1945. In Act I, chorus members sing of their hopes and fears about the invention—a twenty-one-kiloton atomic weapon; the scientists are already voicing concerns over the morality of creating the bomb. We learn here from Oppenheimer that Japan is on the list of projected targets for the first strike. A touching love scene intervenes between the lead scientist and his wife Kitty, who sing a rapturous duet that borrows texts from American poet Muriel Rukeyser and French writer Charles Baudelaire. Meanwhile, at the test site, the military commander, General Leslie Groves, pressures meteorologists to carry out the test as scheduled, despite concerns that poor weather might spread dangerous radiation. Clearly, all the participants are suffering psychological stress.

At the end of Act I, Oppenheimer, struggling with his conscience, sings the stunning aria "Batter my heart" (LG 67), to a sonnet by the English metaphysical poet John Donne. Just as the poet implores God to free him from his sins, so does the tortured Oppenheimer seek godly intervention. He had taken the test site's name, Trinity, from the poetic reference to a "three-person'd God," and the poem's forceful tone and violent images ("break, blow, burn, and make me new") suggest that the mighty force will change all in its wake. Donne's imagery of a citadel under siege ("like an usurp'd town") must have resonated with Oppenheimer's feeling of helplessness and despair against an unthinkable force.

Krishna displayed in his universal form as Vishnu, from the Sri Srinivasa Perumal Temple in Singapore.

This powerful yet elegiac aria takes us to the depths of Oppenheimer's soul. Throughout, Adams exploits a Baroque sighing motive—a two-note descending idea typical of laments—to portray the scientist's anguish ("break," "blow," "burn"). Although Adams didn't follow the original sonnet form in his setting, he looked toward Baroque aria structures, framing the two solemn vocal sections (which are dark and lean in accompaniment) with an animated and jittery orchestral ritornello. We are left with a final dramatic orchestral statement as Oppenheimer looks with awe and trepidation on his creation.

In Act II, we learn that the test will go on while scientists worry about fallout: no one really knows what to expect, but one team member speculates that the atmosphere itself might catch on fire. Tension mounts as the chorus sings, "At the sight of this," a dramatic text from the Hindu scripture *Bhagavad Gita* describing the moment when Krishna, an avatar (or incarnation) of Vishnu, reveals himself as the Supreme God, the all-powerful creator and destroyer of the world. Adams's spine-chilling chorus conveys the apprehension and terror of those about to witness the historic blast. The fearsome text is declaimed on repeated notes in short phrases, punctuated with offbeat brass and percussion accents. An unsettling refrain ("O master") recurs with even shorter, more dissonant tones. At the close, the crowd responds to the immense buildup of tension with mere utterances over distorted electronic sounds. The effect is thoroughly compelling.

Act II

The opera's last scene depicts the moments before the detonation, when a rocket sends out a two-minute warning and Oppenheimer sings, "Lord, these affairs are hard on the heart." The scientist recalls the Hindu text again to describe the explosion: "If the radiance of a thousand suns were to burst at once into the sky, that would be like the splendor of the mighty one."

In *Doctor Atomic*, Adams has taken a hugely complex subject that draws together science and art, and presented it in a multilayered, eclectic score that offers much to the imagination as well as to the ears. The topic of the opera also raises complex moral (and perhaps political) questions: What does it mean to make art about such a destructive and lethal technology? Do we run the risk of losing track of the horrors that followed these experiments (the bombing of Hiroshima and Nagasaki) by focusing on an individual's struggles through beautiful music?

Several of Adams's works have caused controversy, including his opera *The Death of Klinghoffer*, based on an episode in which Palestinian militants hijacked a

LISTENING GUIDE 67   11:35

Adams: *Doctor Atomic,* excerpts

Date: 2005

Genre: Opera

Setting: Los Alamos, New Mexico, 1945

Librettist: Peter Sellars

Characters: J. Robert Oppenheimer, a physicist (baritone)
Kitty Oppenheimer, his wife (mezzo-soprano)
General Leslie Groves, US Army engineer (bass)
Edward Teller, a physicist (baritone)
Robert R. Wilson, a physicist (tenor)
Jack Hubbard, chief meteorologist (baritone)
Captain James Nolan, an Army officer (tenor)
Pasqualita, the Oppenheimers' maid (mezzo-soprano)

Performed by: Gerald Finley, baritone; Metropolitan Opera Orchestra and Chorus, Alan Gilbert, conductor

Act I, scene 3, aria: "Batter my heart"   7:30

What to Listen For

Melody	Jittery figurations and repeated notes in the ritornellos; lyrical vocal line with many dotted descending motives.
Rhythm/ meter	Ritornello is animated; vocal sections are slower, with shifting meters; dotted (short-long) figure prominent in the voice.
Harmony	Triadic, with sustained chords below the vocal line.
Texture	Dense in the ritornello; homophonic in vocal sections.
Form	**A-A-B** structure, framed by ritornellos.
Expression	Nervous quality in the ritornellos, with wide dynamic swells; an overall dark mood, with an expressive sighing motive.
Text	Holy Sonnet XIV, by John Donne.

0:00   **Orchestral ritornello**   Sustained tones and dynamic swells; then flickering woodwinds, repeated-note figures, and irregular beats.

A section

1:06   Batter my heart, three-person'd God; for you   Lyrical solo with dotted figure (short-long) over
As yet but knock, breathe, shine, and seek to mend;   sustained string chords.
That I may rise, and stand, o'erthrow me, and bend   Vocal range grows wider.
Your force, to break, blow, burn, and make me new.   Accented rhythmic figure (short-long) on strong words.

Opening of vocal line, with shifting meters:

Sighing motive from **A section**:

2:26	**Orchestral ritornello**	A high string pitch leads to a rhythmic, accented ritornello.
	A section repeated	
2:54	Batter my heart . . .	Repeat of the first quatrain of poem, with richer orchestral accompaniment; dramatic vocal delivery.
	B section	
4:18	I, like an usurp'd town, to another due, Labour to admit you, but O, to no end. Reason, your viceroy in me, me should defend, But is captiv'd, and proves weak or untrue.	Wide-ranging, with short melodic ideas, short-long rhythms; accompaniment is more active.
5:09	Yet dearly I love you, and would be loved fain, But am betroth'd unto your enemy;	Freer vocal line, gently syncopated; very emotional delivery.
5:38	Divorce me, untie, or break that knot again, Take me to you, imprison me, for I, Except you enthrall me, never shall be free, Nor ever chaste, except you ravish me.	Accented with short-long rhythms and wide leaps; accompaniment is less active. Sustained low notes, high-pitched strings lead to the ritornello.
6:47	**Orchestral ritornello**	Agitated and dissonant; offbeats in strings, repeated notes in brass; irregular percussion accents, then a loud timpani blow at the end.

Act II, scene 3, chorus: "At the sight of this"   4:05

What to Listen For

Melody	Short, choppy phrases with declaimed text, much repetition of ideas.	Expression	Fiery mood; mysterious electronic sounds.
Rhythm/ meter	Syncopated, with many offbeat accents.	Timbre	Prominent timpani and brass.
		Performing forces	Chorus and orchestra.
Harmony	Sharply dissonant.		
Form	Verse/refrain structure with repeated sections and text.	Text	*Bhagavad Gita*, Chapter 11.

A section

0:00   At the sight of this, your Shape stupendous,   Loud, fiery mood; offbeat horn accents.
        Full of mouths and eyes, terrible with fangs.   Chorus with short phrases, recitative style.

Opening of chorus, with text declaimed together:

Refrain

0:27   O O O O O.   Regular harsh chords on the main beats against a syncopated accompaniment.

A section, elongated

0:41   At the sight of this, your Shape stupendous,   **A section** repeated with harsh, offbeat, accented
        Full of mouths and eyes, feet, thighs and bellies,   dissonances.
        All the worlds are fear-struck, even just as I am.

continued on next page

Refrain

1:06   O O O O Master.

Single chords again on the main beats.

Choral refrain, invoking Vishnu:

B section

1:19   When I see you, Vishnu, when I see you omnipresent,
Shouldering the sky, in hues of rainbow.

Connected chords, descending and chromatic, against syncopated accompaniment.

Refrain

1:35   O O O O Master.

Single chord interjections again; active accompaniment leads back to the **A section**.

A section

1:48   At the sight of this, your Shape stupendous,
With your mouth agape and flame-eyes staring—
All my peace is gone; O, my heart is troubled.

Repeated choral section; dissonant string chords.

Refrain

2:13   O O O O Master.

B section

2:26   When I see you, Vishnu, omnipresent, flame-eyes staring,
All my peace is gone, is troubled.

Connected chords as in the last **B section**.

B section, with sustained chords:

2:43   **Coda**

Disjunct high woodwinds, with agitated, accented accompaniment.

3:00   Vocables: "Ee ee" (women)/"Do" (men).

Electronically generated sounds accompany the vocables.

cruise ship and killed one of its Jewish passengers. Some saw it as a nuanced treatment of a complex global political problem, others were disturbed at what they felt was too sympathetic a portrayal of the terrorists and their cause. Still, Adams is hailed as one of the most masterful contemporary composers in part because he constantly seeks to make his music relevant to the concerns of the present time.

The *Bhagavad Gita* chorus from a London performance of *Doctor Atomic*.

CRITICAL THINKING

1. What kinds of stories have contemporary composers chosen for their operas?
2. How does *Doctor Atomic* create an artistic reading of the story of Oppenheimer and the Los Alamos atomic-bomb project?

YourTurn TO EXPLORE

Find an opera or other dramatic/multimedia work that takes a historical event as a starting point and provides an artistic interpretation of that event. How are different individuals characterized through music (high or low voice types, instrumental timbre for accompaniment, tuneful or dissonant melodies)? How do you think the composer wants us to interpret the event—is his or her artistic reading an appropriate interpretation given the historical facts? What recent event do you think might lend itself to dramatic treatment, and what kinds of musical choices would you make to convey the story?

Syncretism and Universalism: León and the Intersection of Traditions

"I am who I am, thanks to my mestizo heritage and my ancestors from China, Nigeria, France, and Spain. I'm a citizen of the world with a global consciousness."

—*Tania León*

KeyPoints

- International musical collaborations, sometimes with marginalized cultures, provide new possibilities for expression.
- Cuban-born composer Tania León has successfully blended musical traditions and styles representing

    her diverse backgrounds; she views herself as a global citizen.
- León's ballet *Inura*, drawing on Afro-Brazilian traditions, is an excellent example of her syncretic, or blended, style.

In Their Own Words

❝ For me, movement is music. When I hear music, movement materializes, and vice-versa. . . . There's dance in it. But to me, it's not dance—it's something indigenous and vital that had no connection to dance when I wrote it."

—*Tania León*

Music that arises as the result of cultural encounters has long laid the foundation for dynamic, new expressive possibilities, and these have only increased with modern globalization. This intersectional approach can highlight the creative energy of communities that have historically been marginalized or considered less "artful." One of the most extraordinary musicians who have taken this path is Tania León, whose self-consciously syncretic (blended) style is at once progressive and representative of her remarkable heritage.

Tania León's *Inura*

One of the best examples of León's blended style is her ballet *Inura* (*In Motion*), written for DanceBrazil, an American company focused on Brazilian traditions (LG 68). The text, a combination of Yoruba and Brazilian Portuguese, expresses an invocation to Exu, an important deity in the Afro-Brazilian tradition who is viewed as the messenger between the gods and people; Exu guards the energy that moves the universe and makes natural events occur. The movement called "Understanding" features, along with strings and SATB chorus of twelve voices, a five-person percussion ensemble, only one of whom reads pitch-notated music; the others play traditional Brazilian drums, idiophones, and a musical bow.

A steady rhythmic grid played by percussion instruments in complex intersecting patterns provides continuity within the movement, which otherwise alternates between voices and strings in both predictable and unpredictable ways. The opening appears to set up a recurring four-measure phrase, but then the music moves back and forth between four-measure and more irregular phrases. The first vocal episode returns twice as a sort of refrain, and string episodes are also repeated, as in a rondo-like form. In a call-and-response practice with roots in Afro-diasporic cultures, two tenors periodically break from the singing group to give a speechlike call to which the group responds. The melodies use mostly pentatonic scales but sometimes shift into minor tonality; repetitions of short motives are reminiscent of minimalist works, but also of Afro-diasporic dances.

In "Understanding," as in many recent choral works, the virtuosic vocal writing requires an extraordinary level of rhythmic precision and tuning of dissonant intervals. Though the percussion parts are inherently designed for instruments outside the Western tradition, their rhythms are much more intricate than what we might expect with simple dance-entertainment music.

Traditional Brazilian percussion instruments called for in *Inura* include djembe drums (right), bongo drums, and caxixi shakers.

Inura is a remarkable example of musical syncretism, combining instruments and languages and rhythms from ostensibly "low culture" Afro-diasporic religious practices with compositional approaches from Euro-American concert music. Here, León illustrates the potential of advancing traditions of multiple "ancestors" through mutual conversation, for the benefit (as she writes in the program notes) of "those who have yet to be born."

Tania León (b. 1943)

Born in Havana, Cuba, to parents of mixed African, Asian, and European descent, León began studying piano at age four. In 1967, after formal studies in piano and composition at Havana's National Conservatory, she moved to New York, where two years later she became music director for the Dance Theatre of Harlem and began composing ballets for the troupe.

Shortly thereafter, León began serving as guest conductor for numerous US-based and international ensembles, often promoting contemporary—and especially Latin American—music. In the late 1970s, she turned her energies again toward composition, and developed an individual style influenced by the diverse music of her youth in Cuba as well as modern classical music. As musical director for several Broadway shows (*The Wiz* and *Godspell*), she absorbed influences from jazz and gospel as well.

León has received many prestigious commissions and awards, including a 2021 Pulitzer for her composition *Stride*, inspired by the women's suffrage movement. She currently holds an endowed professorship at Brooklyn College. While some have called her style Afro-Cuban, she rejects such categorization, proclaiming that she is "totally anti-label." (See quote at the beginning of the chapter.) Still, Latin American and jazz rhythms are important to her compositional style, as is improvisation. Her music abounds with rhythmic energy, complex rhythms, dense textures, and colorful orchestration.

MAJOR WORKS: Stage works, including the opera *The Scourge of Hyacinths* (1994) and the ballets *Haiku* (1973) and *Inura* (2009) • Orchestral works, including *Latin Lights* (1979), *Batá* (1985), *Carabalí* (1991), and *Indígena* (1991) • Chamber works, including *Ethos* (2014) for piano quintet • *Four Pieces for Cello Solo* (1983) • *Rituál* (for solo piano, 1987) and other piano works • Vocal works.

LISTENING GUIDE 68 6:51

León: "Understanding," from *Inura (In Motion)*

Date: 2009

Genre: Ballet with mixed choir, strings, and percussion

Performed by: DanceBrazil and Son Sonora Ensemble

Movements:
1. "The Power"
2. "The Sharing"
3. "Teaching"
4. **"Understanding"**
5. "Respect"
6. "The Lust"
7. "Funny Battle"
8. "Manifest"

What to Listen For

Melody	Modified pentatonic, arpeggiated strings and voices with short motives.
Harmony	Pentatonic, with elements of minor; much dissonance.
Form	Rondo-like, with recurring episodes.

Texture	Dense, layered; instruments and voices trade off.
Rhythm/	Regular dance patterns are overlaid with irregular syncopations.
Expression	Strong rhythmic character, with blended Western and non-Western elements.

0:00	First cycle (4 mm.): drums in dialogue with mixed Brazilian percussion; regular duple along with syncopated triple meter.	
0:09	Second cycle (4 mm.): Brazilian percussion set a fast regular pattern.	
0:16	Third cycle (4 mm.): other percussion play slightly off beat from Brazilian percussion's pattern.	
0:23	Fourth cycle (5 mm.): high strings in dialogue, playing an arpeggiated pentatonic scale.	*[Bracketed text below is shouted by the lead tenors.]*
0:32	Low voices enter, then high voices respond; most of the intervals are seconds and fourths.	Ìrunmalè e se ojú lè o,
0:48	String interlude, playing patterns similar to the fourth cycle.	
1:07	Two tenors lead the full vocal ensemble in a call and response.	Òrò, Òrò, nlo o, Òrò, [Ìrunmalè se o] Igba ìmalè e se ojú lè o,
1:20	String interlude, playing similar patterns again, with double bass added; ends with a loud plucked chord.	
1:52	Full vocal ensemble in homorhythm; harmony is mostly pentatonic, moving toward minor.	Òrò, Òrò, nlo o, Òrò, Igba ìmalè e se ojú lè o
2:07	String interlude, with more imitation; pentatonic scale expands to six notes; builds to a high-register, sustained ending.	
2:28	Opening vocal melody, shortened; low voices are answered by high.	Ìrunmalè e se ojú lè o, Òrò
2:47	Percussion instruments intensify their pattern.	
2:57	Two tenors (one at a time) lead a call and response with the full vocal ensemble.	[Ìrunmalè se o] Òrò [Ìrunmalè se o] Igba ìmalè e se ojú lè o, Òrò
3:15	String interlude, ends with a loud plucked chord.	
3:39	Full ensemble in homorhythm, with tenors interjecting.	Òrò Òrò, nlo o Osó ilé e se lè, Ìrunmalè e se ojú lè o Òrò Ò nlo Òrò Igba Òrò [Ìrunmalè e se ojú lè o] Igba ìmalè e se ojú lè o

4:15	String interlude, builds to a high register.	
4:36	Percussion pattern intensifies.	
4:45	Marimba added to percussion; low voices are followed by a marimba solo.	È ní s'ebo l'ore o,
5:07	Opening idea returns in low voices, then all voices sing in slow triplets, with two tenors interjecting.	Ìrunmalè e se ojú lè o, sebo l'ore Epo kété ní òro, [Ìrunmalè se o] Igba ìmalè e se o
5:31	String interlude, builds to a high register.	
5:56	Full homorythmic vocal ensemble, the two tenors interjecting.	Òrò, Òrò, nlo o, Omi ni sparó iná È Bàrá a dúró kò kikà [È Epo lero È sù] s'ebo l'ore Epo kété ní Odára kò je àdín È sù gbè ní
6:25	The two tenors lead the full homorhythmic ensemble; strings enter from low to high before the fade-out (text is interrupted mid-word).	[s' ù ní yióò gbà e / gbà e bo wa] Odára kò je àdín È sù gbè ní È ní s'ebo l'ore ní [s'ebo l'o . . .]

Translation

O spirits, keep your eyes over us, we pray, we pray, we pray here and now.
Keep your eyes over us, we pray, we pray.
Keep your eyes over our house, we pray, we pray.
Exu, you are the one who makes the good offerings.
Exu of the body, keep together with us, please accept our offerings.
Exu, palm oil is the color of all your power.
Exu, help. Exu, you are the one who makes the good offerings.

CRITICAL THINKING

1. What elements—musical and cultural—in León's work are syncretic, or blended? How is her musical voice unique?
2. Why is Tania León considered a "global citizen"?

YourTurn TO EXPLORE

Investigate the creative approach of another composer who has developed a culturally blended style (for example, Godwin Natoh, from Nigeria; Tan Dun, from China; John Tavener, from England) or the performance choices of cross-cultural ensembles like the International Silk Road Project, Vancouver Inter-Cultural Orchestra (Canada), or the National Arab Orchestra (United States). How do these musicians incorporate different traditions into a blended whole? What is the stated purpose of the composer or group (artistic or social), and how do they go about fulfilling it? In what ways do you find the music effective, and in what ways are you unconvinced?

Music in Words

Reviewing Postmodern Style

You have now heard some compositions from the late twentieth and early twenty-first centuries that provide a frame of reference for other postmodern works you may encounter beyond your course. Here are some suggestions for things to listen for when you have the opportunity to hear an unfamiliar work from this period.

MELODY: Consider the range and shape of the melodies. Are they lyrical and singable, or wide-ranging with leaps? Do they require a high level of virtuosity from the performer? What expressive elements do you hear in the melodic lines?

RHYTHM/METER: What kind of rhythmic treatment do you hear? Is the work set in a regular meter, or an irregular or changing meter; or does it move freely, without metric patterns?

HARMONY: In this era, tonality is sometimes clouded by chromaticism and dissonance, or abandoned altogether. In other cases, consonant harmonies are used in unconventional ways—for example, through the systematic repeating of short musical ideas. Listen for moments that are dissonant and unstable: what expressive purpose might they serve? If you hear repetitive consonances, what is their expressive effect?

TEXTURE: How do the instruments and voices (if any) work together? Try to explain the role of each.

FORM: Most compositions feature the basic formal principles of repetition, contrast, and variation. What is the role of repetition? of contrast (that is, new music)? What holds the selection together, or helps it make sense to the listener?

PERFORMING FORCES AND TIMBRE: Postmodern-era works often feature unusual combinations of instruments and/or new timbres achieved by different performance techniques, new technological advances, or non-Western instruments. What sounds traditional and what innovative in the performing forces and timbres?

EXPRESSION: If the work includes text, what techniques give it expression? What mood is established, and how is it achieved? Does the work seem influenced by non-Western or commercial musical traditions? Explain your answer.

Listen and Respond

Let's see how you well you can apply what you have learned to a new example. Be sure to consult the listening suggestions above and the general principles of postmodern music given below. Compare this new orchestral work with others we have heard from this era.

John Adams: *Short Ride in a Fast Machine*

1. Create a simple outline for the piece. Think about melody, rhythm, harmony, texture, performing forces, and expressive devices such as tempo and dynamics. What instruments are most prominent? How is the piece organized? What postmodern traits do you hear?

2. How might you describe this piece to a friend who is not in the class and not familiar with the terminology we've been developing? What general descriptions can you apply to the melody? rhythm? harmony? texture? overall effect of the piece?

3. Now write a short paragraph describing the work as you might for a concert report. Here you can demonstrate your understanding of the terms and concepts you have learned as well as your response to the song's expressive qualities. Refer back to Chapter 13 for ways to frame your perspective.

Some Principles of Postmodernism in Music

- Reacts against modernism of the early twentieth century.
- Moves away from the compositional practices and sounds of the past.
- Is influenced by technology and popular culture.
- Challenges the distinction between "high" and "low" art.
- Displays an interest in free forms and procedures (anti-rationalism, chance, improvisation).
- Is influenced by non-Western styles.
- Presents an underlying cultural, social, and/or political context.

- What are some of the factors that influence the current generation of composers?
- How might trends in the present shape the canons of the future?

Throughout the book you have heard many of the compositions long recognized as central to the Western musical canon; and you have also met some of the talented musicians whose works have been historically underrepresented for many years. Now, in the twenty-first century, we are not only recognizing—and celebrating—some of these past musicians and their works through expanding concepts of canon, but we are also seeing a changing landscape in the classical music world.

Many music organizations are now actively promoting contemporary music and younger composers as yet another revitalization of the established canon, just as important and exciting as the stylistic shifts of the past that we've explored in this book. These younger musicians, with their ears attuned to the postmodern principles of composition you've experienced in Part 7, have embraced and expanded the approaches of postmodernism, forging new paths and inventing new sounds. Modern technology, blended styles influenced by popular and global musics, and an increased interest in new modes of audience reception all contribute to this soundscape.

In one important shift today, composers, and the classical music world in general, increasingly see

social issues as relevant to their mission. Symphony orchestras, opera companies, and other music institutions are reinventing themselves, as they recognize, and attempt to address, underrepresentation of marginalized identities in the music they perform, in their member musicians, and in their audiences. Composers are more influenced than ever by social issues such as civil rights and racial discrimination, gender inequality, poverty and homelessness, and climate change, among many others. In a way this turn to social issues is not new—many times in the past musicians have been intensely involved in the politics of their communities. If anything, the modernist twentieth century was an exception; postmodernism reopened the gates of social engagement.

Audience appeal is another influential factor for many contemporary musicians. While early twentieth-century modernism challenged listeners' ears with new harmonic systems and increased levels of dissonance, some postmodern composers have turned to more accessible styles such as minimalism and neo-Romanticism in an effort to attract and engage audiences. You have recently heard a work by one of these "new voices": Jennifer Higdon's appealing tone poem *blue cathedral*. Higdon is one of a number of younger composers who has been championed in recent years by the Atlanta Symphony Orchestra and its former director Robert Spano through performances, recordings, and commissions. This fostering of contemporary music has created an unofficial "Atlanta School of Composers," dedicated to writing music that is eminently listenable. As composers and music institutions seek further ways to attract audiences to modern music, the benefactors include you, as you refine your preferences in the classical music of today.

In Their Own Words

" The great thing for us has been that the composers we have cared about, championed, and invested in, in so many ways, are now some of the most successful composers in the world and that is thrilling. They got their start here and they say it."

—*Robert Spano*

- How important is audience appeal to the future of musical composition?
- What social issues do you think should be reflected in contemporary compositions?
- What is your role in the future of Western music?

In Their Own Words

" By deepening our interior worlds with timeless, contemplative music and enriching our social lives with inclusive, joyous community, Groupmuse seeks a greater wholeness in your neighborhood and around the world."

—from the *Groupmuse.com mission statement*

Beyond established institutions, much innovation in contemporary composition (as well as new formats for performing and interpreting older repertories) is happening in smaller spaces, often through "house concerts" or performances in spaces that were not designed as concert halls. (As you will recall, this also has precedents in the chamber music and social singing of the past.) One significant development in this respect is the organization Groupmuse, which uses apps and social media to connect would-be hosts of intimate classical music events with rising musicians who are eager to share their talents with a motivated audience. And even before COVID-19 forced closures at most performing venues, many musicians had already moved their performances online, providing streaming concerts and other "virtual events" that can reach ever wider audiences and allow listeners to engage with some of the most inventive performers across the globe. There are substantial shifts happening as audiences expand and reconfigure themselves around contemporary musicians' creative talents—your opportunity to join this dynamic worldwide movement is more open than ever.

This illustration by English artist Colin Elgie, created for the cover of our book, reflects a chamber music house party of the sort fostered by the organization Groupmuse, connecting young classical musicians with their audiences in an informal home setting.

The Online Gallery of New Voices

Building Your Playlist . . . And Shaping the Canon

Contemporary musical composition has something to offer everyone, and it is more relevant and inviting than ever before. The barriers of genre and stylistic demarcation have broken down so that one's choices are not limited but rather open to experimenting with all kinds of music. The world of music is changing rapidly, so much so that we have introduced a new on-line component with this text that will keep pace with new developments. You will hear a sampling of works by diverse composers in our **Online Gallery of New Voices,** where we feature musicians who may not yet be part of any established canon, but whose voices look not only to the present but to the future. Here,

you will find a brief narrative about each composer and work as well as a basic listening outline, to which you can add your own interpretation and reaction.

Composers have always needed informed and thoughtful audiences to build a creative dialogue: now it's your turn to enter that conversation with musicians of your generation. We need your help to renew and revitalize the canon that has evolved over the centuries in our Western tradition, making it inclusive and relevant to the twenty-first century and beyond. It's up to you, with your now-robust listening skills, to continue pursuing and advocating for the enjoyment of music.

YOUR TURN TO CONTINUE EXPLORING

We have offered suggestions chapter by chapter on ways you might explore the repertories and issues presented in that chapter, beyond the Listening Guide. Now you are equipped for your explorations to continue expanding your understanding and enjoyment of music, whether directly related to the repertories we have examined or outside their scope. Our Online Gallery of New Voices will provide you with an up-to-date assortment of contemporary compositions, but there are many other works on which you can base your explorations through both in-person and recorded performances.

Below we remind you of some specifically musical elements that you now are skilled in listening for

as you explore. You now understand that music exists in specific contexts and carries important cultural meanings; considering these will help deepen your understanding of what you hear. For example, as you encounter a musical work (whether newly composed or new to you), you should consider what influences you can determine from:

- Functions of the work (for worship, dancing, stage or chamber performance?)
- Social, political, or cultural issues
- Musical works or styles from the past
- Non-Western compositional procedures, instruments, and performing techniques
- Experiments with technology

WHAT TO KEEP LISTENING FOR

Our Listening Guides and Music in Words exercises have given you many opportunities to build your skills in focusing on musical detail as well as broad expressive qualities in a work. You are now well prepared to continue honing those skills by engaging

with musical works and repertories that are both similar to, and different from, the ones we have studied in depth.

As you listen to the works in our Online Gallery of New Voices as well as other musical selections that you encounter, whether live or in recorded performance, remember to:

Listen for melodies

- Are they short, long?
- Are they narrow, wide-ranging?
- Are they conjunct, disjunct?
- Do they remind you of types of melodies you have encountered in this book, and if so, how?

Listen for rhythm and meter

- Is it regular or irregular?
- Is it emphasized or subtle?
- Is it duple or triple grouping, or some other kind of pattern?
- Does it remind you of approaches to rhythm that you have encountered in this book, and if so, how?

Listen for harmony

- Is it largely consonant or dissonant?
- How is contrast between consonance and dissonance used as an expressive device?
- Is there a feeling of tension or relaxation from the harmony at particular moments during the piece?
- Can you perceive the return of particular harmonies?
- Does this remind you of approaches to harmony that you have encountered in this book, and if so, how?

Listen for texture

- Where do you hear monophony, homophony, polyphony?
- How does the composer accomplish different textural "densities"?
- How do changing textures highlight or complicate your hearing of the melodies?
- As you listen to the work multiple times, can you focus on different musical lines in the texture, and hear more than one musical line as a potentially important melody?
- Does this remind you of approaches to texture that you have encountered in this book, and if so, how?

Listen for form

- Can you hear repeats and returns of musical ideas, or even of whole sections of music, after contrasting ideas?
- How do the kinds of expectations associated with musical form function in this piece?
- Does this remind you of formal procedures you have encountered in this book, and if so, how?

Listen for performing forces

- How does the composer use different kinds and quantities of voices and instruments in this work for expressive effects?
- How do the performing forces emphasize aspects of melody, rhythm, texture, form?
- Does this remind you of performing forces you have encountered in this book, and if so, how?

Listen for text

- What texts does the composer use, if any?
- How does the text setting connect with the musical details above?
- Does this remind you of text setting approaches you have encountered in this book, and if so, how?

Listen for overall style

- What aspects of the work sound entirely new to you?
- Which link this work to the music of the past that you have encountered through this book, and how?

Listen for emotional impact

- What feelings does this music evoke in you, and how do those connect to the musical elements listed above?
- Listen to the work more than once: does your emotional experience change as you notice different things about the music?

Appendix I: Musical Notation

The Notation of Pitch

Musical notation presents a kind of graph of each sound's duration and pitch. These are indicated by symbols called **notes**, which are written on the **staff**, a series of five parallel lines separated by four spaces:

Staff

A symbol known as a **clef** is placed at the left end of the staff to determine the pitch names. The **treble clef** (𝄞) is used for pitches within the range of the female singing voice, and the **bass clef** (𝄢) for a lower group of pitches, within the range of the male singing voice.

Clefs

Pitches are named after the first seven letters of the alphabet, from A to G. From one note named A (or any other letter) to the next is the interval of an **octave**. The pitches on the treble staff are named as follows:

Pitch names

E   F   G   A   B   C   D   E   F

octave

And those on the bass staff:

G   A   B   C   D   E   F   G   A

octave

If you need to notate pitches above and below these staffs, short extra lines called **ledger lines** can be added:

Ledger lines

A   B   C   D   G   A   B   C   C   D   E   F   B   C   D   E

Middle C—the C that, on the piano, is situated approximately in the center of the keyboard—comes between the treble and bass staffs. It is represented by either the first ledger line above the bass staff or the first ledger line below the treble staff. This combination of the two staffs is called the **great staff** or **grand staff**:

C   D   E   F   G   A   B   C   D   E   F   G   A   B   C

Accidentals Signs known as **accidentals** are used to alter the pitch of a written note. A **sharp** (♯) before the note indicates the pitch a half step above; a **flat** (♭) indicates the pitch a half step below. A **natural** (♮) cancels a sharp or flat. Also used are the **double sharp** (𝄪) and **double flat** (𝄫), which respectively raise and lower the pitch by two half steps—that is, a whole step.

Key signature In many pieces of music, where certain sharped or flatted notes are used consistently throughout, these sharps or flats are written at the beginning of each line of music, in the **key signature**, as seen in the following example of piano music. Here, the sharp symbol on the F line in both clefs means that every F in the piece is played a half step higher, the black key F♯. Notice that piano music is written on the great staff, with the right hand usually playing the notes written on the upper staff and the left hand usually playing the notes written on the lower:

🔊

Chopin: Prelude in E Minor

The Notation of Rhythm

The duration of each pitch is indicated by the type of note placed on the staff. In the following table, each note represents a duration, or **value**, half as long as the preceding one:

Note values

| whole note | half note | quarter note | eighth note | sixteenth note | thirty-second note |

In any particular piece of music, these note values are related to the meter of the music. If the quarter note represents one beat, then a half note lasts for two beats, a whole note for four; two eighth notes last one beat, as do four sixteenths.

Notes

Beats
(in quadruple, or 4/4, meter)

whole	4 beats each
half	2 beats each
quarter	1 beat each
eighth	2 to a beat
sixteenth	4 to a beat
thirty-second	8 to a beat

When a group of three notes is to be played in the time normally taken up by only two of the same kind, we have a **triplet**, indicated by a 3.

Triplet

If we combine successive notes of the same pitch, using a curved line known as a **tie**, and the note values are combined, the result is a single note of longer duration:

Tie

beats: 4 + 4 = 8   2 + 4 = 6 $1 + \frac{1}{2} = 1\frac{1}{2}$

A **dot** after a note extends its value by half:

Dot

beats: 2 + 1 = 3 $1 + \frac{1}{2} = 1\frac{1}{2}$ $\frac{1}{2} + \frac{1}{4} = \frac{3}{4}$

Time never stops in music, even when there is no sound. Silence is indicated by symbols known as **rests**, which correspond in time value to the notes:

Rest

| whole rest | half rest | quarter rest | eighth rest | sixteenth rest | thirty-second rest |

The metrical organization of a piece of music is indicated by the **time signature**, or **meter signature**, which specifies the meter: this appears as two numbers written as in a fraction, to the right of the key signature. The upper numeral indicates the number of beats within the measure; the lower one shows which note value equals one beat. Thus, the time signature 3/4 means that there are three beats to a measure, with the quarter note equal to one beat. In 6/8 time, there are six beats in the measure, each eighth note receiving one beat. Following are the most frequently encountered time signatures:

Time signature

duple meter	2/2	2/4	
triple meter	3/2	3/4	3/8
quadruple meter		4/4	
sextuple meter		6/4	6/8

The examples below demonstrate how the music notation system works. The notes are separated into measures, shown by a vertical line called a **bar** (or **measure**) **line**.

Bar line

Mozart: *Ah! vous dirai-je Maman*
(tune of *Twinkle, Twinkle, Little Star* and the *Alphabet Song*)

Clef: Treble
First pitch: C
Key signature: none = key of C major
Meter: Duple (2/4)

What you hear is the original piano version of the tune, composed by Mozart. Notice how the familiar melody is embellished on the recording.

Brahms: *Lullaby (Wiegenlied)*

Clef: Treble
First pitch: A
Key signature: 1 flat (B♭) = key of F major
Meter: Triple (3/4)
Other features: Begins on an upbeat, after two rests.
This is the original vocal version by Brahms, sung in German. You may know the English lyrics.

Yankee Doodle (Revolutionary War song)

Clef: Treble
First pitch: C
Key signature: none = key of C major
Meter: Quadruple (4/4)
This Revolutionary War song is heard played by a nineteenth-century brass band. This text is the one best known today.

Greensleeves (English traditional song)

Clef: Bass
First note: E
Key signature: 1 sharp (F♯) = key of E minor
Meter: Sextuple (6/8)
Other features: Begins on an upbeat, has dotted rhythms and added accidentals.
This Elizabethan-era song is played here on classical guitar.

Appendix II: Glossary

absolute music Music that has no literary, dramatic, or pictorial program or associations. Also called *pure music*.

a cappella Choral music performed without instrumental accompaniment.

accelerando Getting faster.

accent The emphasis on a *beat* resulting in its being louder or longer than another in a *measure*.

accompagnato Accompanied; also, a *recitative* that is accompanied by orchestra.

accordion A musical instrument with a small keyboard and free-vibrating metal *reeds* that sound when air is generated by pleated *bellows*.

acoustic guitar A *guitar* designed for performance without electronic amplification.

acoustic music Music produced without electronics, especially amplifiers.

active chords In the *diatonic* system, chords that need to resolve to the *tonic chord*. These include the *dominant* and *subdominant* chords.

adagio Quite slow.

additive meter Patterns of *beats* that subdivide into smaller, irregular groups (e.g., 2 + 3 + 2 + 3 = 10), common in some Eastern European and non-Western musics.

aerophone Instruments such as a *flute*, whistle, or *horn* that produce sound by using air as the primary vibrating means.

Afro-diasporic Connected to musical traditions of communities whose ancestors left Africa, often as slaves.

agitato Agitated or restless.

Agnus Dei The last musical section of the *Ordinary* of the *Mass*.

alap A free, unmetered, and often improvisational introductory section to an Indian classical composition.

album rock A tradition in *rock* that presents a group of songs as an expressive unit (similar to a *song cycle*, moving away from the single three-minute-song format).

aleatoric music See *chance music*.

alla breve See *cut time*.

allegro Fast, cheerful.

Alleluia An item from the *Proper* of the *Mass* sung just before the reading of the Gospel; *neumatic* in style, with a long *melisma* on the last syllable of the word "Alleluia."

allemande German dance in moderate *duple meter*, popular during the Renaissance and Baroque periods; often the first *movement* of a Baroque *suite*.

alto The second-highest part in a normal four-part vocal texture; in an instrument family (e.g., *clarinet*, *saxophone*), a member with a *range* lower than *soprano*.

ambient music A type of music that emphasizes atmosphere rather than clear melodies or forms.

amplitude See *volume*.

andante Moderately slow or walking pace.

answer Second entry of the *subject* in a *fugue*, usually pitched a fourth below or a fifth above the subject.

anthem A religious choral composition in English; performed liturgically, the Protestant equivalent of the *motet*.

antiphonal Performance style in which an ensemble is divided into two or more groups, performing in alternation and then together.

antique cymbals Small disks of brass, held by the player (one instrument in each hand), that are struck together gently and allowed to vibrate. Also *crotales*.

aria Lyric song for solo voice with orchestral accompaniment, generally expressing intense emotion; found in *cantata*, *opera*, and *oratorio*.

arioso Short, *aria*-like passage.

arpeggio Broken chord in which the individual pitches are sounded one after another instead of simultaneously.

Ars antiqua The "old art" of twelfth- and thirteenth-century French polyphony, displaced by the *Ars nova*.

Ars nova "New art," the refined, complex style of *polyphony* in fourteenth-century France, as exemplified by music of Guillaume de Machaut.

art rock A subgenre of *rock* from the 1970s that uses more complex harmonies and larger forms than most popular songs; see also *album rock*.

art song A song set to a high-quality literary text, usually accompanied, and intended for concert performance. See also *Lied* and *mélodie*.

a tempo Return to the previous tempo.

atonality Total abandonment of *tonality* (which is centered in a *key*). Atonal music moves from one level of *dissonance* to another, without areas of relaxation.

augmentation Statement of a *melody* in longer note values, often twice as slow as the original.

automaton (plural is **automata**) Mechanical device, sometimes musical.

avant-garde French term that refers to new styles and techniques in the arts, especially in the early twentieth century.

ayre See *lute ayre*.

backbeat In rock-and-roll and related *genres*, the second and fourth *beats* of the *measure*.

bagpipe Wind instrument popular in Eastern and Western Europe that has several tubes, one of which plays the melody while the others sound the *drones*, or sustained notes; a windbag is filled by either a mouth pipe or a set of *bellows*.

ballad A form of English street song, popular from the sixteenth through the eighteenth centuries. Ballads are characterized by narrative content and *strophic form*.

ballade French poetic form and chanson type of the Middle Ages and Renaissance, with a courtly love text. Also, a Romantic genre, especially a lyric piano piece.

ballad opera English comic opera, usually featuring spoken dialogue alternating with songs set to popular tunes. Also *dialogue opera*.

ballet A dance form featuring a staged presentation of group or solo dancing with music, costumes, and scenery.

ballet de cour An elaborately staged French courtly entertainment of the sixteenth and seventeenth centuries, featuring dancing, singing, and acting.

banjo Plucked-string instrument with round body in the form of a single-headed drum and a long, fretted neck; brought to the Americas by African slaves.

bar See *measure*.

bar form Three-part A-A-B form, frequently used in music and poetry, particularly in Germany.

baritone Male voice of moderately low range.

bar (or **measure**) **lines** Vertical lines on a staff that separate *measures*, or bars.

bas Medieval and Renaissance category of soft instruments, used mainly for indoor occasions, as distinct from *haut*, or loud, instruments.

bass The lowest part in a normal four-part vocal texture; also, the lowest sounding member in an instrument family (e.g., *trombone, clarinet*).

bass clarinet *Woodwind* instrument, with the lowest range, of the *clarinet* family.

bass drum *Percussion instrument* played with a large, soft-headed stick; the largest orchestral drum.

basset horn An alto-ranged clarinet, pitched a fourth lower than the normal B-flat clarinet.

basso continuo Italian for "continuous bass." See *figured bass*. Also refers to a performance group with a chordal instrument (*harpsichord, organ*) and one bass melody instrument (*cello, bassoon*); also *continuo*.

basso lamento A repeated bass line, or *ground bass*, that descends stepwise or chromatically by at least the interval of a fourth, associated with laments.

basso ostinato A procedure structured with a repeated bass line, or *ground bass*.

bassoon *Double-reed* woodwind instrument with a low range.

bass viol See *double bass*.

baton A thin stick, usually painted white, used by a *conductor*.

beat Regular pulsation; a basic unit of length in musical time.

bebop Complex *jazz* style developed in the 1940s. Also *bop*.

Beijing opera A form of entertainment from Beijing (Peking), China, with music, mime, stylized gestures, and dance as well as colorful masks and costumes.

bel canto "Beautiful singing"; elegant Italian vocal style characterized by florid melodic lines delivered by voices of great agility, smoothness, and purity of tone.

bell The wide or bulbed opening at the end of a wind instrument.

bell tree Long stick with bells suspended from it, adopted from *Janissary music*.

bellows An apparatus for producing air currents in certain wind instruments (*accordion, bagpipe*).

bent pitch See *blue note*.

big band Large *jazz* ensemble popular in the 1930s and 40s, featuring sections of *trumpets, trombones, saxophones* (and other *woodwinds*), and rhythm instruments (*piano, double bass, guitar*, drums).

big-band era See *Swing era*.

binary form Two-part (A-B) form with each section normally repeated. Also *two-part form*.

bluegrass *Country-western* music style characterized by quick *tempos*, improvised instrumental solos, and high-range vocal harmonies.

blue note A slight drop of pitch on the third, fifth, or seventh note of the scale, common in *blues* and *jazz*. Also *bent pitch*.

blues African American form of secular *folk music*, related to *jazz*, that is based on a simple, repetitive poetic-musical structure.

blues scale A scale featuring *blue notes*; that is, with lowered third, fifth, or seventh scale tones.

bongo A pair of small drums of differing pitches, held between the legs and struck with both hands; of Afro-Cuban origins.

boogie-woogie A form of dance music featuring a fast tempo, blues harmonic progressions, and *triplet* rhythms.

bop See *bebop*.

bourrée Lively French Baroque dance type in *duple meter*.

bow A slightly curved stick with hair or fibers attached at both ends, drawn over the strings of an instrument to set them in motion.

brass instrument Wind instrument with a cup-shaped mouthpiece, a tube that flares into a bell, and slides or valves to vary the pitch. Most often made of brass or silver.

brass quintet Standard chamber ensemble made up of two *trumpets, horn, trombone,* and *tuba*.

bridge Transitional passage connecting two sections of a composition; also *transition*.

Broadway musical A work of *musical* theater performed in New York City's major theater district (Broadway).

buffo In *opera*, a male singer of comic roles, usually a *bass*.

bugle *Brass instrument* that evolved from the earlier military, or field, *trumpet*.

cadence Resting place in a musical *phrase*; a musical punctuation.

cadenza Virtuosic solo passage in the manner of an improvisation, performed near the end of an *aria* or a *movement* of a *concerto*.

call and response Performance style with a singing leader who is imitated by a *chorus* of followers. Also, *responsorial singing*.

camerata Italian for "salon"; a gathering for literary, artistic, musical, or philosophical discussions, notably the Florentine Camerata at the end of the sixteenth century.

camp meeting A musical gathering where *hymns, spirituals,* and folk songs were sung; popular in nineteenth-century America.

canon A list of composers and/or works assigned value and greatness by consensus. Also, a type of *polyphonic* composition in which one musical line strictly imitates another at a fixed distance throughout.

cantabile Songful, in a singing style.

cantata Vocal genre for solo singers, *chorus,* and instrumentalists based on a lyric or dramatic poetic narrative. It generally consists of several *movements,* including *recitatives, arias,* and ensemble numbers.

cantor Solo singer or singing leader in Jewish and Christian liturgical music.

cantus firmus "Fixed melody," usually of very long notes, often based on a fragment of *Gregorian chant,* that served as the structural basis for a *polyphonic* composition, particularly in the Renaissance.

caracol Latin American term for a conch, or shell, trumpet; an *aerophone* made from the shell of a large sea snail.

carol English medieval *strophic* song with a *refrain* repeated after each stanza; now associated with Christmas.

castanets *Percussion instruments* consisting of small wooden clappers that are struck together; widely used to accompany Spanish dancing.

castrato Male singer who was castrated during boyhood to preserve his soprano or alto vocal register; prominent in seventeenth- and early eighteenth-century *opera.*

caxixi shaker An ancient African *percussion instrument* popular in Brazil, consisting of a basket with a gourd bottom filled with seeds that is shaken.

celesta *Percussion instrument* resembling a miniature upright *piano,* with tuned metal plates struck by hammers that are operated by a keyboard.

cello Bowed-string instrument with a middle-to-low range and dark, rich sonority; lower than a *viola.* Also *violoncello.*

chaconne Baroque form similar to the *passacaglia,* in moderately slow *triple meter,* featuring *variations* that are based on a repeated chord progression.

chamber choir Small group of up to about twenty-four singers, who usually perform *a cappella* or with piano accompaniment.

chamber music Ensemble music for up to about ten players, with one player to a part.

chance music Music that makes a deliberate use of indeterminacy, or chance, in its performance; also *aleatoric music.*

changing meter Shifting between *meters,* sometimes frequently, within a single composition or *movement;* also *shifting meter.*

chanson French *monophonic* or *polyphonic* song, especially of the Middle Ages and Renaissance, set to either courtly or popular poetry.

character piece A short, lyric piano work often with a descriptive title; popular in the nineteenth century.

chart Colloquial or *jazz* term for a score or arrangement.

chimes *Percussion instrument* of definite pitch consisting of a set of tuned metal tubes of various lengths suspended from a frame and struck with a hammer.

Chinese reflex balls Small metal balls that can be held in one hand and, when rolled or shaken (usually for health or stress-relief purposes), produce a mysterious shimmering sound.

choir A group of singers who perform together, usually in parts, with several on each part; often associated with a church.

chorale Congregational hymn of the German Lutheran church.

chorale prelude Short Baroque *organ* piece in which a traditional *chorale* melody is embellished.

chord Simultaneous combination of three or more *pitches* that constitute a single block of *harmony.*

chordal *Texture* comprised of *chords* in which the *pitches* sound simultaneously; also *homorhythmic.*

chordophone Instrument that produces sound from a vibrating string stretched between two points; the string may be set in motion by bowing, striking, or plucking.

chorus Fairly large group of singers who perform together, usually with several on each part. Also a choral *movement* of a large-scale work. In *jazz,* a single statement of the melodic-harmonic pattern.

chromatic *Melody* or *harmony* built from many if not all twelve pitches of the *octave.* A chromatic scale consists of an ascending or descending sequence of half steps.

church cantata A multimovement work for solo singers, chorus, and orchestra set to a religious text and structured around a Lutheran *chorale,* sung in a Lutheran church service. See also *Lutheran church cantata.*

clarinet A family of *single-reed* woodwind instruments with a predominately cylindrical bore.

clavichord Stringed *keyboard instrument* popular in the Renaissance and Baroque that is capable of unique expressive devices not possible on the *harpsichord.*

clavier Generic word for *keyboard instruments,* including *harpsichord, clavichord, piano,* and *organ.*

climax The high point in a melodic line or piece of music, usually representing the peak of intensity, *range,* and *dynamics.*

coda The last part of a piece, usually added to a standard form to bring it to a close.

codetta In *sonata-allegro form,* the concluding section of the *exposition;* more broadly, a brief *coda* concluding an inner section of a work.

collage A technique drawn from the visual arts whereby musical fragments from other compositions are juxtaposed or overlapped within a new work.

collegium musicum An association of amateur musicians, popular in the Baroque era. Also, a modern university ensemble dedicated to the performance of early music.

col legno *String instrument* technique in which the strings are hit with the wood of the bow.

comic opera Comprising English *ballad opera,* Italian *opera buffa,* French *opéra comique,* and German *Singspiel.*

commedia dell'arte Type of improvised drama popular in sixteenth- and seventeenth-century Italy; makes use of stereotyped characters.

common time See *quadruple meter.*

compound meter Meter in which each main beat subdivides into three rather than two; 6/8 is a common example.

computer music A type of electro-acoustic music in which computers assist in creating works through sound synthesis and manipulation.

concert band See *wind band.*

concertina Small, free-reed, *bellows*-operated instrument similar to an *accordion*; hexagonal in shape, with button keys.

concertmaster The first-chair violinist of a symphony *orchestra.*

concerto Instrumental genre in several *movements* for solo instrument (or instrumental group) and *orchestra.*

concerto form Structure commonly used in first movements of concertos that combines elements of Baroque *ritornello* procedure with *sonata-allegro form.*

concerto grosso Baroque concerto type based on the opposition between a small group of solo instruments (the concertino) and *orchestra* (the ripieno). Also *ensemble concerto.*

concert overture Single-movement concert piece for *orchestra*, typically from the Romantic period and often based on a literary program.

conductor Person who, by means of gestures, leads performances of music ensembles, especially *orchestras, bands,* or *choruses.*

conga Afro-Cuban dance performed at Latin American Carnival celebrations. Also, a single-headed drum of Afro-Cuban origin, played with bare hands.

congregational singing Simple worship music, often monophonic, in which the church congregation participates; often associated with Lutheranism and Calvinism. See also *chorale.* See also *chorale* and *hymn.*

conjunct Smooth, connected *melody* that moves principally by small *intervals.*

consonance Concordant or harmonious combination of *pitches* that provides a sense of relaxation and stability in music.

continuo See *basso continuo.*

contour The overall shape of a melodic line as it moves upward or downward or remains static.

contrabass See *double bass.*

contrabassoon *Double-reed* woodwind instrument with the lowest *range* in the woodwind family. Also *double bassoon.*

contralto See *alto.*

contrapuntal *Texture* employing *counterpoint*, or two or more simultaneous melodic lines.

contrary motion Motion in opposite directions between individual parts in a *polyphonic* work.

contrast The use of opposing musical elements to emphasize difference and variety.

cool jazz A substyle of *bebop*, characterized by a restrained performance with lush harmonies, moderate volume levels and tempos, and a new lyricism.

cornet Valved *brass instrument* similar to the *trumpet* but more mellow in sound.

cornet à pistons French term for a soprano-range *brass instrument* similar to a *trumpet*; it first appeared c. 1830 in Europe when valves (pistons) were developed.

cornetto Early instrument of the brass family with woodwind-like fingerholes; developed from the cow horn but was made of wood.

countermelody An accompanying *melody* sounded against the principal melody.

counterpoint The art of combining in a single *texture* two or more simultaneous melodic lines.

countersubject In a fugue, a secondary theme heard against the *subject*; a countertheme.

country-western Genre of American popular music derived from traditional music of Appalachia and the rural South, usually vocal with an accompaniment of *banjos, fiddles,* and *guitar.*

courante French Baroque dance, a standard movement of the *suite*, in *triple meter* at a moderate tempo.

cover Recording that remakes and reinterprets an earlier, often successful song with the goal of reaching a wider audience.

cowbell Rectangular metal bell struck with a drumstick; used widely in Latin American music.

Credo The third musical section of the *Ordinary* of the *Mass.*

crescendo Growing louder.

crossover Recording or artist that appeals primarily to one audience but becomes popular with another as well (e.g., a *rock* performer who makes *jazz* recordings).

crotales See *antique cymbals.*

Cubism Early twentieth-century art movement begun in Paris, characterized by the fragmentation of forms into abstract or geometric patterns.

cut time A type of *duple meter* interpreted as 2/2 and indicated as ¢; also *alla breve.*

cyclical form Structure in which musical material, such as a *theme*, presented in one *movement* returns in a later movement.

cymbals *Percussion instruments* consisting of two large circular brass plates of equal size that are struck sideways against each other.

da capo An indication to return to the beginning of a piece.

da capo aria Lyric song in *ternary*, or **A-B-A**, form, commonly found in *operas, cantatas,* and *oratorios.*

decrescendo Growing softer.

development Structural reshaping of thematic material. The second section of *sonata-allegro form*; it moves through a series of foreign keys while themes from the *exposition* are developed.

dialogue opera See *ballad opera.*

diatonic *Melody* or *harmony* built from the seven pitches of a *major* or *minor scale.* A diatonic scale encompasses patterns of seven *whole steps* and *half steps.*

Dies irae Chant from the *Requiem Mass* whose text concerns Judgment Day.

diminuendo Growing softer.

diminution Statement of a *melody* in shorter note values, often twice as fast as the original.

disjunct Disjointed or disconnected *melody* with many leaps.

dissonance Combination of tones that sounds discordant and unstable, in need of resolution.

divertimento Classical instrumental genre for chamber ensemble or soloist, often performed as light entertainment. Related to *serenade.*

divertissement Grand genre of the French Baroque, characterized by spectacle and grandeur, intended for light entertainment or diversion.

Divine Offices Cycle of daily services of the Roman Catholic Church, distinct from the *Mass.*

djembe A goblet-shaped drum originally from West Africa, with skin heads struck by the hands, and ropes for tuning; also used in Brazilian traditional music.

dolce Sweetly.

dominant The fifth scale step, *sol.*

dominant chord *Chord* built on the fifth scale step, the V chord.

double To perform the same notes with more than one voice or instrument, either at the same pitch level or an *octave* higher or lower.

double bass Largest and lowest-pitched member of the bowed-string family. Also *contrabass* or *bass viol.*

double bassoon See *contrabassoon.*

double exposition In the *concerto,* twofold statement of the *themes,* once by the *orchestra* and once by the soloist.

double reed A *reed* consisting of two pieces of cane that vibrate against each other.

double-stop Playing two notes simultaneously on a string instrument.

downbeat First *beat* of the *measure,* the strongest in any *meter.*

doxology A prayer of thanks to God, sung after a *psalm* or at the close of the *Magnificat.*

drone Sustained sounding of one or several pitches for harmonic support, a common feature of some folk musics.

dulcimer See *hammered dulcimer.*

duo An ensemble of two players.

duo sonata A chamber group comprised of a string, wind, or percussion soloist with piano. Also, in the Baroque period, a *sonata* for a melody instrument and *basso continuo.*

duple meter Basic metrical pattern of two *beats* to a *measure.*

duration Length of time something lasts; e.g., the vibration of a musical sound.

dynamics Element of musical expression relating to the degree of loudness or softness, or *volume,* of a sound.

electric guitar A *guitar* designed for electronic amplification.

electronic music Generic term for any composition created by electronic means.

elektronische Musik Electronic music developed in Germany in the 1930s that uses an oscillator to generate and alter waveforms.

embellishment Melodic decoration, either improvised or indicated through ornamentation signs in the music.

embouchure The placement of the lips, lower facial muscles, and jaws in playing a wind instrument.

encore *"Again";* an audience request that the performer(s) repeat a piece or perform another.

English horn *Double-reed* woodwind instrument, larger and lower in *range* than the *oboe.*

English madrigal English secular *polyphonic* song (for two to six voices) developed from the Italian *madrigal;* often lighter and less serious, featuring *refrain* syllables (fa-la-la); largely cultivated by amateurs.

ensemble concerto See *concerto grosso.*

episode Interlude or intermediate section in the Baroque *fugue* that serves as an area of relaxation between statements of the *subject.* In a Baroque *concerto,* the free and inventive material that alternates with returns of the *ritornello,* or instrumental refrain.

equal temperament Tuning system (used today) based on the division of the *octave* into twelve equal *half steps.*

erhu Bowed, two-string instrument from China, with its bow hairs fixed between the strings, and played resting on the leg.

espressivo Expressively.

estampie A dance form prevalent in medieval France, either sung or performed instrumentally.

ethnomusicology Comparative study of musics of the world, with a focus on the cultural context of music.

étude Study piece that focuses on a particular technical problem.

euphonium Tenor-range brass instrument resembling the *tuba.*

exoticism Musical style in which *rhythms, melodies,* or instruments evoke the color and atmosphere of far-off lands.

exposition Opening section. In a *fugue,* the first section in which the voices enter in turn with the *subject.* In *sonata-allegro form,* the first section in which the major thematic material is stated. Also *statement.*

Expressionism A style of visual art and literature in Germany and Austria in the early twentieth century. The term is sometimes also applied to music, especially composers of the Second Viennese School (Schoenberg, Berg, Webern).

extended technique An unusual or nontraditional method of singing or playing an instrument, sometimes drawn from a non-Western musical style.

falsetto Vocal technique whereby men can sing above their normal *range,* producing a lighter sound.

fantasia Free instrumental piece of fairly large dimensions, in an improvisational style; in the Baroque era, it often served as an introductory piece to a *fugue*.

fiddle Colloquial term for *violin*; often used in traditional music. Also, a medieval bowed-string instrument.

fife A small wooden transverse *flute*, with fewer holes than a *piccolo*, traditionally associated with the military.

figured bass Baroque practice consisting of an independent bass line that often includes numerals indicating the harmony to be supplied by the *basso continuo* keyboard player. Also *thorough-bass*.

film music Music that serves as either background or foreground for a film.

first-movement concerto form See *concerto form*.

flamenco A musical dance style from Andalusia (in southern Spain), often associated with Gypsy performers, featuring improvisational singing, finger snapping, foot stomping, and guitar strumming.

flat sign Musical symbol (♭) that indicates lowering a pitch by a *half step*.

fluegelhorn Valved brass instrument resembling a bugle with a wide bell, used in *jazz* and commercial music.

flute Soprano-range *woodwind* instrument, usually made of metal and held horizontally.

flutter-tonguing Wind instrument technique in which the player's tongue is fluttered as though "rolling an R" while he or she blows into the instrument.

folk music See *traditional music*.

folk rock Popular-music style that combines folk music with amplified instruments of *rock*.

form Structure and design in music, based on repetition, contrast, and variation; the organizing principle of music.

formalism Tendency to elevate formal above expressive value in music, as in twentieth-century *neo-Classical* music.

forte (*f*) Loud.

fortepiano Forerunner of the modern *piano;* also *pianoforte*.

fortissimo (*ff*) Very loud.

four-hand piano music Chamber music genre for two performers playing at one or occasionally two pianos, allowing for home or *salon* performances of orchestral arrangements.

French horn See *horn*.

French overture Baroque instrumental introduction to an *opera, ballet,* or *suite,* in two sections: a slow opening followed by an *Allegro,* often with a brief reprise of the opening.

frequency Rate of vibration of a string or column of air, which determines *pitch*.

fugato A fugal passage in a nonfugal piece, such as in the *development* section of a *sonata-allegro form*.

fugue *Polyphonic* form popular in the Baroque era, in which one or more themes are developed by imitative *counterpoint*.

fusion Style that combines *jazz* improvisation with amplified instruments of *rock*.

Futurism An early twentieth-century anti-establishment artistic movement that emphasized the machine age and the dynamism of the era.

galliard Lively, *triple-meter* French court dance.

galop A fast-paced, *duple-meter* dance popular in the mid-nineteenth century, with a galloping kind of step.

gamelan Musical ensemble of Java or Bali, made up of *gongs, chimes, metallophones,* and drums, among other instruments.

gapped scale A scale that lacks some pitches of the seven-note *diatonic* scale; for example, a five-note (*pentatonic*) scale.

gat An Indian classical work or section of a work with rhythmic patterns established by a drum; see also *tabla*.

gavotte *Duple-meter* French Baroque dance type with a moderate to quick *tempo*.

genre General term describing the standard category and overall character of a work.

gigue Popular English Baroque dance type, a standard movement of the Baroque *suite,* in a lively *compound meter*.

glass (h)armonica A musical instrument invented by Benjamin Franklin, made from tuned glass bowls of graded sizes that are rubbed on the rim with wet fingers.

glee club Specialized vocal ensemble that performs popular music, college songs, and more serious works.

glissando A rapid slide from one pitch to another.

global pop Collective term for popular third-world musics, ethnic and traditional musics, and eclectic combinations of Western and non-Western musics. Also *world beat*.

glockenspiel *Percussion instrument* with horizontal, tuned steel bars of various sizes that are struck with mallets and produce a bright metallic sound.

Gloria The second musical section of the *Ordinary* of the *Mass*.

gong Percussion instrument consisting of a broad, circular metal disk suspended on a frame and struck with a heavy mallet; produces a definite pitch. See also *tam-tam*.

gospel music Sacred musical style in the US Christian tradition, most closely associated with African American Baptists and Pentecostals starting in the early twentieth century.

grace note Ornamental note, often printed in small type and not performed rhythmically.

Gradual Fourth item of the *Proper* of the *Mass*, sung in a *melismatic* style, and performed in a *responsorial* manner in which soloists alternate with a choir.

grand opera Style of Romantic *opera* developed in Paris, focusing on serious, historical plots with huge choruses, crowd scenes, elaborate dance episodes, ornate costumes, and spectacular scenery.

grave Solemn; very, very slow.

Gregorian chant *Monophonic* melody with a freely flowing, unmeasured vocal line; liturgical chant of the Roman Catholic Church. Also *plainchant* or *plainsong*.

ground bass A repeating *melody,* usually in the bass, throughout a vocal or instrumental composition.

güiro An idiophone of Latin American origin, comprised of a hollow gourd with notches, across which a stick is scraped.

guitar Plucked-string instrument originally made of wood with a hollow, resonating body and a fretted fingerboard; types include *acoustic* and *electric*.

guitarra moresca A strummed string instrument introduced into Spain by the Moors; an early version of the guitar.

guitarrón A large, six-stringed bass *guitar*, common in *mariachi* ensembles.

habanera Moderate *duple-meter* dance of Cuban origin, popular in the nineteenth century; based on a characteristic rhythmic figure.

half step Smallest *interval* used in the Western system; the *octave* divides into twelve such intervals; on the piano, the distance between any two adjacent keys, whether black or white. Also *semitone*.

hammered dulcimer Metal-stringed instrument with a trapezoidal sound box, struck with small hammers; an *idiophone*.

Harlem Renaissance An early twentieth-century cultural and artistic movement centered in New York's Harlem neighborhood and focused on the rebirth of African American arts.

harmonica Mouth organ; a small metal box on which free reeds are mounted, played by moving it back and forth across the mouth while breathing into it.

harmonics Individual, pure sounds that are part of any musical tone; in string instruments, crystalline pitches in the very high *register*, produced by lightly touching a vibrating string at a certain point.

harmonic variation The procedure in which the *chords* accompanying a *melody* are replaced by others. Often used in *theme and variations* form.

harmonium *Organ*-like instrument with free metal reeds set in vibration by a *bellows*; popular in late nineteenth-century America.

harmony The simultaneous combination of notes and the ensuing relationships of *intervals* and *chords*.

harp Plucked-string instrument, triangular in shape with strings perpendicular to the soundboard.

harpsichord Early Baroque *keyboard instrument* in which the strings are plucked by quills instead of being struck with hammers like the *piano*.

haut Medieval and Renaissance category of loud instruments, used mainly for outdoor occasions, as distinct from *bas*, or soft, instruments.

heterophonic *Texture* in which two or more voices (or parts) elaborate the same melody simultaneously, often the result of *improvisation*.

hip-hop Black urban art forms that emerged in New York City in the 1970s, encompassing *rap* music, break dancing, and graffiti art as well as the fashions adopted by the artists. The term comes from the *vocables*, or nonlexical syllables, used by rap artists.

historically informed performance A performance that attempts to recreate the approach, style, and sound of the musical era in which a composition was written, generally using authentic historical instruments (or replicas) from the time period.

holy minimalism See *spiritual minimalism*.

homophonic *Texture* with a principal *melody* and accompanying *harmony*, as distinct from *polyphony*.

homorhythmic *Texture* in which all voices, or lines, move together in the same *rhythm*.

honky-tonk piano A fast-paced country-music style that was a predecessor of *boogie-woogie*; the name refers to the disreputable bars or dance halls where it was performed.

horn Medium-range valved *brass instrument* that can be played "stopped" with the hand as well as open. Also *French horn*.

hornpipe Country dance of the British Isles, often in a lively *triple meter*; optional dance movement of solo and orchestral Baroque *suites*. A type of *duple-meter* hornpipe is still popular in Irish traditional dance music.

hymn Song in praise of God; often sung by a whole congregation.

idée fixe "Fixed idea"; term coined by Berlioz for a recurring musical idea that links different *movements* of a work.

idiophone Instrument that produces sound from the substance of the instrument itself by being struck, blown, shaken, scraped, or rubbed. Examples include bells, rattles, *xylophones*, and *cymbals*.

imitation Melodic idea presented in one *voice* or part and then restated in another, each part continuing as others enter.

Impressionism A French movement developed by visual artists who favored vague, hazy images intended to capture an "impression" of the subject in different lights. Impressionism in music is characterized by exotic *scales*, unresolved *dissonances*, parallel *chords*, rich orchestral tone color, and free *rhythm*.

improvisation Spontaneous creation or elaboration of music through performance, as in Baroque *ornamentation*, *cadenzas* of *concertos*, *jazz*, and some non-Western musics.

incidental music Music written to accompany dramatic works.

inflection Small alteration of the pitch by a microtonal *interval*. See also *blue note*.

instrument Mechanism that generates musical vibrations and transmits them into the air.

interactive performance Collaborative music-making that includes live performers interacting with computers, interconnected performance networks, and online improvisation.

interlude Music played between sections of a musical or dramatic work.

intermezzo Short, lyric piece or *movement*, often for piano. Also, a comic *interlude* performed between acts of an eighteen-century *opera seria*.

interval The distance and relationship between two *pitches*.

inversion Mirror or upside-down image of a *melody* or pattern, found in *fugues* and *twelve-tone* compositions.

Irish harp Plucked-string instrument with about thirty strings; used to accompany Irish songs and dance music.

irregular meter An atypical metric scheme, often based on an odd number of *beats* per *measure* (e.g., 5/4, 7/8, 11/4).

Italian overture Baroque *overture* consisting of three sections: fast-slow-fast.

jam band A group that focuses on live performance rather than commercial recordings. Jam bands, such as the Grateful Dead and Phish, combine different musical traditions, most notably *folk, jazz, rock,* and *country-western,* in a highly improvisational style.

Janissary music Music of the military corps of the Turkish sultan, characterized by *percussion instruments* like the *triangle, cymbals, bell tree,* and *bass drum* as well as *trumpets* and *double-reed* instruments.

jarabe Traditional Mexican dance form with multiple sections in contrasting *meters* and *tempos,* often performed by *mariachi* ensembles.

Javanese gamelan See *gamelan.*

jazz A musical style created mainly by African Americans in the early twentieth century that blended elements drawn from African musics with the popular and art traditions of the West.

jazz band Instrumental ensemble made up of reed (*saxophones* and *clarinets*), brass (*trumpets* and *trombones*), and rhythm sections (*percussion, piano, double bass,* and sometimes *guitar*).

jig A vigorous dance developed in the British Isles, usually in *compound meter*; became fashionable on the Continent as the *gigue*; still popular as an Irish traditional dance genre.

kabuki A genre of Japanese musical theater with elaborate costumes and makeup.

Kapellmeister A German term referring to the leader of a musical chapel, either at court or at a church.

kettledrum See *timpani.*

key Defines the relationship of *pitches* with a common center, or *tonic.* Also, a lever on a *keyboard* or *woodwind* instrument.

keyboard instrument Instrument sounded by means of a keyboard (a series of keys played with the fingers). See also *celesta, clavichord, fortepiano, harpsichord, organ, piano.*

key signature Sharps or flats placed at the beginning of a piece to show the *key* of a work (there are no sharps or flats if the key is C major or A minor).

Klangfarbenmelodie Twentieth-century technique in which the notes of a melody are distributed among different instruments, often in different registers, giving a pointillistic effect.

koto Japanese plucked-string instrument with a long rectangular body, thirteen strings, and movable bridges or frets.

Kyrie The first musical section of the *Ordinary* of the *Mass.* Its construction is threefold, involving three repetitions of "Kyrie eleison" (Lord, have mercy), three of "Christe eleison" (Christ, have mercy), and again three of "Kyrie eleison."

largo Broad; very slow.

Latin jazz A *jazz* style influenced by Latin American music, which includes various dance rhythms and traditional *percussion instruments.*

Latin rock Subgenre of *rock* featuring Latin and African *percussion instruments* (maracas, conga drums, timbales).

legato Smooth and connected; opposite of *staccato.*

leitmotif "Leading motive," or basic recurring *theme,* representing a person, object, or idea; widely used in Wagner's *music dramas.*

librettist The author of a *libretto.*

libretto Text or script of an *opera, oratorio, cantata,* or *musical* (also called the "book" in a musical).

Lied German for "song"; most commonly associated with the *art song* of the nineteenth century, usually accompanied by *piano.* See also *art song.*

Lieder Plural of *Lied.*

lining out A worship practice prevalent in Calvinist congregations of England and America, in which a leader sings each line of a psalm or hymn, and the congregation repeats it, often singing slight variants of the melody as the spirit moves them.

liturgy The set order of religious services and the structure of each service, within a particular denomination (e.g., Roman Catholic).

lute Plucked-string instrument of Middle Eastern origin, popular in western Europe from the late Middle Ages to the eighteenth century.

lute ayre Song for solo voice and lute, popular in England in the late sixteenth and early seventeenth centuries.

Lutheran church cantata A multimovement genre for voices and instruments with a lyric or dramatic religious text, for use in the Lutheran church service. See also *cantata.*

lyre Ancient plucked-string instrument of the *harp* family, used to accompany singing and poetry.

lyric opera Hybrid form combining elements of *grand opera* and *comic opera* and featuring appealing melodies and romantic drama.

madrigal Renaissance secular work (originating in Italy) for voices, with or without instruments, set to a short, lyric love poem; also popular in England.

madrigal choir Small vocal ensemble that specializes in *a cappella* secular works.

madrigalism A striking effect designed to depict the meaning of the text in vocal music; found in many *madrigals* and other genres of the sixteenth through eighteenth centuries. See also *word-painting.*

maestoso Majestic.

Magnificat Biblical text on the words of the Virgin Mary, sung polyphonically in church from the Renaissance era on.

Magnus liber organi *The Great Book of Organum*, compiled by resident composers at Notre Dame Cathedral in Paris during the eleventh and twelfth centuries.

major-minor tonality A harmonic system based on the use of *major* and *minor scales*, widely practiced from the seventeenth to the late nineteenth century. See also *tonality*.

major scale Scale consisting of seven different pitches that comprise a specific pattern of *whole* and *half steps* (W–W–H–W–W–W–H). Differs from the *minor scale* primarily in that its third degree is raised half a step.

mambo A dance of Afro-Cuban origin with a highly syncopated *quadruple-meter* rhythmic pattern.

mandolin Plucked-string instrument with a rounded body and a fretted fingerboard; used in some *traditional musics* and in *country-western* music.

maqam An Arabic mode or scale.

maracas Latin American rattles (*idiophones*) made from gourds or other materials.

marcato A playing style that is marked or stressed, making the melody prominent.

march A style incorporating characteristics of military music, including strongly accented *duple meter* in simple, repetitive rhythmic patterns.

marching band Instrumental ensemble for entertainment at sports events and parades, consisting of wind and *percussion instruments*, drum majors/majorettes, flag bearers, and baton twirlers.

mariachi Traditional Mexican ensemble popular throughout the country, consisting of *trumpets, violins, guitar,* and bass guitar.

marimba *Percussion instrument*, a mellower version of the *xylophone*; of African origin.

martial style Marchlike, with strongly accented beats.

masque English genre of aristocratic entertainment that combined vocal and instrumental music with poetry and dance, developed during the sixteenth and seventeenth centuries.

Mass Central service of the Roman Catholic Church.

mazurka Type of Polish folk dance in *triple meter*.

measure Metric grouping of *beats*, notated on the musical staff with *bar lines*. Also *bar*.

medium Performing forces employed in a certain musical work.

medley A composition built on a series of well-known tunes that may be loosely connected or from different sources.

Meistersinger A German "master singer," belonging to a professional guild. Meistersingers flourished from the fourteenth through the sixteenth centuries.

melismatic Melodic style characterized by many notes sung to a single text syllable.

melodic variation The procedure in which a melody is altered while certain features are maintained; often used in *theme and variations* form.

mélodie An accompanied French art song of the nineteenth and twentieth centuries; the French parallel to the German *Lied*.

melodrama Theatrical entertainment that alternates spoken dialogue and occasional singing with orchestral music.

melody Succession of single *pitches* perceived by the ear as a unit.

membranophone Any instrument that produces sound from tightly stretched membranes that can be struck.

metallophone *Percussion instrument* consisting of tuned metal bars, usually struck with a mallet.

meter Organization of *rhythm* in time; the grouping of *beats* into larger, regular patterns, notated as *measures*.

metronome Device used to indicate the *tempo* by sounding regular *beats* at adjustable speeds.

mezzo forte (mf) Moderately loud.

mezzo piano (mp) Moderately soft.

mezzo-soprano Female voice of middle range.

microtone Musical interval smaller than a *semitone* (*half step*), prevalent in some non-Western musics and some twentieth-century music.

MIDI Acronym for Musical Instrument Digital Interface; technology standard that allows networking of computers with electronic musical instruments.

minimalism Contemporary musical style featuring the repetition of short melodic, rhythmic, and harmonic patterns with little variation. See also *post-minimalism, spiritual minimalism,* and *process music*.

Minnesingers Late medieval German poet-musicians.

minor scale Scale consisting of seven different pitches that comprise a specific pattern of *whole* and *half steps* (W–H–W–W–H–W–W). Differs from the *major scale* primarily in that its third degree is lowered half a step.

minstrel show A late nineteenth-century American entertainment featuring white performers in blackface acting out stereotypes of African American slaves.

minuet An elegant *triple-meter* dance type popular in the seventeenth and eighteenth centuries; usually in *binary form*. See also *minuet and trio*.

minuet and trio An **A-B-A** form (**A** = minuet; **B** = trio) in a moderate *triple meter*; often the third movement of the Classical *multimovement cycle*.

modal Characterizes music based on *modes* other than major and minor, especially the early church modes.

mode *Scale* or sequence of notes used as the basis for a composition; major and minor are modes.

modernism Early twentieth-century movement in the arts and literature that explored innovative, nontraditional forms of expression. See also *postmodernism*.

moderato Moderate.

modified strophic form Song structure that combines elements of *strophic* and *through-composed* forms; a variation of strophic form in which a section might have a new *key, rhythm,* or varied melodic pattern.

modulation The process of changing from one *key* to another.

molto Very.

monody Vocal style established in the Baroque era, with solo singer(s) and instrumental accompaniment.

monophonic Single-line *texture*, or melody without accompaniment.

motet *Polyphonic* vocal genre, often secular in the Middle Ages but sacred or devotional thereafter.

motive Short melodic or rhythmic idea; the smallest fragment of a *theme* that forms a melodic-harmonic-rhythmic unit.

movement Complete, self-contained part within a larger musical work.

mp3 A file-compression format applied to audio files; short for Moving Pictures Expert Group 1 Layer 3.

muezzin A male crier who sounds the Muslim call to prayer from the top of a mosque.

multimovement cycle A three- or four-movement structure used in Classical-era instrumental music—especially the *symphony, sonata, concerto,* and *chamber music*; each movement is in a prescribed *tempo* and *form.* Sometimes called sonata cycle.

multiphonic Two or more pitches sung or played simultaneously by the same voice or instrument.

musical Genre of twentieth-century musical theater, especially popular in the United States and Great Britain; features spoken dialogue and a dramatic plot interspersed with songs, ensemble numbers, and dancing. *Also* Broadway musical

music drama Wagner's term for his operas.

music video Film that accompanies a recording, usually of a popular or *rock* song.

musique concrète Music made up of natural sounds and sound effects that are recorded and then manipulated electronically.

mute Mechanical device used to muffle the sound of an instrument.

nakers Medieval percussion instrument of Middle Eastern origin resembling small kettledrums and played in pairs with the hands.

neo-Classicism A twentieth-century style that combined elements of Classical and Baroque music with modernist trends.

neo-Romanticim A contemporary style of music that employs the rich harmonic language and other elements of Romantic and post-Romantic composers.

neumatic Melodic style with two to four notes set to each syllable.

new age Style of popular music of the 1980s and 90s, characterized by soothing *timbres* and repetitive forms that are subjected to shifting variation techniques.

New Orleans jazz Early *jazz* style characterized by multiple improvisations in an ensemble of *cornet* (or *trumpet*), *clarinet* (or *saxophone*), *trombone, piano, double bass* (or *tuba*), *banjo* (or *guitar*), and drums; repertory included *blues, ragtime,* and popular songs.

ninth chord Five-note *chord* spanning a ninth between its lowest and highest *pitches.*

nocturne "Night piece"; introspective work common in the nineteenth century, often for piano.

Noh drama A major form of Japanese theater since the late fourteenth century; based on philosophical concepts from Zen Buddhism.

nonimitative polyphony A texture with several distinct, independent melodic lines occurring simultaneously, not dependent on the principle of *imitation.*

nonlexical A syllable that does not carry specific meaning; a nonsense syllable often sung in *madrigals, jazz, hip-hop,* and other vocal styles.

nonmetric Music lacking a strong sense of beat or meter, common in certain non-Western cultures.

non troppo Not too much.

notation The practice of writing down music, as opposed to *oral tradition.*

note A musical symbol denoting *pitch* and *duration.*

oblique motion Polyphonic voice movement in which one voice remains stationary while the others move.

oboe Soprano-range, *double-reed* woodwind instrument.

octave *Interval* between two notes eight diatonic pitches apart; the lower note vibrates half as fast as the upper and sounds an octave lower.

octet *Chamber music* for eight instruments or voices.

ode Secular composition written for a royal occasion, especially popular in England.

offbeat A weak *beat* or weak portion of a beat.

opera Music drama that is generally sung throughout, combining the resources of vocal and instrumental music with poetry and drama, acting and dancing, scenery and costumes.

opera buffa Italian comic opera, sung throughout.

opéra comique French comic opera, with some spoken dialogue.

opera seria Tragic Italian opera.

operetta Small-scale operatic work, generally light in tone, with spoken dialogue, song, and dance.

ophicleide Nineteenth-century *brass instrument* (now obsolete) with *woodwind* fingering holes; used by Berlioz, among others; the parts are usually played today on *tuba.*

opus number (Op.) A number, often part of the title of a piece, designating the work in chronological relationship to other works by the same composer.

oral tradition Tradition of transmitting music by example or imitation and performed from memory.

oratorio Large-scale dramatic genre originating in the Baroque, based on a text of religious or serious character, performed by solo voices, *chorus,* and *orchestra*; similar to *opera* but without scenery, costumes, or action.

oratory A prayer chapel within a church; the origin of the genre term *oratorio.*

orchestra Performing group of diverse instruments in various cultures; in Western art music, an ensemble of multiple strings with various *woodwind, brass,* and *percussion* instruments.

orchestration The technique of setting music for instruments in various combinations.

Ordinary Sections of the Roman Catholic *Mass* that remain the same from day to day throughout the church year, as distinct from the *Proper,* which changes daily according to the liturgical occasion.

organ Wind instrument in which air is fed to the pipes by mechanical means; the pipes are controlled by two or more keyboards and a set of pedals.

organum Earliest kind of *polyphonic* music, which developed from the custom of adding voices above a *plainchant*; they first ran parallel to the chant at the interval of a fifth or fourth and later moved more freely.

ornamentation See *embellishment*.

ostinato A short melodic, rhythmic, or harmonic pattern that is repeated throughout a work or a section.

overture An introductory *movement*, as in an *opera* or *oratorio*, often presenting melodies from *arias* to come. Also *concert overture*.

panharmonicon An automatic instrument designed to simulate a whole orchestra using *organ* pipes and mechanical percussion devices. Beethoven's *Wellington's Victory* was originally written for the panharmonicon.

panpipes Wind instrument consisting of a series of small vertical tubes or pipes of differing length; sound is produced by blowing across the top.

parlor song A song, generally accompanied by piano, intended for home entertainment; the term is particular to nineteenth-century America.

part book A bound music book—either print or manuscript —with music for a single vocalist or instrumentalist.

part song Secular vocal composition, unaccompanied, in three, four, or more parts.

pas de deux A dance for two, an established feature of classical ballet.

passacaglia Baroque form (similar to the *chaconne*) in moderately slow *triple meter*, based on a short, repeated bass-line melody that serves as the basis for continuous variations in the other voices.

passepied French Baroque court dance type; a faster version of the *minuet*.

Passion Musical setting of the Crucifixion story as told by one of the four Evangelists in the Gospels.

patron (patroness) A person who supports music or musicians; a benefactor of the arts. See also *patronage*.

patronage Sponsorship of an artist or a musician, historically by a member of the wealthy or ruling classes.

pavane Stately Renaissance court dance in *duple meter*.

pedal point Sustained *pitch* over which the *harmonies* change.

penny whistle See *tin whistle*.

pentatonic scale Five-note pattern used in some African, Far Eastern, and Native American musics, as well as Anglo-American folk music. See also *gapped scale*.

percussion instrument Instrument made of metal, wood, stretched skin, or other material that is made to sound by striking, shaking, scraping, or plucking.

perfect pitch The innate ability to sing any pitch without hearing it first.

performance art Multimedia art form involving visual as well as dramatic and musical elements.

period-instrument ensemble Group that performs on historical instruments or modern replicas built after historical models.

phase music A technique in which musical phrases, recorded or performed live, are first synchronized and then slowly shifted rhythmically in multiple parts so that they create an overlapping "out of phase" effect; associated particularly with composer Steve Reich.

phrase A musical unit; often a component of a *melody*.

pianissimo (pp) Very soft.

piano (p) Soft.

piano Keyboard instrument whose strings are struck with hammers controlled by a keyboard mechanism; pedals control dampers in the strings that stop the sound when the finger releases the key.

pianoforte Original name for the *piano*, usually associated with the early versions of the instrument.

piano quartet Standard chamber ensemble of *piano* with *violin, viola,* and *cello.*

piano quintet Standard chamber ensemble of *piano* with *string quartet* (two *violins, viola,* and *cello*).

piano rag Dance form created by African Americans and featuring highly syncopated melodies structured with contrasting, repeated sections, or *strains*. See also *ragtime*.

piano roll A perforated paper roll that was recorded by a pianist and then was capable of playing back mechanically on a player piano.

piano trio Standard chamber ensemble of *piano* with *violin* and *cello*.

piccolo Smallest *woodwind* instrument, similar to the *flute* but sounding an *octave* higher.

pipa A Chinese *lute* with four silk strings; played as a solo and ensemble instrument.

pipe A medieval *flute* with three holes, blown at one end through a mouthpiece.

pitch Highness or lowness of a note, depending on the *frequency*.

pizzicato Performance direction to pluck a string of a bowed instrument with the finger.

plainchant See *Gregorian chant*.

plainsong See *Gregorian chant*.

player piano An automatic piano with a mechanical device that plays it, usually from a perforated paper roll with holes relating to each piano key.

plectrum An implement made of wood, ivory, or another material used to pluck a *chordophone*.

pluck To sound the strings of an instrument using fingers or a *plectrum* or pick.

poco A little.

polka Lively Bohemian dance; also, a short, lyric piano piece.

polonaise Stately Polish processional dance in *triple meter*.

polychoral Performance style developed in the late sixteenth century involving the use of two or more *choirs* that alternate with each other or sing together.

polychord A single *chord* comprised of several chords, common in twentieth-century music.

polyharmony Two or more streams of *harmony* played against each other, common in twentieth-century music.

polymeter The simultaneous use of several *meters*, common in twentieth-century music and certain African musics.

polyphonic *Texture* resulting from combining two or more melodic lines, as distinct from *monophonic*.

polyrhythm The simultaneous use of several rhythmic patters or *meters*, common in twentieth-century music and certain African musics.

polytonality The simultaneous use of two or more *keys*, common in twentieth-century music.

portative organ Medieval organ small enough to be carried or set on a table, usually with only one set of pipes.

positive organ Small, single-manual organ, popular in the Renaissance and Baroque eras.

post-minimalism Contemporary style combining lush harmonies of neo-Romanticism with high-energy rhythms of *minimalism*; John Adams is a major exponent.

postmodernism A movement in the arts and literature that reacts against early modernist principles through the use of classical and traditional elements. See *modernism*.

post-Romanticism A trend at the turn of the twentieth century in which nineteenth-century musical characteristics like *chromatic* harmony and expansive melodies are carried to the extreme.

prelude Instrumental work preceding a larger work.

prelude and fugue Paired *movements*—the *prelude* in a free form, the *fugue* in a strict, imitative form.

prepared piano Piano whose sound is altered by the insertion of various materials (metal, rubber, leather, and paper) between the strings; invented by John Cage.

presto Very fast.

prima donna The leading female singer, usually in an opera.

process music A compositional style in which a composer selects a simple musical idea and repeats it over and over, as it's gradually changed or elaborated upon. See also *minimalism*.

program music Instrumental music endowed with literary or pictorial associations, especially popular in the nineteenth century.

Proper Sections of the Roman Catholic *Mass* that vary from day to day throughout the church year according to the liturgical occasion, as distinct from the *Ordinary*, in which they remain the same.

Psalms Book from the Old Testament of the Bible; the 150 Psalm texts, used in Jewish and Christian worship, are often set to music.

psaltery Medieval plucked-string instrument similar to the modern *zither*, consisting of a sound box over which strings were stretched.

pure music See *absolute music*.

quadruple meter Basic metrical pattern of four beats to a *measure*. Also *common time*.

quartal harmony *Harmony* based on the *interval* of the fourth as opposed to a third; used in twentieth-century music.

quarter tone An *interval* halfway between two notes a *half step* apart.

quintet *Chamber music* for five instruments or voices. See also *brass quintet*, *piano quintet*, *string quintet*, and *woodwind quintet*.

quotation music Music that cites portions of another work or works, presenting them in a new style or guise.

raga Melodic pattern used in music of India; prescribes *pitches*, patterns, *ornamentation*, and extramusical associations such as time of performance and emotional character.

ragtime Late nineteenth-century piano style created by African Americans, characterized by highly syncopated melodies; also played in ensemble arrangements. Contributed to early *jazz* styles. See also *piano rag*.

range Distance between the lowest and highest *pitches* of a melody, an instrument, or a voice.

rap Style of popular music in which rhymed lyrics are spoken over rhythm tracks; developed by African Americans in the 1970s and widely disseminated in the 1980s and 90s; the style is part of the larger culture of *hip-hop*.

rebec Medieval bowed-string instrument, often with a pear-shaped body.

recapitulation Third section of *sonata-allegro form*, in which the thematic material of the *exposition* is restated, generally in the *tonic*.

recitative Solo vocal declamation that follows the inflections of the text, often resulting in a disjunct vocal style; found in *opera*, *cantata*, and *oratorio*. Can be *secco* or *accompagnato*.

recorder End-blown *woodwind* instrument with a whistle mouthpiece, generally associated with early music eras.

reed Flexible strip of cane or metal set into a mouthpiece or the body of an instrument; set in vibration by a stream of air. See also *single reed* and *double reed*.

reel Moderately quick dance in *duple meter* danced throughout the British Isles; the most popular Irish traditional dance type.

refrain Text or music that is repeated within a larger form.

register Specific area in the range of an instrument or voice.

relative key The major and minor key that share the same *key signature*; for example, D minor is the relative minor of F major, both having one flat.

repeat sign Musical symbol (||:: ||) that indicates the repetition of a passage.

Requiem Mass Roman Catholic *Mass* for the Dead.

resolution Conclusion of a musical idea, as in the progression from an *active chord* to a *rest chord*.

response Short choral answer to a solo *verse*; an element of liturgical dialogue.

responsorial singing Singing, especially in *Gregorian chant*, in which a soloist or a group of soloists alternates with the choir. See also *call and response*.

rest chord A chord that achieves a sense of *resolution* or completion, normally the *tonic*.

retrograde Backward statement of a *melody*.

retrograde inversion Mirror image of the backward statement of a *melody*.

rhapsody In the nineteenth and twentieth centuries, a freely composed, one-movement instrumental work of indefinite form.

rhetorical effect A stylistic effect determined by the flow and delivery of words.

rhyme scheme The arrangement of rhyming words or corresponding sounds at the end of poetic lines.

rhythm The controlled movement of music in time.

rhythm and blues Popular African American music style of the 1940s through the 60s, featuring a solo singer accompanied by a small instrumental ensemble (*piano, guitar, double bass*, drums, tenor *saxophone*), driving rhythms, and *blues* and pop song forms.

rhythmic modes Fixed rhythmic patterns of long and short notes, popular in early medieval polyphony.

rhythmic variation The procedure in which note lengths, *meter*, or *tempo* is altered. Often used in *theme and variations* form.

riff In *jazz* and *rock*, a short *motive* repeated over changing harmonies.

ring shout Religious dance of African American slaves, performed with hand clapping and a shuffle step to *spirituals*.

ritardando Holding back, getting slower.

ritornello Short, recurring instrumental passage found in the Baroque *aria* and *concerto*.

rock A style of popular music with roots in *rock and roll* but differing in lyric content, recording technique, song length and form, and range of sounds. The term was first used in the 1960s to distinguish groups like the Beatles and the Rolling Stones from earlier artists.

rockabilly An early style of rock-and-roll, from the 1950s, that combines elements of *country-western* music ("hillbilly") with *rhythm and blues*; features *twelve-bar blues* progressions and a driving beat.

rock and roll Popular music style first heard in the 1950s, derived from African American *rhythm and blues, country western*, and pop music.

rocket theme Quickly ascending rhythmic melody used in Classical-era instrumental music; the technique is credited to composers in Mannheim, Germany.

Rococo A term from the visual arts that is frequently applied to mid-eighteenth-century French music, characterized by simplicity, grace, and delicate *ornamentation*.

romance Originally a *ballad*; in the Romantic era, a lyric instrumental work.

ronde Lively Renaissance "round dance," usually performed outdoors.

rondeau Medieval and Renaissance fixed poetic form and French *chanson* type with a courtly love text.

rondo Musical form in which the first section recurs several times, usually in the *tonic*. In the Classical *multimovement cycle*, it often appears as the last *movement* in various forms, such as **A-B-A-B-A**, **A-B-A-C-A**, and **A-B-A-C-A-B-A**.

round Perpetual *canon* at the *unison* in which each voice enters in succession with the same melody (for example, *Row, Row, Row Your Boat*).

rounded binary Composition form with two sections, in which the second ends with a return to material from the first; each section is usually repeated.

rubato "Borrowed time," common in Romantic music, in which the performer hesitates here or hurries forward there, imparting flexibility to the written note values.

run Fast passagework, often ascending or descending *scales*.

rural blues American popular singing style with raspy-voiced male singer accompanied by acoustic steel-string *guitar*; features melodic *blue notes* over repeated bass patterns.

sackbut Early *brass instrument*, ancestor of the *trombone*.

sacred music Religious or spiritual music, for church or devotional use.

salon A gathering of musicians, artists, and intellectuals who shared similar interests and tastes, hosted by a wealthy aristocrat.

saltarello A sprightly Italian dance featuring leaping steps, popular in the Renaissance era.

sampler Electronic device that digitizes, stores, and plays back sounds.

Sanctus The fourth musical section of the *Ordinary* of the *Mass*.

sarabande Stately Spanish Baroque dance type in *triple meter*, a standard *movement* of the Baroque *suite*.

SATB Abbreviation for the standard voices in a *chorus* or choir: soprano, alto, tenor, bass; may also refer to instrumental ranges.

saxophone Family of *single-reed* woodwind instruments commonly used in *wind* and *jazz* bands.

scale Series of pitches in ascending or descending order, comprising the notes of a *key*.

scat-singing A *jazz* style that sets syllables without meaning (*vocables*) to an improvised vocal line.

scherzo Composition in **A-B-A** form, usually in *triple meter*; replaced the *minuet and trio* in the nineteenth century.

score The written form of a musical composition.

Scotch snap A reversed rhythmic dotting pattern, in which short notes occur on the beat.

secco *Recitative* singing style that features a sparse accompaniment and moves with great freedom.

Second Viennese School Early twentieth-century group of composers, including Arnold Schoenberg and his pupils Anton Webern and Alban Berg, who developed and wrote in the style known as *twelve-tone music*.

secular music Nonreligious music; when there is text, it's usually in the vernacular.

semitone See *half step*.

septet *Chamber music* for seven instruments or voices.

sequence Restatement of an idea or *motive* at a different pitch level.

serenade Classical instrumental genre that combines elements of *chamber music* and *symphony*, often performed in the evening or at social functions. Related to *divertimento*.

serialism Method of composition in which various musical elements (*pitch, rhythm, dynamics, timbre*) may be ordered in a fixed series.

seventh chord Four-note combination of notes consisting of a *triad* with another third added on top; spans a seventh between its lowest and highest notes.

sextet *Chamber music* for six instruments or voices.

sextuple meter Compound metrical pattern of six *beats* to a *measure*.

sforzando (sf) Sudden stress or accent on a single note or chord.

sharp sign Musical symbol (♯) that indicates raising a pitch by a *half step*.

shape-note notation Music notation system originating in the United States in the early nineteenth century, frequently used in church music, in which the shape of the note heads determines the pitch; created to aid music reading.

shawm A *double-reed* instrument of Middle Eastern origin; the ancestor of the oboe.

shifting meter See *changing meter*.

side drum See *snare drum*.

simple meter *Meter* in which the *beat* is divided into two, as in *duple, triple,* and *quadruple meters*.

sinfonia Short instrumental work, found in Baroque *opera*, to facilitate scene changes.

single reed A *reed* consisting of one piece of cane vibrating against another part of the instrument, often a mouthpiece.

Singspiel Comic German drama with spoken dialogue; the immediate predecessor of Romantic German *opera*.

sitar Long-necked *chordophone* of northern India, with movable frets and a rounded gourd body; used as a solo instrument and with *tabla*.

ska Jamaican urban dance form popular in the 1960s, influential in *reggae*.

slide On a *trombone* or *slide trumpet*, a U-shaped tubing that when moved in and out changes the instrument's length and thus the pitch. Also, an ornament in which the voice or instrument slides from one pitch to another; in particular, on bowed-string instruments, moving between pitches by sliding the finger on the string.

slide trumpet Medieval *brass instrument* of the *trumpet* family.

snare drum Small cylindrical drum with two heads. Also *side drum*.

solfège French term referring to a pedagogical system for learning music by assigning syllables to scale tones (*do, re, mi, fa, sol, la, ti*).

son A genre of traditional Mexican dances that combine compound *duple* with *triple meters*.

sonata Instrumental genre in several *movements* for soloist or small ensemble.

sonata-allegro form The opening *movement* of the *multimovement cycle*, consisting of themes that are stated in the first section (*exposition*), developed in the second section (*development*), and restated in the third section (*recapitulation*). Also *sonata form*.

song cycle Group of songs that are unified musically or through their texts.

soprano The highest part in a normal four-part vocal texture; also, the highest member of an instrument family (e.g., *saxophone, recorder*).

soul An African American style of popular music, incorporating elements of rock-and-roll and *gospel*.

soundscape The total acoustic environment that can be heard by humans.

source music A film technique in which music comes from a logical source within the film and functions as part of the story.

sousaphone *Brass instrument* adapted from the *tuba* with a forward bell that is coiled to rest over the player's shoulder for ease of carrying while marching.

spiritual Folklike devotional genre of the United States, sung by African Americans and whites.

spiritual minimalism Contemporary musical style related to *minimalism*, characterized by a weak pulse and long chains of lush progressions—either *tonal* or *modal*. Also *holy minimalism*.

Sprechstimme A vocal style in which the melody is spoken at approximate pitches rather than sung on exact pitches; developed by Schoenberg.

staccato Short, detached notes, marked with a dot above them.

staff The five parallel lines on which notes are written.

stanza A unit or verse of poetry; also strophe.

statement See *exposition*.

steamroller effect A drawn-out *crescendo* that builds to a climax; an orchestral device used in early symphonic writing, often credited to Germanic composers.

steel drum A *percussion instrument* made from an oil drum, developed in Trinidad during the 1930s and 40s.

stopping On a *string instrument*, altering the string length by pressing it on the fingerboard. On a *horn*, playing with the bell closed by the hand or a *mute*.

strain One of a series of contrasting sections found in *piano rags* and marches; generally in *duple meter* with sixteen-measure themes.

stretto In a *fugue*, when entries of the *subject* occur at faster intervals of time so that they overlap, forming dense, imitative *counterpoint*. Stretto usually occurs at the climactic moment near the end.

stride A flashy, highly rhythmic jazz piano style that evolved from ragtime.

string instruments Bowed and plucked instruments whose sound is produced by the vibration of one or more strings. Also *chordophone*.

string quartet *Chamber music* ensemble consisting of two *violins, viola,* and *cello.* Also, a multimovement composition for this ensemble.

string quintet Standard chamber ensemble made up of either two *violins,* two *violas,* and *cello* or two violins, viola, and two cellos.

string trio Standard chamber ensemble of two *violins* and *cello* or violin, *viola,* and cello.

strophe See *stanza.*

strophic form Song structure in which the same music is repeated with every stanza (*strophe*) of the poem.

Sturm und Drang "Storm and stress"; late eighteenth-century movement in Germany toward more emotional expression in the arts.

style Characteristic manner of the presentation of musical elements (*melody, rhythm, harmony, dynamics, form, texture,* and *tempo*).

subdominant Fourth scale step, *fa.*

subdominant chord Chord built on the fourth scale step, the IV chord.

subject The main idea or *theme* of a *fugue.*

suite A unified series of instrumental movements meant to be performed as a single work; in the Baroque era, a series of contrasting dances, generally in the same key.

surdo A large bass drum used in Latin American traditional music and samba.

swing *Jazz* term coined to describe Louis Armstrong's style; more commonly refers to *big-band* jazz.

Swing era The mid-1930s to the mid-1940s, when *swing* was the most popular music in the United States. Important musicians of the era were Louis Armstrong, Duke Ellington, and Benny Goodman.

syllabic Melodic style of one note set to each text syllable.

Symbolism Literary movement that paralleled *Impressionism,* in which poetic images were invoked through suggestion or symbol rather than literal description.

symphonic poem One-movement orchestral form that develops a poetic idea, suggests a scene, or creates a mood, usually associated with the Romantic era. Also *tone poem.*

symphony Large work for *orchestra,* generally in three or four *movements.*

symphony orchestra See *orchestra.*

syncopation Deliberate upsetting of the *meter* or pulse through a temporary shifting of the accent to a weak *beat* or an *offbeat.*

syncretic style A blended style achieved by a merger of discrete musical practices and traditions.

synthesizer Electronic instrument that produces a wide variety of sounds by combining sound generators and sound modifiers in one package with a unified control system.

tabla Pair of single-headed, tuned drums used in North Indian classical music.

table-book format A music book layout in which all the performers can see their parts in one copy while sitting around all sides of a table; used primarily for English *madrigals* and *lute ayres.*

tabor Cylindrical medieval drum.

tala Fixed time cycle or *meter* in Indian music, built from uneven groupings of *beats.*

tamborin A small Brazilian frame drum originally of African origin.

tambourine *Percussion instrument* consisting of a small round drum with metal plates inserted in its rim; played by striking or shaking.

tam-tam A flat gong of indefinite pitch. See also *gong.*

tape music Type of *electronic music* in which sounds are recorded on tape and then manipulated and mixed in various ways. See also *musique concrète.*

tempo The rate of speed or pace of music.

tenor The second-to-lowest part in a normal four-part vocal texture; also a part, often structural, in early *polyphony.*

tenor drum *Percussion instrument,* larger than the *snare drum,* with a wooden shell.

ternary form Three-part (**A-B-A**) form based on a statement (**A**), contrast (**B**), and repetition (**A**). Also *three-part form.*

tertian harmony *Harmony* based on the *interval* of the third, particularly predominant from the Baroque through the nineteenth century.

text-painting Musical depiction of the meaning, emotions, or actions in the text; similar to, but a broader concept than, *word-painting.*

texture The interweaving of melodic (horizontal) and harmonic (vertical) elements in the musical fabric.

thematic development Musical expansion of a *theme* by varying its melodic outline, *harmony,* or *rhythm.* Also *thematic transformation.*

thematic transformation See *thematic development.*

theme Melodic idea used as a basic building block in the construction of a piece. Also *subject.*

theme and variations Compositional procedure in which a theme is presented and then altered in successive statements; occurs as an independent piece or as a *movement* of a *multimovement cycle.*

theme group Several themes in the same *key* that function as a unit within a section, particularly in *sonata-allegro form.*

third *Interval* between two notes that are three *diatonic* scale steps apart.

thirty-two-bar song form Popular-song structure that divides into four sections (**A-A-B-A**) of eight measures each.

thorough bass See *figured bass.*

three-part form See *ternary form.*

through-composed Song structure that is composed from beginning to end, without repetitions of large sections.

timbales Shallow, single-headed drums of Cuban origin, played in pairs; used in much Latin American popular music.

timbre The quality of a sound that distinguishes one voice or instrument from another. Also *tone color.*

timbrel Ancient *percussion instrument* related to the *tambourine.*

timpani *Percussion instrument* consisting of a hemispheric copper shell with a head of plastic or calfskin, held in place by a metal ring and played with soft or hard padded sticks, or mallets. A pedal mechanism changes the tension of the head, and with it the *pitch.* Also *kettledrum.*

Tin Pan Alley Nickname for the popular music industry centered in New York City from the nineteenth century through the 1950s. Also, the style of popular song in the United States during that period.

tintinnabulation A bell-like style developed by Estonian composer Arvo Pärt, achieved by weaving *conjunct* lines that hover around a central pitch; from the Latin word for bell.

tin whistle Small metal end-blown *flute* commonly used in Irish traditional music.

toccata Virtuoso composition, generally for *organ* or *harpsichord,* in a free and rhapsodic style; in the Baroque era, it often served as the introduction to a *fugue.*

tom-tom Cylindrical drum without snares.

tonal Based on principles of major-minor *tonality,* as distinct from *modal* or *atonal.*

tonality Principle of organization around a *tonic,* or home, pitch, based on a *major* or *minor scale.*

tone cluster Highly dissonant combination of adjacent *pitches* sounded simultaneously.

tone color See *timbre.*

tone poem See *symphonic poem.*

tone row An arrangement of the twelve *chromatic* pitches that serves as the basis of a *twelve-tone* piece.

tonic The first note of the *scale,* or *key; do.*

tonic chord *Triad* built on the first scale note, the I chord.

traditional music Music learned by *oral transmission* and easily sung or played by most people; may exist in variant forms. Also *folk music.*

transition See *bridge.*

transposed row A *tone row,* or sequence of pitches, in *twelve-tone music* that is shifted to another pitch level.

transposition The shifting of a piece of music to a different pitch level.

tremolo Rapid repetition of a note; can be achieved instrumentally or vocally.

triad Common *chord* type, consisting of three *pitches* built on alternate notes of the *scale* (e.g., steps 1–3–5, or *do–mi–sol*).

triangle *Percussion instrument* consisting of a slender rod of steel bent in the shape of a triangle, struck with a steel beater.

trill Ornament consisting of the rapid alternation between one note and the next.

trio A second, contrasting section of a *minuet and trio* or *scherzo* and trio, or a contrasting *strain* in a *march.* Also, an ensemble of three players.

triple meter Basic metrical pattern of three *beats* to a *measure.*

triplet Group of three equal-valued notes played in the time of two; indicated by a bracket and the number 3.

trobairitz Female *troubadours,* poet-musicians of southern France in the later Middle Ages.

trombone Tenor-range *brass instrument* that changes pitch by means of a *slide.*

troubadours Medieval poet-musicians in southern France; such women were called *troubairitz.*

trouser role In Classical *opera,* the part of a young man written for a soprano or mezzo-soprano singer.

trouvères Medieval poet-musicians in northern France.

trumpet Highest-pitched *brass instrument* that changes pitch by means of valves.

tuba Bass-range *brass instrument* that changes pitch by means of a *slide.*

tubular bells See *chimes.*

tumkul A Latin American *idiophone* made from a hollow log; a log drum.

tutti "All"; the opposite of solo.

twelve-bar blues Musical structure based on a repeated harmonic-rhythmic pattern, twelve measures long: I–I–I–I–IV–IV–I–I–V–V–I–I.

twelve-tone music Compositional procedure of the twentieth century based on an ordering of all twelve chromatic pitches (in a *tone row*), without a central pitch, or *tonic,* according to prescribed rules.

two-part form See *binary form.*

underscoring A technique used in films in which the music comes from an unseen source.

unison "Interval" between two notes of the same pitch (for example, two voices on the same E); the simultaneous playing of the same note.

upbeat Last *beat* of a *measure,* a weak beat that anticipates the *downbeat.*

variation The compositional procedure of altering a preexisting musical idea. See also *theme and variations.*

vaudeville A light comedic variety show with music featuring popular song, dance, comedy, and acrobatics; flourished in the late nineteenth and early twentieth centuries.

venue Place where a performance happens; a concert space.

verismo Operatic "realism," a style popular in Italy in the 1890s, which tried to bring naturalism into the theater.

vernacular The common language spoken by the people as distinguished from the literary language, or language of the educated elite.

verse In poetry, a group of lines constituting a unit. In liturgical music for the Catholic Church, a phrase from the Scriptures that alternates with the *response.*

vibraphone A *percussion instrument* with metal bars and electrically driven rotating propellers under each bar that produces a *vibrato* sound, much used in *jazz.*

vibrato Small fluctuation of pitch used as an expressive device to intensify a sound.

vielle Medieval bowed-string instrument; ancestor of the *violin*.

Viennese School The main composers of the Classical era (Haydn, Mozart, and Beethoven), active in Vienna.

vihuela An early version of the *guitar* popular in medieval and Renaissance Spain; also, a type of Mexican guitar with a rounded back, common in *mariachi* ensembles.

villancico Devotional song, often for Christmas, from Latin America.

viola Bowed-string instrument of middle range; the second-highest member of the *violin* family.

viola da gamba Family of Renaissance bowed-string instruments that had six or more strings, was fretted like a *guitar,* and was held between the legs like a modern *cello.*

violin Soprano, or highest-ranged, member of the bowed-string instrument family.

violoncello See *cello.*

virelai Medieval and Renaissance fixed poetic form and French *chanson* type, generally with a courtly love text.

virginal A small keyboard instrument on which the strings run at right angles to the keys; popular in the sixteenth and seventeenth centuries.

virtuosic Demanding remarkable technical ability.

virtuoso Performer of extraordinary technical ability.

vivace Lively.

vocables Nonsense, or *nonlexical,* syllables, lacking literal meaning.

vocalise A textless vocal melody, as in an exercise or concert piece.

voice In a *fugue,* a melodic line. Keyboard fugues of the late Baroque period, such as those by J. S. Bach, commonly have four distinct voices even though they are played by a single musician.

volume Degree of loudness or softness of a sound. See also *dynamics.*

Wagner tuba A *tuba* developed specifically for Wagner's opera cycle *The Ring of the Nibelung;* the instrument was adopted by other late nineteenth-century composers.

wah-wah A musical effect on a *brass instrument* achieved by opening and closing a *mute,* making a "wah-wah" sound; also used on electric guitar.

waltz Ballroom dance type in *triple meter;* in the Romantic era, a short, stylized piano piece.

West Coast jazz A *jazz* style developed in the 1950s, featuring small groups of mixed-timbre instruments playing *contrapuntal* improvisations; similar to *cool jazz.*

whole step Interval consisting of two *half steps.*

whole-tone scale Scale pattern built entirely of *whole-step* intervals, common in music of the French Impressionist composers.

wind band Instrumental ensemble ranging from forty to eighty members or more, consisting of wind and *percussion instruments.* Also *concert band.*

woodwind Instrumental family made of wood or metal whose tone is produced by a column of air vibrating within a pipe that has holes along its length.

woodwind quintet Standard chamber ensemble consisting of *flute, oboe, clarinet, bassoon,* and *horn* (not a woodwind instrument).

word-painting Musical pictorialization of words as an expressive device; a prominent feature of the Renaissance madrigal.

work song Communal song that synchronized group tasks.

world beat See *global pop.*

xylophone *Percussion instrument* with tuned blocks of wood suspended on a frame, laid out in the shape of a keyboard and struck with hard mallets.

yangqin A Chinese hammered *dulcimer* with a trapezoidal sound box and metal strings that are struck with bamboo sticks.

zapateado A lively Spanish and Latin-American dance style that features foot-stomping patterns.

zither Family of string instruments with a sound box over which strings are stretched; they may be plucked or bowed. Zithers appear in many shapes and are common in traditional music throughout Europe, Asia, and Africa.

Appendix III: Reporting on the Concert Experience

Have you ever been to a live classical music concert? If so, you have some idea what to expect, although each type of concert has its own conventions.

First, you need to decide which concert to attend. Did you ever play an instrument in a band or orchestra or sing in a choir? Most universities have all these ensembles, and more. The quality of the groups is usually very good, since the student participants are often music majors who have been performing for several years. So try one of these for your first concertgoing experience. There are all kinds of other groups to hear, some specialized: jazz bands and combos, early- and new-music ensembles, chamber groups such as brass or woodwind quintets and string quartets, percussion ensembles, and perhaps even some groups that specialize in repertories from an unfamiliar part of the world.

The performers, whether in promotional material or onstage, may appear formal in their dress and actions; these are part of the traditions of the concert hall. Here are a few other conventions of classical concertgoing that you should heed:

- Arrive early enough to get seated before the program starts, as late seating only occurs between works.

- Hold your applause during a multimovement work until the end—study the program to figure out how it's organized.

- Don't talk or make other unnecessary noise during the concert, as this can be disruptive to those around you—and, more important, to the performers, who need to concentrate on the music.

- Stay seated until the intermission or end of the concert, again in order not to be disruptive.

Try to follow the program, noting the differences in musical style of the various selections. Even the movements of one large-scale work—such as a symphony, sonata, or concerto—will present varied melodies, harmonies, meters, and textures. This is what you will need to write about in a concert report. Hearing and describing these varied styles using the terminology you are learning can be a challenge, but do your best. Some elements will be easier to discern than others.

A sample concert report is provided below to give you an idea of what musical characteristics you might try to describe. This student took good notes on each movement and did a little extra reading from the textbook as well. The comments here pertain to all the basic elements of music (Chapters 1–11)—melody, rhythm/meter, harmony, texture, form, dynamics, tempo, and instruments—using the terms defined in these chapters. The composers' dates (or date of the composition) will help you place the music in a particular style period; be sure to consult the style charts at the end of each part, and look over the writing tips provided in

---

Program

Overture to *The Marriage of Figaro (Le nozze di Figaro)*	W. A. Mozart (1756–1791)
Symphony No. 4 in A Major, Op. 90 ("Italian")	Felix Mendelssohn (1809–1847)

    Allegro vivace
    Andante con moto
    Con moto moderato: Scherzo and trio
    Presto: Saltarello

Intermission

Piano Concerto in A Minor, Op. 54	Robert Schumann (1810–1856)

    Allegro affettuoso
    Intermezzo: Andantino grazioso
    Allegro vivace

Barbara Allen, piano

University Symphony Orchestra
Roger Hickman, conductor

Chapter 14 ("Putting Music into Words"), to help you frame your ideas. Finally, we have suggested some criteria your instructor might use in evaluating your report.

So find a concert that looks appealing to you (or that is recommended by your instructor), invite a friend to go along, and enjoy!

Sample Concert Report

I attended the University Symphony Orchestra concert on October 16, 2021, in the Daniel Recital Hall. The hall was much more crowded than I expected. At the beginning of the concert, the orchestra was seated on the stage; the men wore tuxedos, and the women wore black dresses or pants. The concertmaster came out to tune the orchestra, and then the conductor made his entrance and gave brief comments about each piece that was about to be played.

The concert opened with an overture from an opera by Mozart. Fortunately, we had studied several scenes from this opera, which helped relate the music to the opera's plot. The fast-paced opening suggested the hustle and bustle of wedding preparations. The strings' busy, scurrying idea was answered by the woodwinds. These ideas came to a halt in a strong cadence (and likely a modulation), after which a new idea was introduced, with notes emphasized in the strings with a quick *forte*, then *piano* (*fp*), which added to the drama. One more singing melody was heard briefly before the whole section repeated. As explained by the conductor, this overture is basically in a sonata-allegro form, but without a real development of the themes. After hearing this, I'd like to see more of the comic opera that it introduces.

The next work was a symphony, nicknamed the *Italian*, by the early Romantic-era composer Felix Mendelssohn. The conductor explained that Mendelssohn wrote this work upon his return from a trip to Italy. Although I had expected some deviations from the "standard" four-movement symphony structure we studied, this work seems entirely classical to me. The composer even set the third movement more like a slower minuet and trio than a fast-paced scherzo/trio, as

Beethoven did in his Fifth Symphony. But the use of an old Italian folk dance type, the saltarello, in the last movement was unique.

The first movement of the symphony began with a very dynamic dancelike theme. After the action died down a bit, the woodwinds were featured in a calmer second melody, after which the exposition closed vigorously. Next I think I heard yet another theme, and some hints at the ones from the opening section. This was certainly a sonata-allegro form, with the expected recapitulation. The second movement was much darker, probably in a minor key with a lovely, singing melody over a kind of moving ("walking") bass line. The third movement was in triple meter, as expected, with short repeated sections and a different, more relaxed mood for the trio section. The last movement was the crowning achievement of the symphony—it was a wild-paced dance that featured the flutes and piccolos with the main tune. The drama of this movement made me wonder what the composer had seen or heard on his trip to Italy to inspire this dance.

The second half of the concert was a Romantic-era piano concerto by Robert Schumann. As is typical, it had three movements, alternating fast-slow-fast, but I also noticed some changes from the standard concerto form we studied with Mozart. First, the piano entered almost immediately with a dramatic introduction, after just one chord from the orchestra. Then came a lovely and flowing melody played by the oboe. When the piano entered again, it played the same enchanting melody. The motion then picked up, as the volume increased. Suddenly, the music became marchlike, played staccato. The piano had long passages by itself which varied in tempo and dynamics. The clarinet got the motion moving faster again with a second theme, which instead of being a contrasting idea, was very similar to the first. The instruments exchanged short ideas, leading to a triumphant orchestral section that felt like a closing. This moved, however, into a slower and very expressive section—the beginning of the development—where the melodies we heard at first were varied. Throughout this section, the mood shifted from dramatic to sweet and back. The oboe brought back the main theme, just as in the opening, to begin the recapitulation. Once again, the piano worked with, and sometimes against, the orchestra. A long and flashy solo piano passage—the cadenza—sounded almost improvised, after which the orchestra played a quick, marchlike version of the main theme we had heard numerous times.

In the slow movement, called Intermezzo, the solo piano took up a dialogue with the string section. A contrasting middle section featured a touching melody in the cellos, after which the opening conversation returned—in all, it seemed to be a three-part structure. Surprisingly, the second movement flowed directly into the vigorous last one, without a pause. Here, the solo piano introduced the main melody, after which the orchestra repeated it. The next idea seemed slower and more static, but very rhythmic. In the middle, the themes were varied, leading to a repeat (a recapitulation) of the first section that seemed to stretch out. This last movement featured fast passages for the soloist—it was amazing watching her fingers fly over the keys. I read that Schumann wanted to be a concert pianist, but after injuring his hand, he settled on composing. In fact, the conductor told us that the composer's talented wife Clara performed the premiere of the first movement.

I enjoyed the concert and was really surprised at how the organization and the performance took place. As this was my first classical music concert, I was intrigued to see how the concertmaster came out to prepare the orchestra and to see the conductor at work with all the players at his command. All in all, it was a very positive experience.

Analysis

This student's description of the overture relates principally to the changing moods and the instrumentation. For both the symphony and the concerto, the discussion is based on the structure of Romantic-era works, and how these pieces are similar to and different from works studied in the text. The student's focus is on form and genre, noting the main events rather than trying to describe everything heard. (See Chapter 14.)

Now here is how an instructor might assess the report:

- Uses terms accurately.
- Shows understanding of concepts.
- Considers many different elements of music (melody, meter, harmony, form, dynamics, tempo, instrumentation).
- Shows an understanding that elements change as a piece progresses.
- Discusses all works and movements from the concert, recognizing differences in styles.
- Includes some information about the work from lecture/book/program notes.
- Attempts to describe the music in their own terms, with a genuine reaction.

Credits

Photos

Music

Index

Page numbers in **boldface** indicate definitions; page numbers in *italics* indicate illustrations or musical examples.

Dudamel, Gustavo, 6, *50*
Duke Ellington. *See* Ellington, Edward Kennedy ("Duke")
Duke Ellington Orchestra, *Take the A Train*, 341
dulcimers, 38
Dumas, Alexandre, *père*, 237, 288
duo sonatas, 48, 187
duple meter, **11**, *12*, *51*, 341
duration (rhythm), **7**
Dvořák, Antonín, 320–24, *322*, 325, 327
 life and music of, 322
 New World Symphony, 320
 String Quartet Op. 96, 320, 321–24, *323–24*
Dylan, Bob, 140, 412, *413*
dynamics, 30–32, **30**, *31*, *32*, 174, 334

The Earl of Essex Galliarde, 103
earthworks, **409**
East African drumming, 438–39, *438–39*
Eastern Orthodox Church, 88
Easter Parade (Berlin), 340
Echoes of Time and the River (Crumb), *422*
Ecstasy of Saint Teresa (Bernini), 129
Edison, Thomas, *327*
Edwards, Edward, *149*
Egozy, Eran, 416
Eichheim, Henry, 424
Eine kleine Nachtmusik (A Little Night Music) (Mozart), 195–200, *199–200*
Einstein on the Beach (Glass), 446
Eleanor of Aquitaine, 87
Electric Counterpoint (Reich), 434, 436–37, *437*
electric guitar, **41**
Electric Light Orchestra (ELO), *444*
 Roll Over Beethoven, 443, *444*
elektronische Musik, **413**
Elf-King (Erlkönig) (Schubert), 243, 244–46, *245–46*, 250–51, 422
 by Corona Schröter, 250–51
El Greco, 124
Ellington, Edward Kennedy ("Duke"), 365, 369–72, *369*, 374, 461
 Black and Tan Fantasy, 369
 Caravan, 370
 Conga Brava, 370
 life and music of, 369
 Ko-Ko, 369
 Mood Indigo, 369
 Sophisticated Lady, 369
 Take the A Train, 369–72
embellishments, **114**, **116**
embouchure, **43**
The Empire Strikes Back (film), *456*, *457*, 460
Empress of the Blues (Bearden), 366

England, opera in, 137–39
English horn, **42**, *49*
English madrigal, **96–97**, 100, 101, *101*
English national school, 278
Enlightenment, **178–79**, 180, 250
Eno, Brian, 416, 445–46
ensembles, **47–53**. *See also* bands, orchestra
 big band, 369–70
 ensemble vocal music, 72
 gamelan, 424–25
 mariachi, 398–99
 New Orleans jazz, 366–67
 standard chamber, *48*
Ensiraba ya munage Katego (East African drumming), 38, 438–39
entries, order of (in fugue), 172
environmental art, 409
episodes (in concerto), **170**
equal temperament, **126**
erhu (Chinese instrument), *460*
Erlkönig. See Elf-King
Essays Before a Sonata (Ives), 385
estampie, **86**, 87, 90–91
Esterházy family, 187
Eszterháza Palace, *185*
ethnomusicologists, **401**
E.T.: The Extra-Terrestial (film), 454, *455*
Étude, Op. 10, No. 12 (*Revolutionary*) (Chopin), *57*, *256*, 258–59, *260*
études, of Chopin, **256**, 258–60
euphonium, **45**
Europe, map of, *182*
Europe, James Reese, 340
Ewe drumming, 435, *436*
exoticism, **307**, 309, 316
 in Baroque music, 127
 in Impressionist era, 316
 in Romantic music, 309
experimental music, mid-twentieth-century American, 418–25
"An Experiment in Modern Music," (Gershwin), 379–80
exposition (form), **170**, **195**, *197*
expression, 30–32, *478*
 in Romantic symphony, 283
 tempo and dynamic as elements of, 31–32
Expressionism, **339**, 344–47, **344**, *359*
Expressionist opera, 358–64

Fair Phyllis (Farmer), *57*, 100, 101, *101*
Fanfare Ritmico (Higdon), 450
Farmer, John, 96, 100
 Fair Phyllis, *57*, 100, 101, *101*
 life and music of, 100
Fats Domino, 441

Faust et Hélène (Boulanger), 355
Fel, Marie, *182*
Fellini, Federico, 410
feminism, musical, 413
Fernandes, Gaspar, 156–57
figured bass, **125**
film, music for, 413–14, 454–62
Final Fantasy VII, 459
The Firebird (Stravinsky), 348, 350
First Book of Songes or Ayres (Dowland), 102–3, *102*
The First Emperor (Tan Dun), 461
first-movement concerto form, **202–3**, *203*
Fisk Jubilee Singers, 326, *326*, 327–28, 329
fixed forms (chanson), 93–94
flat (in music notation), **16**, *17*
Florentine Camerata, 125
Flow My Teares (Dowland), 103
fluegelhorn, **45**
flutes, 38, 39, **42**, *42*, 48, *49*, 100
flutter-tonguing, **421**
folklore, 238, 250–51, 316, 394
folk music, 279, 316, 400–2
 Greensleeves (English folk song), 11, *12*, *28*
 nineteenth-century, 250–51
form(s), 26–29, **26**, *55*, 61, 174, 232, 334, 404, 478
 bar form (A-A-B), **143**
 A-B-B form, **154**
 binary form (A-A-B-B), **158**, *159*
 binary form (A-B), **26**, 27, *28*, 186
 building blocks of, 27–29
 Classical-era forms, 185–87, 191–92, 196–98
 first-movement concerto form, **202–3**, **203**
 larger forms, 195–200
 minuet and trio form, 197–98
 modified strophic form, **242**, *243*
 musical form, 26–29
 orchestral forms, 239–40
 ritornello form, **149**, **163**, *164*
 Romantic-era, 239
 Romantic form, 239
 rondo form (A-B-A-C-A), **186**
 rounded binary form, **188–89**
 sonata-allegro form, **195**, **196–97**, *197*, 283
 song form (A-A-B-A), **370**
 strophic form, **26**, **35**, *55*, **242**, *243*, 251
 ternary form (A-B-A), **26**, 27, *28*, **158**, *159*, 186
 thirty-two bar song form, 370
 through-composed form, **26**, **242**, *243*
 twelve-bar blues form, 367–68
forte, 30, *31*, 126

Mexico

GREENLAND

Nuuk

Bering Sea

ALASKA

Fairbanks

Hudson Bay

Gulf of Alaska

Labrador Sea

C A N A D A

Calgary

Vancouver

North Pacific Ocean

Ottawa   Montreal

Chicago

North Atlantic Ocean

U N I T E D   S T A T E S

New York

San Francisco

Washington D.C.

Los Angeles

Dallas

Mexico City

Cihuatlan

M E X I C O

Gulf of Mexico

THE BAHAMAS

HAWAII

Mexico City

Havana

CUBA

DOM. REP

Cihuatlan

GUATEMALA   BELIZE   JAMAICA   HAITI

HONDURAS   *Caribbean Sea*

EL SALVADOR   NICARAGUA   Caracas

COSTA RICA   VENEZUELA   GUYANA

PANAMA   Bogota   SURINAME

                                      COLOMBIA   FRENCH GUIANA

ECUADOR

Quito

B R A Z I L

PERU

Lima   Brasilia

BOLIVIA

La Paz   Rio de Janeiro

Sucre   Saõ Paulo

PARAGUAY

CHILE   Asuncion

ARGENTINA

Santiago

Buenos Aires   URUGUAY

Montevideo

FALKLAND ISLANDS

SOUTH GEORGIA IS.

Canada

Beaufort Sea

GREENLAND (DENMARK)

UNITED STATES

Dawson

Yukon Territory

Great Bear Lake

Victoria Island

Baffin Bay

Whitehorse

Nunavut

Baffin Island

Pacific Ocean

Northwest Territories

Yellowknife

Labrador Sea

Great Slave Lake

Lake Athabasca

British Columbia

Alberta

Saskatchewan

Churchill

Hudson Bay

Labrador

Victoria   Vancouver

Edmonton

Calgary

Saskatoon

Regina

Manitoba

Lake Winnipeg

Winnipeg

Thunder Bay

Ontario

Quebec

Newfoundland

New Brunswick

Prince Edward Is.

Quebec   Fredericton

Sydney

Montreal

Halifax

UNITED STATES

Lake Superior

Lake Huron

Ottawa

Lake Ontario

Nova Scotia

Toronto

Lake Michigan

Atlantic Ocean

Lake Erie

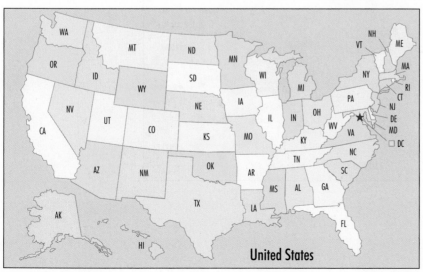

WA

MT

ND

MN

NH

VT   ME

OR

ID

SD

WI

NY

MA

WY

MI

PA

RI

CT

NV

NE

IA

IL   IN   OH

NJ

UT

CO

WV

DE

CA

KS

MO

KY

VA

MD

DC

AZ

NM

OK

AR

TN

NC

MS   AL   GA

SC

TX

LA

FL

AK

HI

United States

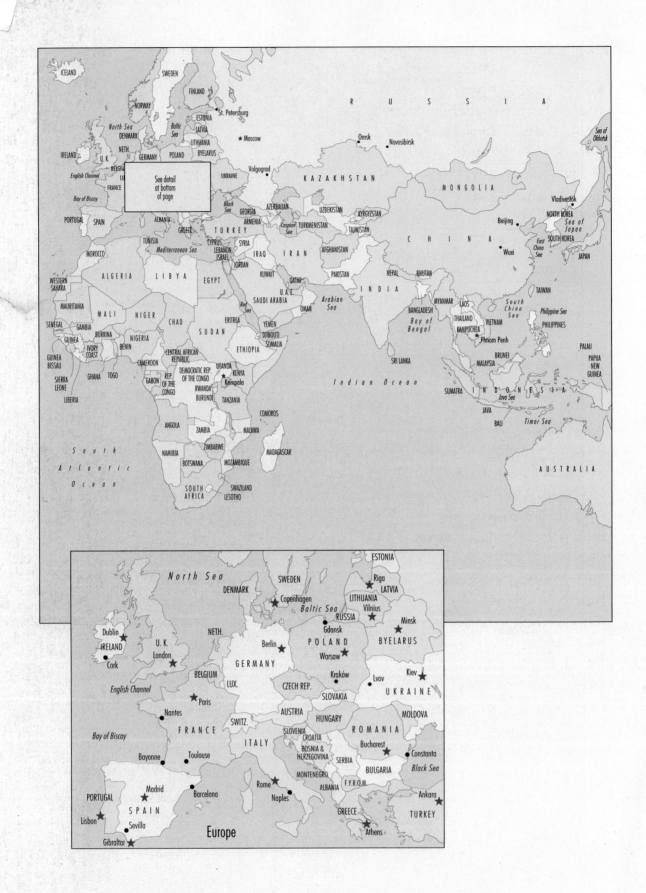

Europe